GLOBAL RHETORICAL TRADITIONS

LAUER SERIES IN RHETORIC AND COMPOSITION
Editors: Thomas Rickert and Jennifer Bay

The Lauer Series in Rhetoric and Composition honors the contributions Janice Lauer has made to the emergence of Rhetoric and Composition as a disciplinary study. It publishes scholarship that carries on Professor Lauer's varied work in the history of written rhetoric, disciplinarity in composition studies, contemporary pedagogical theory, and written literacy theory and research.

RECENT BOOKS IN THE SERIES

Writing in the Clouds: Inventing and Composing in Internetworked Writing Spaces (Logie, 2022)

Pedagogical Perspectives on Cognition and Writing (Rifenburg, Portanova, & Roen, 2021)

Feminist Circulations: Rhetorical Explorations across Space and Time (Enoch, Griffin, & Nelson, 2021)

Creole Composition: Academic Writing and Rhetoric in the Anglophone Caribbean (Milson-Whyte, Oenbring, & Jaquette, 2019). MLA Mina P. Shaughnessy Prize 2019-2020, CCCC Best Book Award 2021.

Retellings: Opportunities for Feminist Research in Rhetoric and Composition Studies (Enoch & Jack, 2019)

Facing the Sky: Composing through Trauma in Word and Image (Fox, 2016)

Expel the Pretender: Rhetoric Renounced and the Politics of Style (Wiederhold, 2015)

First-Year Composition: From Theory to Practice (Coxwell-Teague & Lunsford, 2014)

Contingency, Immanence, and the Subject of Rhetoric (Richardson, 2013)

Rewriting Success in Rhetoric & Composition Careers (Goodburn, LeCourt, & Leverenz, 2012)

Writing a Progressive Past: Women Teaching and Writing in the Progressive Era (Mastrangelo, 2012)

Greek Rhetoric Before Aristotle, 2e, Rev. and Exp. Ed. (Enos, 2012)

Rhetoric's Earthly Realm: Heidegger, Sophistry, and the Gorgian Kairos (Miller) *Winner of the Olson Award for Best Book in Rhetorical Theory 2011

Techne, from Neoclassicism to Postmodernism: Understanding Writing as a Useful, Teachable Art (Pender, 2011)

Walking and Talking Feminist Rhetorics: Landmark Essays and Controversies (Buchanan & Ryan, 2010)

Transforming English Studies: New Voices in an Emerging Genre (Ostergaard, Ludwig, & Nugent, 2009)

Ancient Non-Greek Rhetorics (Lipson & Binkley, 2009)

Roman Rhetoric: Revolution and the Greek Influence, Rev. and Exp Ed. (Enos, 2008)

Stories of Mentoring: Theory and Praxis (Eble & Gaillet, 2008)

Networked Process: Dissolving Boundaries of Process and Post-Process (Foster, 2007)

Composing a Community: A History of Writing Across the Curriculum (McLeod & Soven, 2006)

Historical Studies of Writing Program Administration: Individuals, Communities, and the Formation of a Discipline (L'Eplattenier & Mastrangelo, 2004). Winner of the WPA Best Book Award for 2004–2005

Rhetorics, Poetics, and Cultures: Refiguring College English Studies Exp. Ed. (Berlin, 2003)

For more titles, visit the series page: http://bit.ly/lauerseries

GLOBAL RHETORICAL TRADITIONS

Edited by

Hui Wu and Tarez Samra Graban

Parlor Press
Anderson, South Carolina
www.parlorpress.com

Parlor Press LLC, Anderson, South Carolina, USA
© 2023 by Parlor Press
All rights reserved.
Printed in the United States of America on acid-free paper.

SAN: 254-8879

Library of Congress Cataloging-in-Publication Data on File

978-1-64317-316-0 (paperback)
978-1-64317-335-1 (hardcover)
978-1-64317-317-7 (pdf)
978-1-64317-318-4 (epub)

1 2 3 4 5

Cover image: Marjan Blan on Unsplash.
Book Design: David Blakesley

Parlor Press, LLC is an independent publisher of scholarly and trade titles in print and multimedia
formats. This book is available in paper and ebook formats from Parlor Press on the World Wide
Web at https://parlorpress.com or through online and brick-and-mortar bookstores. For submission
information or to find out about Parlor Press publications, write to Parlor Press, 3015 Brackenberry
Drive, Anderson, South Carolina, 29621, or email editor@parlorpress.com.

Contents

ACKNOWLEDGMENTS

This book would not have come into being without the input of several communities. First, we offer special thanks to all members, both past and present, of the Global and Non-Western Rhetorics Standing Group of the Conference on College Composition and Communication. Their earnest and well-informed concerns about the lack of primary sources for teaching non-Western rhetorical traditions, and their innovative ideas about how to teach and learn them, have compelled us to design and complete this book project. Next, we offer sincere thanks to our wise and talented contributors who are eager to change, and to see changes in, rhetoric's place in diversifying histories, enhancing communication practices, and creating new understandings of the world. We are especially grateful to Professor Patricia Bizzell for composing a foreword in which she offers additional retrospective insights into researching and teaching rhetorical traditions. Finally, we are indebted to the manuscript's reviewers and to the editorial team at Parlor Press, all of whom received this project with the right combination of enthusiasm and criticism, helping to make it all the stronger. Series editors Jennifer Bay and Thomas Rickert, along with managing editor David Blakesley, have buoyed this project with exceptional support from start to finish. We are honored to have this book included alongside the excellent titles already populating the Lauer Series in Rhetoric and Composition.

ILLUSTRATIONS

FOREWORD

Patricia Bizzell

In his discussion of Hebraic Mediterranean rhetorics in this volume, Jim Ridolfo cites Janice Fernheimer's observation that "Jewish rhetorics disrupt the typical binary of Western/non-Western" rhetorics. The same could be said for all the other rhetorics under consideration here. In their rich multiplicity, they defy the distribution of traditions into only two simplistic categories.

Not that I think "disruption" is the primary motive of the contributors. Many contributors note that the rhetorics they discuss have received little scholarly attention, but I do not sense that these rhetoricians are primarily interested in the kinds of defensive recovery work that were so often referenced in critiques of the first edition of Bruce Herzberg's and my *The Rhetorical Tradition: Readings from Classical Times to the Present,* published in 1990. Indeed, we expected push-back from the title's implication that there was only one "rhetorical tradition" of any interest, that being the traditional Western canon. Through three editions of our anthology (the third having appeared in 2020), we have tried to diversify our selections. For example, in the third edition, the Jewish treatise that Ridolfo analyzes in this collection, *The Book of the Honeycomb's Flow*, appears for the first time. There is no denying, however, that the implied focus centering on the Western tradition still obtains in what we called in-house "RT3."

I was honored to see, in Tarez Samra Graban's introduction, that the editors consider *Global Rhetorical Traditions* to be a "counterpart" to *The Rhetorical Tradition*; I might rather say, *The Rhetorical Tradition* is a counterpart to the present volume. Graban is wise to acknowledge that *Global Rhetorical Traditions* is in no way comprehensive. How could it be? At the same time, the goal of representing as many global rhetorical traditions as possible leads to a plethora of mostly short excerpts of the rhetorics under analysis. The volume's units plant flags on the sites where future scholarship can develop further, and they stimulate that work in multiple ways—a great benefit.

Browsing happily through *Global Rhetorical Traditions*, I speculate that the contributors are motivated primarily by a desire to share their enthusiasms. Every chapter provided me with fascinating new insights. To mention just a few examples: Hui Wu discusses the advent of paper as a writing medium influencing the career of the early Chinese woman rhetorician

Ban Zhao. Leonora Anyango fleshes out the concept of "orature" to explain the development of rhetoric in multilingual East Africa (where there are over three hundred documented languages). Anne Melfi explains how much is lost when eloquent hymns from the Rig Veda are translated into English: who knew how many meanings could be packed into the word translated as "cow"?

At the same time, the present contributors have guided their scholarship by the most current concepts of rhetorical historiography, beginning with the definition of "comparative rhetoric" in the introduction. As Graban elucidates, many of the sub-chapters here employ interpretive vocabularies specific to the cultures that have produced the rhetorical texts they consider. One striking example comprises Shreelina Ghosh's analysis of traditional Indian dance as a rhetorical medium. Or, consider Gregory Coles's treatment of the "familial" language in a twenty-first-century address by Megawati Sukarnoputri.

And yet classical Western rhetorical terms are not strictly quarantined. Sometimes, their use is historically and culturally appropriate, as in the complex discussion by several scholars of the interweavings of classical Greek and Arabic terminologies that Graban orchestrates in the chapter on Arabic and Islamic rhetorics. Sometimes, a classical term is admitted to the discussion where it is useful if approached with careful cultural grounding. Georganne Nordstrom and ku'ualoha ho'omanawanui offer such an admission in their use of *kairos* and other classical concepts when analyzing the Polynesian-Hawaiian genre of the name chant, which has retained its cultural distinctiveness in postcolonial times up to the present day. (One contemporary example even honors Hawaiian-born Barack Obama.)

Decisions that the contributors have made in this collection, including the choice to use or not use classical Western terminology, express the meanings of Jerry Won Lee's concept of "semioscape," taken up by Graban in the introduction. This concept helps rhetoricians understand that, while global rhetorics are certainly situated in particular geographic and temporal locations, analysis can cut across boundaries of time and space. Ideas migrate and flow. I'm reminded of the Talmudic principle of Biblical analysis such that "there is no time in Torah," so readers do not balk at Abraham's separating milk and meat when he serves his angelic visitors in Genesis, even though the laws of kashrut are not given by G_d until the Sinai event in Exodus. With the contributors' careful theoretical cautions in mind, I found myself beginning to generate teaching ideas, such as a course on comparative epideictic, based in this volume.

Having served as the editor of several collections, too, I have to applaud the heroic labors of Wu and Graban in shepherding into print a collection that will be of such immense usefulness to contemporary scholars. Every unit in this volume begins with an introductory essay that sets the unit's sometimes disparate elements into historical and theoretical relation to each other. Each sub-chapter that follows—typically focusing on an individual rhetorician, text, or genre—adds a more detailed introduction to its subject matter and a more sophisticated analysis of its examples. Each unit concludes with not only the substantive bibliography we would expect, but also a helpful glossary of terms to assist us with unfamiliar vocabulary in the relevant languages. I actually read this anthology for pleasure, but if I were looking for a topic to spark a research project, here is where I would turn first.

Introduction: Renewing Comparative Methodologies

Tarez Samra Graban

Global Rhetorical Traditions was conceptualized in response to three needs. First, our shared interest in recovering rhetorical treatises in traditions and cultures that are not primarily Pan-Hellenic at their core or European in their influence has led us to redefine origins, locations, and circulations of rhetorical traditions on a global scale in the twenty-first century. While much of our existing scholarship in comparative rhetoric necessarily focuses on secondary sources, the bilingual and multilingual contributors in our collection present translations of primary sources and commentaries to guide the study and teaching of global rhetorical traditions. Their efforts not only result in more recoveries of rhetorical treatises, they also further enrich the curriculum of rhetoric, composition, and communication. By including as many contributions as currently possible, this collection showcases the ways in which our contributors' translations and analyses offer renewed insights into how rhetoric has been taught in the past, how it influences communicative practices today, and how it can continue to do so in different regions around the world.

Second, our shared interest in teaching global rhetorical traditions has led us to appreciate the linguistic challenges of building pedagogy around practices that have not historically been circulated or performed in Anglo-American English. As a result, the chapters in this book discomfit the binary distinction between actions that serve language maintenance and actions that serve language change. Implicit in the global study of rhetorical treatises is a relationship between "stable" and "unstable" conceptualizations of language that James Clackson,[1] Joshua Fishman,[2] and George Schmidt-Rohr[3] have encouraged historians to consider. Whereas "stable" conceptualizations of language imply maintenance and preservation, "unstable" conceptualizations imply fluctuation and change based on the same circulatory factors that occur when dominant tongues become replaced by or subsumed within their modern variants. However, as the contributors to this volume aptly demonstrate, recovering rhetorical treatises

1. Clackson 2001, 37.
2. Fishman 1972, 407–34. See also Fishman (1964, 32–70).
3. Schmidt-Rohr 1933.

in various languages does not necessarily mean tracing when and how a dominant language has given way to its variants, or establishing one language's dominance over another. Rather, it means attending to the periods of textual mobility that allowed certain rhetorical practices to become vigorously and concurrently coopted or shared among diverse cultures and geographical spaces.[4] Thus, our project not only accommodates both processes—language maintenance and language change—but also presumes that rhetorical histories are best found where these processes occur in tandem, with or without ancient Greece at their center.

The third need addressed by this collection is to develop analytic methodologies from rhetorical realignments[5] and alternative frameworks for study[6]—frameworks that can be accessed by comparatists and non-comparatists alike. Our twenty-eight contributors examine rhetorical treatises to reveal intricate terminologies that may or may not bear resemblance to the so-called Western rhetorical tradition, disrupting the persistent dominance of a Pan-Hellenic core. While this collection is by no means the first to suggest such disruption, we uniquely consider how the study of global rhetorical traditions can inform past, present and future notions of comparative work, especially where work occurs between Englishes, as well as between languages, and especially in support of scholars who many not speak, write, or read in multiple languages. In doing so, we have adopted an approach that neither privileges nor defaces conceptualizations of "West" or "non-West" in its mission.

In short, this collection serves a dual function. On the one hand, it offers a global counterpart to Patricia Bizzell and Bruce Herzberg's now-classic *The Rhetorical Tradition*, which has been adopted extensively as a textbook at both graduate and undergraduate levels, and whose richness has emerged from the editors' curation of primary source texts. On the other hand, it troubles neat distinctions between non/Western and ancient/modern rhetorical traditions, highlighting contributors' language-informed historical narratives of rhetorical traditions and commentaries that accompany their translated source texts. In both cases, *Global Rhetorical Traditions* pairs well with this and other prior work. While Bizzell and Herzberg identified a rhetorical period of "flourishing" during the rise of Greek democracy (in the fifth century BCE), they also acknowledged the difficulty, or impossibility, of discerning an authentic rhetorical history, and argued for the careful handling of cultural origin stories in their various obscurities. Similarly, while we begin with an assertion that there is more for the classical rhetorical scholar to do than revise Greco-Roman systems, we also anticipate that Classical scholars will use this collection to broaden and expand the traditions they study by filling in the gaps with less represented works, by redefining their tradition according to different landmarks and trajectories and translated instances, and by presenting rhetorical antiquity through its complex interdependence with other globalized movements.

---

4. In much the same way that Clackson disrupts the stable-unstable binary by accounting for the presence of complex bilingual influences on the ancient texts he studies, the contributors in this volume help us to account for the presence of complex circulatory principles in how rhetorical lessons have become inherited or conveyed.

5. Borrowman 2010, 97–118.

6. Lyon 2009, 176–96.

The translations and commentaries throughout this book point to renewed methodologies for comparative studies of rhetoric. These methodologies both differ from and realign existing scholarship so as to empower marginalized research and teaching in global rhetorical traditions and practices, and they make it obvious how different rhetorical traditions have developed in tandem with Pan-Hellenic rhetoric, with or without its direct influence. To help these renewed methodologies unfold, in this introduction I demonstrate the significance of our collection in three ways. I begin by arguing for the nature of and need for more primary source work in the teaching of global rhetorics, by critiquing extant scholarship in the field and by delineating "comparative" approaches from those that are more broadly cultural, postcolonial, and/or transnational. Then, I articulate the principles underlying the design of the book. Finally, I describe the layout of the chapters by addressing the availability of some non-Pan-Hellenic sources and the paucity of others, arguing not only for ways to overcome paucity but also for helping the comparative study and teaching of global rhetorics to endure.

CALLING FOR PRIMARY SOURCE WORK

Our collection joins a critical conversation already underway about the nature of comparative rhetorical scholarship, which has gotten notably richer and deeper in the past three decades, mostly in the form of anthologies of secondary scholarship. Indeed, we admire the breadth and depth of available texts that have formed around the rhetorical analysis of discourses, historical examinations of rhetorical traditions and practices, and observations of rhetorical development in particular regions or cultures. Carol S. Lipson and Roberta Binkley, in *Ancient Non-Greek Rhetorics* and *Rhetoric Before and Beyond the Greeks*, have organized collections that both celebrate and question appropriate methods and ethical practices surrounding what it means to study rhetorical traditions comparatively, urging comparatists to adopt what Lu-Ming Mao calls a more *emic* approach by learning to view rhetorical phenomena from within their unique cultural contexts rather than without.[7] Shane Borrowman, Robert L. Lively, and Marcia Kmetz, in *Rhetoric in the Rest of the West*, have assembled a collection of essays that defy an understanding of rhetorical histories as a straight-line "between ancient Greece and the modern world, between the lessons of the Sophists and the rhapsodes of Attic Greece."[8] Instead, their collection presents histories of rhetoric as "memor[ies]" or "shared sense[s] of our common heritage,"[9] and thus as cultural intricacies and temporal complexities that fall into or out of the comparative purview. More recently, Damián Baca and Victor Villanueva, in *Rhetorics of the Americas: 3114 BCE to 2012 CE*, have assembled a collection of "uniquely Western Hemispheric rhetorics," extending comparative approaches toward the rhetorical reading of material life prior to the Discovered West.[10] Moreover, they emphasize how a range of schol-

---

7. Mao 2013, 171, as qtd. in Lipson and Binkley 2009.
8. Borrowman et al. 2010, ix.
9. Borrowman et al. 2010, xi–xii.
10. Baca and Villanueva 2010, ix–x.

arship from rhetoric, composition, and comparative literature can be studied together across translations of indigenous texts, artifacts, and even non-textual (or embodied) performances to push the boundaries on what constitutes "America" and "the West" in their globalized and circulating notions. Finally, Keith Lloyd and forty-three contributors in *The Routledge Handbook of Comparative World Rhetorics* look historiographically away from the notion of a stable and linear rhetorical tradition, instead reflecting the proliferation of transcultural practices that make such historiography necessary.[11] In doing so, they have constructed the most expansive collection of perspectives (to date) on the critical, historical, philosophical, and pedagogical dimensions of comparative rhetorics, proving its *longue durée*.

We have also seen specific arguments work to productively confound stark distinctions between east and west in their appropriation of global rhetorical perspectives. For example, Richard Enos, in *Roman Rhetoric: Revolution and the Greek Influence*, bucks the traditional expectation that Rome and Greece are vital only when historicized in respect to one another.[12] Mary Garrett and Xing Lu have argued for a Chinese tradition of suasory discourse based on the use of key terms for argumentation and persuasion during the fourth century BCE (overlapping with Greek's sophistic period), such as *bian* (dialectical disputation taking the form of definition); *shuo* (an explanation that could be introduced into bian); *shui* a speech act intended to be persuasive to a particular audience.[13] And Maha Baddar[14] and Shane Borrowman[15] have argued that in the Middle Ages, Arab writers would become more significant to western historians because their work was central to the understanding of ancient Greek texts, as "the West" had not yet obtained these texts or solidified their communicative traditions around them. In medieval histories, especially, this migration of text and tradition is enveloped in debates about the origins of Islamic philosophy. There, it reflects the recurrent discovery of remnants of Greek intellectual traditions (through Plato and Aristotle, among others) in what became known as *bala'gha* (rhetoric and eloquence) and *falsafa* (philosophy in the Arabic and Islamic world), terms and traditions that scholars now know are not geographically bound.

Furthermore, Susan Jarratt has argued for a kind of thinking that "make[s] contemporary use of rhetoric's heterogeneous pasts, a comparative practice to which histories from every time and place can contribute."[16] Kermit Campbell [17] and Omedi Ochieng[18] have brought classical and contemporary examples of African philosophy to bear on contemporary rhetorical theory to argue that there is no African philosophy without some positioning in respect to "the west," in fact making "the west" a more metonymic concept than we realize. And Lyon and Borrowman encourage us to reread Chinese and Medieval Arabic traditions in light of new

---

11. Lloyd 2020.
12. Enos 2008.
13. Kennedy 1998, 159–60. See also Garrett (2013, 243–55). See also Liu (2015, 375–83).
14. Baddar 2015, 59–70.
15. Borrowman, "Recovering" 2010.
16. Jarratt 2015, 252.
17. Campbell 2006, 255–74. See also Ochieng (2011).
18. Campbell 2010; Ochieng 2011.

evidence about their actual geographic or geopolitical spread, as keen reminders of how *both* "western" and "non-Western" texts from Antiquity through the Middle Ages had already experienced a kind of globalization, taking up new influence with each translation, circulation, and re-distribution.

These whole collections and individual arguments, punctuated by special issues of *College English, Rhetoric Society Quarterly, College Composition and Communication,* and *Rhetoric Review*, have, over the decades, transformed comparative rhetorical studies into a vital pursuit— one that limns historically marginalized or underrepresented perspectives beyond the merely contrastive study of hemispheric traditions, cultures, and texts. In their 2015 symposium on "Manifesting a Future for Comparative Rhetoric," nine participating scholars offered the following definitions of *comparative rhetoric* and *comparative rhetorician* for our current century:

> Comparative rhetoric examines communicative practices across time and space by attending to historicity, specificity, self-reflexivity, processual predisposition, and imagination. Situated in and in response to globalization, comparative rhetoricians enact perspectives/performances that intervene in and transform dominant rhetorical traditions, perspectives, and practices.[19]

Their manifesto concludes with an admission of the wide-ranging methodologies that are now required to practice comparative rhetoric as "a navigation [both] among and beyond."[20] This way of conceptualizing comparative work—as methodological innovation—is what we hope to renew.

Global Rhetorical Traditions is predicated on the argument that translated primary sources and diverse terminologies help expand the horizon of global rhetorics and inform their critical methodologies even for non-translational work—and moreover, that "comparative" rhetorical study deserves to become a commonplace approach, even for non-comparatists. In spite of the growing scholarship in comparative rhetorical studies, there exists a scarcity of primary sources that can adequately address the needs of those who teach and study non-Western rhetorical traditions in the United States. To wit, at the 2018 and 2019 Conferences on College Composition and Communication, the consensus of the Special Interest Group formed around global and non-Western rhetorics[21] was twofold: while there is a growing body of secondary scholarship from which rhetorical scholars can draw for some traditions, there are still too few primary sources available to teach about global terminologies and traditions in languages other than English. A common refrain among participants at this conference each year has been an over-reliance on Greco-Roman terminologies as universal standards for studies of global rhetorics and communication, despite latent and recent developments of other linguistic or regional works, along with the complaint that, for most teacher-scholars engaged

---

19. Mao et al. 2015, 273.

20. Ibid., 274.

21. As of Summer 2020, this group is now the Global & Non-Western Rhetorics (GNWR) Standing Group with the Conference on College Composition and Communication.

in global rhetorical study, even authentic primary-source work remains inaccessible to them if they cannot acquire multiple languages.[22] If Anglophone teachers and students must rely heavily on secondary sources and primary texts in philosophy and literature (not rhetoric) to teach the traditions that interest them, it seems likely that this perceived scarcity will endure.

Out of both the richness of this prior scholarship and the vexation of what sources we still lack, we offer this anthology for scholarly research and reference in global and non-Western rhetorics, and also for teaching historical and methodological questions related to *the global* in composition and communication at both undergraduate and graduate levels. In doing so, we hope to equip specialists and non-specialists alike with a new rhetorical vocabulary that can help them to "talk the comparative talk" in communication with colleagues from different cultures. Our twenty-eight contributors have committed to broadening their horizons by undertaking non-Western rhetorical study in ways that foreground methodological innovation and by extending cross-cultural rhetorical inquiry into previously understudied regions and traditions, both in an effort to expand our extant rhetorical terminology and in an effort to realize more diverse rhetorical terms. The challenge to more systematically expose these available methods is what ultimately inspired this book.

Some of this work remains inaccessible for reasons not only related to scarcity or linguistic dominance. An additional barrier to making comparative rhetorical work accessible for many non-comparatists may be found in the fine lines and thin boundaries (perhaps, even, in certain misconceptions) that occur between the monikers of *comparative, cultural, postcolonial,* and *transnational* when they are used to describe rhetorical study. What differentiates their agendas from one another? When are those agendas conflated or confused?

Several chapters in this volume reflect an investment in theorizing the transnational as a critical space, and we see the transnational occupying an important part of our contributors' work, even if they do not directly take up the arguments about neoliberalism, development, citizenship, or human rights that characterize transnational rhetorical work. The linkage between comparative and transnational is prevalent when we realize that chapters dedicated to articulating more contemporary indigenous practices—such as East African and Polynesian rhetorics, for example—disrupt our assumptions about who or what needs representation at all. This linkage is productively blurred inasmuch as our contributors seek alternatives to the same Afro-Eurasian *longue durée* frame that has traditionally dominated post-, anti-, and decolonial scholarship.

Put differently, questions about what can be historicized through translation and translational politics are important for more than comparative work, yet not always central in cultural and postcolonial studies. As such, this anthology is for scholars working in explicitly non-Pan-Hellenic rhetorical traditions as well as for scholars invested in re-assembling the Pan-Hellenic through a more informed witnessing of different languages. It has emerged from

---

22. Hany Rashwan challenges this issue, especially when imposing or inviting the negative cultural attachments of the term *rhetoric* in analyzing Arabic and ancient Egyptian texts. See Rashwan (2020, 335–70).

many conversations about using translation to move comparative rhetorical studies beyond post-colonizing readings, stark polarities, and contrastive principles, toward more globalized epistemologies for the twenty-first century. Thus, the work of this collection is pan-historical at its core—not only rooted in the past, but also residing in present-day activities and events.

CHARTING RHETORICAL REGIONS

Complicating the distinction between foreign and vernacular is central to our collection, and we follow in the footsteps of other scholars who have sought similar complicating frameworks. Like the work of those prior scholars, the scholarship represented in this collection does not necessarily reject or deny Western influences on rhetorical histories or on critical perspectives; rather, it considers "the West" in its globalized and circulating notions. However, it encourages reflection on how scholars might reinvent key terms, identify critical dilemmas, and express new desires by distinguishing between "comparative," "cross-cultural," "indigenous," and "nomadic" approaches to rhetorical studies in the coming historical moment. Lipson and Binkley have called for scholars to extend their examinations of ancient rhetoric outside of the dominant Western tradition—more specifically, to analyze ancient cultural rhetorics without "reify[ing] classical rhetoric as the culmination in the development of ancient rhetorical systems,"[23] thus spotlighting other ways of being, seeing, and making knowledge through comparative rhetorical work. We agree, and ultimately we choose to understand global rhetorics as more than a combination of non-Western subject areas and more than a mode of analysis. Instead, we understand them as a frame of thought guiding our research.

The principal methodology driving this book is in the concept of *rhetorical regions*, which encompass more than language or geography or politics alone. What we present here as "regional" distinctions between chapters draws attention to how various rhetorical practices are not bound to a single nation, country, language, or culture, even if the practices are stabilized by one or more of those constraints at a time. Instead, a region's rhetoricity is demonstrated through its *utility* and *deployment*—through the conscious re/construction of how time, space, history, and memory all interact to form what we recognize as a functioning rhetorical tradition (e.g., "Arabic and Islamic," "Chinese," or "Mediterranean"). This approach is one we have not yet seen employed in prior comparative scholarship. We invite readers to recognize the shifting possibilities of various rhetorical regions by examining them through their own terms of engagement—around acts of identifying, sharing, and considering underrepresented or under-recognized terms through which to engage a historical rhetorical practice.

We believe this causes our collection to act distinctively from other intercultural works. For example, in *The Global Communication Intercultural Reader*, editors Molefi Kete Asante, Yoshitaka Miike, and Jing Yin advocate for a "distinctly non-Eurocentric approach to the study of communication and culture." They note that the intercultural communication enterprise—like most other critical enterprises—has striven for an outcome of "interpreting 'other'

---

23. Lipson and Binkley 2009, 2.

cultures in search of the most productive pathways to the consumers of those societies."[24] Communicating successfully across differences is one prerogative of what they and we understand as global communication, yet we take a markedly different approach to this task. While Asante et al. study the "links and nexuses between macro-level communication contexts and micro-level communication behaviors,"[25] we ask how scholars can locate sources of culturally specific rhetorical traditions by avoiding the representational traps that often occur when comparative associations are driven by binary logic and by acknowledging that "border-crossings of all kinds are unfolding on an unprecedented scale."[26]

Here, I draw on Jerry Won Lee's "semioscape" as an operative concept for our own work—a phenomenon that describes the reinvention of nation-ness among globally mobile communities.[27] While Lee developed this concept by examining how "Koreanness" gets built into physical environments through multiple semiotic systems (e.g., language practice, signage, and other public language artifacts), the idea of semioscapes guides our collection's methodology in three ways. First, the semioscape is more than simply a linguistic or spatial territory; it is powerful testament to the many linguistic and cultural identifications that are exercised by ethnic groups when and wherever they settle, and it extends beyond, or cuts across, purely national or political lines.[28] LuMing Mao has argued that rhetorical traditions may not be tethered to place but to semioscape; we agree, but we argue further that they are more productively bound by historicization. As Asante, et al. write,

> To claim that there is something of Tokyo in every city and something of Lagos in every city is to make a claim for international connectedness based on the exchange of ideas, thoughts, myth, and goods. We are participants in a world running full speed toward a common language transmuted, but not because it becomes a language embedded with world ideas rather than those of a single culture. . . . The global cannot mean the prosecution of a single cultural reality as if it is global. It must mean the acceptance of an integrative global system where those who communicate are able to bring into consideration the *yuan-fen* and *nkrabea* as well as Western concepts. (Asante et al., 2010, 11).

It is precisely this kind of "bringing into consideration" that we see the scholars in this volume striving to accomplish.

Second, the semioscape implies movement, migration, and flow.[29] The nuanced frame of thought guiding the research in this collection is intended to give readers a taste of global rhe-

24. Asante, et al. 2014, 1–2.

25. Ibid., 2.

26. Mao and Wang 2015, 240.

27. Lee 2017, 111.

28. Ibid., 109–10.

29. Ibid., 109.

torical theories and vocabularies, encouraging them to recover even more traditions on their own. At the same time, this collection complicates existing notions of comparative rhetorics by treating "global" as a critical lens, "bring[ing] the game on" as the editors of the 2015 *Rhetoric Review* comparative symposium have invited us to do.[30] Global rhetorical cultures emerge when we focus, as Lyon and Mao argue, "on the politics of representation through the art of recontextualization and methods of developing the rhetorical vocabularies of specific culture in their own discursive fields."[31] While they (and others) have been motivated by a desire to "avoid simple or narrow appropriation [of culture] and begin to represent . . . culture on its own terms," we also want to trouble simple acts of naming and appropriating rhetorical heritages. In this collection we accept their challenge to build on the already excellent work of looking beyond or differently at non/Western rhetorics. We accept their challenge to consider alternative sources of what we are calling the "traditions" underlying common regional distinctions between various language groups.

Finally, and most significantly for our project, the semioscape accounts for diasporic rhetorical traditions,[32] highlighting that a rhetorical region is best recognized in the constellation of moments showing how its particular traditions have spread, rooted, and grown.[33] Thus, we settled for naming rhetorical regions in this book according to various semioscapes as they have emerged through *historical practice*: Arabic and Islamic, Chinese, East African, Indian and Nepali, Indonesian, Irish, Mediterranean, Polynesian/Hawaiian, Russian, and Turkish. These semioscapes, or rhetorical regions, reflect what LuMing Mao and Bo Wang call the "coevalness" of "the indigenous and the exogenous, the past and the present, and the local and the global."[34]

We hope that the regional organization of this collection can enable classical and non-classical scholars alike to rediscover what is inherently foreign about any of the traditions they study. We also hope the regional nature of this collection makes visible when and where English-speaking scholars can intervene in traditions not their own. In our collaborations with the contributors in the following pages, we have seen their work reflect several goals from Lyon's and Mao's explicit call for the field to "develop the rhetorical vocabularies of specific cultures in their own discursive fields so that we can avoid simple or narrow appropriation and begin to represent the culture in its own terms."[35] We have seen them illuminate how tra-

---

30. Mao and Wang 2015, 239.

31. This is drawn from Arabella Lyon's and LuMing Mao's "The Rest of the World" syllabus, which guided a comparative rhetoric workshop at the Rhetoric Society of America Institute in 2017. Our collection follows on the heels of this syllabus, along with excellent primary scholarship in selected traditions.

32. Lee 2017, 111.

33. Here, "region" may trouble historians' labeling of some traditions as "sovereign" or "indigenous," when those traditions are more accurately understood as diasporic or nomadic.

34. Mao and Wang 2015, 241.

35. This is drawn from Arabella Lyon's and LuMing Mao's "The Rest of the World" syllabus, which guided a comparative rhetoric workshop at the Rhetoric Society of America Institute in 2017. Our

ditions both "constitute and are constituted by their rhetorical heritage," investigate how to "approach rhetoric through its culture, using the words and practices within the culture," and raise the difficult question of how to "include non-Western traditions of political discourses in rhetorical education without making them an extension of what we already know." Bringing to the forefront of our research the intersecting knowledges of "these other (constructed) rhetorical traditions and our own (otherwise hidden) limitations"[36] is both a principal goal and a principal limitation of this anthology. In other words, we do not try to achieve full coverage, in any sense, of all global rhetorical traditions; we merely pinpoint a few new spaces in which to intervene.

FROM SCARCITY, INNOVATION

The regional nature of this volume intentionally deviates from other geographical and temporal[37] frameworks, such as those that trace practices derived within major language families (e.g., Indo-European, Afro-Asiatic, and Sino-Tibetan) or by epistemological histories (e.g., Middle East, Egypt, Indus Valley, China, Mesoamerica, Andean civilizations). The latter reflects Lipson and Binkley's approach in *Rhetoric Before and Beyond the Greeks*, as a way of texturizing how rhetorical societies with a clear hierarchical state organization left behind clues of new forms of culture ("civilizations"). While we admire this approach, it is our desire to join Mao and Wang (and others) in achieving a more "dialogic" process for comparative work;[38] to join C. Jan Swearingen in searching for "interdependence and heterogeneous resonance;"[39] and to join Susan Romano in achieving a more "nuanced comparison analyzing the dynamic relations between and among lived experience, ethics, and rhetoric."[40] To accommodate these desires, we have featured traditions that scholars inform us have had insufficient

---

collection follows on the heels of this syllabus, along with excellent primary scholarship in selected traditions. For example, Lahcen Ezzaher's translation of *Three Arabic Treatises on Aristotle's* Rhetoric (2015) offers a concrete demonstration of the idea that Aristotle's *Rhetoric* has in some ways always already functioned as a multinational text, contrary to narratives about its historical reappearance in Renaissance discussions of authorship or later. As well, Hui Wu and C. Jan Swearingen have offered a new translated critical edition of the work of *Guiguzi* (2016), Chinese author of the culture's first treatise in rhetoric, as a way of inciting dialogue about the origins of particular stylistic practices.

36. Mao and Wang 2015, 240.

37. Because most early treatises and sources lack the precise date(s) they were compiled or came into being, lifecycles of historically recognized authors in certain cultures supersede the importance of dates. Where possible, we include both Gregorian and non-Western calendars and temporal notations so as to encompass paradigms alongside one another. Where that is not possible, we attempt to date the treatise author's career or identify the time frame most often associated with the global recirculation of the treatise in question.

38. Mao and Wang 2015, 241.

39. Swearingen 2015, 252.

40. Romano 2015, 256.

primary treatment in their own right, sometimes in spite of sufficient secondary scholarship. Many chapters attend uniquely to text technologies or manuscript traditions, considering how those technologies bear on the oral, literate, and social spaces of their traditions. Additionally, many chapters are made coherent by a critical through-line in problems of framing or inter-sections—for example, in questions of how best to reframe or unframe their legacies, and how best to determine stabilities or origins to look between.

At the same time, our selection of regions acts as an admission of the uneven representation of translated primary-source work *in rhetorical studies*—studies whose methods primarily deal with the teaching or theorizing of rhetorical roles, practices, education, or literacies. In this work, some regions are much less well represented than others in terms of available sources. We are the first to admit that the rhetorical regions are not in themselves complete, and we hope this collection provides a snapshot representation of that un/availability as a siren's call for the work yet to be done. For example, our collection lacks a chapter on sources for Syriac rhetorical traditions, in spite of their centrality to both Arabic and Greek traditions, or a chapter that distinguishes Egyptian from Arabic traditions, or a chapter on sources for Jewish rhetorical traditions, in spite of vital distinctions between Jewish and Judeo-Christian scholarship. In addition, our collection lacks adequate representation of African rhetorical traditions writ-large, owing to Africa's complex demographics and distribution of seven so-called "major" language families and over twenty-five "official" languages, not to mention hundreds of ethnic languages and dialectical families, and over 150 cultural groups active across fifty-four bordered nations.[41]

Indeed, the list of exclusions could continue, and many chapters have only one or two treatises on which to build or demonstrate their methodological insights, in part a circumstance of our attempting this work in a slimmer anthology than a textbook. As a result, this is not a collection that accounts comprehensively for global or world rhetorics. This *is* a collection that reflects the critical possibilities of translation, highlights internal debates between and within traditions and, where possible, offers alternatives to the competing fundamentalisms that typically accompany translational work. In other words, we are not aiming for, nor have we ever aimed for, canonical girth in demonstrating these regions. Instead, in the spirit of Bizzell and Herzberg we offer selective methodological moments—exemplary demonstrations of the possible ways to reread, recover, and re-translate alternative sources for rhetorical traditions.

Of course, any region is contestable.[42] The rhetorical regions that organize this collection are at best placeholders for our contributors' work. Who decides the region, at what point, and in what temporality? How does the region convey or not convey communicative power? And how does the region emerge from the interstices between precolonial, postcolonial, and deco-

---

41. While "Africa" cannot be represented in any sense as a singular entity, we regret that this volume does not offer more insight into regional practices beyond the excellent work on Nilotic contained herein. However, readers will want to consult Ige, et al., eds (2022) for a comprehensive introduction to the scope of both primary and secondary scholarship in African rhetorical traditions, including its theoretical origins, practices, languages, and literatures.

42. Lloyd 2020.

lonial frameworks? We address these complicated questions by introducing our contributors' translations through both chronology and geography, though we do so with an understanding that the prolific recirculation of their primary source texts has made it difficult to stabilize the precise time and place of their initial publication with any certainty. Ultimately, each region is derived from the challenge of naming a tradition or fitting a culture within a particular argumentative label—from the tensions between analyzing them and placing them.

Practically speaking, each region constitutes a single chapter in this volume, and includes a prefatory introduction, translated primary sources, critical notes on both past and present scholarly commentary, a comprehensive bibliography,[43] and a glossary of rhetorical terms.[44] We have arranged them alphabetically rather than geographically, first, to avoid the implication that each tradition only ever occurred or only does occur in a particular geospace; and second, to convey an encyclopedic expectation of this volume and of the volumes we hope will soon follow. Within each chapter, readers may notice some variations among how contributors treat diacritical markings, transliterations, and titles of holy texts. Our decision to encourage these variations stems from our commitment to value the different translational approaches required by each primary text. Moreover, these variations point to rich pluralisms in how the traditions are studied, conveyed, and understood; rather than flatten the nuances, we invited contributors to heighten them. We hope readers will use them to better understand the linguistic, cultural, and historiographic richness of the traditions they study.

GLOBAL RHETORICAL TRADITIONS IN BRIEF

Without making claims to uniformity across traditions or practices, the alphabetic and encyclopedic organization of this collection helps establish a basis for more modern rhetorical study, given that many of the treatises and practices illuminated here are translated into English for the first time. The opening chapter on Arabic and Islamic rhetorics emphasizes the evolution of these practices through, and even beyond, the Medieval vehicles of transmission, interpretation, and recirculation. It features contributions under three sections helping to delineate Arabic and Islamic rhetorics according to chronology and genre, texturizing what Bernard

---

43. Comprehensive bibliographies at the end of each chapter mostly reflect the contents therein. However, in some cases, contributors provided additional references that they felt could round out readers' investigation of the methodological moments they discuss. We trust that our readers will find these bibliographies to be indispensable resources for both teaching and learning, and we are grateful to all our contributors for their work in this regard.

44. By nature, glossaries tend to stabilize language, yet the decision to include glossaries in this volume was motivated by our desire to show the pluralities inherent in each tradition. This reflects one way of speaking back to the flattening that occurs when linguistic and rhetorical traditions are aligned with overly simplistic or fundamentalist ideals about how a tradition *should work*. In the chapters with multiple contributors, when there have been duplicated glossary entries with differing definitions, we have asked contributors to contextualize their definitions carefully enough that readers might appreciate and honor the differences.

Lewis[45] and Brandon Katzir[46] understand as the "Arabization" and "Islamization" of translations. The chapter's contributors—Tarez Graban, Lana Oweidat, Lahcen Ezzaher, Maha Baddar, Robert Eddy, Raed Alsawaier, and Rasha Diab—consider the actual and potential influences of Qur'anic instruction on the development of rhetorical actions, and reflects the vast reach of both Arabic and Islamic worlds.[47] Contributors argue that observing how to derive a rhetorical history from in-depth examinations of Qur'anic scholars illuminates the Arabic linguistic tradition extant before the reception of Aristotle's treatises via Syriac influences. With a lexicon centered on *rhetorikha* (persuasive logic), *senaha* (art), *assabieh* (solidarity), *tabligh* (propagation), *quias* (syllogisms), and *dunn* (commonplaces), we see a philosophical tradition forming in geospatial contexts other than Greco-Roman.

The chapter on Chinese rhetorics highlights the culture's long history through transmission and recirculation of masters and texts, from *Analects* to *Wen Ze*, with an emphasis on the complexities of authorship and some insight into the mis/representation of women in this lineage. Notably, the chapter features contributions in four sections helping to delineate Chinese rhetorics according to their principal dynasties or periods—the Classical or Warring States Period; the Han Dynasty, Six Dynasties or Early Medieval Period, and Tang Dynasty; the Song Dynasty, Yuan Dynasty, and Ming Dynasty; and the Modern Period. In so doing, Hui Wu, Haixia Lan, and Andrew Kirkpatrick reveal how various epistolary and argumentative traditions from the Medieval periods to the twentieth century may be indebted to—or have developed in tandem with—Confucian and Daoist practices of transcription, interpretation, and social systematization. In all these things, language becomes a way of moving closer to attaining the Dao, while translation becomes a mechanism by which the masters of one dynasty accessed or intervened in the texts of another.

In both singular and plural forms, "African" rhetorical traditions remain a conundrum.[48] In response, the chapter on East African rhetorics provokes key critical differences in understanding African rhetorics as rhetorics of community, resistance, and reaffirmation.[49] More

---

45. Lewis 1995.

46. Katzir 2018, 28–48.

47. Mowlana 2014, 238. Mowlana indicates that this geopolitical area stretches from Indonesia and the Pacific Ocean in the east to Morocco and the Atlantic coast in the west, from central Asia and the Himalayas in the north to the southern African nations and the Indian Ocean.

48. For example, some African scholars claim African rhetorics emerge only through a return to Yoruba cultural thought, while others claim that rhetorics emerge out of young democracies and out of a culture's coming to terms with those democracies over time. When argued historically and terministically, these regions challenge our assumptions about pre- and postcolonialized discourse, because much of their retrospective beauty has grown from intellectual hybrids, making it difficult to know what was "pre" and "post" the "colonial" influence, especially in countries or nations where the pluralisms are prevalent and hybrid at any historical moment. See Ige, et al., eds. (2022) for further complications of African rhetorical traditions.

49. See Dadugblor (2020, 255). See also Omedi Ochieng's blog post, "What Is African Rhetoric?" on the Association for African Rhetoric website (www.afrhet.org/post/what-is-african-rhetoric), in which

specifically, in this chapter Leonora Anyango engages with African oral literature as a way of confronting both absences and presences in available histories of African communication practices as they advance pre-, post-, and decolonial perspectives.[50] To demonstrate how East African writers have "sought to harmonize their world of writing without leaving their oral culture behind," the chapter highlights the Luo and Acholi, two Nilotic communities whose rhetorical legacy reveals an inherent complexity of African translation: the idea that writing in English may not diminish the richly indigenous oratorical practices that are transmitted through proverbs, idioms, and songs, but better amplify the political tensions within them. By recapturing the Nilotic writer as simultaneously "entertainer, historian, and orator," this chapter neither overlooks nor excuses the historic sense of privilege that comes with inscribing African stories into English. Rather, it draws our attention to a long tradition of "transacting"—transforming oral performances into text domains, showing how criticism and creativity are meaningfully combined. Offering a perspective on sources of African rhetorical traditions that operate somewhat distinctly from African-American critical theories of race, this chapter also presents alternative ways of thinking about colonial rhetorical hybrids and presents alternatives to Maulana Karenga's[51] and Molefi Kete Asante's[52] signature work on Kemet as an originary construct.[53]

The chapter on Indian and Nepali rhetorics reflects a shared interest in Sanskrit and Hindu texts and follows the progress of etymological study done by key scholars in the field. Indeed, the contributions in this chapter reveal as much about preservation and circulation as they do about invention. More specifically, the chapter features contributions under three sections that delineate Indian and Nepali rhetorics according to their relations to sacred and secular practices, as well as their emergence from Christian, Vedic, and Colonial encounters: Indian-Poetic, Indian-Logical, and Hindu. Through this tripartite organization, Indian and Nepali rhetorics can be understood as both a presumed and an actual rhetorical culture they

---

he accounts for the indeterminacy of the tradition as a result of its multiplicity, polyvocality, and intertextuality, and of AAR's attention to all of Africa's various rhetorical traditions.

50. Karenga 2014, 213–14. See also the contemporary critical scholarship in *African Journal of Rhetoric*, especially volume 10, whose emphasis on "Media, Rhetoric, and Development in Africa" draws simultaneously on pre-, post-, and decolonial readings of critical texts, reflecting not only how the classical and the decolonial co-reside as intellectual influences, but also how the intellectual and the political co-reside as textual influences.

51. Karenga 2014.

52. Asante 2015.

53. To be clear, both Asante's exploration of the Kemet as antecedent to rhetoric in antiquity and Kanga's work to recover *nommo* are essential to the conscious formation of the plurality of African rhetorics. Inasmuch as Kanga argues for the unnecessary (Western) conflation of Aristotle's notion of *techne* with scientific technique, or instrument for routine manipulation, rather than a more deliberative and localized practice (Karenga 2014, 218). Karenga argues that there has been a tendency in the US to theorize, practice, and preach a "degenerative" rhetoric more like political oratory most likely because of modern interpretations of what it means to attain persuasion by any and all available means (219).

have helped to promote. All the chapter's contributors—Uma Krishnan, Anne Melfi, Shreelina Ghosh, Keith Lloyd, Shuv Raj Rana Bhat, Trey Conner and Richard Doyle—would agree that, while etymologies are important for studying Hindu and Indian traditions, so too are questions of agency and access. Thus, the entries in this chapter take up different orientations to pedagogy by reclaiming the sacred as a site for inquiry. From hymns to dance to poetry to song, this chapter effectively conveys rhetorical knowledge-making as a multimodal and ambient experience.

The chapter on Indonesian rhetorics is based on a collection of underexamined and underserved national and post-national texts, defined by scholars as having emerged from the fusion of comparative and postcolonial critiques since the 1980s. An examination of these and others is important for theorizing the complex "voice" of Indonesia's rhetorical identification.[54] Characteristics of such a recent rhetorical tradition are based on a historic demonstration of Megawati Sukarnoputri's presidential speeches as agents of circulation, due to their negotiation of national and cross-national contexts. According to Gregory Coles, since Megawati is the chair of the political party under whose banner Jokowi ran for the presidency, she occupies a uniquely authoritative stance within this large gathering of influential Indonesian politicians. Furthermore, although the speech is not unique among Megawati's speeches in its style or content, it includes telling examples of Megawati's most important rhetorical strategies, including her navigation of gender and religious tensions, and her invocations of her father Sukarno, Indonesia's first president. Finally, the speech's availability online (albeit in untranslated form) makes it possible for readers to witness Megawati's speech for themselves, giving scholars access not only to her words but also to her tone, gesture, and physical appearance as matters of rhetorical interest.

In the chapter on Irish rhetorics, Brian J. Stone emphasizes the ways in which medieval Irish-Gaelic texts could be understood as markedly non-Western.[55] Both "The Cauldron of Poesy" and the Hiberno-Latin grammar text serve minority perspectives on Celtic grammars and native learning, demonstrating one theoretical and historical possibility behind the adage that the Irish were not always "white." While Hiberno-Latin grammatical handbooks are of interest for a student of Irish rhetoric, the metaphors, imagery, and concepts revealed in this poetic text provide a view of an oral, vernacular rhetorical tradition at the very least distinct from, if not opposed to those of the western, Christian church. The "Cauldron of Learning" is an example of a local reflection"[56] of a western rhetorical tradition preserving native learning traditions within budding monastic communities in early medieval Ireland, and that "prompt us to consider how European scholars transferred and adapted ideas and concepts from the

---

54. Engelson 2020, 195–205.

55. Richard Johnson-Sheehan also promotes the study of ancient Irish rhetorics as a window into how some European rhetorics did and could differ from inherited Greco-Roman rhetorical traditions. See Johnson-Sheehan (2009, 268).

56. Corthals 2013, 85.

authoritative tradition of classical Greece and Rome to suit the pedagogical and ideological needs of their own languages and cultures."[57]

The chapter on Mediterranean rhetorics combines two traditions that have typically been understood as disparate, arguing that our field reconsider the umbrella term "Western rhetorical tradition" with more precise cultural and geographic discussions of cultural and regional designations, especially in regard to Mediterranean traditions.[58] While this is an unusual combination, it better serves this volume's attempts to illuminate the cross-currents that move between and among various linguistic and rhetorical traditions. It may also remind us that Byzantine and Judeo rhetorical traditions have been historicized as both "Eastern" and "Western," and at the same time neither one nor the other exclusively. Ellen Quandahl's and Jeffrey Walker's contributions on the Byzantine tradition primarily emphasize how Byzantinists and classicists work in tandem to expose complications in the eastern/western divide, while Jim Ridolfo's contribution on the Hebraic Mediterranean has historic and geographic significance beyond the outer reaches of the Fertile Crescent. As a result, the chapter focuses its work on three long contributions, in which we see demonstrated the performative and ekphrastic aspects of a rhetorical education that would influence mimetic and iconographic study for several centuries in both hemispheres of the charted world, as well as in historians' memories and understanding of the Mediterranean. In traditions that have been so long reliant on verbal mimesis, it becomes important to observe the stylistic revivals that occurred at various political moments. In Byzantium, these stylistic politics inform historical assumptions about audience and reveal key representational difficulties that historiographers worked through in the eleventh, twelfth, and fifteenth centuries respectively. In the Jewish and Hebraic diaspora, these stylistic politics reveal the unique challenges in transmission and remediation of holy texts, owing in part to a long, complex and shifting dynastic tradition. Aided by Steven B. Katz's critical prefatory introduction, the chapter helps align the differences between *Halaha'* and Talmudic law with the stases of definition and conjecture, demonstrating the value of rhetorical intelligence in working with an interpretive practice that lacks a written corpus, as does *Halaha'*.

Our chapter on Polynesian-Hawaiian rhetorics presents them as new-world and non-European practices, that can inform the application of indigenous and authentic methodologies even in twentieth- and twenty-first-century texts, where new expressions of indigeneity can still be realized. This chapter achieves what Aluli-Meyer calls a demonstration of "old *and* new, cycled *and* creative, ancient *and* developed-this-moment."[59] In a rhetorical culture where

---

57. Hayden and Russell 2016, 2.

58. We feature both Byzantine and Jewish and Hebraic in this chapter because it complicates the non/Western binary in more than one sense. In many ways, Byzantine hybridity helps to characterize the complexities of translation work, while Jewish and Hebraic texts "historically, socially, culturally, philologically, [and] philosophically" transcend geographical time and space (cf. Katz's prefatory introduction in this volume), and yet both of these qualities help to illuminate "Mediterranean" as a site for investigative work.

59. Aluli-Meyer 2014, 134.

"[g]enuine knowledge must be experienced directly,"[60] Hawaiian "holographic" epistemology—a way of knowing that challenges the dominant research worldview based on the Newtonian notion of space—is constructed through the triangulation of body, mind, and spirit, "extend[ing] through our objective/empirical knowing (body) into wider spaces of reflection offered through conscious subjectivity (mind) and, finally, via recognition and engagement with deeper realities (spirit)."[61] In their examination of rhetorical strategies of the Kanaka Naoli (or Native Hawaiians), Nordstrom and ho'omanawanui offer insight into how physical, spatial, cultural, and sensual categories of knowing all help to organize authentically Hawaiian "systems of consciousness."[62] Ultimately, they reveal the rhetorical importance of Native Hawaiian texts as ones that resist contemporary notions of agency built on Cartesian separation of body and mind, self and culture, stomach and brain, feeling and thinking, knowing and cognition, intention and reality.

In the penultimate chapter, Maria Prikhodko introduces a homiletic style, the "eloquent" tradition of Russia's Kievan Rus', made popular between the ninth and the thirteenth centuries, in a linguistic and cultural moment when there were no accurate equivalences to the term "rhetoric." As a result, the latent references for this tradition—euphemism, conferring, cunning/clever grappling of words, and encompassing—instead offered guidance for rhetorical agents to morally grow, given their closely circumscribed relationship to sacred texts. In arguing for Kievan Rus's historic influence on Russian literacy practices, Prikhodko argues that the tradition might inform more contemporary rhetorical pedagogies of difference. Through the idea of "super-addresses," or metaphorical ways of preaching and educating about moral standards and ethics of communication, this chapter portrays Russian rhetorics as a metacritical practice that was traditionally opposed to the revived Greco-Roman ideals of the Middle Ages.

Our final chapter on Turkish rhetorics emphasizes how this tradition reflects the challenges of recovering the practices of non-Western cultures. While Turkic refers primarily to the pre-Islamic period (4000 BCE to 11th CE), and Turkish to more contemporary traditions in and beyond the twelfth century, Elif Guler argues that differentiating the traditions in this way is less important than recognizing how they frustrate binary distinctions between oral and written, ceremony and politics, and Orkhon and Runic. In defining commonplaces of the traditions that she studies, Guler explores themes of responsibility, interconnectedness, humility, and balance, asking us to consider whether Turkic ceremonial speeches could enlarge historians' understanding of other non-Western community formations. Moreover, through translation she reveals the ways in which the syllabic and stress-timed nature of Turkish makes it both more and less compatible with the many other linguistic traditions through which it was delivered.

---

60. Ibid., 142.
61. Ibid., 134, 142.
62. Ibid., 135.

In witnessing the circulations and uptakes of different languages, we resist reproducing the essentializing moves of other comparative or contrastive projects and believe this project, and comparative scholarship will retain its epistemic value—will endure. Such an anthology cannot be complete, but it can resist reductive or flattening notions of regionalism, and it should promote critical historiography even as it enables historical recovery. If we have done our work well as contributors, then our ability to illuminate global rhetorical traditions is neither dependent on English as a single mode of deportment, nor tied to arguments about rhetorical sovereignty. We hope this anthology equips scholars to recognize what Mary Louise Pratt might call various "translinguistic battlefields" and "hemispheric inter-imperial experiences"[63] that become flattened or made opaque when the politics of a particular language, including its administration and its subjectification, cannot be accessed by its historians.

"Bringing the Game On": Responding to Cultural Moments

It is worth mentioning that, while these sources are timeless, our contributors were responding to specific cultural moments. For the editors and contributors of this volume, *Global Rhetorical Traditions* engages directly with critiques on comparative rhetoric and engages critically with disciplinary activism. While most chapters do not explicitly take up dialogues about race, they embody an unmistakably and enduring antiracist ideology by privileging diverse rhetorics on their own merit. And while the length of time it takes to produce and enact translations outlives most disciplinary conversations and social trends, much of the work in this particular volume was borne from actual need—from scholarly and lived situations marked by intolerances and fundamentalisms, at home and abroad. This became evident during the earliest responses to our call for papers, when we saw in contributors' responses that their colleagues in comparative literature, classics, and religion held a greater ideological tolerance for cultural and linguistic variation than did colleagues in their closer disciplines of rhetoric, literacy, composition, or communication studies. Thus, alongside Pratt's framework—and alongside Mao's, Lyon's, and Lee's agendas—this anthology is poised to offer rhetoric and communication scholars a fresh examination of the discipline.

Ultimately, the linkage between comparative scholarship and disciplinarity becomes evident in the many aims out of which this collection has emerged: there is our aim to include "non-Western traditions of political discourses in rhetorical education without making them an extension of what we already know," as Lyon and Mao articulated in their 2017 Rhetoric Society of America workshop; there is our aim to represent the other without diminishing the otherness or necessarily making that representation "mirror" the West (or the dominant culture); there is our aim to consider the "politics of representation and the ethics of methodology in articulating other traditions especially when we lack the appropriate vocabularies and terms of engagement and when power asymmetry is being most acutely felt"; and there is

---

63. Pratt 2015, 350.

our desire to grapple with the realities of shifting rhetorical geospaces.[64] As one contributor, Robert Eddy, might say, this volume "looks toward openness to and tolerance of unassimilated otherness." We trust this is the beginning of many more such works.

REFERENCES

Aluli-Meyer, Manulani. 2014. "Indigenous and Authentic: Hawaiian Epistemology and the Triangulation of Meaning." In *The Global Intercultural Communication Reader*, edited by Molefi Kete Asante, Yoshitaka Miike, and Jing Yin, 2nd ed., 134–50. New York: Routledge.

Asante, Molefi Kete. 2015. *African Pyramids of Knowledge: Kemet, Afrocentricity and Africology*. Brooklyn: Universal Write Publications LLC.

Asante, Molefi Kete, Yoshitaka Miike, and Jing Yin. 2014. "Introduction: New Directions for Intercultural Communication Research." In *The Global Intercultural Communication Reader*, edited by Molefi Kete Asante, Yoshitaka Miike, and Jing Yin, 2nd ed., 1–14. New York: Routledge.

Baca, Damián, and Victor Villanueva, eds. 2010. *Rhetorics of the Americas*. New York: Palgrave MacMillan.

Baddar, Maha. 2015. "Toward a New Understanding of Audience in the Medieval Arabic Translation Movement: The Case of Al-Kindi's 'Statement of the Soul.'" In *Rhetoric Across Borders*, edited by Anne Teresa Demo, 59–70. Anderson, SC: Parlor Press.

Borrowman, Shane. 2010. "Recovering the Arabic Aristotle: Ibn Sina and Ibn Rushd on the Logic of Civic and Poetic Discourse." In *Rhetoric in the Rest of the West*, edited by Shane Borrowman, Robert L. Lively, and Marcia Kmetz, 97–118. Newcastle, UK: Cambridge Scholars.

Borrowman, Shane, Robert L. Lively, and Marcia Kmetz, eds. 2010. *Rhetoric in the Rest of the West*. Newcastle, UK: Cambridge Scholars.

Campbell, Kermit E. 2006. "Rhetoric from the Ruins of African Antiquity." *Rhetorica* 24 (3): 255–74.

Clackson, James. 2012. "Language Maintenance and Language Shift in the Mediterranean World during the Roman Empire." In *Multilingualism in the Graeco-Roman Worlds*, edited by Alex Mullen and Patrick James, 36–57. London: Cambridge University Press,.

Dadugblor, Stephen Kwame. 2020. "Usable Presents: Hybridity in/for Postcolonial African Rhetorics." In *The Routledge Handbook of Comparative World Rhetorics*, edited by Keith Lloyd, 250–58. New York: Routledge.

Engleson, Amber. 2020. "'I Have No Mother Tongue': (Re)Conceptualizing Rhetorical Voice in Indonesia." In *The Routledge Handbook of Comparative World Rhetorics*, edited by Keith Lloyd, 195–205. New York: Routledge.

---

64. Wu 2002, 81–98.

Enos, Richard Leo. 2008. *Roman Rhetoric: Revolution and the Greek Influence.* Anderson, SC: Parlor Press.

Ezzaher, Lahcen. 2015. *Three Arabic Treatises on Aristotle's Rhetoric.* Carbondale, IL: Southern Illinois University Press.

Fishman, Joshua A. 1964. "Language Maintenance and Language Shift as a Field of Inquiry." *Linguistics: An Interdisciplinary Journal of the Language Sciences* 2 (9): 32–70. doi. org/10.1515/ling.1964.2.9.32.

—. 1972. "Domains and the Relationship between Micro-and Macrosociolinguistics." In *Directions in Sociolinguistics: The Ethnography of Speaking*, edited by J. Gumperz and D. Hymes, 407–34. New York: Holt, Rinehart and Winston.

Galvany, Albert. 2012. "Sly Mouths and Silver Tongues: The Dynamics of Psychological Persuasion in Ancient China." *Extrême-Orient Extrême-Occident* 34 (1): 15–40.

Garrett, Mary. 2013. "Tied to a Tree: Culture and Self-Reflexivity." *Rhetoric Society Quarterly* 43 (3): 243–55.

Hayden, Deborah, and Paul Russell eds. 2016. *Grammatica, Grammadach and Gramadeg: Vernacular Grammar and Grammarians in Medieval Ireland and Wales.* Amsterdam Studies in the Theory and History of Linguistic Science.

Hesford, Wendy S., and Eileen E. Schell. 2008. "Configurations of Transnationality: Locating Feminist Rhetorics." *College English* 70 (5): 461–70.

Ige, Segun, Gilbert Motsaathebe, and Omedi Ochieng, eds. 2022. *A Companion to African Rhetorics.* Lanham, MD: Lexington/Rowman & Littlefield.

Jain, Nemi C., and Anuradha Matukumalli. 2014. "The Function of Silence in India: Implications for Intercultural Communication Research." In *The Global Intercultural Communication Reader,* edited by Molefi Kete Asante, Yoshitaka Miike, and Jing Yin, 2nd ed. 248–54. New York: Routledge.

Jarratt, Susan C. 2004. "Beside Ourselves: Rhetoric and Representation in Postcolonial Feminist Writing." In *Crossing Borderlands: Composition and Postcolonial Studies*, edited by Andrea A. Lunsford and Lahoucine Ouzgane, 110–28. Pittsburgh, PA: University of Pittsburgh Press.

Johnson-Sheehan, Richard. 2009. "Orality, Magic, and Myth in Ancient Irish Rhetorics." In *Ancient Non-Greek Rhetorics*, edited by Carol S. Lipson and Roberta Binkley, 267–92. West Lafayette, IN: Parlor Press.

Karenga, Maulana. 2014. "*Nommo, Kawaida,* and Communicative Practice: Bringing Good into the World." In *The Global Intercultural Communication Reader,* edited by Molefi Kete Asante, Yoshitaka Miike, and Jing Yin, 2nd ed. 211–25. New York: Routledge.

Katzir, Brandon. 2018. "Paths of Virtue: Legal Rhetorics in Judaism and Islam." *Rhetoric Society Quarterly* 48 (1): 28–48.

Kennedy, George. 1998. *Comparative Rhetoric: An Historical and Cross-Cultural Introduction.* New York: Oxford University Press.

Lee, Jerry Won. 2017. "Semioscapes, Unbanality, and the Reinvention of Nationnes: Global Korea as Nation-Space." *Verge: Studies in Global Asias* 3 (1): 107–36.

Lewis, Bernard. 1995. *The Middle East: A Brief History of the Last 2,000 Years.* New York: Touchstone.

Lipson, Carol S., and Roberta A. Binkley, eds. 2004. *Rhetoric Before and Beyond the Greeks.* New York: SUNY Press.

—, eds. 2009. *Ancient Non-Greek Rhetorics.* West Lafayette, IN: Parlor Press.

Liu, Lydia H. 2015. Scripts in Motion: Writing as Imperial Technology, Past and Present." *PMLA* 130 (2): 375–83.

Lloyd, Keith, ed. 2020. *The Routledge Handbook of Comparative World Rhetorics.* New York: Routledge.

Lyon, Arabella. 2009. "'Why Do the Rulers Listen to the Wild Theories of Speech-Makers?': Or *Wuwei* (non-action), *Shi* (position/power) and Methods of Comparative Rhetoric." In *Ancient Non-Greek Rhetorics*, edited by Carol Lipson and Roberta Binkley, 176–96. West Lafayette, IN: Parlor Press.

Mao, LuMing. 2003. "Reflective Encounters: Illustrating Comparative Rhetoric." *Style* 37 (4): 401–24.

Mao, LuMing, Bo Wang, Arabella Lyon, Susan C. Jarratt, C. Jan Swearingen, Susan Romano, Peter Simonson, Steven Mailloux, and Xing Lu. 2015. "Symposium: Manifesting a Future for Comparative Rhetoric." *Rhetoric Review* 34 (3): 239–74.

Mowlana, Hamid. 2014. "Communication and Cultural Settings: An Islamic Perspective." In *The Global Intercultural Communication Reader,* edited by Molefi Kete Asante, Yoshitaka Miike, and Jing Yin, 2nd ed. 237–47. New York: Routledge.

Ochieng, Omedi. 2010. "The Ideology of African Philosophy: The Silences and Possibilities of African Rhetorical Knowledge." In *Silence and Listening as Rhetorical Arts*, edited by Cheryl Glenn and Krista Ratcliffe, 147–62. Carbondale, IL: Southern Illinois University Press.

O'Malley, John W. 2013. "'Not For Ourselves Alone': Rhetorical Education in the Jesuit Mode with Five Bullet Points for Today." *Conversations on Jesuit Higher Education* 43 (4) : 1–5.

Perelman, Chaim, and Lucie Olbrechts-Tyteca. 1971. *The New Rhetoric: A Treatise on Argumentation.* Notre Dame, IN: University of Notre Dame Press.

Pratt, Mary Louise. 2015. "Languages and the Afterlives of Empire." *PMLA* 130 (2): 348–57.

Rashwan, Hany. 2020. "Arabic Jinas Is Not Pun, Wortspiel, Calembour, or Pranomasia: A Post-Eurocentric Comparative Approach to the Conceptual Untranslatability of Literary Terms in Arabic and Ancient Egyptian Cultures." *Rhetorica: A Journal of the History of Rhetoric* 38 (4): 335–70.

Schmidt-Rohr, Georg. 1933. *Mutter Sprache – Vom Amt der Sprache bei der Volkwerdung.* Jena: Eugen Diederichs.

Wu, Hui. 2002. "Historical Studies of Rhetorical Women Here and There: Methodological Challenges to Dominant Interpretive Frameworks." *Rhetoric Society Quarterly* 32 (1): 81–98.

Wu, Hui, and C. Jan Swearingen. 2016. *Guiguzi, China's First Treatise on Rhetoric: A Critical Translation and Commentary*. Carbondale, IL: Southern Illinois University Press.

Zondi, Siphamandla. 2014. "The Rhetoric of *Ubuntu*: Diplomacy and Implications for Making the World Safe for Diversity." *African Journal of Rhetoric* 16 (1): 103–42.

GLOBAL RHETORICAL TRADITIONS

1 Arabic and Islamic Rhetorics

Prefatory Introduction

Tarez Samra Graban

In his concise overview of "Arabic Rhetoric" in the *Encyclopedia of Rhetoric*, Muhsin al-Musawi constructs a terministic understanding of the tradition, using *balāghah* to roughly connote the suite of practices that include rhetoric, eloquence, and the purity and perfection of language (*faṣāḥah*).[1] This same focus is reinforced in Basil Hatim's landmark text, *Arabic Rhetoric*, through his use of *balagha* as a convenient label when deciding upon a single discipline that can subsume three Arabic rhetorical sciences: *'ilmu alma'anee* (science of meaning, esp. focusing on word order), *'ilmu albayan* (science of eloquence, esp. focusing on allegorical and non-allegorical figures of speech) and *'ilmu albadee'* (science of embellishment, especially focusing on teaching language users how to bestow particular elements onto their speech activity).[2] Moreover, al-Musawi historicizes Arabic rhetoric in both its pre-Islamic and Islamic usages as a practice concerned with "inclusiveness of manner and matter, clarity and brevity of address for the purpose of communicative efficiency."[3]

Still other contemporary scholars center their studies of "Arabic Rhetoric" on the vital relationships between *balāghah* and *khitābah* (oral public speech and philosophical argumentation), and how those traditions have been transformed both within and without Euro-American scholarship.[4] These relationships are important. The Arabic *'ilm al-balāghah* deals with Arabic eloquence from a standpoint that covers stylistic and epistemological conventions derived from the analysis of Qur'anic and pre-Islamic poetry. It is referred to in Arabic as *'ilm*, or science. On the other hand, *fan al-khataba,* or rhetorica, is the field of knowledge that emerged in the wake of the Graeco-Arabic Translation Movement, covering translation, com-

---

1. al-Musawi 2001, 29–33.
2. Basil Hatim 2010, 10. Also, Hussein 2006. This is not necessarily a universal view. Hany Rashwan argues that, historically, philosophers in the pre-modern Islamic world favored *khitabah* for its explicit associations with Greek practices of oral public speaking. See Rashwan (2021, 171–96).
3. al-Musawi 2001, 29.
4. Rashwan 2016, 849–63; Rashwan 2020, 386–403.

mentary, and innovative rhetorical theories based mostly on Aristotle's rhetoric.[5] As a tradition, then, Arabic rhetoric has been both "linked to political notions of debate and dialogue"[6] and linked to Islamic religion and culture in specifically Arabic contexts.

Of course, there are other ways of historicizing "Arabic rhetoric," including but not limited to the following: (1) by naming contributions from major philosophers during the four major Caliphates (or dynasties) following the death of the prophet Muhammad in 632 CE; (2) by delineating between classical and modern pragmatics; (3) by identifying the evolution of its sub-disciplines—*ma'ani* (linguistic pragmatics), *bayan* (imagery and figurative language), and *badi'* (rhetorical embellishments); and (4) by offering a trace of the various purposes of utterances derived from Qur'anic texts. Hatim's *Arabic Rhetoric* follows an approach much like the latter, with his emphasis on conceptualizing what he calls "the 'rhetoric of the unexpected'— the purposes for which utterances are used and the effects achieved when norms are flouted."[7] Ezzaher's and Borrowman's works focus on the former, raising questions about the history of the discipline, and emphasizing the rich qualities and characteristics of a deliberative tradition that demonstrates the wisdom of dispensing justice and the value of jurisprudence.[8] The influences of Ibn Sina—to whom Borrowman refers to, not inappropriately, as a "celebrity of Islamic philosophy"[9]—on Ibn Rushd, on the Arabo-Islamic uptake of Aristotle's corpus, and on the Graeco-Arabic tradition in general, are irrefutably significant. Indeed, Medieval Arabic scholars facilitated the emergence of Arabic *hitab* (or discourse) through public speaking for the purposes of persuasion, and through syllogistic speaking for the purposes of art. Two of our contributors highlight the intellectual contributions of Al-Farabi and Ibn Sina, yet our chapter offers fresh methodological insights not only into the "diffusion" and "codification" of Greco and Persian texts through the "culturally unified world of classical Islam,"[10] but also into the growth and evolution of key Arabic rhetorical constructs beyond the treatises of Aristotle. As such, this chapter reinforces the view that Arabic and Islamic rhetorical scholars have been more than merely the caretakers and translational handmaidens of Greco-Roman traditions.[11]

---

5. In fact, Ibn Sina's *Long Book on Rhetoric* is referred to as ريطوريكا, an Arabic transliteration of the word *rhetorica*. *Al-khataba* is referred to in Arabic as *fann*, or art, as in the Greco-Roman tradition with which it is identified. Both chapters on Al-Farabi and Ibn Sina in this chapter cover the latter field, *fann al-khataba*. In addition, see Baddar (2018).

6. Smyth 1992, as qtd. in al-Musawi 2001, 29.

7. Hatim 2010, 4–5. For comparative linguistics and language theorists, a principal concern is recovering what Hatim calls an interrelationship between language and thinking that is not only at the core of Arabic rhetoric but also "at the heart of serious misunderstandings of the perceptions and attitudes of the Arabs on the part of those who interact with them via culture, trade and, more recently, politics."

8. Ezzaher 2008, 347–91. See also Ezzaher (2015), and Borrowman (2010, 97–118).

9. Borrowman 2010, 101.

10. Fletcher 1993, 8.

11. Borrowman 2010, 103. See also Ezzaher (2008), Comas (2019), Ezzaher (2015). Prince (2002), Haddour (2008), and Yucesoy (2009) have argued especially that the reciprocity between transna-

The chapter's main organizing principle is a somewhat pragmatic delineation between Early Islamic, Medieval Islamic, and Arabic-Islamic. The Early Islamic contribution offers insights from seventh-century Iraq, the Medieval Islamic contributions offer insights from tenth-century Damascus, and eleventh-century Persia and Spain, and the Arabic-Islamic contributions offer insights into eleventh-century Persia and fifteenth-century Egypt that focus especially on the influence of Arabic stylistics and pragmatics on chancery practices and translation debates, as well as peacemaking and conciliatory discourse.[12] This tripartite organization reflects neither stark temporal divisions within the tradition nor strict alignments with the three rhetorical "sciences" (meaning, eloquence, embellishment) that underscore al-Musawi's and Hatim's work. Nor is it strictly chronological, as by most accounts early (or classical) Islamic scholarship spans from 640–900 CE (roughly 19–287 AH) while Medieval Islamic scholarship spans from 915–1700 CE (roughly 303–1112 AH). Instead, this organization reflects pragmatic shifts in global influences on the study of Arabic rhetorics, as well as historic debates about the inimitability of the Qur'ān (*i'jāz*) to Arabic rhetorics.[13] It also implies a discussion of the progress of the study of Arabic rhetorics as both historical *and* theoretical. That is, Arabic rhetoric's relationship to medieval vehicles of transmission, interpretation, and recirculation offers a way to both delineate the Arabic from the Islamic and appreciate their comity.[14] Whereas other authoritative and comprehensive studies of Arabic rhetoric focus almost methodically (sometimes exclusively) on three medieval scholars—Al-Farabi, Avicenna (or Ibn Sina), and Averroes—we hope our readers will find here a fluent and provocative look into methodological moments that extend the study of Arabic and Islamic rhetorics beyond even those vital historical figures.

In addition, the methodological moments in this chapter are varied and rich, showing us how an entire practice of dispensing justice can emerge from the translation and circulation of a first/seventh-century letter (see Oweidat's "Letter from Omar bin Al-Khattab") and demonstrating how to teach students to construct their own pluralist perspectives based on the translation and re-historicization of a fifth/eleventh-century text (see Eddy and Alsawaier's "Foundations of Rhetoric in Ibn Hazm"). By intensifying their methodological moments, our six contributors in this chapter provide an essential backdrop for understanding three things.

---

tional and transcontinental movements of Aristotle's texts through 'Abbadic commentary are altered in ways that extend beyond mere appropriation; Islamic contributions to the genealogy of western knowledge typically go unnoticed, except through the careful recovery work demonstrated in chapters like this one.

12. Where possible, dates are included from both Hijri and Gregorian calendars.

13. al-Musawi 2001, 30.

14. For example, the ninth century CE brought an interest in "style as craft" and in *majaz* (metaphor) as a trope, while the thirteenth century CE brought an interest in centralizing Arabic discourse around the growth of common knowledge and cultural milieu (al-Musawi 2001, 31), as well as an interest in "aesthetic criticism justified by psychological argumentation" (Ritter 1954, as qtd. in al-Musawi 2001, 32). Al-Musawi further argues that the twentieth century brought about a Hellenizing influence on *balaghah,* which becomes evident in increasing references to Greek rhetors and philosophers over the Indian and Persian scholars in Arabic scholarship (2001, 32).

First, they equip our understanding of classical (or Qur'anic) Arabic rhetoric as distinct from modern Arabic rhetoric in its reliance on provincialism as theoretical knowledge. Second, they help to complicate the modern assertion that Arabic rhetoric has grown only due to its Hellenizing influence, as their analyses demonstrate an Arabic and Islamic rhetorical tradition that did not consist wholly of translating Greek texts into Arabic. Third, they equip our understanding of modern Arabic rhetoric as a tradition still "concerned with the semantics of stylistics" and with "linguistic eloquence,"[15] even when employed in secular or non-Qur'anic contexts. Together, their contributions draw readers' attention to the vital ramifications of the Graeco-Arabic Translation Movement,[16] which saw its greatest development in the eighth and ninth centuries CE during the Abbasid period, yet without constraining all of Arabic and Islamic rhetoric to the exegetical discoveries of that Movement.[17] This chapter strikes a balance between explaining these works as part of a coherent (though vast) tradition while retaining as many of these nuances as possible, in celebration of the pluralisms that necessarily underscore contemporary rereadings of Arabic and Islamic rhetorics.

Yet, even in their togetherness, the contributions in this chapter still reflect critical disagreements on both macro and micro scales. Such disagreements range from differing assessments of the role and historical evolutions of Qur'anic influence, to the im/propriety of using the term "Arabo-Islamic" versus "Arabic-Islamic," to the role of Ibn Sina as either a bridge-builder or purveyor of a uniquely Arabic tradition of persuasion and stylistics, to varying opinions about preferred diacritical markings (e.g., *Qur'an* vs. *al-Qur'ān*). Ultimately, the following chapter presents the study of *balāghah* as a phenomenon closely imbued with spiritual practices in Arabic culture even in its civic instruction, and one that includes recurrent philological, grammatical, and theological investigations of poetry and oratory as a way of preserving ancient traditions while also resisting cultural subversion. At a time when anti-Islamic sentiment runs high, Alsawaier, Baddar, Diab, Eddy, Ezzaher, and Oweidat all work to reveal the intricate dimensions of texts that ultimately promote wisdom, pluralism, reflection, and peace.

---

15. Hussein 2006, xiii.

16. The Translation Movement is often described as a relationship between two periods: (1) the early Islamic empire and Umayyad period (632–750 CE), which represented the second of four caliphates established following the death of Islam's first prophet Muhammad; and (2) the Abbasid period (750–1258 CE). The four caliphates comprising the Islamic empire during the medieval period include the Rashidun Caliphate (632–661 CE), the Umayyad Caliphate (661–750 CE), the Abbasid Caliphate (750–1258 CE) and the Ottomon Caliphate (1362–1924 CE). See Kadi and Shahin (2013, 81–86).

17. While the Translation Movement was centered in Baghdad, the Abbasid Caliphate encompassed at its height a vast geographical region from Algeria to Afghanistan, making Arabic translation a historically multiethnic and ecumenical endeavor.

1.1 Early Islamic, c. 18 AH/639 CE, Basrah (Iraq)

Letter from Omar bin Al-Khattab to Abu Musa Al-Ash'ari

Lana Oweidat

INTRODUCTION

This letter to Abdulla bin Qais (also known as Abu Musa Al-Ash'ari)[18] belongs to the early Islamic period (*sadr al-islam*), which spans from the early seventh century (the rise of Islam) to approximately the beginning of the medieval period of Islam starting in the eighth century (the Islamic Golden Age). As the Islamic state was expanding under the reign of Omar bin Al-Khattab (the second Caliph of Islam, 584–644 CE), it was necessary to appoint governors (*wulah*) to oversee the provinces (*wilayat*).[19] Therefore, Omar bin Al-Khattab appointed Abu Musa Al-Ash'ari governor to Basrah in 639 CE and sent him this letter to provide him with the basic concepts of jurisdiction and ruling that stem from Islam's religious teachings.[20]

Since that time, the letter has been mentioned, praised, and analyzed by many historians, writers, and scholars, such as Al-Jahiz, Ibn Taymiyyah, Ibn Qayyim Al-Jawziyyah, Al-Bayhaqi; translated into different languages (English, German, French, etc.); and extensively examined by modern Islamic scholars, such as Nasir Bin Aqeel Al-Tareefi, Ahmad Sahnoon, and Ahmad Bazmoul. This piece is celebrated in the Arab-Islamic tradition as a valuable document. It demonstrates the wisdom of dispensing justice and the value of deductive analogy (*qiyas*) and interpretive judgment (*ijtihaad*). In its time, it established legal precedents and expectations, including the burden of proof. Readers up through the present day have noted that it does so while emphasizing the human factor in the process of jurisdiction, especially in relation to the judge's ethos. This document provides some of the most effective guidelines that exist in the annals of rhetorical theory on dealing with bias in one's judgment.

The letter appears in different renditions (*riwayat*) with minor changes of meaning, and it has been transmitted through multiple chains of authority (*isnad*). Some renditions of the text refer to this letter as a formal document (*kitab*). Al-Sarkhasi, an Islamic scholar and jurist, refers to the letter as a seminal work about the "politics of jurisdiction and managing regulations."[21] The Arabic text I am adopting appears in Abu Uthman Amr ibn Bahr Al-Jahiz's book, *Al-Bayaan wa Al-Tabyeen (Book of Clarity and Clarification).*[22] Al-Jahiz (776–868 AD), the author of the book, was a Muslim writer who lived in the medieval era and was well-

---

18. Abu Musa Al-Ash'ari was one of Prophet Muhammad's Companions.
19. As-Sallabi 2007, 25.
20. As-Sallabi 2007, 38.
21. Al-Sarakhsi 1989, 66 (translation mine).
22. The text appears in the second part of the book, pp.48–50.

known for his clear and concise prose. There are two different renditions of the text in this book. I chose to translate the one that gives the chain of transition/authority (*isnad*).

The letter was most likely orally transmitted (only one narrative describes it as transmitted through writing).[23] Likewise, scholars from the medieval Islamic period like Ibn Hazm and more recent ones like D. S. Margoliouth questioned whether it was indeed composed by Omar bin Al-Khattab, but many other Islamic scholars from that period to the present (al-Mubarrad, al-Jahiz, Ibn Taymiyyah, al-Bulqini, al-Tareefi, Sahnoon among others) have examined its historiography and reached the conclusion that it was Omar's. Regardless of the controversy surrounding it, this letter sheds light on different aspects of jurisdiction in the underappreciated early Islamic era, while also exemplifying cultural connections between legal theory, persuasion, and rhetorical practice.

The closest term to rhetoric in the Arab-Islamic tradition is *ilm al-balagha* (the science of eloquence), which was primarily shaped by "theological concerns,"[24] especially those pertaining to the Qur'an.[25] Although this science of eloquence flourished in the thirteenth century in medieval Islam,[26] its seeds can be traced to the early Islamic period where the Qur'an, its preservation, and its interpretation occupied the minds of early Muslims under the leadership of Prophet Muhammad and the caliphs after him. Influenced by the Qur'an's communicative eloquence (*balagha*), Arab and Islamic rhetors have strived for centuries to communicate clearly using elegant prose. Poets and rhetors had a high status in the early Islamic period and onward. Hassan ibn Thabit, whose poetry focused on praising Islam, was called the poet of the prophet (in reference to Prophet Muhammad) (Okasha 2006, 23). Poetry, which was transmitted orally in the early Islamic period, has significant historiographical value, as poets commented on events and praised leaders. Prophet Muhammad, however, was instructed in the Qur'an not to use poetry: "We have not instructed the Prophet in poetry, nor is it suitable for him" (36:69).[27] Islamic scholars believe that instruction, in addition to the fact that proph-

---

23. In his book *Al Talkhees Al-Habeer*, Ibn Hajar Al-Asqalani refers to a narrative in which one of the transmitters pulled out a written letter (1995, 385).

24. Halldén 2005, 680.

25. The Qur'an is considered the holy book of Muslims, revealed to Prophet Muhammad by the angel Gabriel over a period of twenty-three years (610–632 CE). Its recording became a priority to prevent it from alteration and interpolation; as a result, Prophet Muhammad assigned scribes to write it after verifying the chains of narration. The compilation of a manuscript was kept by the two first caliphs: Abu Bakr Al-Siddiq and Omar bin Al-Khattab. While the process of compiling the Qur'an was rigorous and went through phases, Prophet Muhammad prevented his followers from writing down the hadith (the sayings and doings of Prophet Muhammad) for fear that it might get mixed up with the Qur'an (the words of God). The writing of the hadith took place after completing the writing of the Qur'an and two centuries after the death of prophet Muhammad (Alak 1986, 6).

26. Halldén 2005, 680.

27. If prophet Muhammad had composed poetry, "the miraculous eloquence of Qur'an could have been attributed to the Prophet (SAS) [Sallallahu Alayhi wa Sallam, Peace be upon him]'s poetic talents, thus reducing the Divine Book to a humble human endeavor" (Galander 2002, 62). The Qur'an's poetic resonance, rhymed prose (*saja'*), and eloquence have facilitated its transmission and preservation

et Muhammad was an unlettered man, contributed to proving that the Qur'an is God's (*Allah's*) words and not Muhammad's. In studying the following letter, rhetorical scholars might gain a better understanding of Arab-Islamic rhetoric's simultaneous deep roots and modern relevance. The translation is presented in three parts, each followed by a respective commentary, though the letter itself does not delineate parts or sections.

Translation: Part 1

A Letter from Omar bin Al-Khattab to Abu Musa Al-Ash'ari (May God Have Mercy on Him)

Recorded by Ibn Uyainah and Abu Baker al-Huthali and Maslamah bin Muharib, after Qatadah. And by Abu Yusuf Yacoub bin Ibrahim after Ubaid Allah bin abi Humaid al-Huthali after Abi[28] Al-malih Usamah al-Huthali. Omar bin Al-Khattab wrote a letter to Abi Musa Al-Ash'ari:

In the name of God, the most Gracious, the most Compassionate,

Hereafter,

Jurisdiction (*al-qada*) is a firm religious obligation (*farida*) and a prevailing tradition (*sunnah*).[29] Contemplate when a matter is put forward to you.[30] There is no use in speaking justly without then taking action upon your words.[31] Do not show bias to any of the conflicting parties, and be fair in your gestures and your court, so those with high status will not covet more than their rights, and the weak will not despair from your justice.[32] The burden of proof is on the plaintiff while the obligation of the oath (*al-yameen*)[33] is required from the respondent.

---

in the early Islamic period through oral tradition before it was written down during the lifetime of prophet Muhammad.

28. Ab (meaning father) is one of the Five Nouns in Arabic. When "Ab" is the doer of the action, "Abo" is used and when it is a governed noun, we say "Abi".

29. *Sunnah* is the Prophet Muḥammad's example, deeds, and customs.

30. In Al-Jahiz's other rendition of the text, the following phrase appears "and issue a just verdict when revealed to you." The Arabic word for revelation is *bayan*.

31. *Ibn Qayyim* Al-Jawziyyah highlights that Omar bin Al-Khattab not only urges his judge to know what is right from wrong, but he also emphasizes the importance of having the courage and the strength to execute the judgment (2002, 167).

32. Ibn Kutaibah's rendition of the text differs slightly here: "nor will the humble despair of justice from you" (Margoliouth 1910, 311).

33. Taking an oath in Islam should only be by God (*Allah*), and it has its own rules. The oath usually starts with "Wallahi" or "Uqsimu bil-laah" (I swear by Allah).

COMMENTARY: PART 1

Omar's letter starts by providing *isnad*, which developed as a "science in hadith study,"[34] and is defined as the chain of transition/authority that indicates the reliability of a particular saying or doctrine by the Prophet Muhammad or one of his Companions (*sahaba*) (Omar was one of the Companions).[35] *Isnad* precedes the actual text (*matn*), and lists the names of all transmitters. A transmitter is considered most reliable (*thiqa*) in *isnad* when possessing a moral character and religious piety. An uninterrupted *isnad*, in addition to the reliability of transmitter guarantees the validity of that transmitted tradition. *Isnad* "takes the form, 'It has been related to me by A on the authority of B on the authority of C on the authority of D (usually a Companion of the Prophet) that Muhammad said. . . .'"[36] This method was crucial to the early Islamic historiography, as it was integral in preserving Prophet Muhammad's example, deeds, and customs (*sunnah*) and the sayings and doings of his Companions.

All the renditions of the text capture the essence of this letter, and the differences for the most part are minor: switching word order, adding a conjunction, deleting a word, etc. While, for example, the rendition I am using starts with the chain of authority (*isnad*), al-Mubarrad's[37] rendition as it appears in his book *The Perfect One (Al-Kamil)* starts by highlighting the importance of the letter: "Abu Abbas said: and there is his [Omar's] letter in jurisdiction to Abi Musa al-Ash'ari in which he compiled the best regulations, summarized them with eloquent prose, and people after him took his letter as legal law. A just person will not find a better alternative and the unjust cannot escape its regulations."[38] While the letter's significance stems from its content, a close examination of its form provides a valuable glimpse into the early Islamic prose style.

Letter writing in the early Islamic period reveals the culture's rhetorical and stylistic features.[39] Starting with "In the name of God, the most Gracious, the most Compassionate" (*al-basmalah*) is a common formulaic expression and a distinguishing element of Islamic discourse. Muslims start their writing and actions by either saying it verbally or writing it, depending on the situation. The translation does not do justice in capturing the poetic resonance of the expression as it invokes the divine presence in the action that is being conducted. This convention of Islamic discourse is still relevant in our modern times, as letters usually start with *al-basmalah* and end with another formulaic expression: "Peace be upon you" (*as-salamu alaykum*). Although persuasion is at work in this letter, letter writing in the early Islamic period "was driven by . . . stylistic and aesthetic considerations and appreciation."[40] Arabic epis-

---

34. Here, *hadith* refers to the words of the Prophet Muhammad, not to be confused with the Qur'an, which were considered the words of God.
35. "Isnad," *Oxford Islamic Studies Online*, accessed January 21, 2019.
36. "Isnad," *Britannica Encyclopedia of World Religions*, accessed January 22, 2019.
37. al-Mubarrad (826–898 CE) was an Arab grammarian and a literary scholar.
38. al-Mubarrad 1997, 15 (translation mine).
39. Gully 2008, x.
40. Gully 2008, 7.

tolary style, such as letters sent to leaders inviting them to Islam (*da'awa*) and others, like this one, sent to governors, are characterized by an appeal to logic with a great attention to style and aesthetic prose, which, unfortunately in this case, for the most part gets lost in translation. "Hereafter" is another commonly used expression that comes after the greeting in Arabic letter writing that is still used in our modern time. In another rendition of the text in al-Jahiz's book the following appears before "Hereafter": "From the Servant of God, Omar bin al-Khattab, Commander of the Faithful to Abdulla bin Qais, Peace be upon you."[41] Abdulla bin Qais is better known as Abu Musa al-Ash'ari and is one of Prophet Muhammad's Companions.

The Qur'an's influence on this genre of communication is evident in the use of the standard salutation among Muslims: Peace be upon you (*al-basmalah*), which was first introduced in the Qur'an. This rendition of the text follows the conventions of letter writing during the early Islamic period, starting with *al-basmaleh* (In the name of God, the most Gracious, the most Compassionate), followed by mentioning the name of the addressee and the addresser, and then the greeting. Letters were transmitted orally at that time through transmitters. This letter can be of great pedagogical significance; students of rhetoric can be asked to compare and contrast the epistolary conventions in the early Islamic period to the rhetorical and stylistic conventions of letter writing in other traditions, highlighting how the central rhetorical role of religion and the medium of transmission have shaped this genre in the early Islamic era.

From the first line after the salutation, Omar makes a strong statement about the importance of jurisdiction: "Jurisdiction (*al-qada*) is a firm religious obligation (*farida*) and a prevailing tradition (*sunnah*)." His rhetorical purpose is to help his judge understand the great responsibility he is tasked with, while encouraging him to take pride in it. There are five religious duties (*fara'id,* plural of *farida*) that are considered obligatory for all Muslims: The Profession of Faith, Prayer, Alms, Fasting, and Pilgrimage. Giving jurisdiction the status of a religious duty shows its great importance in Islam. Omar, after all, wants his judges to rule with fairness and compassion rather than perceive their roles as sources of prestige or opportunities to abuse their power.

This emphasis on fairness goes as far as instructing the judge to sit in the same proximity of both parties. Ibn Khaldoun's rendition of the text adds the word "fairness" after "court" while al-Mubarrad adds the word "fairness" as one of the items that the judge needs to be fair about: "gestures, fairness, and court." Fairness in your court (*majlisik*) can be translated as "fairness in the distance by which they sit from you." Islamic scholars, such as Ibn Qayyim al-Jawziyyah, believe that Omar's perception of justice stemmed from the Qur'an and Prophet Muhammad's example, deeds, and customs (*sunnah*). Justice assumes a central role in the Qur'an, and Muslims are encouraged to be custodians of justice in all aspects of life, including in providing evidence without bias: "O you who have believed, be persistently standing firm in justice, witnesses for Allah, even if it be against yourselves or parents and relatives. Whether one is rich or poor, Allah is more worthy of both. So follow not [personal] inclination, lest you not be just. And if you distort [your testimony] or refuse [to give it], then indeed Allah is ever, with what you do, Acquainted."[42]

---

41. al-Jahiz 1987, 225 (translation mine).
42. Sahih International 1997, 4:135.

Additionally, there is ample evidence from Prophet Muhammad's example, deeds, and customs (*sunnah*) showing the legal necessity of evidence:[43]

Ali[44] said: The Messenger of Allah[45] (May peace be upon him) sent me to Yemen as a judge, and I asked: O Messenger of Allah, are you sending me when I am young and have no knowledge of the duties of the judge? The Prophet replied: Allah will guide your heart and keep your tongue true. When two litigants sit in front of you, do not decide till you hear what the other has to say as you heard what the first had to say; for it is best that you should have a clear idea of the best decision. Ali said: I had been a judge (for long), or he said (the narrator is doubtful): I have no doubts about a decision afterwards.[46]

Translation: Part 2

Reconciliation (*al-sulh*) is permitted (*ja'iz*) among Muslims[47] except for one that permits what is prohibited (*haram*)[48] or one that prohibits what is lawful (*halal*).[49] There is no problem in revisiting a decision, in order to uphold truth, if you were later shown guidance (*hidayah*), [50] as nothing invalidates justice; [51] correcting the judgment is better than for the void to continue.

Understand, understand[52] what is in your heart when litigants seek a decision on a matter that is not mentioned in God's book (*Qur'an*)[53] or his prophet's *Sunnah* [54] (peace be upon him).[55]

---

43. Hussain 2011, 185.

44. Ali ibn Abi Talib (601–661 CE) was the cousin and son-in-law of Prophet Muhammad. He was among the first to convert to Islam and was known for his bravery.

45. The reference here is to Prophet Muhammad.

46. Hussain 2011, 185. (Hussain quotes this Prophet Muhammad saying (*hadith*) from Mahmud Saedon Awang Othman's *The Importance of Evidence* (1992), who, in turn, quotes it from *Sunan Abu Dawud*, vol. 3 *Kitab al-Aqdi*)

47. Ibn Kutaibah's rendition of the text uses "people" instead of "Muslims."

48. What is *haram* (prohibited) in Islam is determined by God (*Allah*). Muslims rely on Islamic jurisprudence to distinguish between what is Prohibited (*haram*) and what is Lawful (*halal*).

49. The order is switched here in Ibn Kutaibah's rendition: prohibits what is lawful (*halal*) and permits what is prohibited (*haram*).

50. *Hidayah* also means the correct path in Arabic.

51. There is a slight difference in word use and structure in Ibn Kutaibah's rendition (Margoliouth's translation): "for justice may not be annulled" (1910, 312).

52. "Understand" is repeated twice in the original text for emphasis.

53. The Qur'an is the holy book of Muslims

54. The Prophet Muḥammad's example, deeds, and customs

55. God instructs Muslims in the Qur'an to address Prophet Muhammad respectfully and to wish blessings upon him: "Allah and His angels send blessings upon the Prophet. Oh you who believe! Send blessings upon him, and salute him with all respect" (33:56). Therefore, Muslims follow the mention of Prophet Muhammad with the phrase: "peace be upon him."

COMMENTARY: PART 2

Reconciliation (*al-sulh*) is an important concept in the Arab-Islamic rhetorical tradition. Rasha Diab notes that the term is "grounded in investment in restorative justice as a modality for the realization of relational responsibilities toward oneself and others."[56] In this context, reconciliation (*sulh*) is encouraged, but it is conditional on maintaining *huddod Allah* (embracing the lawful (*halal*) and avoiding the forbidden (*haram*)). While Muslims submit to God to achieve personal inner peace,[57] they strive to achieve *sulh* and to live in harmony with others. Islam emphasizes restorative justice and building relationships as key elements to have a harmonious society.

This text has value for its pedagogical possibilities, especially for teaching students about different rhetorical traditions. Students can examine a number of primary texts, such as a chapter in the Qur'an called "The Narrations" (*Surah Al-Qasas*) and different examples from the *hadith* that provide more details in how Islam deals with restorative justice. They can also explore the term *qasas* (law of retaliation) within the Islamic discourse and its current and past practices in some Muslim-majority countries. Although at first glance *qasas* might seem encouraging retributive justice, it can provide insight into a "victim-centered" restorative justice system, as the victim plays a significant role in determining the punishment or forgiving the perpetrator.[58] Additionally, students can compare the Arab-Islamic concepts of *qasas* and justice to those in the western rhetorical tradition, especially in Plato's *Republic* and Aristotle's *Politics*, or to those theories of medieval Christianity found in the works of Augustine and Aquinas. There is ample room for such comparison, since the latter rhetorical tradition, like the early Arab-Islamic rhetorical tradition, is grounded in theological concerns. Finally, students can identify the rhetorical appeals used in the text and discuss the different techniques Omar utilizes to appeal to his judge. Although Omar constructs his argument and frames his instructions to the judge in an imperative tone to emphasize the importance of taking these instructions seriously, he comes across as a rhetor who is skillful in utilizing different rhetorical tools.

Translation: Part 3

Resolve to use your knowledge of examples (*al-amthal*) and analogy (*al-ashbah*) that are alike, and make your decision based on what is closer to God and true to your own perspective. And for those who claim injustice, give them a deadline; if they provide clear evidence (*bayyinah*), grant them the justice they deserve. If they cannot provide evidence, then contemplate the matter and decide what is just,[59] as this will suspend

---

56. Diab 2015, 125.

57. The word Islam means submission to God.

58. Hascall 2011, 38.

59. Ibn Kutaibah's rendition of the text replaces the verb here, which slightly changes the meaning. Margoliouth's translation of this phrase reads: "you will be entitled to give judgment against him"

doubt in your judgment; provide insight into your own judgment; and when you make a mistake, it will not be because you rushed to judgment.

Muslims are equal to one another when testifying (*shahada*) except those who have been flagged for committing an offense (*hadd*),[60] or those who were found guilty of providing a false testimony (*Shahadat al-zur*),[61] or those who serve the interests of family and friends.[62] God (*Allah*), Almighty and Exalted, knows what is in the hearts and chooses not to expose their offenses except when evidence is presented.

Do not you dare[63] be anxious, lose your patience with, get bored of, or hurt the litigants, or deny them their rights in places of justice[64] where Allah confers on you a reward[65] and makes a decent store.[66] A person with sincere intentions between him and God (blessed and exalted be he)[67] even at the person's own expense, Allah will reconcile between him and the people. And the person who pretends before the world what Allah knows that he has not, Allah will expose him and reveal his actions.[68] Allah the Almighty will not reward him in his livelihood and his mercy. And Peace be upon you.[69]

---

(312). I disagree with this translation. Although at first glance the phrase can be literally translated as "you will be entitled to give judgment against him," there is a level of complexity that is not addressed in his translation. My preference is for a much more literal understanding of the verb *istahllalta* (استحللت). My translation highlights that the judge should resort to jurisdiction, which entails asking the respondent to take an oath since the plentiful cannot provide clear evidence (*bayyinah*). The rest of this paragraph as it appears in Al-Jahiz's rendition is omitted in Ibn Kutaibah's text.

60. *Hadd* is an Arabic word that means "a punishment fixed in *the Qur'an* and hadith for crimes considered to be against the rights of God" (*Oxford Islamic Studies Online*).

61. Bearing, including providing, false evidence or assisting in fraud.

62. In Ibn Kutaibah's text (Margoliouth's translation): "or one whose pedigree is suspected." The emphasis on family affiliation should be read in the historical context of the piece, as this letter was sent to a governor of a tribal society—a society that valued kinship.

63. Margoliouth's translation leaves out the Arabic word "Iyyaka," which is crucial to the understanding of this point. Margoliouth's translation in Serjeant's piece, on the other hand, translates it as "have care." My translation captures the sense of threat associated with this word to indicate the importance of not committing the act.

64. The literal translation is "places of justice;" however, I agree with Margoliouth's translation that for this context, the reference is most probably for the court.

65. The word "confer" is closest to the meaning.

66. Reputation and a good place in judgment day.

67. An expression used in the Islamic tradition to praise God (*tabaraka wa ta'ala*).

68. This part is omitted in Ibn Kutaibah's text: "Allah will expose him and reveal his actions. And Allah the Almighty will not reward him in his livelihood and his mercy" (my translation) and is replaced with "will take care of him" (Margoliouth's translation).

69. "Peace be upon you" (*as-salamu alaykum*) is a formulaic expression in Islamic discourse that Muslims use to greet one another or upon parting company. The Qur'an emphasizes the importance of reciprocating the Islamic greeting in the Chapter "The Women" (*surah An-Nisa*): "When a courteous

COMMENTARY: PART 3

Omar was among the first to instruct judges to use analogy (*al-ashbah*) and one's knowledge of examples (*al-amthal*) to derive regulations on matters that are not mentioned in the Qur'an or the sunnah. This form of analogical reasoning (*qiyas*) was exercised by jurists in the early Muslim community. These jurists had to possess an ethos "resulting from the knowledge, reputation, and character" to be considered for this position.[70]

Although these judges are held to high standards, the possibility of making an error in judgment is discussed; there is always room for revisiting one's decision and accepting appeals. Ibn Taymiyyah, a Muslim theologian, highlights that if the plaintiff does not provide proof, then the judge should make the plaintiff aware that he can ask the respondent to take an oath (*al-yameen*).[71] He uses the following saying by prophet Muhammad (*hadith*) to extract this information and show the influence that the prophet's teachings had on Omar's instructions to his judge:

> A man from Kenda and another from Hadramout came to Prophet Muhammad. The man from Hadramout said: God's prophet, this man took my father's land from me. The other man said: it is my land and I planted it; you have no right to it. Prophet Muhammad asked the man from Hadramout: Do you have any evidence? He said: No. Prophet Muhammad said: then you can ask him to take an oath (*yameen*). The man from Hadramout said: This person is a licentious; he does not mind giving me a false oath. He does not fear God. Prophet Muhammad said: that is all that you can get from him. When the man left, prophet Muhammad said: if he gave a false oath, he will meet God and God will shun him.[72]

As can be concluded from the *hadith*, taking a false oath in Islam is unlawful and sinful. Using this *hadith*, students exploring the Arab-Islamic rhetorical tradition can further examine how justice operates at two levels within this rhetorical tradition: the legal and the divine.

For a religion that has been negatively stereotyped as rigid, inflexible, violent, and barbaric, this letter shows a sophisticated understanding of justice, transparency, and reconciliation. Students can be asked to identify places in the text where this nuanced understanding surfaces. This letter paired with verses from the Qur'an or/and the sunnah (such as the aforementioned *hadith*) can help students develop their theories in response to the questions: What does Islam teach about justice? How do these teachings about justice and the traditions of law in the Islamic rhetorical tradition shape current practices in Muslim-majority countries?

---

greeting is offered you, meet it with a greeting still more courteous, or at least of equal courtesy. Allah takes careful account of all things" (4:86).

70. Tomeh 2010, 145.

71. Taymiyyah 2004, 393 (translation mine).

72. Taymiyyah 2004, 339 (narrated by Muslim and Tirmidhi, translation mine).

How are they put/not put into practice? Asking students to ponder these texts and questions can go a long way toward greater understanding of rhetoric beyond the limits of the western rhetorical tradition.

1.2 Medieval Islamic, c. 10th Century CE, Damascus

Al-Fārābī's *Book of Rhetoric*: An Arabic-English Translation of Al-Fārābī's Commentary on Aristotle's *Rhetoric*[73]

Lahcen E. Ezzaher

INTRODUCTION: MEDIEVAL ARABIC TRANSLATION

The noted medieval translators who rendered Greek works from Syriac translations into Arabic were Yaḥyā ibn al-Biṭrīq (770–830 CE), Ḥunain ibn Isḥāq (809–877 CE), his son Isḥāq ibn Ḥunain (845–910 CE), and Abū Bishr Mattā ibn Yūnus (870–940 CE). The translations into Arabic of Porphyry's *Introduction (Eisagoge), Categoriae, De Interpretatione, Analytica Priora, Analytica Posteriora, Topica, Sophistica, Rhetorica, Poetica, Physica, De Generatione et Corruptione, Liber Animae, Liber Sensus et Sensati, Liber Animalium, Metaphysica,* and *Ethica,* as well as Plato's *Republic,* were mostly done by these Syriac-Christian scholars. In his bibliographical work *Kitāb al-Fihrist,* Ibn al-Nadīm paid tribute to them and called them "the encyclopedists," thus emphasizing the disciplinary character of translation and its important contribution in cultural production. Commenting on the effects of this cultural activity on Greek philosophy in general and Aristotle's work in particular, scholar of Renaissance humanism Paul Oskar Kristeller acknowledges that Aristotle attained in medieval Arabic-Islamic culture "an authority and doctrinal preponderance that he had never possessed in Greek antiquity to the very end."[74]

In the twelfth century, most Latin translations from the Greek came through the Norman kingdom of Sicily. As Carolyn Prager notes, the Sicilian court under Roger II of Sicily around 1152 CE was a place frequently visited by famous English scholars such as Adelard of Bath and John of Salisbury. The work of these scholars, Prager maintains, served as "an important conduit of knowledge about Greek and Arabic culture to Europe in general and to England in particular."[75]

The school of translation in Toledo in Spain was yet another important center in the West actively involved in the rendering into Latin of the Arabic translations and commentaries. Hermannus Alemannus did most of the translations of the Arabic commentaries by Averroes and Alfarabi on Aristotle's *Poetics* and *Rhetoric* into Latin between 1243 and 1256 CE. In a

---

73. Reprinted in sections from Ezzaher 2008, 347–91, with permission from University of California Press. Ezzaher's piece contains excerpts from an Arabic-English translation of Al-Fārābī's short commentary on Aristotle's *Rhetoric.* This is the first English translation of a significant medieval Arabic text made available to English-speaking scholars in rhetoric, philosophy, and logic.

74. Kristeller 1979, 35.

75. Prager 1990, 52.

very informative essay titled "Pratique de la traduction en Espagne au Moyen Age: les travaux tolédans," translator and critic Clara Foz describes the Toledan population in the twelfth and thirteenth centuries—composed of Spaniards, Arabs, and Jews—as a rich multilingual and multicultural environment that offered an important site for dialogue among diverse cultures.[76] Foz informs us that Latin was introduced later in Toledo after Alphonse VI conquered the city. This rich linguistic and cultural contact in medieval Spain should have an important implication in our understanding of medieval history in the sense that it defeats the existing view of medieval Western society as something essentially European and Christian.

A careful study of the complex character of the textual transmission of Aristotle's treatises on the *Rhetoric* and the *Poetics* from Greek into Arabic and then into Latin, for example, would certainly expand horizons for fruitful research in rhetoric and literature programs. The inclusion of such works will constitute a tremendous contribution to the history of rhetoric and poetics in the humanities because it will indicate a good appreciation of the academic effort that Arabic-Muslim philosophers demonstrated by working closely with Greek commentators such as Themistius and John the Grammarian, with whom they engaged in an academic debate over Aristotle's works.

Abū Naṣr Al-Fārābī

Most biographies indicate that Abū Naṣr al-Fārābī was born in the district of Fārāb (Turkestan) in 870 CE. Although his family was Muslim, he received his education in philosophy and logic under two well-known Nestorian masters of logic in Baghdad. The first one was Abū Bishr Mattā ibn Yūnus (870–940 CE), who translated Aristotle's *Posterior Analytics* into Arabic from a Syriac translation by Isḥāq ibn Ḥunain. Abū Bishr Mattā ibn Yūnus also rendered into Syriac the *Poetics* and the *Sophistics*. The second one was Yuḥannā ibn Ḥailān (860–920 CE), who was knowledgeable in philosophy, Christian theology, and logic. Al-Fārābī was also a contemporary of Yaḥyā ibn 'Addi (893–974 CE), who translated *Categories, Topics,* and *Sophistical Refutations* from Syriac into Arabic. It is worth pointing out that these Nestorian masters of logic and philosophy, who knew Syriac and Arabic, had inherited the Christian Neo-Platonic tradition handed down to them by the last representatives of the school of Hellenistic Alexandria. This educational background puts Al-Fārābī, to use Nicholas Rescher's words, in the position of "a continuator of the logical work of the Syrian Christian logicians."[77]

Al-Fārābī knew Turkish, Persian, Kurdish, and Arabic. He did not know Syriac or Greek, but still he is considered in Islamic philosophy the first to have rendered Greek logic into Arabic, for he brought Aristotle's logical scheme close to the Arabic-Islamic mind, which made him known as the "Second Teacher," after Aristotle, who was known in Arabic-Islamic philosophical circles as the "First Teacher" (al-Mu'allim al-Awwal). Al-Fārābī was also known for his talent in music theory, for he composed a monumental piece titled *The Great Book of Music*

---

76. Foz 1991, 29.
77. Rescher 1963, 19.

(Kitab al-Musiqa al-Kabir). He traveled extensively around the Islamic world, visiting academic circles of linguists, dialecticians, literary critics, and commentators on Greek philosophical works in Baghdad, Aleppo, Damascus, and Cairo. He received benefits at the court of Sayf al-Dawla (d. 967 CE), the Hamadani ruler of Aleppo and a great patron of the arts and letters. After a lengthy stay in Aleppo, where he wrote and taught, he went to Damascus with his patron, where he died in 950 CE.

Al-Fārābī's Work on Aristotle

In his monumental work on the Aristotelian tradition, Al-Fārābī is particularly concerned with the universality of logic. For example, in his introduction to his short commentary on Aristotle's *Prior Analytics*, he explains: "to follow in [Aristotle's] footsteps in this regard is to explain the canons found in his books to the people of every art and of every science and to the scholars in every age by means of examples which are familiar to them."[78] For Al-Fārābī, just as scientific truth is unique and universal, so is the end of logic, for despite the differences of time, place, and people, it reaches one universal truth. It is worth mentioning that in addition to his interest in Aristotle, Al-Fārābī also drew upon Plato and Plotinus and the result of this intellectual effort is a synthesis of diverse philosophical views based on his notion of the unity of philosophy. This explains his concern with reconciling Plato's philosophical ideas with those of Aristotle, and ultimately religion with philosophy. Al-Fārābī closes his treatise *The Attainment of Happiness* by drawing the reader's attention to the following conclusion: "So let it be clear to you [the reader] that, in what they [Plato and Aristotle] presented, their purpose is the same, and that they intended to offer one and the same philosophy" (I, sec. 64). The same idea is reiterated in the opening section of *The Philosophy of Aristotle* when he states: "Aristotle sees the perfection of man as Plato sees it and more" (III, sec. 1). The notion of the unity of philosophy would later be the basis of the intellectual effort of Avicenna and Averroes. As to the relation between religion and philosophy, Al-Fārābī brings the two together by presenting the philosopher as the supreme ruler and lawgiver whose duty is to teach and lead his people to happiness by his mastery of "theoretical virtues, deliberative virtues, moral virtues, and practical arts" (I, sec. 1).

Al-Fārābī was aware of the deep divisions in the Islamic state and his effort to reconcile Aristotle with Plato was motivated by his concern for establishing unity. The Islamic world was more complex and diverse and multicultural. And since Al-Fārābī believed in the unity of the human mind, the unity of philosophy, according to his view, will pave the way for the unity of reason and revelation, and ultimately the future of the Islamic state depends on this unity. Thus, we can recognize three levels of this reconciliation: Plato and Aristotle, Greek philosophy and the Islamic faith, and reason and revelation. The third level is the most significant one since it announces the unity of a political state that stands on both reason and religion. This intellectual effort clearly made Al-Fārābī earn the reputation of the founder of Islamic philosophy.

---

78. Mahdi 1962.

In his book *Kitāb Iḥṣā'al-ᶜ Ulūm* (*The Book of the Enumeration of Sciences*), which is a sort of encyclopedia in which he gives a brief account of all branches of art and science, Al-Fārābī classified Aristotle's works into two categories.[79] In the first one, he listed eight studies, each corresponding to a treatise by Aristotle: *Categoriae, De Interpretatione, Analytica Priora, Analytica Posteriora, Topica, Sophistica, Rhetorica,* and *Poetica.* Following the late Alexandrian commentators on Aristotle, Al-Fārābī treated the *Rhetoric* and the *Poetics* as part of Aristotle's *Organon.* That Al-Fārābī included the *Rhetoric* and the *Poetics* in this first category is quite significant because, as Deborah Black explains, "Aristotle's *Organon* represented the main source of logical speculation for the philosophers of the Middle Ages, and was a major inspiration for their epistemological doctrine as well."[80] In the second category, Al-Fārābī put Aristotle's books on physical matters and also included the three books on *Metaphysics, Ethics,* and *Politics.*

In this short commentary on Aristotle's *Rhetoric,* Al-Fārābī is reconstructing a Greek text for a Muslim-Arabic speaking audience, and so in his reading of Aristotle's treatise he does not follow it word for word. Rather he looks for appropriate topics and issues and treats them as totally independent of their cultural context. Thus, those issues and topics are immediately put into contemporary context. Knowing that he is dealing with a text from a pagan culture, Al-Fārābī picks and chooses what he deems useful from the Aristotelian corpus. He treats logic as an instrument totally independent of who is speaking and of its cultural context. Logic is seen here as a universal instrument free of ideology. But this instrument is manipulated for ideological purposes. It is put side by side with revelation to clear the Islamic state from any internal contradictions and strife that threaten to bring it down.

This translation is based on an excellent critical edition prepared by Langhade and Grignaschi, who used two manuscripts recently discovered: manuscript N0 812 of Hamidiye Library in Istanbul and manuscript N0 231, TE 41, of the University of Bratislava Library.[81] In their critical edition, titled *Al-Farabi: Deux ouvrages inédits sur la rhétorique,* Langhade and Grignaschi included punctuation and paragraph division to make the text clear to read. In my effort to render the Arabic text into English, I have frequently resorted to their French translation for help, especially when I arrived at some passages in which Al-Fārābī's style seemed very obscure. Al-Fārābī's commentary may be divided into the following sections:

I. Introduction
II. Things That Cause the End of Belief and Certainty
III. Opinion Is of Two Types
IV. Strong Opinion
V. Definition of Doubt
VI. Composition of the Enthymeme
VII. The Example
VIII. Three Types of Listeners

---

79. Al-Fārābī' 1996.
80. Black 1990, 1.
81. Langhade and Grignaschi 1971.

Translation

II. Things That Cause the End of Belief and Certainty

There are various things that cause the end of belief: death; that is, when the person who believes dies; or corruption of the mind; or forgetfulness; or forgetfulness of proof; or the end of the matter about which there was belief, through destruction, or transformation into the opposite of what it had been, or a fallacy that gets into it and which the person who believes does not detect, or a true opposite that shows him the error of his belief. The same with certainty: it ends with the death of the person who believes, the corruption of his mind, or his forgetfulness. But it does not cease with the end of the matter or the end of opposites, as has been shown in *Kitab al-Burhan* (*The Book of Proof*) [*Posterior Analytics*]. Considered in an absolute manner, of the properties of certainty, when it occurs, is that it never ends as long as the person who believes is sane and his mind is sane. However, temporary certainty ceases with the end of the matter, or when it changes into its opposite, despite the fact that the person who believes is sane and his mind is sane. Of the properties of opinion, there is the fact that it can end in the future, despite the sanity of the person who believes, the sanity of his mind, and the integrity of the matter, and without forgetting it.

In sum, every belief that is acquired at a certain time and which can end in the future by opposition is an opinion. And every belief that stood for a while and then ended by opposition was an opinion before it ended. And the person who held that belief did not feel that it was an opinion. Some ancients raised the question about the subject of point of view that is particular to each individual person and said: "Are you confident that the points of view in which you believe today, you are not going to turn away from them and embrace their opposite?" A similar question: "Did you not have a point of view in the past which you believed was true? And then you turned away from it so that its opposite has become today what its opposite was yesterday? What guarantee do you have that you are not going to turn away from this point of view in favor of its first opposite?" There are other similar questions among these ancient issues. The purpose of all these was simply to show that such points of view were opinions and insufficient in speculative matters, by means of which points of view were at the level of certainty, and that they should not be considered of the level of certainty.

Insufficient answers have been suggested to these questions because of their poor knowledge of the ways of certainty. Thus, some of them said: "I do not turn away from this specific point of view as long as I am in this state of mind." This is not an answer to make his points of view certain, because there is no difference between this statement and the following one: "I do not turn away from them [points of view] as long as I do not know of an opposite that will destroy them, or as long as the proofs that make them appear true in my mind are not proved wrong." Such is the state of opinions. For when an opposite to an opinion does not appear, that opinion is like certainty for the person who believes it.

Others among the ancients thought that there should not be an answer to this question and that it should be dropped because it was a false question. Earlier they had claimed that these questions and other similar ones involved the invalidation of the point of view of every person asking questions with the aim of invalidating the point of view of another person, and that they made invalid all points of view and did not allow a person to have any point of view. Not to allow this is impossible, since every person has a point of view, to the extent that when someone says: "There is absolutely no point of view," his statement is a point of view. These ancients' claim that such questions must be dropped and are not worth answering, for the reasons that they suggested, and also their claim that the questions are invalid because they are related to the points of view of the person who raises questions about them are erroneous and absurd, because if the points of view of the questioner were all opinions and if he felt or admitted they were opinions, they would not turn against him and invalidate his points of view. The questioner will have simply committed to the implications of his questions, before he asks those questions. His aim is to show that to the person who does not feel or acknowledge that his points of view, as they are, are indeed opinions, but thinks that they are certainty or makes people believe that they are certainty. Moreover, the questioner's points of view, if they were certainty, or there was an element of certainty in them, they would not turn against him by invalidating his points of view—because certainty can never be removed by an opposite—or by invalidating each particular point of view or all the points of view or the points of view of everyone, but they are only invalidated for the person who does not see or acknowledge, regarding points of view in this state, that they are opinion and should remain opinion. As to the person whose point of view is certainty, or an opinion that he acknowledges is an opinion, these questions do not invalidate his point of view.

Why do such questions not deserve an answer? Does this not resemble the case in which a statement widely known authenticates a proposition, and a syllogistic statement authenticates its opposite, to the degree that the widely known statement and the syllogistic statement oppose each other? Does this not resemble the case in which there are two syllogistic statements, one of which implies the opposite of what the other implies? Do we reject one of the two statements? Do we not listen to it or to the person using it in his discourse? Are we going to be content and say that there is another proof here to confirm what that statement invalidates? And then we will look for ways to make it invalid and show the place of error in it, if there is an error, by using the testimony of someone against the truth of a point of view, by his fame and by the testimony of other people on his behalf. As to the other argument by a syllogistic statement against the truth of the opposite of that statement, it is like the opposition of two proofs, one of which implies the opposite of what the other one implies. The same with the issue brought up by a person who asks: "Is it possible that what you believe in a matter is different from what the matter is?" He only means by that: "Is it possible that what you believe in a matter is in opposition to what the existence of the matter is outside the soul or not?" By this question, we seek to prove also, in such points of view as these, that they are opinions and not certainty.

Some of those who test their points of views in speculative matters by stretching them further to the point that they do not find any opposites against them exaggerate the value of their points of view to confess that they are opinions, but when they contemplate the matter, they find that their points of view are such, or that they are not certain that such points of view are in opposition to what the existence of the matter is. They respond to the question by giving the illusion that their opinions are certainty, and they reject by their views what the questioner wants to impose. They do this by referring to the words used by the questioner and not to the meaning of the words in the questioner's mind.

And if someone asked them: "Is it possible that what someone believes to be such or not such is in opposition to what he believes?" they would provide a vague answer that gives the illusion that their point of view is certainty, which is: "It is not possible that what I believe to be such or not such is different from what I believe." This is an ambiguous statement that can be used in different ways, one of which is that the meaning of the statement "It is not possible" is that it is not in the capacity or power of his mind to believe in that thing differently from what he has believed, given the fact that he has done his best to find true the opposite to his point of view, and that he has not found it true. This is not an answer that will make his point of view a certainty, even if he was sincere.

It is also probable that he means by "It is not possible" (that it is not possible) that the belief of a person that something is such is identical to his belief that it is not such. This does not mean anything more than two opposites cannot be identical to the same thing. This answer also does not prevent the point of view from being opposite to the matter itself. This was exactly the object of inquiry from the part of the questioner, and they have not answered "no" by one of the two opposites of the question; they have only pushed away what the question aimed to imply.

It is also probable that the ambiguous statement "It is not possible" means that it is not possible that when we believe that something is such, we believe in that thing itself at one and same time that it is not such. In such case, there is nothing more than this: that it is not possible that we have two opposite beliefs about the same thing at one and same time. This is an answer about something different from what they have been asked.

III. Opinion Is of Two Types

There are two sorts of opinion. One for which a person does not know an opposite, either because he did not look for it at all; or he did not examine it; or he did not try to find one; or because he attempted to find an opposite, but did not find one. Or because he refuted, according to his ability, whatever opposite he encountered. As to the other type of opinion, the person knows the opposite. The opinion whose opposite is known relates to a particular person, or a particular group, or to all, at a certain time; or it relates to a person or a group at a certain time. It is not impossible that the opposite of a point of view is hidden from a person at a certain time and appears to him at another time, or that it appears to another person at that time or after that time. The same thing goes with the group. It is not impossible also that a point of view, which is commonly known to everyone, is such that no one among them is aware of its opposite, and that some of them recognize that opposite at a later time.

IV. Strong Opinion

Strong opinion in every person is one to which there is no opposite. This type has various degrees: the weakest is one of which we do not know the opposite, because we have not looked for one, for negligence, inattentiveness, distraction, or good faith. The strongest is one we have worked hard to examine and compare with its opposite and refute whatever opposites we have found.

An opinion that has more support than opposition prevails. An opinion whose support is less, or less apparent, and whose opposition is more, or more apparent, is called doubt and suspicion and is discarded. An opinion whose support is equal to its opposition in number and clarity is used with its opposite in the arts of conjecture, not that they are used in one thing at one time, but in two different situations and two different times; and from such opinions doubt and confusion may result, whenever they are used in sciences and we are not aware of what falsehood they may contain.[82]

V. Definition of Doubt

Doubt is when the soul stops between two opposite opinions, resulting from two things that are equal in clarity and firmness. Equal firmness is when the two opinions are equal in the necessity of the consequence of what is deduced from each one of them and that they are equal regarding the necessity or the possibility of their existence. Their clarity is equal when they are commonly known, or when a person knows about them, or has an opinion about them in an equal manner. And if a person does not have an opinion on either one of the opposite propositions, this calls for research and it is not a doubt.

An opinion is authentic when it is an object of inquiry and is examined until we do not sense any opposite to our point of view. This may be done by rhetorical as well as dialectical means. A person is aware of rhetorical means before he is aware of dialectical means because he is used to rhetorical means since childhood and since his first experience observing first things that a person can see. As to dialectical means, he is aware of them later. Demonstrative means are even less apparent than dialectical means, because a person is almost not aware of them spontaneously. Philosophers in antiquity used in their study of speculative matters rhetorical means for a long period of time because they were not aware of any other means, until

---

82. Cf. Plato, *Philebus* 55e.

they finally became aware of dialectical means, and as a result, they rejected rhetorical means in philosophy and used dialectical means instead. Several of these philosophers used sophistry and continued to use it until Plato, who was the first to become aware of demonstrative means, for he distinguished them from dialectical, sophistic, rhetorical, and poetic means. However, he only distinguished them one from the other in usage, in diverse disciplines, and according to what spare time and higher instinct advise, without prescribing any universal laws for them. Aristotle did this in his [*Kitāb al-Burhān*] *Book of Proof* and its canons [*Posterior Analytics*].

In fact, Aristotle was the first to possess these means, for which he framed universal laws, arranged in a technical manner, and which he firmly put in logic. Philosophers refused since then the old ways that the ancients used in speculative matters as a means of seeking certainty. They used dialectic in mathematics, sophistry for tribulation and warning, and they used rhetoric in the general matters common to all the arts, namely those matters in which we cannot use a method proper to an art without the other arts. Thus rhetoric is common to all the arts and it is for teaching the public several speculative matters, and for teaching a person who is not versed in a particular art those things that are proper to this art, whenever he needs that, and also in the discourses used for civic matters.

The arts of conjecture are those from which opinions are obtained in their topics that have been determined. Those are rhetoric, prudence, and practical arts, such as medicine, agriculture, navigation, and other similar arts. Each of these arts, except rhetoric, works hard and pursues what is right in everything that a person has to do or where he has to do it. The right point of view is a sort of true opinion. Each of these arts has a special topic. He only invents what is right or persuades in its special topics. Rhetoric is a separate art.

In fact, rhetoric has been instituted for persuasion only, not for reflection, nor even for discovering the matter about which one persuades. The other arts of conjecture use reflection in discovering the thing that is their object of persuasion. Rhetoric does not have a special domain for persuasion; but we look for persuasion in all types of matters. Also, the business of rhetoric is the invention of opinions either in the domain where there are opinions, that is the things possible in themselves, or in the domain where there is certainty, that is the things necessary. From the other arts we only have opinion in matters of opinion, not certainty, since their topics are about things possible.

Each of these arts is used in a person's reflection when he seeks to discover the right point of view in what he should do in such and such thing concerning a particular topic, which is governed by the laws that he has acquired from his art only. When he wants to persuade others, if those others are versed in his art and have the same degree of knowledge of the laws governing that art, the means that he has available is to use, in order to persuade, those same laws by which he discovered that right point of view. If they are not versed in his art, he will need to use rhetoric, which is common to all. He will not use the particular method of that art, unless it is agreed that that art is also common to all. If he is not able to follow the method that is common to all and wants to persuade others, he will commission a rhetorician to do the job for him.

As to rhetoric, it uses, for persuasion, the means common to all, since it aims at persuasion in all types of matters. It does not use particular means, except when those are also common to all. That is why it is possible to use persuasion in medical matters, not by the means that are particular to a doctor, but by those means that are shared between the doctor and those who are not doctors. The same goes with each of the other arts. That is why it [rhetoric] has the power to persuade all people in all matters. That is why when someone who professes an art, speculative or practical, aims at correcting one of the points of view that he has discovered by his art to someone who is not versed in that art, does not have free time or is not fit to study that art, he will need to be a rhetor, or commission a rhetor.

A point of view that is prior and shared is a point of view that, when it suddenly presents itself to a person, will appear as it is, before the person conducts any inquiry about it. To conduct an inquiry about a point of view is for a person to search, with all his capacity, the things that reinforce and strengthen that point of view. If he finds those things, his point of view will be stronger and he will grow confident in it. If he encounters things that are opposite to his point of view, he will seek to refute them. If he refutes them, his initial point of view will confirm itself. If they are not refuted, he either totally rejects his initial point of view, or his attention is drawn by the opposites regarding his initial point of view to the condition or conditions that may have been neglected in the first place. This is what we mean by examining the initial point of view.

Rhetoric has this in common with dialectic and sophistic, for they all proceed with investigation and, as a consequence, false points of view are exposed.

VIII. *Three Types of Listeners*

Listeners are of three types: those we want to persuade, the opponent, and the judge. Those we want to persuade, either they have started the dispute and demand that the speaker persuade them in a given matter, or the speaker started the dispute, demanding that the others accept something or listen to what he has to say. The goal of the person demanding persuasion is to hear the arguments so that he hears an argument that confirms a matter that he likes or to accept the most effective argument from two opposed arguments.

IX. *The Opponent*

The opponent is either an adversary who stands up against the speaker whose discourse aims to persuade the listener, impeding persuasion, or an apparent adversary, examining what the speaker says and giving profound thought to what the speaker advances. His intention is to make the arguments the speaker advances more persuasive.

X. *Conditions for Being a Judge*

One of the conditions for being a judge is the ability to distinguish well which one of the two opposing arguments is more persuasive. It is clear that the manner in which the judge addresses each of the two opponents is different from the manner in which they address each other. A judge who does not conform well to what judges use may well become a hostile opponent, and this happens when he uses in his discourse by which he judges one of the adversaries the arguments which each of the adversaries use with the other. This is why a person who does not have the ability to conform to the condition of judgment must not be raised to the status of judge.

If the argument of one of the opponents about an issue was less persuasive because of the weakness of that opponent, and if the judge had things about the issue by which he could reinforce the argument of that opponent, so that it could become more persuasive, and if he [the judge] wanted to judge for that opponent by what he knew to be persuasive about that matter, not by what was apparent in the argument of the opponent, that would be a place for doubt. Will he judge according to what is apparent from the argument of the opponent, or according to what he knows about the force of persuasion in that matter? But if the judge is judge in that matter only according to those two opponents, he must not judge according to what he knows about the matter without the two opponents. If he is judge in that matter according to the matter itself, or according to what is considered good in the city, or according to what is better for the two opponents in addition to what is good in the city, and what he knows is the best, he will judge according to what he knows in that matter.

All this must be known from the position of the judge exercising his power of judgment. It must be known from his rank in the judiciary. At that moment what is entrusted to the judge from the judgment in this case will be according to the rank of the judge. By what power and by what faculty and art a person becomes judge between two opponents by means of rhetoric is what we will summarize as follows: Of the things that constitute persuasion we have enthymemes and examples. The status of the enthymemes in rhetoric is like the status of proofs in the sciences and syllogisms in dialectic. The enthymeme is a rhetorical syllogism and the example is a rhetorical induction.

The enthymeme is a proposition composed of two joint premises and gives us by itself, first according to the apparent point of view, persuasion about the conclusion resulting from the premises. It becomes persuasive since the speaker hides one of the two premises and does not state it. For this reason, it is called the enthymeme or that which is hidden, since the fact of hiding one of its two premises has been the reason for making it persuasive.

1.3 Medieval Islamic, c. 428 AH/1037 CE, Persia (Buyid Dynasty)

Ibn Sina (Avicenna) on Style: Article Four from His Book on *Rhetoric*

Maha Baddar

Introduction: Ibn Sina's Book on Rhetoric from Al-Shifa' (The Cure)

Abu Ali al-Husayn Ibn Sina, known in the west as Avicenna, was a medieval Arabic scholar (980–1037 CE) best known for his work on medicine but who has written extensively on philosophy, logic, mathematics, and mysticism. His *Rhetoric* is derived from his encyclopedic work *al-Shifa'* (الشفاء), or *the Cure*, a multivolume compendium that covers philosophy, metaphysics, mathematics, and the different logical arts following the order of the *Organon*. The title, *al-Shifa'*, metaphorically signifies that the book is meant to *cure* the reader's quest for knowledge by providing answers to their questions.

Ibn Sina's disciple and biographer, Abu Ubayd al-Juzjani, reported that Ibn Sina did not keep copies of the works that were commissioned of him. According to his biography, al-Juzjani explicitly asks Ibn Sina "to comment on the books of Aristotle," to which Ibn Sina responds by saying that commentary involved "debating with those who disagree or occupying [oneself] with their refutation" which Ibn Sina refused to do.[83] Ibn Sina ultimately calls the *Cure* a compendium, or *jumla* (جملة).[84] The *Cure* follows the order and the titles of the Aristotelian curriculum; however, at least as far as the *Rhetoric* is concerned, the content, approach, and organization are notably different from Aristotle's version and offer a more comprehensive approach to rhetoric that includes theories of government, law, and style relevant to Ibn Sina's immediate cultural and religious contexts. Gutas describes Ibn Sina not as necessarily anti-Aristotelian, but as a "reformer of the Aristotelian tradition."[85] In the Prologue Ibn Sina mentions:

> There is nothing of account to be found in the books of the ancients which
> we did not include in this book of ours; if it is not found in the place where
> it is customary to record it, then it will be found in another place which I
> thought more appropriate for it. To this I added some of the things which
> I perceived through my own reflection and whose validity I determined

---

83. Gutas 2014, 104.

84. Gutas 2014, 105. "Compendium" is a problematic labelling because the works within the multi-volume text are quite lengthy. For example, the Arabic edition of *Rhetoric* that I used is 247 pages in length and covers topics that extend far beyond those in Aristotle's *Rhetoric*.

85. Gutas 2014, 115.

through my own theoretical analysis, especially in the Physics, Metaphysics—and even in Logic if you will.[86]

The book's genre is not easy to identify. Ibn Sina refuses to call it a commentary, yet it fits within a series of books that follow the organization and titles of Alexandrian-Aristotelian canon. On the other hand, Ibn Sina himself calls it a compendium, but the sheer number, size, and scope of the topics covered contradict this classification. I claim here that this is an independent book on rhetorical theory that happens to be in dialogic engagement with Aristotle's logical curriculum.

At hand is a book that combines well-organized comprehensive sections, with rushed sections that are difficult to follow even for the trained reader of medieval Arabic, and sections that seem to have been inserted post-hoc from lecture notes taken by students. Despite these challenges, the book provides valuable contributions to political theory, the nature of legal discourse and documents, as well as style all under the larger umbrella of rhetoric.

RHETORIC AS PART OF A LARGER LOGICAL CURRICULUM

In the first article of the book, Ibn Sina compares rhetoric and dialectic, indicating that they share certain similarities, namely the lack of a specific subject matter and the same purpose, persuasion. According to Ibn Sina, however, rhetoric is based on probability, conjecture, and what is commonly believed to be good. Additionally, rhetoric relies on the manipulation of the audience's short-term memory and the rhetor's ability to mask disputable claims through the enthymeme. For Ibn Sina, unlike al-Farabi, the enthymeme's missing premise is not eliminated because it is obvious and does not have to be directly mentioned; rather, it is a questionable claim that is eliminated to avoid having the audience question the rhetor's credibility. Ibn Sina compares rhetoric to mathematics when he claims that a rhetor is better off refuting the doubt in the audience's soul by preparing to solve it in advance like a mathematical problem.

Early on in the treatise, Ibn Sina provides a traditional definition of persuasion as psychological process: the audience "leans" towards believing the rhetor; they "dispel" possible contradictions to what the rhetor says, and persuasion occurs when as a result of the tendency of the audience's "soul" to believe the rhetor. Unlike Aristotle, the audience play a prominent, active role in Ibn Sina's rhetorical situation and are referred to as more sophisticated than the simple masses, who are easily swayed. The rhetor uses topoi that are either ready-made or are created by him for persuasion; these make up a large component of Ibn Sina's book where all examples are rooted in an Islamic worldview, further distinguishing his work from that of the Greco-Roman tradition.

The tools of persuasion are specified in the *Rhetoric* and they all belong to the overarching notion of the Good. *Tathbit* (تثبيت), or proof, is the most general term used. Ibn Sina's most preferred means of persuasion is *al-i'tibar* (الاعتبار) or *al-tamthil* (التمثيل), which is the

---

86. Gutas 2014, 43.

use of examples. He also mentions the syllogism which he divides into nine types and the enthymeme, which he refers to using the Farabian term, *damir* (ضمير), as well as his own coined expressions, *tafkir* (تفكير) which is derived from the Arabic word for thinking.

Ibn Sina lists the following as kinds of rhetoric: praise, criticism, complaint, apology, and advice. These classifications may seem similar to the three Aristotelian types of rhetoric but the rest of the book shows some different interpretations for the use of rhetoric in society. For example, the focus on advice (or consultation) as an approach to governing a city is a clear diversion from Aristotle and positions rhetoric as a political art, especially that the advisor in the book is presented as a high-ranking government official, military leader, and even as a ruler in different contexts.

Ibn Sina refers to persuasion as the pillar of rhetoric, a reading of Aristotle's content through an Islamic lens (the term pillar invokes the five pillars of Islam in an Arabic reader's mind). The pillar, persuasion, has a list of assistants or tools that include persuasive statements, preparing the scene for the audience to be persuaded, and the use of witnesses. The latter topic, the introduction of witnesses, is quite different from Aristotle's. The word "witness" acquires various meanings when translated into Arabic; its meaning now includes citing a prophet, an imam, a philosopher, or a poet. To accommodate these meanings, Ibn Sina uses an Arabic derivation of the root *shahad* (شهد), namely, *istishhad* (استشهاد), that has the connotation of citing or quoting someone and does not necessarily refer to the witness as a person in the way it is presented in Aristotle's book. A typical outcome of the Translation Movement, this connotation reflects one way that Arabic scholars have added depth to the different fields of knowledge through translation. Other terms that have acquired newer connotations when translated into Arabic include logic, enthymeme, and persuasion.[87]

Ibn Sina's book uses Islamic law and the needs of an Islamic society as the foundation for his theory of rhetoric. He concludes the opening chapter of the first book by forcefully situating demonstration and rhetoric in an Islamic context by interpreting a verse from the Qur'an as referring to both arts. The verse says, "Invite to the way of your Lord with wisdom and good advice, and debate with them in the most dignified manner."[88] He interprets wisdom as demonstration and good advice as rhetoric. While some Arabic linguists and Islamic scholars may find this connection outlandish, this conclusion of the first article sets the tone for a rather extensive theory of rhetoric that serves the needs of a Muslim society.

One of the main contributions of Ibn Sina's rhetorical theory is the presentation of rhetor as political advisor. The responsibilities of the advisor vary in the different sections of the book, ranging from political leader, to military leader, to the ruler himself. Ibn Sina makes the original claim that "rhetoric is a beneficial talent in maintaining the well-being of cities and is a tool for governing the masses." Along these lines, a substantial part of the book covers what he calls *mashureyat* (مشوريات), or advisory rhetoric. It is one of the main branches of rhetoric and is not the equivalent of any of the three traditional Aristotelian classifications. *Mashureyat*

---

87. See Baddar (2010, 230–42).
88. Chapter: "An-Nahl," verse 125

is derived from the Islamic term *shura* (شورى) which means negotiation and consensus and was the foundation of Islamic politics in the early days of Islam.

IBN SINA'S ARTICLE ON STYLE

It was likely an awareness of the difference between the Arabic ʿ*ilm al-balagha* (علم البلاغة) and the Greek *fann al-khataba* (فن الخطابة), two different rhetorical traditions informing the discursive conventions of two different languages and cultures, that led Ibn Sina to incorporate elements from both fields into a comprehensive theory of style for Arabic speakers and writers. The Arabic ʿ*ilm al-balagha* deals with Arabic eloquence from grammatical, Qur'anic, and pre-Islamic poetic standpoints. It is an ancient, sophisticated field that was known to share little if anything with the art of rhetoric, *fann al-khataba* or the Greek *rhetorica*, which was hybridized with mostly Arabic-poetic stylistic elements. Because Arabs relied predominantly on poetry to fulfill rhetorical functions, the rules of eloquence in ʿ*ilm al-balagha* became rooted in Arabic poetics. Ibn Sina finds himself negotiating rules that belong to one field, poetics, and adapting them to another, rhetoric, while accommodating the immediate needs of his contemporary, cosmopolitan society that the rules of both fields were not initially created for.

As well, it was likely an awareness of linguistic and cultural contexts that made Ibn Sina continuously highlight some of the incompatibilities between the Arabic and Greek rhetorical traditions because of the differences in the morphological and syntactic nature of the two languages; this led him to openly reject certain Greek stylistic rules and substitute them with ones adapted from the Arabic tradition. This goes beyond setting clear rules of grammar to covering topics such as decorum. Due to the widespread use of writing within the different institutions of the Islamic empire at the time, Ibn Sina focuses not only on spoken discourse in speeches, but also on written discourse. He highlights its permanent nature, the rules that would guarantee the coherence of the written document, and the importance of writing and preserving documents in sensitive fields such as court documents.

While many rules from poetics are incorporated into Ibn Sina's theory of style, he clearly distinguishes poetry as not simply rhyming rhetoric. For Ibn Sina, rhyming statements with proper meaning do not qualify as poetry because they do not include metaphor and do not appeal to the imagination. They are poetic rhetoric—that is, persuasive utterances that convey acceptable, persuasive content. Certain stylistic decisions serve the goals of both rhetors and poets, namely persuasion and imagination.

Metaphor plays a minor if not non-existent role in rhetoric, or so claims Ibn Sina until he contradicts himself. He puts himself in numerous awkward situations throughout the article regarding the role of metaphor in rhetorical discourse. On more than one occasion, Ibn Sina declares the incompatibility between metaphor and rhetoric, yet he finds himself recommending the use of metaphor in certain situations related to decorum and sensibility. Ibn Sina's resistance to metaphor in rhetoric seems to stem from an emphasis on clarity and simplicity in rhetorical utterances because metaphor could be interpreted in different ways, hence jeopardizing this sought-after simplicity.

One discussion covered in the chapter on style that was not covered in Aristotle's rhetoric relates to the advancement in literacy in the Islamic empire during that reign of the Abbasids. Ibn Sina covers stylistic elements that work for written discourse as well as speeches. He differentiates between the difference types of written discourse and ranks them according to importance. Documents that merit attention in Ibn Sina's book are legal documents; as a result of writing a book on rhetoric almost a millennium after Aristotle, the focus shifts from memory and delivery in the oral Greek legal tradition to refined style and preservation in the Arabic written legal tradition. He recommends clarity, avoiding overgeneralizations, and variation in written discourse, all elements a speaker is not held accountable for.

Deciding on whether to adopt a simple or complex style in writing or speaking is another discussion covered in Ibn Sina's theory of style. He calls for an analysis of one's audience and context as well as an evaluation of the seriousness of the topic covered before a poet or rhetor decide on the level of complexity of their style. Audience and context awareness are also highlighted when he points out that the stylistic and grammatical rules of one language are not transferable to another.

In addition to the theorizing rhetoric as a political art, Ibn Sina's second main contribution is his theory of style, which he achieves by bridging two previously irreconcilable arts, the Arabic *'ilm al-balagha* and the Greek *fann al-khataba*. Ibn Sina does not hesitate to substitute the content of Greek stylistic norms with more culturally relevant material. In the article on style, Ibn Sina breaks with convention and uses the rules from both fields to help rhetors hone their style to better persuade their audiences.

A simple descriptive approach of the highlights on the article on style shows that the *Rhetoric* is neither simply an interpretation of Aristotle's *Rhetoric* nor a repurposing of it for a different time and place. Instead, Ibn Sina created his own version of the *Organon*, not to refurbish an ancient art for more contemporary uses, but to establish rhetorical rules that better serve the cultural, political, and legal needs of his society. His own ethos—and that of a highly cultured, cosmopolitan Islamic empire—are reflected in the ease with which he draws on several rhetorical traditions while acknowledging what could work from each tradition, and what would not or should be dismissed as obsolete.

Translation of Selections from Article Four: Style

Chapter 1, On Refining Style and Word-Choice

Some rhetors use intonation as a tool to persuade. Examples include using intonation to highlight an idea, emphasize it, make it sound wise, announce it, or imply it. Intonation is appropriate for expressing emotional actions as well as morals. For example, anger produces a certain intonation, while fear produces another; a different emotion will produce a completely different intonation. Emphasis and declaration show elegance, while a nervous or low intonation reflects weakness of the soul. All these are used by rhetors either so that the audience imagine what the rhetor's goal is through that intonation, or so that the soul of the listener emulate what the intonation invoked be it anger and harshness, cruelty, or tenderness and lenience.

Emphasis through tone is one kind of intonation. It is a form of intonation characterized by emphasis [of an expression or phase verbally]; it is non-literal. A rhetor can start a speech with it, or use it in the middle or the end. Emphasis could be used extensively or scarcely in a speech; the tone includes pointers toward the purposes of the rhetor. These pointers may be designed to satisfy [the audience], to define the parts of the speech, or to prepare the audience for imagination. They are also used to emphasize certain words. Emphasis could be delivered through strong pitch to reflect the state of the speaker, such as being confused or angry; or it could indicate that the speech includes threat or imploring, etc.

You should know that meaning may vary according to difference in tone. For example, it could change a statement [into a question]; or it could change a question into an exclamation, and so forth. Tone could be used to illustrate meter and balance. It could also be used to indicate that an expression is a conditional statement, a hypothesis, a predicate, or a subject.

Difference in intonation is characterized by three aspects: pitch, emphasis, and tone. Rhetors acquire this skill through emulating poets; they copy what works for poets to their art. They could also learn these skills from politicians who govern cities. But these things were not documented during the time of the First Teacher.[89] Even more important topics such as word-choice were not mentioned at all by him. These topics balance the statement so that it is better-rooted in the soul of the listeners and to cause belief in their soul. In reality, these characteristics of intonation have nothing to do with morphology and conjugation because the latter deal exclusively with utterances but the former are employed as useful artifices.

You should know that working on polishing utterances in rhetoric and poetry is an endeavor of great importance. However, in providing instructions, the question of choosing utterances is an easy task; it is sufficient that they be comprehensible, not confusing, non-metaphorical, and their meaning is clear.[90] Belief occurs in instruction using any statement as long as it conveys the meaning. On the other hand, with persuasion in rhetoric and imagination in poetry, one meaning can have several interpretations depending on the choice of utterance that covers it. Therefore, more effort is put into rhetoric and poetry to create belief and imagination respectively. A clear utterance makes the meaning clear while a nonsensical utterance creates a nonsensical meaning. Additionally, a solemn statement conveys a meaning that is seemingly firm while a quick statement makes the meaning flow. Therefore, those who deal with the truth have a strong command of knowledge, are honest, and do not embellish utterances.

---

89. Aristotle is referred to in Arabic scholarship from this time period as the First Teacher. Al-Farabi is referred to as the Second Teacher.

90. This reference to "instructions" could be referencing absolute facts in demonstration.

Deception and attracting people's attention are the product of character, but the use of linguistic artifices is the product of art.[91] This is why those who are able to master expression are better at argumentation than those who cannot, even if the meaning is the same. Those who can attract people's attention succeed in accomplishing what a naïve person cannot succeed in, even if the meaning is the same.

Written rhetorical messages are strongly effective only as far as the utterance itself is concerned, not based on deception since it cannot be written; it often weakens the meaning and a clear utterance makes up for it.

The first group to use what is outside the norm of accurate discourse are the poets because their structures are not based on either truth or a firm foundation, but only on imagination. Because of that, they took up exaggerating utterances and made recitation as equally important as every other aspect of the poem's purpose. From there they arrived at inventing civic rhetorical and narrative arts. Therefore, if a poet is able to invoke imagination without resorting to singing, musical composition, or through attracting attention and deception, they are worthy of admiration and their artifact is considered significant. For this reason, belief does not precede imagination in time. The well-known statements and debates from the past follow the poet's path of imagination. Some of the first things that people listen to are poetic examples that resemble imaginary sayings. After some time, they graduate to rhetoric, followed by dialectic, sophistry, and, finally, demonstration.

Those in charge of eloquence in every time period exert effort to understand and master mundane speech. This does not work in every situation or with any kind of poetry. Oftentimes, similar effort it used with discourse other than poetry. Short and light poems that deal with weak and ludicrous meanings should not be made grand but, banal ones should be used instead. This is why, when the propositions used by the Greeks for a certain meaning were modified and followed by other propositions, the grandeur of style involved within them was modified as well.

The rhetor should not express simple matters as having deep knowledge in every situation through the use of language that is extremely eloquent. Instead, the strength and fluidity of an expression should reflect the strength and fluidity of the content.

An utterance is made more graceful through variety. Variety includes not only the use mandated by the meaning but the use of metaphor, simile, and substitution. This is because discourse and utterances signify meaning. If an utterance does not signify something, it is not satisfactory. It should independently possess a certain allure so that appropriate imagination is invoked and adds to its significance. Therefore, utterances should not base or vulgar, on the one hand, or exceed in strength the meaning of the topic they refer to, on the other. Similarly, creative poets who utilize good, informal language in their poetry still choose from a discursive repertoire that is well-known and dignified instead of using base or affected

---

91. In this translation I use the expressions "attracting the audience's attention" or enticing the audience to refer to the Arabic expression *al-akhthi bilwojouh* (الاخذ بالوجوه), which, if literally translated, means "taking by the faces." The closest interpretation to the medieval expression is to "dishonestly attract or entice the audience."

language that oversteps social norms in its lack of decency. These middle utterances that go above colloquial language, but are not too affected, are called appropriated utterances. Types of utterances are referred to in the *Poetics*.[92]

Note that the splendor gained through the use of metaphor and variation is caused by the surprise they invoke that is followed by a sense of awe and charm. This is similar to how people feel when they meet a stranger; they feel shy and in awe around them than around relatives. A rhetor should adopt this approach when the need for invoking awe and surprise is needed. Meter is a great tool to accomplish this effect. Using metaphor and imagery in statements with meter is more appropriate in poetry than using them in prose. But they are more appropriate for free prose than in poetry. Yet it varies from one situation to another. For example, addressing someone you do not know as "a man" is not the same as calling them "a little child" because the latter is not appropriate at all.[93] This is a situation that requires appropriate language use to go with it. One should not follow poetic conventions in such situations because rhetoric is designed to persuade, unlike poetry whose goal is invoking imagination.

It should be known that use of metaphor in rhetoric is not a foundational element but a kind of artifice used to promote something to those who are deceived and cheated by weak persuasion and imagination. This is similar to cheating food and drink by adding something to make them taste better or to make them seem to possess good qualities and are thus promoted as good and pure. Some of these actions [in rhetoric] could lead to repugnant expressions such as the actions of a man known as Edros who used to falsify his language and voice; he spoke in a language different from his native language in order to imitate foreigners. The experts were repulsed by these actions because he deviated from the norm whereas the arrogant and ignorant were fascinated by him.

It is accidental to use poetic rhetoric or rhetorical poetry. It is possible for a poet to use rhetoric while not reciting poetry if regular meanings and proper sayings free of imagination or simile are put together in a rhyming pattern. However, this is foolish and perceptive people do not consider this to be poetry. It is not sufficient for poetry to rhyme only. The person who does this is similar to a thief because they unnecessarily steal belief. The first person to do so was Orephedes.

The basic foundation of rhetoric is that the words from which a speech is constructed be original and appropriate and that metaphor be introduced as adornment. Similarly, the use of foreign languages and compound, coined expressions that are not commonly used should be sparsely introduced. However, poets and those who emulate them are the ones who create these coined combinations such as saying, "this person *yatakahsham* (يتكشحم)."[94] This is looked down upon in rhetoric because it is suited for use in imagination rather than belief. You should know that there is a difference between *beautiful* and *agreeable*, between *strong*

---

92. He likely refers to his own book, which precedes the *Rhetoric* in *al-Shifa*.

93. This is an awkward transition from the appropriate use of meter to the appropriate use of words. The awkwardness may be caused by the nature of the lecture setting. Or, it may be due to an interruption in writing, or that this was the beginning of a new lecture on a different day.

94. This is a coined verb in the original text, with no obvious meaning.

and *great* as well as between *shape* and *form*. It is recommended in rhetoric to use known, appropriated terms as well as language that is commonly used in the community; these are words that reflect meaning. Variations only work to a certain extent and agile rhetoricians use these variations.

Metaphor and variation use a known expression to indicate something else; they include the use of strange expressions, or expressions that are neither known nor strange but are pleasant. A pleasant expression is an appropriated one, especially if it is not made up of letters that are not repulsive in their distinction or composition. In any case, synonyms, metaphors, and other imagery should be used in a matter appropriate to the thing they seek to express, not be necessary according to convention. This could also be accomplished through the use of opposites since a thing's qualities could be learned through contrasting it with its opposite. For example, an elderly man can use *kohl* (كحل), whereas a child uses other ways to improve their appearance.[95] When one sees the child, it is known that what they used for improving their appearance is not appropriate for an older person. Similarly, if a rhetor wants to use metaphor and variation to adorn their speech, they should use ones that are appropriate and that are not far-removed from the genus of the topic. If they want to belittle someone and make them seem repugnant, they should not describe them using similes that are far-removed from the genus of their bad deeds. Therefore, if a rhetor wants to put down a petitioner, they should say, "This person is imploring." Similarly, if a rhetor wants to praise a strong matter, they should not use a farfetched simile, but instead describe the matter or person as proficient. Also, for example, a swindler or thief could be described using a simile that would not miss the original meaning but would either exaggerate or minimize their qualities depending on the purpose. This is similar to undermining the state of an oppressor by describing them as *mistaken*; on the other hand, the actions of someone who committed an error could be exaggerated through describing them as an oppressor or transgressor. Other examples of minimizing or exaggerating a quality include describing someone who stole as having taken or acquired with the intention of lightening the issue, or describing them as having raided or looted to exaggerate the matter.

If a rhetor cannot find a specific term to express a certain meaning, they should borrow [or use metaphor] but the borrowing should be from appropriate and similar matters. The meanings from which the rhetor borrows should be pleasant, known, and commended as well as used in familiar speech. Metaphors that are not widely spread and known are contrary to rhetorical conventions.

It is a sign of decorum in rhetoric that if a rhetor wants to express something that is considered inappropriate that they not mention the simple, straightforward term that reflects the literal, inappropriate meaning without the use of a compound expression, that is, without the mediation of metaphor. Instead, they should avoid the straightforward meaning and use metaphor or replace it with something else. Even though this is lying, it is good lying. It is possible to allude to meaning without the use of a clear expression. But this is not an honest trend in a speech because a rhetor should express meaning in such a way that they are understood.

---

95. *Kohl* is an eye liner made from a ground black mineral.

Therefore, if they omit a term and allude to it instead, it is as if they abandoned delivering a speech. It is preferable that, instead of utilizing what is inappropriate, that the rhetor mention and recommend its opposite. The rhetor should use statements that reflect what is preferred and recommended. For example, if a rhetor wants to defame a person, they should say that honor is better than injustice or that chastity is better than promiscuity. Instead of using the direct reference, the rhetor, for example, could say, "moderation is no less than greed in bringing about affluence." A rhetor could mention the opposite of what is unacceptable and recommend the more acceptable alternative as these examples have illustrated. Alternatively, they may not mention the opposite and only focus on what is recommended and preferred alone; that would suffice in this particular topic. For example, they would say; "Acquiring chastity is recommended" or, "Acquiring more friends is preferred." This approach could also work to defame those who are not chaste or do not have friends, but it is mainly a tool for conciseness in style.[96]

All metaphors are created from topics that they share certain aspects with such as the expression itself, a similarity in emphasis, a similarity in action, or a similarity to the senses, seen or otherwise.

A metaphorical transitional expression has different levels in influencing the audience. For example, in a courtship poem describing the beloved's fingers, it is more realistic to describe them as rosy rather than red or crimson. Metaphorically using "rosy" to refer to a shade of red invokes in the imagination the pleasantness of a rose; such a connotation would never be invoked in the audience's imagination by simply using "red." Using "red" does not indicate praise and commendation. Additionally, using "crimson" invokes imagining a dirty crimson worm. The same applies to non-metaphorical, fabricated names, some of which are better than others. It is better to use a term with positive, dignified connotations than one with negative, lowly ones, even if both refer to the same meaning. For example, a mule could be described as the offspring of a horse even though it is not a horse. This has a better connotation than saying that it is the offspring of a donkey but is not a donkey. Both statements aim superficially at expressing the same meaning. But an analysis of both leads to different conclusions, one of them is more appealing than the other. This is close to what Abu at-Tayyeb said: "O Ibn Karous, you are half-blind/ but you pride yourself on being half-seeing."[97] Superlative and diminutive statements are used in the same manner.

Simile follows the same path as metaphor.[98] However, metaphor makes something become another whereas simile indicates that it is similar to another, not the different thing itself. An example of simile is saying, "Achilles leapt like a lion." Simile works in rhetorical discourse like metaphor if it is used in moderation. But its original use is in poetry. If both simile and met-

---

96. I added *not* here, because it seems to have been dropped as a scribal error.

97. This references Abu at-Tayyeb al-Mutanabbi, the famous Arab poet.

98. This paragraph begins with a sentence that says, "Expressions that are very farfetched use اطراغودية" (*itraghoudiyya*). I have not been able to locate this term for translation, which may signal that it was a scribal error, as the editor of the Arabic edition has provided several alternative spellings. It may have been unclear in the original manuscript.

aphor are used together, they are compatible. For example, if one needs to refer to Venus and Mars at the same time through the use of metaphor, simile, or imitation and refers to Venus the "cup holder," one should refer to Mars as the "spear holder." Even if they are opposed in meaning to each other, they are figuratively represented in ways that are similar in certain aspects but different in others.

Chapter 2, On Satisfactory Discourse: On avoiding Hybrid Terms; On Choosing what is Recommended in Rhetoric

Let us now discuss word choice. I say: Words should first and foremost be accurate and eloquent. They should not have a trace of another language pronunciation because this weakens the discourse and makes it unpleasant. Moreover, conjunctions should be used whenever they are needed.

It is important to note that different languages have different rules, so nothing said about these rules is universal or absolute. It is important, when choosing words free of simile or metaphor, to use special terms that do not have a common meaning with others. They should not be confusing by invoking a certain meaning as well as its opposite. These terms are sugar-coated and erroneously used such as Empedocles's use of the term "sphere," saying that one day the world will become one while also saying that the world started as one.

It may be beneficial to elaborate when the goal is to stress persuasion or exaggeration. In this case, individual words are substituted by statements. A noun could be replaced by a statement if saying the noun directly may be offensive, such as the reference to a woman's vagina; in this case it is better to substitute it by using "a woman's private parts" instead. One should also substitute the reference to menstruation by saying ,"women's blood" and the direct reference to intercourse by saying, "touching women."[99] A noun could be substituted by a specific attribute, such as substituting intercourse by "lying down with." The same applies to referring to genitals. It is also possible to not use an attribute and resort to using simile and metaphor.

Poets avoid using the set meaning of a term and are eager to use metaphor. If there are two meanings for a term, one set and the other includes variation, they tend to use the latter. For example, if something is referred to as a "rest place" or a "house," poets tend to call it a "rest place" even though it is more accurate to call it a "house" because it is the person's own place and home. They use "rest place" because it introduces variety in meaning and invokes the imagination of resting. Poets also move from using nouns to using adjectives. For example, they refer to buildings and houses as the "multi-windowed," or as the "double-faced" and "double-doored."

Emotional discourse is the motivator at emotional times even if it is contrary to ethics. Such discourse a wise person would be embarrassed of and avoid mentioning using direct terms as a result of being stuck between ethics and emotions. An example of such emotional sayings is when a speaker says, "every rational person knows 'x.'" In this case, the listener

---

99. Ibn Sina was a renowned medical scholar in the Medieval period; hence these medical references likely came from his own experience.

would feel too embarrassed to deny such a statement. Another example is a person telling their opponent, "do you think people yield to your boring statements and listen to your equivocation?" Or someone could say, "you disrespect the ruler and the audience and neglect them and do not critically examine what speech you propose to them." Such speech or what is similar to it aggravates mediators and leads them to chastise the opponent.

It is necessary to carefully choose the appropriate time for every action according to what suits it. This is a prevalent rule for all discourse. Claiming accuracy also follows these guidelines. This occurs through accompanying each utterance by saying, "there is no doubt that," and "it is obvious that."[100] It is also necessary to preface utterances by listing numbers.

It is not always necessary for the rhetor to only use moderate expressions. It may sometimes be necessary to use others such as leaning toward the use of overstatements or understatements. The rhetor should persuade through a variety of ways. If they do not do so, the speech on face value would be naïve and would not improve through the use of artifice. In such a case, persuasion would not work. If something gentle is expressed through harsh expression or vice versa, this is considered reparation accomplished through good art that leads to persuasion. Spurious terms, as well as exaggerated and strange ones, are useful in emotional cases, especially if they are accompanied by emotional meanings and expressions of praise, defamation, modesty, and cordiality. This is similar to what Socrates said: "my aim will be fulfilled because I have put forth my patience and effort." Indeed, one who puts in effort accomplishes their goal. This is more relevant to poetry. Socrates said that this used to be the practice of ancient poets. This is why no ancient poet had come across as foolish; their sayings were persuasive, and their wisdom and their predictions were believed if they made their claims using these techniques. As for rhetoric, if such techniques are licensed, meter and rhythm should not be used because people will view the discourse as artificial and affected. However, the rules of the art should be followed and, within this framework, what could cause surprise or imagination, not persuasion, should be avoided. A rhetor should not be led through enthusiasm to focus on words and conveying their purpose prematurely. Such haphazard speech is unpleasant to the audience and sounds redundant. If they present such a speech against an opponent, it will sound like the argument of young boys in the marketplace. Such discourse sounds redundant to the public.

I say, habit and customs mandate issues that cannot be fully mastered in creating speech, conjugating it, presenting it as rhymed prose, and so forth. It is worth noting that the Greeks in this category used cases that we did not learn, or stop at, and we do not believe they are beneficial today. Arabs have different rules to make prose closer to poetic composition.

---

100. This is an antiquated rhetorical rule that contradicts current conventions.

Chapter 3, On Meter in Rhetorical Discourse; On Using Tools that Include Intonation; On what is Required in Rhetorical Speeches; On what is Recommended when a Speech is Addressed Orally to an Audience; On what is Recommended in Specialist Settings; On what is Recommended in Speech and what is Recommended in Writing

It has been mentioned in the *First Learning* that rhetorical discourse should be detailed; this means it should include sections.[101] A detailed section should not stand alone but should lead to the following section that completes the meaning. This is similar to what the eloquent among the Arabs say, "Avoid saying what the soul [of the audience] would deny, even if you have a justification for it/ Not all who deny it will have the open mind to accept the justification.[102] Each hemistich needs the following one to be fully understood. Such details are recommended in spoken rhetoric that includes tone that signals pauses and connections. Rhetorical discourse should use conjunctions to link clauses; this means conjunctions and transitions should join the beginning and the end of an utterance either for repetition or alliteration. The repeated word should signify a different meaning. This makes the speech pleasant through including clear boundaries at which the audience's mind would pause. They also make memorizing the speech easier because its sections are numbered. Similarly, metered discourse can be memorized through repeated transitions. Overall, utterances that include rhyme, meter, and conjunctions are more likely to be stored in the memory than utterances that do not. The length of rhyming prose should be done in such a way that it does not separate the beginning and end of an utterance in a way that hinders remembering the first rhyme. Additionally, it shouldn't be too short and ends quickly. Joining the parts of an utterance through conjunction should not be dissimilar or separated in a way that makes it incoherent. Coherent discourse includes sections that include pauses in between like in rhymes joined with conjunctions.

One of the pleasant metaphorical variations is to attribute a quality to the subject while omitting the subject itself, especially when this quality is integral to the meaning. For example, one should not say, "older people do good deeds," but say, instead, "old age does good deeds." This is a quality in general and works like genus. One should avoid metaphors that are too intertwined, which is using a metaphor within a metaphor. Unfamiliar expressions should also be avoided. Overdoing an art is a disadvantage. Moreover, indulging in the use of foolish and vulgar expressions is despicable; these are expressions that are instantly understood by everybody. What is difficult to understand is also despicable. An utterance should be composed in such a way that it is understood by exemplary people, not the base commoners, and it should only be understood if they contemplate its meaning without having to examine it closely. This is not infrequent. Well-balanced discourse, especially that which includes oppositional sections, is pleasant. Well-balanced discourse also includes pleasant metaphors that are not farfetched. The rhetor should examine, contemplate, and choose the most appropriate of terms and metaphors.

---

101. Most likely, this references Aristotle's *Rhetoric.*
102. These are rhyming lines in Arabic.

Variation should be used for clarity and to attract attention. Three factors are key to this, namely variations, oppositions, and verbs. As for variations, the most successful of these is when a metaphor is identical in meaning to its source and includes nothing that expresses a deviation from the meaning intended. There are four kinds of variation. One is the use of similes. Another is to use metaphors based on opposition (such as referring to the sun as "the radiant," or to refer to black as "the father of whiteness." Another kind of variation it to use metaphors based on similarity (such as referring to the king as the commander or pilot of the nation). The fourth are metaphors made up of one word, such as referring to the Dog Star as "the barking in the sky" or referring to Aries as "the butter (that who butts horns) in the sky".

It is unpleasant to use rhetorically rare, uncommon metaphors in writing. This includes exaggerating utterances, such as saying, "All people agree that . . . ," and saying, "You and that person. . . ."[103] Pleasant variation includes referring to a noun using a pronoun in such a way that the reference to the noun is inferred. That way the speaker can avoid having to mention the noun explicitly. The opposite is also a pleasant kind of variation; in this case, the speaker will say something explicitly, but it will be clearly inferred from the context that the opposite is the intended meaning. This could be accomplished through the use of a similar noun.

You should know that the written utterance should be verified and well-scrutinized for accurate signification. On the other hand, the spoken utterance is more inaccurate because of the use of deception and the tendency to attract the audience's attention that were previously mentioned. This could be accomplished through ethical or emotional means. Such deceptive speakers are very adept at reading books on how to attract an audience's attention and books on improving style. Poets do the same. What is heard but not read is easily forgotten so it is not subject to critical thinking and it is not necessary to correct it the way written discourse is. This is why many good writers do not excel at persuasion in speeches while many creative, persuasive speakers are not good at working with their hand, writing to persuade. The reason is that deception works well in arguments and negotiations as well as in other cases where conjunctions are ignored through summarizing and repeating the same words from memory. None of this is appropriate for writing.

Combining methods of persuading an audience through variation works well in persuasion because they all work on misleading the mind. Abandoning the use of deception is taking the stronger path to persuasion, whereas being deceptive includes the use of courtesy and entreaty. Additionally, if terms are used without any conjunctions, it is considered a type of deception. Examples include saying, "I kept" or "I requested" without signifying the object through speech but through gesturing, form delivery, and intonation, as well as through symmetrical emphasis and rapid acceleration. Note that summary through avoiding the use of conjunctions is only verbal, but not mental. Using transitions makes long utterances coherent and avoiding their use makes an utterance verbose causing the possibility for different interpretations. For example, "I kept, found, and requested." This gives the illusion that the person has done a lot.

---

103. The reference is unclear in the original text.

It is recommended that a speech begin with an introduction that presents the rhetor's purpose, especially in advisory rhetoric. Most speeches are argumentative. Arab rhetoricians have known that as illustrated by their speeches after conquests.[104] They would say, "Praise be to God who supports His followers, the Conqueror of His enemies." This gesture is like presenting a mental picture setting the scene before the description of the purpose.

The bigger the audience, the more explanation and less persuasion are needed. This is because persuading large groups, the general public, and the masses is an easy endeavor. However, persuading specialists is difficult. Explaining things to the general public is difficult but it is easy to explain them to specialists. It is necessary that forensic rhetoric be phrased in a way very close to the purpose. Each word used should be identical to the intended meaning, especially that it is not a general speech but is addressed to one judge and a special council. By contrast, faking disputes is easy in front of large audience. One particular thing is needed in forensic rhetoric: good utterances that are free of many metaphors, similes, and exaggerations that are used in speeches at the pulpit (mosques) and in celebrations. Working on a dispute for a special council should focus on specifically expressing the purpose of the topic as closely as possible. That way, the person presenting the cause does not deviate from their goal because judging in a special council is a straightforward, civil, honest work that does not require the affectation needed in celebrations. This is why those rhetoricians who are accustomed to speaking to large groups are not successful in special councils as they are at the pulpit, since deception and attracting the audience's attention work better in the latter setting than in the former. What is used to address a large audience could be far removed from the truth because what is used to help a big group should be at the level of the lowest in intellect among them, but explaining something to a group of specialists is a different matter. If the purpose of a general speech is quantity, not verification, then deception works better in it than close scrutiny.

As for the seen discourse, i.e., the written, not the spoken discourse, which includes epistles, it only requires reading. This discourse also includes records that judges and rhetors make permanent. Such discourse does not require exaggeration or glorification; this is despised. Instead, a part of the discourse should be refined. If it includes praise and advice, utterances should follow the same criteria. It should be closely corrected because an official record is more distinct than a letter. It is also more permanent and more needed to fulfil the purpose of the rhetor. Therefore, its terms should be well-known, not unfamiliar or strange, and it should be free of vulgar terms. It should not include ellipses because they make the discourse regress into being unfamiliar, and such abbreviation makes it lose its purpose. It should still be combined with agreeable gestures such as familiar variations as well as a few unfamiliar ones and some rhetorical meter in the persuasive sections.

---

104. His discussion of advisory and argumentative rhetoric followed by an example that deals with ceremonial rhetoric is a bit confusing here.

Chapter 4, On Parts of the Rhetorical Utterance: Organization of the Three Kinds; On Audience Response

We should now learn about composing and organization. I say: Rhetoric is concerned with two matters: the topic of the discourse and the proof used to explain the topic. In general, rhetoric includes a claim and proof. Rhetorical utterances include an introduction, a narrative, and the conclusion. The introduction outlines the persuasive appeals and informs the audience of what needs to be done overall. Persuasion is precision.[105] The conclusion puts together what has been proven and reminds the audience of it in one piece as an ending to the utterance.

Narrative is not needed in advisory rhetoric because it is a narration of a real, current topic so it is concerned with what is pleasant and unpleasant such as in dispute, or what is fair or not fair, such as in argument. Advisory rhetoric does not include content to be narrated for argumentation, praise, or defamation; neither does it include disputation or challenge. Instead it includes proof for a future benefit. If such elements of narration are introduced, it becomes a complaint. It is recommended to include an introduction in advisory rhetoric so that the audience is aware of the purpose in one of the statements then continues to evaluate its value through comparing the proof presented by the different contestants. Having a conclusion is also recommended in advisory rhetoric, such as saying, "I have said all I have about the benefits of my proposal, and you can now decide." Some complaints should not be prolonged by narration if the goal is to be brief. The introduction, narrative, and conclusion are presented to the audience, not the opponent in the case of complaint. Opponents are addressed through persuasion. Persuasion could be prolonged and repeated to remind and explain not necessarily because repetition is part of the composition of a speech.

The introduction works well in praise and defamation, such as saying, "People should be amazed at the Greeks' virtue." Afterwards, the rhetor would list these virtues and confirms them. The introduction also works in advising, such as saying, "It is one's duty to treat virtuous people reverently." Then the rhetor would transition to referring to the particular person whom one should treat reverently.

As for the artifices that are not part of the topic, you have learned about their usefulness earlier. These include the speaker praising themselves, enticing the listeners, making them imagine the topic the way the rhetor wants them to, and showing the flaws of the opponent, and vice versa. A person who has a complaint definitely uses these artifices. They should emphasize their virtue as well as the baseness of their opponent. The respondent to the complaint should start by honestly responding to the complaint at the beginning because this is what is expected. Then they should use artifices. For example, those who defame the opponent to contradict their praise of themselves should introduce persuasion immediately to exaggerate the opponent's repulsiveness.

While considering organization, opening with what is pleasant for praise is good, or what is ugly for defamation as a surprise is more realistic. Only after that can the artifices be used.

---

105. It could be inferred here that he is referring to the narrative section where the persuasion takes place.

The person presenting a complaint should use a lengthy introduction. Attracting the audience's attention happens through making the topic closer to their mind, familiar, or simplifying it while at the same time making it seem unfamiliar. Making the topic familiar should be done in a moderate manner so that the audience do not notice. Enticing the audience could also be accomplished through familiarity and affection at times and through the opposite at other times. Affection makes the audience imagine the good in what the speaker says. It should be accomplished through closeness, status, and good appearance.[106] All of this occurs through illusion. If affection does not work for the speaker, it is recommended that the rhetor rely exclusively on persuasion. A foolish listener is more malleable to enticing than to persuasion. Therefore, the speaker should use appeasement rather than persuasion. Appeasement is accomplished through an introduction that would capture their attention and that is ornate and grand.

You should know that, while presenting a complaint, it is unpleasant to open with very base attributes or statements that evoke feelings of sadness and alienate the listener. Doing so makes the speaker lose their splendor. The introduction is intended for capturing the attention of the audience. This is why many people tend to prolong it. If they overdo it, however, the souls of the listeners yearn for the truth. Dwelling on the introduction and prolonging it is an act of cowardice, and a sign of weakness and the inability to declare the topic. Praising the audience is useful in enticing them. If the speech is prepared for complaint, it does not need a substantial introduction, because most of the topic is about known matters. However, if the listener or opponent does not understand the importance of the topic, then their attention to it should be drawn through an introduction.

Countering a complaint can occur by two means. The opponent can deny the occurrence of the incident, or they can admit its occurrence and deny its harm.

In praise, the rhetor should use persuasion derived from the actions and qualities of the person to be praised. It is through these that virtue is emphasized. Outside factors and qualities that are agreed upon to be virtuous should be used to confirm persuasion, such as saying, "It is befitting to say that, being the son of virtuous people, he was virtuous."

As you have so far learned, advisory rhetoric and praise share certain qualities. Praise can become advice using minimal change in wording. For example, saying, "He is virtuous because he does 'x' and 'y'" is praise. But saying, "Do 'x' and 'y' to become virtuous" is advice.

Moral speech is related to choice. That is why the teachings do not include any moral sayings attributed to something beautiful or ugly, or beneficial or harmful, except among some of Socrates's companions. Moral sayings could be used as proof of the moral character of the opponent.[107] For example, if it is said, "he both talks and walks at the same time," this proves that he is heedless and rash and that he does not speak through perception but depends on taking risks. Moral statements depend on the choice of form. If persuasion is not achieved through that, they lead to it through signs, reasons, and examples of the person's actions. The

---

106. Reference to delivery.
107. This is a reference to the *topoi* or maxims mentioned in the *Rhetoric*.

respondent should represent attracting the audience's attention (through deception) as despicable by saying, "this is a trick and it is like the pretense to weep done by muggers."[108]

Argumentation in advisory rhetoric is as follows: either the topic does not exist or is not useful; it exists but is not useful; it is useful but not just; what is referred to is not needed in the issue; or it should not be one way, but another.

Proof is useful. Examples are more useful in advisory rhetoric to compare what was with what is. Enthymemes are more useful in disputation, whereas examples are of little use because the object of complaint exists. Therefore, the system of enthymemes should be changed from what was mentioned in *Dialectic*. In some situations, they should be mentioned in order if the utterance is strong and the organization further clarifies it. You should remember from the science of dialectic what you need to rely on in order to achieve that. If you aim to cause an emotional reaction, you should not use an enthymeme at all; they are mutually exclusive. The emotional reaction distracts from the enthymeme. It is accomplished through imagination and pain and sways choice to a certain direction. An enthymeme informs without offering any options.

Advisory rhetoric is more difficult than argumentation forensic rhetoric because talking about what exists is easier than talking about what does not. Stressing Islamic law in forensic rhetoric is a strong resource because using it as proof is certain to be believed and no one dares to contradict or reject it as with other propositions, unless the opponent themselves doubt an aspect of Islamic law itself.

Topoi of praise work well in praise. Chastising is more effective than proof because it includes inflicting pain and diminishing the status of the opponent addressed.

As for the speech of the opponent, some of it can be opposed, as you have learned, through resistance, while some is opposed by another measure. If you oppose in advisory and forensic speeches, you are better off beginning by criticizing what the opponent has said. You should then proceed to prove the opposite of what they tried to say. If an advisor proves the advice of their opponent to be wrong, this increases the possibility that their own speech will be better listened to than if they started simply with their own advisory speech, especially if what they recommend leads to success, is sound, and is persuasive.

It is useful for a speaker to respond to an opponent presenting a complaint by saying, "a person who insists on complaining pays no heed to apology. You are sharp-tongued and eloquent; you quarrel about or exaggerate everything; you blow things out of proportion; additionally, are able to win and are articulate, so people believe you to be truthful but God does not." Or they could say, "you are insistent and you entice through long speeches." Or they could say, "you are a fool who does not know what they are saying and it is a wonder I busy myself with you."

---

108. Most likely, this references an idea similar to crocodile tears.

Chapter 5, On the Rhetorical Question and when it Should be Used; On Response; On Concluding a Rhetorical Text

Posing questions in rhetoric does have benefits in some situations. These include: yes-no questions that, if they are answered by yes, the opponent is obligated to fulfill what they specifically say in their speech. If answered by no, the opponent's response would be received as repugnant and would be renounced by the listeners, or vice versa. Next, the speaker should be confident enough to respond with a term that corresponds to a pronoun that results in the desired result, such as saying, "Hasn't he entered the house without permission? Then after his entrance things were lost?" In this case, the speaker knows that the opponent believes them and admits the deed. When they respond with "yes," it is taken against them and it is believed that the person is a thief. The first case differs from this because the former response leads to vilification while the latter leads to the required result. This is beneficial because the speaker would not be able to prove the accusation without the opponent's confession.

In dealing with questions, if the opponent provides a contradictory response, the speaker can ridicule their foolishness. If the question is multi-faceted, the respondent has the right to provide a very detailed answer. If they are asked such a question, and they do not provide details, then they have adhered to what is expected, but if they prolong their response, they bore the listeners and give the impression that they are confused. After all, the general public does not discern details; instead, a response persuades them if it is brief and determined through the use of "yes" or "no." If a respondent is tested by providing a response to a group of commoners, and responds briefly, then they are cut off.[109] If, on the other hand, they provide a detailed response, they show the illusion they are clinging to interpolation and talking incoherently. This makes the situation of the speaker difficult.

It may be necessary to use jesting and joking at times. I have covered joking elsewhere and mentioned how its use varies whether the person is noble or base. A noble person uses it for allusion, to imply the meaning without explicitly mentioning it. It is used in cases such as praising oneself, belittling the enemy, or enticing the audience.

The conclusion is how to end a speech; it should be detailed and not part of what was said before it, just like the introduction, especially in advisory discourse. An example is saying, "this is what I said and you heard. The judgment is yours, as we Muslims say, I say this speech of mine and I ask God forgiveness for myself and you. He is merciful and gracious."[110]

---

109. Unclear statement in the original text.

110. It is standard rhetorical practice in Arabic to open and close both spoken and written discourse with such religious notes.

1.4 Medieval Islamic, c. 442 AH/1050 CE, Spain

Foundations of Rhetoric in Ibn Hazm: Selections from *Ring of the Dove* and *A Treatise on the Cure of Souls and the Improvement of Manners*

Robert Eddy and Raed Alsawaier

INTRODUCTION

Ibn Hazm was born in tenth-century CE Islamic Spain. More precisely, Abu Muhammad Ali Ibn Hazm was born on 30th of Ramadan in November 994 CE. He died in August 1064 CE. Ibn Hazm's own account of his birth reads: "I was born in Cordoba, in the eastern part, . . . before sunrise and after the imam's morning call to prayer . . . at the end of the night of Wednesday, the last day of the moon in the magnificent month of Ramadan, which corresponds to 7 November . . . 994, with Scorpio in the ascendant."[111] He lived in a remarkably multicultural, multireligious environment and mixed with people of many different races and ethnicities. Ibn Hazm comes from a mixed heritage of both Arabic and Persian descent, although the Persian connection might be a false claim of political motive chosen by his ancestors and believed by him.[112] In addition to being familiar with other languages, Ibn Hazm was fluent in Arabic and Hebrew. He was influenced by the works of Plato and Greek philosophy in general, although Vilchez sees no evidence that Ibn Hazm knew Aristotle's *Rhetoric*.[113] Understanding this cultural and philosophical background is essential in appreciating the multiple identities and roles that the polymath Ibn Hazm represented. Vilchez lists some of Ibn Hazm's rich complexity of roles: "genealogist, religious historian, theologian, philosopher, great theoretician of Zahirism and the famous author of *The Ring of the Dove*.[114]

In addition to being a philosopher, theologian, physician, and a poet, he was also a pioneer in publishing about topics rarely addressed such as the art of love as manifested in his *The Ring of the Dove*. Unlike Ibn Sina (Avicenna) who in his *Treatise on Love* never quotes the Qur'an or Hadith, Ibn Hazm has frequent references to both.[115] He wrote mostly in prose but a significant part of his writing is also Arabic poetry. He was a preeminent historian who was a prolific author of more than a hundred books, of which only about 40 survive. His rhetorical style uses argument and counter argument in an inventive manner to emphasize his views and respond both to his proponents and opponents. As a politician, philosopher, and Islamic jurisdictionist, Ibn Hazm focused on language and rhetoric. He established his rhetorical

111. Vilchez 2013b.
112. Wasserstein 2013, 69–72.
113. Vilchez 2013b, 290.
114. Vilchez 2013a, 4.
115. Ghazi Bin Muhammad. *Love in the Holy Quran*. Cambridge: Islamic Texts Society, 2013, 6.

foundations in his book: *An Approximation of Logic's Extremities.*[116] His views on rhetoric are based on the following foundations:

- He posited that successful rhetorical language had to be founded on two things: clarity, and accessibility. Clarity referred to comprehensibility and accessibility included freedom from unnecessary elaboration and laconic expressions. He commented: "Rhetoric should be as comprehensible to the average as it is appreciated by the knowledgeable" [117]
- Ibn Hazm used arguments based on numerous references to and with figurative language. For example, his poetry was unique because he would use three, four, and five images in one or two lines of poetry; a technique unique even among the best poets in Arabic literature. An example of this in this line of poetry from *The Ring of the Dove*[118]:

ن النوى والعتبَ والهجرَ والرضا   قرانٌ وأندادٌ ونحسٌ وأسعدُ كأ

Desertedness, blame, abandonment, and content;
Are like friends, foes, misery, and happiness

CONTEXT OF RAED ALSAWAIER'S TRANSLATION

Alsawaier's translation includes two parts. The first part, a selection from the *Ring of the Dove*, was previously translated to English by A. J. Arberry in 1953.[119] While Arberry's translation focuses on preserving the original text and creating a Shakespearean English equivalent, Alsawaier focuses on creating a translation from an Arabic speaker's perspective, which is accessible and teachable in contemporary American learning spaces in schools and colleges.

The uniqueness of Alsawaier's translation is reflected by the choices he made in texts selected for translation which center rhetorical elements of Ibn Hazm's writing. Ibn Hazm continuously uses *Logos* to appeal to his audience's intellect by supporting his argument with historical and literary evidence aiming at principles of reason and logic above all else; many are influences of Greek tradition. This is evident in both selected translations as Ibn Hazm cites others and advances his argument with an unusually complete focus on logical reasoning.

Certainly, however, Ibn Hazm is not exclusively engaged with *Logos*. The second element of rhetoricity in Ibn Hazm's writing, particularly unique to *The Ring of the Dove*, is *Pathos* where he intrigues his audience's interest and emotions. This element of rhetoric is not only

---

116. Ibn Hazm 1900.
117. Ibn Hazm 1980, 204–05.
118. Ibid., 204–05.
119. Arberry 2013, 4.

elaborate and prominent in this specific selection, but also appropriate to the theme of sublime love and its complexities.

The purpose of Alsawaier's choice of *A Treatise on the Cure of Souls and the Improvement of Manners* is to share with the reader the third element of Ibn Hazm's rhetoric: *Ethos*. Whether intrinsic and stemming from Islamic tradition which he quotes heavily, or extrinsic and pertaining to his lived human experience and character, Ibn Hazm charms his audience's ethical system to advance his argument and persuade his audience; the essence of rhetoric. He rhetorically tempts readers to be close to him through sharing literacies of thought and emotion.

THE METHODOLOGY OF ALSAWAIER'S TRANSLATION AND ARBERRY'S INFLUENCE

Alsawaier's translation relies directly on the original texts of Ibn Hazm's writing as collected by Abbas.[120] Alsawaier shows indebtedness to Arberry's translation, particularly in sections including Arabic poetry in Ibn Hazm's writing. However, the selection from *The Ring of the Dove* that Alsawaier translated is not a reproduction of Arberry's, but is rather original as indicated in the following typical examples:

> The story where the name Khalwa appeared on page 28 in Arberry's translation is not annotated with any explanation, although it is part of the foundation of Ibn Hazm's rhetorical writing using complex images and highly symbolic language. The word appears in my translation on page 5 and the explanation of the name's meaning on page 20.

> Arberry translated Ibn Hazm's chapter *Of the Slanderer* (58) while Alsawaier translated the title of this chapter as *The Maligner* because it better captures the evil motivation of the one spreading mischief among lovers.

> Arberry quoted a Shakespearean translation of the Qur'an as in this example: "Obey thou not the contemptible, back-biting perjurer, who goeth about with slander, and is a hinderer of good, being a transgressor, a criminal, a lowborn churl withal"[121]

> Arberry relied on a biblical style of translation of the Qur'an which was intended to add a sense of familiar holiness to it. Raed's translation is addressed to modern readers and students who prefer direct and accessible language. Raed's translation

---

120. Alsawaier describes his translation methods and process as follows: "I worked directly with the original text and I read the entire selections in Arabic in the beginning to get a literary taste of Ibn Hazm's writing (which I enjoyed a lot). I then translated the text word by word to English sometimes consulting with an Arabic-Arabic dictionary. The part I compared the most to Arberry's translation was the poetry Ibn Hazm authored or cited. I wanted to preserve the poetic text and Arberry's translation informed mine in this sense. Other than that, the translation is uniquely mine. The second selection has never been translated to the best of my knowledge, and is a private conversation between Ibn Hazm and me made public."

121. Arberry 2013, 14 (Qur'an LXVIII 10-13).

intends to be unique in its originality and departure from archaic to communicative English while preserving accuracy of translation. Alsawaier's translated the above verse as: "And do not yield to any contemptible swearer, the fault-finder who goes around slandering, the hinderer of good, the transgressor, the sinful; the coarse-grained, and above all mean and ignoble"[122]

The second part of Alsawaier's translation, *A Treatise on the Cure of Souls and the Improvement of Manners*, is previously untranslated to the best of his knowledge. This text was chosen for its highly rich content as a source of Arabic rhetoric with important information on Islamic moral and belief systems. Alsawaier left out parts of the original text which he thought needed a stronger background knowledge of Islam than glossary items could clarify. Consequently, he focused on translating statements discussing Islamic manners and morals as in Ibn Hazm's general discussion or Qur'anic verses easily understood (relatively) without knowing the context. Finally, Alsawaier's translation keeps interpretation to a minimum and aims at revealing the original meaning of Ibn Hazm. Due to the richness and compactness of Arabic, the ratio of the translated text is disproportionate with Ibn Hazm's original text, as in the following visual example, which renders six stanzas into ten lines:

فأرسَلَ الدَمْعَ مُقتصًّا من البَصر   عيني جَنت في فؤادي لوعَة الفِكَر
منها بإغراقها في دَمعها الدِرَرِ (٢)   فكيف تُبصرُ فعلَ الدَمْع مُنتصفاً
وآخرُ العهد منهـا سَاعـةُ النظر   لم ألقها قبل إبصاري فأعـرفَها

My heart plotted against my eye,
Great mischief, also anguish to my intellect.
How ought my eye view indeed,
This justice that my sorrow demands?
Perceiving that for their surge profound,
My weeping eye is wholly drowned.
Since I've never seen her since,
I might not know her, when we meet;
The last thing from remembering her I knew,
Might have been what I saw at first gaze.

In addition to the rhetorical elements previously mentioned, there are other reasons for selecting these excerpts from among Ibn Hazm's work: the uniqueness of his multicultural background and the topics he addressed (i.e., the art of love), which had previously been considered insignificant to the Islamic rhetorical tradition, work in tandem here. Most of the known publications in the tenth century, about 400 of which are by Ibn Hazm, were focused on

---

122. Almawdudi 1979, 881.

medicine, algebra, science, Islamic jurisprudence, and theology.[123] Ibn Hazm was influenced by Plato's *The Symposium* and another symposium, similar to Plato's, by Albarmaqee, a Muslim minister at the court of Alrasheed (803 CE). Albarmaqee had thirteen philosophers and authors in his symposium and complained about the scarcity of publication on the protocols and etiquettes of love. This was one of the motivations that inspired Ibn Hazm to publish his book in addition to a request by a dear friend who asked Ibn Hazm for guidance in this area. The second translated excerpt is a collection of Ibn Hazm's ruminations on life and ethics that he presented in the form of advice on various topics related to manners.

Plato's Influence on Ibn Hazm's Philosophy of Love in *The Ring of the Dove*[124]

Ihsan Abbas compiled and edited four letters by Ibn Hazm: "The Ring of the Dove," "A Treatise on the Treatment of the Souls," "A Treatise on Distracting Singing," and "A Treatise on Being Ignorant about One's Self and Knowledgeable about Others." His editing of Ibn Hazm's letters was seminal since he relied on the critique of two scholars before him and made corrections based on their recommendations. Abbas's compilation of Ibn Hazm's work was translated into French in 1980.

Plato's *The Symposium* was known to Muslim intellectuals in the third Hijri century (816 CE–913 CE). The dialogue in *The Symposium* concerns the topic of love and passion. Five speakers discuss their views on the nature of love as they indulge in eating and drinking. When the turn comes for the sixth speaker, Socrates presents a less eloquent rhetoric in support of his views. This was his way of critiquing the grandiloquent speeches of the others as he shifted to a progressive dialogue. Socrates narrates a conversation with a woman knowledgeable in the art of love named Diotima. When Socrates finishes, Alcibiades walks in with a group of drunken men and the conversation takes a pragmatic shift. Alcibiades, the seventh speaker, praises Socrates's knowledge of the nature of love and refers to the love between him and Socrates as an example. More drunken men walk in and chaos follows ending the symposium.

In a similar vein, another symposium inspired by Plato's was held in 805 CE where thirteen Muslim philosophers met in the presence of Albarmaqee, a court minister appointed by the Muslim caliphate of Alrasheed. The speakers present their views on love and critique the lack of research and publications on this subject. Not only the framework of the gathering resembled Plato's *The Symposium*, but also the content. The main theme was how pure love mandates a sacrifice for the beloved citing the example of Alcestis's sacrifice, as mentioned in *The Symposium*. Alcestis scarified herself for her husband out of love when everyone had abandoned him including his parents.

Both Plato and Albarmaqee's symposiums influenced Ibn Hazm and shaped his philosophy on love as manifested in his book, *The Ring of the Dove*. Ibn Hazm had published this

---

123. Garcia-Sanjuan 2013, 683–760.
124. Ibn Hazm 1980, 23–25.

book as a request from a friend who fell deeply in love and sought Ibn Hazm's advice on its complexities.

Selections from *The Ring of the Dove*

On the Signs of Love, Ibn Hazm

Love has signs well-observed by the clever and discerned by the intelligent.[125] The first is the prolonged observation of the beloved. The eye is the wide-open gate of the soul; the revealer of its secrets; the expression of its conscience; the reflection of its inner thoughts. The beholder blinks not moving the eyes in tandem with those of the beloved, similar to a lizard moving its body with the rotation of the sun.

Among the signs of love is the deep engagement in the beloved's conversation and becoming oblivious to others. This entails excessive attention to the beloved and suspending disbelief in the lover's story even when it challenges common sense and the laws of nature. It entails siding with the beloved even when wrong, testifying in the beloved's favor even when distant from the truth. Love dictates that the lover seeks to be in the same place as the beloved, getting as close as possible, becoming heedless of other responsibilities, and departing slowly from this reunion.

Other signs include absent mindedness and a feeling of awe at the sight of the beloved's sudden presence. Furthermore, a feeling of confusion and anxiety at the moment of hearing the beloved's name or seeing the beloved's resemblance.

Another sign of love is sacrifice. A lover will sacrifice everything precious for the sake of his beloved. Even when doing so, the lover feels no favoritism to his beloved but an overwhelming joy and happiness. All this sacrifice at the altar of love is to gain the beloved's satisfaction. Inspired by love, how often misers become generous, the stern become gentle, cowards gain courage, the ill-mannered become courteous, the foolish acquire understanding, the old behave like the young, the pious lose piety, and the chaste desecrate one's chastity. This is even before love becomes more intense and its fire more engulfing. I created poetry to describe this condition:

> I long for the words of the one,
> Whose aroma is pushed by the wind's musk.
> When my beloved speaks, I listen not,
> Except to her melodious well-tuned words.
> I sway not from her presence,
> Even to that of the prince.

---

125. Ibn Hazm 1980, 103–14.

I leave. Compelled. Looking behind.
Looking behind and lame-walking,
My eyes pinned on her. Our bodies depart,
Like the drowning seeking land.
In the middle of a sand storm,
I struggle for a breath as I remember her.

Among the signs of love is feeling unfettered even in a confined place and feeling confined in the vastness of space. The lover seeks to drink the leftover of the beloved, placing his lips where she left hers. There are some conflicting signs of love, the intensity of which depends on the causes and symptoms, similar to the contradictions that God placed in nature. Consider the burning sensation of the one holding snow in his hand, the overwhelming joy that might kill, the tears of joy, and many other contradictions. When lovers share the strength of love, meaningless desertedness often happens for no apparent reason. Arguments follow pursuit. But this is different from non-lovers' disputes. Soon after, all disagreements are brushed aside, and all tensions ease leading to better companionship between the lovers.

Love at First Glance

Falling in love at first sight happens frequently and it falls into two categories.[126] The first one is different from the latter one (in reference to falling in love with a specific person) in the sense that one would fall in love with a mental image with no specific reference in time or space. This has happened to more than one:

Story

I was told by Abu Baker Mohammad bin Ahmad bin Ishaq who narrated that Yousef bin Haron, the poet, was walking through the Perfumery[127] gate in Cordoba[128] which was an ideal meeting place for women. He saw a young woman walking who immediately captured his heart and the chill of love went down his spine. He diverted from his path and followed her towards Cordova Bridge leading to a place known as Rabeth. She looked back at him knowing that he had no intention except to follow her. "Why you are in my pursuit?" she said to him who had no answer except his deep obsession with her.

"Please leave me alone and don't disgrace me. You have no way of getting what you want from me"

"I am satisfied with your sight." He said in an assuring manner.

---

126. Ibn Hazm 1980, 120–23.
127. Arberry 2013, 4. Gate of the Perfumers: A place where perfumes were sold and a gathering place of ladies in the Islamic Spanish city of Cordoba
128. Watt and Cachia 1965. Cordoba, a city in the southern region of Andalusia and the capital of the province of Cordoba, was a major Islamic center in the Middle Ages.

She said: "That is permissible for you."[129]
He said: "Madam." "Are you a slave or a free person?"
"I am a slave."
"What is your name?" he said to her.
"My name is Khalwa."[130]
"Who is your master?"
"By Allah, knowing what is in the seventh heaven is more possible for you than knowing this, so mind your business."
"But Madam, where shall I see you next time."
"Same place and same hour every Friday. So now, either you leave or I leave?"
"You go with the protection of Allah." [131]

Yosef said after this incident: "By Allah, I have committed myself to the Perfumers' gate from that point on and I have never again seen her or heard anything about her. I do not know if she vanished up in heaven or was swallowed by which earth. In my heart there is burning hotter than coal!"

Khalwa became the love theme in all of Yosef's poetry after that. For example, he said:

> My heart plotted against my eye,
> Great mischief, also anguish to my intellect.
> Which sin my soul to compensate,
> Has caused these mournful against my sight?
> How ought my eye view indeed,
> This justice that my sorrow demands?
> Perceiving that for their surge profound,
> My weeping eye is wholly drowned.
> Since I never saw her since,
> I Might not know her, when we meet;
> The last thing remembering her I knew,
> Might be what I saw at first gaze.

The second category under discussion is contrary to the section which will immediately follow this one, Allah willing. This is about falling in love at first glance with a specific woman in a known place and time. This is set apart by the speed at which love fades. Whoever loves at first sight is evidence of a person with thin patience, inconsistent feelings, and showing

---

129. "That is permissible for you." It was believed that gazing at slave women was not an equal sin as gazing at noble ones.

130. A female name which ironically means being alone in the company of someone. Ibn Hazm is famous for using complex images and symbolism, which are part of his rhetorical foundations.

131. *Allah* (Arabic): A non-gender, non-plural noun derived from "Ilah," which means, the One to be worshipped.

fickleness, with quick boredom. This applies to everything in life. The faster their responses grow, the faster they decay.

Story

A young man who is the son of a clerk was one day seen by a lady of respectable birth, high position and adhering closely to strict rules. She saw him cruising by, while peeping out from a vantage point in her home, and envisioned an association for him which he also desired in the same manner. They exchanged letters for a period, by ways more touchy than the edge of a fine sword; and because it is not my purpose in this composition to uncover such plots and discuss such tricks, I could have set down here such things as I am certain would have puzzled the shrewdest and stunned the most canny of men. I implore that Allah in His extraordinary abundance will draw over every Muslim and us the veil of His compassion. He is indeed all sufficient to fulfill our needs.

The Maligner, Ibn Hazm

One more of the setbacks of Love is the maligner who is of two sorts.[132] The main kind of maligner is the one who just wants to part the adoring couple. He is the less wicked of the two; yet for all that, he is a savage toxic substance, a sharp bitter fruit, an inevitable fate and an approaching catastrophe. Here and there, his weavings are inadequate. The maligner would deliver himself to the beloved not so much for the lover who is overwhelmed by love as in the sayings "Choked by his own saliva," or "The clash of war spoiled all delights."[133] The lover is unreasonably involved with his own inconveniences to tune in to what the maligner needs to state. Maligners are very much aware of this, and in this way coordinate their endeavors just toward those whose brains are free of different considerations, and who are accordingly prepared to jump with the rage of a strong mastermind, arranged to discover blame in any incitement.

Maligners have different techniques for gossiping. For example, they will convince the beloved that the lover is not keeping secrets. That is troublesome to manage, and difficult to cure unless it so happens by chance that the beloved shows no interest in the lover's advances—a situation which regardless makes dislike inescapable. There is no way out of this situation unless fate be on the lover's side exposing his inner feelings to the beloved who might delay judgment on the lover for a short while. At the point when the beloved finds, in the wake of acting with due lack of approachability and hold, that the maligner's story was a lie, and that the lover has in certainty not unveiled the secret by any means, she obviously understands that the story was a creation from start to finish, and all her suspicions disappear.

---

132. Ibn Hazm 1980, 170–77.

133. "Choked by his own saliva," or "The clash of war spoiled all delights": two sayings in Arabic suggesting a state where someone is completely absorbed in an activity and oblivious to everything else and everyone else.

An instance of this enactment between two lovers was observed by me. The loved was very watchful, and excessively discreet; but many defamatory memories were carried about, and in the long run visible signs of this were showing on the lover's expression. He stated "a love that by no means was realized"; he has become a prey to conjectures and so dumbfounded and distraught that he could not contain his emotions; sooner or later he will disclose what has been reported to him. If you can be in the company of the lover when he provides his excuses, you will find that passion is certainly a tyrant who should be obeyed, a unity most strongly bound together, a sharp penetrating spear. His apologies were an amalgamation of humility, confession, denial, shame, and unconditional submission. Soon after, all commotion is over and the pair is happy again.

From time to time, the maligner alleges that the affection, which the lover is protesting, is not proper, and that his real motive is to satisfy his sensual impulses. That is a form of malignancy which, even as dangerous when spread around, is easier to deal with than the previous example. The reality of a lover is certainly varied from the one in pursuit of lust. This subject has been discussed amply enough in the section on obedience.

On occasion, the maligner reports that the lover is not devoted in his love: This is like a raging fire, and a pain saturating all relationships. Often the rumor which the maligner is spreading involves a handsome, attractive, good-mannered young man with an inclination for sensual desires. At the same time, the beloved is a prestigious lady of high position and influence. Most probably, she will strive to be the tool for his demise. How often a truthful young lover has been killed in this account! or been given poison to drink, or had his belly cut open, for a reason like that! In the same manner was the end of Marwan Ibn Ahmad Ibn Hudair, the father of Ahmad the virtuous and of Musa and 'Abd al-Rahman, better known as the sons of Lubna: he met his doom at the hands of his slave-girl Qatr al-Nada. This is my reason for writing a cautionary poem for a friend of mine, from which I quote.

> Only a blind man puts his trust in Womankind!
> What a fool he must be
> So to flirt with calamity!
> How many fools have come,
> To the gloomy pool of doom!
> Believed it clean, and wholesome too,
> And drunk up the deadly potion!

The second kind of maligner works to part the loving couple and have her for himself. This is the most troublesome, dangerous and conclusive sort of all, due to the immense endeavor the maligner will make considering the personal gain he attempts to achieve.

There is yet a second-rate class of maligners: the man who slanders both the lover and the beloved alike, trying to expose the supposed private life of both. Such a sort might be neglected, if the lover is mature. I have put this issue into a lyric.

> I wonder about the maligner,
> Trying to let our secret out.
> He just has our news to manage,
> Nothing else to gab about.
> Why should he stress my unhappiness,
> Or the inconvenience if I black out and worry?
> Myself the pomegranate ingest,[134]
> The youngsters' teeth tense are set!

I am obliged to set down a few perceptions firmly comparable to the subject now under discussion, despite the fact that they might be somewhat off the point. I want to state several clarifications about maligners and backbiters. In talking, one thing dependably leads on to another, as we visualized toward the start of this paper.

There are no individuals on earth more terrible than slanderers and backbiters. Defaming is a trademark demonstrating' the tree to be spoiled, and the branch infected; it demonstrates that nature itself is degenerate, and that childhood is additionally corrupted. The backbiter lies; defaming is one of the branches, one of the bona fide types of lying. Each backbiter is a liar.

I have never adored a liar. In spite of the fact that I am prepared to be liberal, and to be benevolent with each man whatever his sin, regardless of the possibility that it be a grave one, conferring his case to the delicate kindness of his Creator and loving him for his other good attributes. I cannot stomach anybody whom I know to have the tendency for lying: that for me wipes out every one of his good deeds, decimates his benefits, and discredits any worth there might be in him. I search for no great qualities in such a man at all. Of every bad sin a man shows repentance; he tries to conceal it or quit the activity. However, with respect to telling a lie, there is no turning once again from that, and that can never be covered up, wherever it might be. I have not found in all my life, neither have I got notification from any man, an instance of a liar who shunned lying and did not come back to the propensity once more. I have never stepped up with regards to severing relations with a colleague, aside from when I have identified him in a lie; in such a case it is I who venture out, make a special effort to stay away from and to spurn him. Lying is a check which I have never observed on any man, without his being associated with having some dull corruption in his spirit and analyzed as torment from some repulsive profound deformation. I supplicate that God may never forsake us, nor prevent us the assurance from claiming His bounty!

A shrewd man of old has stated, "make companions with whom you wish, yet maintain a distance from three sorts of men—the ignorant, whose craving to help you just harms you; the tired, on the grounds that in the hour when you depend upon him most, by virtue of the long and firm fellowship between you, in that very hour he disappoints you; and the liar, since the more you have confidence in him, the more clearly he will do you a filthy trap when you

---

134. An Arabic saying meaning, "Why should others pretend to show pain when I am the one experiencing it firsthand?"

expect it the least." The Prophet of Allah is accounted for to have stated, "To keep one's agreement is a piece of belief"; and once more, "No man is a true believer, if he has not surrendered lying even jokingly."

I got these two Traditions[135] from Abu 'Umar Ahmad Ibn Muhammad Ibn Muhammad Ibn 'Ali Ibn Rifa'a, who had them from 'Ali Ibn 'Abd al-'Aziz, from Abu 'Ubaid al-Qasim Ibn Sallam, from his educators. The second of them is a definitive report of 'Umar Ibn al-Khattab, and of his child 'Abd Allah (God be all around satisfied with them both). Allah says, "O you who have believed, why do you say that which you do not do? Most hateful it is in the sight of Allah that you should say that which you do not do."[136]

The Prophet of Allah was once asked, "May a believer be a miser?" He answered, "Yes." "And may an adherent be a coward?" "Yes." "And may a devotee be a liar?" "No." I got this Tradition* from Ahmad Ibn Muhammad Ibn Ahmad Ibn Ahmad Ibn Sa'id, who had it from 'Ubaid Allah Ibn Yahya, from his dad, from Malik Ibn Anas, from Safwan Ibn Sulaim. By a similar chain of narrators, I am informed that the Prophet of Allah[137] additionally stated, "There is no greatness in lying." This announcement was in a similar manner issued in reply to an inquiry. Another Tradition, which I have on a similar narration to Malik, detailing for this situation from Ibn Masud, cites the Prophet of Allah as saying, "A man will continue lying, and making one dark spot after another on his heart, until the point when his heart is entirely dark, and his name will be recorded in God's book as one of the liars." This chain, contingent on Ibn Masud, cites the Prophet of Allah further as saying, "Practice honesty; for honesty leads on to devotion, and devotion leads on to Paradise. What's more, be careful with lying; for lying leads on to evil, and corruption leads on to Hell."

It is said that a man went to the Prophet of Allah and said to him, "O Prophet of Allah, I have three plaguing sins—drinking, sex (outside of marriage), and lying. Summon me which of these I should surrender." The Prophet of Allah stated, "Give up lying." The man left him, and after that coveted to confer sex; however, he thought a while and after that said to himself, "I will go to the Prophet of Allah, and he will ask me, 'Have you had sex?' And in the event that I let it be known, he will rebuff me as the law requires; yet in the event that I deny it, I might break my promise. I will in this manner surrender this wrongdoing." Thereafter he was enticed similarly to drink, and contemplated after a similar way. Finally, he came back to the Prophet of Allah and stated, "O Prophet of Allah, I have surrendered each of the three sins." Lying is in this manner seen to be the base of each plague, and to contain all that is detestable; it draws in the disdain of Almighty God.

On the authority of Abu Bakr al-Siddiq the Prophet of Allah stated, "That man is without faith, in whom faith can't be put." Ibn Masud is a reliable source of narration on the Prophet

---

135. Afzal Iqbal, "The Qur'an and the Sunnah: The Two Main Sources of Legislation in Islam." This is in reference to the sayings of Prophet Muhammad, which were subjected to meticulous scrutiny based on a science that Muslim scholars established, called the science of Hadith, to ensure authenticity.

136. Qur'an 61, 2-3.

137. Goldman 1995. "Prophet of Allah:" In reference to Prophet Muhammad who lived in Arabia between 570 and 632 CE.

of Allah's expression, "The adherent is subject to every intrinsic demeanor, aside from betrayal and lying." The Prophet of Allah additionally pronounced, "Three qualities there are which, in the event that they stay with a man, that man is a wolf in sheep's clothing: to promise and break his promise, to lie when talking, and to betray the trust when trust is set in him."

What is unbelief, on the off chance that it is not lying against Almighty God? Truth has a place with God, and God adores truth; by truth, the sky and the earth stand quick.

I have never observed any man more disgraceful than a liar. Domains do not die, kingdoms are not wrecked, blood is not shed unjustifiably, and respect is not damaged, aside from through defaming and lying. It is lying, which generates destructive antipathy. The fortune of the backbiter is only disdain, disgrace and mortification; he should be looked down on by the individual to whom he conveys his foulness and all the more by others—as one looks down on a dog.

God the All-knowing says, "Woe unto each offensive defamer!'[138] Again, Allah says, "Believers, if an evil doer brings you news, ascertain the correctness of the report fully, lest you unwittingly harm others, and then regret what you have done.'[139] Here God calls the gossip an evil doer. Allah likewise says, "And do not yield to any contemptible swearer, the fault-finder who goes around slandering, the hinderer of good, the transgressor, the sinful; the coarse-grained, and above all mean and ignoble."[140]

The Prophet of Allah stated, "No defamer might enter Paradise." He likewise stated, "Beware of the three babblers!" By this last saying, he implied the gossip, the man who gets stories, and the man who issues them. Al-Ahnaf[141] stated, "The reliable man does not convey reports about, and the hypocrite man should be held in no respect by God." Such is the weight of abomination and evil with which he is stacked.

A friend once conveyed a lying report about me to Abu Ishaq Ibrahim Ibn `Isa al-Thaqafi, the poet (God show mercy to him!), as a joke. Be that as it may, the poet, being exceptionally imaginative, trusted the story, which infuriated him. I should include that both were great companions of mine; the previous was not by any stretch of the imagination a backbiter, yet he was an awesome entertainer and adored joker. I consequently sent to Abu Ishaq, who was greatly vexed by the report, a message in verse, which incorporated the accompanying lines:

---

138. Qur'an 104, 1.
139. Qur'an 49, 6.
140. Qur'an 68, 8–13.
141. Shepard 2014. Alahnaf: One of the four schools of thought in Islamic jurisprudence.

Substitute not a lie with the truth
A story you have heard men tell,
At the point when you cannot choose well
Like a man in excessively incredible scramble,
Seeing a mirage, spill out
The valuable drops he carries about,
And die in the crying waste.

COMMENTARY

Before we transition to the second translation, we need to reflect on the rhetorical commitments of this important text from Ibn Hazm. This translation highlights a multicultural and pluralist "rhetoric of possibility" in which individual and group divisiveness is overcome by a sense of our desperate need for a compact of shared fate and mutual understanding across difference. Ibn Hazm was surely not thinking only of the frequent internecine combative politics of his country of Muslim Spain and his time period, which so disrupted his work and the location of his residence. His context thinking and his sense of an attainable ideal was almost certainly the remarkable Constitution of Medina which effectively ended the bitter inter-tribal conflicts, blood feuds and blood money of Yathrib, before it became Medina in 622 CE with the Hijra.[142]

This unique and evocative "rhetoric of possibility" as conflict resolution through a compact of understanding across difference is focused first and last on love and its endless re-directions and instabilities. Rhetoric at its heart is the attempt to create viable possibilities and functioning unity. But this desire for unity is the desire for unattainable perfection. The main challenge to a rhetoric of love and relationship, a pluralist overcoming of conflict in this dynamic text is the challenge of the endlessly corrupting rhetoric of liars. Ibn Hazm does more in this text than provide vivid narratives of lying and its devastations to relationships, politics, and the rhetoric of possibility itself. Since there are very few people who can say 'I have never lied,' unless they want to add to the number, this moving text is indicting all of us with attacks on love, on relationship, and attacks on compacts of pluralist group life. The heart of destructiveness in Ibn Hazm's rhetoric of lying involves two massive indictments: 1) lying's instabilities against love: "Domains do not die, kingdoms are not wrecked, blood is not shed unjustifiably, and respect is not damaged, aside from through defaming and lying. It is lying, which generates destructive antipathy." But the second indictment at the heart of the rhetoric of lying is its "endless re-directions": For Ibn Hazm, the only proper direction for love and the only way to overcome lying is to understand the following: "I implore that Allah in His extraordinary abundance will draw over every Muslim and us the veil of His compassion. He is indeed all sufficient to fulfill our needs."

---

142. The best recent essay on the pluralism of Islam's foundation legal document and rhetoric is Diab 2018.

Selections from *A Treatise on the Cure of Souls and the Improvement of Manners*

1. The reward and pleasure of the intelligent in his understanding, the scholar in his science, and the wise in his choices, are greater than the pleasures of food, sex, money, and playfulness.[143] As evidence of this claim, you will find many scholars, researchers, and people of intelligence turning their backs on materialistic and sensual pleasures in pursuit of what they are passionate about.

2. If you chase all of your objectives at once, you will achieve nothing and lose all. The true meaning of work is to seek the hereafter. Every hope we fulfilled is followed by sadness either because of its very nature as being transient, or by your final demise. There is no way out of these two except seeking the pleasure of Allah the glorified in His majesty. If you do things for His own sake, you win both in this life and on the Day of Judgment. In this life, you will be stress free of what people compete for gaining as a result respect in the heart of both friend and foe. The ultimate reward is of course Paradise.

3. I sought something in common that all human beings strive for regardless of beliefs, opinions, and the level of their commitment. This common goal is the pursuit of happiness and the desire to live stress-free. Every action and endeavor people make is to banish stress out of their lives. Some of them seek this in the wrong manner and others barely miss the path of happiness while very few attain this ultimate goal. Attaining happiness and living stress free is a sort of denomination that all nations agreed on since Allah created the universe until the Day of Reckoning. However, there are people who do not believe in the hereafter and consequently never seek happiness by preparing for it; others who are evil seek not the truth, the good, or tranquility; some are lazy short-sighted people who prefer to reside in their worldly desires than attaining a sublime goal, and finally there are those who seek not the worldly possessions and actually rather not have them at all such as the prophets (peace be upon them) and those who followed in their path such as monks and philosophers. The majority of people prefer ignorance to knowledge, yet everyone shares one common objective: driving away stress and attaining happiness.

    When this knowledge of people's common goal settled in my heart and this treasure of knowledge was revealed to me, I thought of the best means to drive away this enemy of us all: stress. To fulfill this precious highly sought-after goal by the ignorant and knowledgeable, the virtuous and the sinful, is to seek a path leading to Allah and plan for the hereafter. The only reason for the one who seeks to accumulate wealth is to drive away the stress of poverty, the one who strive to attain fame is to drive away the stress of inferiority, the one who indulges in desires is to drive

---

143. Hazm 1980, 335–42.

away the stress of missing out, the one who tries to become a scholar is to avoid the stress of ignorance, the one who likes company and socializing is to keep away the stress of loneliness. This endeavor of fighting stress is the motivation for everyone who engages in eating, drinking, traveling, and playing. It is their purpose to drive away the opposites of such actions and the various kinds of stress and misery. Relevant to every endeavor we mentioned before are obstacles interrupting these actions causing failure or partial fulfillment and generating new stresses of their own. There is the fear of losing what one accumulated or missing opportunities to multiply it, which generates stinginess. In addition, there is the stress of envious competitors striving to take over what others have. There are the many other forms of stress associated ironically with the endeavor to be stress free. I found seeking the hereafter to be the only stress-free endeavor leading to a state of real happiness. The one who works diligently for attaining happiness in the life after death cares not about tests along the way as his motivation in winning the final reward is urgently pushing him to carry on. I find the person in pursuit of such high goal is happy in every situation; if he experiences fatigue along the path of achieving his goal, he is pleased; if he is being tested with difficulties, he is still pleased. The only path to happiness is working for the sake of Allah and everything else is nonsense and illusion.

4. Do not exhaust yourself except in a cause higher than yourself, which is seeking the pleasure of Allah by inviting people to the right path, by protecting oppressed women, by elevating a state of humiliation imposed on you, by establishing justice for someone oppressed. The one spending all his energy in worldly matters is exchanging rubies for stones.

5. The one with no chivalry has no faith.

6. The only reward worthy of the intelligent is Paradise.

7. Lucifer plays some tricks connected to fear of showing off. How many instances are there where a good person refrained from doing a good deed for fear of boasting. If this fear creeps upon you, fear not and carry on with your good deeds causing a great pain for Lucifer.

8. A great source of joy and inner peace is to be heedless of what others say and be more caring about the words of the Creator; this is truly the ultimate gate for wisdom and peace. The only one safe from people's criticism and backbiting is the insane. Whoever contemplates and trains the self to accept life's realities even when painful, especially in early stage of shock, will be more pleased with people's criticism than with their praise. Their commendation, even when true, and reaches the praised one, might lead to degrees of self-admiration and corruption.

If praising someone is not substantiated, then it might lead to a delusional state of happiness and a form of incompetence. When people offer substantiated critique of someone, then this might result in improving behavior by encouraging the avoiding of the cause of such criticism. Such an outcome is of great benefit that only the base will overlook. If one is condemned based on falsehood, then he will get credit on the Day of Judgment for being unlawfully wronged. On that day, he will be rewarded for deeds he has not really done but will get credit from the good deeds of those who have wronged him. This is a great status only the fortunate attains. It is all the same for the one who never accesses others' criticism or praise. However, when someone backbites him, he will still get credit by way of taking from the good deeds of those who practiced this against him. Had not prophet Muhammad commended the good words as immediate glad tidings for the believer, one should be more inclined to be falsefully accused (to get the reward) than rightfully praised. The saying of the prophet: "a good word is an immediate glad-tiding for the believer," does not mean praising someone, but literally carrying good news to him.

9. There is no difference between sins and virtues except in the inner state of acceptance or rejection. The happy is the one whose soul settles in virtues and refrains from sins and the wretched is the one whose soul is inclined towards sins and immoralities.

10. The one who aspires towards Allah's reward in the hereafter resembles the angels, and the one seeking evil deeds resembles the devils. The one in pursuit of dominance and control resembles predators, and the one seeking pleasures and desires resembles animals. The one who dedicated his life to collecting money and kept it in a miserly fashion is baser than any animal, and resembles barren isolated places, such is the effect of money not spent in righteousness.

11. A person of intelligence does not rejoice at gaining an attribute that animals have mastered. He finds triumph in achieving a virtue that makes him transcend the animal nature. Whoever is deceived by his valor, let him know that lions and tigers are braver. Whoever is fooled by his strength let him know that mules, oxen, and elephants are stronger. Whoever is arrogant about how much weight he can lift then let him know that donkeys can carry more weight than him. So, what pleasure is there in achieving a quality or honor shared with animals that mastered it more effectively? Compare animal strength to the acquisition of knowledge and the performance of good deeds; how they excel and rejoice in such qualities unique to the best of the people!

12. The words of Allah: "But he who feared to stand before his Lord, and restrained himself from evil desires"[144] is a statement encompassing every virtue. For he who

---

144. Qur'an 79, 40.

restrained himself from evil desires is safe from the trials of anger and lust. Transcending these evil traits elevates the soul from animalistic qualities.

13. The prophet's advice (Peace be upon him) to those who sought it: "Do not get angry!" and his statement that a "believer should love no other believer except for the sake of Allah" are two pieces of advice which encompass every virtue. In his command not to get angry is an admonishment for every animalistic inclination. The only thing left to do if such impurities are dismissed is to dedicate oneself to more sublime things which elevate us from animals.

14. I saw the majority of people, except for a few whom Allah has guided, rush to their doom and dwell in stress-causing conditions which eventually lead them into committing grave sins leading to Hellfire. They have ill intentions hoping for the misery of others and overall difficult conditions for other people with no distinction. They wish calamities would inflict those whom they hate. Yet, they know that their ill intentions will not make anything they hoped for be realized. If they purify their intentions and clear their hearts, they would attain inner peace leading them to focus more on their best interests. Only then would they achieve tranquility and qualify for the great reward on the Day of Judgment. There is no state of deception like that of those with ill intentions and no better condition than achieving inner peace.

15. If you investigate the length of the worldly life as we know it, you will see that it falls between two moments. Whatever is past and whatever is about to happen; both of which are equal to non-existent. Who would exchange the time in between which goes as a blink of an eye with eternity?

16. When one sleeps, he leaves the boundaries of life and becomes oblivious to the extremes of excessive joy and overwhelming sadness. If one disciplines himself during his sobriety and protects himself from these extremes, he will achieve ultimate happiness.

COMMENTARY

This Ibn Hazm text offers the "improvement of manners" as the rhetoric of the "cure of souls," as changes in consciousness. This rhetorical labor is literally enumerated and in an important sense is linear, as a rhetoric of following the path outside of conflict and competition for goods and titles to improved manners by seeking well-being for all. Ibn Hazm describes that numbered goal this way: "I find the person in pursuit of such high goal is happy in every situation; if he experiences fatigue along the path of achieving his goal, he is pleased; if he is being tested with difficulties, he is still pleased. The only path to happiness is working for the sake of Allah and everything else is nonsense and illusion." The previous translation was about the devastating effects of the rhetoric of lying, while this text elucidates the nuances of the deeply related action and disease of boasting, the lie of claiming as one's own what is a gift from God. To those committed to group well-being, fear of boasting can interrupt intended actions of group generosity: "Lucifer plays some tricks connected to fear of showing off. How many instances are there where a good person refrained from doing a good deed for fear of boasting. If this fear creeps upon you, fear not and carry on with your good deeds causing a great pain for Lucifer." The rhetoric of following the path leads Ibn Hazm half a millennium before Shakespeare to his own version of "There is nothing either good or bad but thinking makes it so." Ibn Hazm puts it this way: "There is no difference between sins and virtues except in the inner state of acceptance or rejection."

The consciousness that Ibn Hazm wants to change most of all in this work is the consciousness of time: "If you investigate the length of the worldly life as we know it, you will see that it falls between two moments. Whatever is past and whatever is about to happen; both of which are equal to non-existent. Who would exchange the time in between which goes as a blink of an eye with eternity?" What is the possible benefit of such a change in consciousness and its attendant rhetoric? The moment outside time when change takes place.

TEACHING IBN HAZM IN CONTEMPORARY NORTH AMERICAN LEARNING SPACES

As Adam Sabra makes clear in "Ibn Hazm's Literalism: A Critique of Islamic Legal Theory (I)," Ibn Hazm was a pluralist in his commitments to individualism in rhetoric and religion and especially in his desire "to curtail the claims made by Muslim jurists to speak on behalf of God's law."[145] His literalism was a commitment to return power to the people against its abuse by specialist legalistic scholars. Ibn Hazm can be taught dynamically in the context of competing fundamentalisms in the contemporary US. Here is one such collaborative task for an undergraduate class on rhetoric, fundamentalism and pluralism.[146]

Context for the Assignment

The divisiveness in the US between religions, races, and political parties is so full and intense that all we have in the present national reality is a binary choice between Fundamentalism and Pluralism. There are no longer any other choices. Fundamentalism is the conviction that your religion, race, or political party has one hundred percent of the truth and that those outside your group are less than fully human. Pluralism is an openness to unassimilated otherness and is the heart of democracy, shared fate, and the possibility of mutual survival. The differences between fundamentalism and pluralism can be further clarified in these two ways:

> Fundamentalists perceive religions, cultures, and races as discrete and self-contained while Pluralists see them as interactive and as constructed in relation to others; Ibn Hazm often quotes this line of scripture: "O Humankind! We have created

---

145. Sabra 2007, 7. See also Gleave 2012, 150–74.
146. For the theory and methodology of this course see Eddy and Espinosa-Aguilar 2019.

you from a male and a female, and we made you nations and tribes that you may come to know one another."[147] For Muslims this is a divine injunction: cherish the others: "come to know one another."

Fundamentalists perceive themselves as strictly inside one and outside the rest of religions and cultures; Pluralists see Humankind—and, by comparison, Fundamentalists see only their own kind. This is where we stand in our country.

Accordingly, interfaith dialogue embodies pluralism and is an alternative to fundamentalist monologues of delusional totalizing claimed knowledge.

Assignment Task

In groups of three or five students, so that there cannot be tie votes, use the pluralist rhetorics in Ibn Hazm's *Ring of the Dove* and *Treatise on the Cure of Souls and the Improvement of Manners* to construct an argument urging Ibn Hazm-like pluralist perspectives for resisting the fundamentalist stances implied by one of the following three issues: (1) the systemic racism of the fundamentalist position against immigration to the US from countries of color; or (2) the hatred of Muslims that manifests in routine contemporary American Islamophobia; or (3) the increase of antisemitism connected to the proliferation of white supremacist groups in the US (see www.splcenter.org/fighting-hate/extremist-files/groups).[148] Construct an Ibn Hazm pluralist rhetoric to engage one of these four kinds of pluralist dialogues:

Inter-faith Dialogue

Inter-race Dialogue

Inter-cultural Dialogue

Inter-political Dialogue[149]

You have only twenty minutes to complete this assignment, after which each group's "Recorder" will present their Ibn Hazm pluralist rhetoric to the class and invite questions from the front of the room or from the digital space, where all group members will be present.

---

147. Qur'an 49, 13.
148. See Benhabib 2018, Dorrien (2018), Giroux (2018), and Learner (2019).
149. See Pluralism Project at Harvard, pluralism.org.

1.5 Arabic-Islamic, c. 11th Century CE, Persia

Abū Ḥayyān al-Tawḥīdī's "Night 8": No Place for Greek Logic in Arabic Language and Thought

Lahcen E. Ezzaher

INTRODUCTION TO THE DEBATE

Kitāb al-Imtāᶜ wa-l-mu'ānasa (The Book of Enjoyment and Conviviality), by ᶜAli Ibn Muḥammad Ibn al-ᶜAbbās Abū Ḥayyān al-Tawḥīdī (922–1023 CE),[150] is composed in the manner of a cycle of a total of forty nights, during which Abū Ḥayyān al-Tawḥīdī witnesses in the presence of Vizier Ibn Saᶜdān a series of conversations covering a number of literary and philosophical topics. The art of conversation makes the spirit of enjoyment and conviviality dominate during these nights of intellectual engagement. As Ṣalāḥ Nātij puts it, the art of conversation in the book plays an important role since it constitutes a space for social interactions.[151] The enjoyment that comes from a pleasant intellectual exchange is manifest throughout the book.

Perhaps it is worth pointing out the significance of the physical sphere in which and the time during which these conversations take place. *Al-Majlis,* or sitting-place, conveys an image of a salon where a group of dignitaries observe a number of social conventions, such as sitting cross-legged, putting aside what is cumbersome, returning salutations, participating in what is good, and avoiding what is evil.[152] In fact, *al-majālis* represented an intellectual space that was characteristic of the most productive period of Arabic classicism. These *majālis* were hosted by monarchs, princes, and men of state and the audiences grouped mainly men of letters and scientists who desired to be under the patronage of the royal prince.[153]

Ibn Saᶜdān, an important government official as well as the host of these gatherings, fulfills the function of the initiator of the debates by proposing the topics to be discussed. "'Al-layla al-Thāmina" or "Night 8" opens with the mention of Jewish philosopher Ibn Yaᶜīsh's epistle (*risāla*) in which he indicates that true philosophy is the way to achieve happiness. The philosophical way is clear and those who follow it feel no pain and no hardship in their pursuit of wisdom, happiness, and salvation in the hereafter.

Ibn Yaᶜīsh denunciates those logicians from Baghdad, whom he calls *aṣḥābunā* (our friends), saying that they have sewn the way with their misleading principles. In fact, Ibn

---

150. Kitāb al-Imtā ᶜwa-l-mu'ānasa (922–1023 CE), a famous man of letters who composed *Kitāb al-Imtāᶜmu'*ānasa (*The Book of Enjoyment and Conviviality*) between 983 and 985 CE. For an extensive study of the life and work of Abū Ḥayyān al-Tawḥīdī, see Bergé (1974).

151. Nātij 2008, 228.

152. For details about the various meanings of the term *al-majlis/al-majālis,* see Lane (1865, 443).

153. For more details on this point, see Urvoy (2003).

Yaᶜīsh claims that those mathematicians and logicians have closed the door to truth and wisdom. The debate during this "Night 8" is between two major figures in the Arabic literary and philosophical tradition. The first one is Nestorian logician Abū Bishr Mattā ibn Yūnus (d. 950 CE), under whom Abū Naṣr al-Fārābī (d. 950 CE) studied logic. He was also known for his Greek-Arabic translation through Syriac of Aristotle's *Poetics*. The second one is grammarian Abū Saᶜīd al-Sīrāfī, who was known for his work on grammar, especially his *Sharḥ Kitāb Sibawayh* (Commentary on the book of Sibawayh) and his *Kitāb akhbār al-naḥwiyīn al-baṣriyīn* (Book of Stories of the Grammarians of Baṣra).[154] Al-Sīrāfī died in Baghdad in 979.

Translation of "Night 8"

What follows is an Arabic-English translation of a major section in "'Allayla al-Thāmina" or "Night 8".[155]

He said to me [qāla lī] on another occasion: "Jewish philosopher Wahb ibn Yaᶜīsh composed a letter in which he said, after a lengthy eulogy: there is a way by which to understand philosophy, that is easy to follow, succinct and wide open. Those who take it will not encounter any toil or exertion in their pursuit of wisdom and happiness and they will gain their wish in the hereafter. Indeed, our friends[156] (*aṣḥābunā*/ the logicians) have spoken in an extensive and alarming way about this subject and they have sewn the way with thorns and have put obstacles in a deceitful, stingy, and spiteful manner and, out of envy, they have given little advice and more hard work to discourage those who seek wisdom. They have used logic and geometry and things related to them as a means to make a living and they have turned these disciplines as hard as an iron wall to break the spirit of those who seek wisdom and love the truth and explore the secrets of the world. This is what I mean by this discourse."

The answer was: I know the approach that Ibn Yaᶜīsh follows in this matter. It is a current one. He composed this epistle in this manner and forwarded it to the Happy King in the year 370 H. He used it to get closer to the King and it turned out to be beneficial for him and drew attention to him. Indeed, he was very poor. What he claimed in this epistle was based on clear evidence. What our friends (*aṣḥābunā*/ the logicians)—that is, his opponents, claimed was another argument. The two arguments have their respective supporters.

He said: Let us hear what you have to say—with the blessings of Allah! I wish to hear everything that has been said about this subject and everything related to it.

The answer was that Ibn Yaᶜīsh intended to say that human life was short and knowledge of the world was plentiful and its secret concealed. How could it not be this way when its broad stones are arranged in a sound manner and put one on top of the other in a perfect

---

154. See Gérard Troupeau's essay "Le commentaire d'al-Sīrāfī sur le chapitre 565 du *Kitāb de Sībawayhi*," *Arabica* 5, 1958, pp. 168–82.

155. There is an Arabic-English translation of "Night 8" in an essay by Margoliouth 1905, 97–129. There is also an Arabic-French translation of "Night 8" by Abderrahmane 1978, 310–23.

156. The term *aṣḥābunā* (our friends) is used, in a sarcastic way, in reference to the logicians of the period.

fashion? The person seeking to know the mystery of the world and what the world contains has a limited capacity, is faced with obstacles, and is provided with weak arguments. However, in spite of these conditions, he is intuitively attentive, a dreamer with reason, a lover of evidence, amazed by what is hidden, at home in the land with which he is familiar and where he has been raised. He is afraid of a land to which he has not traveled and from which he has not come. He has no steady knowledge of that or complete trust in that. The best thing a person characterized by this weakness can do is to seek the nearest way to happiness and salvation and hold onto the easiest means according to his ability. The nearest ways and the easiest means are found in the knowledge of nature, of the soul, of the mind, and of Allah, the Exalted. When he has known all these things in detail and has known the details of all these things, he will achieve the greatest success and will gain the noblest power. And he will be rewarded with the greatest supply of information in reading the great volumes of books, with the continuous care in study, and establishing the validity of the question and answer, and the search for truth. The thing that Ibn Yaʿīsh has said does not stray outside the realm of truth, although the question is a very difficult one to examine. But not everybody has this intense power, this rising expertise, this excellent perception, this sharp nature, this critical mind, [...] that he possesses, for this [intellectual] power that he has is divine. If it is not divine, then it is beatific; if it is not beatific, then it is at the highest level of humanity. A man of this quality can rarely be found [...].

* * *

When the Majlis met in the year 326 AH, Vizier Ibn al-Furāt addressed those present, saying, "Will anyone answer the call to engage Mattā in a debate over his claim on the significance of logic? He says that there is no way to tell fact from falsity, truth from untruth, good from evil, evidence from dubiousness, and certainty from uncertainty, except with what we gather from logic, what we possess from the practice of this art, and what we learn from the master who laid down the classifications and definitions of its parts and understand the facts from the name of this art." Those present drew back and bent down their heads.[157] Then Ibn al-Furāt said, "By God, there must be among you someone who knows his words and who can bring Mattā to a debate and refute his views. I consider you men of extensive knowledge, defenders of the faith and of its people, a beacon of light for truth and seekers of truth. What does this exchange of glances among you mean?" Abū Saʿīd al-Sīrāfī raised his head and said:

Forgive me, Oh, Vizier. Knowledge that is preserved in the heart is different from the kind of knowledge that is presented at this meeting to the attentive ears, the watchful eyes, the sharp minds, and the critical thinking of this quiet audience. This matter is associated with awe and awe is a place where one is defeated; it brings shame and shame is a place where one

---

157. The names of the most noteworthy public figures that constitute the learned audience in this gathering (*Majlis*) are Al-Khālidī, ibn al-Akhshād, al-Kutbī, ibn Abī Bishr, ibn Rabāḥ, ibn Kaʿb, Abū mru Qudāma ibn Jaʿfar, al-Zuhrī, ibnʿIsā al-Jarrāḥ, ibn Firās, ibn al-Rashīd, ibnʿAbd al-Azīz al-Hāshimī, ibn Yaḥyā al-ʿAlawī, Rasūl ibn ṭaghj from Egypt, and al-Marzabānī Ṣaḥib Al-Samān.

is overcome. To encounter someone in a private battle is not the same as to meet him in an open field.

Ibn al-Furāt said: "Let us hear what you have to say, Abā Saʿīd. The excuse that you advance on behalf of others makes it obligatory for you to win for yourself. And your victory will benefit the group." Abū Saʿīd said: "To go against the Vizier's plan is a disgrace. To avoid his point of view makes one inclined to fall short of doing what one ought to do. We seek God's protection against slipping into error and we ask for His assistance in war and in peace."

Then Abū Saʿīd turned to Mattā and said: "Tell me, what do you mean by logic? If we understand what you intend to show about it, we shall agree with what is correct and refute what is incorrect in a proper manner." Mattā said: "By logic, I mean an instrument [ʾāla] of discourse by means of which we tell what is sound from what is not sound, the meaning that is corrupt from the meaning that is good to use. It is similar to the weighing scale by which I can tell the surplus from the shortfall and what is upright from what is sloping."[158]

Abū Saʿīd said, "You are wrong because it is by way of familiar composition and traditional grammar that we tell what is correct from what is incorrect when we are speaking Arabic. We tell a corrupt meaning from the right meaning by way of reason, if we examine that meaning through reason. Suppose you can tell excess in weight from shortage by means of a weighing scale, how do you know the nature of that which is weighed? Whether it is iron or gold or brass or copper? I see that after you know the weight, you still lack the knowledge of the substance of that which is weighed. You still lack the knowledge of its value and all its characteristics, which are numerous. In the end, weight, on which you count and for which you spent your effort, is no good to you, except for a slight benefit in one way and yet several other ways remain. As the poet said:

You have known one thing, but you have missed several things.[159]

And so, you have missed one thing here. Not everything in this world is weighed. In fact, there are things that you weigh, things whose capacity that you measure, things whose length you measure, things whose area you measure, things whose quantity you measure, and this is with respect to visible bodies. The same thing applies to established abstract concepts. The shadows of the minds more or less reflect feelings, with similarities and apparent analogies kept.

Put this aside. If logic was laid down by a man from Greece,[160] based on the language of the Greeks; if it was based on Greek terminology and on its shared definitions and its characteristics, where does the obligation come from for the Turks, the Persians, and the Arabs to

---

158. In the Arabic philosophical tradition, the term *"organon"* is generally rendered as *"al-ʾāla"* or "instrument."

159. This is the second part of a line attributed to Abbasid poet Abū Nuās (756–814 CE). The first part is as follows: "Tell the person who claims he knows" and the whole line is "Tell the person who claims he knows: [You have] known one thing, but you have missed several things." Grammar is seen here as the way to have access to correct knowledge. Without prior knowledge of the Arabic language, any form of knowledge is flawed.

160. This reference is to Aristotle.

study it and adopt it as a judge and arbiter for them and about them so that they accept what it approves and reject what it disapproves?"

Mattā said: "The obligation comes from the fact that logic is the study of rational things; it is the examination of thoughts occurring in the mind. With respect to rational things, people are the same. Do you not see that 4 and 4 make 8, and that they are equally the same among all nations, and so on and so forth?"

Abū Saᶜīd said: "If the things that the mind seeks and the things put in words are taken with their different branches and distinct ways to this plain level of 4 and 4 making 8, there will no longer be a difference and concord will set in. But that is not the case. By this example, you have been deceitful and you, logicians, are used to this type of deceptiveness."

Abū Saᶜīd continued, "However, if rational things are reached only through language, which includes all the nouns and verbs and particles, is it not obligatory to know language?"

Mattā replied, "Yes [*Naᶜam*]."

Abū Saᶜīd corrected him, saying, "That is incorrect. In this context, you say, 'Nay' [*Balā*]."[161]

Mattā said: "Nay [*Balā*]. In this context, I do as you say."

Abū Saᶜīd said: "Then you are not asking us to learn the science of logic; you are asking us to study the Greek language, which you do not know.[162] So how come you ask us to study a language that you do not know? A language that ceased to exist a long time ago? A language whose speakers passed away? A language of negotiation and communication whose people perished? You translate from Syriac, so what do you say about meanings rendered from the Greek into Syriac? And then from Syriac into Arabic?"[163]

Mattā said: "Even when Greece has perished, translation has preserved its language and has rendered its true meanings."

Abū Saᶜīd said: "If I grant you that translation has been truthful and that it has not lied; that it has straightened up meaning and has not altered it; that it has given the right measure, not an excessive measure; that it has not added anything superfluous or taken out anything essential; that it has not moved anything forward or backward; that it has not diminished the

---

161. The word *Balā* [Nay] is used as a reply to a question with the negative. For further details on this meaning of this word, see the entry on *Balā* in Book I, Part I, page 257, in *An Arabic-English Lexicon* by Edward William Lane.

162. Here Abū Saᶜīd echoes a verse in the Qu'ran that says "wa-mā 'arsalnā min rasūlin 'illā bi-lisāni qawmihi li-yubayyina lahum" (Ibrāhim: 4) when he argues that the Aristotelian logic for which Mattā ibn Yūnus speaks is a Greek language, good only for the Greeks. [We never sent any messenger except in the language of his people, to make things clear for them."]

163. As Jacques Langhade explains in his essay "Mentalité grammairienne, . . ." "Pour les grammairiens la vérité est celle de la langue, elle est dans l'adéquation de l' énoncé, dans la correction de cet énoncé" (113). [For grammarians, truth is in the language; it is in the adequate utterance, in the correct utterance.] For the philosopher, this truth is not a given; it is elaborated progressively. This means the need to construct little by little a system that is organized differently from the system elaborated by grammarians. . . . The first principles themselves are not initially given, but the fruit of an enquiry, the end of research" (113).

meaning of the specific and the general or the meaning of the specific of the specific or the meaning of the general of the general—even if this does not happen and it is not in the nature of languages or the levels of meaning—this is as if you were saying: "There is no evidence, except what the Greek minds have advanced; there is no demonstration, except what they have put forth; there is no truth, except what they have demonstrated."

Mattā said: "No, but the Greeks are known among the nations for being scrupulous with philosophy and for being thorough with the examination of the visible as well as the invisible characteristics of the world, of what is connected to the world and what is disconnected from the world. Thanks to their careful examination, different branches of science and different types of arts have emerged, have been disseminated, have been revealed, and have been established. We do not find this in any other nation."

Abū Saᶜīd said: "You are mistaken, prejudiced, and carried away by flawed opinion. Knowledge has been disseminated respectively among all the nations in the world. For this, the poet has said:

> Knowledge is in the world disseminated;
> And towards knowledge the mind is urged.

In the same way, the arts have been distributed proportionately among all those living on the plain surface of the earth. Thus, one science is superior to other sciences in one place and one art is more practiced than other arts in another place. This is evident and to say more about it is simply unprofitable work. However, what you have said would have been correct and what you have advocated would have looked sound if Greece had been known among all nations for having a firm hand on power, clear sagacity, and a unique structure. If the Greeks had wanted to err, they would not have been able to do that; and if they had intended to tell lies, they would not have been able to do that; and that gravity had come down to them; and truth had been their sponsor; and error would have stayed away from them; and excellences would have been attached to their origins and their branches; and vices would have stayed away from their quintessence and their veins. This is ignorance on the part of those who think so of them and stubbornness on the part of those who claim such things about them. The Greeks, just as other nations, were right in some particular things and wrong in other things; they were knowledgeable in some particular things and ignorant in other things; they were truthful in some particular matters and dishonest in other matters; they were good in some particular cases and bad in other cases. Not all Greece is the founding authority in logic. Only one man among the Greeks is.[164] He learned from those who came before him as those who came after him learned from him. He is not an authority over this multitude of creatures and this mass of people. There are Greeks and non-Greeks who differ from him. Yet in spite of this, difference of views, of understanding, of examination, of asking questions and answering questions is a natural principle of things. So how can a person come up with something by which he removes or unsettles or influences this difference? Alas, this is quite impossible! The world has remained the same after Aristotle's logic as it had been before his logic. Therefore,

---

164. The reference is to Aristotle.

forget about something that is impossible to do since that is something tied with intuition and instinct. If you had applied your mind and devoted your interest to the study of this Arabic language that we have been using in this debate and in which we have been conversing; if your friends, the logicians, had studied the meaning of things in Arabic; and if they had explained the books of the Greeks in the language of Arabic people, you would have realized that you would not need the concepts of the Greeks as you would not need the language of the Greeks.

Here is a problem that says: People have different minds from which they draw in different ways."

[Mattā] said: "Yes."

[Abū Saᶜīd] asked: "Is this difference and variance gained through nature or is it gained through acquisition?"

[Mattā] answered: "Through nature."

[Abū Saᶜīd] asked: "Then how is it admissible here that something is brought up by this natural difference and original variance?"

[Mattā] answered: "You have mentioned this before."

[Abū Saᶜīd] asked: "Have you reached this conclusion in an incisive and clear way? Leave this point aside. I ask you about one particle, which goes around in the language of the Arabs. The meanings of this particle are distinct among men of reason. Then draw the meanings of this particle, using Aristotle's logic, which you boast about and use for evidence. The particle is 'wāw'.[165] What are the rules that govern it? How is it distributed? Is it used in one way or is it used in several ways?"

Mattā looked perplexed and said: "This is grammar. I have not looked into grammar because a logician has no need for it. But a grammarian very much needs logic since logic searches for meaning, whereas grammar searches for the word. If a logician goes by a word, it is by coincidence. If a grammarian comes across a meaning, it is by coincidence. Meaning is nobler than the word and the word is lower than meaning."

[Abū Saᶜīd] said: "You are wrong, for discourse, pronunciation, language, lexis, eloquence, perspicuity [*al-'iᶜrāb*],[166] clarity, conversation, informing, seeking information, offering, wishing, admonishment [al-nahyi], inciting, imploring, calling, demanding, all these are from the same source showing antonyms and synonyms. Do you not see that if a man said: "Zayd uttered the truth, but he did not speak the truth; and he spoke obscenity, but he did not say anything obscene; and he expressed himself, but he did not speak eloquently; and he showed what he wanted to say, but he did not clarify; or he uttered something, but he did not put it in words; or he gave information, but he did not notify," he would be altering, contradicting, putting words in the wrong place, and using words without evidence from his mind or the minds of others. Grammar is logic, but it is drawn forth from Arabic; logic is grammar, but it

---

165. The Arabic particle "*wāw*" corresponds to the conjunction of coordination "*and*" in English.

166. In this particular context, the term *al-'iᶜrāb* coveys the meaning of perspicuity and clarity. The science *al-'iᶜrāb* in Arabic syntax is what Arabic grammarians refer to as "the science of the various inflections of words, literal or virtual, by reason of the various governing words." See Book I, 1992 in *An Arabic-English Lexicon* by William Lane.

is understood in Arabic. The difference between word and meaning is that the word is a natural thing and meaning is rational. This is why the word perishes with time, for time follows the course of nature in a divine way.

The material from which the word is made is clay and everything made of clay is destructible. You have remained without a term for the art that you appropriate and the instrument about which you boast, except that you borrow from the Arabic a term for it and for which you are indebted [*tu ᶜ ār*]. And you are permitted to use this term to a degree. And if you had to use a little amount of this language for the sake of translation, then you must also need much of it to edit the translation to earn the trust of your audience and to avoid the criticism of future translators."

Mattā said: "It is sufficient for me to know the terms 'noun,' 'verb,' and 'particle' in your language. With this amount of knowledge, I get to achieve goals that have been polished for me by Greek logic."

[Abū Saᶜīd] said: "You are wrong because you need to know the descriptive characteristics of the noun, of the verb, and of the particle; you need to know the structure of the noun, of the verb, and of the particle, according to their classification in the speakers' intuitions. Also, you need to know the vocalizations [*ḥarakāt*] of nouns, of verbs, and of particles. The wrong and altered vocalizations are just as bad as the errors committed in the words undergoing vocalizations [*al- mutaḥarrikāt*]. This is a chapter of which you and your folk and your people are unaware. There is a secret that does not occur to your mind; that is, you should know that a language is not the same as another language with respect to the characteristics of its nouns, its verbs, and its particles; that is, their structure and distribution; their connotation and denotation; their stressed and unstressed elements; their expansion and restriction; their composition in verse and prose and rhyming; their measure and deviance [*maylihā*]; and so on and so forth. I do not think there is a person with intelligence and fairness who will oppose this rule or who will have doubts about its right characteristic. Therefore, based on what I have described to you, how can you trust something that has been translated to you? In fact, you need to know the Arabic language more than you need to know Greek semantics, for meanings are neither Greek nor Hindu. Also, languages are Persian or Arabic or Turkish. And yet you claim that meaning happens by way of reason, examination, and thought. Only the rules of language remain, so why do you scorn the Arabic language while you explain the works of Aristotle in it, and you do not even know the true character of the Arabic language?

"Tell me about someone who said this to you: 'With regard to knowing the facts and carefully considering them and examining them, I am in the same situation as those people who lived before the founder of logic. I understand things the way they did, and I think the way they did because I acquired the language by birth and inheritance. I pecked for meanings by way of examination, thought, sequence, and effort.' What do you say to him? Do you say that his judgment is not sound and that he is not on the right path with respect to this matter because he does not know these things the way you do? Perhaps you will be happier to see him emulate you—even if in error—more than you will be happy to see him stick to his views even if he is in the right. This is plain ignorance and bad judgment.

"However, tell me about the coordinate conjunction '*wāw*' and the rule that governs it, for I want to show you that your exaggeration of logic does not give you anything. You do not know one particle in the language by which you advocate for Greek logic. A person who does not know one particle may not know particles; a person who does not know particles may not know the entire language. If he knows some of the language, but does not know part of it, he may not know what he needs. Knowing what he does not need will not be of any use to him. This is the rank of the common people or the rank of those who are a little above common people, so why withstand that and show arrogance towards it and imagine himself of the elite, of the elite of the elite? Why should he pretend that he knows the secret of discourse and the obscure side of philosophy [*al-ḥikma*] and the hidden things of the syllogism and the sound part of demonstration?

"I only asked you about the meanings of one particle, so what would it be like if I scattered all the particles on you and asked you to explain their meanings and their proper and figurative distribution? I heard you, logicians, say: 'Grammarians do not know the positions of the particle '*fī*' [in]. They simply say it is for the meaning of 'container.' They also say the particle '*bī*' [by/with] is for linking. The particle '*fī*' is used in many ways. It is said: 'the thing is in [*fī*] the container.' 'The container is in [*fī*] the place.' 'The politician is in [*fī*] politics.' 'Politics is in [*fī*] the politician.'

"Do you see this derivation coming from the minds of the Greeks and from the Greek language and that the Hindus, the Turks, and the Arabs cannot think this way? This is ignorance on the part of those who make this claim and confusion on the part of those who expand on it. When the grammarian says that '*fī*' [in] is for the meaning of container, he clearly shows the correct meaning in the sentence. He uses metonymy based on the ways that show specificity. There are many cases such as this one and it is sufficient in the place of metonymy."

Ibn al-Furāt turned to Abū Saᶜīd and said: "Brilliant wise man, answer the question for [Mattā] with eloquence about the distribution of the particle '*wāw*' and make him tongue-tied; check with the group what he is unable to say in an Arabic language that he dislikes."

Abū Saᶜīd said: "The particle '*wāw*' has many characteristics and positions, one of which is coordination, as when you say, 'I honored Zayd *wa* [and] ᶜAmr.' It is used to convey the meaning of 'oath' [*al-qasam*], as when you say, '*wa-llāhi* [By God] such and such a thing happened.' It is used to convey the meaning of sequence, as when you say, 'I went out *wa* [and] Zayd was standing' since what comes afterward is a subject and a predicate. It is used to convey the meaning of 'few', which is used to render the meaning of reducing the number, as when they say,

Wa [And few are] its dark depths and empty [is] its wide space.

The particle 'wāw' can also originally be part of a noun, as when you say, '[w]āṣil, [w]āqid, [w]āfid.' And it can also be part of a verb, as in '[wa]jila, ya[w]jalu . . . .'"

CLOSING COMMENTARY

Abū Saʿīd emerges the winner in this debate, while Mattā is reduced to silence. The translation of this text was both a challenge and an immense source of pleasure. The style of al-Tawḥīdī's writing is, as Franz Rosenthal put it, "at times heavy and overloaded" and yet "it bristles with sparkling phrases." This makes him "one of the foremost representatives of Arabic prose literature."[167]

---

167. Rosenthal 1948, 1.

1.6 Arabic-Islamic, c. 791 AH/1389 CE, Egypt

The Tongue of Sovereignty and the Weaver of Wise Words: A Partial Translation of al-Qalqashandī's *Maqāmah on the Chancery Writer*

Rasha Diab

INTRODUCTION

In the Middle Ages, an erudite and skilled writer was carefully recruited to be, among other things, "the tongue of sovereignty" and the weaver of wise words.[168] The famed writer al-Ḥarirī (446–516 AH/1054–1122 CE)[169] describes the official writer as "the confidant of the mighty" whose "pen . . . bears good tidings and warnings alike, . . . intercedes and acts as an envoy."[170] Detailed descriptions like this of the qualities of the (official) writer or secretary proliferate in Arab-Islamic texts. The training of the perfect writer/secretary preoccupied medieval Arab scholars. The text translated here was written by Aḥmad ibn ʿAlī ibn Aḥmad ibn ʿAbd-Allāh ibn Shihāb ibn al-Jammāl Abi-al-Yaman al-Fazārī al-Qalqashandī (756–821/1355–1418), a well-known medieval scholar and writer. al-Qalqashandī was hired to work for the Mamlūk chancery (*dīwān al-inshāʾ*)—the official bureau responsible for all matters related to correspondence and the production of documents—in Egypt. He eventually became the head of the chancery. Early on in his career, he wrote a narrative text (*maqāmah*) that describes the status, potential, and reach of the writer.[171] And, al-Qalqashandī's narrative centers on Nāthir ibn Naẓẓām (literally, prose writer the son of a composer or poet; al-Qalqashandī's mouth piece and representative), who reflects on his future. Nāthir wonders whether to continue his studies or to pursue a professional career. Serendipitously, he meets a sage who responds to varied questions concerning chancery writing/writers.

This translated text is relevant to rhetorical studies for many reasons. In addition to manifesting a keen awareness of *al-maqāmah* literary tradition, this text sheds light on chancery writing, testifies to the elevated expectations of medieval chancery writing/writers at the time, and provides a glimpse into literature on epistolography. Regrettably, this text can be dismissed as *just* an entertaining narrative. The significance of this text, however, becomes

---

168. al-Ḥarirī as translated by Bosworth; Bosworth 1964, 131.

169. Whenever Hijrī (AH) and Gregorian (CE) calendars are used, dates are assigned in this order.

170. Bosworth 1964, 131.

171. *Maqāmah* (plural, *maqāmāt*) refers to a literary genre originated by al-Badiʿ al-Zamān al-Hamadhanī (969–1008 AH) that comprises a narrative episode or a short, entertaining narrative. Characteristically, *al-maqāmah* blends poetry and rhymed prose (*sajʿ*). *Maqāmah* is often translated as "assembly" since the narrative is typically narrated in a *majlis* (i.e., assembly). For more, see Mattock's "Early History."

evident when read in the context of Arab-Islamic rhetorical practices and the burgeoning handbook tradition that aimed for training writers. Since, Arabic rhetoric handbooks and Arab-Islamic epistolography seem under the radar of rhetoric scholars, I first shed light on epistolary rhetoric and writers' handbooks; then, introduce al-Qalqashandī and his narrative text; and subsequently, provide a translation of the first part of Essay Ten, "On Genres—Unrelated to Institutional Writing—That Writers Compete to Compose and Circulate."

Epistolary Rhetoric and Chancery Writers

Outside rhetorical studies, evidence of Arab-Islamic epistolary rhetoric abounds both in terms of anthologized epistles and handbooks.[172] Drawing on this evidence, elsewhere, I demonstrate that epistles realized social, political, intellectual, and administrative goals and that distinct epistles were remembered, quoted, and anthologized.[173] Relatedly, epistolary rhetoric was studied under the domain of artistic prose (*inshā'*), which covers varied rhetorical practices like essayistic writing (*maqālah*), oratory (*khatābah*), and narrative (*qissah*). Generally, *inshā'* "came to encompass any form of composition written in an ornate style, but it was applied particularly to letters and epistolary models."[174] Those who excelled in *inshā'* were esteemed, and their rhetorical skills were sought. Chancery writers were deemed superior to other writers and were often praised for their work. For example, chancery writers were described as "the tongue[s] of sovereignty" and the weavers of wise words as noted earlier, a statement that underscores their potential and reach.

Concomitantly, specialized literature on the arts of letter-writing and the writer (*adab al-rasā'il* and *adab al-kātib*) was in demand and flourished. Handbooks written to guide and train writers are compendia of knowledge.[175] This specialized literature systematically (1) classified letters and documents; (2) provided compendia of words and terms, especially those often unknown or confused; (3) enumerated and distinguished between writers' tools (e.g., inks, paper types, paper cuts); (4) detailed writers' linguistic and rhetorical resources (e.g. quotable proverbs, poetry, and Qur'ānic verses); (5) identified wide ranging areas of knowledge to be diligently pursued (e.g., governance systems, history, jurisprudence), and (6) catalogued terms, ranks, and titles needed for official correspondence.

The detailed exposition of these technical skills and areas of knowledge is not, however, the most striking facet of this literature. Equally intriguing, there is a conspicuous vision of the writer (*al-kātib*) as a person (a man in this historical context) of both moral and intellectual excellence. This vision can be seen in the writings of chancery exemplars and handbooks written to guide future chancery writers like Ibn al-Athīr (538–637/1163–1239) and Ibn Qutaybah al-Daynawarī's (213–c.276/828–889) who are (in)directly referenced in al-Qa-

---

172. See for example, Hämeen-Anttila (2006); Ṣafwat (1937); Serjeant (1983).
173. See Diab (2020).
174. Gully 1996, 147.
175. See, for example, Durūbī (1992); al-Athīr (1959); Qutaybah (1900).

lqashandī's *maqāmah*.[176] To illustrate, I shed light on Ibn Qutaybah, who is recognized as one of four pillars of *adab*—literature identifying standards of learning and conduct in varied spheres and activities like playing chess as well as poetic and official writing.

In the introduction of *Adab al-Kātib* (i.e., *The Writer's Handbook*), Ibn Qutaybah articulates a vision for the writer.[177] This vision is bidimensional. The writer is expected to be both well-rounded and erudite as well as a person who strives for moral excellence. To realize the intellectual dimension of this vision, the writer needs a life-long study, which is guided by writer's handbooks like Ibn Qutaybah's. The goal is to acquire different areas of knowledge, including lexicology and morphology, orthography, grammar, spelling, inflection, pronunciation, styles, and figures of speech. Ibn Qutaybah also expects the writer to be familiar with history; al-Qur'ān, *ḥadīth* (prophetic sayings), and *isnād* (chain of transmission); geometry; calendars; and jurisprudence, for example.[178] More importantly, these intellectual excellences are matched with ethical ones. Ibn Qutaybah asserts that a refined tongue demands a refined character, which mandates investing in integrity, honesty, forbearance, discernment, and guarding against excesses (e.g., indecorousness, glibness, conceit).[179]

Far from being an anomaly, Ibn Qutaybah's vision is consistent with that articulated by prominent writers like Ibn al-Athīr, al-Ḥarīrī, who paved the way for al-Qalqashandī, and al-Qalqashandī. In their works, we preview their training of the perfect writer or secretary and their perceptive and preceptive description of the lofty art. In this translated excerpt from al-Qalqashandī's work, this vision of and investment in training the perfect writer endures. al-Qalqashandī does not just seek this noble profession but also proves himself to know well its long and enduring tradition.

AL-QALQAṢHANDĪ AND *"AL-KWĀKIB AL-DURRĪYAH"*

Well-recognized as a virtuoso, al-Qalqashandī (756–821/1355–1418) was a multilingual (Arabic, Turkish, and Persian) scholar, writer, and mathematician.[180] al-Qalqashandī was born in Qalqashandah (also Qarqashandah)—a small village in al-Qalyūbīyyah, Egypt. In Alexandria, he studied under the well-known scholar ibn al-Mulaqqin. Certified (777/1376) in the Shāfiʿī tradition of Islamic law (*sharīʿah*) and jurisprudence (*fiqh*), he became eligible for *fatwa* (i.e., providing legal opinion based on Islamic law) and teaching.[181] Because he wrote books

---

176. Ibn al-Athīr was a literary critic and prolific writer, and Ibn Qutaybah al-Daynawarī was a judge, linguist, philologist, theologian, and writer of *adab*.

177. Ibn Qutaybah 1900, 1–21.

178. Ibid., 11–12.

179. Ibid., 12–20.

180. In the West, al-Qalqashandī is more recognized as a cryptologist. *Ṣubḥ al-Aʿshá*, his most known work, has a section on cryptology. For more, see al-Kadit (1992).

181. Ḥamzah 1962, 32–54. Ḥamzah notes that al-Qalqashandī aspired to be a judge and was recognized as a scholar. However, other scholars state that al-Qalqashandī worked as a judge and then worked in *dīwān al-aḥbās*, or the Endowments Diwan (Abdelhamid and El-Toudy 2017, 10).

on *fiqh* and literary epistles, his scholarship was noted. He was recruited to join the Mamlūk Chancery in Cairo as an entry-level writer (*kātib darj*) in 791/1389.[182]

Celebrating his appointment to the Mamlūk Chancery as chancery writer/secretary (*katib inshā'*), al-Qalqashandī wrote the aforementioned *maqāmah* titled "*al-Kwākib al-Durrīyah fī al-Manāqib al-Badrīyah*," or "The Glistening Stars Illuminating the Virtues of al-Badr Family" (hereafter "*al-Kwākib al-Durrīyah*"). "*al-Kwākib al-Durrīyah*" is a simple autobiographical narrative about and written by his much younger self. Then, al-Qalqashandī (speaking through the character/voice of Nāthir ibn Naẓẓām) reflected on and weighed his professional options. An opportune encounter with an old sage facilitated his decision-making process. Their dialogue included a comparison between the skills, professional and ethical responsibilities, and socio-political standing of accounting and chancery writing (*kitābit al-inshā'* and *kitābit al-ḥisbah*, respectively). By the end of *al-maqāmah* the ideal *kātib* is described as an erudite scholar, and al-Qalqashandī's choice is clear. He should become a chancery writer. In *al-maqāmah*, al-Qalqashandī showcases his knowledge of numerous literary genres, rhetorical practices, and their histories.

al-Qalqashandī fuses *al-maqāmah*, which the Arabs excelled in, and *adab al-kātib*—or literature developed to train secretaries.[183] He produces a rhetorically rich text that blends panegyric poetry, comparison, autobiographical narration, argumentation, and epistemic dialogue. In such a blend, the skills and responsibilities of the writer are explicitly identified. To illustrate, *al-maqāmah* is a comparison between *kātib al-inshā'* and *kātib al-ḥisbah* (chancery writer and accountant, respectively) and an argument for the prestige and far-reaching impact of *kātib al-inshā'*, who is the "tongue of sovereignty," "repository for secrets," and wielder of power. Both comparison and argument further an epistemic dialogue wherein the learned sage answers al-Qalqashandī's (or Nāthir's) inquisitive probing on the best professional pursuit to undertake. The question-answer series highlight the chancery writer's skills and responsibilities, for example. Their epistemic exchange results in a précis of information typically produced in writers' handbooks: writers are expected to excel in language and rhetoric in general (e.g., semantics, grammar and declension, embellishments, stylistics, genres) and especially in oratory and epistolary rhetoric; Qur'ān and Prophetic sayings (*Ḥadīth*); poetry; proverbs and wise sayings; customs and traditions of Arabs; geography, history, and governing systems and institutions, and so forth. *Al-kātib*'s enumerated skills and responsibilities make him "a walking and talking encyclopedia."[184] Therefore, by writing *al-maqāmah*, al-Qalqashandī proves his knowledge of and looms large in the epistolary and artistic prose traditions.

However, al-Qalqashandī's knowledge exceeds technical knowledge of institutional writers and writing, for his writing abilities also contend with noted *maqāmāt* writers who finessed the art of weaving poetry and rhymed prose. *Al-maqāmah*'s plot line is intriguing, the fusion

---

182. *Kātib al-darj* (often translated as entry-level or minor secretary, scribe, or writer) is one of the writer's professional ranks, which are described briefly in the glossary. For more on professional ranks, see Ḥabashī (1976); Abdelhamid and El-Toudy (2017).

183. See, for example, van Berkel (1997).

184. Van Berkel 1997, 163.

of the narrative and the epistemic dialogue is captivating, the technical account of the skills and responsibilities of writers is gracefully and easefully laced with poetry and rhymed prose. As such, *al-maqāmah* is a performative argument that showcases al-Qalqashandī's ability to seamlessly weave prose with praise (*madīh*) and invective (*hijā'*) poetry, merge voices of literary and writing forefathers, all while explicating the knowledge, skills, and ethical responsibilities of chancery writers. Proving to be a rhetor par excellence, al-Qalqashandī does not shy away from a symbolic jab at al-Ḥarīrī, renowned originator of *al-maqāmah* when al-Qalqashandī refers to al-Ḥarīrī's alleged failure in chancery writing in al-Qalqashandī's own *maqāmah*.[185]

Though written decades earlier, al-Qalqashandī's *maqāmah* is included in volume fourteen of al-Qalqashandī's fourteen-volume encyclopedia titled *Ṣubḥ al-A'shá fī Ṣinā'at al-Inshā'* (hereafter *Ṣubḥ*).[186] *Ṣubḥ* comprises approximately 6,500 pages and was composed over twenty years to be completed in 814/1411.[187] *Al-maqāmah* anticipated and was a blueprint of *Ṣubḥ*, which is widely recognized as a compendium of knowledge needed by official writers, an authoritative source on different types of epistles and documents, and the peak of institutional writing.[188] With astounding detail, *Ṣubḥ* reveals medieval, Arab-Islamic institutional rhetoric. For example, in Essay 9, al-Qalqashandī explains legal-political principles that inform the writing of peace agreements, reproduces exemplars of agreements and correspondence between political dignitaries, presents textual formulae that chancery writers use, explicates the arrangement of and typically used discursive moves in letters and varied documents, and underlines legal, historic, social, political, and jurisprudential knowledge needed to compose peacemaking agreements, for example.[189] Like other handbooks, *Ṣubḥ* provides insight into different writing tools and materials; lists *al-kātib's* skills and knowledge; covers classifications of ink, titles, honorifics, and even ice imported or referenced in mercantile transactions.

Many of the lines of Arab-Islamic rhetorical development are invisible to rhetoric studies and, therefore, understudied. This includes epistolary rhetoric, handbooks to guide and train writers, and literary genres that praise the writer. There is so much to unearth and to know about institutional rhetoric. This translation of the first section of al-Qalqashandī's *maqāmah* can introduce this line of rhetorical development and expand our current knowledge of institutional rhetoric beyond medieval Europe.

---

185. For more on *al-maqāmah* genre and it originators, see Mattock (1984).

186. Al-Maqāmah is included as the first example of serious texts relevant but not directly related to the work of the chancery. For the Arabic text, see al-Qalqashandī (1922, 110–28).

187. van Berkel translates the title *as The Daybreak for the Sufferer of Night Blindness in Composing Official Documents* (van Berkel 1997).

188. See, for example, 'Abd al-Karīm (1973); Ḥamzah (1962); van Berkel (1997).

189. Rulers often recruited legal experts like al-Qalqashandī to work at their chancery. For more on the legal expertise of chancery writers, please see Tillier (2012). For more on legal-political, peacemaking instruments, see Diab (2015).

Translation of al-Qalqashandī's *Maqāmah*: An Excerpt from *Ṣubḥal-A'shá fī Ṣinā'at al-Inshā'*

Essay Ten

On Genres—Unrelated to Institutional Writing—That Writers Compete to Compose and Circulate

(Addresses Two Subjects)

Subject 1: On Serious Matters

Chapter 1: On Maqāmāt

Maqāmāt is the plural of *maqāmah*. In terms of the study of the origin of [words in the Arabic] language, the word refers to an assembly and congregated people.[190] And a short story is termed a *maqāmah* as if it is iterated in one session as people congregate to listen. However, *al-muqāmah* refers to taking residence or *al-iqāmah*.[191] Using a Qur'ānic illustration, this meaning is exemplified in Allāh's reference—Exalted is He—to the people of heaven, who assert that ". . . out of His bounty, [He] settled us in a home [*al-muqāmah*] that will last."[192]

Know that the originator of *maqāmāt* is the literary genius and leading scholar al-Badi' al-Hamadhanī. His famed, well-composed, exceptionally eloquent *maqāmāt* manifest exemplary literary workmanship. He was then followed by Imām Abū-Moḥammad al-Qāsim al-Ḥarīrī, who composed the fifty renowned *maqāmāt*. His *maqāmāt* exemplify finesse. They were so well-received that they were popular among specialists and general readership. This positive regard rendered al-Badi''s *maqāmāt* no longer welcome, and eventually they sank into oblivion. However, Minister Ḍiyā' al-Dīn ibn al-Athīr, in his *Al-Mithāl al-Sā'ir* ["The Current Knowledge or Model"], neither gave al-Ḥarīrī due credit nor celebrated his writing abilities when he [ibn al-Athīr] noted that al-Ḥarīrī excelled *only* in *maqāmāt*. And he even mentioned that Shaīykh Abū-Moḥammad Aḥamd ibn al-Khashāb noted that al-Ḥarīrī specialized in *maqāmāt*, implying that al-Ḥarīrī excelled in writing prose *only* when he composed *maqāmāt*.[193] And, if he composed something else in prose, it amounted to nothing. ibn al-Athīr also reported that when al-Ḥarīrī went to Baghdād and his *maqāmāt* were known and studied, people assumed that he could be employed for institutional writing in the Caliphate

---

190. The reference is to *glottogony* or *glossogeny*. In contrast to etymology, which focuses on the genesis of a word, *glottogony* focuses on the genesis of language. Since the focus is on the word *maqāmah* and how it differs from *muqāmah*, I translate the Arabic text as "the origin of words in the Arabic language."

191. In Arabic script, *maqāmah* and *muqāmah* look the same. The difference is in inflection.

192. This statement quotes verse 35 of Faṭir (chapter 35) in al-Qur'ān.

193. ibn al-Khashāb (492–567 CE/1099–1172 AH) is a famed poet, scholar, and grammarian.

Diwan [*Dīwān al-Khilāfah*]. He was recruited and charged with composing a document. Confounded, al-Harīrī's claims to excellence were confuted, for al-Harīrī was so dumbstruck that he could articulate neither short nor long utterances. Recounting this incident, some wrote,

> An elder, of our own, from Rabī'aht al-Faras [tribe],[194]
> In his usual pensive craze, pulls his beard.
> In al-Mashān, Allāh endowed him the gift of eloquence.[195]
> In Baghdād, he's become bridled and dumbstruck.[196]

al-Harīrī recused himself from this charge [to write official correspondence] by explaining how all *maqāmāt* revolve around a purposive story. Conversely, correspondence, like a shoreless sea, is boundless, for meanings evolve as daily events alter our perception, and meanings vary as often and as frequently as the breaths we take.

I composed the aforementioned *maqāmah* in the preface of this book [*Ṣubḥ al-A'shá fī Ṣinā'at al-Inshā'*], circa 791 AH, when I was hired by Dīwān al-Inshā' in the royal courts.[197] This *maqāmah* comprises a précis on the art of composition [institutional writing], which I titled "al-Kwākib al-Durrīyah fī al-Manāqib al-Badrīyah" ["The Glistening Stars Illuminating the Virtues of al-Badr Family"], which I wrote as a panegyric of al-Maqarr al-Badrī ibn al-Maqarr al-'Alāī ibn al-Maqarr al-Maḥiawī ibn Faḍl Allāh, who was the Master of Dīwān al-Inshā' in the Sultān's Courts in the Egyptian Governmental Bureaus at the time.[198] My *maqāmah* centers on a human being's need for a profession to affiliate with and a life to hold onto. *Kitābah* [writing] is the only profession befitting the pursuer of knowledge, and it is impermissible to refrain from its pursuit for others. Special preference is to *kitābit al-inshā'*, which

---

194. The phrase refers to al-Harīrī, who belongs to al-Rabi'ah tribe. The tribe's forefather—ibn Nizār ibn 'Adnān—inherited horses (*faras*). Ismā'īl ibn 'Alī Abū al-Fidá 1870, 2: 247.

195. Al-Mashān is a small village near Baṣrah. See ibn al-Athīr 1959, 39.

196. ibn al-Athīr 1959, 39-40. These verses comprise a direct invective (*hijā'*) of al-Harīrī and are attributed to the poet Abū al-Qāsim ibn Aflaḥ. The verses, al-Harīrī's response, and the comparison between *maqāmāt* and chancery writing have been used (almost verbatim) by Ibn al-Athīr (al-Qalqashandī's predecessor), who is critical of al-Harīrī. However, their use by al-Qalqashandī can be considered not just a pointer to the preeminence of chancery writing but also an indirect praise of the self (*madīḥ*): al-Qalqashandī parades his knowledge of critiques and limitations of his predecessors while underlining his own rhetorical agility.

197. This is approximately 1389 CE. At the time, al-Ẓāhir Sayf al-Dīn Barqūq ruled. He ruled from 783/1382 to 801/1399) and was the first Sultan of the Mamlūk Burjī dynasty (1382–1517 CE). For more, see Bosworth (1996, 76–80).

198. *Manāqib* can be translated as virtues or feats. al-Maqarr is an honorific, formerly used as a title for political sovereigns (e.g., *sultān* or *amīr*) who rule a territory, but later it was mainly used to refer to dignitaries like Badr ibn Faḍl Allāh al-'Umarī, the Master, or head, of Dīwān al-Inshā' (783/1382–801/1399). Following Abdelhamid and El-Toudy, I use the title "Master of Dīwān al-Inshā.'" It is worth noting that *saḥib* was a title for ministers or secretaries, which points to the noble position of heads of the chancery at the time. For more, see Abdelhamid and El-Toudy 2017, 394.

is outweighed and favored, for it transcends and surpasses *kitābit al-daīūnah*. *Al-maqāmah* comprises a statement clarifying the materials *kātib al-inshā'* needs and the excellences he cultivates, while heeding a compilation of terminology that clarifies the goals and principles of *kātib al-inshā'*; all in addition to other areas of knowledge to be known by studying what's between *al-maqāmah's* folds, God willing. *Al-maqāmah* follows:

Nathīr ibn Nazzām narrated . . .

* * *

As I strolled in abundant gardens, . . . I puzzled over how earning a living disrupted my diligent study. . . . Adamant and well-founded arguments for both interests—in seeking employment and pursuing knowledge—clashed. Because none would abate, I was left amiss. Ruffled, I could not tell which would be more beneficial. If I forsook knowledge to earn a living, I would perilously backtrack. If I refrained from work, I would ruin what I established and perish from hunger.

Realizing that these two interests are interdependent . . . , I rummaged around for a career consistent with learning . . . to find an art or profession that matches my aspiration . . . .

As I walked and perused a garden's scenes, I discerned a mournful, yearning voice. Claiming my attention, I took heed and traced the voice to find a handsome, wise man reciting,

> If you are intentionally unjust to me,
> You will lose the friendship of writers.
> They, who usher abundant prosperity to friends,
> They, who free friends from their own failings,
> They, who bear cumbersome responsibilities,
> They, who clear complexities and conciliate quarrelers.[199]

* * *

Deferentially, I listened to his recitation and description of writers. With trepidation, I approached and sat with an inquisitive stance. I said, "These are not just the traits of kings but also the kings of traits, the noblest of virtues, and the most cherished values. I did not know that writing had such grave consequences or that writers are endowed with such dexterity." Angrily, he looked away. Then, with an upward gaze, he reflectively said, "Nay, you missed the judiciousness and prudence [required to appropriately interpret the lines of verse recited] as well as misidentified the purpose of writing. It is the noblest of professions. It is the most esteemed profession. The Holy Qur'ān expounded its eminence, and the honored prophetic *sunnah* [norms or traditions] recognized writers."

"The Almighty—exalted is His praise and blessed are His names—said, 'Proclaim [or Read]! And thy Lord is Most Bountiful. He, who taught [the use of] the pen, taught the

---

199. These lines seem to draw on al-Ḥarīrī's description of *al-kātib* in his Twenty-Second *maqāmah* on scribes. al-Ḥarīrī 1867, 229–34.

human that which he knew not.'"[200] Thus, the Omnipotent stated that He [, providing us with knowledge,] taught us about the use of the pen. Describing Himself as the Most Bountiful indicates that this teaching is an immense blessing. . . . And said He, whose Power is Exalted, "[By the power of the Letter] Nūn, the pen, and the records [i.e., that which the angels record]."[201] So, God made an oath using [a reference to] the pen and that which is recorded by the pen, and this oath was made using the most emphatic avowal. And the Almighty, holy is His glory, avowed, "Verily, over you are those [appointed angels] who protect [you]. Kind and honorable, writing down [your deeds]."[202] Hence, He made writing [skills] a description of the kind and noble ones. The same was done with a group of the prophets—peace be upon them.[203] Prophet Muḥammad—may the blessings and the peace of Allāh be upon him— was precluded from its practice as a sign, which Allāh, the Exalted and Glorified, clarified when He noted the disbelievers' incredulity in "And they say: Tales of the Ancients, which he (Prophet Muhammad) has caused to be written."[204]

* * *

Know that Prophet Muḥammad—may the blessings and the peace of Allāh be upon him—invested in hiring a lot of *kuttāb*. It's reported that he—may the blessings and the peace of Allāh be upon him—had over thirty writers who were the best of companions, the most dependable and trustworthy of cohorts. They [were those] he entrusted with the mysteries of revelations and [revealed message or] scripture. They [were those] whose pen tips he used to communicate with the kings of the world who conceded despite distance and long duration [it takes to correspond]. And kings also initiated and responded to his correspondence. He corresponded with his associates, and they corresponded with him; he charitably [or attentively] listened and soundly refuted. Thus was the tradition of the Righteous Caliphs and their successors.[205] The kings of Islām and their counterparts followed his way.

---

200. The reference is to verses 3–5 of al-'Alaq (chapter 96) in al-Qur'ān. The phrase " *'alama bilqalam*" is often translated as "taught using the pen," "taught by/through [what is recorded by] the pen," and "taught (the use of) the pen" to point to three different gifts, namely the discovery of the pen, what the pen allows to be revealed by God, and that which is preserved and shared.

201. Nūn is an Arabic consonant. Exegetes recognize the use of letters to begin chapters of al-Qur'ān, which is beyond the scope of this chapter, as a feature of al-Qur'ān's inimitability. The reference is to verse 1 of al-Qalam (chapter 68) in al-Qur'ān.

202. The reference is to verses 10–11 of al-Infiṭār (chapter 82) in al-Qur'ān. Other verses communicate that angels protect humans, and the word protect ("*ḥāfiẓīn*") here may not just refer to protection. It can refer also to angels' dedicated work to account for, record, safeguard, or "memorize" all deeds.

203. This statement, which is an honorific and a prayer, typically follows reference to Prophet Muḥammad.

204. The reference is to verse 5 of al-Furqān (chapter 25) in al-Qur'ān.

205. The reference is to the four Righteous/Rightly-Guided Caliphs who succeeded Prophet Moḥammad, namely Abū Bakr al-Ṣidīq, 'Umar ibn al-Khaṭṭāb, 'Ali ibn Abi Ṭālib, and 'Uthmān ibn 'Affān.

Writing is the law that regulates political acts. The status of a writer is a sought-after leadership position, for writers are sought by dignitaries and high-ranked officials serving the caliph. Writers are the caliph's insightful eyes, judicious ears, articulate tongues, repository of knowledge and secrets, and are undoubtedly pure and truth-seeking. Kings need writers more than writers need kings. People of the sword and flag compete with the people of the pen, but they don't compete with the people of the sword and flag in their domain.[206]

Generally, writers embody all graceful attributes and noble affairs. Beneficence is their slogan; equanimity is their mantle; magnanimity is their avenue; goodness is their custom; decorum is their vessel; and courteousness is their way. It is said [in their description]:

> Wine as if distilled
> From writers's moral strengths.

When the sage finished and his point became clearer, I said: "You mentioned people whose descriptions delighted me and whose courteousness I yearn for. The fine qualities of the people described inspire delight and their courteousness stir yearnings. Their approving depiction, fine attributes, appealing traits invite me to join their societies, nestle in their valley to make their occupation my livelihood, and to apply myself to their art. This will reunite me with learning and reweave [the loosened] chords of my occupation. Thus, I will realize my dreams and attain my goals."

"But, which order of scribes do you refer to? Which kind of writing do you point to? Is it accounting (*kitābat al-amūal*) or is it official writing (*kitābat al-inshā'*)?" The sage looked at me with a smile, and recited as if chanting,

> People, if angrily they take hold of their pens,
> Then filled their inkstands with the waters of death,
> From afar, they conquer those enemies
> They didn't defeat with their swords.

So, I said, "It seems you are pointing to the art of composition (*al-inshā'*). . . ."

* * *

"al-Ḥarīrī, though, endowed the writing of finances the best of attributes and noted the virtues and meritorious traits of its scribes."

Then the sage said, "This claim is refutable using the same text. Actually, the claim is false, for al-Ḥarīrī declared at the beginning:

---

206. This is a metonym for the military. The competition directs our attention to literary debates wherein the merits of a contestant (e.g., person, concept, profession) are paraded and "invective poured on [their] adversary." Hämeen-Anttila, "The Essay and the Debate," 142. al-Qalqashandī also wrote literary debates. One was a literary debate between the sword and the pen, which was written in 794/1392. This literary debate is also published in volume 14 of his encyclopedia. For more on literary debates, see Hämeen-Anttila (2006 14: 231–40).

. . . the art of Composition is the more lofty, though the art of Account may be the more useful. –The pen of correspondences is a choice orator, but the pen of account-keeping picks up phrases carelessly: —And the fablings of eloquence are copied to be studied, but the ledgers of accounts are soon blotted out and razed.—And the Composer is the Johayneh for information, and the post-bag of secrets, and the confidant of the mighty, and the great among guests.—And his pen is the tongue of sovereignty, and the knight of the skirmish; a Lokmân of wisdom, and the interpreter of purpose: it carries glad news, and it warns, it is the intercessor and the envoy.—By it fortresses are won, and foes are vanquished, and the rebel is made obedient, and the distant is brought near; —And its master is free from suits, secure from the malice of accusers, praised in the assemblies, not exposed to the drawing up of registers.[207]

---

207. Nāthir quotes verbatim al-Ḥarirī's twenty-second *maqāmah* titled *"al-Maqāmah al-Furātīah."* This section is excerpted from Chenery's translation.

COMPREHENSIVE BIBLIOGRAPHY

Abd al-Karīm, Aḥmad 'Izzat. 1973. Abū al-'Abbās al-Qalqashandī wa Kitābuhu Ṣubḥ al-A'shá [Abū al-'Abbās al-Qalqashandī and His Book Ṣubḥ al-A'shá]. Cairo, Hay'āt al-Kitāb.

Abdelhamid, Tarek Galal, and Heba El-Toudy. 2017. Selections from Ṣubḥ Al-A 'shā by Al-Qalqashandī, Clerk of the Mamluk Court: Egypt: "Seats of Government" and "Regulations of the Kingdom," From Early Islam to the Mamluks. 1st ed. London: Routledge.

Abderrahmane, Ṭ. 1978. "Discussion entre Abū Sa'id al-Sirāfi, le grammarien, et Mattā b. Yūnus, le philosophe." Arabica 25: 310–23.

Abū-al-Fidá, Ismā'īl ibn 'Alī. 1870. Tārīkh al-Malik al-Mu'ayyad [The History of al-Malik al-Mu'ayyad]. 4 vols. Constantinople: Dār al-Ṭibā'ah al-'Āmirah al-Shāḥanīyyah. http:// sites.dlib.nyu.edu/viewer/books/columbia_aco003613/7.

Alak, Khaled Abel Rahman. 1986. *Tareekh Tawtheek Nas Al Qur'an Al Kareem* [The History of Documenting the Noble Qur'an]. Damascus: Dar Al-fikr.

Almawdudi, S. A. 1979. *Towards Understanding the Qur'an: English Only Edition.* Kano: Kube Publication.

Alon, Ilai. 2002. *Al-Farabi's Philosophical Lexicon.* 2 vols. Wiltshire: Aris and Philips Ltd.

al-Asqalani, Ibn Hajar. 1995. *Al Talkhees Al-Habeer.* Vol. 4. Riyadh: Mu'asasat Kurtuba.

al-Farabi, Abu Nasr. 1976. *Kitab Fi Al-Mantiq: Al-Khataba*, edited by Mohamed Salim. Cairo: Dar Al-Kutub.

al-Jahiz, Abu Uthman Amr ibn Bahr. *1987. Al-Bayaan wa Al-Tabyeen* [Book of Clarity and Clarification], part 2. Beirut: Dar Al-jeel.

al-Jawziyyah, Ibn Qayyim. 2002. *I'lam Al-Muwaqqi'in an Rab Al-Alamin.* Vol. 2. Dammam: Dar Ibn Al-Jawzi.

al-Ḥarīrī, Abū Moḥammad al-Qāsim. 1867. "al-Maqāmah al-Furātīah." In *The Assemblies of Al Harîri.* Vol. 1 Containing the First Twenty Six Assemblies. Translated by Thomas Chenery. Edinburgh: Williams and Norgate.

al-Kadit, Ibrahim A. 1992. "Origins of Cryptology: The Arab Contributions." *Cryptologia*, 16 (2): 97–126.

al-Mubarrad, Abu-l Abbas Mohammad bin Yazid. 1997. *Al-Kamil* [The Perfect One], part 3. Cairo: Dar Al-fikr Al-arabi.

al-Musawi, Muhsin J. 2001. "Arabic Rhetoric." In *Encyclopedia of Rhetoric*, edited by Thomas O. Sloane, 29–33. London: Oxford University Press.

—. 2003. "Vindicating a Profession or a Personal Career? Al-Qalqashandī's Maqāmah in Context." *Mamlūk Studies Review* 7: 111–35.

al-Qalqashandī, Aḥmad ibn 'Alī. 1992. Ṣubḥ al-A'shá fī Ṣinā'at al-Inshā'. 14 vols. Cairo: Dār al-Kutub al-Miṣrīyah.

al-Sarakhsi, Shams Al-deen. 1989. *Kitab Al-Mabsut.* Vol. 16. Cairo: Dar Al-Ma'rifa, 1989.

al-Sirāfi, Ḥasan b. 'Abd-Allāh. 1897. *Sharḥ Kitāb Sibawayh*, excerpts in the edition of the *Kitāb Sibawayh*, Cairo.

—. 1955. *Kitāb akhbār al-naḥwiyīn al-baṣriyīn, ed. F Krenkow*, Beirut-Paris, 1936; ed. M. ʿA. Khafājī, Cairo.

Arberry, A. J. 2013. *Aspects of Islamic Civilization: As Depicted in the Original Texts*. Vol. 19. London: Routledge.

Aristotle. 1991. *On Rhetoric: A Theory of Civic Discourse*. Translated by George A. Kennedy. New York: Oxford University Press.

As-Sallabi, Ali Muhammad. 2007. *Omar Ibn Al-Khattab: His Life and Times*. Vol. 2, translated by Nasiruddin Al-Khatib. Riyadh: International Islamic Publishing House.

Baddar, Maha. 2010. "The Arabs Did Not 'Just' Translate Aristotle: Al-Farabi's Logico-Rhetorical Theory." In *The Responsibilities of Rhetoric*, edited by Michelle Smith and Barbara Warnick, 230–42. Long Grove, IL: Waveland.

—. 2010. "From Athens (Via Alexandria) to Baghdad: Hybridity as Epistemology in the Work of Al-Kindi, Al-Farabi, and in the Rhetorical Legacy of the Medieval Arabic Translation Movement." PhD diss., University of Arizona.

—. 2015. "Toward a New Understanding of Audience in the Medieval Arabic Translation Movement: The Case of Al-Kindi's 'Statement on the Soul.'" In *Rhetoric Across Borders*, edited by Anne T. Demo, 59–70. Anderson, SC: Parlor Press, 2015.

—. 2018. "Texts that Travel: Translation Genres and Knowledge-Making in the Medieval Arabic Translation Movement." In *Travel, Time, and Space in the Middle Ages and Early Modern Time: Explorations of Identity Formation*. Fundamentals of Medieval and Early Modern Culture. Vol. 22, edited by Albrecht Classen, 95–119. Boston: De Gruyter.

Benhabib, Seyla. 2018. *Exile, Statelessness, and Migration*. Princeton, NJ: Princeton University Press.

Bergé, Marc. 1974. *Essai sur la personnalité morale et intellectuelle d'Abū Ḥayyān al-Tawḥīdī*. 2 vols. Damas: Institut français de Damas.

Black, Deborah L. 1990. *Logic and Aristotle's Rhetoric and Poetics in Medieval Arabic Philosophy*. New York: E. J. Brill.

Borrowman, Shane. 2010. "Recovering the Arabic Aristotle: Ibn Sina and Ibn Rushd on the Logic of Civic and Poetic Discourse." In *Rhetoric in the Rest of the West*, edited by Shane Borrowman, Robert L. Lively, and Marcia Kmetz, 97–118. Cambridge: Cambridge Scholars.

Bosworth, Clifford Edmund. 1964. "A Maqāma on Secretaryship: Al-Qalqashandī's 'al-Kawākib al-Durriyya fi'l-Manāqib al-Badriyya.'" *Bulletin of the School of Oriental and African Studies* 27 (2): 291–98.

—. 1996. The New Islamic Dynasties: A Chronological and Genealogical Manual. Edinburgh: Edinburgh University Press.

Britannica Encyclopedia of World Religions. 2006. Encyclopedia Britannica, Inc.

Comas, James. "Medieval Arabic-Islamic Rhetoric and Poetics: Selected Bibliography of Work in English." Accessed August 15, 2019. capone.mtsu.edu/jcomas/rhetoric/arabic.html.

Copeland, Rita and Ineke Sluiter, eds. 2009. *Medieval Grammar and Rhetoric: Language Arts and Literary Theory AD 300–1475*. New York: Oxford University.

Diab, Rasha. 2015. "Peacemaking and the Chancery in Medieval Cairo: Revisiting Medieval Arabic Rhetoric." In *Rhetoric Across Borders*, edited by Anne Teresa Demo, 121–33. Anderson, SC: Parlor Press.

—. 2018. "Legal-Political Rhetoric, Human Rights, and the Constitution of Medina." *Rhetorica* 36 (3): 219–43.

—. 2020. "Epistolary Rhetoric." In *Routledge Handbook of Comparative World Rhetorics*, edited by Keith Lloyd, 144–54. New York: Routledge.

Dorrien, Gary. 2018. *Breaking White Supremacy*. New Haven, CT: Yale University Press.

Durūbī, Samīr Maḥmūd. 1992. *A Critical Edition of and Study on Ibn Faḍl Allāh's Manual of Secretaryship 'al-Taʿrīf bi'l-Muṣṭalaḥ al-Sharīf*. Jordan: Publications of the Deanship of Research and Graduate Studies, Muʾtah University.

Eddy, Robert, and Amanda Espinosa-Aguilar. 2019. *Writing Across Cultures*. Logan, UT: Utah State University Press.

Elamrani, Jamal. 1983. *Logique aristotélicienne et grammaire arabe*, Paris: J. Vrin,.

Endress, Gerhard. 1997. "The Circle of al-Kindi: Early Arabic Translations from the Greek and the Rise of Islamic Philosophy." In *The Ancient Traditions in Christian and Islamic Hellenism*, edited by Gerhard Endress and Remke Kurk, 43–76. Leiden: CNWS.

Endress, Gerhard and Dimitri Gutas, eds. 1995. *A Greek and Arabic Lexicon (GALEX): Materials for a Dictionary of the Medieval Translations from Greek into Arabic*. 3 vols. Leiden: Brill.

Escovitz, Joseph H. 1976. "Vocational Patterns of the Scribes of the Mamlūk Chancery." *Arabica* 23 (1): 42–62.

Ezzaher, Lahcen E. 2008. "Alfarabi's Book of Rhetoric: An Arabic-English Translation of Alfarabi's Commentary on Aristotle's Rhetoric." *Rhetorica* 26 (4): 347–91.

—. 2015. *Three Arabic Treatises on Aristotle's* Rhetoric. Carbondale: Southern Illinois University Press.

Fletcher, Richard. 1993. *Moorish Spain*. Berkeley: University of California Press, 1993.

Galander, Mahmoud M. 2002. "Communication in the Early Islamic Era: A Social and Historical Analysis." *Intellectual Discourse* 10 (1): 61–75. journals.iium.edu.my/intdiscourse/index.php/islam.

Garcia-Sanjuan, Alejandro. 2013. "Ibn Hazm and the Territory of Huelva: Personal and Family Relationships." In I*bn Hazm of Cordoba: The Life and Works of a Controversial Thinker*, edited by Camilla Adang, Maribel Fierro, and Sabine Schmidtke, 51–65. Leiden: Brill.

Ghazi, HRH Prince (Ghazi Bin Muhammad). 2013. *Love in the Holy Qur'an*. Cambridge: Islamic Texts Society.

Giroux, Henry. 2018. *American Nightmare: Facing the Challenge of Fascism*. San Francisco, California: City Lights Books,.

Gleave, Robert. 2012. I*slam and Literalism: Literal Meaning and Interpretation in Islamic Legal Theory*. Edinburgh: Edinburgh University Press.

Goldman, E., Believers: 1995. *Spiritual Leaders of the World*. New York: Oxford University Press.

Gully, Adrian. 1996. "Epistles for Grammarians: Illustrations from the Insha' Literature." *British Journal of Middle Eastern Studies* 23 (2): 147–66.

—.2008. *The Culture of Letter-Writing in the Pre-Modern Islamic Society*. Edinburgh: Edinburgh University Press.

Gutas, Dimitri. 1993. "Aspects of Literary Form and Genre in Arabic Logical Works." In *Glosses and Commentaries on Arabic Logical Textx: The Syriac, Arabic and Medieval Latin Traditions*, edited by Charles Burnett, 29–76. London: Warburg Institut.

—. 1998. *Greek Thought, Arabic Culture: The Graeco-Arabic Translation Movement in Baghdad and Early 'Abbāsid Society (2nd-4th/8th-10th Centuries)*. New York: Routledge.

—. 2002. "The Study of Arabic Philosophy in the Twentieth Century: An Essay on the Historiography of Arabic Philosophy." *British Journal of Middle Eastern Studies* 29 (1): 5–25.

—. 2014. *Avicenna and the Aristotelian Tradition: Introduction to Reading Avicenna's Philosophical Works, Including an Inventory of Avicenna's Authentic Works*. Leiden: Brill, 2014.

Ḥabashī, Ḥasan. 1973. "Dīwān al-Inshā': Nash'atuhu wa Taṭawwuruhu [The Chancery: Its Establishment and Development]." In *Abū al-'Abbās al-Qalqashandī wa Kitābuhu Ṣubḥ al-A'shá* [Abū al-'Abbās al-Qalqashandī and His Book Ṣubḥ al-A'shá], edited by Aḥmad 'Izzat 'Abd al-Karīm, 81–96. Cairo: Hay'āt al-Kit.

Haddour, Azzedine. 2008. "Tradition, Translation and Colonization: The Graeco-Arabic Translation Movement and Deconstructing the Classics." In *Translation and the Classic: Identity as Change in the History of Culture*, edited by Alexandra Lianeri and Vanda Zajko, 203–26. Oxford: Oxford University Press.

Halldén, Philip. 2005. "What Is Arab Islamic Rhetoric? Rethinking the History of Muslim Oratory Art and Homiletics." *International Journal of Middle East Studies* 37 (1): 19–38. JSTOR, www.jstor.org/stable/3880080.

Hämeen-Anttila, Jaakko. 2006. "The Essay and the Debate (al-risāla and al-munāzara)." In *Arabic Literature in the Post-Classical Period*, edited by Roger Allan and D. S. Richards, 134–44. Cambridge: Cambridge University Pres.

Ḥamzah, Abd al-Laṭīf. 1962. *Al-Qalqashandī Fī Kitābihi Ṣubḥ Al-A'shá: 'Arḍ wa Taḥlīl* [al-Qalqashandī in His Book Ṣubḥ al-A'shá: An Exposition and Analysis]. Cairo: al-Mū'sasah al-Miṣrīyah al-'Āmah lil-Tarjamah wa al-Ṭibā'ah wa al-Nashr.

Hascall, Susan C. 2011. "Restorative Justice in Islam: Should Qisas Be Considered a Form of Restorative Justice?" *Berkeley Journal of Middle Eastern & Islamic Law* 4 (2): 35–78.

Hatim, Basil. 2010. *Arabic Rhetoric: The Pragmatics of Deviation from Linguistic Norms*. Muenchen: LINCOM.

Hussain, Jamila. 2011. *Islam: Its Law and Society*. Alexandria: The Federation Press.

Hussein, Abdul-Raof. 2006. *Arabic Rhetoric: A Pragmatic Analysis*. Abingdon, Ontario: Routledge

Ibn al-Athīr, Ḍiyā'al-Dīn. 1959. *Al-Mathal al-Sā'ir fī Adab al-Kātib wa al-Shā'ir* [Exemplars: On the Arts of the Writer and Poet]. Vol. 1, 1st ed., edited by Aḥmad al-Ḥufi and Badawī Ṭabanah. Cairo: Nahḍat Masr Lil-Ṭibā'ah wa al-Nashr. ia902607.us.archive. org/14/items/FP4441/mtsa1.pdf

Ibn Hazm. 1900. *The Approximation of Logic's Extremity*. Beirut, Lebanon: House of Life Publications.

—. 1929. *Detailed Accounts of Nations, Denominations, and Beliefs*. Cairo: Khanji Library.

—. 1980. *The Letters of Ibn Hazm*. Edited by Ihsan Abbas. Beirut, Lebanon: Institute for Arabic Publications.

Ibn Hazm of Cordoba. 2013. *The Life and Works of a Controversial Thinker*. Edited by Camilla Adang, Maribel Fierro, and Sabine Schmidtke. (Handbook of Oriental Studies; section 1, the Near and Middle East; v.103). Leiden: Brill.

Ibn Qutaybah, Abū Muḥammad 'Abd Allāh. 1900. *Kitāb Adab al-Kātib (Ibn Kutaiba's Adab al-Kātib)*. Edited by Max Grünert. Leiden: Brill. archive.org/details/ ibnkutaibasadaba00ibnquoft/page/n5

Ibn Sina, Abu Ali Al Husayn. 1954. "Rhetorica." In *Al-Shifa'*, edited by Mohamed Selim Salem, 1–249. Vol. 4 of Al-Shifa'. Cairo: Al-Amireyya.

Ibn Taymiyyah, Ahmad. 2004. *Majmou' Fatawa Shaikh Al-Islam Ahmad bin Taymiyyah*. Vol. 16, organized by Abdil Rahman bin Muhammad bin Kasim. Riyadh: Maktabat Al Malik Fahid Al-watanieh.

Iqbal, Afzal. 1960. "The Qur'án and the Sunnah-The Two Main Sources of Legislation in Islam." *Islamic Review* 48 (12). search.proquest.com/docview/1291864062/.

Kadi, Wadad, and Aram A. Shahin. 2013. "Caliph, Caliphate." In *The Princeton Encyclopedia of Islamic Political Thoughts*, edited by Gerhard Bowering, et al., 81–86. Princeton: Princeton University Press.

Lane, Edward William. 1865. *An Arabic-English Lexicon: Derived from the Best and the Most Copious Eastern Sources*. London: Williams and Norgate. www.tyndalearchive.com/ tabs/lane/.

Langhade, Jacques. 1985. "Mentalité grammairienne et mentalité logicienne au IVe siècle." *Zeitschrift für Arabische Linguistik* [Studies in the History of Arabic Grammar], (15): 104–17.

Learner, Michael. 2019. *Revolutionary Love: A Political Manifesto to Heal and Transform the World*. Berkeley: University of California Press.

Lloyd, G. E. R. 1968. *Aristotle: The Growth and Structure of His Thought*. Cambridge: Cambridge University Press.

Lyons, M. C., ed. 1982. *Aristotle's* Ars Rhetorica: *The Arabic Version*. 2 vols. Cambridge: Pembroke Arabic Texta.

Mahdi, Muhsin. 1970. "Language and Logic in Classical Islam." In *Logic in Classical Islamic Culture*, edited by Gustave E. von Grunebaum, 51–83. Wiesbaden.

Mao, LuMing. 2013a. "Beyond Bias, Binary, and Border: Mapping out the Future of Comparative Rhetoric." *Rhetoric Society Quarterly* 43 (3): 209–25.

—. 2013b. "Writing the Other into Histories of Rhetorics: Theorizing the Art of Recontextualization." In *Theorizing Histories of Rhetoric*, edited by Michelle Baillif, 41–57. Carbondale, IL: Southern Illinois University Press.

Margoliouth, David Samuel. 1905. "The Discussion between Abu Bishr Matta and Abu Saʿid al-Sirafi on the Merits of Logic and Grammar," *Journal of the Royal Asiatic Society*: 97–129.

—. 1910. "Omar's Instructions to the Kadi." *The Journal of the Royal Asiatic Society of Great Britain and Ireland* 42 (2): 307–26.

Mattock, John Nicholas. 1984. "The Early History of the Maqāma," *Journal of Arabic Literature* 15 (1): 1–18.

Meri, Josef W., ed. 2005. *Medieval Islamic Civilization: An Encyclopedia*. Vol. 1. London: Routledge.

Merriam, Allen H. 1974. "Rhetoric and the Islamic Tradition." *Today's Speech* 22, no. 1: 43–49. doi:10.1080/01463377409369129.

Natij, Salah. 2008. "La nuit inaugurale de Kitāb al-Imtāʿ wa-l-muʾānasa d'Abū Ḥayyān al-Tawḥīdī: une leçon magistrale dʾadab" *Arabica*, T. 55: 227–75.

Okasha, Mahmoud. 2006. *Alshiʾir fi Asr Alnobowa* [Poetry at the Time of the Prophet]. Cairo: Maktabit Dar Al-Maʾrifeh.

Oxford Islamic Studies Online. 2007. Oxford University Press.

Peters, F. E. 1968. *Aristotle and the Arabs: The Aristotelian Tradition in Islam*. New York: New York University Press.

Pluralism Project, The. Harvard University. N.d. pluralism.org/

Prince, Chris. 2002. "The Historical Context of Arabic Translation, Learning, and the Libraries of Medieval Andalusia." *Library History* 18 (2): 73–87. doi:10.1179/lib.2002.18.2.73.

The Qur'an. Mujam' Al-malik Fahid li tiba'it Al-Mushaf Al-Shareef.

Rashwan, Hany. 2016. "Philosophical and Literary Argumentation Methods in the Ancient Egyptian Rhetorical Systems." In *Argumentation and Reasoned Action: Proceedings of the First European Conference on Argumentation*, edited by D. Mohammad and M. Lewinski, 849–63. College Publications.

—. 2020. "Comparative Balāghah: Arabic and Ancient Egyptian Literary Rhetoric through the Lens of Post-Eurocentric Poetics." In *Routledge Handbook of Comparative World Rhetorics*, edited by Keith Lloyd, 386–403. New York: Routledge.

—. 2021. "Against Eurocentrism: Decolonizing Eurocentric Literary Theory in the Ancient Egyptian and Arabic poetics," *Howard Journal of Communications*, 32 (2): 171–96. doi:10.1080/10646175.2021.1879695.

Rosenthal, Frank. 1948. "Abū Ḥaiyān al-Tawḥīdī on Penmanship" *Ars Islamica* 13: 1–30.

Sabra, Adam. 2007. "Ibn Hazm's Literalism: A Critique of Islamic Legal Theory (I)." *Al-Qantara: Revista de Estudios Arabes* 28 (1): 7–40.

Ṣafwat, Aḥmad Zakī, ed. 1937. *Jamharat Rasāʾil al-ʿArab fī ʿIsūr al-ʿArabīyah al-Zāhirah* [A Compilation of the Arabs' Letters during the Prosperous Periods]. Vol.1. Beirut: Al-Maktabah Al-ʿIlmīyah.

Sahih International. 1997. *The Qur'an (Arabic Text with Corresponding English Meaning)*. Riyadh: Abul-Qasim Publishing House.

Serjeant, Robert Bertram. 1984. "The Caliph Umar's Letters to Abu Musa Al-Ash'ari and Mu'awiya." *Journal of Semitic Studies* 29 (1): 65–79.

—. 1983. "Early Arabic Prose." In *Arabic Literature to the End of the Umayyad Period*, edited by Alfred Felix Landon Beeston, T. M. Johnstone, R. B. Serjeant, and G. R. Smith, 114–53. Cambridge: Cambridge University Press.

Shepard, William E. 2014. *Introducing Islam*. Second edition. New York: Routledge.

Tamcke, Martin, ed. 2007. *Christians and Muslims in Dialogue in the Islamic Orient of the Middle Ages*. Würzburg: Ergon Verlag.

Tillier, Mathieu. 2012. "Le Cadi et le Sauf-Conduit (Amān): Les Enjeux Juridiques de la Diplomatie dans l'Orient Abbasside," *Islamic Law and Society* 19 (3): 201–21.

Tomeh, Mamoud Munes. 2010. "Persuasion and Authority in Islamic Law." *Berkeley Journal of Middle Eastern & Islamic Law* 3 (3): 141–71.

Troupeau, Gérard. 1958. "Le commentaire d'al-Sīrāfī sur le chapitre 565 du Kitāb de Sībawayhi," *Arabica* 5: 168–82.

Urvoy, Dominique. 2003. "La tradition vivante de l'Antiquité dans la philosophie arabe" *Pallas*, (63): 89–95.

van Berkel, Maaike. 1997. "The Attitude towards Knowledge in Mamlūk Egypt: Organization and Structure of The Subh Al-A 'shā by Al-Qalqashandi (1355-1418)." In *Pre-Modern Encyclopedic Texts. Proceedings of the Second COMERS Congress*, edited by Peter Binkley, 159–68. Leiden: Brill.

—. 2001. "A Well-Mannered Man of Letters or a Cunning Accountant: Al-Qalqashandī and the Historical Position of the Kātib," *Al-Masāq* 13: 87–96.

Versteegh, Kees. 1997. *The Arabic Linguistic Tradition*. New York: Routledge.

Vilchez, Jose Miguel Puerta. 2013. "Ibn Hazm: A Biographical Sketch." In *Ibn Hazm of Cordoba; the Life and Works of a Controversial Thinker*, edited by Camilla Adang, Maribel Fierro, and Sabine Schmidtke. (Handbook of Oriental Studies; section 1, the Near and Middle East; v.103), 4–24. Leiden: Brill.

Vilchez, Jose, Miguel Puerta. "Art and Aesthetics in the Works of Ibn Hazm of Cordoba." In Ibn Hazm of Cordoba; the Life and Works of a Controversial Thinker, edited by by Camilla Adang, Maribel Fierro, and Sabine Schmidtke, 253–372. Leiden: Brill, 2013.

Vilchez, Jose, Miguel Puerta. 2013. "Inventory of Ibn Hazm's Works." In *Ibn Hazm of Cordoba; the Life and Works of a Controversial Thinker*, edited by by Camilla Adang, Maribel Fierro, and Sabine Schmidtke, 683–760. Leiden: Brill,.

Wasserstein, David. 2013. "Ibn Hazm and Al-Andalus." In *Ibn Hazm of Cordoba; The Life and Works of a Controversial Thinker*, edited by by Camilla Adang, Maribel Fierro, and Sabine Schmidtke, 69–85. Leiden: Brill.

Watt, W. M., and Cachia, P. 1965. *A History of Islamic Spain*. New Brunswick, NJ: Transaction Publishers.

Yücesoy, Hayrettín. 2009. "Translation as Self-Consciousness: Ancient Sciences, Antediluvian Wisdom, and the 'Abbāsid Translation Movement." *Journal of World History* 20 (4): 523–57. doi:10.1353/jwh.0.0084.

Glossary of Terms

Term		Translation
adab	أدب	literature identifying standards of learning and conduct in varied spheres and activities like playing chess as well as poetic and official writing
adab al-kātib	أدب الكاتب	specialized literature developed to guide and train prospective writers
AH		short for *al-taqwīm al-hijrī* (التقويم الهجري)؛ refers to a lunar calendar widely used in Muslim countries along with the Gregorian calendar; takes the *hijrah* (migration of Prophet Muḥammad from Mecca to Medina) as its starting point (622 CE)
al-amthāl	الأمثال	examples
ash-shabah	الشبه	analogy
al-basmalah	البسملة	a phrase with which Muslims begin their writing and actions, either verbally or in writing, depending on the situation. It translates as "In the name of God, the most Gracious, the most Compassionate"
al-inshā'	الإنشاء	institutional or chancery writing
al-istiᶜārah	الإستعارة	metaphor
al-kātīb	الكاتب	singular of *kuttāb*, translated as scribe or writer; refers to both *kātib al-inshā'* and *kātib al-hisbah*
al-qaḍā'	القضاء	jurisdiction
al-ṣulḥ	الصلح	reconciliation and peace
at-tashbīh	التشبيه	simile
al-yamīn	اليمين	taking an oath
as-salāmu ᶜalaykum	عليكم السلام	"Peace be upon you"; a formulaic expression in Islamic discourse that Muslims use to greet one another or upon parting company
al-bayān	البيان	revelation; or, in the context of rhetoric, "eloquence" (cf. the work of al-Jaḥiz "*al-bayān wa al-tabyīn*" as one example)
bayyinah	بينة	clear evidence

da'wa	دعوة	inviting people to Islam
dīwān al-inshā'	ديوان الإنشاء	chancery or the official bureau delegated with all matters related to correspondence
fann al-khaṭābah	فن الخطابة	the art of oratory
farīḍah	فريضة	religious obligation or duty in Islam
faṣāḥah	فصاحة	eloquence
ḥadd	حد	crimes committed against God's rights
ḥalāl	حلال	what is lawful in Islamic jurisprudence
ḥarām	حرام	what is prohibited in Islamic jurisprudence
hidāyah	هداية	religious guidance
hijā' and madīḥ	مديح و هجاء	literary terms referring to the genre of panegyric; *madīḥ* refers to praise and *hijā'* refers to invective poetry
ḥudūd Allah	حدود الله	embracing the lawful (*ḥalāl*) and avoiding the forbidden (*ḥarām*)
ʿilm al-balāgha	علم البلاغة	the science and art of rhetorical/communicative eloquence
ʿilm al-bayān	علم البيان	the science of figures of speech; or, eloquence
jā'iz	جائز	permitted
kātīb al-ḥisbah/ al-amwāl	كاتب الحسبة/ الأموال/	refers to the governmental employee responsible for accounting, recording debts, or finances, respectively
kātib inshā'	كاتب الإنشاء	refers to secretary or chancery writer
kātib/kuttāb al-darj	كاتب / كتاب الدرج	*darj* is a large composite scroll or sheet of paper, which is rectangular and made out of numerous scraps (*'ausāl*) (Ḥamzah 80). The title points to a professional tiered system: *kātib al-darj* was assigned the task of writing down what *kātib al-dast* (pedestal or seat) who sat with *kātib al-sirr* (secret) *or kātim al-sirr* (keeper of secret) had previously written. Both *kātib al-dast* and *kātib al-sirr* were higher in rank. Unlike *kātib al-dast*, for example, *kātib al-darj* did not have the authority to sign in the margins upon receiving grievances (80). El-Toudy and Abdelhamid translate these titles as the Scribe of the Scroll, the Scribe of the Pedestal, and the Scribe of the Secret. See Abdelhamid and El-Toudy, *Selections from Ṣubḥ Al-Aʿshā*, (379–81).

khilāfah	خلافة	caliphate, a system of governance wherein a Muslim leader (Caliph, *khalīfah*) is charged to govern the community in succession of Prophet Muḥammad
majlis	مجلس	assembly or gathering at a conference hall
maqāmah	مقامة	a literary genre; a short, entertaining narrative that blends poetry and prose; *saj'* (rhymed prose) is one of its characteristic features
matn	متن	the actual wording of a text, sometimes referring to a text or a saying by prophet Muhammad or one of his companions
qāḍī	قاضى	judge
qiṣāṣ	قصاص	law of retaliation (requital)
qiyās	قياس	deductive analogy
Qur'ān	قرآن	the holy book of Muslims
riwāya	رواية	narration
rūwāh	رواة	narrators or transmitters of the sayings and actions of Prophet Muhammad and his companions
Sajᶜ	سجع	rhymed prose
sanad or isnad	إسناد او سند	chain of authority; *isnad* precedes the actual text (*matn*), and lists the names of all transmitters
shahādah	شهادة	testimony; or, the profession of faith (one of five pillars in Islam)
shahādat al-zūr	شهادة الزور	bearing, including providing, false evidence or assisting in fraud
sunnah	سنة	Prophet Muhammad's practices, including words, deeds, and silences
tabāraka wa taᶜlā	تبارك وتعالى	an expression used in the Islamic tradition to praise God (Allah)
tafsīr	تفسير	the science of explaining and interpreting the Qur'an
thiqa	ثقة	trustworthy; in the context of narration transmission, the more trustworthy the narrator, the more reliable the narration

2 Chinese Rhetorics

Prefatory Introduction

Hui Wu

"Rhetoric" was translated into *xiuci* (修辭) in the early twentieth century under the influence of Japanese academics.[1] According to Chen Wangdao, *Xiu Ci Jian Heng* (修辭鑑衡 *Rhetorical Assessment and Criteria*) by Wang Gou (王構 1245–1310 CE) was the first treatise that used *xiuci* to mean "rhetorical study" or "rhetoric." Before Wang, *xiu* and *ci* were two separate words to mean "polishing/studying the word."[2] Whether the translation accurately represents what *xiuci* signifies in the Chinese context remains debatable. Thousands of years ago, China started its own rhetorical tradition almost in parallel to, if not earlier than, ancient Greece.[3] All along, rhetorical theories, philosophies, concepts, terminologies, and praxis emerged and evolved. Such a long history, evidently, cannot be studied merely from a Western rhetorical view nor can be fully presented within the limit of this book. The chapters that follow introduce representative figures who have influenced both ancient and modern rhetorics but exclude Guiguzi, the alleged author of China's first treatise on rhetoric, whose full translation is in circulation.[4] The carefully chosen excerpts reflect the mosaic of Chinese rhetoric on its own right. With attention to the close relationship between rhetoric and literacy, contributors examine Chinese educational systems, writing technologies, and genres to track the trajectory of rhetorical ethics, principles, and practices. In a chronical order, readers can access rhetorical theories and instructions ranging from Confucius (551–479 BCE) to the author of the modern rhetorical canon, Chen Wangdao (1891–1977 CE). This approach can provide a model for comparative studies of rhetoric. The introduction here illustrates interconnections among audience, purpose, and ethics of rhetoric, as well as key rhetorical concepts and major classical canons cited frequently in the primary treatises.

---

1. See Chen Wangdao in this book.
2. Wu 2020, 86.
3. Garrett 1991, 295–306; Lu 1998; Wu 2016, 1–31; Wu 2020.
4. *Guiguzi*, 2016.

First, unlike rhetors in ancient Athens who usually spoke in public, persuaders in ancient China had to convince the single-person audience, the ruler or a superior, often in a private setting and sometimes at life risk. Classical Chinese rhetoric emerged during the Spring-Autumn and Warring States period (771–212 BCE) when states were constantly at war for conquest or self-protection. Kings needed highly skilled learned men to provide advice on political, diplomatic, and military strategies.[5] In response, almost all learned men who wished to move upward socially tried to master rhetorical strategies in order to be hired by the kings. Accordingly, Chinese educational systems aimed to prepare such learned men to win imperial appointments. The selected rhetorical treatises reflect such a tradition of literacy and talent hiring, as well as rhetorical ethics, principles, and strategies.

Next, many Chinese rhetorical terminologies overlap in the primary texts but sometimes differ in references, for example, *ci* (辭), *yu* (語), *yan* (言), *ci* (詞), and *wen* (文). They can all be translated into "discourse," but the single word does not represent their evolving, nuanced, and sometimes distinct meanings in different historical contexts. Take 辭 (*ci*), for example. It is a combination of two characters to mean "tongue's labor." On oracle bones, 辭 appeared in dialogues of divine prophecies.[6] All lines in the scripts were named 辭. Later, the meaning of 辭 evolved from a dialogue to "a spoken word," to "speech/oratory," to "prose or poetry," and finally to "oral or written composition" in modern times. It is recommended that readers pay attention to the glossary and notes on how the above terms are translated.

Furthermore, "*wen* (文)" is worth a special note because it is often said to mean aesthetic literature. The rhetorical treatises in this book prove that "*wen*" variedly means "literacy and learning," "eloquent speech or writing," or "knowledge of rhetorical culture and conventions," rather than exclusively literature. Originally, it mainly referred to broad knowledge of nature, science, history, culture, and humanity, including subjects, such as astronomy (*tian wen*), topography (*di wen*), and humanity (*ren wen*).[7] Confucius defines *wen* as literacy and rhetorical articulation, saying that *wen* is the first of the four attributes of a well-educated ethical person.[8] The other three are *xing* (行 self-presentation, conduct), *zhong* (忠 royalty, honesty), and *xin* (信 trustworthy, creditable). In *Zuo Zhuan* (circa 300 BCE), which covers the events between 722 BCE and 468 BCE, *wen* signifies an elaborate means to modify a speech. For instance, "Confucius inspected the record [of the practice of rites] and believed that the speech was too elaborate (*wen*)."[9] In *Guiguzi*, *wen* in "*cheng wen zhang*" (成文章) means developing eloquent composition.[10] In *Lun Heng* (論衡 *On Critical Criteria*) by Wang Chong (王充 circa 27–97 CE), *wen* represents not only classics, biographies, arguments, treatises, petitions, and propositions, but also the "six arts"—rituals, music, arrow-shooting, civil service, literacy (reading

---

5. Lu 1998, 10–11.

6. Li 2003, 32–33.

7. Cheng 2011, 191. Owen 1992, 186–87.

8. *Analects*, 1999, 7–25.

9. *Zuo Zhuan* 2013. Chapters, instead of page numbers, are used for citations, regardless of editions.

10. *Guiguzi,* 2016, 66.

and writing), and math.[11] The first Chinese dictionary, *Shuowen Jiezi* (說文解字 *Illustrating Writing and Decoding Characters*) by Xu Shen (許慎58–147 BC), uses *wen*" to refer to all sorts of writing, and not merely aesthetic literature.[12] In Wang Gou's *Rhetorical Assessment and Criteria*, *wen* means "treatise" or "critical prose." Later, *wen*'s rhetorical references were expanded, but not limited, to belletristic composition and criticism. Today some modern phrases containing *wen* refer specifically to literature (*wenxue* 文學) and performing and fine arts (*wenyi* 文藝). The evolving meanings of *wen* confirm that it indicates the origin of Chinese rhetoric, including diverse genres of discourse, spoken and written, rather than merely aesthetic literature.[13] Whenever needed, the chapters explain varied translations of *wen* in a specific context.

Last but not least, readers may notice that the rhetorical figures after Confucius repeatedly point to his *Analects* and the five classics: *Book of Changes* (*Yi Jing* 易經), *Book of Poetry* (*Shi Jing* 詩經), *Book of History/Shang* (*Shang Shu* 尚書), *Spring and Autumn Annals* (*Chun Qiu* 春秋) and *Book of Rites* (*li ji* 禮記). They remind us of Confucius's impact on the development of rhetorical philosophies, ethics, and principles as well as the rhetor, all of which constitute the foundation for Chinese rhetoric. Considering Confucian's impact, Haixia Lan's translation of *The Analects* contains some similar rhetorical terms in a system of its own, such as *dao*-the-way and *yan*-the-dao. However, no knowledge or teaching can be transmitted without oral and written records. For this reason, the chapters chronologically present carefully selected excerpts as sources for the Chinese rhetorical tradition.

---

11. Chen and Wang 1998, 251.
12. Xu 2005.
13. Garrett 1991, 297. Lu 1998, 163.

2.1 Spring-Autumn Period and Warring States Period (Classical)

Rhetorical Teachings by Confucius (551–479 BCE): A Partial Translation of the *Analects* with an Introduction

Haixia Lan

BIOGRAPHY AND INTRODUCTION

The name Confucius is the Latinized transliteration of *Kong fuzi*, the appellation for an ancient Chinese thinker. *Kong* is the family name, and *fuzi* is like a title, meaning "venerable teacher," and is the way Confucius's students addressed him but also a way the Chinese people refer to those whom they deem honorable and wise. In China, Confucius is also known as *Kong*zi, where *Kong* is again the family name and *zi* is a suffix attached to the names of those who are much learned and respected. Some similarly well-known people in Chinese history who are referred to this way include *Lao*zi, *Zhuang*zi, *Hanfei*zi, *Zhu*zi, and others. Most Chinese people do not refer to Confucius by his actual name, which is *Kong Qiu*, *Qiu* being his given name. All of these ways in which Confucius is or is not addressed and referred to reflect how deep Confucius's influence is on the Chinese culture, including its rhetorical culture.

Confucius's insights into the art of rhetoric are neither completely different from nor absolutely the same as those insights into rhetoric in the West, thus providing an alternative. This means that to understand this alternative, we need to examine the contested meaning of rhetoric in Chinese but also be aware that the West, too, has various views of it. To understand this alternative, in other words, we need to avoid overgeneralization and attend to specifics. Like in the West, for example, although *rhetoric* in Chinese is taken variously, the most common translation is *xiuci*—style, the style of speaking or writing. But Lu and Frank use the Chinese concept *bian* "as a synonym (not equivalent) of 'rhetoric.'"[14] They explain that in classical Chinese, *bian* is defined as making argumentation, distinction, changes and "achieving justice and order," while in modern Chinese *bian* does not contradict these classical meanings although it focuses more on disputation.[15] Drawing upon their insights and based primarily on the teachings of the *Analects*,[16] I would like to emphasize the broader sense of *bian* and translate Confucian rhetoric as *yan*-the-*dao*/ways-of-discourse. As such ways, rhetoric was important to Confucius who lived in a time when Chinese civilization was experiencing tumultuous changes and when the need for discursive activities to be an integral part of the change was

---

14. Lu and Frank 1993, 451.

15. Lu and Frank 1993, 452.

16. Confucius taught many students but did not write any book. *The Analects* is a collection of mainly dialogues between Confucius and his students, who compiled *The Analects* during the early Warring States period (453–221 BCE) after his death.

felt more palpable than usual. While Confucius certainly deemed rhetoric an art of eloquence, disputation, or persuasion, he also taught it as a meaningful part of the human effort to interpret and to know (*tianming*) the-cosmic-order and to form provisional decisions accordingly in the midst of socio-cultural changes. In this regard specifically, Confucius's view of rhetoric is both similar to and different from the teachings of rhetoric by Aristotle, an ancient Greek thinker whose treatise on rhetoric is influential in the West and who teaches that the function of rhetoric "is not simply to succeed in persuading":[17] "rhetoric exists to affect the giving of decisions,"[18] the forming of judgments, and the actualizing more and more fully the human potentiality to know. In what follows, I introduce Confucian rhetoric by focusing on this one important similarity between Aristotelian and Confucian rhetoric and then a difference between the two. Such a comparative and contrastive endeavor can help show that it is possible for cultures to enrich each other with their differences as alternatives through theories and practices they have in common.

A few details of the historical context could help shed some light on Confucius's rhetorical thinking and teaching. Confucius lived in the period known as Spring and Autumn (770–481 BCE), a time when "the concept of Chinese (*huaxia*) nation was formed and articulated."[19] Spring and Autumn followed the Zhou Dynasty where the Zhou royal power, which had been deemed the power of the Son of Heaven, was in decline, so much so that the Zhou King was forced to share that power with the dukes of the peripheral states by letting them be the hegemons (*ba*)—the overlords of the states. As the royal power was waning, however, not only did the outer states gain hegemonic opportunities, but marginalized individuals whose lineages were unrelated to royalty or state rulers also gained upward mobility. In the end, Spring and Autumn witnessed an aristocratic society gradually giving way to the new bureaucratic states.

These deep social changes called for rhetoric, which played its role especially in the rise of one social group: the lower elites *shi*—state officeholders both military and civilian. The rise of *shi*-state-officials meant that no longer could those who were born into wealth and with social status monopolize the interpretation of *tianming* (the-cosmic-order); *shi* (state-officials), more and more of whom of humble origin, became an interpretive and disputing force to be reckoned with. The *shi* class grew rapidly: from obscurity to between sixty and seventy percent of the offices in a matter of just four hundred years.[20] With such a swift rise of the *shi* class, the interpretation of *tianming* suddenly was open to the interpretive deliberation and negotiation by more people than ever before. And, in revising who were legitimate interpreters, the *shi* class necessarily introduced revisions to, and therefore more debates over, what made interpretations more appropriate and probable. Indeed, debating about *tianming* in such socially and politically volatile times would require skills of effective expression *to* and persuasion *of* one's audience. However, it would require also the ability to form probable judgments and

---

17. Aristotle 2001, 1355b 10.
18. Aristotle 2001, 1377b 21.
19. Li 2013, 180.
20. Li 2013, 171.

interpretations of *tianming* in particular circumstances *with* one's audience. Confucius lived during the end of Spring and Autumn and the third century into the four-hundred-year rise of the class of *shi*-state-officials. With more than two hundred years of history behind it, the *shi* class by then had a relatively stable presence in the society of Spring and Autumn. Confucius therefore both engaged in and taught disputation and deliberation. This can be seen clearly in the *Analects*, where fifteen passages discuss the meaning of *shi*-state-officials and how to become good ones.

COMMENTARY

In this historical context, Confucius taught rhetoric by highlighting one of its most vital aspects: an art of discursively inventing probable knowledge. Probable knowledge is obtained with the assistance of the use of ordinary language and therefore has a degree of truthfulness to it but is not true always and everywhere. In other words, against a background of genuine and deep disputations over the interpretations of *tianming* during Spring and Autumn, Confucius did not emphasize rhetoric simply as a set of tactics for winning the debate; rather, he taught it as the intertwining of expressing and thinking. Confucius advanced a rhetorical education that emphasized *zhongxing* (riding-the-middle),[21] a concept that is similar to *kairos* and is a characteristic of Confucius's teaching of how to walk *dao*-the-way towards understanding, speaking, and living *tianming* in everyday lives. More concretely, Confucius's rhetorical curriculum may be illustrated as shown in Figure 2.1.

Diachronically, Confucius's teaching resists glibness (*ning*) and underscores the importance of trustworthiness (*xin*) on the one hand while, on the other, treats appropriateness (*yi*)[22] as highest accomplishment; in between is the art of rhetoric or *yan* (the-*dao*-of-discourse). According to these ways in between or in "the middle," glibness, pretention, and trustworthiness are understood and judged often according to given situations or time. In the *Analects*, for instance, Confucius describes those who speak with no sense of appropriateness or timing as difficult people[23] and adjusts his replies to the same questions that come from different students.[24]

---

21. Though the expression *zhongxing* (riding-the-middle) appears in the *Analects* only once (13.21), it is central to Confucius's teaching. The expression does not mean the way it sounds (i.e., it does not mean "middle-of-the-road"); in a way, it is the opposite in that it means "not in the middle." Commenting on "now roaring, now yielding" (13.21), Qian Mu explains that in the bigger picture of things "the middle" does not always stay in the middle and that this is why Confucius is saying that being now haughty ("roaring") now timid ("yielding") could be sagely (478), the real way of the middle.

22. This is one of the major concepts that I borrow from Roger Ames and Henry Rosemont Jr. For their discussion on *yi* as appropriateness, see Ames and Rosemont Jr 1998, 53–55.

23. Confucius 1971, 15.17. All passage numbers correspond to the ones in James Legge's translation, a version of which is available online ctext.org/confucianism.

24. Confucius 2003, 11.22.

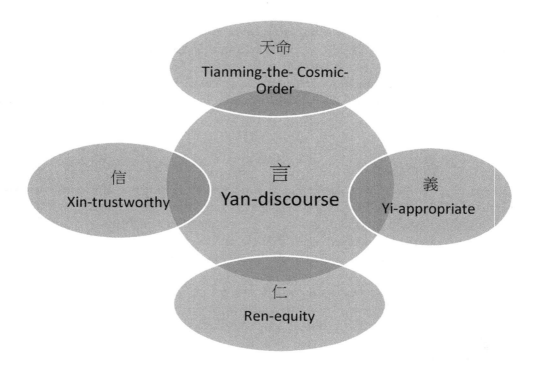

Figure 2.1: Model of Confucius's Rhetorical Teaching, by Haixia Lan

Synchronically, the Confucian *yan* (the-*dao*-of-discourse) are situated in a more in-depth context. As said above, in the process of understanding and discoursing according to *tianming*, people must use ordinary language and abide by human standards. One of the more prominent of these standards, for Confucius, is *ren* (equity),[25] a concept that embodies knowledge of probability. Repeatedly, for instance, Confucius is seen in the *Analects* guiding his students to different ways to discourse, between the ideals of *tianming*-the-cosmic order and *ren*-equity, in persuading one's parents,[26] friends,[27] subordinates, superiors, and equals.[28] The

_____

25. *Ren* is often translated as *benevolence, humaneness*. While both do describe *ren*, *equity* is more rhetorical a translation in that it makes more explicit the relation of *ren*-equity to *yi*-appropriateness and *li*-propriety. Here I use *equity* in the sense Aristotle develops it in *Rhetoric*: it is "the sort of justice which goes beyond the written law" (1374a 27-28). He explains, if "a precise statement is impossible and yet legislation is necessary, the law must be expressed in wide terms" (1374a 34); and, when we interpret this kind of law in forming judgment in everyday situations, "equity bids us be merciful to the weakness of human nature" (1374b 9).

26. Confucius, 2003, 4.18.

27. Confucius 2003, 4.26.

28. Confucius 2003, 10.2.

idea is that despite the differences, these different ways to discourse can all be meaningful interpretations or probable knowledge of *tianming* given the forgiving scope of the human ideal of *ren*. Confucius illustrates this point well in his judgment of Guan Zhong, a famous minister. Even though Confucius disapproves of Guan Zhong for not observing *li* (propriety),[29] he also twice judges Guan Zhong's failure to keep his word, in the unfolding of the historical contexts, as exemplifying true *ren*[30] and as showing the ways of speaking according to *tianming*. Synchronically, in short, Confucius emphasizes both the changing (*ren*) and the continuous (*tianming*) aspects of the rhetorical invention of probable knowledge, a focus of Aristotelian rhetoric as well.

What do the Confucian ways to discourse have to offer as an alternative, the *yan*-the-*dao* that emphasizes *zhongxing* (riding-the-middle)? Admirable and valuable efforts have been made to address this question, but when rhetoric is viewed as including not only effective expressing but also probable thinking, rhetorical differences remain elusive. To continue our efforts to understand these differences, again, we need to reconsider the assumption that we can find some coherent rhetorical difference between the entire West and all of China. Instead, we should acknowledge that each culture's rhetorical conceptions and practices are genuinely diverse. In the case of Confucius, this means we need to understand the difference as well as similarities between rhetorical teachings by Confucius and by other Chinese philosophers. When we focus specifically and comparatively on particular figures—such as Confucius and Aristotle, for example—we may find it easier to recognize distinct approaches to rhetoric and to discover alternative views. In the remainder of this introduction, I will first examine critically two lines of inquiry in comparative rhetorical studies and then offer some thoughts on how Confucian rhetoric may offer an alternative to Aristotelian rhetoric in both approach and conception.

Some scholars have focused on different ways of reasoning and observe that the Chinese tend to draw inductive conclusions, by which they mean reasoning from particular examples to generalizations.[31] Others have complemented this observation by suggesting that "deductive argument in the form of enthymemes," consequently "argument from probability," is yet to be found and seems to be undeveloped in ancient Chinese rhetoric.[32] This focus on whether all Chinese emphasize one mode of reasoning, compared to all Westerners who emphasize the other, risks oversimplification of the complex relation between the two modes of reasoning. Induction and deduction do differ in important and useful ways. Aristotle, for example, characterizes the enthymeme, rhetorical deduction, as the substance of rhetoric.[33] Yet, deduction and induction are not mutually exclusive, and deduction operates indispensably within induction. To generalize inductively through repeated experience that certain measures are

29. Confucius 2003, 3.22.
30. Confucius 2003, 14.16, 14.17.
31. Kirkpatrick 1995, 271–95. Kirkpatrick and Xu, 2012.
32. Kennedy 2001, 151.
33. Aristotle 2001, 1354a 15.

inducive to public health, for example, necessitates deductive thinking: repeated results are meaningful results; Xs are repeated results; Xs are meaningful results. Similarly, we can see why to see examples as examples requires deductive moves, so examples are established as such "through the use of syllogism [deduction]."[34] Aristotle himself also describes deduction as that which "springs out of induction,"[35] lists examples as one of the four kinds of material for the enthymeme,[36] and is explicit about the enthymematic deduction leading to probable reasoning[37]—as does induction. Given this connection between deduction and induction, we cannot conclude that enthymematic deduction is deemphasized and undeveloped in Confucius's teaching just because he highlights induction when, for example, he describes the way to *ren* as analogical[38] or inductive—since inductive thinking is both deductive and inductive. Therefore, at least Confucius's view of rhetoric as *yan* (the *dao*-of-discourse) problematizes the characterization that deduction and therefore the enthymematic kind of probable thinking are deemphasized by the entire Chinese rhetorical teaching, ancient or otherwise.

Other scholars have reflected on the argumentativeness, or the lack of it, in Chinese rhetoric. They observe that a characteristic of Chinese rhetoric is its emphasis on correlating differences,[39] as opposed to dichotomizing them. Some have taken the point further, characterizing Confucian rhetoric as displaying "a valuing of amicable relationships and kinship."[40] Indeed, these observations reflect a reading of the Chinese *yin-yang* cosmology that is part of Confucius's thinking.[41] The view is also consistent with a conventional image of the *ru*, a sobriquet for Confucians: that they prioritize harmony and are not combative. Like the first view above, however, these comparative observations face challenges when examined against *The Analects* of Confucius and the *Rhetoric* by Aristotle. On the one hand, Aristotelian rhetoric does not focus exclusively on dichotomies. One example of this can be the important rhetorical concept of *stasis*, the art of identifying central issues in a discussion, deliberation, or debate. Some rhetorical scholars of *stasis* have shown how Aristotle in the *Rhetoric* deliberately does not stress, as much as many in the West, the confrontation of dichotomized differences;[42] others have even advanced the argument that Aristotle hardly focuses on it at all.[43] At the very least, therefore, we may say that Aristotle emphasizes both the complex and dichotomized characteristics of differences. On the other hand, Confucius is seen in *The Analects* repeatedly taking strong, often polemical, stands against what he deems wrong, not merely—or even mainly—recon-

---

34. Benoit 1980, 188.

35. Aristotle 2001, 68b 15.

36. Aristotle 2001, 1402b 15-16.

37. Aristotle 2001, 1357a 15. Rapp 2010, sec. 5 para 6. Schaberg 2002, 612. Burnyeat 2015, 18.

38. "Making progress from things close by to those farther away, from self to others—that is called the way of *ren*-equity" (Aristotle, 2010, 6.30).

39. Mao 2007, 233.

40. Lyon 2013, 42.

41. For example, Confucius 2003, 7.17.

42. Thompson 1972, 134. Nadeau 1964; Dieter 1950.

43. Liu 1991, 53-59.

ciling differences. For example, his polemical views appear regularly in *The Analects* regarding filial piety,[44] certain ritual practices,[45] personal conduct,[46] and military actions.[47]

Does Confucian rhetoric offer us an alternative then? I think so. When we take seriously the obvious—that Confucius didn't treat rhetoric separately from other subjects as Aristotle did—we come to see that perhaps the way we have been searching for differences and alternatives reflects a difference between the two views of and approaches to rhetoric. Having been educated in the West, we are familiar with the important issues of whether rhetoric is an art or not, whether the reasoning is deductive or inductive, whether the function is harmonizing or distinguishing, so we look for them. None of these issues that guides our search for an alternative may be chosen by us deliberately, but that may just be the point: unquestioned presuppositions can reveal certain differences and may be a reason we run into impasses when it comes to understanding differences in comparative rhetoric. In contrast, however, if we retrain ourselves and refrain from expecting to find the familiar system of the know-how, we may see a less technical view of and thus approach to the know-how of rhetoric, of *yan* (the *dao*-of-discourse), in Confucius's discussions of life in general, as shown in Figure 2.2.

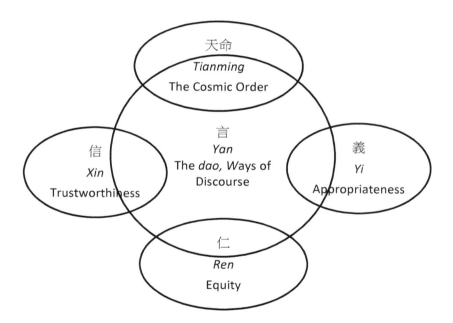

---

44. Confucius,2003, 2.7 and Book X.
45. Confucius 2003, 3.1, 3.2, 3.22, 11.17, 12.1.
46. Confucius 2003, 5.10, 5.24, 5.25, 14.43.
47. Confucius 2003, 14.21.

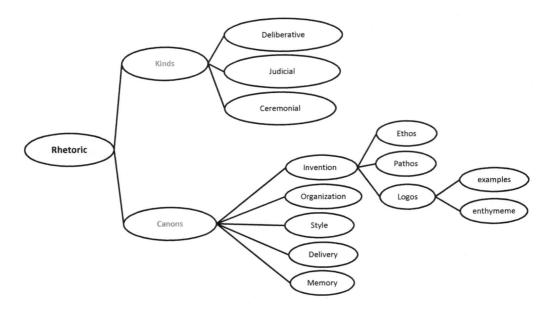

Figure 2.2: Model Comparing Confucius's and Aristotle's Rhetorical Teachings, by Haixia Lan

Before attempting a conclusion on Confucian and Aristotelian rhetoric as alternatives, we must take care not to overlook yet another complication these graphs do not illustrate explicitly: Aristotle's rhetorical teaching is also contextual. For instance, Aristotle defines rhetoric as "the counterpart of dialectic,"[48] "and also of ethical studies."[49] At one point, he even states that "[rhetoric] is a branch of dialectic."[50] He also repeatedly in the *Rhetoric* relies on his discussions in other works, including *Nicomachean Ethics*, *Topics*, but also more implicitly in *On Interpretation*, *Sophistical Reasoning*, the *Analytics*, *Categories*, *Politics*, and *Metaphysics*. We should not dismiss this complication and focus exclusively on how Aristotle defines rhetoric as the power to find means of persuasion,[51] how he delineates the "scope" of rhetoric to distinguish it from politics,[52] and how he classifies different subject matters including rhetoric by authoring separate treatises on them. When we focus only on these, we risk misinterpreting Aristotelian rhetoric as merely instrumental and simply dualistic, misinterpreting it as focusing only on how the subject or the orator persuades or resolves disputes with the audience, missing how the interlocutor must also work with the audience to resolve dilemmas facing all members of the community. This eclipsed view distorts Aristotle's actual teaching of rhetoric and, as a re-

---

48. Aristotle 2001, 1354a 1.
49. Aristotle 2001, 1356a 25.
50. Aristotle 2001, 1356a 30.
51. Aristotle 2001, 1354a 13.
52. Aristotle 2001, 1356a 26–37.

sult, compromises the insights that comparative rhetoric can help provide to foster meaningful cross-cultural understandings.

It is only when we take both Aristotelian and Confucian rhetoric in context that we can conclude that the overall more contextualized way Confucius conceptualizes and approaches rhetoric, compared to Aristotle's approach, is less likely to give rise to such a decontextualized reading. Agreeing with Aristotle that there are truths of things or there is *tianming*, agreeing also with Aristotle on the instrumental aspect of rhetoric,[53] Confucius nevertheless focuses on walking *dao*-the-way, approaching *yan*-the-*dao* through his teaching of life as a whole. While Aristotle focuses on what rhetoric is and approaches its practice through such an understanding, Confucius does not focus on that technical aspect of rhetoric so much as to approach rhetoric as a part of the art of life.

As I see it, these two different views of and approaches to rhetoric—more analytic and more synthetic—are alternatives in the sense that they each have their strengths, can complement each other, and make the main difference between Aristotelian and Confucian rhetoric one of emphasis. I hope that understanding Confucius's rhetorical teaching in context and also as an alternative to the Aristotelian rhetorical tradition can help readers appreciate the sophistication of the Confucian insights into *yan* (the *dao*-of-discourse) and to use those insights to further cross-cultural understandings.

Finally, I would like to leave the readers with a note on my translation below. I am deeply indebted to many existing translations including those by James Legge, Arthur Waley, Roger Ames and Henry Rosemont, Edward Slingerland, and Robert Enos. At the same time, I also find that most translations emphasize the theistic, philosophical, and literary aspects of Confucius's teaching. Therefore, I tried to incorporate more directly the rhetorical aspect. My understanding of Confucian teaching has also benefited greatly from two influential Chinese Confucian scholars: Qian Mu and Yang Bojun. They translated the *Analects* from classical Chinese into modern Chinese, and their perspectives, approaches, and translations, in my view, are more rhetorical.

Translation of Selected Passages from *The Analects* of Confucius

[1.3] The Master said, "Those who are fond of using crafty speeches and putting on pretentious appearances can hardly be *ren* (equitable)."

[1.13] Master You said, "Those whose trustworthiness is close to *yi* (appropriateness) [i.e., *kairos*] can keep their words. Those who respect in ways close to *li* (propriety) can keep humiliation at a distance. Those who in need can turn first to those near and dear can be respected."

---

53. See, for example, 14.4 below.

[1.14] The Master said, "Fond of learning are *junzi* (the-deferential person)[54] who focus, not on a full stomach and comfortable residence, but on acting diligently, speaking prudently, and consulting frequently with others so as to walk *dao*-the-way."

[1.15] Zigong asked, "Some people are poor yet not obsequious, and others, affluent yet not haughty. What do you think of people like these?" The Master said, "They are good, but even better are those who are poor but also fond of *dao*-the-way and affluent but also fond of *li* (propriety)." Zigong reflected, "Isn't it like what's said in *The Book of Songs* '[Cultivate by] cutting, polishing, carving, and grinding'?" The Master said, "Zigong, now I can speak with you about the *Book of Songs*; you can bring to bear what you have learned from it and infer correlations."

[2.13] Zigong asked about how to become a *junzi*-deferential-person. Confucius told him, "Try to act faster than you speak, and then let your words reflect your actions."

[2.18] Zizhang inquired about the wherewithal to become a successful *shi*-state official. The Master told him, "Listen carefully to minimize doubt, and speak prudently about what remains doubtful; you will then make fewer mistakes. Be observant to reduce uncertainty and act judiciously on what remains uncertain; you will have fewer regrets. The secretes to becoming a successful *shi*-state-official lie in prudent words and therefore fewer mistakes, judicious actions and therefore fewer regrets."

[2.22] The Master said, "I don't know if one who has no credibility can accomplish much. Can carriages, big or small, work without the linchpin connecting the wheel axle and the crossing shaft?"

[4.10] The Master said, "In dealing with affairs of the world, *junzi* do not form judgment obstinately; rather, they observe *yi* [i.e., *kairos*]."

[4.16] The Master said, "*Junzi*-the-deferential judge by *yi* [i.e., *kairos*], while petty persons, by personal gain."

---

54. *Junzi* used to be translated as *gentlemen*, a translation that has obvious limitations. Ames and Rosemont, among others, have tried to improve the translation by using the more specific and gender-neutral phrase *exemplary persons*. I make the translation even more specific by using *deferential*, and I do so for two reasons. First, *deferential* describes *junzi* as one kind of good people, not the best of all people, just as *ren*-equity is a very important quality but it alone does not make one the best of all people for Confucius. This can be seen when *Zigong* asked if philanthropists were *ren*-people and Confucius replied, "How could *ren* be enough for that? Even sages *Yao* and *Shun* could find themselves inadequate" (6.30). Second, *deferential* meets the level of specificity with which Confucius once said about *junzi*: "Those who are both polished and unpretentious are *junzi*" (6.18); *deferential* characterizes those who are both polished and unpretentious. Also see Xunzi in this book.

[4.18] The Master said, "In persuading your parents, be thoughtful and charitable with your words. If you fail, remain respectful and do not be affrontive. Though frustrated, do not be resentful."

[4.22] The Master said, "The ancients did not take discourse (*yan*) lightly and were ashamed when they could not keep up with their words."

[4.24] The Master said, "*Junzi*-the-deferential speak slowly but act diligently."

[4.26] Ziyou said, "Nagging the ruler, ministers bring humiliation to themselves; nagging friends, they alienate themselves."

[5.5] Someone said, "Ranyong are *ren* (equitable) but is not good at *ning* (glib-talk)" The Master said, "Why should he be? Being too ready with the tongue in talking back to others is off-putting to many. I don't know if he is *ren*-equitable, but why should he be *ning*?"

[5.25] The Master said, "Using *qiaoyan* (crafty-speeches), putting on pretentious appearances, and fidgeting the feet calculatedly to feign awestricken reverence, these are self-mortifying behaviors in the eyes of Zuo Qiuming; they are so to me, too. Hiding disagreements to maintain sham friendships is shameful in the eyes of Zuo Qiuming; it is so to me, too."

[6.21] The Master said, "It is appropriate to engage in thorough *yu* (discussion) with those above average. With those who are not, it is inappropriate to do so."

[7.3] The Master said, "Not cultivating virtue, not discussing learning, not pursuing *yi* [i.e., *kairos*], and not facing up to one's mistakes, these are my worries."

[9.30] The Master said, "Those who study together may not be able to aspire to walk *dao* (the-way) together. Those who aspire to walk *dao* together may not be able to persist on it together. Those who persist on walking *dao* together may not be able to *quan* (weighing) together."

[10.1] In both of Confucius's hometowns, Confucius acted reverential and humble, *yan* (speaking) as if he could hardly do so. At the ancestral temple and state court, he *yan* (spoke) clearly, unambiguously, but also cautiously.

[10.2] At the state court, the Master *yan* (spoke) to lower officials amiably and joyously, and he *yan* (spoke) with higher officials justly and candidly. On the arrival of the Duke, he acted with respect and poise.

[11.22] Zilu asked, "On learning about something, should I act on it right away?" The Master replied, "Your father and older brothers are still alive for you to consult with.

Why would you act right away?" Ranyou asked, "On learning about something, should I act on it right away?" The Master replied, "Yes, you should." Gongxi Hua said, "Zilu inquired whether he should act immediately on knowing about something, you told him to consult his father and older brothers, but when Ranyou asked the same question, you told him to act right away. I am confused, so may I ask why?" The Master replied, "Ranyou is of the hesitant kind, and that's why I encouraged him, but Zilu is rash in temperament, and that's why I cautioned him."

[11.26] Zilu, Zengxi, Ranyou, and Gongxi Hua were visiting with the Master. The Master said, "Although I am your senior, I do not want you to let this factor prevent you from speaking your minds. Often you say, 'no one knows me,' but if someone does know [and employ] you, what would you do?" Zilu replied quickly, "Give me a state that is the size of a thousand chariots, bordering on larger states, and pressured from the outside by constant military threats and from inside by continued poor harvests. In three years, I can make the people brave and respectful." The Master smiled . . . . After three of them left, Zixi asked, . . . "Why did the Master smile after Zilu spoke?" The Master explained, "Running a state requires *li* (propriety). Zilu is incapable of *rang*-yielding to others in discourse (*yan*), and that's why."

[12.1] Yan Yuan asked about *ren*-the-equitable. The Master said, "Disciplining yourself to practice *li* is *ren* (the-equitable). When people practice *li* this way for a day, they are *ren* [because both originate from the same place, the heart]. To be *ren* depends on oneself, not others." Yan Yuan asked again, "Could you please advise more specifically?" The Master said, "Do not look at, listen to, talk about, or act on what is not *li*." Yan Yuan said, "I am slow but will continue to improve accordingly.

[12.3] Sima Niu asked about *ren* (equity). The Master explained to him, "The *ren* (仁 equitable) are *ren* (訒 slow-at-*yan*-discoursing)." "Are all those *ren* (slow-at-*yan*-speaking) *ren* (equitable)?" The Master said to him, "Following up on one's words (*yan*) is hard; how can one not be *ren* (slow-at-*yan*-discoursing)?"

[12.23] Zigong asked about friendship. The Master said, "Advise friends in good faith and be good at persuading them. On seeing that they are unreceptive, let up to avoid humiliation."

[13.3] Zilu asked, "If the Duke of Wei let you manage the state of affairs in Wei today, where would you start?" The Master said, "I would have to start with rectification of names!" Zilu exclaimed, "Indeed? The Master has become such a pedant! How would you conduct such rectifications?" "How foolish, Zilu!" The Master reproved, "*Junzi* do not approach so recklessly things they don't know. If names are not rectified, then one cannot discourse (*yan*) coherently; if *yan* is incoherent, work does not get done; if work doesn't get done, *li* won't flourish; if *li* suffers, punishment will be off the mark; if the law is not carried out fairly, people will not know how to behave. Therefore, *junzi* must use names in ways that can be *yan* coherently and must *yan* in ways that can be effected in everyday life. [This is why] when *junzi yan* (speak), they never do so carelessly"

[13.27] The Master said, "Those who are strong, perseverant, unpretentious, and *ne* (slow-at-speaking) are close to being *ren (*equitable)."

[14.3] The Master said, "When *dao*-the-way prevails within the state, speak (*yan*) and act forthrightly. When *dao*-the-way ebbs away from the state, act the same way but *yan* circumspectly."

[14.4] The Master said, "The virtuous have the wherewithal to *yan*, but those who are skilled at *yan* may not be virtuous. The *ren* (equitable) persons are brave, but those who are brave may not be *ren* persons."

[14.8] The Master said, "[In the State of Zheng,] diplomatic documents were drafted by Bi Chen, conferred by Shi Shu, edited by Zi Yu, Head of all diplomats, and polished by Zi Chan of Dong Li."[55]

[14.12] Zilu asked about those who are perfect. The Master replied, "Those who are perfect have the wisdom of Zang Wuzhong, the austerity of Gong Chuo, the bravery of Bian Zhuangzi, the artistic versatility of Ranqiu, and are cultivated in *li*." Then the Master added, "Today's perfect people can no longer reach that level. They think of *yi* when dealing with self-interest, are willing to sacrifice their lives in dangerous situations, and always keep their words. These are the people who can be considered perfect today."

[14.17] Zigong asked, "Isn't Guan Zhong un-*ren*? After Duke Huan killed [his elder brother] Prince Jiu, not only did Guan Zhong not protest by committing suicide and dying with his master Prince Jiu, but he later even served Duke Huan [the murderer of his master Prince Jiu]." The Master said, "With the assistance of the Minister Guan Zhong, Duke Huan became the leader of the vassal states and corrected their wrong doings [without relying on the military force[56]]. People today are still benefiting from what they did. If it were not for Guan Zhong, we would be wearing our hair down and button our garments on the left [as we would be ruled by other cultures]. Do you actually think that Guan Zhong should have stuck to the so-called honor according to the standard of some petty persons, killed himself, and died in some ditch in the wild without a trace?"

---

55. The writers were Confucius's contemporaries and were all senior officials serving the State of Zheng, with Zi Chan being one of the most accomplished and well-known statesmen during Spring and Autumn. See Confucius (2003, 5.16).

56. Confucius 2003, 14.16.

[14.20] The Master said, "*Buzuo* (boastful-talk) makes acting on it difficult."

[14.27] The Master said, "*Junzi* deem it shameful to have their actions lagging behind their words (*yan*)."

[14.32] Wei Shengmu said to Confucius, "Qiu! Why do you move from state to state, like a bird that skips from one tree branch to another? Are you really becoming a *ning* (glib) talker [whose trustworthiness depends on words]?" Confucius replied, "Not wanting to be a *ning* talker, I do dread being *gu* (inflexible)."

[15.8] The Master said, "Not *yan* (speaking) with those whom one should *yan* (speak) with, one misses [the opportunity to know] them; *yan* with those whom one shouldn't *yan* with, one misspeaks. The wise do not miss people, nor do they misspeak."

[15.17] The Master said, "Those who gather together day in and day out, not *yan* with *yi* [i.e., *kairos*] but showing off their cleverness at resorting to trickery: this kind of people are difficult!"

[15.23] The Master said, "*Junzi*-the-deferential do not commend others merely based on their *yan*-words, nor do they reject others merely based on them."

[15.37] The Maser said, "*Junzi*-the-deferential are true to *dao*-the-way but do not rigidly adhere to some *liang* (petty-honor)."

[15.41] The Master said, "When words (*yan*) can accomplish what they are meant to accomplish, they are good enough."

[16.6] Confucius said, "In conversing with *junzi*, one wants to avoid three mistakes. *Yan* (speaking) out of turn is called disrespectful and impatient. Speaking (*yan*) not when spoken to is called secretive and dishonest. And speaking (*yan*) without taking into consideration of the mood and attitude of the audience is called blind."

[16.8] Confucius said, "What *junzi* hold in awe are three in number: *tianming*-, those in higher positions, and words (*yan*) by the sages. Petty persons do not know *tianming*-the-cosmic-order, so they do not hold it in awe, affront those in higher positions, and insult sages's words (*yan*)."

[16.13] [The Master said,] "Not studying *The Book of Songs* one won't know how to speak (*yan*) with others!"

[17.19] The Master said, "I would not *yan* (speak) any more." Zigong asked, "If so, what would we students pass on to future generations?" The Master said, "What does the cosmos (*tian*) say (*yan*)? The four seasons move along and hundreds of things live on; what does say (*tian yan*)?"

[17.23] Zilu asked, "Do *junzi* emphasize bravery?" The Master replied, "They prioritize *yi* [i.e., *kairos*]. *Junzi* who are brave without *yi* become agitators, and petty persons who are brave without *yi* become thieves."

[19.10] *Junzi* only assign work to people after they have established credibility (*xin*) with them; otherwise, they come across as wanting to harm the people. *Junzi* persuade (*jian*) their rulers after they have established *xin* with them; otherwise, they come across as wanting to vilify the rulers."

[20.3] The Master said, "Not knowing *tianming*, one cannot become a *junzi*. Not knowing *li*, one cannot establish oneself within human communities. Not knowing *yan*, one cannot know people."

2.2 Spring-Autumn Period and Warring States Period (Classical)

Rhetorical Treatise by Xunzi[57] (荀子) (316–208 BCE): A Partial Translation of *Xunzi* with an Introduction and Commentary

Hui Wu

INTRODUCTION

Little is known about Xunzi's life. *The Grand Scribe's Records* (*Shi Ji*) records his full name as Xun Kuang (荀況), a native of the State of Zhao (趙).[58] It is said that Xunzi lived from 316 BCE to 208 BCE about a hundred years after Mengzi (孟子Mencius circa 372–289 BCE or 385–302 BCE).[59] Xunzi was a contemporary of students of Guiguzi (circa 400–320 BCE), alleged author of China's first book on rhetoric.[60] He also traveled from state to state, trying to provide counsel to state kings and promote his ideas about governance and socio-political system. But not until when he was almost fifty years old was Xunzi hired by the State of Qi (齊).[61] Being slandered, he had to move to the State of Chu (楚), where he was appointed to the post of magistrate of Lanling, a region in today's southern Shangdong where he taught and lived for the rest of his life.[62]

Xunzi successfully advanced his doctrine through private teaching, an educational system developed by Confucius. His philosophical impact was not as prominent as that of Confucius and Mencius, but Xunzi was an equally renowned teacher with Hanfeizi (韓非子) and Li Si (李斯) being his students (see chapter on Hanfeizi). While Confucius's method of teaching in the *Analects* is dominated by dialogues, Xunzi's is primarily a systematic account of his own critical theories and rhetorical ethics in relation to human nature, state governance, and key Confucian concepts, such as *junzi* (君子 exemplary person), *li* (禮 rites or rituals), and *xue* (学 learning or education).[63] During his last years, Xunzi "collated and organized his writings, which amounted to several tens of thousands of characters."[64] However, Xunzi's teaching would not have appeared in a book format without his students' assistance and the effort of

---

57. See honorific naming of "*zi*" in the previous section on Confucius.

58. Ssu-Ma 1994, 179.

59. Watson 2003, 1; Yong and Bo 2011, 1; Dan and Tian 2007, 1.

60. *Guiguzi,* 2016.

61. Hutton 2014, xix–xx.

62. Watson 2003, 2.

63. "Exemplary person" is borrowed from the *Analects* translated by Roger Ames and Henry Rosemont (*Analects*). Both Hutton and Knoblock translated *junzi* into "gentleman." See also Lan's translation of *junzi* and *li* in Confucius.

64. Ssu-Ma 1994, 184.

later compilers.[65] Liu Xiang (劉向 77–76 BCE) compiled the definitive collection of Xunzi's writings from his findings of some 322 manuscripts scattered on bamboo strips and silk scrolls in the Imperial Library.[66] Finally, Xunzi's philosophical and rhetorical treatises were arranged in thirty-two chapters in a book named after him, *Xunzi*.

Like *Guiguzi*, the *Xunzi* is written in rhymed verse and is an instructional text, which has initiated the rhetorical genre of essay for argumentation and explication.[67] Throughout *Xunzi*, all sentences are structured in perfect parallelism with matching numbers of characters. One of the syntactic patterns in chapter 25, "*Cheng Xiang* (成相)," is allegedly influenced by popular folk songs whose lines are composed of three, three, and seven characters.[68] Some sentences imitate those in Confucius's *Book of Poetry*.[69] Poetic and artistic, each of the first twenty-six chapters is a complete essay itself with coherent logical reasoning to develop an argument. For example, passage one in chapter one, "Encouraging Learning (*quan xue* 勸學)," begins with the proposition that "learning must not end." Then Xunzi uses analogies and cites the *Book of Poetry* to develop it. An analogy says, "Without climbing the high mountains, one does not know how high the sky is; without looking down a fathomless gorge, one does not know how unfathomable the earth is; without listening to the ancient king's words, one does not know how expansive learning and inquiry are."[70] As we shall see later, Xunzi's rhetorical genres of argumentation and instruction have been inherited and expanded by Hanfeizi, Lu Ji, Liu Xie, and women teachers.

Furthermore, Xunzi is credited for originating another rhetorical genre, *fu* (賦 exposition, explicatory/expository verse).[71] As the second element of Confucius's *Book of Poetry*, *fu* initially signifies arrangement, "arranging and selecting diction to compose, to represent objects, and express the mind."[72] This explanation is verified in *Zuo Zhuan* (左傳), where *fu* means to compose or deliver (a poem or verse). For example, "Prince [Zhong] delivered [verse titled] 'River,' and Lord [Qin Mu] delivered 'June.'"[73] Xunzi transformed *fu* into a rhetorical genre in chapter 26 titled "*Fu* (賦)," where he uses questions and answers alternately to elaborate, sometimes playfully but always philosophically, on his ideas about *li* (rites), learning, nature, family, kindness, and governance.[74] Each of the five pieces of *fu* verse starts with a riddle and ends with a solution. One riddle reads, "There is a great thing. It is not silk thread nor silk

---

65. Shen 2000, 454; Knoblock 1988, 115–18.

66. Knoblock 1988, 105–07.

67. Shen 2000, 486.

68. Fang and Li 2022, 5; Shen 2000, 488–89.

69. Hutton 2014, xv.

70. Fang and Li 2011, Chapter 1.1. Translations are mine unless indicated otherwise. Modern Chinese condense the statement to "not knowing the height of the sky and the depth of the early (*buzhi tiangao dihou* 不知天高地厚), meaning "having little knowledge or experience."

71. Fang and Li, 2011, 5; Shen, 2000, 488–89.

72. Liu Xie 2016, Chapter 8.1.

73. The original is "公子賦《河水》公賦《六月》" (*Zuo Zhuan* 2013, 61).

74. Fang and Li 2011, Chapter 26.

scroll. Yet, it is composed of prose and reason. It is not the sun nor the moon. Yet, it illuminates the world."[75] The solution is *li*. The allegory is intended to explain the great power of *li* in the development of an individual. As Liu Xie (劉勰) observes, the basic features of *fu* are already evident in Xunzi's "Fu."[76] In the Han dynasty (206 BCE–220 CE), *fu* became a popular hybrid rhetorical genre of poetry and verse to illustrate a philosophical idea or argue for a proposition. It is also said that *fu* was shaped into the Song Prose (*Song Ci* 宋辭) in the Song Dynasty (960–1279 CE) that has long-lasting impact on the modern essay.[77]

As a philosopher, Xunzi's holds that humans are born evil but can be transformed or changed through learning, which enables one to practice rites and rituals and embrace kindness. He says that "People's nature is bad. Their goodness is a matter of deliberate effort."[78] Although Xunzi is said to be critical of his predecessors' notions and theories,[79] he adheres to Confucian doctrines in his instruction. For example, Xunzi encourages students to begin their learning by reciting the Confucian classics—*The Book of Poetry, Book of History (Book of Shang), Spring and Autumn Annals,* and *Book of Rites.* Their learning should result in a full understanding of the Confucian notion of *li* to develop themselves into *junzi,* an exemplary person.[80] Xunzi believes that to correct and transform humans' inborn bad dispositions, they must be trained by teachers to internalize *li* (rites) and *yi* (morality or justice) conceptualized by ancient sages. A learned man conscientious of self-improvement can become a *junzi,* who accumulates historical knowledge of eloquence and literacy (*wen xue* 文学) to practice what he has learned about *li* and *yi*.[81]

In Xunzi's teaching of rhetoric, a *junzi* is a rhetorical practitioner in speech and writing. Becoming a *junzi* requires self-development (*xiu shen* 修身). Chapter 2 of the *Xunzi* is devoted to the concept and process of self-development, a theory inherited by male and female teachers centuries later (see chapters on Queen Xu and Song Ruozhao). Xunzi teaches that a person who wishes to understand what constitutes kindness (*shan* 善) must develop him/herself through self-reflection, saying, "When you observe goodness in others, then inspect yourself, desirous of cultivating it. When you observe badness in others, then examine yourself, fearful of discovering it."[82] A developed *junzi* "loves goodness tirelessly, and can receive admonitions and take heed."[83] According to Xunzi, self-development is only possible by following the Confucian *li* and one's teacher. He asks rhetorically, "If you don't follow *li*, how can you develop yourself? If without my teachers, how could I have learned how to direct my conduct with *li*?"[84]

---

75. Fang and Li 2011, Chapter 26.1.

76. Liu 2016, Chapter 8.2.

77. Fang and Li 2011, 5.

78. Hutton 2014, 248.

79. Watson 2003; Lu 1998, 185.

80. Watson 2003: 19; Fang and Li 2011, Chapter 1.6.

81. Fang and Li 2011, Chapter 24.1.

82. Hutton 2014, 9.

83. Ibid.

84. Fang and Li 2011, Chapter 2.10.

Self-development is key to cultivating a human because Xunzi believes in the human faculty of making distinctions in language, saying that "A human is human because he [or she] has the capability of making distinctions (*bian* 辨)."[85] Humans are different from other creatures not because they have two legs and no fur but because they can differentiate things.[86] Xunzi does not relate the human capability of classification and categorization explicitly to language use or to orality and literacy, but his reasoning implicitly forms a preliminary to conceptualization of human cognitive and linguistic power of naming things. His epistemology, however, is hierarchical. On the top is the sagacious king (*sheng wang* 圣王). *Li* is the second highest. Under the *li* are ranks (*fen* 分) or social status. At the bottom is distinction-making (*bien* 辨).[87] This order is what Xunzi calls the law (*fa* 法), which decrees that one serves a state king by following the *li* to differentiate right from wrong.[88] Then what was Confucian codification of rites and morals has assumed the status of linguistic and logical realities by Xunzi's redefinition. For example, he points out that only humans can name the emotional bond between son and father, not other creatures; while other creatures have both male and female, only humans define them into men and women.[89]

Furthermore, in chapter 22, "Correcting Names (*zheng ming* 正名)," emerges a linguistic theory that continues Guiguzi's teaching of "naming the reality" to connect the sensory processing of things and name them in language. While Guiguzi envisions words that signify reality based on virtues,[90] Xunzi's system focuses on the correlation between the sensor and the object, which reminds us of Ferdinand de Saussure's definitions of signifier and signified in his *Courses in General Linguistics*. Like Saussure's definitions, Xunzi's signifier and signified are also arbitrary bound by agreement. To Xunzi, "Names have no intrinsic appropriateness. They are bound to something by agreement in order to name it. The agreement becomes fixed, and custom is established, and it is called 'appropriate.' If a name is different from the agreed name, it is called 'inappropriate'."[91] Put rhetorically, Xunzi means that "if names are used in an agreed upon manner, communication takes place. Otherwise misunderstandings and confusions are likely to occur."[92] An ethical speech should appropriately define things and name them properly because to avoid confusion one should give each different reality a different name."[93] Persons who can correctly name the reality according to the rites and morality can help bring order to the state. These persons represent what Xunzi calls the *junzi*.

---

85. Fang and Li 2011, Chapter 5.6.
86. Ibid.
87. Fang and Li 2011, Chapter 5.7.
88. Ibid.
89. Fang and Li 2011, Chapter 5.6.
90. *Guiguzi*, 2016, 88.
91. Knoblock 1988, 130.
92. Lu 1998, 189.
93. Knoblock 1988, 130.

Commentary on Xunzi's Rhetorical Teaching

The concept of *junzi* dominates Xunzi's philosophy and ethics of rhetoric. The *junzi* is what Xunzi imagines to be a fully developed rhetor, who does "Nothing Improper."[94] A comparison between *Xunzi* and its predecessor, *Guiguzi*, can deepen our understanding of their different philosophies on the rhetor. First, Xunzi's *junzi* differs from Guiguzi's sage in rhetorical practice. While the sage of rhetoric in *Guiguzi* upholds the *Dao* to be connected to Heaven and Earth to deliver persuasion through seamless *yin-yang* moves,[95] "A *junzi* only holds what is proper in the highest regard" without compromising his speech based on random examinations.[96] Xunzi's *junzi* speaks to argue (*yan bian* 言辯) but does not manipulate eloquence (*bu ci* 不辞).[97] Xunzi "was contemptuous of scholars arguing on minutiae" as well as those who were good at "smooth talk."[98] He accused those speakers, including Guiguzi's students, of confusing the public and the rulers they served with treacherous speeches.[99] Xunzi was even disappointed that Li Si, one of his students well known for intriguing persuasion, quit learning from him and became the Prime Minister of the State of Qin.[100] Like Confucius, Xunzi was not against rhetorical practice that aimed to achieve goodness for the state through propriety. But he did not trust treacherous speeches (*jian yan* 奸言) that disagreed with ancient kings and *li* and *yi* (rites and morality).[101] Xunzi's *junzi* is willing to speak and is committed to argument.[102] As such, "the *junzi* has good will, acts peacefully, and enjoys speaking."[103]

Next, Xuniz's *junzi* is a secular independent practitioner of rhetoric with his own *Dao* of propriety. While the sage of rhetoric in the *Guiguzi* is an inseparable part of *Dao* related to Heaven and Earth,[104] Xunzi's *junzi* forms his own *Dao* that is independent of Heaven and Earth. He explains that "The *Dao* is not the *Dao* of Heaven, nor is it the *Dao* of Earth. It is what humans make their *Dao,* and it is what the *junzi* makes his *Dao.*"[105] In secularizing the *Dao*, Xunzi's *junzi* is as not as omniscient as Guiguzi's sage who can "persuade the world."[106] Nonetheless, the *junzi* accumulates knowledge and can deliver a proper speech, for "What a *junzi* calls knowledge is not what everybody else calls knowledge. What a *junzi* calls an ar-

---

94. Hutton 2014, 16.
95. Wu 2016, 25-26; *Guiguzi* 2016, Chapter I.1.
96. Fang and Li, 2011, Chapter 3.1. Also see the translation by Hutton (2014, 16).
97. Fang and Li 2011, Chapter 3.2.
98. Ssu-Ma 1994, 184.
99. Lu 1998, 187.
100. Ssu-Ma 1994, 184; also see chapter on Hanfeizi in this book.
101. Fang and Li 2011, (Chapter 5.9)
102. Ibid.
103. Ibid.
104. *Guiguzi* 2016, 101–02.
105. Fang and Li 2011, Chapter 8.3.
106. *Guiguzi* 2016, 42.

gument [*bian* 辯] is not what other arguers [*bian ren* 辯人] call an argument."[107] Xunzi gives examples to explain what the *junzi* selects to do properly. A *junzi* cannot farm as well as a farmer does. He cannot handle finances or tell the value of some commodity as well as a merchant does. What the *junzi* does well is his cogent speech and pragmatic business conduct.[108]

Xunzi's *junzi* is also different from a sage in the method of speech, for "a sage speaks a lot but with analogies; a *junzi* speaks little but with propriety."[109] It seems that Xunzi recognizes the ethic and power of the sage, but the rhetorical purposes and methods of a sage and a *junzi* are different. As Xunzi says, "There are junzi's ways of argument; there are sage's ways of argument."[110] As such, "Sages do not need to deliberate or plan beforehand. They deliver their arguments properly and compose them according to their genera. They adjust and move to meet changes with countless measures."[111] In comparison, "a *junzi* deliberates and plans in advance. His speech is concise but pleasant to the ear, composed to tell truth."[112] The core value of the *junzi* is his boundless knowledge and adherence to propriety. Put differently, Xunzi's *junzi* is an exemplary rhetor who follows what is proper in a rhetorical situation, according to the Confucian orthodoxy of *li*. The exemplary person is, therefore, independent to develop his mind and capability of speech through learning rites and morality.[113]

Xunzi teaches rhetoric specifically in chapters five and twenty-two, which are retranslated hereafter. There are three preexisting translations respectively by John Knoblock in 1988, Burton Watson in 2003, and Eric Hutton in 2014. Knoblcok's translation consists of 1,153 pages in three volumes, a scholarly contribution aimed to be "precise and literal" but produced a translation difficult to follow.[114] Burton's bridged translation, however, leaves out chapter five specifically on rhetoric. Hutton's translation is intended to appeal to general readers, specifically undergraduate students. As a result, Hutton had to make "certain compromises" to provide a translation not too literal, [115] making Xunzi's treatise on rhetoric easily escape the reader's attention. None of the three translations, regardless of readability or accurateness, present Xunzi's teaching of rhetoric, erasing him from Chinese rhetoric. The newly translated excerpts fill this gap by showcasing Xunzi's philosophy and teaching of rhetoric, particularly his ideas about the development of the ethical rhetor. By positioning Xunzi as an important teacher of rhetoric in classical China, the excerpts reflect the trajectory of historical development of rhetorical terminologies, concepts, and genres.

The retranslation is based on the edition by Fang Yong and Li Bo published by the China Press, the most reputed press for classics, in consultation with other Chinese editions. Since

---

107. Fang and Li 2011, Chapter 8.3.

108. Fang and Li 2011, Chapter 8.4.

109. Fang and Li 2011, Chapter 26.94.

110. Fang and Li 2011, Chapter 5.13.

111. Ibid.

112. Ibid.

113. Fang and Li 2011, Chapter 5.12.

114. Hutton 2014, xii.

115. Hutton 2014, xii-xiii.

classical Chinese writing contains no punctuation nor separation of sentences and paragraphs, the division of passages and paragraphs follows the Chinese editions that are consistent in this regard. They are numbered as well for convenient cross-reference.

Translation of Xunzi's Rhetorical Treatise

*Chapter 5 Refuting Physiognomy (*Fei Xiang 非相*)*

5.9 Any statement that disagrees with what ancient kings have said and does not accord with the rites (*li*) and morality (*yi*) is called a treacherous speech. It may constitute an argument (*bian* 辯), but a *junzi* refuses to heed it. A person who follows the ancient kings and befriends learned men but does not like speaking (*yan* 言) or does not enjoy speaking is definitely not a sincere man. Thus the *junzi* resorts to good speeches (*yan* 言). He has good will, acts peacefully, and enjoys speaking. It is, therefore, said that the *junzi* is committed to argument (*bian* 辯). All humans are fond of speaking about goodness. The *junzi* is specially so. Thus, a speech as a gift to others is more precious than gold, gems, pearls, and jade; observing a speech is more beautiful than seeing embroidered gowns; listening to a speech is more enjoyable than hearing music of bells, drums, zithers, and lutes. Therefore, the *junzi* is never tired of advocating speeches. Unlearned men are the opposite. They prefer a speech's practicality to its rhetorical composition (*wen* 文). Their whole life is inescapably low, filthy, indecent, and vulgar. Hence says *Yi Jing* (*Book of Changes*):

An all-purpose sack contains nothing blamable or honorable.
This explains corrupt scholars of Confucianism (*ru* 儒).

5.10 All the difficulties of persuasion (*shui* 說) reside in talking about lofty causes to advance the low-class and talking about ideal states to address chaos. They are outright unachievable. Illustrations without immediate relevance are considered disconnected; down-to-earth ones are considered tasteless. Good persuaders situate themselves in the middle. They can illustrate the lofty without sounding disconnected and the practical without sounding unrefined. They move and walk with times; they lower themselves to see the world as it is. They speed up or slow down according to the highs and lows. They are like reservoirs and carpentry tools in their favor. The results are achieved along the curves without harm or damage. It is thus said that the *junzi* disciplines himself like a carpenter's measuring line, while accommodating others like a boat. His strict self-measurement should become the criteria across the world. Accommodating others like a boat magnifies tolerance, with which great undertakings of the world are accomplished. As such, the *junzi* is virtuous and tolerant. Though educated, he understands the uneducated. Though knowledgeable, he tolerates shallowness. Though pure, he accommodates mixtures. This is called the art of adaptability (*jian shu* 兼術). The *Book of Poetry* says,

Agreements gradually reached across the board are the success of the Son of Heaven.[116]
This explains what I said.

5.11 The art of speech and persuasion: Situate it with dignity and respect. Practice it with integrity and honesty. Adhere to it with consistence and fortitude. Delineate it with analogies. Clarify it with allegories and definitions. Deliver it with visible joyfulness and natural sweetness. Treasure it, cherish it, and value it like a divine bequest. Such persuasion is never unaccepted. Even if it does not convince people, it is still regarded highly. This is called enabling others to see what one values. An ancient saying has it:

> Only a *junzi* can enable others to see what he values.
> This explains what I said.

5.12 A *junzi* is committed to argument. Nobody dislikes speaking about what he (she) calls goodness (*shan* 善), the *junzi* is especially so. When petty persons argue, they emphasize risks; when the *junzi* argues, he emphasizes benevolence (*ren* 仁). If one's speech does not hold benevolence in the core, it is better to be silenced. This type of argument is worse than speaking clumsily. When benevolence is the core of a speech, good speakers become superior, and bad speakers inferior. Hence benevolent speeches are great. What is originated from the top to direct the inferior is an official decree. What is originated from below to show loyalty to the superior is a plan to avert dangers. Hence, the *junzi* is never tired of practicing benevolence. He has good will, acts peacefully, and enjoys speaking. It is thus said that the *junzi* is committed to argument. Debating about trivial matters is not as beneficial as seeing their roots. Seeing their roots is not as beneficial as seeing them identified and ranked. Debating about trivial matters helps investigate them; seeing their roots clarifies them; identifying and ranking them set them in order. This (practice) establishes the differences among a sage, good man, and *junzi*.

5.13 There are petty person's way of argument; there are *junzi*'s way of argument; and there are sage's ways of argument. A sage does not need to deliberate or plan beforehand. He delivers his argument properly and composes them according to their genera. He adjusts and moves to meet changes with countless measures. The *junzi* deliberates and plans in advance. His speech is concise but pleasant to the ear, rhetorically composed with credibility, profound knowledge, and righteousness. This is the argument by a good man or the *junzi*. Another type of speaker is heard playing with the word for argument without coherent unity. When appointed, he engages in multiple treacherous games to achieve nothing. He can neither follow the wise king above him nor unite and harmonize subjects under him. Nonetheless, his mouth and tongue serve his purpose. Talking eloquently with pauses and in control, he seems to belong among

---

116. The original is "許方既同天子之功 (*xu fang ji tong tyanzi zhi gong*)." 許 (*xu*) means "gradual" here. Some interpret it as a state, for example, Fang and Li's commentary (2011: 64). However, Hutton points out that in the original context of the *Book of Poetry*, "it is less clear that the poem interprets [the state of] Xu's submission this way" (2014, 38, Note 29). The Son of Heaven refers to the king of a state.

those worthy of awe and pride. Such persons are called vile men's advocates. Rising sage kings execute them first and then robbers and thieves. Robbers and thieves can be transformed, but not this type of people.

Chapter 22 Correct Naming

22.6 Assertions, such as "Insults are not humiliations," "Sages do not love themselves," or "Killing a robber is not killing," are cases where names (definitions) are used to confuse nomenclature. The reasons for the misnaming should be examined against the consequences. Only by this method can they be stopped. Assertions, such as "Mountains and abysses are both flat," "Human desires are few," or "Fine meats have no better taste; chiming does not bring more delight," are cases where realities are used to confuse nomenclature. The reasons for likes and dislikes should be examined to see what questions and adjustments may arise. Only by this method can they be stopped. The assertion that "there are oxen and horses; but horses are not horses" is a case where naming is used to misinform reality. It should be examined against the agreed names to reveal the erroneous argument (*ci* 辭). Only by this method can it be stopped. Almost all heresy (*xie shuo* 邪說) and hearsay (*pi yan* 辟言) that depart from the right *Dao* are fabricated recklessly. They can be categorized in the three aforesaid dissident types. For this reason, a wise *junzi* knowing the differences refuses to be engaged in these arguments.

22.7 The mass of people is to be united easily by means of the *Dao* but not to be enlightened with reason. Thus, the wise king uses power to govern them, applies the *Dao* to guiding them, issues decrees to order them, praises them to make a point, and controls them with penalty. Thus, his subjects are transformed with the *Dao* in divine spirits. What need does he have for argument? Nowadays sage kings are all dead; the world is in chaos, and treacherous eloquence arises. The *junzi* has no authority to govern people. There is no punishment to deter them. This is why he is engaged in differentiation (*bian* 辨) and persuasion (*shuo* 說). If reality (*she* 实) is not apprehended through analogy (*yu* 喻), he resorts to naming (*ming* 命). If naming is not enough to illustrate it, he tries to reach an agreement (*qi* 期). If the agreement is not reached, he engages in persuasion (*shuo* 說). This is why agreement, naming, argument, and persuasion are used in grand composition (*da wen* 大文) to launch kingly enterprises. When a name is heard to illustrate reality (*shi* 實), the naming is functional. When names are accumulated to compose a discourse (*cheng wen* 成文), they are in accord (*li* 麗).[117] When both the function and accord are achieved, naming is understood. What is called naming is expected to contain reality. Eloquence (*ci* 辭) delineates the names of different types of reality (*shi* 實) to illustrate an idea. The so-called differentiation and persuasion are to illustrate motion and silence without changing the names of realities. Agreement and naming are utilized in differ-

---

117. 麗 also means beauty, but here it means the match between a name and what it signifies for rhetorical effectiveness.

entiation and persuasion, which mirror the heart[118] that follows the *Dao*. The heart serves as the craftsman for the *Dao*, the doctrine and dogma of good order. When the heart and *Dao* are in accord (*he* 合), persuasion accords with the heart, and eloquence with the persuasion. Then naming is in agreement, and substance and feeling are illustrated. When telling differences (*bian yi* 辨異) commits no error, and allegorizing categories draws no disagreement, a speech heard is in accord with the composition (*wen* 文), and the differentiation fully illustrates all the reasons.

Using the right *Dao* to reveal treacheries is like using the carpenter's measuring line to tell if a piece is straight or not. This way, no treacherous speeches can bring about disorder, and the hundred schools (*bai jia* 百家) have nowhere to hide.[119] With brilliant minds, they listen to all but show no excitement or conceitedness on their countenances. With generosity, they accommodate different sides without displaying self-righteousness. When their persuasions work, the whole world is in order; when their persuasions do not work, they explain the *Dao* in plain language and quietly bow out. This is the way sages make distinctions and speak. The *Book of Poetry* has it:

> Full of gracious humility and honorable dignity,
> A jade emblem and symbol he is,
> Compelling to be heard and seen.
> So peaceful and composed the *junzi* is,
> Who models everywhere all good deeds.

This explains what I said.

22.8 He balances eloquence and deference properly. He pays respect to seniors and juniors in the right order. He never makes improper claims or utters graceless words. He delivers persuasion with a heart of benevolence; he listens with a heart for learning; he makes distinctions with a heart for the common good (*gong* 公). He is not swayed when out of the favor of the masses. He does not shadow his audience's ears and eyes. He does not bribe patricians to acquire power and status. He does not help spread hearsay. As such, he is situated in the *Dao* without uncertainty. He does not force his speech when it encounters challenges. He speaks fluently but does not follow trends. He values morality and justice and despises immorality and infight. This is how good men and *junzi* make distinctions and deliver speeches. The *Book of Poetry* has it:

> As the long night is passing,
> I am engrossed in thinking.
> I never neglect ancient teaching
> Nor digress from the *li* and morality,
> Why should I mind others talking?

---

118. Here "the heart" refers to the mind. See note 1 in *Guiguzi* (2016, 39).

119. The hundred schools refer to different types of thought in the classical period (475–221 BCE), including Laozi, Kongzi, Mozi, Mengzi, Zhuangzi, Guiguzi, Xunzi, Hanfeizi, and others.

This explains what I said.

22.9 The speech (*yan* 言) of the *junzi* is thorough and yet refined. He is pragmatic and yet clear in definition. He moves high and low alternately and yet maintains the order. He uses correct names and is responsible for eloquence (*ci* 辭) for the purpose of demonstrating the mind (*zhi* 志) and morals (*yi* 義). He names types of eloquence according to his mind and duty (*yi* 義), making them correspond with one another effortlessly (*she* 舍).[120] A speech incompliant with this practice is treacherous. That said, names must agree with reality; eloquence must satisfactorily demonstrate outcomes. Then it is effortless indeed. Semblance (*wai* 外) results in unintelligibility (*ren* 訒), which the *junzi* disdains. But unlearned persons hold it as a treasure. This is why their speeches sound groundlessly crass, seemly profound and yet indistinct (*bu lei* 不類), clamorous and yet passionless. They resort to seductive naming and show off their dazzling eloquence without deep concerns about the mind and morality. For this reason, their long-winding speeches are of no significance. They work to achieve nothing. They are greedy but achieve no fame. As for wise men's words, dwelling on them makes learning effortless, acting on them brings security, and upholding them helps one establish oneself. All the successes fulfill one's wishes and steer him away from what disgusts him. Unlearned persons are the opposite. The *Book of Poetry* says:

> If you were a ghost or a monster,
> I could not see your true figure.
> If you have an image and a face,
> I can fully reveal your shape.
> This good song is a composition
> To uncover your circumvention.
> This explains what I said.

---

120. As a verb, 舍 means "to give up" or "to leave something alone." Hence the translation.

2.3 Spring-Autumn and Warring States Period (Classical)

A Treatise on Rhetoric by Hanfeizi[121] (韓非子 295–233 BCE): A Partial Translation of Hanfeizi with an Introduction and Commentary

Hui Wu

INTRODUCTION

Hanfeizi (280–233 BCE) was one of the princes of the State of Han and a student of Xunzi (荀子). Hanfeizi was fond of studies of epistemology, law, and statecraft and is known for his intellectual contribution to the Legal School (*fa jia* 法家) with the goal to strengthen the state and governance by law. As "the first Legalist" representing one of the five major schools of philosophy in Classical China, or the Warring States period,[122] Hanfeizi distinguished himself by trying to persuade rulers to lead their states through a legal system of rewards and penalties based on their own wisdom and conscience.[123] His thinking, Hanfeizi claimed, was derived from the Yellow Emperor and Laozi. A stutterer, Hanfeizi was unable to speak as eloquently as his contemporaries, but he was said to be good at writing books. Wang Gou (王構 1245–1310 CE), an editor for the School of Chinese History in the Hanlin Yuan (which was similar to a National Academy), commented that "Han Fei's books are exhaustive arguments (*shui* 說) on occurrences and their causes."[124] Hanfeizi wrote twenty books[125] containing fifty-five chapters that later appeared as a collection entitled *Hanfeizi*, whose main purpose was to persuade the King of Han to lead his state through a legal system.[126]

In addition to his advocacy for legal governance, Hanfeizi was said to write his treatises to criticize ministers and *zhong-heng* persuaders (a school of vertical and horizontal military strategies) who, he believed, "beguiled lords and people to gain their own advantages and benefits. As a result, wicked and villainous men were looting and committing violence at their will."[127] Outraged by corrupt officials with power who had done nothing to restore peace and security, Hanfeizi took it upon himself to write books "laboriously to clarify his propositions" yet with

---

121. See honorific naming of "*zi*" in the chapter on Confucius.

122. Lu 1998, 267.

123. Lu 1998, 258–87; Ma 2011, 2–3.

124. Gou 1937, 31. All translations are mine unless indicated otherwise.

125. He likely wrote these codices on bamboo slips or on silk. By the Warring States period, both types of materials were used for brush-writing (Xi 2002, 28–31).

126. Ma 2011, 2–5.

127. Yu and Shi 1999, 2.

an understanding that his connection to the royalty was not close enough to advance him to serving the King in person."[128]

Hanfeizi did provide some service, but briefly, for the State of Han and met the King of Qin (秦) after writing his treatises. It is recorded that when the King of Qin saw Hanfeizi's work, he said, "Alas, if we could only see this man and make his acquaintance, we would not regret it even if it meant death."[129] For this reason, the King of Qin attacked the State of Han. When the situation became critical, the King of Han sent Hanfeizi as an emissary to the State of Qin. The King of Qin was pleased to meet Hanfeizi but did not fully trust him. Li Si (李斯), the lead advisor for the King of Qin and also a former student of Xunzi who felt inferior to Hanfeizi, used the King's suspicion as an opportunity to slander Hanfeizi, calling him "one of the Noble Scions of Han," who would always "work for Han, not Ch'in [Qin]," and thus would not remain faithful to the king. He said to the king, "This is simply leaving yourself open for trouble. . . . [B]etter to punish him [now] for breaking the law."[130] Hanfeizi wished to present his case but could not win the audience of the King of Qin who had been convinced by the slander. Upon the permission of the King of Qin, Li Si sent someone to force Hanfeizi to poison himself. Later, the King of Qin regretted his own decision and sent someone to pardon Hanfeizi, who by this point was already dead.[131]

COMMENTARY ON HANFEIZI'S RHETORICAL TREATISE

The newly translated texts presented hereafter are based on the edition prepared by Wang Xianshen in 1896, the authoritative edition of *Hanfeizi*. There are two preexisting translations. One is by Burton Watson, presenting twelve chapters out of fifty-five in the original Chinese. It contains "The Difficulties of Persuasion" (*shui nan* 說难) but leaves out the other three chapters specifically on rhetoric. The other translation is by W. K. Liao in two volumes with Volume I published in 1939 and Volume II in 1959. A new translation is needed for two reasons. First, it replaces missing chapters, and second, to render a more accurate translation from a comparative rhetorical perspective, showing a consistent trajectory of rhetorical terminologies in cross-reference to other texts, enabling readers to make meaningful associations and develop reasonable interpretations.

The translated excepts here provide complex cultural and political insights into the private rhetorical setting where a persuader spoke to the single-person audience, the ruler. Those before Hanfeizi, such as Kongzi (Confucius), Xunzi, and Guiguzi, all addressed rhetorical concepts, principles, and methods. Research results also conform that rhetorical terms in *Hanfeizi,* such as *bian* (辯), *yan* (言), *yu* (語), *shui* (說), *shuo* (説), have evolved from the trea-

---

128. Ibid.
129. Ssu-Ma 1994, 29.
130. Ibid.
131. Ibid.

tises by his predecessors.[132] As Haixia Lan (in this book) and Xing Lu argue, like Confucius, Hanfeizi did not reject all speeches but made distinctions in speeches or persuasion (*yan* 言). Kongzi denounced those who used speech in a demoralized way to confuse their audience,[133] and so did Hanfeizi, who aimed to rectify the inadequacy of a statecraft founded on the leaders' virtue and relationships.[134] Xunzi emphasized *zheng ming* (正名) to define things clearly to represent truths or true reality, and so did Hanfeizi, who encouraged rulers to examine words and demand facts.[135]

Additionally, Hanfeizi's perspectives on rhetoric and his petition to the King of Han provide concrete scenarios for comparative studies of classical Chinese rhetoric, where persuaders were overpowered by their audience—a superior or a ruler—in a private setting. In other words, *Hanfeizi* explains complex Chinese rhetorical practices in which the unprivileged was trying to persuade the privileged. The power imbalance posed challenges to persuaders whose lives depended on the mood of the king to whom they provided counsel. The chapters entitled "The Difficulties of Speech (*nan yan* 难言)" and "The Difficulties of Persuasion (*shui nan* 說难)" reveal Hanfeizi's dilemma as a persuader and a critic of rhetoric. Aware of risks faced by persuaders, Hanfeizi warns that "advisors who engage themselves in proposition (*jian* 諫), persuasion (*shui* 說), discussion (*tan* 談), or argument (*lun* 論) cannot leave unexamined the likes and dislikes of the masters they serve before speaking."[136] He strengthens his point by contrasting twelve genres of eloquence that a king may reject for no good reason, arguing, "Should His Majesty distrust a speech, . . . the speaker would be found guilty of defamation, or at least, slander; or he would be charged with death penalty, suffering from the worst misfortune."[137]

Hanfeizi's warning also illustrates the complexities and nuances of rhetorical strategies prevalent in *Guiguzi*, particularly his teaching of tactics of listening and building connections with the audience.[138] While Hanfeizi warns persuaders of the mood swing of the single-person audience,[139] he also asks the audience, the top authority (*shang* 上), to listen to a speech carefully for its consequences, saying, "All words have consequences; speeches are responsible for their usefulness. For this reason, words spread among friends and groups should not gain their superior's ears."[140] As a rhetorical principle, Hanfeizi believes that both the persuader and the audience should be accountable, arguing, "If persuaded by a speech (*yan* 言) without examining it, one has no way to hold the subordinate accountable. If a speech is not held re-

---

132. Garrett 1993a, 13–39. Garrett 1993b, 105–15. Lu 1998. Lyon 2010, 350–66.

133. Lu 1998, 163.

134. Lyon 2010, 360.

135. *Hanfeizi* 2016, Chapter XVII.41.1.

136. *Hanfeizi* 2016, Chapter IV.12.7.

137. *Hanfeizi* 2016, Chapter IV.12.1.

138. Wu 2016, 26–28.

139. *Hanfeizi* 2016, Chapter IV.12.3–4.

140. *Hanfeizi* 2016, Chapter XVIII.48.6.

sponsible for its usefulness (*yong* 用), then vicious speeches (*xie shuo* 邪説) prevail."[141] Similar to Guiguzi who believed that the goal of rhetoric is building human connections, Hanfeizi believes that a long-term relationship is the key to successful persuasion[142]. Furthermore, Hanfeizi's legalist political strategies are said to have been dominated by three components, *fa* (法 penal law or standard), *shu* (術 strategy or strategic method), *shi* (勢 power position), which form Hanfeizi's own theory on politics and communication.[143] Not coincidentally, these terms appear in *Guiguzi*, with *fa* signifying a method or the principle of *Dao*,[144] *shu* rhetorical art or technique,[145] and *shi* authority, status, or situation of an affair.[146]

Following Guiguzi's theory of reflective listening (*fan ting zhi dao* 反聽之道), Hanfeizi devotes a passage titled "Examination of Speech (*can yan* 参言)" to rhetorical listening (*ting dao* 听道) and relates rhetorical principles to a legal system of reward and punishment, saying, "The master of the people [king] upholds the *Dao* to examine a speech for its usefulness and study its merit for reward. When the merit is rewarded, principles of reward and penalty are born."[147] Perhaps wishing to regulate persuasion by the reward-penalty system, Hanfeizi wrote another passage titled "Inquiries into Debate (*wen bian* 問辯)" to designate rhetorical power to a king's speech. He posits that "in a state ruled by scruples, His Majesty's decrees are the most venerated speech (*yan* 言); his laws are the rightest measures for all matters . . . [a]ny speech or conduct that deviates from the law must be forbidden."[148] In support of the ruler's authority of judging eloquence, Hanfeizi distinguishes him from his predecessors by imagining "the law as a speech act, a communicative act" "to warn rulers and ministers that rhetorical acts are dangerous."[149] The four excerpted translations of *Hanfeizi* presented below demonstrate the abstract and technical complexities of Chinese rhetorical practice in the Classical Period. In making correlations and responses among theorists of rhetoric as a comparative method, I hope scholars and non-specialists in rhetoric can form a coherent historical understanding of the development of and debate about rhetoric in antiquity.

141. Ibid.

142. *Hanfeizi* 2016, Chapter IV.12.5.

143. Lu 1998; Lyon 2010, 360.

144. *Guiguzi* 2016, Chapter III.1.1–7.

145. *Guiguzi* 2016, Chapter III.1.1.

146. *Guiguzi* 2016, Chapter I.5.1, II.8.

147. *Hanfeizi* 2016, Chapter XVIII.48.6.

148. *Hanfeizi* 2016, Chapter XVII.41.1.

149. Lyon 2010, 360–61; *Hanfeizi* 2016, Chapter IV.12.4.

Translation

Book I, Chapter 3

The Difficulties of Speech (nan yan 难言)[150]

I.3.1 Your servant, Fei, has no difficulty in delivering a speech (*yan*). The reason for the difficulties in speaking (*yan*) is that a fluent smooth speech, eloquent and orderly, would be considered ostentatious and inessential, while an honest courteous speech, straightforward and comprehensive, would be considered awkward and disorganized. A speech with many references and citations, full of illustrations and analogies, would be considered superfluous and useless. A speech that generalizes deliberative details, succinct and unembellished, would be considered blunt and unmindful. A speech that is acute and quick to the point, provoking private feelings, would be considered self-assured and bellicose. A speech that is erudite and extensive, visionary and profound, would be considered boastful and impractical. A speech about family planning and household trivia, numerating details one by one, would be considered tasteless. A speech that sounds worldly without critical words (*ci* 辭) and insight would be considered timid and ingratiating. A speech far from the conventions, uncompliant and eager for changes of social norms, would be considered preposterous. A speech of adroit witty argument (*bian* 辯), elaborate and exquisite, would be considered pleonastic. A speech that does not draw upon classical canons, a simple and sincere speech (*xin yan*信言), would be considered unlearned. A speech that occasionally quotes the *Book of Poetry* and *Book of History*, following the principles and referring to the ancients, would be considered a recitation. For these reasons, your servant, Fei, worries about the difficulties of speech.

I.3.2 Therefore, while estimates and measures are right, they may not be used; while reasons and principles are flawless, they may be not followed. Should His Majesty distrust a speech for any of the aforementioned reasons, the speaker would be found guilty of defamation, or at least, slander; or he would be charged with death penalty, suffering from the worst misfortune.

Book IV Chapter 12

The Difficulties of Persuasion (shui nan 說难)

IV.12.1 Generally speaking, the difficulties of persuasion are not that I do not know the facts needed to persuade others; nor is it that I have no reasoning ability to make myself understood; nor is it that I do not have the audacity to exercise my persuasive power to the fullest. The difficulties of persuasion, on the whole, reside in reading the mind of the audience and in choosing proper persuasive words.

---

150. W. K. Liao translated 难言 (*nan yang*) as "On the Difficulty in Speaking: A Memorial." This chapter is missing from Burton Watson's translation (1964).

IV.12.2 If the superior[151] pursues fame and high status but is being persuaded of big monetary gains, he would look down upon the persuader, considering him low-bred and detestable who should be shunned from afar. If the superior wants monetary gains quietly but is being persuaded of fame and high status, he would consider the persuader insincere and ignorant of worldly affairs and reject him. If the superior seeks monetary gains quietly and yet openly expresses interest in fame and high status, when persuaded of fame and high status, he would accept the persuader in public but draw distance in private. Reversely, when persuaded of monetary gains, he would accept the persuasion privately but reject the persuader in public. These [complexities] should not be unexamined.

IV.12.3 Therefore, success is achieved secretly; divulging it in words (*yu* 語) brings failure. Sometimes it is not that the persuader intentionally leaks the information but that his speech (*yu* 語) happens to uncover the secret of his superior. If so, the persuader is in danger. When he [the superior] openly declares to pursue a business but intends to accomplish it secretly through a different task, if the persuader knows not only the purpose of the declared business but also that of the undeclared one, then the persuader's life is in danger. When the persuader devises an extraordinary plan that meets the needs, if other wise men know about it through weighing (*chuai* 揣) surrounding situations and divulge it, he [the superior] would assume that it is the persuader's own doing. If so, the persuader is in danger. When closeness and friendship are not fully developed, if the persuader's words convey intimate knowledge and has brought success, his persuasive effectiveness is recognized, but his reward (*de* 德) is neglected. If the persuasion does not take effect, while failure looms, the persuader would arouse suspicion to himself and put his life in danger. With regard to high-ranking officials' faults, if a persuader honestly speaks of rites and justice thereby to point out misconducts, he puts his life in danger. Sometimes high-ranking officials[152] have acquired a certain scheme that leads to success. They give credit to themselves. If the persuader knows all about it because of his own participation, his life is in danger. When the persuader tries to impose what is beyond capability and to stop what cannot be stopped, he puts himself in danger. Therefore, a persuader who discusses men of power[153] rouses suspicion of dividing people. A persuader who discusses men of trivial influence rouses suspicion of showing off his own power. A persuader who appeals to his superior's likes is considered seeking favors; a persuader who addresses his superior's dislikes is considered probing feelings. A persuader who speaks concisely and straightforwardly is considered unwise and incompetent. A persuader who argues on and on about rice and salt

---

151. Like classical Chinese prose, *Hanfeizi* seldom specifies the subjects of sentences. Although the audience of the persuader can be read as the ruler (*Hanfeizi* 2016; Liao 1939, 1959; Watson 2003 73–79), the text does not specify it, hence "the superior" in translation to refer to any audience who holds power over the persuader.

152. The original is 貴人 (*gui ren*) to mean "persons with honorable titles". The term indicates that the audience of the persuasion refers to a superior, and not merely to the ruler.

153 The original is 大人 (*da ren*), which means ancient sages or men of power. Liao translates it as "great men" (1939, 107).

[trivial matters] is considered obsessive and uninteresting.[154] A persuader who speaks of only the main point without detailed elaboration is considered a coward who dares not to express himself fully. A persuader who speaks incessantly is considered rude and arrogant. These difficulties of persuasion should not be unrecognized.

IV.12.4 After all, the business of persuasion is about knowing how to polish a speech to dignify what the superior is proud of and to play down what he is ashamed of. If he acts urgently out of a selfish motive, the persuader should encourage it in the name of public responsibility. If he cannot help but act upon a dishonorable intent, the persuader should emphasize its positive side and minimize its negative side to derail the act. If the superior holds a high goal in mind but has no adequate capacity to realize it, the persuader should point out the faults and help him see bad consequences, making it a virtue to take no action. If he [the superior] wants to show off his intelligence and ability, varied instances should be used to supply him with more of the similar ideas and provide more evidence for the purpose of making him borrow you [the persuader] as resources yet without showing your awareness. This way his intelligence is further enhanced. If you wish to propose a policy of peaceful coexistence, be sure to name (*ming* 名) and clarify (*ming* 明) it in honorable words and imply that it satisfies his personal interests as well. If you wish to speak about risks of an undertaking, then show how it would invite destruction and censure, while implying how detrimental it is to himself as well. Praise other men whose deeds are similar to his; strategize various matters that meet his plan. If other men are involved in the same vices as he is, make effort to camouflage them and demonstrate their harmlessness. If other men have encountered failures as he has, make sure to ameliorate them and downplay the losses. If he shows off his strength, do not propose matters beyond his overall capability. If he is daring in decision making, never talk about his past faults to anger him. If he is smart at scheming, never talk about his past failures to embarrass him. Your overall intent should draw no resistance or antagonism; your word (*ci* 辭) and speech (*yan* 言) should cause no criticism or friction. This way, you can rise high with any intelligent argument (*zhi bian* 智辯). Acquire this method, and you can dispel any suspicion of your devotion and intimacy to deliver any eloquence (*ci* 辭) without reserve.

IV.12.5 Yi Yin (伊尹)[155] was a cook, and Bai Lixi (百里奚) a captivated slave. Both pleased their superiors through their positions. Both became sages later but could not avoid using their bodies in hard labor to advance themselves. What a degradation they went through! Today what I am saying (*yan* 言) could be regarded as an utterance by a cook or a slave. However, if heard and adopted to change the world, then my speech is no disgrace a learned man should be ashamed of. A person who has provided service for a long time gains deep knowledge of his

154 The original is 交 (*jiao*), meaning 猥交 (*wei jiao*, boring company).

155. According to *Chinese Encyclopedia*, Yi Yin was also named Yi Zhi (伊挚1649–1549 BCE), the cook as part of the dowry of Lady Xin (*Xin Shi*莘氏) when she married Shang Tang (商湯), founder of the Shang Dynasty (1600–1048 BCE). Yi Yin later was appointed as a critical minister who helped Shang Tang conquer the Xia Dynasty (夏, 2070–1600 BCE).

superior. The plan he proposes causes no suspicion; the argument (*zheng* 争) he puts forward draws no blame. This way, he can clearly demonstrate benefits and harms to help achieve success; he can directly speak about the right and wrong to glorify himself. With this type of support on both sides, persuasion (*shui* 說) is decidedly successful.

IV.12.6 Legend has it that King Zheng Wu (鄭武公) of Zheng intended to attack the State of Hu (胡). So he first married his daughter to the King of Hu to make him happy. Then he asked his ministers, "I want to exercise my military power. Which state should I invade?" The highest official, Guan Qisi (關其思),[156] replied, "The State of Hu could be attacked." Upon the words, King Zheng Wu lashed into rage and had Guan executed,[157] saying, "Hu is a brother state. How could you suggest to attack it?" King Hu, upon hearing of this, believed that King Zheng was his true friend and took no defensive measures. Then King Zheng made a surprise attack to occupy Hu. Once upon a time, there was a rich man of Song (宋).[158] A heavy rain damaged a wall of his house. His son said, "If not repaired, we would have a break-in." The father of his next-door neighbor also said so. When night fell, there was indeed a break-in, which costed the rich man a big fortune. His family then praised his son for his wisdom but casted suspicion about their neighbor. Both men made right comments. Yet, the favorite advisor was executed, while the other caused suspicion to himself. For this reason, it is not difficult to acquire knowledge; what is difficult is how to apply the knowledge. Similarly, Rao Zhao (繞朝)[159] said the right thing. He was esteemed as a sage by [State] Jin (晉) but executed by [State] Qin (秦). These [cases] should not be unexamined.

IV.12.7 In ancient times, Mi Zixia (彌子瑕) was favored by His Majesty Wei (衛). According to the state law of Wei, anyone who secretly rode in His Majesty's carriage would have the feet amputated. One night, Mi Zixia was told that his mother was ill. Without asking permission, Mi rode in His Majesty's carriage to go home. Upon hearing of it, His Majesty praised Mi, saying, "How filial! For the sake of his mother, he forgot that his feet might be amputated." On a stroll around an orchard with His Majesty, Mi took a bite of a peach. Savoring its sweet juice, Mi stopped eating to give the rest of it to His Majesty, who then exclaimed, "He loved me so much that he forgot his own craving and gave me his food." Later, Mi Zixia's looks faded, so did His Majesty's affection. Then when His Majesty felt unpleased, he said, "Just like this, he neglected my permission to ride in my carriage and let me eat what was left from

---

156. King Zheng Wu's most favorite advisor.

157. It probably took place in 763 BCE (Watson 2003, 77).

158. Song should be Zheng (Wang 2016, 99).

159. It was said that in 614 BCE, Shi Hui (士會), an official of Jin, defected to Qin and that Jin sent a man to Qin as a defect to retrieve Shi Hui for fear that Qin would employ him. Rao Zhao unsuccessfully advised the King of Qin against letting Shi Hui return. When Shi Hui was about to leave for Jin, Rao Zhao said to him, "It was not that Qin had no wise man; it was because my advice was not adopted, even though it was right." Upon his return to the State of Jin, Shi Hui sent a spy to pass Rao's words to the King of Qin, who then felt insulted and executed Rao as a result (Gao 2015: 122; Liao 1939, 113; Watson 2003, 78; *Hanfeizi* 2016, 91–92).

the peach he had bitten into." Mizi [Master Mi] never changed his demeanor and was consistent from the very beginning. That a merit became a fault was decided by the change from favor to disfavor. If you gain the favor, you are praised for your intelligence and endowed with affection. Disfavor makes your wisdom forgotten and your fault worsened, casting you in estrangement. Therefore, advisors who engage themselves in proposition (*jian* 諫),[160] persuasion (*shui* 說), discussion (*tan* 談), or argument (*lun* 論)[161] cannot leave unexamined the likes and dislikes of the masters they serve before speaking (*shuo* 說).

IV.12.8 It is said that a dragon can be a harmless worm, whose back can serve as a saddle. However, a-foot-long scales on his neck can kill anybody who chances to rub them the wrong way. The ruler of people also has killing scales. If a persuader (*shui zhe* 說者) can avoid rubbing them the wrong way, then he can have opportunities.

Book XVII Chapter 41

Inquiries into Debate (wen bian 問辯)[162]

Somebody asked, "Where does debate (*bian* 辯) come from?" Somebody answered, "It comes from a superior's lack of scruple." The inquirer asked, "How can the superior's lack of scruple give rise to debate?" The answer was that "in a state ruled by scruples, His Majesty's decrees are the most venerated speech (*yan* 言); his laws are the rightest measures for all matters. There are no two equally venerated speeches; there are no two equally rightest measures. For this reason, any speech or conduct that deviates from the law must be forbidden. Without law, when considering suggestions to counter conspiracies, adapt to disruptions, generate profits, or plan business, the top authority (*shang* 上)[163] must pay attention to words (*yan* 言) and demand facts. If the words (*yan* 言) are true, grant a rich reward; if they are false, impose a severe penalty. Given the demand, unintelligent persuaders may stay silent for fear of penalty; intelligent ones then would have nobody to whom they can deliver a counterargument (*song* 訟). This is why there is no debate (*bian* 辯). In an unruly state, however, when the top authority issues decrees, his subjects draw upon classics (*wen* 文) and learning (*xue* 學) to criticize them. When his ministries issue laws, citizens alter them as they wish. His Majesty neglects his own laws but honors learned men's wisdom and conducts. Such is the reason that men of letters and learning are everywhere in this world. Indeed, words (*yan* 言) and conducts have their functions and practicalities. When one uses a newly sharpened arrow to take a random

---

160. See Xing Lu's nuanced study of *jian* (諫) (1998, 78-80).

161. 論 can also mean "discussion," depending on the context.

162. 辯 means to argue, debate, reason, or dispute. Liao translated it into "dialectic" (1959, 207), which deviates from its roots in persuasion. See Lu's study of 辯 (1998, 84–90) and Lu and Frank (1993, 445–63).

163. 上 (shang above or up) here means a ruler or a king. The translation follows Hanfeizi's choice of diction.

shot, its pointed head may hit the tip of a flying feather by chance. This type of shooter cannot be called skillful archers because of the lack of consistency. Just image a target that is five inches in diameter and an arrow that is shot at it from a hundred feet away. Nobody but Yi[164] and Feng Meng can hit the target consistently. The consistency with which Yi and Feng Meng hit the target of five-inch diameter is called skillfulness, while the inconsistency of random shots which may hit the tip of a flying feather by chance is called incompetence. Today when listening to the word (*yan* 言) and observing a conduct, if one does not use function and practicality as the target, he would accept persuasion (*shui* 說) that shoots randomly in intelligible words with powerful action. In an unruly world, people, when listening to speeches (*yan* 言), take unintelligible words as intelligence and extensive quotations (*bo wen* 博文) as debate (*bian* 辯). When observing conducts, they regard divergence from the norm as excellence and offense to the top authority as resistance. Even the master of his people (*ren zhu* 人主) delivers persuasion (*shui* 說) and argument (*bian* 辯) whose diction requires deciphering and esteems resistance as good conducts. Those, who craft laws and strategies (*shu* 術) and who ought to establish criteria for acceptable and unacceptable behaviors, do nothing to differentiate and rectify argument (*lun* 論), eloquence (*ci* 辭), and dispute (*zheng* 爭). For this reason, men wearing ropes of literati and carrying swords are abundant, while farmers and soldiers are few. Speeches (*ci* 詞) and verse (*zhang* 章) about "Hard and White (*jian bai* 堅白)"[165] and "Mercilessness (*wu hou* 無厚)"[166] prevail, while constitutions and decrees stand still. This is why it is said, "When the top authority is unscrupulous, debate comes into being."

---

164. Yi (羿) or Hou Yi (后羿), is said to be the teacher of Feng Meng (逢蒙). Both were known for their divine archery in the Xia Dynasty (2205–1766 BCE). Descending from Heaven to be commissioned by King Yao (堯), Yi shot down nine of the ten suns to end their scorching heat that had brought drought and deprived people of food and water.

165. It is said that Gong Sun Long (公孫龍) in the State of Zhao (趙) put forward an argument about the difference between "hard" and "white" that are used to describe of a stone to prove that "hard" and "white" could be two separate characteristics, because "white" can only be seen, and "hard" can be only felt. So even if both are part of a stone, they are independent of each other (Ssu-Ma 1994, 185).

166. 厚 (hou) here means affection or mercy. 無厚 (wu hou) can mean "lacking mercy" or "lacking depth". There are two versions about the origin of 無厚. One claims that Dengxizi (鄧析子) wrote a piece titled "On Mercilessness" (wu hou pian 無厚篇) in the Spring and Autumn Period (770-403 BCE). It uses the analogy of merciless natural disasters to bemoan injustices and punishments that a ruler mercilessly inflicts on the people who have committed theft due to poverty, while the ruler and his officials were living a luxury life (Wang 2016, 430; Liao 1959; 209). The other tale claims that Hui Shi (惠施 circa 370-310 BCE) was the one who pointed out that the flat surface on earth had no depth (Hanfeizi 2016, 465). But Liao insists that it was Dengxizi who wrote the piece (1959, 209).

Book XVIII. Chapter 48

Eight Principles (ba jing 八經)

XVIII.48.6 Examination of Speech (can yan 參言) [167]

If persuaded by a speech (*yan* 言) without examining it, one has no way to hold a subordinate accountable. If a speech is not held responsible for its usefulness (*yong* 用), then vicious speeches (*xie shuo* 邪說) prevail.[168] A speech that sounds true is because numerous people believe it; the untrue (*bu ran zhi wu* 不然之物), if believed by ten people, may still be subject to doubt. If believed by a hundred people, then it becomes true. If believed by a thousand people, then it is difficult to dispel (*bu ke jie ye* 不可解也). A stutterer's words are susceptible to doubt; an eloquent debater's words sound believable. Treacherous persons who take advantage of their superiors use the mass of people as sources and rely on their beliefs in embellished arguments to cover up personal agendas. If the master of the people (*ren zhu* 人主) is not indignant and does not conduct examinations, his power would only support his inferiors. The master upholding the *Dao* examines a speech for its usefulness and study its merit for reward. When the merit is rewarded, principles of reward and penalty are born. For this reason, whoever delivers useless arguments are never kept by the court; those who are appointed but conduct faulty business would be removed from their positions and deprived of power. Those who deliver exaggerated grand eloquence would be driven to their wit's end; rewarded treacherous speeches would rouse indignation. Disappointing business outcomes without extraneous hindrance are considered frauds for which ministers can be indicted. All words have consequences; speeches are responsible for their usefulness. For this reason, words spread among friends and groups should not gain their superior's ears. According to the way of listening (*ting dao* 听道),[169] honest speeches by people and ministers should be used to tell if a speech is malevolent. Extensive arguments should be heard prior to an action. When the master of the people lacks wisdom, perpetrators would take advantage of him. According to the way of an astute wise master (*ming zhuzhi dao* 明主之道),[170] when pleased, he would seek what meets his needs; when outraged, he would critically examine what constructs the proposition. When not swayed by emotions anymore, reexamine the argument in order to understand damages and honors and draw lines between public and personal motives.[171] Numerous advices may be presented to

---

167. 參 (can or 糝) means to examine, inspect, review, or test as a verb; as a noun it means a subordinate. Liao translated 參言 into "Comparing Different Speeches" (1959, 269).

168. Wang Xianshen notes, "Listening to a speech without paying attention to its usefulness, His Majesty would be pleased by malevolent vicious eloquence" (Hanfeizi 2016, 478).

169. See Wu, (2016, 27-29) and Guiguzi (2016, I.2.3) for the way of listening.

170. See *Guiguzi* for the way to be "a wise conscientious master" (2016, II.12).

171. Wang Xianshen quotes Wang Xianqian to say, "When an argument sounds pleasant, the ruler should examine if it is true or false; when outraged by a speech that exposes evils (*jie yan* 訐言), he should investigate if it holds truth or untruth. When his emotions die down, he should examine the

show off intelligence and force His Majesty to select one so that the advisors can avoid consequences. For this reason, when multiple types of counsel are presented simultaneously, only a fallen ruler would take them. Speeches that speculate the future should not be delivered to His Highness to prevent ill outcomes; today's proven word (*fu yan* 符言)[172] can only be testified by the future to know if it is a falsified or honest speech.[173] The way of an astute wise master never tolerates minsters' contradictory propositions (*jian* 諫) but make them responsible for one. Language (*yu* 語) should not have a free rein but must be tested by examinations. Thereupon perpetrators have no way to advance.

---

arguments again. Hereby their damages or honors and private or public motives can be detected" (*Hanfeizi* 2016, 480).

172. See note 150 of Chapter 12 in *Guiguzi* for the original meaning of 符言 (*fu yan*) (83).

173. Wang Xianshen notes, "Speeches proven true by the future are honest; otherwise they are falsified. '符' indicates consistency" (*Hanfeizi* 2016, 480).

2.4 Han Dynasty

Rhetorical Instruction by Ban Zhao (班 昭 49-120 CE): A Partial Translation of *Lessons for Women* (女誡 *Nü Jie*) with an Introduction and Commentary

Hui Wu

INTRODUCTION

The previous section shows that males and their instructions dominate Chinese rhetoric. Yet, women also taught and performed rhetoric. Although her *Lessons for Women* was allegedly the first book for women, Ban Zhao referred to two previous books by women—*Principles for Women* (*Nü Xian* 女憲) and *Rules for Women* (*Nü Ze* 女則). However, both authors remain unknown, and their texts lost. Ban's book became the first on record. Known for her classical learning and writing, Ban was summoned by Emperor He (*Han he di* 漢和帝) of the late Han Dynasty (25–220 CE) to teach classics, poetry, and historiographies to the queen, concubines, and court ladies to develop a virtuous environment for the emperor. At forty years of age, she assisted his brother, Ban Gu (班固) to complete the *Book of Han* (*Han Shu* 漢書) left unfinished upon the death of their father, Ban Biao (班彪), the court historian tasked with the book. Also called the *Book of Former Han*, or *Book of West Han*, the book presents a detailed complete history of the early Han Dynasty. In recognition of her talent and integrity, Ban was called Cao Dagu (曹大家 Master Cao), a combination of her husband's last name "Cao" with the honorific title "master" to distinguish her from a male master, "*zi*" (子). Ban's *Lessons for Women* was born when the Han Dynasty, or neoclassical period,[174] was going through a renaissance of classical learning and revival of Confucianism, after Qin Shi Huang (秦始皇 First Emperor Qin) ruling in 246 BCE–210 BCE burned books and persecuted Confucian scholars to stop debates about his ordinances.[175] The late Han Dynasty saw 853 books consisting of 6,437 volumes being collected without political bias.[176] While persuasion in a private setting dominated rhetorical practices in the classical period, varied writing genres rose in the neoclassical period in an effort to edit and collect classics, such as documentations, commentaries, and historiographies, all commissioned by emperors. For instance, in 94 BCE, Sima Qian under the auspices of Emperor Wu of Han (*Han Wudi* 漢武帝) completed *Shiji* (史記 *The Grand Scribe's Records*) to record 2,500 years of history. Liu Xiang (劉向 77–6 BCE) also compiled biographies and historiographies, including *Biographies of Exemplary Women*

---

174. Philosophers often call it the neo-Confucian period, because of the exclusive learning of Confucian classics. However, the commentaries and historiographies were not limited only to Confucian classics.

175. Ssu-Ma 1994, 341.

176. Yu and Shi 1999, 204–207.

(*Lie N ü Zhuan* 列女傳), a collection of legacies about women who followed Confucian rites. The neoclassical period further revived Confucianism to strengthen central control and uniformity of thought, while denouncing traveling persuaders' eloquence as amoral and dangerous.[177] Meanwhile, a new writing genre similar to Western expository writing emerged. Dong Zhongshu (董仲舒 179–104 BCE) wrote *Luxuriant Gems of the Spring and Autumn* (*Chun Qiu Fan Lu* 春秋繁露)[178] to articulate his interpretations of Confucius's thought. Dong's "novel cosmology" unknown before his time incorporated "Daoist, Legalist, and *Yin-Yang* naturalist teachings into Confucianism," literally institutionalizing it as the governing orthodoxy.[179]

Moreover, Confucian learning was reinforced through formal education thanks to advances of writing technologies. Compared with writing on bamboo slips, wood boards, or silk before, writing on paper was easier and faster, resulting abundant production of writing and large scale of literacy development. The first Imperial University (*tai xue*大學) was established in 124 BCE; an annual civic service examination system was also created to select promising males for state service.[180] In other words, in the classical period, it was possible for learned men of rhetoric to develop a career of government service through advising and persuading the king. Now they had to memorize and explicate Confucian classics in writing for the highest test scores possible before being selected for civic service.

The state needs for promising officials made it compelling to ensure that boys received superb education to cultivate their minds early on for the service career. But this demand also created a paradox for women's education. On the one hand, women, who bore the responsibility of educating their young sons at home, should have access to rhetorical and classical learning. On the other hand, although women bore the responsibility, their education was not formalized into a system. It was for this reason that Ban wrote her book near the end of her life. She felt that she had yet to teach her daughters how to perform rhetoric to survive as wives and daughters-in-law in a severely unequal gendered society and to advocate for young women's education.

Ban's book began circulating to Japan in the Ming Dynasty (1368–1633 CE). Japanese women read it in a set of four women's books from China, except that the last one was *Women's Filial Duties* (*Nü Xiao Jing* 女孝經).[181] During the years of Emperor Kangxi (康熙1654–1711 CE) in the mid-Qing Dynasty, *Lessons for Women* became the first of the four "women's classics" compiled by Wang Xiang (王相). The first three books in his collection are the same as those in the Japanese edition—*Lessons for Women*, *Women's Analects*, *The Doctrine of the Inner Chamber*. But the last one in Wang's edition is *A Brief Survey of Exemplary Women* (*Nü*

---

177. Wu 2016, 19.

178. The author of the book remains controversial. But most scholars have accepted the authenticity of the author and the text (Queen 1996, 5).

179. Wang 2015, 219; Queen 1996, 3.

180. Doran 2017, 97.

181. *Nü si shu* 2016, 4.

Fan Jielu 女范捷录) compiled by his mother, Wang Jiefu, or Madam Liu (Liu Shi 劉氏).[182] These four books for women were meant to serve as the counterpart to *sishu* (四書), the four Confucian classics for men—*Great Learning* (*Da Xue* 大学), *The Analects* (*Lun Yu* 論語), *The Doctrine of the Mean* (*Zhong Yong* 中庸) and *Mencius* (*Mengzi* 孟子). Although they are called "women's books" in China and "conduct books" or "instruction texts" in the West,[183] the four books for women are rhetorical instruction books, because of their teaching of a women-centered philosophy of rhetoric and reconceptualization of rhetorical terms and strategies in the dominant male tradition. The following commentary will demonstrate how Ban performs rhetoric and how she overturns the gender hierarchy to teach rhetoric to young women.

COMMENTARY ON BAN'S RHETORICAL TEACHING

Although many Chinese scholars read Ban's primary concerns as those about women's virtues, duties, and status to meet societal expectations,[184] their reading tends to overlook her embodiment and teaching of a re-gendered rhetoric that counterbalances male power. Also, a modern feminist perspective may misread her recommendation of women to humble themselves as support for gender subordination. Her encouragement of women's humility shows her keen awareness of a gendered reality and her *yin-yang* rhetorical motions "help women exercise agency within their marital families and respect and influence."[185]

A careful reading proves that Ban was familiar with the rhetorical tradition to practice multifaceted *yin-yang* rhetoric, specifically through the strategy and teaching of self-degradation, or female humility, to broker space for women to perform rhetoric. In other words, Ban teaches and preforms an embodied rhetoric that enables women "to deploy *yin* to acquire the gain of *yang*."[186] The opening sentence in her book serves as an example. It reads,

> I, the unworthy writer, am unsophisticated, unenlightened, and by nature unintelligent, but I am fortunate both to have received not a little favor from my scholarly father, and to have had a mother and instructresses upon whom to rely for a literary education as well as for training in good manners.[187]

Her strategy—yielding herself to traditional expectations of women and then presenting herself as a beneficiary of women's education—is what Guiguzi calls "deploying *yin* to acquire

---

182. Shi was often used to indicate the maiden name of a married woman who loses her first and surname upon marriage. Hence no record on Madam Liu's first name.

183. These books are hardly equivalent to conduct books in the Western context that have guided women's social, non-academic lives. While instructional, as Lisa Raphals identifies (1998, 249), these books specifically teach rhetorical performance to women.

184. Wen 2013, Chapter 1.

185. Bacabac 2018, 169.

186. *Guiguzi* 2016, Chapter II.10.3.

187. Wang 2003, 178.

the gain of *yang*."[188] In Ban's performance, *yin* is lowering her female self, even in disparaging terms, to "yield to the inside" and "to shape situations;"[189] then when the situation shaped by *yin* naturally intersects with *yang*, she moves on to credit her parents with her own education. This recognition involves both *yin* and *yang* moves. On the one hand, she yields to the traditional expectation of the humble female through *yin*; on the other hand, she grasps the interactive moment of *yin* and *yang* to lead to an implied recognition of her as a female sage with 'literary talent" and "moral integrity."[190] The motion of *yang* allows Ban to "reach out' and "take action."[191] In other words, the *yin-yang* moves interact to give her authority to speak out and share wisdom. Her rhetorical performance embodies a *yin-yang* tactic Guiguzi recommends—embracing virtues to acquire *yin* through *yang* and adding force to acquire *yang* through *yin*.[192]

This *yin-yang* rhetorical principle is constantly and consistently exemplified in Ban's rhetorical performance paired with her keen awareness of the gender hierarchy wherein women are born subordinate to men. For this reason, even after she has established herself as a highly respected sagely teacher and even after she has brought up her son and educated him successfully to become a high-ranking officer who "has unprecedentedly received the extraordinary privilege of wearing the Gold and he Purple."[193] Ban makes a self-diminutive *yin* motion to say that "Being careless, and by nature stupid, I taught and trained (my children) without system."[194] The *yin* motion allows her to acquire *yang*, with which she then presents her son's achievement as a result of her education. Although sounding self-debasing, Ban implies that she was the first woman who trained her son successfully and who was ready to establish a system of education for women. Her rhetorical performance involves sophisticated *yin-yang* strategies to establish authority to argue against tradition that has excluded women from formal education. She now adds force to acquire *yang*, saying, "Yet, only to teach men and not to teach women—is that not ignoring the essential relation between them? According to the *Rites*, by the age of eight, boys begin to learn to read. At the age of fifteen, they should begin great learning. Why can't it be the principle (for girls)?"[195] She then teaches women the same rhetorical strategy. By humbling themselves, she believes, women can build personal reputations through *yin* to achieve *yang*, which makes their long speeches possible without causing others to detest them.[196]

---

188. *Guiguzi* 2016, Chapter II.10.3.
189. *Guiguzi* 2016, Chapter I.1.6.
190. Wang 2003, 177.
191. *Guiguzi* 2016, Chapter I.1.6.
192. Ibid.
193. Wang 2003, 178.
194. Ibid.
195. Shen 2012, 8. All quotations of Ban in Shen's edition are my translations to show correlated lexicons in Ban and *Guiguzi*.
196. Shen 2012, Chapter 4.

Once she has established her authority, Ban re-genders the *yin-yang* concept against the unequal *yin-yang* gender positions established by Dong Zhongshu in his *Luxuriant Gems of the Spring and Autumn*. Dong integrated *yin-yang* into Confucianism, not to guide rhetorical performance as Guiguzi had done, but to form a new philosophy of nature, the human , and gender.[197] The new genre of expository writing gave Dong means to not only explicate concepts in Confucian classics to form his own theory on state governance but also define *yin-yang* into a hierarchical relationship that subordinated women as a result.[198] He labels the sun, superiors, and males as *yang*, and the moon, subordinates, and females as *yin*, with *yang* having authority over *yin*.[199] Dong's prescription of *yin-yang* has perpetuated unequal gender stratification in Han China at large. In other words, while Guiguzi established *yin-yang* as the foundational philosophy in the male rhetorical tradition, Dong reshaped the concept into signifiers of gender hierarchy. Within this severe gender hierarchy and with an understanding of *yin-yang* in the rhetorical tradition, Ban established her authority through humility, she argues, "The Way of man and wife is intimately connected with *yin* and *yang* to lead to the full achievement of omniscient intellectual conscience (*shen ming* 神明)."[200] Her redefinition of *yin-yang* enabled her to argue that "*Yin* and *yang* are of different natures, so are different behaviors (*xing* 行) of men and women. The virtue of *yang* is fortitude (*gang* 刚); the virtue of *yin* is resilience (*rou* 柔)."[201] Here she reshapes Dong's sexually unequal *yin-yang* theory into an interdependent and interactive notion of equity to bestow positive traits and characters upon the female. Then Ban suggests, "Should a husband be unworthy, then he possesses nothing by which to manage (*yu* 御 or serve) his wife; should a wife be unworthy, then she possesses nothing by which to serve (*shi* 事) her husband . . . The purpose of these two is the same."[202] In so doing, Ban reveals the *Dao* [truth] of gender relations and conceptually places two sexes on an equal ground.

Having outlined women's social position, Ban Zhao establishes four canons of women's rhetoric—morality, language use, self-presentation, and diligent work in Chapter 4, where she stages a female authoritative figure who upholds moral principles to discipline the family. She is "calm, peaceful, faithful, and poised to maintain chastity and order" and performs as a sage of rhetoric who chooses the right word for the right occasion. These qualities strengthen a woman's authority at work and in society as a result. She can put the house and social activities in order because she is the head and the center of the family. It is reasonable to point out that Ban takes advantage of the Confucian notion of "state family" (*guo jia* 國家) to place the woman on the central stage. The notion of "state family" regards the public and domestic domains as equally important. Because the family is the foundation of the state, women's work is as important as men's. The Confucian teaches that "the ancients who wished clearly to exemplify illustrious virtue through the world would first set up good government in their

---

197. Dong 2016, 163–78, 289–326, 371–422.
198. Wang 2003, 209.
199. Wang 2003, 215–16.
200. Shen 2012, 7; Ban's term corresponds with that in *Guiguzi* (2016, Chapters II.12.3, III.1.1).
201. Shen 2012, 9.
202. Shen 2012, 7.

states. Wishing to cultivate their persons, they would first rectify their families . . ."[203] Ban's employment of the interconnection between state and family to give rhetorical space—the family—to women.[204] As the last statement in Chapter 4 shows, Ban's familiarity with classical teaching and ability to form her own philosophy of rhetoric enable her to establish not only herself but also other women as authoritative persons who exercise benevolence (*ren* 仁) to function in the state by managing the home, where they assume exclusive responsibilities to manage their husbands and educate their sons for state service.

Lessons for Women consists of seven chapters. The newly translated Chapter 4 that follows is based on the edition prepared by Wang Xiang, which is the authoritative version for later editions, English translations of Ban's book are available in *Image of Women in Chinese Thought and Culture* by Robin Wang and *The Confucian Four Books for Women* by Anna A. Pang-White. The new translation of Chapter 4 highlights Ban's rhetorical teaching from a historical perspective, particularly the terms that have appeared in previous male rhetorical treatises.

Translation of Ban's Rhetorical Teaching to Women

Chapter 4 女行 (Nü Xing)

Women's Self-Presentation

The female presents herself according to four principles. The first is womanly virtue (*de* 德). The second is womanly speech (*yan* 言). The third is womanly presence (*rong* 容). The last is womanly work (*gong* 功). As for womanly virtue, it does not mean brilliant gift or exceptional distinction. Womanly speech does not mean eloquent mouth (*ban kou* 辯口) or acute words (*li ci* 利詞). Womanly presence does not mean glowing colors or glimmering beauty. Womanly work does not mean better skills and craft than those of others. Be calm, peaceful, faithful, and poised to maintain chastity and order. Know what types of self-presentation bring shame. Master principles to present yourself and handle business. These are called womanly virtue. Choose words (*ci* 辭) with care before speaking (*shuo* 說). Never use offensive language (*e yü* 惡語). Select a proper speech for a right moment to cause no aversion. These are called womanly speech (*yan* 言). Wash and scrub away dirt and filth. Keep your garments and ornaments refreshed and spotless. Wash your hair and bathe your body regularly to be rid of abhorring grime. These are called womanly presence. Complete all weaving and craft work in diligence without fooling around. Serve food and wine in an orderly arrangement to entertain guests. These are called womanly work. These four principles are the most important attributes of a woman. No woman can afford to neglect them. They are not difficult to master, as long as you bear them in mind. The ancient said: "Benevolence (*ren* 仁) is not unreachable. When I set my mind on it, it comes to me naturally."[205] This saying tells all.

---

203. de Bary 1960, 129.
204. Wu 2005, 176–77.
205. Although some online Chinese sources claim that the saying is from Confucian *Analects*. No printed edition of *The Analects* contains it. It is possible that Ban recalled it from her memory. Maybe

2.5 Six Dynasties or Early Medieval Period

Rhetorical Treatise by Lu Ji (陸 機 261–303 CE): A Translation of "An Exposition on Writing" (*Wen Fu* 文賦) with an Introduction and Commentary

Hui Wu

INTRODUCTION

Lu Ji was born in the period of the Three Kingdoms (220–280 CE) controlled by the States of Wei (魏 or Jin 晋), Shu (蜀), and Wu (吳) after the Han Dynasty (206BCE–220 CE) or "shortly after the end of Hellenistic Greece."[206] His grandfather and father, reputed for their arts of warfare, served as generals for the State of Wu. Lu's birthplace, Hua Ting (today's Songjiang district in Shanghai), was an estate rewarded by the grateful emperor of Wu to his grandfather for his loyal service.[207] Following the family tradition, Lu and his younger brother Lu Yun (262–303 CE) also serviced as military officers. When Lu was twenty years old, the State of Wu was conquered by the State of Jin. He and his younger brother fled to Hua Ting, where they lived in seclusion fully devoted to classical education and writing. It is said that Lu wrote over "three-hundred compositions," and his brother "three-hundred and forty-nine."[208] After over a decade of seclusion, the bothers decided to move north to Luoyang (洛陽), capital of the State of Jin, fearing that Jin's tight control would not allow them to keep their estate.[209] Their southern accent was mocked by the northern people, but their writing talent and family connections won them posts in the imperial court. Lu served first as a literary secretary and later headed an army detachment. His talent and good service won him the position of personal secretary to the emperor.[210]

However, Lu's case only reinforced the warnings of Guiguzi and Hanfeizi about dangers of providing service to the ruler. There are several versions about Lu's death. The consensus was that Li could not protect himself as a talented learned man.[211] His career ambition and obligation to the powerful top without compromising moral principles were constant at war within him. Like Hanfeizi, he was a victim to treacheries and suspicion. The historical record shows that the State of Jin was plagued by incessant infighting among the princes of the im-

---

for this reason, she did not identify it as a Confucian saying.

206. Hamill 2000, xvii.

207. *Chinese Encyclopedia,* 1979, 415; Hughes 1951, 31.

208. Hughes 1951, 34.

209. Hughes 1951, 38.

210. Hughes 1951, 39; Hamill, 2000, xxi.

211. Also see Hughes 1951, 46–49; Yang 2016, 3–4.

perial court. Between the years of 300 and 306 CE, frequent warfare amongst them to usurp the throne caused social disorder and disastrous economy.[212] Lu was invited to lead troops for Prince Yin on the promise that Lu would be rewarded with a fief and dukeship if winning the war. Lu offered resignation instead, saying that his employment should be for the public welfare, but not for his personal benefit.[213] His response, however, was purposely conveyed to Prince Yin as an insinuation of disloyalty and insult. Lu unwillingly went to the battlefield at Prince Yin's insistence. As he feared, he and his troops were compromised treacherously by those above and around him. Lu lost heavily in the battle whose goal was seizing the capital for Prince Yin. Consequently, he was slandered for revolting against his employer. Convinced that Lu was playing treason, Prince Yin ordered that Lu be killed secretly, neglecting his repeated written pleas.[214] Upon his death at forty-two years old, Lu lamented that he would never hear again the honks of cranes at Hua Ting, the family estate he failed to protect.

COMMENTARY ON LU JI'S RHETORICAL TREATISE "AN EXPOSITION ON WRITING"

Lu is celebrated as one of the most accomplished literary writers.[215] Such appraisal stems generally from an aesthetic perspective. Indeed, all of Lu's recorded 233 compositions, including fragments, are written in poetic patterns with perfect line-by-line rhythmical parallelism and antithesis. Colorful and metrical, his writing incorporates newly minced phrases and words, many of which allude to classical canons, to articulate his sentiments and emotions. Although adopting classical sentence patterns of four or six characters, Lu intersperses five, seven, eight, or nine characters into his sentences, projecting vivid images of interactions between human and nature, sensation and environment, triumph and defeat, reward and loss. Lu's transformation of the rhetorical tradition led to inventions of new patterns for poetry and composition of verse and essays.[216] Powerful, moving, and aesthetic, Lu Ji's writing is elegant, genuine, and irresistibly appealing to the ear and eye.

Yet, reading Lu exclusively as a poet and his writing as literature from the aesthetic perspective disregards his practice of other rhetorical genres. He wrote not only poems but also prose, or essays, on state politics and policies as well as on rhetoric. For example, he analyzes the death of a state in a two-essay sequel titled "On the Death of a State (*Bian Wang Lun* 辨亡論)." In an argumentative essay, "A Recommendation for Fieldwork (*Da Tian Yi* 大田議)," he proposes changes of state policies to benefit merchants and farmers and attract talents to the state.[217] Furthermore, he also comments on the aristocratic hierarchy in another essay, "On

---

212. Hughes 1951, 42–45; Hamill, 2000, xxi–xxii.
213. Hughes 1951, 43.
214. Hughes 1951, 42–44.
215. Yang 2016, 5–14; Owen, 1992, 73–75; Chen, 1952, vii–iv.
216. Yang 2016, 13.
217. Yang 2016, 687–88.

the Five Classes of Lordship" (*Wudeng Zhuhou Lun* 五等諸侯論).[218] Lu's most famous essay, "*Wen Fu*" (文賦), can further illustrate the point. It is often considered a work on literature, literary thought, or literary criticism.[219] "*Fu*" is often translated as "rhapsody" or "rhapsodic exposition,"[220] while its English versions all appear in the genre of poetry. However, these, and other similar pieces cannot, and should not, be read exclusively for their aesthetic value.

First, like his poetry, Lu's other writings follow the classical patterns of prose or verse, which Chinese scholars call the essay and categorize it as such.[221] In this genre, all sentences are composed of parallelisms and antitheses in rhythm and rhyme, just like the compositions by Guiguzi, Xunzi, and others whose works are not read primarily as poetry. In other words, most, if not all, writings before Lu and in his time, regardless of genre or purpose, read as elegant, metaphoric, and analogical as poetry. Strictly, the prose or essay ought to be composed of lyrical metrical lines. Readers, and scholars in later periods, make distinctions among genres by understanding their purposes. For this reason, Lu himself lists several genres in "*Wen Fu*" to clarify their purposes and recommends all writing genres create "melody" (see paragraph 7). Again, all these rhetorical genres contain poetic features and read like poetry in rhyme and rhythm, but their purposes are distinctively different from that of poetry.

Furthermore, like classical writing and poetry before and during his period, Lu's writings, including "*Wen Fu*," do not contain any punctuation to separate sentences or lines and paragraphs or stanzas. In other words, a written composition with the brush on bamboo or wood strips or on a piece of silk looks like a piece of print fabric without spatial breaks. By Lu's time, paper was widely used for writing.[222] Still, writing, regardless of the genre, was presented without punctuation. Readers rely on combinations of phrases, antitheses or parallelisms, and grammatical functional characters to divide words into lines or sentences as well as stanzas or paragraphs. Scholars and modern readers are often controversial on how to separate paragraphs and where to put periods or commas in modern editions. From this grammatical point, Lu's "*Wen Fu*" should not be read exclusively as poetry.

Therefore, the translation of Lu's "*Wen Fu*" in this book adopts the genre of prose, or the so-called essay, according to Chinese scholars,[223] in contrast to other extant translations in the genre of poetry.[224] This is because translating the original prose into a poem makes its English version dominate Lu's original choice of genre as well as his voice, ideas, and style. One of the translators, Sam Hamill, says, "My goal is to use paraphrase or interpolation as judiciously as possible."[225] Yet, translating is not paraphrasing. Translating means representing the original

218. Yang 2016, 688–784.

219. Owen 1992, 73–74; Chen 2013, vii; Hughes 1951, 93.

220. Kern 2003, 304; Owen 1992, 75.

221. Yang 2016; Liu 1992; Xiao 2002.

222. Paper was invented in China in the early second century CE.

223. Yang 2016; Liu 1992; Xiao 2002.

224. Owen 1992, 73–181; Chen 1952; Hughes 1951, 94–108; Barnstone and Ping 1996, 3; Hamill 2000.

225. Hamill 2000, xxix.

in a foreign (target) language by keeping the original meaning as faithful as possible, including its ambiguity and genre, while paraphrasing means expressing the meaning of the original by using different words in the same language to achieve greater clarity. Consequently, paraphrasing results in discrepant translations. Take the conclusion in "*Wen Fu*" as an example. Placed side by side, the translations of the first two sentences differ to such an extent that anglophone readers have difficulties to recognize the same text. Hamill's translation reads, "Consider the use of letters./All principles demand them./ Though they travel a thousand miles or more,/nothing in this world can stop them."[226] The same sentences in Shi-Hsiang Chen's translation read, "The use of literature/lies in its conveyance of every truth/It expands the horizon to make the space infinite,/And serves as a bridge that spans a myriad years."[227] E. R. Hughes's translation is that "Behold now the utility of letters, a utility endorsed by every kind of principle./It extends over a thousand miles and nothing can stop its course; it penetrates a million years, the ferry from one to the other."[228] Stephen Owen's translation is that "The functioning of literature lies in being/The means for all natural principle./It spreads across ten thousand leagues, nothing bars it;/it passes through a million years, a ford across."[229] Evidently, the translators' effort to "paraphrase" or "interpolate" the original essay to fit their own poems results in varied translations of the same sentences.

The chosen genre for this translation matches Lu's original form of prose. According to him, *fu* is a different genre than poetry, or songs. He says, "Poetry (*shi* 詩) expressing sentiments is beautiful and elaborate. Expository prose (*fu* 賦) explaining matters is clear and brilliant" (paragraph 7). Based on Lu's definition, *fu* explains a subject matter, while *shi* expresses feelings. As Owen points out, in its early stages, "(*fu*) was an epideictic form (i.e., the rhetoric of verbal display) that made extensive use of catalogues and lists. Its aim was ". . . to say all that would be said about its topic."[230] In other words, Lu inherited the genre of *fu* from the antiquity. for example, Xunzi already employed *fu* to discuss a serious topic through questions and answers (see chapter on Xunzi). Later, in the Han Dynasty, "writers wrote *fu* as advice to their rulers and tools of statecraft . . . *Fu* were [sic] a form of rhetoric."[231] In fact, "*Fu* as an expression of the writer's feelings and aspirations became a widespread Han concept," or a genre for political advice, a way to praise virtue, and sometimes a forum for personal feelings.[232] By the late Han Dynasty, *fu* meant elaborate beautified expressions different from poetry.[233] In his treatise *Fa Yan* (法言*Remarks on Methodology*), Yang Xiong (楊雄 53 BCE-18 CE) wrote, "Poets who use *fu* for beauty obey the rule. Prose writers who use *fu* for beauty are superfluous."[234]

---

226. Hamill 2000, 39.
227. Chen 1952, xxx.
228. Hughes 1951, 108.
229. Owen 1992, 179.
230. Owen 1992, 75.
231. Zhang and Pease 1999, 16.
232. Ibid.
233. Guo and Wang 2001, 91.
234. Ibid.

Evidently, both poetry and prose writers adopted *fu* as a genre but for different purposes. According to Yang Xiong, *fu*'s purpose is "indirect admonition" (*feng* 風) mostly through adducing analogies (*tui lei* 推類).[235] Stylistically, most Chinese scholars think that in the form of the essay, *fu* presents things in different colors, varies its ways of expression, demonstrates witty ideas, and employs words elegantly.[236] As such, Lu follows not only Xunzi's model of *fu*—playful, sometimes contradictory and yet complementary—but also the classical features for which *fu* is known— analogical, allegorical, vivid, and refined.[237] Accordingly, all Chinese editions of "*Wen Fu*" retain its original form of prose or the essay. "*Wen Fu*" in this chapter is, therefore, translated in the genre of prose to remain faithful to Lu's original genre wherein he attempts to explain the challenges and joys of the writing process.

My translation of "*Wen Fu*" into "An Exposition on Writing" as a rhetorical treatise, and not as poetry, helps clarify the key terms, particularly the term *wen* in the title. Extant translations are incoherent in presenting the title of "*Wen Fu*," for instance, "The Poetic Exposition on Literature," "The Essay on Literature," "Poetic Prose on the Art of Letters," or "The Art of Writing."[238] As the "Prefatory Introduction to Chinese Rhetorics" in this book suggests, *wen* holds broad meanings of literacy, eloquence, writing, and knowledge of history and rhetorical cultures and conventions, rather than a narrow sense of aesthetic literature. Specifically, *wen* in "*Wen Fu*" should be read as "the art of writing" or "written composition," and not general literature. When it is treated as a rhetorical treatise, the title "An Exposition on Writing" naturally embraces implication of purported rhetorical effect in the writing process.

As the first treatise on the writing process in Chinese rhetoric, "An Exposition on Writing" sheds light on Lu's recognition of difficulties, joys, and success as a writer. Many Chinese scholars suggest that "'*Wen Fu*' vividly describes various stages of the writing process" and is a treatise on rhetoric.[239] Lu uses analogies, metaphors, and allusions to ancient canons to explain some elements of invention, arrangement, and style. For example, the first five paragraphs foreground his description of invention. The beginning paragraph sets up the tone for an exposition on the writer and the craft, taking into consideration challenges and spontaneity in composition. Lu believes that invention relies on the writer's repertoire of classical knowledge and language use. He draws upon classical odes, eulogies, and virtues to empower his writing with exquisite elegance.

In terms of arrangement, Lu focuses on coherence, sometimes in newly coined rhetorical terms. For example, he says that the essence of a written composition should form a structure (*gan* 幹) to tie up complex ideas and coordinate credibility (*xin* 信), sentiment (*qing* 情), and wording (*mao* 貌) (paragraph 4).[240] Considering difficulties in revision with the brush and

---

235. Kern 2003, 390.

236. Yang 2016, 48; Liu 1992; and Xiao 2002.

237. Also see Owen 1992, 75.

238. Owen 1992, 73; Chen 2013; Hughes 1951, 94; Barnstone and Chou 1996, 3; Hamill 2000.

239. Yang 2016, 5; Zheng 1979, 58–59.

240. These terms may remind us of ethos, pathos, and logos in Western rhetoric. However, a simple comparison may lead to applying Western rhetoric as the universal framework.

paper in Lu Ji's time, we can further understand his recommendation of planning the arrangement (*shi ci* 識次) before composition. Li recommends that writers seize the opportunity in the beginning to coordinate the whole piece (paragraph 8). Otherwise, he warns, the composition would lose its color and appeal in the end. Adaptions and selections of details, deletions, and retainment, to Lu, ought to fit application and criteria. All these strategies depend on establishing key words in essential places to "realize effect" and ensure adequacy without change. Although Lu does not list any key words, he emphasizes that they are essential to significant lines and the order of a written composition (paragraph 10).

Furthermore, Lu suggests that coherent arrangement results in appealing delivery. Given that all writers in his time mastered calligraphy, a written composition in parallelism and antithesis appealed to the eye. To the ear, it ought to sound like music in beat and tune. In composition, Lu emphasizes that images and sounds are intertwined with natural scenes to achieve sensual impact. For example, a writer "knocks on silence to seek resonance," and his/ her thoughts "spread around aromatic fragrance of overhanging blossoms." Lu deems it important that "sounds and utterances respond to one another in echoes" like rich colors bouncing off one another vibrantly (paragraphs 5 and 8).

Lu also pays attention to rhetorical ethics in terms of the purpose and function of writing. Ethics in Chinese rhetoric has been dominated by the Confucian virtue to judge the integrity of a speaker or a writer. In *the Analects*, Confucius judged a speech based on the criteria of *de* (德 virtue), *li* (礼 rites), *ren* (仁 kindness), *shu* (恕 reciprocity), *zhong*, (忠 loyalty), *xin* (信 credibility).[241] He believed that "a cunning speech [*qiao yan* 巧言] undermines virtues."[242] In saying so, Confucius established "*wen de*" (文德), the virtue or ethics of eloquence. In the late Han Dynasty, the ethics of rhetoric developed mainly into concerns about whether the writer upheld integrity and whether writing had pragmatic value to the state. Yang Xiong maintained that the function and purpose of *ci* (辭 speech or writing) should be tied to the success it brought to the state. He explains, "When endeavors are successful, *ci* is beautified; when *ci* is successful, endeavors become *fu* [beautified]."[243] Wang Chong also said, "A learned man's writing should promote kindness and condemn malevolence."[244] Lu follows these teachings of his predecessors. In invention, he recites classical odes to learn "ancient virtues" and savors nourishment from the Confucius canons (paragraphs 1 and 2). To him, the goal of writing is to uphold moral principles. In "An Exposition on Writing," the word "principle" appears six times. For example, "the intent of using accurate words is to bring forth principles" or to illustrate principles (paragraph 7). The essentials in composition are supported by the principles to coordinate credibility, sentiment, and deportment or delivery (paragraph 4). Lu's use of "principle" reminds us of Guiguzi, who says that speakers "who hold principles do not look for

---

241. Lu 1998, 174-194; Lan 2017, 145–63.

242. *Analects* 1999, Chapter 15.27.

243. Guo and Wang 2001, 91.

244. Chen and Wang 1998, 241.

anything improper," because their speeches always draw upon Confucian books.[245] It seems that Guiguzi and Lu agree that ethical principles are fundamental to rhetorical practice because they enable a rhetor to maintain justice.[246] As Lu reflects near the end of "An Exposition on Writing," the function and cause of writing are grounded on the principles.

The above rhetorical reading is reflected in the translation hereafter. It presents Lu as a writer in the first-person point of view to foreground his thought about invention, arrangement, style, and delivery and to keep the rhetorical terminologies consistent with those in other treatises. As said previously, rhythmic and sensual, Lu's style, like those of Guiguzi, Xunzi, and others, amplifies visual and audial effects. To preserve these stylistic features, this translation sometimes repeats paralleled phrases with an awareness that they may sound redundant. In the genre of prose, the following translation, "An Exposition of Writing," identifies "*Wen Fu*" as a rhetorical treatise on the writing process.

TRANSLATION OF "AN EXPOSITION ON WRITING"

1. Each time I read works by talented men, I feel for them and understand their arduous endeavors. Their delivery of the language (*fang yan* 放言) and employment of words (*qian ci* 遣辭) differ in a variety of ways. Still, it is possible to tell (*yan* 言) the beautiful from the ugly, the appealing from the unappealing. Each time I am composing, I can discern their dispositions. There are always worries about what is intended fails to name (*cheng* 稱) the thing (*wu* 物) and what is written (*wen* 文) fails to capture the meaning (*yi* 意). It is not that writers do not understand how difficult writing is but that they cannot overcome the difficulties. Therefore, I write "An Exposition on Writing" to recount the sublime craftsmanship of past writers and thereby to illustrate why a written composition (*zuo wen* 作文) is a success or a failure in hopes that in the future it can be appreciated like music for its meticulous articulation. In carving an axe handle with an axe, the model is ready at hand. But if it (the craft) involves spontaneous variations, it is often beyond words (*ci* 辭). Hereafter is whatever can be said in words (*yan* 言).

2. I stand at the center[247] to speculate on the unknown (玄 *xuan*),[248] cultivating my disposition (*qing* 情) and will in ancient canons. With the four seasons passing, I lament the fleeting time. Observing the myriad things (*wang wu* 万物), I am full of thoughts. I bemoan the falling leaves in the buoyant autumn and rejoice in supple sprigs in the blossoming spring, my heart embracing the frost and my will soaring to high clouds. I recite odes to the unshakable power of the ancient virtues and read aloud eulogies to pure-spirited predecessors. Roaming around

---

245. *Guiguzi* 2016, 108.
246. *Guiguzi* 2016, 112.
247. The "center" means the human's location between the Heaven and Earth. See Guiguzi's explication of the relationship among human, Heaven, and Earth (*Guiguzi* 2016, 92–93).
248. 玄 can mean darkness, myths, marvels, or wonders. Some translated it as "in the darkness," "nothing," or "the whole universe" (Owen 1992, 87; Barnstone and Chou 1996, 8; Chen 2013, xx).

the forest and treasure house of eloquent compositions (*wen zhang* 文章), I admire their exquisite embellishment and unfailing elegance. Full of inspirations, I lay the books aside and take the brush to express myself in writing (*wen* 文).

3. To begin, I turn blind to what I see (*shou shi* 收視) and deaf to what I hear (*fan ting* 反聽).[249] I am engrossed in thinking, making inquiries from different angles. My spirit gallops beyond the boundaries of the world; my heart roams thousands of miles. When attained, feelings (*qing* 情) ascend like sunrise, gradually revealing their brilliance and ingenuity. Things (*wu* 物) are illuminated, moving one another forward. With so many words flowing out like dripping water, I savor the sweet enrichment of the six classical arts.[250] I drift between Heaven and the abyss, riding streams at ease. I bathe and submerge myself in the waterfalls. Then, words (*ci* 辭) in the depth struggle to surface, like swimming fish biting the hook to emerge from the deep water. Floating thoughts are interconnecting and sinking into places, like birds hit by stringed arrows whirling down from layered clouds. I gather written compositions (*wen* 文) lost for a hundred generations; I adopt rhymes (*yun* 韻) neglected for a thousand years. Farewell to the splendid flowering dawn that is employed exhaustively. Initiate the burgeoning beauty of the dusk that awaits exploration.[251] I see the past and the present for a fleeting moment; I touch the whole world in a fraction of a second. Afterward, I select ideas to arrange them in proper genres, while examining words (*kao ci* 考辭) to classify their meanings. Compound vividly all the ideas containing images; stroke ideas containing sounds as if they were musical notes. Sometimes I utilize a branch to shake down leaves; sometimes I follow flows to seek the beginning of a stream. Sometimes my intended obscurity becomes manifest; sometimes my simple attempt encounters difficulties. Sometimes changes of a tiger agitate other beasts; sometimes a jouncing dragon shocks birds into waves. Sometimes they are proper and fitting for easy employment; sometimes they are unsmooth and unsuitable.

4. I purify my heart (*xin* 心) for concentrated thinking and delineate various considerations with words (*yan* 言). I fold Heaven and Earth into certain shapes and forms, gathering the myriad things on the bristle of my brush. In the beginning, they stumble and pause in my dry mouth; but in the end they flow freely from my ink-drenched brush. The essentials (*zhi* 質) are supported by principles (*li* 理)[252] to establish the structure (*gan* 幹); the writing (*wen* 文) branches out to tie up complexities (*jie fan* 結繁).[253] The creditability (*xin* 信), sentiment

---

249. Although the meaning of *fan ting* is changed over time, the phrase still retains the meaning of reflection as in "the *Dao* of reflective listening" (*fan ting zhi dao* 反聽之道) in *Guiguzi* 2016, 46.

250 The six arts refer to the Confucian classics, *Book of Poetry, Book of History, Book of Changes* (or *Yi Jing*), *Spring and Autumn Annuals, Book of Rites,* and *Book of Music.*

251. These three sentences mean that Lu does not want to repeat any clichés or oft-used expressions.

252. *Li* can refer to "common sense, reason, matter, or justification" and not exclusively "truth or orthodox" (Yang 2016, 13; Chen 1952, xxii).

253. Some translators continue the metaphors in this couplet (Owen 1992, 113). The translation here foregrounds Lu's reference to the development of writing.

(*qing* 情), and deportment (*mao* 貌) are never in discordance. Thereby each modification shows on the face (*yan* 顏).[254] Thoughts of joy elicit laughter; expressions of sorrow evoke sighs of sadness. Sometimes I press the tablet to write on it rapidly;[255] sometimes I hold the brush but feel distanced.

5. This matter of composition can be enjoyable. This is why sacred sages held it in high regard. One starts out with nothing to grasp something; one knocks on silence to seek resonance. Miles of distant land are enveloped by the leaves of writing silk;[256] volumes of torrent are gushing out of the heart. Words come forth to expand the sphere; thoughts recur to become deeper. They spread around aromatic fragrance of overhanging blossoms; they grow young green twigs into heavy woods. The bright breeze, gaining power, upswings into whirlwinds; swelling dark clouds hover over the forest of writing brushes.

6. Physiques take thousands of unique shapes; objects have no single measure. Diverse and different in constant change, their configurations hardly fit any frames. Decisions on diction (*ci cheng* 辭程) require the talented to vary the craftsmanship (*xiao ji* 效伎); articulating accurate meanings demands him to be a wordsmith. He toils no matter if it is nothing or something. He never yields no matter if it is superficial or profound. Although the shapes are neither square nor circular, he hopes to fully explore their forms and reveal their visages. Thus, those who prefer hyperboles (*kua* 誇) esteem superfluity; those who want to satisfy the heart value propriety (*dang* 當). Those who use the language (*yan* 言) to the fullest extent have no limit; those who deliver sensible arguments (*lun da* 論達) revere broadness.[257]

7. Poetry (*shi* 詩) expressing emotions is beautiful and elaborate. Expository verse (*fu* 賦) explaining matters is clear and brilliant. Stele inscription (*bei* 碑) publicizing a writing (*wen* 文) reflects facts (*xiang zhi* 相質). Eulogy (*lai* 誄) pronouncing sentimental reminiscence shares pain and sorrow. Maxim (*ming* 銘), general and brief, is kind and aspiring. Admonition (*zhen* 箴) that exerts influence is honest and powerful. Ode that romanticizes the good and idyllic (*you you* 優遊) is elegant and refined. Argument (*lun* 論) that illustrates essence and subtlety is candid and fluent (*lang chang* 朗暢). Proposition (*zou* 奏) to the throne that shows equilibrium and deference is impartial and clear. Persuasion (*shui* 說) that sounds charming and brilliant is deceitful and delusive. Though distinctions are made hereby, they prohibit misuse and unconstrained application. The intent is using accurate words to bring forth principles. Thus, writing should not be tedious and long.

8. Subjects (*wu* 物) of writing vary in shape; genres (*ti* 體) of writing change frequently. Meanings of writing are exquisite and ingenious; words of writing are allusive and beautiful. Then

---

254. "*Yan*" literally means facial color. Lu uses it as a metaphor to refer to how writing reads.

255. The original 操觚 (*sao gu*) and 率爾 (*shuai er*) have become a fixed phrase in modern Chinese to refer to writing activities.

256. The phrase of "leaves of writing silk" is a metaphor for sheets of writing.

257. "Those" is used to translate "*zhe*" (者), which can mean the writing or the writer.

sounds and utterances respond to one another in echoes like the five colors bouncing off one another in vibrance. It is not regular when to delete or halt, for challenges and crafts never make it easy. If mutation is achieved by understanding arrangement (*shi ci* 識次), it is like opening an aqueduct to welcome the stream. If the opportunity is missed and everything has to be worked out near the end, then the ending is forced to correspond to the beginning. This error turns the arrangement of an account (*zhi xü* 袟敘) dark and brown.[258] It then becomes muddy water devoid of freshness.

9. Sometimes a digression happens to an earlier section; sometimes a diversion happens to a later section. Sometimes the wording (*ci* 辭) is awkward, but the reasoning (*li* 理) is in order; sometimes the language (*yang* 言) flows fluently, but the meaning (*yi* 意) stops short. Eliminating the two problems doubles the delicacy (*mei* 美); combining the two causes twice the detriment (*hai* 害). Considerations of what serves the best depend on small details; decisions on what to delete and what to retain rely on fine tuning. If adaptions and selections are tailored to fit, then applications and criteria are surely appropriate.

10. Sometimes a writing is luxuriant with fully illustrated principles, but its meaning is unprecise and unfitting. The final point (*ji* 極) does not allow two unmatching ends; excessiveness (*jin* 盡) is not rewarded.[259] Establishing key words in essential places to foreground significant lines of a whole piece. Although many phrases (*zhong ci* 眾辭) are in order, they rely on key words to realize the effect. Demonstrating many achievements then becomes effortless. Thereby adequacy is achieved without changes.

11. Sometimes sophisticated thoughts presented in flowery coherence are lucidly bright in lovely colors. Their cheerfulness shines through like elaborate embroidery. Their sadness echoes in resonance like a monody. An imitation is certain to have no distinction. It quietly follows former models. Even if the shuttle and loom suit my needs, I fear that others may have already used them before. Should integrity suffer in transgression, I would give up my preference.

12. Sometimes a blossom opens and a new bud spikes up, uniquely exquisite. Its shadow cannot be followed; its reverberation is hard to reproduce. The section stands alone above the ordinary, to which normal utterance is irresponsive. The imprisoned heart is sinking for no parallel can be found. The idea wanders in hesitation for it cannot recede.

13. Rocks containing jade make the mountain glisten; waters bearing pearls make the river delightful. In instances where overgrown trees remain untrimmed, their glory is reflected by

---

258. A metaphor to mean that a writing loses its vividness and brilliance like withering dark leaves.
259. The final point refers to the theme or the topic of a composition. This couplet means that the beginning and ending of a writing should be coherent to develop the main point and that writing with too much embellishment does not make it better.

the bushy green. Integrating the commonplace (*xia li* 下裏) with the sublime (*bai xue* 白雪) may also glorify magnificence.

14. When composing a rhyming short piece, exhaustive use of the pattern manifests an individual's interest. Looking down at the quiet expanse, he finds no companion; looking up at the vast void, he finds no direction. It is like a rarely used musical instrument struck in solo wherein a clear song evokes no response.

15. When a writing (*ci* 辭) is delivered in a tired voice (*cui yin* 瘁音), luxurious words achieve no grandeur. Blending the beautiful with the ugly to develop a style (*ti* 體) damages quality with defects, giving the impression that pipes down the hall are being played too fast to react in harmony.[260] When the principles are disregarded to accommodate oddity; the pursuit of trifles is a search for nothing. The words are devoid of sensation and affection. The writing drifts and roams to no end, as if tiny strings were being struck to emit rapid shrills. It follows the sequence but without elegiac solemnity.

16. When the bold and unrestrained are at play to create harmony and unity, boisterous intonations must form enchanting allurement. When an attempt to please the eye accidentally contributes to vulgarity, the sound is voluminous, but the music is inferior. A comparison between *Clear of the Dews* (*Fang Lu* 防露) and *Among the Mulberries* (*Sang Jiang* 桑間) reveals (the former's) intense, yet undignified, sensations.[261] When pure transcendence is at play to achieve graceful calmness, complexities must be eliminated to avoid indiscriminate misuse. Or it will lack the lingering flavor of the ceremonial soup just like music played on a red-stringed instrument without tunes and focus. Even though a singer is accompanied by three others, they attain dignity, but not allure.

17. If a sumptuous work calls for trimming (*cai* 裁), view the pattern up and down to make proper adjustment. Melodies express nuanced emotions.[262] Sometimes they are written in simple words but with clever metaphors. Sometimes the principles are plain, and the words light. Sometimes they quote the old to refresh the new. Sometimes they apply ambiguity to enhance clarity. Sometimes a study is conducted to refine them. It is like dancers who step to the beat to fling their sleeves or vocalists who sings in response to the accompanying music. All cannot be described by Wheelwright Bien (*Lun Bien* 輪扁) in words; nor can all brilliant splendid eloquence (*hua shuo* 華說) pinpoint the essence.[263]

---

260. "Pipes" (*guan* 管) refers to musical instruments.
261. "Clear of the Dews" is said to be a poem with sexually charged allusions, while *Among the Mulberries* is a poem in the *Book of Rites* that expresses despair and melancholy at the loss of a state. Lu uses them as a contrast between low and high tastes in writing (Yang 2016, 33; Owen 1992, 163–64).
262. Here melodies (*qu* 曲) allude to writing.
263. Zhuangzi describes a dialogue between Mr. Lun Bian and Duke Huan of the State of Qi, where Bian said that it was impossible to pass on his craft because he could not describe his intuitive skills thoroughly in words (also see Barnstone and Chou 1996, 17, note 3; Owen 1992, 168–69).

18. All sentence patterns (*ci tiao* 辭條) and rules of composition (*wen lu* 文律) I bear well in mind. Familiar with oft-committed faults in worldly affairs, I understand the virtues learned in the past. Although ideas may emerge from the witty heart, they may sound ridiculous in the eyes of the unlearned. Exquisite embellishments and jade-green elegance, like crops and grains in the central plain and blowing bellows in blank oblivion, stay nurtured along with Heaven and Earth. They are abundant in this world, but deplorably, I can grasp only a handful. It is lamentable that the bottle in hand is almost empty. It is disappointing that a masterpiece (*changyan* 昌言) is hard to produce. Thus, jumping and limping, I come up with short rhymes; mumbling commonplace notes, I complete songs. I always have some regret at the end of composition (*pian* 篇); I have not achieved any fulfillment to satisfy myself, terrified that this dust-muffled jar will be tapped and destined to be mocked by tinkling jade.[264]

19. When reaction (*ying* 應) and perception (*gan* 感) interact, when passage and blockage converge, what comes cannot be suppressed, what departs cannot be stopped. If it is hidden, the scene vanishes; if it moves, the sound echoes. This is a Heaven-endowed opportunity of speedy advantage. Why disorders are not being arranged (*li* 理)? The wind of thought comes forth from the depth of the heart; a fountain of words (*yan* 言) flows through lips and teeth. Vibrance and lethargy whirling in abundance can be only portrayed by the writing brush and silk. Writing (*wen* 文) makes marks, overflowing the eye. Its tunes carry tinkles, overflooding the ear. However, the Six Senses falter deep down. The will moves forward, but the spirit lags. They are like perched leafless trees and exposed waterless rivers. One collects the soul to explore all mysterious sources; he shakes up the spirit to pursue the self. Thoughts (*li* 理), implicit and vailed, lie down asleep; ideas, obscure and buried, are pulled out like threads. As such, sometimes I feel exhausted emotionally, ending up with many regrets; sometimes I dash ideas, feeling particularly resourceless. Although the thing is within me, I have no power to harness it. Hence, at times, with an empty heart, I pity myself. I have yet to learn how to overcome the block.[265]

20. One composes writing for its function (*yong* 用). Hence, many principles constitute its cause. It reaches the myriad miles without obstruction; it passes through millions of years to develop its core. Looking down to quest (*dai* 殆), one finds purpose for the coming generations (*lai ye* 來葉). Looking up for models (*xiang* 象), one finds them in ancients. It prevents scholars (*wen* 文) and generals (*wu* 武) from falling. It promotes trends and reputations to make them last. No place is so far that it cannot permeate. No principle (*li* 理) is so subtle that it cannot extract. It brings mist from rainy clouds. It transforms its presence like a phantom or an apparition. Inscribed on gold and stone, it spreads virtues widely. Sung through flutes and strings, it renews itself each day.

---

264. "Dust-muffled jar" and "tinkling jade" refer to ordinary and high-quality writing. Lu uses the former to show humility as a writer who always want to improve.
265. Meaning writer's block.

2.6 Six Dynasties or Early Medieval Period

Rhetorical Treatise by Liu Xie (劉勰 465–522 CE): A Partial Translation of *A Heart for Eloquence and the Invention of Dragons* (*Wenixin Diaolong* 文心雕 龍)[266] with An Introduction and Commentary

Hui Wu

INTRODUCTION

Liu Xie spent over twenty years studying orthodox classics in different genres, from *Yi Jing* (*Book of Changes*) to Confucian treatises, to *Guiguzi*, to well-known historiographies, such as *Shi Ji* (*Grand Scribe's Record*) (Ssu-Ma) and *Zhan Guo Ce*, or *Intrigues* (Crump) to "An Exposition on Writing" by Lu Ji, and others. It is recorded that when Liu was twenty years old, he became a disciple of a famous Buddhist monk, Zeng You (憎佑) of Ding Lin Temple (定 林寺) in today's Zijing Mountain (紫金山) in Nanjing. After a decade, he became a master of major Buddhist canons by working on commentaries and editions and then completed a treatise on Buddhism titled *Elimination of Confusion* (滅惑論 *Mie Huo Lun*). Meanwhile, he continued his study of Confucian and other classics in hopes to follow the tradition of scholar-official career in the imperial court.

Wenxin Diaolong resulted from Liu's reception of the Confucian classics and reflection on eloquent speeches and writings by his predecessors. Liu completed this treatise around 501 CE, when he was in his thirties.[267] At this point, Liu was faced with life choices. Should he continue as a secular scholar in a monastery or pursue an imperial office that would bring wealth and honor? According to the "Biography of Liu Xie" in *Liang Shu* (梁書), Liu sough sponsorship from a leading scholar, Shen Yue (沈約), who, after reading Liu's *Wenxin Diaolong*, had him placed on the waiting list of official appointments by Emperor Liang Wu (梁武帝).[268] In 504 BC, Liu had the opportunity to serve as a scholar-official in charge of documentation and record for a local managerial. Quickly, Liu climbed up the ranks and was appointed by Emperor Liang Wu as the history and literacy advisor for Prince Xiao Tong (蕭統), who, following the quoted works in *Wenxin Diaolong*, compiled the well-known *Selected Eloquent Works* (*Wen Xuan* 文選). Afterwards, Liu gained an opportunity to serve the Emperor himself. His recommendation of using produce instead of meats as ceremonial sacrifice based on his monastery life was enthusiastically adopted by the Emperor, who even accepted Buddhism as his own

---

266. See 50.1 where Liu explains the title. My translation of "*wen*" into "eloquence" relates it to the arts of oratory and writing. For evolving meanings of "*wen*," see the "Prefatory Introduction to Chinese Rhetorics" in this book.

267. Wang and Zhou 2016, 1; Qi 2008, 12.

268. Qi, 2008, 3-4.

religion. The conversion prompted the Emperor to revitalize the religion by sending Liu back to the Ding Lin Monastery to edit and collect Buddhist canons.[269] It remains a myth if Liu was happy to return after thirty years. However, it was confirmed that he completed the imperial task but wrote little on classics and eloquent composition. Liu died a monk at fifty-six.[270]

COMMENTARY ON *WENXIN DIAOLONG*

In fifty chapters, *Wenxin Diaolong*, which literally means "rhetorical composition, heart, carve, and dragon," critiques more than 180 authors and cites over 500 works produced during the pre-Qin and Han periods (500BCE–220 CE).[271] It is studied primarily as the first systematic treatise on literary aesthetics, literary criticism, or literary creation in China and in the West.[272] The literary reception impacts translations. Zhao Heping notices that the translated titles mostly agree with scholars' own disciplinary interests and interpretations, for example, Vincent Yu-cheng Shih's *The Literary Mind and the Carving of Dragons*, Wang Zuoliang's *The Literary Mind, or the Carving of the Dragons*; Hsien-yi Yang and Gladys Yang's *Carving a Dragon at the Core of Literature*.[273] Some scholars leave the original Chinese title in romanization due to the lack of an English equivalent. However, almost all scholars read Liu's book as a treatise on literary thought or literature, agreeing that it is "the first and unquestioned, systematic compendium of Chinese literary thinking, and the first categorization of literary knowledge."[274] Scholars notice that *Wenxin Diaolong* is also a guide to writing well by modeling and teaching. Stephen Owen recognizes that Liu applies analytical rules to some objects, and his rhetoric is close to the formal expository procedures of his Western counterparts.[275] Yet, he reads and translates Liu's book as "a systematic treatise on literature," a conclusion that dominates studies of *Wenxin Diaolong*.[276]

   Wenxin Diaolong is, in fact, a rhetorical treatise on oral and written discourses and their composing process. Zhao notices that Liu uses "*wen*" over 500 times.[277] Under Liu's pen, "*wen*" means broadly the rhetorical culture, tradition, and practice. It is reflected in the person who practices it, the genre in the context, the chosen style, and the proper diction. "*Wen*" includes, but is not limited to, aesthetic literature. Most of the classics Liu cites and critiques serve as examples for eloquent composition or as models or criteria for rhetorical genres. For example, his reference to *Guiguzi* and *zong-heng* strategists can be read as illustration of effec-

---

269. Qi, 2008, 5-6.
270. Qi, 2008, 7.
271. Guo and Wang 2001, 1.
272. Guo and Wang 2001, 1; Qi 2008; Wang and Zhou 2016; Zhao 1990, 8–9; Owen 1992, 183–298.
273. Zhao 1994, 2.
274. Lavagnino 2017, 1007.
275. Owen, 1992, 185.
276. Owen 1992, 183–298.
277. Zhao 1990, 70.

tive persuasion (18.11). His delineation of rhetorical genres before and in his time directs his audience's attention to their origins and their criteria set up by the classical canons (3.10). The rhetorical genres evidently include not only poetry and expository verse but also argumentation, persuasion, speech, proposition, biography, chronicle, etc. (3.10). Liu also tracks the transmission of Confucius's *Analects* from oratory to a written record by his disciples to show the development of the genre of argumentation (18.1). Hence, "*wen*" in *Wenxin Diaolong* signifies far more than literary writing and should be examined from a rhetorical point of view.

Using the classical canons as models for genres and criteria, Liu delivers his rhetorical instructions based on his perception of the *Dao*, the source of eloquence (1.1). In this regard, Liu has inherited and enhanced Guiguzi's philosophy of rhetoric, in which the *Dao* is the principle of eloquence while the composer or rhetor belongs in the Triad together with Heaven and Earth.[278] Liu holds, as Guiguzi does, that words can mobilize people because their eloquence (*wen*) comes from the *Dao*, which is the purpose of sages' rhetoric (1.8). When Liu reveals his belief that all classical canons manifest the heart embracing the *Dao* (1.8), he extends Guiguzi's philosophy of rhetoric focusing on oratory to one that guides different genres of oral and written composition. Guiguzi believes that the *Dao* is the goal of eloquence and the rhetor, as part of the Triad, is the agency to realize the goal.[279] Guiguzi sees eloquence and humans as two vehicles for upholding the *Dao*. In contrast, Liu sees oratory and writing as embodying virtue, which is the *Dao* itself, envisioning eloquence, humans, and the *Dao* as one entity (1.2). Throughout the book, Liu's notion of the *Dao* and virtue is concretized into the principle (*li* 理) taught by the orthodox classics. Humans, as instrumental to eloquence as they are, do not form the Triad. It is eloquence that is part of the Triad with Heaven and Earth. Put differently, "*wen*" embodies humans to represent the principle, the heart of Heaven and Earth, the virtue, *Dao*, nature, sound, and landscape (1.2).

Liu's notion of eloquence constitutes his ethics of rhetoric, namely, for what eloquence serves and who can compose it. As Liu understands, in a hierarchical society, eloquence is indispensable to maintain the state order and to promote practical affairs and one's career.[280] Writing about the functionality of eloquence, Liu confesses, "He composes eloquent works to help with the governance of the military and the state. When he bears important responsibilities, he is dependable as a pillar and a beam to hold the duties."[281] To him, eloquence is instrumental to state affairs. Liu quotes an ancient saying to relate ideas of the composer to his dream of life—he lives an ordinary life but aspires to serve in the imperial court someday (26.1). Furthermore, Liu places composers of "*wen*" on a hierarchy with sages on the top, recounters or teachers of classics in the middle, and exemplary persons, or *junzi*, at the bottom. Only these humans can create eloquence. The sages' eloquent works serve as models and criteria; teachers of classics transmit them by speaking or writing about the classics, and the *junzi*

---

278. *Guiguzi* 2016, 91–92.
279. *Guiguzi* 2016, 39.
280. Zhao 1994, 1.
281. Liu 2016. Wang and Feng 2016, Chapter 49.6.

(exemplary person) creates eloquence by following the classics to incorporate the *Dao*, virtue, and principle. Thereby, Liu returns to the ethics of rhetoric in Kongzi and Xunzi, arguing that an ethical person creates effective eloquence (see chapters on Kongzi and Xunzi). It seems that Liu thinks that Lu Ji can be regarded as a *junzi* but not a wise teacher yet. He comments, "It is claimed that Lu Ji's 'An Exposition on Writing' exhausted all the fine points. But what he really accounted was general argumentation about tiny details without touching the real essence."[282] His critique reveals that Liu wishes to be regarded as a teacher of eloquence without losing the status of *junzi*. Liu says, "An exemplary person living in this world is committed to developing the virtue and language. I have no choice but present my argument" (50.1). Indeed, he spent his life practicing his philosophy of rhetoric as a *junzi*. He wrote *Wenxin Diaolong* in hopes to hold an advisory position in the imperial court. His description of *junzi* reads like a self-representation—"When appointed, he utilizes the opportunity to provide state service and strives for achievements. This is a man of eloquence (*wen ren* 文人), a man of talent to be a state pillar" (49.6).

A rhetorical reading shows that Liu uses "*wen*" to address the art of composing oratory and writing. He calls the art *shu* (術). Some scholars in literature also notice that Liu might compose his book to delineate the principle and method of composition.[283] The composing process addressed in *Wenxin Diaolong* is, to some degree, different from the five canons in Aristotelian rhetoric—invention, arrangement, style, memory, and delivery—but similar to modern composition theory on the writing process. The steps in Liu's book may not be clearly organized in such an order as in Aristotelian rhetoric nor delivered in the same terminologies as those in today's composition theory, but the composing process is taught to address invention, arrangement, genre, style, and diction. Sometimes, Liu's teaching sounds like that of a modern composition instructor. He describes three steps from brainstorming to selection of a genre based on the theme or the sentiment, to categorization of contents, and finally to utilization of proper words for key points (32.2).

In chapters 1–5, Liu advises students to "learn certain sets of inventive acts appropriate for the rhetorical goals."[284] Specifically, Liu's theory of eloquence as invention consists of content-oriented and form-oriented inventive acts.[285] Put differently, Liu uses classical examples to teach where to find sources and how to learn different genres. The first two chapters speak of the *Dao* as the source of eloquence and the importance of classical learning to cultivate the will and mind for invention. Chapter 3 directs attention to classical models of eloquence in different genres with different stylistic features. To prevent errors, Liu reminds readers to follow closely the rhetorical tradition to develop their own eloquence. Furthermore, eloquence learners should devote their hearts to displaying their sentiments and depositions and apply intuitive stylistic features and genres in the classics.

---

282. Liu 2016, Chapter 44.3. My translation.
283. Wang and Zhou 2016, 3; Qi 2008, 27-41.
284. Zhao 1994, 2.
285. Ibid., 2-3.

Also, Liu teaches arrangement to make the ending echo the beginning and to present rich contents coherently (43.1). Effective eloquence should express a complex theme without digression. In persuasion, *yin* and *yang* coordinate to unite eloquence coherently (43.1). Liu sees arrangement as the bones of a body of words (18.1). The sentence and diction are the flesh on the bones in a style with flair. Liu describes eight graceful, grand, and sublime styles for powerful eloquence (30.1). For delivery, all compositions should go through careful deliberations. Specifically, Liu uses "melting" to refer to the techniques of adopting genres and sources from the *Dao*, while comparing "tailoring" to trimming redundant sentences and superfluous words (32.1). The principle for an eloquence with style and flair is that eloquence and its contents are in unity, just like what he calls the "eloquent composition" by sages and honorable persons (31.1).

Moreover, stylistic features and the composition process stem from the composer's sentiment and character. Sentiment represents the contents controlled by the theme. Complementing the *Dao*, sentiment is a critical source of style. Character is the composer's *ethos* manifested in the choice of genre, or form (30.1). Embodied by composers, sentiment and character reflect their ideas and ideals, their ambitions and aspirations, their accomplishment in learning, their ethics, and their rhetorical techniques. All these are expressed in *wen*, the classical inspiration to the composer, the *junzi*, who, in turn, embraces *wen* in his/her heart to create powerful eloquence, or dragons, for the purpose of becoming a state pillar.

The rhetorical reading presented above leads to the selection of passages in the following translation with a focus on Liu's ethics of rhetoric, philosophy of rhetoric, and instruction of the composition of oral and written eloquence. Though not as complete as we wish due to the limited scope, the translated passages provide adequate resources for the study of Liu Xue's rhetorical teaching.

Partial Translation of *A Heart for Eloquence and the Invention of Dragons*

Chapter 1. Originality from the Dao (Yuan Dao 原道)

1.1 Eloquence (*wen* 文) is as great as virtue (*de* 德). It is said to be born together with Heaven and Earth. Why?

1.2 Because all colors are mixtures of black and yellow, and all shapes are differentiated through square and round. The sun and moon are like layered jade to illuminate the beauty of the sky and natural phenomena. Radiant divine mountains and rivers are the outlines of the order and landscape. These are *Dao*'s eloquence (*wen*) itself. Look up to see radiance above; look down to observe inherited rules below. High and low positions are thus determined, and two agencies (*liang yi* 两儀) are born.[286] Only humans, endowed with the character and spirit, participate to

---

286. Heaven and Earth

form the Triad. The human stands out among the five elements[287] to manifest the mind (*xin* 心) of Heaven and Earth.[288] The mind establishes the language, and the established language brings forth eloquence and wisdom (*wen ming* 文明) to develop the *Dao* naturally.

Chapter 2. Drawing Upon the Sage (Zheng Sheng 征聖)

2.1 Creators are sagacious; recounters are wise. The development of the character (*xing* 性) and sentiment (*qing* 情) is credited to ancient sages. All masters' eloquent compositions (*wen zhang* 文章) are available and known. Yet, sages' sentiments are seen only from their words (*ci* 辭). The oral teachings of ancient kings are in the books; the masters' stylistic grace permeates their aphorisms. . . . Confucius, when commending his disciple, Zi Chan, said, "his speech (*yan* 言) strengthens his will, and his rhetoric (*wen*) strengthens his speech." When Confucius talked generally about exemplary persons (*junzi* 君子), he said, "sentiments must be creditable; words must be deft." This is the source upon which self-development (*xiushen* 修身) and honorable eloquence (*wen*) draw. Thereby the will is strengthened for speech (*yan*) and writing (*wen*); sentiments become trustworthy, and speeches (*ci* 辭) deft. These are the precious stones in composition (*zhang* 章) and the golden rule for understanding eloquence (*wen*).

Chapter 3. The Orthodox Classics (zong jing 宗經)

3.10 Argumentation (*lun* 論), persuasion (*shui* 說), speech (*ci* 辭), and preamble (*xu* 序) began in *Yi Jing* (*Book of Changes*). Decree (*zhao* 詔), edict (*ce* 策), acclamation (*zhang* 章), and memorial (*zou* 奏) originated in the *Book of Shang*. Expository verse (*fu* 賦), ode (*song* 頌), poetry/lyric (*ge* 歌), and appraisal (*zang* 贊) were defined in the *Book of Poetry*. Maxim (*ming* 銘), eulogy (*lai* 誄), admonition (*zhen* 箴), and prayer (*zhu* 祝) first appeared in the *Book of Rites*. Chronicle (*ji* 記), biography (*zhuan* 傳), treaty (*meng* 盟), and declaration (*xi* 檄) are rooted in the *Spring and Autumn Annuals*. Visionary and far-reaching, they have established models of high standards. Hundreds of schools have attempted to sprint out of the bound but eventually return to the prescribed scope (of the classical canons).

3.12 Eloquence (*wen*) is built on action, which in turn transmits eloquence. The four areas of teaching are headed by eloquence, enriching and supporting one another.[289] Promoting virtues and establishing reputations cannot but follow the sages' teaching. But in developing the language (*jian yan* 建言) and polishing the speech (*xiu ci* 修辭),[290] few follow the classics. For

---

287. Wood, fire, earth, metal, and water.

288. The heart was believed to control thinking and spirit. See *Guiguzi* for detailed explanation (2016, 39).

289. The four areas of education include eloquence or literacy (*wen*), action or conduct (*xing*), loyalty (*zhong*), and credibility (*xin*).

290. Liu uses "*xiu ci*" in chapter 10 as well to mean polishing the word or speech (2016, 10.13).

this reason, the gaudy Chu prose and overly elaborate Han expository verse are repeated over again.[291] Wouldn't it be beautiful to just return to the roots?

Chapter 18. Argumentation and Persuasion (lun shui 論說)

18.1 The philosophical teachings by the sages are called classics. The recounts of the classics and the explications of their principles are called arguments. Argumentation means ethics (*lun*倫). When ethical principles are not compromised, the sages' messages do not go amiss. The astute speeches (*wei yan* 微言) by Confucius were recorded by his disciples who humbly excluded their own work from the classics and named it "*Lun Yun (Analects* 論語)." Since then, argumentation (*lun*) has been established as a name for this type of works. Before the *Analects*, the classics did not have a name for argumentation.

18.7 Argumentation (*lun*) is regarded as a genre because its function is to tell right from wrong. It exhausts the tangible to seek the intangible thoroughly with perseverance and adherence. As an instrument, its hook goes to the bottom of things to capture hundreds of deliberations and balance a myriad of things. Hence, its values reside in accommodating and coherent meanings; it prohibits incoherent and fragmented words (*ci* 辭). The principle and the heart are in perfect accord without any seam or gap. The speech is put together intimately with the heart, leaving no information or chance to the enemy. This is the essence (of argumentation).

18.10 Persuasion (*shui* 說) means to please (*yue*悅). The character "*dui* (兌)" means the mouth and tongue.[292] The speech depends on pleasure and appeal . . .

18.11 When the warring states were fighting to conquer one another, numerous persuaders rose like clouds, providing advice on *zong* (vertical) and *heng* (horizontal) intrigues and competing with long-short tactics for victory.[293] "Rotation of Small Shots" (*zhuan wan* 轉丸) rode on deft speeches; "Captivate-Capture" (*fei qian* 飛鉗) manifested superior skills.[294] The eloquence of one man is weightier than precious nine tripods; a tongue three inches long is stronger than a million troops.

18.15 Conclusion: The principle (*li* 理) is shaped by the language (*yan* 言), which articulates the principle to develop argumentation. Profound remarks (*ci* 詞) connect human with Heaven, reaching far into the heart. *Yin-yang* leaves no doubt; ghosts and spirits have no way to hide. Persuasion captives and captures the target to stop evil doings instantly.

---

291. Liu criticizes writers who extend the styles of *Chu Verse* (楚辭) by Qu Yuan (屈原373–278 BCE) and expository verse in the Han Dynasty (206 BCE-–220 CE) to such an elaborate degree that the quality of their writing deteriorates.
292. The *Book of Changes* equalizes "*dui*" with "*shui* (說)" (Qi 2008, 217; Shih 1969, 105).
293. See scholarship on rhetoric during the Warring States Period (Lu 1998; Wu,2016).
294. "Rotation of Small Shots" and "Captivate-Capture" are chapter titles in *Guiguzi* (2016, 88–89, 56–58).

Chapter 26. Aspiration and Idea (shen si 神思)

26.1 An ancient said, "The body stays above rivers and seas, but the heart focuses on the court of the State of Wei."[295] This speaks to aspirations and ideas. The ideas for eloquence are inspired to reach far. Therefore, concentrated thinking in solitude connects one's ideas back to thousands of years ago . . .

26.2 Incessant learning results in a collection of treasures. Deliberations on the principle enrich talent. Study readings to reach a thorough understanding and gradually grasp how words are employed. Thereby resolve the unknown before commissioning the cut like a butcher. Trace sound patterns to decide what to write in accord. Conduct independent reflections to become a wordsmith. Detect the moves of the mind to exercise skills for the cut. This, in short, is the primary technique to drive eloquence and the great beginning to develop a piece of work (*pian* 篇).

Chapter 27. Style and Character (ti xing 體性)

27.1 Excited sentiments (*qing*) manifest in the form of language (*yan*). Enlightenment from the principle reflects eloquence (*wen*), which transforms from invisible to visible and from internal to external . . .

27.2 The ways that have been followed can be generalized in eight styles. The first is elegant and exquisite, the second far-reaching and profound, the third refined and concise, the fourth lucid and linear, the fifth convoluted and elaborate, the six splendid and sublime, the seventh novel and unusual, and the eight light and delicate.

27.3 The eight styles interchange constantly. Successful applications require accomplished learning. The talent and power are then centralized in the blood and energy (*qi* 氣). The energy fulfills the will; the will determines the language. Absorbing and contributing to the finest splendor (of eloquence) are not but sentiment and character.

Chapter 28. Flair and Bones (feng gu 風骨)

28.1 The *Book of Poetry* speaks of six appeals. The first is flair.[296] It is the original source of emotional appeal in correlation with the will and energy. Expressions of disconsolate moods and sentiments always come with flair. Deep thoughts in arranged words (*ci* 辭) never begin

---

295. Meaning that living as an ordinary person, one has the ambition to hold state offices (Liu 2016, 274; Qi 2008, 321). Liu implies that the mind is not limited to one's living conditions.

296. Six appeals include flair (*feng* 風), beauty (*fu* 賦), analogy (*bi* 比), exhilaration (*xing* 興), grace (*ya* 雅), and praise (*song* 頌). *Fu* in antiquity was not a genre, as the chapters on Xunzi and Lu Ji demonstrate.

without bones. Hence, words depend on bones like the human body depending on its skeleton. When the will and energy are vigorously revitalized, the flair in eloquence is distinct . . .

28.2 Therefore, eloquence known for its bones elaborates in refined words; eloquence known for its flair foregrounds sentiments. Words tempered with unmovable strength in unstoppable deep resonance manifest the power of flair and bones.

Chapter 30. Decision on Power (ding shi 定勢)

30.1 When sentiments (*qing* 情) involve different forms, eloquence varies techniques. All depend on nothing but the sentiments to develop style. The style then exerts power. Power means utilizing opportunities to structure the form. . . .

Chapter 31 Sentiment and Coloration (qing cai 情采)

31.1 The books and speeches by the sages and honorable persons are generally called "eloquent composition (*wen zhang* 文章)." . . . Eloquence (*wen*) is entwined with substance (*zhi* 質) . . . Substance depends on eloquence.[297] . . . Hence, the way to develop eloquence is based on three principles (*li* 理). The first is the form of eloquence, which has five colors.[298] The second is the sound of eloquence, which has five tunes.[299] The third is the sentiment (*qing* 情) of eloquence, which has five temperaments (*xing* 性). . . .[300] The five temperaments contribute to the words of composition (*ci zhang* 辭章). This counts as the principle of omniscient intellectual conscience (*shenming* 神明).[301]

31.2 Laozi criticizes falsehood, saying "appealing words (*yan*) are untrustworthy." . . .

31.3 . . . the color of eloquence (*wen*) is a means to adorn words (*yan*), but the elegance of argumentation (*bian*辯) originates from sentiment and character (*qing xing* 情性). Therefore, sentiments are warps of an eloquence (*wen*), and words (*ci* 辭) its wefts. When warps are lined up correctly, wefts are in place. When the principle is confirmed, words (*ci* 辭) become fluent. Hereby the original source of eloquence (*wen*) is established.

---

297. The original of the two sentences is "文附質也, 質待文也," which is often quoted by later generations as a criterion for composition.
298. Blue, yellow, red, white, and black.
299. The five common tunes played by ancient string musical instruments.
300. Joy, anger, desire, fear, and anxiety.
301. See *Guiguzi* (2016, 84) and the chapter on Ban Zhao for "omniscient intellectual conscience."

Chapter 32 Melting and Tailoring (rong cai 熔裁*)*

32.1 When sentiments and the principle are in order, the color of eloquence (*wencai* 文采) flows across them with fortitude (*gang* 刚) and resilience (*rou* 柔), which are the fundamental source (*ben* 本). They remain adjustable and accommodating in accord with momentum . . . The established source offers choices of genres (*ti* 體). If contents run too long, the momentum loses directions. Then words (*ci* 辭) tend to be redundant and confusing. Regulating the fundamental source and genre is called melting; cutting and trimming superfluous words (*ci* 詞) is called tailoring . . .

32.2 . . . at the beginning of brainstorming (*caochuang* 草創), go through three stages. The first and foremost is deciding on the genre (*ti*) based on the sentiment. The middle stage is weighing things to know their categories. The final stage is collecting words (*ci* 辭) to recount important points . . .

32.3 After the three stages are set up, deliberate on characters (*zi* 字) and sentences (*ju* 句). Sentences that can be shortened are too loose. Characters that cannot be removed are tightly knit. Refined arguments (*lun*) and important remarks (*yu*) are expressed in concise manners. The active mind (*xin*) and flowing sentences enrich styles (*ti*). It is said that concise complex expressions come from different preferences . . .

Chapter 43. Arrangement and Coherence (fu hui 附会*)*

43.1 What is arrangement and coherence? It is the general order of an eloquence and its principle (*li* 理). It correlates the beginning with the ending, determines the contents, and weaves warps and wefts together to present complex rich contents without digression . . . Although words are abundant, they never fall into the disorder of tangled threads. Hold *yang* to lay out lines; follow *yin* to hide traces. The start and the end are carefully planned; the interior and exterior are a body of unity. This is the art (*shu* 術) of arrangement and coherence.

Chapter 49. Moral Standards and Talent (cheng qi 程器*)*

49.6 An exemplary person (*junzi*) keeps his talent hidden and awaits the right time to take action. . . . He composes eloquent works to help with the governance of the military and the state. When he bears important responsibilities, he is dependable as a pillar and a beam to house the duties. When disappointed (by the court), he secludes himself peacefully to immortalize his eloquent works (*wen*); When appointed, he utilizes the opportunity to provide state service and strives for achievements. This is a man of eloquence (*wen ren* 文人), a man of talent to be a state pillar.

Chapter 50. Epilogue (xu zhi 序志)

50.1 A heart for eloquence (*wen xin*) means devoting one's heart to transforming words (*yan*) into eloquence. . . . The heart is beautiful. The eloquent compositions (*wen zhang* 文章) from the antiquity have developed genres (*ti*) thanks to the thriving art. Isn't it fitting here to borrow "*diao long* (to carve a dragon)" from Zou Shi (鄒奭)?[302] . . . An exemplary person (*junzi*) living in this world is committed to establishing the virtue (*de*) and language (*yan*). I have no choice but present my argument (*lun*).

---

302. Zou Shi was a scholar in the State of Qi (齊) during the Warring State period (475–221 BCE) (Liu 2016, 513; Qi 2008, 565). In his work titled "Caving a Dragon," Zou compares the art of composition to that of making a dragon out of a piece of wood.

2.7 Tang Dynasty

Rhetorical Instruction by Song Ruozhao (宋若昭, c. 9th Century CE): Chapter One in *The Analects for Women* (*Nü Lun Yu* 女論語) with an Introduction and Commentary

Hui Wu

INTRODUCTION

Song Ruoxin (?–820 CE) was the original author of *The Analects for Women* that followed the dialogical form of *The Analects* by Kongzi.[303] but her text was lost. It was rewritten and noted by one of her four younger sisters, Song Ruozhao (?-825). Their father, Song Tingfen (宋廷棻), was a reputed Confucian scholar in the Tang Dynasty (618–907 CE).[304] All the five Song sisters received education of Confucian classics, poetic composition, and history. Their knowledge and literary talents were so well known that they were summoned as masters by Emperor De Zong (德宗780–805 CE) to participate in court literary events. The Emperor also invited them to court antiphonal events[305] exclusive to high-ranking male officials. It was said that all the Song sisters greatly appreciated the opportunities, except Song Ruozhao.[306] Comparing herself to Ban Zhao, Song Ruozhao would rather read and write in her own living quarters than participate in these events. The Emperor, instead of being offended, commended her for her will of learning and bestowed her with the title of "Female Scholar" (*nü xueshi* 女学士). As such, Song Rouzhao was responsible for court literacy and literary development, teaching the princes and princesses as their Court Master (*gong shi* 宮師).[307] Both Song Ruoxin and Song Ruozhao remained unmarried. Through her life, Song Ruozhao composed several collections of poetry and expository verse, while rewriting her oldest sister's book, *The Analects for Women*.

When this book was composed, the Tang Dynasty (618-907 CE) witnessed great advancement in educational system, architecture, arts, and literature enhanced by woodblock printing on paper. The era is best known for Tang poetry represented by Li Bai (李白 701–762 CE), Du Fu (杜甫712–770 CE), Han Yu (韓愈768–842 CE), Li He (李賀790–816 CE), Bai Juyi (白居易 772–846 CE), Yuan Zhen (元稹 779–831 CE), and many more.[308] Meanwhile, many

---

303. Wang 2011, 3.
304. Wang 2015, 327; Wang, 2011, 74.
305. An antiphonal event (*geng he* 赓和) in ancient China was a banquet where attendees improvised lyrical poems in tune to certain music.
306. Shen 2012, 98.
307. Wang 2011, 74.
308. Rouzer 2017, 248–49.

anthologies and encyclopedias were produced "in a more robust fashion than any previous era."[309] Literary scholars "know the names of over a hundred anthologies compiled during the Tang."[310] Encyclopedias were compiled under imperial auspices, for example, *Pearls and Blossoms of the Three Teachings* (*Sanjiao Zhuying* 三教珠英), a collection of poetry completed in the year 699 CE, *Old History of Tang* (*Jiu Tang Shu* 舊唐書) and *New History of Tang* (*Xin Tang Shu* 新唐書), as well as many private collections.[311]

The Tang Dynasty renewed its interest in Confucianism as its ruling orthodox and welcomed students from neighboring regions. The mandated readings for all schools were the same as in the Han Dynasty that included the five Confucian classics (*wu jing*五經)—*Book of Poetry, Book of History (Book of Shang), Book of Rites, Book of Changes,* and *Spring and Autumn Annuals.* Students from Japan, Persia, Tibet, Turkey, Mongolia, and regions consisting of the now South and North Koreas traveled to Chang'an (now Xi'an), capital of the Tang Empire. They could enjoy free boarding and clothing.[312] In particular, Japan embraced Chinese architecture, writing system, literature, Confucian learning, Buddhism, and other cultural influences. As part of the four books for women, *The Analects for Women* was introduced centuries later to Japanese women for their education.

The high literate and literary productivity resulted from vibrant complementary state and private educations of Confucian classics and history. The government continuously improved schooling for men, though strictly based on social status or official ranks of their fathers. Boys of fourteen years old had to pass entrance examinations before being accepted into a state academy. They were required to complete the state schooling in six years or in no more than nine years.[313] Afterwards they could participate in the annual civic service examination held in the capital. The exam required candidates to explicate the Confucian orthodox and books in restricted verse patterns, such as six antitheses in perfect rhyme and rhythm, each constituting no more and no less than twelve characters that must be divided equally into six characters in half of each antithesis.[314] If participants scored high enough, they could be selected as ranking officials for the state or for the local government. For this reason, late Tang rulers continued to improve the civic service examination system to discover talents.[315] For example, in the mid-Tang period, the first female empress, Wu Zetian (武則天 624–705 CE), who ruled China from 690–705 CE and commissioned the composition of *Pearls and Blossoms of the Three Teachings,* tried to perfect the examination system to select the most talented to serve her empire. Since then, all young men, except those with criminal records or sons of merchants,

---

309. Kroll 2017, 303.

310. Ibid.

311. Tian 2017, 140–42.

312. Song and Wang 1999, 541–42.

313. Ibid., 330–31.

314. Ibid., 487.

315. See chapter on Ban Zhao for the exam's beginning.

could participate in the exam, even though many of them were not allowed to attend state academies due to their low social status.[316]

The open examination without an open educational system to supply participants strengthened private education that followed the long Confucian tradition. By the late Tang period, many highly learned men, mostly self-educated due to lack of social status, offered private teaching in isolated locations to encourage concentrated study for the civic service exam.[317] Male scholars with high official titles also taught their sons and daughters at home. The Song sisters' education by their father became a model for home schooling.[318] Another type of private education is offered by learned men and women who were connected to families of high social status or the court.[319] This explains why the Song sisters were summoned by Emperor De Zong to teach princes, princesses, and court ladies, while participating in court antiphony and poetry composition.

Furthermore, since boys from families of higher social status were not allowed to attend state academies until they were fourteen years old, teaching sons at home gave women opportunities to be educators. Many married women of families of higher social status educated their sons at home in hopes that they could attend a state academy and launch successful state service careers.[320] In particular, educated widows, who were discouraged to remarry to maintain chastity in the Confucian tradition, educated their sons and daughters at home and served as household heads to keep the social status of their families.[321] Chapter 8 of *The Analects for Women* confirms a mother's significant role in educating children at home, saying, "As they [children] grow older there is a sequence in teaching them. The right to instruction belongs, in fact, to the mother."[322] Indeed, the Tang Dynasty is known not only for women's education of the Confucian classics and history in general but also for children's education by exemplary mothers, such as mother of Liu Zongyuan (柳宗元), a famous Tang poet who passed the civic service exam with high scores to become a top-ranking official.[323]

In terms of rhetorical practice, the state and private education systems taught young men and women to compose poetry and verse in rhythm and rhyme to present their explications of history and Confucian classics. The practice expanded composition of poetry and verse to poetic rhapsody or poetic expository verse (*shifu* 诗赋), which became a popular genre near the end of the Tang Dynasty.[324] Although scholars in literature often consider *shifu* a literary genre, it is, in many cases, a rhetorical genre in poetic patterns to document history, teach, or express wishes and requests; they were also composed to present opinions, critical thoughts,

316. Song and Wang 1999, 440–41.
317. Ibid., 390–406.
318. Ibid., 413–14.
319. Ibid., 414–16.
320. Ibid., 416.
321. Ibid.
322. Zhan and Bradshaw 1996, 265.
323. Song and Wang 1999, 416.
324. Rouzer 2017, 247–48.

and advocacy about social and political affairs. For example, *The Analects for Women*, notwithstanding its aesthetic values in terms of style and form, purports to teach rhetoric to women. Therefore, it has never been considered literature in the pure aesthetic sense, even though it is written in the perfect pattern of *shifu*. Indeed, it meets all the genre's stylistic and aesthetic requirements. There are eight Chinese characters in a sentence that is divided into two halves with each containing four characters in perfect parallelism. The written form demonstrates Song Ruozhao's adept mastery of the genre and her advanced education comparable to, if not better than, her male counterparts.

COMMENTARY ON SONG'S RHETORICAL INSTRUCTION

The historical backdrop helps us read *The Analects for Women* from a contextualized rhetorical feminist perspective. Much like Ban Zhao, the Song sisters were aware of women's lower social position than men's with a strong wish to maintain women's leading roles within the domestic domain—the home and the family, particularly those of married women who could become household heads to manage their husbands and sons. The Confucian orthodox indeed set restrictive expectations of women's behaviors to subordinate them socially and institutionally to men in general, by limiting women to the home and excluding them from state education and civic service. However, educated women took advantage of the private educational system to occupy the home, even though they had to follow Confucian gendered teaching.

This narrow performing space seemingly forced Song to be careful and smart when teaching women how to preform rhetorically under severe social restrictions and gender hierarchy. In the "Preface" she practices and recommends humility recommended by Ban as a rhetorical strategy. Instead of claiming her teaching authority directly, she calls this book an inspiration by "Cao Dagu" (Ban Zhao). While confessing that she has not learned any womanly craft defined as part of women's work by Ban (see chapter on Ban), Song unapologetically states that she has observed all the four proprieties and is well-read in history.[325] This statement naturally reinforces her authority as a teacher and legitimizes her authorship of the book. She finds "many heroines praiseworthy and some virtuous women admirable," but Song feels that their models are not followed. Thus, she writes the book "in the hope of teaching women to inherit the good and guard against the evils."[326] Meanwhile, while Ban wished to fill gaps in young women's education, Song ensures the learning outcomes of her teaching, saying, "Those who follow these teachings will be regarded as virtuous women, whose names will rank among those of their predecessors and be passed down to future generations."[327] At the end of her book, Song emphasizes the importance of her instruction, promising that if women take "unquestioned guidance from it" persistently, they will enjoy "boundless happiness."[328] From this

---

325. Zhan and Bradshaw 1996, 261.
326. Ibid.
327. Ibid.
328. Ibid., 268.

rhetorical perspective, Song's recommendation of womanly rhetorical behaviors in Chapter 1, such as speaking without revealing the teeth or sitting without moving the knees, reveals her teaching of humility as a strategy for rhetorical performance, an embodied performance through life-long learning and development. Her rhetorical appeal under the restricting gender hierarchy ultimately made her book a classic for women's education.

Again, neither Ban's *Lessons for Women* nor Song's *the Analects for Women* is a conduct book in the Western sense (see chapter on Ban Zhao). Both teach rhetoric to women to develop agency and occupy the home as the head and master. For this reason, Song believes that it is important for a woman to be recognized as a human (*ren* 人) (see Chapter 1 hereafter). In *Guiguzi*, the sage of rhetoric, who develops omniscient intellectual conscience (*shen ming* 神明) to upholds the *Dao* for persuasion, is One with Heaven and Earth—a true human being (*zhen ren* 真人).[329] In Confucian teaching, "the human (*ren*) is a realized person that has established himself/herself socially through self-learning and self-cultivation with full understanding of human relations and the fulfillment of the duties these relationships entail."[330] Becoming a recognized *ren*, therefore, is the goal for a woman's education, says Song. A women's self-establishment ultimately decides her status and reputation inside and outside the home. Therefore, Song emphasizes purity and chastity, which, though echoing restriction and suppression of women in the Confucian tradition, demonstrates how intimately Song understands the consequences to a woman without compliance. Purity means integrity and decency free of immorality and evil deeds. A pure and honorable woman must demonstrate benevolence (*ren* 仁) or kindness (*shan* 善), two qualities in the Confucian teaching regarding how to develop learned men into exemplary persons (*junzi*).[331] Therefore, women should not be in contact with unbenevolent females who may compromise their purity. This part of Song's teaching demonstrates her strong desire for women's self-establishment. Her encouragement of women to follow principles to regulate their behaviors prescribed by the Confucian rites is meant to promote their reputation and bring them honor, the key components of being a recognized human. In the narrowly restricted space, Song tries to help women develop rhetorical agency to gain power in the inner space they are allowed to occupy, yet only when they have become recognized humans. This contextualized feminist point of view reveals her rhetorical strategies and the purpose of her rhetorical instruction.

The *Analects for Women* contains twelve chapters. A newly translated Chapter 1 is provided hereafter. Readers who wish to read the full text in English translation can consult "Texts and Contexts: Book of Analects for Women" or its reprinted version in *Images of Women in Chinese Thought and Culture*.[332] Another full translation can be found in *The Confucian Four Books for Women*.[333] The retranslation below tries to fulfill two purposes. The first is to keep consistent

---

329. *Guiguzi* 2016, 92–93; also see chapter on Ban.

330. Wu 2005, 176.

331. *Analects* 15.18, 15.33.

332. Zhan and Bradshaw 1996, 262–68. Wang, 2015, 327–340.

333. Pang-White 2018, 71–116.

rhetorical concepts in the Chinese tradition, and the second aim is to align the parallelisms in Song's poetic verse with the choice of diction to relate her teaching of rhetoric to the larger historical context of literary and literate development.

Partial Translation of *Analects for Women*

Chapter 1

On Self-Establishment (lishen zhang 立身章*)*

All women must learn how to establish herself. The utmost important principle for self-establishment is the practice of purity (*qing* 清) and chastity (*zhen* 貞). Purity leads to flawless reputation; chastity brings honor.

When you are walking, do not turn your head back or around. When you are speaking (*yu* 語), do not show your teeth. When you sit, do not move your knees. When you stand, do not sway your skirt. When you are happy, do not laugh out loud. When you are angry, do not yell.

The inside and outside are two different worlds. Men and Women are separate groups. Do not try to look beyond the outer wall. Do not step out of the courtyard. When you must go outside, hide your face.[334] When you look outside, make yourself invisible.

Males who are not your relatives should not know your name. Females who are not benevolent and reputable should not be your friends. Only by establishing yourself squarely on the principles can you be recognized as a human (*ren* 人).

---

334. Hiding the face here means avoiding eye contact or seeing a male directly face to face, according Wang Xiang's commentary (2011, 76).

2.8 Song Dynasty

The *Rules of Writing*[335] in Medieval China by Chen Kui (陈騤 1128–1203 CE): Partial Translation with Commentary

Andrew Kirkpatrick

In this chapter I discuss the *The Rules of Writing* (*Wen Ze*文则) which was written by Chen Kui (陈騤 1128–1203 CE). *The Rules of Writing* has been called the first systematic account of Chinese rhetoric[336]. Its author, Chen Kui, was born at the beginning of the Southern Song dynasty (1127–1279 CE). He lived at a time of great change, being born one year after the beginning of the Southern Song period. The Northern Song emperors had ruled from 960 CE but had been forced to flee south in 1127 CE in face of invasion from the north.

Chen Kui was a member of the intellectual elite and passed the extremely prestigious and competitive metropolitan exam to become a *jinshi* (进士) at the comparatively early age of twenty-four. This was no mean feat. John Chaffee (1985) has eloquently recorded the trials and tribulations of being a scholar in Song China.[337] During the Song dynasty, the number of people taking the series of exams that culminated in the *jinshi* exam increased dramatically. There were two major reasons for this. First, the Song emperors desired to create a meritocracy by increasing the number of able men in the civil service. Exams replaced privilege as the main gateway into the civil service. Chen Kui himself held a number of senior official positions. In 1190 CE, during the reign of the Emperor Guang Zong, he was appointed secretary of the Imperial Library and was the author of *The Record of the Library of the Southern Song*. Second, the advent of printing opened up education to more people: "The spread of printing transformed Chinese book culture."[338] *The Rules of Writing* may thus well have been stimulated to provide a writing and rhetorical guide for the many thousands of men who were now preparing for one of the imperial civil service exams.

Here, I first briefly summarize how Chinese scholars have evaluated *The Rules of Writing* and then provide translations and discussion on excerpts from the book. The first excerpts are taken from Chapter 1 and illustrate Chen Kui's comments on the classics and their style. I then focus on three topics that are of particular relevance to rhetoric and the teaching of writing: the first topic concerns Chen Kui's advice on the use of simple and contemporary language; the second concerns his advice on the sequence of argument when writing discursive texts; and the third, concerns the use of citations.

---

335. Much of this chapter draws on two previously published articles, namely Kirkpatrick (2004, 27, 1, 1–14) and Kirkpatrick (2005, 103–52), where a fuller translation and more detailed commentary is provided.
336. For example, Liu (1988).
337. Chaffee 1985.
338. Cherniack 1994, 5–125.

THE RULES OF WRITING

The Rules of Writing is primarily concerned with the study of "essays" (*wenzhang*文章), which, in another context, Bol has translated as "literary composition."[339] *The Rules of Writing* is concerned with literary composition of a particular type—the writing of compositions suitable for the examination system as it was during the Southern Song. These compositions were based on the *guwen* (古文) style of the classics and presented the messages of the classics in contemporary language. The type of composition that Chen Kui is concerned with is *lun* (論), discourse or discussion. In summary *The Rules of Writing* is concerned with the composition of *lun* for use in the Song civil service exams.

The Rules of Writing is accepted by contemporary Chinese scholars as the study of Chinese classical rhetoric. Indeed, it has been described as the benchmark for the study of Chinese rhetoric as a whole.[340] Chen Kui's major aim in writing *The Rules of Writing* was to identify and summarize the rules of writing literary composition, using classical texts as his source material. *The Rules of Writing* thus discusses and exemplifies principles of composition and rhetoric, including aspects of genres, styles and methods of composition at the levels of word, sentence and text.[341] The book comprises five main topics: genre, 'negative' rhetoric, 'positive' rhetoric, syntax and style.[342]

Chen Kui's research method is also praised. Tan discusses this in detail and classifies Chen's use of the comparative method into seven categories. I list them in the order Tan does:[343]

> comparing the beginnings and endings of texts;
>
> comparing different genres;
>
> comparing one book with another;
>
> comparing works written at the same time;
>
> comparing contemporary texts with classical texts;
>
> comparing different ways of expressing the same or similar meanings;
>
> comparing the use of the same method to convey different meanings.

Tan also praises Chen for his use of what he calls the inductive method, *guinafa* (歸納法) and gives as an example Chen's classification of metaphor into ten categories based on count-

---

339. Bol 1992, 16.

340. Two Chinese scholars who have expressed this view are Wang (1988, 283–95) and Zhou (1999).

341. Liu 1988.

342. Negative rhetoric deals with such aspects of rhetoric as text structure and argument sequencing. Positive rhetoric deals with rhetorical tropes. George Kennedy makes a comparable division of Classical Western rhetoric into primary rhetoric, the art of persuasion, although this was primarily oral, and secondary rhetoric, the study of tropes and figures of speech (1980).

343. Tan 1978.

less examples. As a further example of Chen's use of induction, Tan identifies his elucidation of the rhetorical pattern of balanced parallelism based on the study of forty-four separate words, each supported by numerous examples.

The Rules of Writing is made up of ten chapters which themselves each comprise a number of sections, ranging from one (Chapter 10) to ten (Chapter 5). As Chapter 10 is actually the longest, it follows that the number of sections per chapter has little to do with the overall length of each chapter. There are sixty-three sections in all and these are listed in the Appendix. The numerical references used below refer to the chapter of *The Rules of Writing* and section within it. So (1/3) refers to Chapter 1, Section 3. In the selections below, I first give excerpts from Chapter 1 and then excerpts which are of particular relevance to rhetoric and persuasion.

Excerpts from Chapter 1 and the Style of the Classics

Chapter 1 Section 1. The Similarity between the six Classics

The principles upon which the six Classics[344] are based are fundamentally the same, and so there are few differences in the types of texts themselves. The texts of the *Book of Changes* are similar to those of the *Book of Poetry* which, in turn, are similar to those of the *Shang Histories* which are similar to those of the *Rites of Zhou*. The *Book of Changes* says "When the crane in the tree softly calls, the young bird must respond. When my cup is full of excellent wine, I want to drink with you." There is little difference between the dynastic hymns in the *Book of Poetry* and those in the *Book of Changes*.

Chapter 1 Section 2. Originality and mimicry in the six Classics

It has been argued that the original intention of the six Classics was not the same and that they did not model themselves after each other. But having thoroughly studied the six Classics, the evidence demonstrates this theory to be incorrect.

Chapter 1 Section 5. Descriptions can be implicit.

Compiling written records can be difficult; making the meanings implicit can be a good thing. For example, the *Gong Yang commentary*[345], in recording the episode of the catastrophic defeat in battle of the Qin army, simply says, "Not even one horse, not even one wheel, returned to Qin." A further example from the *Gong Yang commentary* occurs when it records

---

344. It is customary to refer to the "FiveClassics and Four Books.'" The five Confucian Classics are *The Book of Changes, The Book of Poetry, The Shang Histories* or the *Book of History, The Rites of Zhou* and the *Spring and Autumn Annals*. Chen Kui's sixth Classic is probably the *Book of Music*, which has been lost. For further discussion see de Bary and Bloom (1999).

345. *The Gong Yang* commentary is a commentary on the *Spring and Autumn Annals*.

the episode of the Qi State sending men to welcome Xi Ke and Zang Sun. "The approaching visitors were lame and blind in one eye, so the Qi State sent a lame person to meet a lame person and a one-eyed person to meet a one-eyed person.

Chapter 1 Section 6. Repetition, roundaboutness and tact.

Repetition is sometimes used in the Book of Poetry and the Shang Histories to express meaning in the roundabout and respectful way. For example, the Shang Histories say, "From this day on, a young man like you needs to exercise caution in making friends and must be aware when acting in concert with people; young people must be cautious in making friends and when acting in concert."

Chapter 1 Section 7. On balance.

Texts use contrast to combine ideas. For example, "An arrow can kill a small piglet, yet it can also kill a large rhinoceros," "I tirelessly advise you, yet you carelessly ignore me," and "As schemes and intrigues develop, so military conflicts and disputes break out." Such sentences link ideas. In general, the language of these sentences can be considered exquisite.

COMMENTARY

In the next sections of the chapter, I have translated excerpts that are of direct relevance to rhetoric and the art of writing. The first topic concerns Chen Kui's advice on the use of language.

Advice on Language Use

As a fervent advocate of the *guwen* style, Chen Kui identifies the general overriding principle that language should be simple, clear, succinct and contemporary. "To be good, things need to be simple and easy; to be appropriate, language needs to be simple and clear" (1/4). "Good texts need to be succinct and concise. However, being succinct, texts must also be complete and logical. If the reader feels that a text has gaps and omissions, then it cannot be considered succinct, but rather one that has been constructed carelessly." Chen Kui praises the brevity and clarity of the example below from the *Spring and Autumn Annals* and criticizes the *Gong Yong commentary* of the same event. The criticized Gong Yong version reads: "Hearing the sound of falling meteorites, as soon as I realized these were stones that were falling, I examined them carefully and found that they were five meteorites." The praised version in the *Spring and Autumn Annals* reads: "Five meteorites fell on Song territory." Chen Kui exalts; "This is a succinctness that is hard to achieve" (1/4).

   It is interesting to compare Chen Kui's treatment with the ways other scholars have analyzed this passage. For example, Francois Jullien cites the same excerpts in his discussion on the *Wen Xin Diao Long* as an example of how a commentator "scrutinizes every notation, for nothing in the mention of an event is seen as either fortuitous or innocuous."[346]

Why does it say "fell" before "stones?" The falling of stones repeats the way it is heard: one hears the noise of something falling, and in looking at the thing that has fallen, one sees that it is stones; in looking at them closer, one can count that there are five. . .

Rather than the commentator scrutinizing every notation, however, I suggest that the *Wen Xin Diao Long* commentary stresses the logical, chronological, and natural order of the events. This notion of "logical" order is an accepted principle of sequencing in Chinese. Here, however, Chen Kui's focus is on the importance of clarity and succinctness. He further illustrates this in the example below, in which he compares the relative economy in the use of characters in three different texts all expressing the same idea.

TRANSLATIONS INTERSPERSED WITH COMMENTARY

Xie Ye (洩冶) is recorded as saying: "The guidance and help a ruler gives to his subjects is like wind blowing among grass; when the wind blows from the east, the grass bends to the west, and when the wind blows from the west, the grass bends to the east; when the wind blows the grass bends."

This excerpt needs thirty-two characters to make its meaning clear.

The Analects say: "The behavior of people of position can be compared to the wind, while the behaviour of normal people can be compared to the grass; when the wind blows through the grass, the grass bends accordingly."

This uses half the number of characters that Xie Ye used, but its meaning is clear.

The Shang Histories say: "Your behaviour can be compared to the wind, and the behaviour of the people can be compared to the grass."

This uses nine fewer characters than *The Analects* but its meaning remains very clear (1/4). Chen Kui also calls for writing that is both natural and coherent.

> If a musical performance is not harmonious, then music is unpleasant; if a text is not coherent, then it cannot be read . . . classical texts were natural and coherent and were without adornment and embellishment. (1/3)

> To help ensure this, writers should use the language of the people and the time. "The use of language that was the common speech of one period will be found abstruse and difficult by people of later periods. (1/8)

He continues:

> Although classical texts used classical language, classical language cannot be fully understood by later generations, unless there are explanatory notes.

---

346. Jullien 2004, 105–06.

> Reading classical books without notes is like scaling a tricky peak, after each step you need to take several deep breaths. If, after arduous study, one picks up some classical language and uses it to record contemporary events, one can be compared with maidservants who tried to act like their mistresses, but whose attitudes and postures were very unnatural and did not look right. (1/8)

As an example of the use of the language of the time, Chen Kui cites excerpts from The *Book of Rites*. As he points out, this often used plain and simple language. It is also completely straightforward and to the point. There is no indirection or obliquity here. For example:

> Use your hand to cover your mouth when speaking to avoid breathing over people;

> When dining as a guest in someone's house don't toss your leftover bones to the dog, so showing that you do not give a fig for the things of your host;

> Even when eating the leftover sauce from the vegetables still use chopsticks;

> When men and women meet, they should observe the proprieties;

> If you have an itch do not scratch it in front of your relatives.

Chen Kui explains:

> Although the meaning of these extracts is complex and is concerned with preventing people violating the rites, there is very little literary embellishment. The language used is plain and simple. Writers who study historical literary forms and who adopt classical language to write texts frequently produce muddled gibberish. (5/1)

Chen Kui concludes Section 5 of Chapter 1 with a striking metaphor:

> The old saying says, "Dimples on the face are very attractive, but on the forehead, they are very ugly." This saying is absolutely right. Ever since the Jin dynasty (265-420 CE), there have been far too many people who have longed to imitate the classics when they pick up their pens to write. (5/10)

Chen's main concern here is with the language of the classics and its influence on contemporary (Song) writing. He realized that, as language changed with the times, writers should not slavishly mimic classical texts. They should not use classical language to write about contemporary events. He pointed out that the language used in the classics was, at the time, contemporary language, and was language that could be easily understood by the people. Simply put, he opposed the misuse of classical language and promoted the use of common and contemporary language. He cites many examples from different texts to show how the simply expressed text is more effective than the more complex or embellished one. He championed the use of the vernacular and spoken language.

These principles are stressed throughout *The Rules of Writing*. He fully understood the phenomena of language change and language variety. "The language used in the *Pan Geng* section of *The Shang Histories* was contemporary and vernacular. It was the common language of the people and language, therefore, that everyone could understand" (5/2).

He also advocates the use of regional varieties and low-brow genres. He quotes, with approval, this builder's ballad:

> Within the city's Southern gate, the people's skin is white,
> Urging us to work hard
> Within the city, the people's skin is black,
> Consoling us. (9/5)[347]

Coupled with these principles of language use is Chen Kui's belief that form should serve meaning. Throughout the Chinese rhetorical and literary tradition there has been a constant debate about the relative importance of *dao* (道) (meaning) and *wen* (文), language and/or literature, or form. This is obviously closely linked with the debate over the relative merits of the flowery literary form known as *pianwen* (駢文) and the simpler classical form known as *guwen* (古文). In *The Rules of Writing*, *dao* (content) is primary and *wen* (form) is subordinate to *dao*. Words must serve meaning. This notion held true, whether Chen Kui was discussing the use of words, syntax and sentence construction, or rhetoric itself.

I now turn to the second topic directly concerned with rhetoric and writing, the arrangement of ideas.

The Arrangement of Ideas

A second topic that Chen Kui discusses in *The Rules of Writing* that is of direct relevance to rhetoric concerns the sequence or arrangement of argument. There are, says Chen Kui, three ways in which texts can enumerate the conduct and deeds of people:

> The first is that they can they first state the summary or overall point, and then list the individual details. For example, when judging Zi Chan, Confucius said, "Zi Chan had four aspects of behavior fitting for the way of a ruler: his own moral conduct was dignified and respectful; he waited upon the ruler in a dignified way; he nurtured the people kindly; and he made sure that the people followed the truth. (4/4)

---

347. The reference to the color of people's skins reflects the belief that workers and farmers developed dark faces as they worked outside in the sun, while people with white faces were indoor workers (and therefore seen to be of higher class).

The second method of sequencing information is to list individual details first and then summarize and explain. For example, when enumerating the charges against Gong Sun Hei of Zheng, Zi Chan said,

> Your turbulent heart cannot be satisfied, and the State cannot condone this. Usurping power and attacking Bo You, this is your first charge; coveting your brother's wife and resorting to violence, this is your second charge; setting up local factions on the pretext of being ruler, this is your third charge. With these three charges, how can your behavior be condoned? (4/4)

The third way is to provide the overall or main point at the beginning, then list the individual details and then conclude with the overall point again. For example, Confucius said,

> Zang Wenzhong did three cruel-hearted and stupid things: he gave a low official position to Hui 'beneath the willow'; he set up a toll-gate and collected taxes; and he allowed his concubines to sell their woven mats on the open market. These were the three cruel-hearted things. Zang exceeded the bounds of his duty. He kept a giant turtle; he failed to stop Xia Fuji when Xia violated the rituals of sacrifice; and he ordered the entire country to make sacrifices to some seabird. These were the three stupid things. (4/4)

In the next section of the same chapter (4/5) Chen Kui continues this theme of sequencing by saying that when writing about events, one can first introduce the argument or judgment and then write about the events, or one can write about the events and then make some judgment about them. As an example of first introducing the argument, Chen Kui cites the excerpt in *The Zuo Zhuan* where it records Jin Linggong's imposition of tax revenues, using money obtained through usury to paint and decorate the palace walls.

It firmly states at the beginning: "Jin Linggong had no principles and did not have the moral conduct of ruler" (4/5).

An example of drawing a conclusion after describing the events also comes from the *Zuo Zhuan*.

> First, the noble deeds of Duke Wen are recorded, including how he trained the people and then put this training to use. The passage concludes: "one battle caused the Jin State to become a hegemony, this was the result of Wen's training! (4/5)

The striking aspect of this advice about sequencing is that it is not dissimilar to the advice given by Anglo teachers of rhetoric today. In providing three ways of arranging argument, Chen gives cause to doubt that the commonly expressed view that the rhetorical structure of Chinese argument and writing is somehow uniquely Chinese. In fact, the three methods of sequencing information identified by Chen Kui will appear familiar to many. The first was to summarize the main point(s) and then provide the details, and this looks very much like a deductive pattern; the second was to provide the details first and then summarize, and this looks very much like an inductive pattern; and the third was to use a three-part structure whereby the main points were stated at the beginning and recapped at the end, with the details being provided in the middle. This looks very much like the three-part structure of introduction—body—conclusion. This is of particular interest as it would appear that Chen Kui is promoting a "marked" "main-frame" rhetorical structure, rather than the unmarked "frame-main" sequence, which might be expected and which I have myself argued to be the preferred default rhetorical structure.[348] The advice to adopt this main-frame sequence is, however, linked to the type of text *The Rules of Writing* is aimed at producing. It needs to be remembered that Chen Kui was adamant that a return to the plain and simple *guwen* style was needed, and that this style should not encumber itself with obscure classical language, but be written in a way which would be clear to contemporaries. We should also remember that the Song empire of the time was keen to establish a meritocracy and therefore to employ only deserving people in the civil service. This was a relatively open time in which people felt they could express their ideas 'up' without too much fear of retribution if they displeased the emperor. Nevertheless, Chen Kui himself appears to have overstepped the mark on a number of occasions in his own memorials to the emperor, of which he penned thirty or so. On one occasion, for example, he wrote to criticize the extravagance of the imperial court, and for this he was demoted and sent to cool his heels for a time in an official position in the provinces.[349]

There is some evidence that Chen Kui's influence was felt throughout later periods of Chinese history and can be traced through later handbooks. For example, his influence upon Gui Youguang's (1506–1571 CE) *Guide to Composition Writing* (文章指南) is clear. Gui's handbook advises the writer that three arrangements for an essay are possible:

> Present the main idea at the beginning, then break the idea into several points/aspects devoting one paragraph to the elaboration of each; discuss the component points first one by one, then present the main idea in the end; or, best of all, on the basis of the first layout, add a summary of the main idea at the end.[350]

A much more recent text which shows apparent influence from Chen Kui—although it is impossible to verify this—is the twentieth century reformer Hu Shi's promotion of the vernacular as the medium of educated discourse. Hu Shi formulated eight famous rules for writers, which bear a striking similarity to Chen Kui's advice:

> Language must have content.
>
> Do not (slavishly) imitate classical writers.
>
> Make sure you pay attention to grammar and structure.

---

348. See, for example, Kirkpatrick and Xu (2012).
349. Zhang 1998, 465.
350. Liu 1996.

Do not complain if you are not ill—in other words, don't overdo the emotion.

Cut out the use of hackneyed clichés.

Don't cite or rely on the classics.

Don't use parallelism.

Embrace popular and vernacular language.[351]

It is commonly assumed that Hu Shi was influenced by his time in the United States—he studied at Cornell and did his PhD at Columbia where he studied under John Dewey, and with whom he maintained a lifelong professional relationship—and that it was his experience in the United States that led him to promote the use of the vernacular and *bai hua* Chinese in place of the literary *wenyan* (the classical language) style. But it is at least possible that Hu Shi was also influenced by traditional Chinese scholars such as Chen Kui.

I now turn to the third topic to be considered here, namely Chen Kui's advice on citation

Chen Kui's Advice on Citation

Chen Kui's advice on the use of citation is also relevant to rhetoric and persuasion, as citation gives authority or support for an argument or claim. He starts by pointing out that *The Book of Poetry*, *The Shang Histories*, and the many books that explain the classics and histories all contain many citations. There were definite rules for citing and, generally speaking, there were two methods:

> The first was to use citation as evidence about an event or action that had taken place, or to exemplify appropriate behaviour; the second was to use citation to prove one's argument. (3/2)

> At the same time, copying without acknowledgment, plagiarism, was not condoned. (5/5)

Chen Kui illustrates ways of using citation to provide evidence that an event has taken place and gives examples. One reads,"The Zuo Zhuan records: "The Book of Poetry says: 'A person who sought for himself worry and sadness,' this was really talking about Zi Zang!" (3/2).

Among the many examples provided by Chen Kui of using citation to explain or promote actions and behaviour are these two.

The Zuo Zhuan records:

> The Book of Poetry says: 'Where does one go to pick wormwood? By the banks of a pond or on a small sand bar. Where can you use it? At the funeral ceremony of a duke.' Tai Mu Gong did this. (3/2)

---

351. Hu Shi 1917, Vol 1, 5–16.

Work hard and do not let up at dawn or dusk to pay respect to someone. Meng Ming did this. (3/2)

Chen Kui also gave three ways of using citation to prove one's argument. It could be done by citing widely from the Classics, or by presenting one's argument and then using citations to support it, or by analyzing the cited excerpts and showing that they supported one's argument. As an example of citing from the Classics, Chen Kui provides this excerpt:

> Shang Tang says, "If one day you can get rid of the old customs and renew yourself, with this new foundation, by renewing daily and constantly, you can arrive at a brand new realm." Kang Gao says, "Education stimulates the masses, makes them get rid of old customs, and become new people."
>
> *The Book of Poetry* says, "Although Zhou was an ancient state, (by the time of King Wen), it received the mandate of heaven in a further renewal of virtue and replaced Shang. Therefore, we say that a ruler, in order to build a good state, must try all methods and must explore all paths" (3/2).

Finally, the method of analyzing cited text to support one's argument is illustrated with this passage from *The Zuo Zhuan*:

> The Zuo Zhuan says, "Appoint people you can use, and respect men worthy of respect." This extract is discussing the Duke of Jin's rewarding of those who render outstanding service. It also says, "Although the last ruler of the Shang dynasty had millions of subjects, dissension and discord was in them all; The Zhou dynasty had ten great officials who helped in ruling and they were all united and in accord." The point of this passage is that virtue can serve the people. If the emperor has virtue, the masses must come together and turn to him. (3/2)

Chen Kui's discussion of the use of citation suggests that the claim that Chinese do not acknowledge sources as frequently or as comprehensively as Western scholars does not have a historical origin.[352] Chen Kui shows that citation was an important part of scholarly writing at the time and gives a detailed explanation of the ways in which this could be done and for what purposes. He also explicitly states that copying another person's work without acknowledgement cannot be condoned. I should make it clear that I am not claiming that this means that Chinese scholars used citation in the same way as Western scholars do today. On the contrary, certain styles of Classical Chinese writing required the listing, one after the other, of many citations from the Classics, with the author providing little of his own voice, or, at least, providing his voice in characters of smaller size than those of the citations themselves.[353] Chen

---

352. See for example, Bloch and Chi (1995, 231–74).
353. Moloughney 2002, 23.

Kui's comments do show, however, that Chinese scholarship has been familiar with the practice of citation for centuries and that plagiarism is understood and condemned. Moloughney provides further evidence of this when he translates a witty aphorism of Zhang Xuecheng, a Chinese scholar of the late eighteenth century: "The plagiarist fears only that people would know of his source; the creative user that they would be ignorant of it."[354] It is also worth noting that the importance we currently attach to citation and acknowledgement has at least as much to do with copyright law as with a genuinely altruistic wish to acknowledge the work of others.[355] Writers in medieval Europe were notorious for not acknowledging the work of others. For example, St Jerome "borrowed" complete excerpts from Quintilian.[356]

There is much more to *The Rules of Writing* than can be summarized here. Chen Kui made an extraordinary contribution to the study of Chinese rhetoric. In addition to his advice on clarity, the arrangement of ideas, and the importance and use of citation, he categorized metaphor for the first time, and many of his categories are still used today. He showed how a whole range of function words were used. He illustrated the rhetorical effect of tropes, such as inversion, repetition and balance. He discussed the relative merits of sentence length. He identified and discussed a number of genres and took genre theory forward. His method distinguished him as an original thinker and ground-breaking rhetorician. For the first time, rules of writing and principles of rhetoric were identified from a close study of real texts. Chen Kui compared texts and deduced rules from a close study of numerous examples. *The Rules of Writing* is peppered with examples that illustrate the points Chen Kui is making. In this way, he provides hard linguistic and rhetorical evidence for all of his claims. Finally, this is all presented in a non-prescriptive way, in that the final determiner of use has to be the context and the rhetorical effect the writer wishes to make.

Appendix

List of the contents/subsections of the *Wen Ze* (文則) (My translations of chapter/section titles)

Chapter 1 (eight sections) Classical and Contemporary Language

Section 1: The similarity between the six Classics.

Section 2: Originality and mimicry in the six Classics

Section 3: Good texts are natural and coherent

Section 4: Textual Simplicity

---

354. Ibid., 136.
355. Scollon 1995, 1–28.
356. Lanham 2001, 79–121.

Section 5: Descriptions can be implicit

Section 6: Repetition, roundaboutness and tact

Section 7: On balance

Section 8: When recording contemporary events, classical language is inappropriate.

Chapter 2 (six sections) The Use of Words

Section 1: The use of function words

Section 2: Inversion

Section 3: Word formation

Section 4: Lexical errors and solecisms

Section 5: Relative importance and emphasis

Section 6: Ornateness.

Chapter 3 (four sections) Metaphor and Citation

Section 1: Ten types of metaphor

Section 2: The function and methods of citation

Section 3: Methods of and examples of the use of citations from the *Discourses of the States* (*guo yu* 國語) and the *Zuo Zhuan* (左傳)

Section 4: Methods of recording *Fu* (賦) poetry in the *Zuo Zhuan* (左傳)

Chapter 4 (eight sections) Rhetoric and Argument

Section 1: Rhetoric and progression

Section 2: Rhetoric and repetition

Section 3: Cohesion as repetition

Section 4: Three ways of sequencing information

Section 5: Two methods of argumentation

Section 6: Repetition and avoiding repetition

Section 7: Rhetoric and the style of question and answer

Section 8: Ways of citing surnames

Chapter 5 (ten sections) Plain Language and the Classics

Section 1: The use of plain language in the *Book of Rites* (禮記)

Section 2: The use of contemporary and vernacular language in the *Pan Geng* (盤庚)

Section 3: Local color in the language of the *Book of Songs* (詩經)

Section 4: Linguistic characteristics of the *yi li* (儀禮 rites) and *the Analects* (論語)

Section 5: Following old customs in the *Classic of Filial Piety* (孝經)

Section 6: Examples modelled on the "Er Ya" (爾雅) and "Shi Fa" (諡法)

Section 7: A comparison on language use in the *Analects* (論語), *Zuo Zhuan* (左傳) and other books

Section 8: Rhetoric and irony

Section 9: A text that misuses classical language must have faults

Section 10: Thoughtlessly applying hackneyed phrases makes a text absurd.

Chapter 6 (seven sections) Classical Language Use

Section 1: The language of the "Tan Gong" (檀弓) is simple but not sparse, the ideas profound but not obscure

Section 2: Sentence length in the *Tan Gong* (檀弓)

Section 3: Exquisitely crafted sentences in the *Tan Gong* (檀弓)

Section 4: 3 beautiful qualities of the language of *the Kao Gong Ji* (考工記)

Section 5: Language in the *Spring and Autumn Annals* (春秋) and the *Book of Songs* (詩經)

Section 6: Function words in the *Book of Songs* (詩經)

Section 7: Kong Yingda's (孔穎達) discussion on the method of composition of the *Book of Songs* (詩經)

Chapter 7 (two sections) Balance and Parallelism

Section 1: Rhetoric and the use of balance and parallelism

Section 2: Examples from the Classics of sentences that are similar

Chapter 8 (eight sections) The Eight Genres of the Zuo Zhuan (左傳)

Section 1: Edicts;

Section 2: Vows;

Section 3: Treaties;

Section 4: Prayers;

Section 5: Critical remarks;

Section 6: Notes of censure;

Section 7: Letters;

Section 8: Responses

Chapter 9 (seven sections) 7 More Genres

Section 1: Admonition;

Section 2: Praise;

Section 3: Inscriptions;

Section 4: Lyrics;

Section 5: Ballads;

Section 6: Threnodies and eulogies;

Section 7: Eulogistic prayers.

Chapter 10 (one section) Edicts

2.9 Ming Dynasty

Rhetorical Instruction by Queen Xu (徐皇後 *Xu Huanghou,* 1362–1407 CE): A Partial Translation of the *Doctrine for the Inner Court* (內訓 *Nei Xun*) with an Introduction and Commentary

Hui Wu

INTRODUCTION

Queen Xu (1362–1407 CE), officially known as Queen Renxiaowen (仁孝文皇後), took her royal title as her formal name upon marriage. She was the empress consort of Emperor Mingcheng (明成帝1360–1424 CE) who occupied the throne from 1402 to 1424 CE as the third ruler of the Ming Dynasty (1368–1644 CE). Queen Xu (hereafter Xu) completed *Doctrine for the Inner Court* in 1404 CE based on her education by Queen Xiaocigao (孝慈高皇後 1332–1382 CE), Xu's mother-in-law and empress consort of the first Ming emperor, Zhu Yuanzhang (朱元璋 1328–1398 CE). Highly educated with full knowledge of history and Confucian classics, Xu expressed concerns about the shortage of teaching materials for women's education. First, available books for women's education either repeated some sayings in Confucius's *Book of Rites* or retold the tales of chaste widows and legendary mothers who maintained the honor of the family by educating their sons.[357] Second, two early books for women—*Principles for Women* (*Nü Xian* 女憲) and *Rules for Women* (*Nü Ze* 女則)—had been lost, while Ban Zhao's book was too brief for a full women's education.[358]

Furthermore, given the long-established dominant male education of women, we can further understand Xu's concerns. Prior to her era, books for women's education were mostly written by men, for example, the *Book of Rites* by Confucius, the *Biographies of Exemplary Women* by Liu Xiang (see chapter on Ban), and "*Jia Fan* (家范 *Family Rules*)" by Sima Guang (司馬光 1019–1086 CE), a high-ranking scholar-official known for his 294-chapter *Zizhi TongJian* (資治通鑒) to record the history from 403 BCE to 960 CE. Particular attention should be paid to Sima's quotation and interpretation of Ban Zhao's definitions of womanly virtue, speech, deportment, and work. In his book, *Jia Fan* (家范 *Family Rules*), while he shows belief in women's education, Sima utilizes the Confucian rites to twist Ban's teaching of women, reinforcing Dong Zhongshu's gender hierarchy that subordinated women (see chapter on Ban). A careful reading shows that Sima's scheme of things with regard to familial propriety is a ladder where the father is on the top rung, and the daughter-in-law at the bottom.[359] In terms of gen-

---

357. Wang 2011, 24–25.
358. Wang 2011, 25; Pang-White 2018, 12–125.
359. Wang 2003, 415.

der relations, he strongly recommended total sex separation, except for married couples.[360] For example, men and women should not sit together on the same mat. Single men and women should not contact the other sex before accepting engagement gifts. Married woman should wear a colorful ribbon and should not go outside unless for serious matters.[361] The deficiency in proper teaching materials and male dominant education of women compelled Xu to write her own book based on what she has learned and observed from her mother-in-law.

Xu witnessed the further development of educational systems based on the Confucian orthodox in the Ming dynasty (1368–1644 CE), including women's private education and the civic service examination system, all for the benefit of serving the empire. The Ming dynasty enjoyed its inheritance of poetry writing from the Tang Dynasty (618–907 CE) and verse composition from the Song Dynasty (960–1279 CE). The Song verse (*song ci* 宋詞) developed Tang poetry to a new subjective genre for social and political purposes. Many Ming scholar-officials modified the genre of Song verse into expository prose to document history, write biographies of legendary figures, and articulate ideas about state governance, education, familial matters, as well as institutional and social functions of women's education. Sima Guang's *Family Rules* and Xu's *Doctrine for the Inner Court* are prime examples. Also, the new writing style for the civic service examination in the Ming dynasty deviated from *shifu* (poetic exposition) that required perfect rhyme and rhythm in the past (see chapters on Song Ruozhao and Lu Ji). Ming examinations required a smooth flow of words for reasoning in response to a prompt based on the Confucian four classics and five books.[362] The changed requirement almost perfected *Baguwen* (八股文), the eight-legged essay, which had undergone full-fledged development in the previous Song dynasty.[363] The *Baguwen* in the Ming dynasty was composed of eight units of antithesis—opening the subject, elaborating the subject, identifying its origin, beginning the discussion, extending to associated ideas, repeating what has been said, narrowing it down, and concluding the essay.[364] *Baguwen* also required expressions of genuine ideas based on Confucian's teaching in elegant proper diction and style with logical reasoning and interpretation of classical teaching.

However, *Bagumen* hardly influenced women writers who were excluded from the civic service examination. For instance, Xu had completed her *Doctrine for the Inner Court* in the genre of poetic expository prose established in the Han dynasty (206 BCE–220 CE). The sentence structure in rhythm with clear beats and pauses makes her book easy to read aloud for memorization and recitation, thus enhancing the effect of teaching. Instead of being restricted by *Baguwen*, Xu adopted the genre of expository prose to present, at her own will, new definitions, ideas, and reinterpretations of the classics, as we shall see in the following commentary and translation.

---

360. Ibid.
361. Ibid.
362. Wu 2000, Vol. 4, 509.
363. Ibid. 509–11, 534; also see chapters on Song Ruozhao and Chen Kui.
364. Ibid. 515.

COMMENTARY ON QUEEN XU'S RHETORICAL INSTRUCTION

In *Family Rules*, Sima focuses on gender roles and family relationships, believing that "A woman's position is inside. A man's position is outside. The male and female balance is the order of the world."[365] Sima might not mean letting women fully occupy the domestic domain, but his restatement of Confucian's teaching about the state and the family gave Xu freedom of interpretation that women is the central pillar of family and should be respected as such. Women's roles at home, Xu believes, are more important than men's outside the home, because women are responsible for the education of their sons and daughters. Prior to Xu, books on women emphasized chastity, the character, behavior, self-presentation, and work due to gender restrictions. Xu's *Doctrine of the Inner Court*, however, foregrounds virtue (*de* 德) and self-development (*xiushen* 修身), two aspects of women's attributes that were implied but not fully discussed before. As she notes in the preface, "Nobody can become a sage without cultivating virtue (*de*) in self-development. Therefore, virtue is the primary focus followed immediately by self-development, which depends entirely on scrupulous speech and deed."[366] In other words, Xu orients speech and conduct to virtue and self-development, two fundamental attributes that shape rhetorical performance. For this reason, Xu devotes the first three chapters to virtue, self-development, speech and conduct to lay the foundation for her teaching to women who, she hopes, can grow into sages embodying prudent speech and deed to manage the family and educate children.[367] When reading Xu, readers must keep in mind that despite her high royal position, she was a woman, after all, in an oppressive patriarchal society, where all male teaching of women aims to restrict and tame women's activities. It is, therefore, no surprise that we find some of her comments on women's speech contradictory. Some of them may even be considered a ban of women's speech. A careful reading, however, reveals that her caution is not meant to forbid women from speaking but to enhance their awareness of rhetorical ethics and situations. Her quotation from the *Book of Rites* proves that Xu wants women to deliver prudent and proper speeches. As she says in chapter one "On Virtue," "Actions stem from the *Dao*, speeches are grounded on trust."

Interestingly, although Xu's book was written much later than Song's *The Analects for Women*, somehow Chinese scholars always place Queen Xu's as the second women's book, including Wang Xiang's edition, maybe because of Xu's royal position. But the reasons remain unknown. This book presents all four women's books in the chronological order, with Xu's being the third.

The retranslated excerpts of Xu's book hereafter present consistent terminologies and concepts in the Chinese rhetorical tradition. Readers can find a full translation in *The Confucian Four Books for Women* by Anna A. Pang-White. Xu's book contains twenty chapters. In the introduction, Xu wrote about her own education by her parents and mother-in-law, while expressing her concerns about the scarcity of teaching materials for women's education

---

365. Sima n.d., Chapter 1.2. All translations are mine unless indicated otherwise.
366. Wang 2003, 25.
367. Ibid., 28.

and male-dominated teaching of women. The introduction also outlines logical correlations among virtue, self-development, speech, and deed, the important aspects of managing finances and resources, and the ways of extending benevolence and kindness to family members, relatives, and others. Xu believes that virtue and self-development are fundamentals of women's speech, deed, and work, enabling women to demonstrate good habits of benevolence and kindness. Immediately following the introduction are three chapters respectively on virtue, speech, and deed. The next four chapters are on the importance of diligent work, self-awareness, benevolence, and exemplification of good speech and deed. The rest of the book lays out the methods for maintaining good relationships with the parents, husband, relatives, children, and friends, as well as those for ceremonial events planning and management. The following excerpts present chapters two and three based on the first edition of four women's classics compiled by Wang Xiang.

Translation of Queen Xu's Rhetorical Instruction to Women

Chapter 2

On Self-Development (xiu shen zhang 修身章)

If someone asks whether Tai Ren (太任)[368] had refused to gaze at evil scenes (*e se* 惡色), listen to grotesque sounds (*yin sheng* 淫聲), and utter arrogant words (*ao yan* 傲言),[369] is this a question about practice of self-development?

The answer is yes. This is a recognized practice since antiquity. It is said that gazing at evil scenes causes confusion; listening to grotesque sounds muddles the mind; uttering arrogant words inflames self-conceitedness. They are all harmful to selfhood. Therefore, women must balance their minds to stop evils and conduct righteous deeds to embody the virtue (*de*).

For this reason, lavishly designed colorful clothing does not bring dignity and honor. Only chastity, resilience, and observance of the *Dao* can foster a woman's virtue. Negligence of one's self-development and inattention to one's virtue lead to evils and misconducts.

A proverb says, "Killing weeds to nourish young sprouts suppresses the growth of the weeds; cutting bushes and trimming the edges open up the road." This method applies to self-development and cultivation of virtue (*de*).

It is said those who refuse to develop themselves do not establish the virtue (*de*). Without embodying the virtue (*de*), few people can teach a whole family, much less the whole state.

---

368. Tai Ren was wife of Lord Xibo (西伯, or Ji Li 季曆) in the Shang Dynasty (1600–1046 BCE) and mother of King Wen (*ji chang* 姬昌 1152–1056 BCE) during the Zhou Dynasty (1046–256 BCE).
369. The general interpretation is that when Tai Ren was pregnant with her son who later became King Wen, she tried to keep her mind and body pure without being affected by evil deeds, over-indulgence in entertainment, and self-conceitedness (Wang 2011, 31). Xu quotes the story from Confucius's *Book of Rite*.

Thus, it is said that women are behind others. The relationship between the husband and wife follows the law of fortitude and resilience.[370] Prior wise emperors made prudent selections to begin their marriages and emphasized continuing the tradition, which determined if the family was strong or weak for generations to come and if the state was in prosperity or decline. How significant it (marriage) is! At home, women should be taught attentively and purposefully to develop themselves.

Chapter 3

On Prudent Speech (shen yan zhang 慎言章)

Of the four aspects of women's education, speech (*yan*) is the first.[371] How can the mind (*xin*) that reacts to the myriad of things stop its expression in speech? A proper speech prevents regrettable mistakes; an improper speech causes adversity.

A proverb says that "Being pleasant and equable (*yinyin jianjian* 闇闇謇謇) can turn an unmovable rock around. Being iniquitous and antagonistic (*zizi xuanxuan* 訾訾諼諼) is like blazing wildfires." Another proverb says, "A speech (*yan*) from a mouth that seldom opens itself demands trust. A speech from a mouth that constantly pours out utterances loses credibility." True indeed. Speech (*yan*) should never be imprudent.

A woman esteemed for her calmness and peacefulness is not expected to speak much. The more she speaks, the more mistakes she makes. She had better not speak. Thus, the *Book of History* condemns doomed families where hens chuck restlessly in the morning. The *Book of Poetry* derides loquacious women who caused misfortunes. The *Book of Rites* warns strictly against indiscretions about interior and exterior speeches. Good at self-discipline, women must follow the teaching to develop prudence, which cannot be more emphasized.

Is there a way to develop prudence? The answer is yes. Just learn from Nan Gong Tao (南宮紹).[372]

Be quiet and attentive to mindful development. Do not make promises that cannot be fulfilled. Pacify the heart (*xin*), fortify the will, and harmonize the *qi*.[373] Preserve benevolence and courteousness, maintain dignity and respectfulness; build trust and loyalty. Whether in speech (*yü*) or in silence (*mo* 默), be tranquil, mindful, and affable to follow the *Dao*. These qualities fit the essential female attributes of humility and serenity and provoke no damaging scandalous rumors for a thriving and harmonious family.

---

370. See chapter on Ban Zhao.

371. See chapter on Ban Zhao for the components of women's education.

372. Also called Nan Gong Kuo (南宮適). A disciple of Confucius's, Nan Gong Tao was known for being reserved and reminding himself of his master's teaching in the Book of Poetry, which said "A defect on pure white jade could be ground away; a defected speech could not be corrected" (Wang 2011, 34).

373. See *qi* (氣 energy) as a key component of being a sage of rhetoric and its function in developing the mind in *Guiguzi* (2016, 91, 94–95).

Therefore, a woman should not dwell on beauty. Her deed is grounded on virtues (*de*). Wu Yan (無鹽),[374] though not pretty, used her words (*yan*) to bring peace to the State of Qi. Confucius said, "A virtuous person (*you de zhe* 有德者) always has speeches to deliver; a person who speaks eloquently may not embody virtue (*de*)."[375]

---

374. Wu Yan, a single uncomely forty-year old woman, delivered an admonition to King Qi Xuan (奇宣) of the State of Qi to point out security threats caused by his flawed political policy and diplomacy as well as his unscrupulous lavish spending. Moved by her courageous and insightful speech, King Qi Xuan married her as the Queen who later helped govern the state.

375. See Chapter 14.4 in Confucius's *Analects*.

2.10 Ming Dynasty

Rhetorical Instruction by Wang Jiefu (王節婦, c. 17th CE): Excerpt from
A Brief Survey of Exemplary Women (*Nü Fan Jie Lu* 女範捷錄) with an
Introduction and Commentary

Hui Wu

INTRODUCTION

Madam Liu (Liu Shi 劉氏) lost her name upon marriage and was renamed officially Wang Jiefu (Chaste Woman Wang) to exemplify the virtue of chastity. While her birthdate is not recorded, it is known that Wang, widowed at thirty, remained unmarried for the next sixty years of her life. Her book, *A Brief Survey of Exemplary Women*, was allegedly written near the end of the Ming Dynasty (1368–1644 CE). A well-educated woman, she not only educated her son, Wang Xiang (王相), to be a reputed scholar but also guided his compilation of the four women's books, including hers. Thanks to his mother's guidance and education, Wang Xiang restored many more books for educational purposes. The well-known ones include his editions of *Three-Character Doctrine* (*san zi jing* 三字經) by Wang Yinglin (王應麟 1223–1296 CE) for children's education in Confucian virtues and exemplary historical figures and *Hundreds of Family Names* (*bai jia xing* 百家姓) that records the origins of 504 family names. His edition of *Four Women's Books* remains the most authoritative today and serves as the basic text for the translation presented here.

Wang Jiefu's era saw stabilized private education of girls in well-to-do families. While now boys began state or private education when they were eight years old, girls started home schooling when they were ten. All male learners were taught to read and memorize four Confucius books and five canons and practice *Baguwen* in preparation for the civic service examination (also see chapters on Song Ruozhao and Queen Xu). Young women were educated by reading not only the books for men but also those for women, including Ban's, Song's, and Queen Xu's, to understand the ethics of state governance to help their husbands and to educate their children in the future. Perhaps because women were excluded from the civic service examination that required the genre of *Baguwen*, their writing rarely deviates from the classical genre of expository verse composed of sentences in prefect parallelism or antitheses in perfect rhythm and rhyme (see chapters on Ban, Lu Ji, and Queen Xu). They were not influenced by the male trend of *Baguwen* nor its transformed genre of "popular composition (*shi wen* 時文)" in response to prompts in the civic service exam.[376] A comparison shows concrete differences. Tang Shunzhi (唐順之1507–1560 CE) originated the "popular composition" in

---

376. Wu 2000, 520–21.

his famous exam essay, "The Exemplary Person's Sense of Justice" with neither parallelism nor antithesis. It begins, "The sage tells the sense of an exemplary person from that of a petty person to demonstrate a way to understand one's will for learning."[377] In contrast, Wang's book begins with a statement in perfect antitheses (see translation hereafter) that shows features of the classical genre of poetic expository verse.[378] While Tang draws upon Confucius to meet the requirement of the civic service examination, Wang paraphrases *Book of Changes* to rationalize gender relations and positions, again, in perfect antitheses. Coming of age as a legendary learned chaste widow more than two hundred years after Queen Xu, Wang's mastery of classical knowledge and rhetorical genre gave her a distinct voice and philosophy in terms of women's education and rhetorical performance for the purpose of strengthening their position as the manager of their families and their husbands, as is shown in the following commentary and translation.

COMMENTARY ON WANG'S RHETORICAL TEACHING TO WOMEN

Wang's *A Brief Survey of Exemplary Women* has been fully translated under the title of *Short Records of Models for Women*.[379] The retranslated excerpts that follow maintain the consistency in rhetorical terms and concepts throughout the history. Wang's book contains eleven chapters. Chapter one lays out the philosophical foundation for her standpoint of gender relations to argue for women's education and proper rhetorical performance. The next four chapters use historical female role models to develop Wang's philosophy of women's leading roles in educating children, fulfilling filial duties, and maintaining chastity. The rest of the book delineates Wang's philosophical perspectives on women's rhetorical practice, through illustrating moral concepts and recommending actions, including loyalty and justice, affection and love, deed and propriety, wisdom and intelligence, diligence and frugality, as well as education and virtue. All chapters use historical legendary women as examples to explain Wang's rhetorical theory and recommended rhetorical practices. Wang's rhetorical philosophy exemplified by women's models enables her to negotiate space for women to perform embodied rhetoric to govern their husbands and sons.

The introduction, "On General Principles," begins with Wang's understanding of the concept and theory of *yin-yang* in *Book of Changes* and her seamless incorporation of Ban's re-gendered concept to establish complementary balanced gender positions and roles. Despite her reception of the separated external and internal roles for men and women, Wang clarifies spaces for men and women to perform different, but equal, roles. Men perform duties outside; and women inside to "begin the myriad of things." Her revision of Confucian patriarchal perspectives on the sexes intends to equalize (conceptually) gender roles and uplift women to

---

377. Ibid. The original title is "君子喻于義" The opening reads "聖人論君子小人之喻以示辨志之學."
378. Wang's beginning statement is "乾象乎阳坤象乎阴日月普两仪之照" (2011, 103).
379. Pang-White 2018, 211–94.

take total charge of the family. The historical examples she provides in chapter twelve testify that men's career future depends on whether they follow wise women's advice. Furthermore, Wang's articulation of the *yin-yang* balance strengthens her argument for not only women's position at home but also women's education. Like Ban, Wang criticizes Confucius's *Book of Rites* that emphasizes men's education for state service to argue that women's education is more important than men's because they are the ones who manage their husbands and educate their sons at home. Her argument, again, utilizes the Confucian teaching that the family is the foundation for the state.

Adapting the rhetorical moves of female humility by her predecessors, Wang downplays herself as an exemplary chaste widow. Instead, she defers to exemplary deeds of legendary women in history to illustrate her rhetorical theory and practice. All the female legends are from men's books. She uses them to her advantage to turn men's rhetoric on gender against their subordination of women and Confucian devaluation of women's education. In chapter 10, Wang recognizes men's duties to defend the state, but, in a quick turn, she tells the world that women are superior to men in preventing disasters and wars thanks to their ability to foreknow situations and responsive actions. The twenty-one exemplary women who saved men from their self-destructions provide evidence for Wang's proposition that women's intellect and wisdom are superior to men's; hence their assistance in state governance should be emphasized.

For this reason, women must be educated. Chapter 12 is devoted to Wang's counterargument to the Confucian statement that a woman must be virtuous but not necessarily educated. She explicitly opines that the statement is wrong because a virtuous woman has already received education. Wang's counterargument is perhaps the first in Chinese rhetoric to demonstrate a woman's ability of logical reasoning. Her point is that virtue and education are mutually related to achieve benefits on both fronts. They cannot exist without the other. Exposing contradictions in Confucius's teaching, Wang notes that women's words, like men's, can benefit state governance. The same reason applies to virtue. If women are susceptible to evil deeds and injustice, so are men. Then the logic follows to answer her question that "[i]f men can be educated to become exemplary persons, why cannot women?" The twelve examples in chapter twelve showcase historical women who offered help to save their men or the state. They prove Wang's argument that women's virtue and education are not mutually exclusive as Confucius has said. Indeed, "women who achieved literacy, observed propriety, and understood the classical canons established their fame in their time." An important truth.

Partial Translation of A Brief Survey of Exemplary Women

Chapter 1

On General Principles (tonglun pian 統論篇)

1.1 The phenomena of *Qian* (乾) represent *yang*, and those of *Kun* (坤) represent *yin*. The light from the sun and the moon represents both types of phenomena.

1.2 Men's proper position is outside; women's proper position is inside. The husband and wife are the beginning of a myriad of things.[380]

1.3 The five virtues (*de*) are the basic general principle.[381]

1.4 When the three guiding relations are understood, a person's virtue is developed.[382]

1.5 Therefore, persons who wish to develop themselves (*xiushen*) must hold the family as the priority. Persons who wish to be educated must understand the fundamentals of ethics.

1.6 The right way to harmonize the family relies solely on proprieties (*li* 禮) between men and women. The moment their education begins they should be taught the dining ritual.

1.7 Uneducated youths will not know propriety when they become adults. A man may cultivate virtues (*de*) under the influence of his teachers and friends; where can a home-confined woman find models of benevolence and integrity to rectify her flaws?[383]

1.8 Therefore, methods of educating women are more important than those of educating men. Establishing propriety for women has priority over that for men. That said, it is obvious that teaching women is more important than teaching men.

1.9 The bronze mirror is used to perfect the appearance; the past is used to teach through examples.

---

380. Zisi (子思), a decedent from Confucius, once said that "the beginning of the *Dao* for an exemplary person has originated from the husband and wife" (Wang 2011, 103; also see Ames and Hall 2001).
381. The five virtues refer to benevolence (*ren* 仁), justice (*yi* 義), propriety (*li* 禮), intellect (*zhi* 智), and credibility (*xin* 信).
382. The three guiding relations are the king and his commissioners, the father and sons, the husband and wife.
383. Wang Xiang comments, "It is said that both men and women, if not educated properly, will not understand propriety. While men may have friends and teachers to mend their flaws, home-confined women who, if missing early education, would receive no teaching of principles to understand benevolence when they grow up" (2011, 104).

1.10 Where there is capability to learn from ancient examples, there is no worry about developing virtues (*de*) and setting the family order.

Chapter 9

On Observation of Propriety (bingji pian 秉禮篇*)*

9.1. Virtue (*de* 德), appearance (*mao* 貌), speech (*yan* 言), and work (*gong* 工) are four women's virtues.

9.2 Propriety (*li* 禮), justice (*yi* 義), incorruptibility (*lian* 廉), and repentance (*chi* 恥) are four state conduct codes.

9.3 Persons of misconduct terminate their lives instantly.[384] The rites for speech (*yan li* 言禮) should never be overlooked.

Chapter 10

On Intelligence and Wisdom (zhi hui pian 智慧篇*)*

10.1 Guarding security and peace of the state is a man's duty.

10.2 An intelligent woman is superior to men.

10.3 She plans with a futuristic vision and premeditates responsive actions. No unexpected changes or emergencies can exhaust her resourceful measures.

10.4 Sought after from their deep internal living quarters, they are the most outstanding women.

10.18 Le Yangzi (樂羊子) listened to his wife's remonstrant speech (*jian* 諫) and established his fame as a result;[385]

---

384. According to Wang Xiang, it is a paraphrase of the *Book of Poetry* that says that persons of improper conducts are unworthy of the status of human (2011, 133). See Hui Wu's "The Paradigm of Margret Cavendish" for explanation of the Chinese notion of human.

385. According to Wang Xiang's commentary, Master Le in the Han Dynasty (202 BCE–220 CE) returned shortly from a brief journey for his advanced education. When his wife, who was weaving, asked him why he was home so soon, Le said that he missed her. Upon his word, Le's wife cut the thread on the weaving machine to say, "A piece of fabric takes work inch by inch to make a yard. Only through constant progress can a long piece be completed. Your return to home before finishing your study is like cutting this fabric to jeopardize its progress." Following his wife's words, Le set back onto

10.19 Ning Chenhao (甯宸濠) refused to follow his wife's words (*yan* 言) and lost his kingdom consequently.[386]

10. 24 In their contributions to strong state governance, all of these women showed female wisdom and sensibility. They could understand a person to prevent him from adversity. By assisting their husbands and sons, they safeguarded the family and state.

Chapter 12

On Intellect and Virtue (cai de pian 才德篇)[387]

12.1 The statement that a man who is virtuous has intellect (*cai* 才) is right.

12. 2 But the statement that a woman who has no intellect is virtuous is wrong.[388]

12.3 This is because virtue is the fundamental principle of education (*cai* 才) in cultivating the ability to tell right and wrong.

12.4 Virtue enables the development of intellect (*cai* 才), which further cultivates virtue.

12.5 Therefore, virtuous women may not be highly intellectual (*cai* 才), but well-learned (*cai* 才) women are honored for their virtues.

12.6 That virtue is fundamental to education (*cai* 才) is the obvious truth. This is the reason that misconduct cannot blame education (*cai* 才) for its sins.

12.7 With regard to state management and governance, a woman's speech (*fu yan* 婦言) is useful. To evil and wrong deeds men are susceptible.

---

the journey of study again and eventually became a reputed scholar-official for the state (Wang 2011, 134).

386. Prince Ning Chenhao, a great-grandson of the Ming Emperor, Zhu Yuanzhang (朱元璋 1328–1398 CE), tried several times to overthrow the regime, neglecting his wife's repeated warnings. He was caught at insurgence and was prisoned for life. Upon his death, he expressed his regret for not following his wife's advice.

387. 才 can be translated as talent or gift, as Pang-White has done. But here it refers mainly to knowledge or advanced literacy, hence its varied English translations—intellect, education, learning, learnedness, knowledge, etc.

388. The original of these two Confucian statements is "男子有德便是才, 女子無才便是德."

12.8 The *Book of Rites* says that slanderous utterances and disoriented images block sensible eyes and acute ears. Excessive sex and entertainment violate propriety, weakening the heart (*xin*) and will.[389]

12.9 If men can be educated to become exemplary persons (*junzi*), why cannot women?

12.10 In antiquity, from court ladies and queens to ordinary concubines and wives, all of them received learning from the *Book of Poetry*. Were they all women of no virtue?

12.11 In recent history, from treacherous women and obscene misses to shrews and querulous wives, all of them violated propriety. Were they all educated (*cai* 才) women?

12.17. The *Canon for Women's Filial Duties* (*Nü xiao jing* 女孝經) was written by Madam Chen, and the *Analects for Women* by the Song sisters.[390]

12.18 *Lessons for Women* by Cao Zhao (Ban Zhao), and *The Doctrine for the Inner Court* by Queen Renxiao (Xu).

12.23. These legendary models for court ladies and ordinary young women have set the criteria for women's education (*xue* 學). From this perspective, women who achieved literacy, observed propriety, and understood the classical canons established their fame in their time. They will be followed for years to come. A truth that is indeed so important.

12.24. If wicked books are banned from the family and villainous speeches are not heard, daughters and sisters whom their fathers and elder bothers wish to protect can be educated to hold justice and become talented. They will follow past examples to develop virtues to their perfection.

---

389. The heart (*xin* 心) refers to the mind (see *Guiguzi* 2016, 39 note 1). Also see *Guiguzi* for cultivating the mind and will in a rhetor (2016, 93–95, 97–100).

390. The *Canon for Women's Filial Duties* was based on *Canons of Filial Duties* by Zengzi (曾子 505–436 BCE) that uses the Confucian doctrine to recommend filial propriety for senior family members to maintain family harmony (Feng 2008).

2.11 The Modern Period (the 20ᵗʰ century)

Rhetorical Treatise by Chen Wangdao (陳望道 1891–1977 CE): Partial Translation of *An Introduction to Rhetoric* (*Xiucixue Fafan* 修辭學發凡) with an Introduction and Commentary

Hui Wu

INTRODUCTION

Chen Wangdao was born to a farmer's family in Yiwu City, Zhejiang Province. Public records show that Chen graduated from Waseda University, the center for modern Japanese rhetoric, and returned to China in 1919 to teach in college. Chen's enthusiasm about language reform made him receptive to Marxism. In 1920, he translated Marx and Engels's *The Communist Manifesto*, which was reprinted seventeen times and was enthusiastically applauded by Mao Zedong, ruler of China from 1949 to 1976. Teaching in Fudan University in Shanghai, Chen led the Communist Party's underground activities in the 1920s as one of the five founders of the Chinese Communist Party and the Director of the Shanghai Chapter. While teaching language arts and rhetoric, he promoted the vernacular (modern Mandarin) language in writing and education in defiance of the rhetorical tradition of writing in the classical language, which, composed of single-syllable words, is incomprehensible when spoken and difficult to read without punctuation and paragraph division. The language movement leaders, most of whom received democratic ideas from their college education in Japan and the West, believed that writing in the vernacular could advance literacy. As Chen notices, "Chinese language studies are often associated with socio-political movements. Whenever our country faces disasters, academics would turn their attention to language issues and make efforts to enhance literacy of the people."[391] In 1952, Chen was officially nominated by Mao Zedong as the President of Fudan University, a position he held for twenty-five years until his death at eighty-seven.

An Introduction to Rhetoric has been recognized as the canon of modern Chinese rhetoric. First published in 1932 and reprinted twelve times by 1942, its two new editions were published in 1960 and 1976 during Mao's era. Although critically acclaimed as a native breed, Chen's book is a hybrid that integrates concepts from Japan and the West to illustrate Chinese rhetorical praxis.[392] Some of Chen's frequently used terminologies, such as "rhetorical artifacts/phenomena (*xiuci xianxiang* 修辭現象)," "active rhetoric (*jiji xiuci* 積極修辭)," and "inactive rhetoric (*xiaoji xiuci* 消極修辭)," are borrowed directly from modern Japanese rhet-

---

391. Chen 1976, 1.
392. Wu 2009, 161–63.

oric.[393] Some of them are borrowed from books influenced by Western rhetoric, for example, Tang Yue's *Figures of Speech* (*Xiucige* 修辭格), which borrowed heavily from figures of speech in J. C. Nesfield's *Senior Course of English Composition* (1903), and James C. Fernald's *Expressive English* (1918).[394] Tang has created most modern Chinese figures of speech in parallel to English ones, which Chen uses in his book. For example, Chen's terminologies for simile are the same as those in Tang's book, such as 如 (*ru*), 好比 (*haobi*), 猶 (*you*), 若 (*ruo*), 像 (*xiang*), 似 (*si*).[395] From chapter 5 to chapter 11, Chen's classification of analogies and styles also follows Tang's models.

Apart from its academic intervention, Chen's book reflects the geo-politics of rhetoric studies. Before and when it was published, many books on rhetoric were used extensively. For example, Hu Huanshen's *On Rhetorical Schemata* (*Xici de Fangfa* 修辭的方法) was published in 1930, two years before Chen's book, and reprinted three times by September 1932. Yang Shuda's *Study of Chinese Rhetoric* (*Zhongguo Xiucixue*中國修辭學) was published in 1933 and was adopted as a major textbook in Taiwan in the early 1950s. Zhang Yiping's *Lectures on Rhetoric* (*Xiucixue Jianghua* 修辭學講話) dominated secondary education in the 1940s. There were also Xu Gengsheng's *The Course in Rhetoric* (*Xiucixue Jiaocheng* 修辭學教程 1933), Jin Zhozi's *Practical Rhetoric* (*Shiyong Guowen Xiucixue* 實用國文修辭學 1934), and more. However, none of them gained the same dominance as Chen's book in mainland China. One reason might be the endorsement by Liu Dabai (劉大白), an established poet, scholar, and social activist, as well as a colleague of Chen's at Fudan University. Liu praises it as "the first systematic treatise of rhetoric that examines both ancient and modern Chinese writings," which evolved from Chen's diligent study and practice for more than ten years.[396] The second reason might be Chen's political leadership before and under Mao's ruling, which always placed him on the cutting-edge of language reform, an advantage his predecessors and contemporaries might not have. Chen's critical acclaim was strengthened by his double roles as a scholar and leader in language reform and social movements, which may also explain why his book continues to be the canon of modern Chinese rhetoric that still directs the rhetorical practice in today's mainland China.[397]

However, whether this modern rhetorical canon has had impact on rhetoric studies in Taiwan remains largely unknown. In the beginning of the 1950s, Taiwan and mainland China were separated. Yang Shuda's book, *A Study of Chinese Rhetoric*, was reprinted five times as a college textbook in Taiwan by 1988.[398] But in mainland China, Yang's book became invisible by the early 1950s. Unlike Chen's book, Yang's does not show any impact by modern Japanese rhetoric. Does the difference in Yang's book mean that modern rhetoric in Taiwan and mainland China differs in conception, terminology, and pedagogy? Have other books, besides

---

393. Ibid., 150–54.
394. Ibid., 157–58.
395. Tang 1923, 45.
396. Liu 1999, 289.
397. Wu 2009, 163.
398. Wu, 2009, 160–61.

Chen's, been read and used in Taiwan's college classrooms since the separation? Chen's book is now available in some libraries of Taiwan universities since the two regions started direct trades and tours after the 1980s. How has the book impacted rhetoric instruction in Taiwan now? These questions point out not only geo-politics but also limitations of current studies of Chinese rhetorics. When a region is not included, an area of the study is left out. For this reason, *An Introduction to Rhetoric* holds special significance in the study of Chinese rhetoric.

COMMENTARY ON *An Introduction to Rhetoric*

An Introduction to Rhetoric was developed from Chen's teaching notes and was classroom-tested by several professors at Fudan University during the 1920s. Written in the vernacular with many classical and modern examples, the book, as Chen claims, aims to illustrate the theory and principles of Chinese rhetorical artifacts, schemata, and devices in hopes to help students study rhetoric, learn about classical rhetoric, and improve written and oral composition. The twelve chapters cover the definition of rhetoric, features of speech, passive and active forms of rhetoric, figures of speech, rhetorical artifacts, and styles. Chen defines "rhetoric" in two ways. First, rhetoric means to beautify composition in written and oral forms. Second, it is an effort to express meanings through writing and speech. Chen emphasizes the commonality between speech and writing and the three rhetorical modes they share: the narrative, the expressive, and the integrated.[399] Chen believes that the purpose of rhetorical study is to learn models of language use, or rhetorical artifacts, and rhetorical concepts. A student of rhetoric should examine, investigate, generalize, categorize, and explain various forms of rhetorical use in both spoken and written languages. Second, s/he should study treatises on rhetoric. Furthermore, rhetorical study should have three pragmatic functions: to determine meanings, to serve as hermeneutics for classics, and to gain respect for spoken language.[400] Throughout the book, Chen holds that speech is as worthy of studying as writing and that the two forms of language share many rhetorical devices. Most important, Chen emphasizes pragmatic application of rhetoric, focusing on the functionality of rhetoric in communication. That is, it must befit the theme and context of a discourse, regardless of whether it is in written or spoken form.

In the translation presented hereafter, Anglophone readers may notice some redundancies, as in "word composition" and "language and word use." They are purposely translated as such to indicate the transitional period when the classical and vernacular languages intersected. It was during this period that Chen was writing the book. Not until after the 1950s was the modern vernacular language used exclusively in writing. The phrase, "word composition," stands for both writing and speech in Chen's book, but it is now a linguistic concept referring to speech only. The same can be said about "language and word use." The phrase is to retain the repetitiveness of the original meaning—"the uses of the spoken language and written

---

399. Chen 1999, Chapter I.3.
400. Chen 1999, I.6–I.7.

word." The translation, though sounding redundant, cannot leave either part out without losing some meaning.

Moreover, Chen's rhetorical treatise include many examples in classical canons to explain Chinese rhetorical praxis. Unfortunately, when translated into English, many of them would lose meanings, stylistic features, and tastes. For this reason, the translation leaves out examples that require detailed long narratives of cultural or historical connotations but retains some that make sense in English. The omissions are indicated by ellipses.

Chapter one is presented below to introduce modern Chinese rhetorical concepts and definitions. It is based on the 1997 edition, a special edition for the sixty-fifth anniversary of *An Introduction to Rhetoric*, which is based on the 1976 edition, for which Chen wrote a preface in December 1975, saying that the revised edition is similar to the first 1932 edition, except for some changes in examples and wording.[401] As the reader shall see, the concluding paragraph of the "Introduction" has incorporated some political terms of the Cultural Revolution (1966–1976) under Mao, for example, "the proletarian worldview" and "revolutionary social practice." The translation keeps them for the purpose of reserving the history behind the text.

Translation of Chen Wangdao's Rhetorical Instruction

Chapter One

Introduction

I.1. An Examination of the Common Use of "Xiu (修)" and "Ci (辭)"

Xiuci has become a familiar term. *Yijing* (*Book of Changes*) said that "polish a composition to establish one's integrity (*xiu ci li qi sheng* 修辭立其誠)." Since then the two words are often used together. Combined as such for a long time, whenever *ci* is mentioned, *xiu* naturally appears. The two words are bound so tightly that they seem unable to be separated. Yet, whenever they are explained, *xiu* still means "to polish" and *ci* "word," They are regarded as two separate characters. This is still the case whenever *xiuci* is under discussion.

Yet, people give the two words different definitions and explanations. Generally, they can be divided into two categories—broad and specific. A. specific view: It defines *xiu* as "to polish" and "to beautify" and *ci* as "the word of written composition (*wenci* 文辭)." *Xiuci* then means to polish and beautify written composition. B. broad view: It defines *xiu* as "to adjust" and "to appropriate," and *ci* as "the word of speech (*yüci* 語辭)." *Xiuci* means to adjust or appropriate the word of speech. Together, they generate four functions:

Polish and beautify words of written composition

Modify and appropriate words of speech

---

401. Chen 1976, 284.

Modify and appropriate words of written composition

Polish and beautify words of speech

All are now in use, sometimes consciously and sometimes unconsciously. When speaking of rhetoric (*xiuci*), we must briefly examine the applications of the two characters.

First, does *ci* refer to written composition or spoken language? The answer used to be, of course, it means the former because it is what *ci* stands for. Gu Tinglin's statement that "Those who begin their learning from the spoken language are not good at rhetoric" is an example for this answer (Chapter 19).[402] A cursory inquiry reveals some discrimination in an age when the classical language was highly esteemed while the vernacular language (*yüti* 語體) was looked down upon, being called a "slang" or "vulgar" language and mocked for its worthlessness in various manners. The classical language was valued as the only linguistic model. Yet, classical Chinese was also a form of vernacular when it was born. Also, notions of rhetoric (*xiuci*) were developed from the spoken language in China and other countries alike. For some time, controversies about language use arose. Writers became linguistic cleansing agents as if they were sacred guardians of classical Chinese. In reality, however, phrases that have evolved from the vernacular are respectfully accepted. For example, *yütu* (於菟 tiger) and *adu* (阿堵 this or this one) in the vernacular are now considered ornate words (*ci zao* 辭藻). Also, the phrase of *xieyin* (諧讔 enigma) is now an accepted lantern riddle at festivals, a rhetorical choice for the learned class. Thus, (1) rhetorical devices (*xiuci fangshi* 修辭方式) in written composition (*wenci* 文辭) are often influenced by trendy spoken words (*kouto yüci* 口頭語詞). If lower trendy rhetorical devices in written composition are recognized, then there is no reason to reject higher rhetorical devices in speech composition (*yüci* 語辭). (2) Rhetorical devices for written and oral compositions are almost identical. If the former is recognized, there is no reason to reject the similar trend in the latter. (3) Since rhetorical devices for both written and oral compositions share similarities, there is no reason to find where they have originated or to believe they work only for written composition. When rhetorical artifacts (*xiuci xianxiang* 修辭現象)[403] are studied from the same point of view, we ought to recognize that *ci*, in fact, includes all types of word composition (*yüci*), not merely writing on the paper, whose trend returns to its source—the spoken language that serves as a vehicle of ideas and sentiments. Nowadays when we hear "rhetoric of speech" or a similar phrase, we do not think it is unusual. This means that we have recognized that word composition (*yüci*) is a rhetorical instrument.[404]

---

402. Gu Tinglin (顧亭林1613-1682), also named Gu Yanwu (顧炎武), was known for his philosophical and scholarly treatises on all sorts of topics ranging from governance, military affairs, politics, and sciences to rhetoric, literature, and arts. They are included in his thirty-two-chapter book, *A Record of Everyday Knowledge* (*Rizhi Lu*日知錄).

403. The phrase is translated alternately into "rhetorical artifacts" or "rhetorical phenomena," depending on the context.

404. From this point on, Chen refers to all types of word composition, as *yüci*, regardless if it is written or spoken.

Second, does rhetoric mean "to polish" or "to modify"? The answer used to be that since it is about rhetoric (*xiuci*), of course, it refers to polishing and embellishing. . . Yet, this answer shows a preference to written composition and is limited only to one of its areas. Rhetoric originated from the purpose of articulating ideas and emotions, and mainly for these. Therefore, rhetoric reflects an effort to appropriate word composition (*yüci*) for accurate articulation of ideas and emotions. It is not merely embellishing and ornamenting; nor is it an approach separated from ideas and feelings. Rhetoric for rhetoric's sake is rooted in (1) a focus on written composition (*wenci*), which is believed to be suitable for embellishment and ornamentation and (2) an emphasis on flowery deft words in written composition (*wenci*) because of a genre's demand. In fact, no matter whether it is writing or speaking and whether its words are deftly flowery or plain awkward, the most ideal composition is always one where "ideas meet words" and "words deliver ideas." The latter means utilizing word composition (*yüci*) to communicate ideas and emotions fully and properly. It is not merely about embellishing the word. Rather, it is about its adjustment and appropriation. Even when needs for deliberation and revision arise, for example, the story about "push or knock [the door]" (*tuiqiao* 推敲),[405] the goal is appropriating the word to articulate sentiments and ideas. It is, in fact, not about embellishing and polishing merely the written word (*wenzi* 文字).

I.2 *Three Areas of Applications of Rhetoric (xiuci) and Word Composition (yüci)*

To know if or not flowery deftness (*huaqiao* 華巧) can represent all aspects of rhetorical phenomena, we can investigate and illustrate word composition (*yüci*) from a rhetorical viewpoint.

Our rhetorical observations reveal roughly three general genres in written and oral composition:[406]

A. Narrative mode: its purposes are describing or explaining the processes and reasons of something. The writing genres include legal documents, decrees, scientific reports, records of oral business discussions and negotiations, etc. They represent the typical forms of an account.

B. Expressive mode: its purposes are reflecting life experiences. The genre is represented by poetry in writing and folk songs in oral delivery.

C. Integrated Mode: its composition typically combines writing genres and oral conversations.

The first two modes are different in their language and word use (*yüci*). Rhetorically speaking, the practices in category A are called passive schemata (*xioji de shoufa* 消極的手法), and

---

405. In the story, Jia Dao (賈島) in the Tang Dynasty (618–907 CE) replaced "push" with "knock" in one of his poems to foreground the sound effect after a careful deliberation. *Tuiqiao* now stands for careful consideration or deliberation.

406. The original is 境界 (*jingjie*). Chen used it to refer to rhetorical genres in composition. See studies of rhetorical genres in Bawarshi and Reiff (2010); Miller et al., (2018, 269–77); Miller (1984, 151–67); Bazerman (1994, 67–84).

those in category B active schemata (*jiji de shoufa* 積極的手法). . . . Active schemata generally constitute two components: (1) the contents that reflect life experiences and individual cases; (2) The diction that enhances audial and visual effects, in addition to the consideration of a word's meaning. An ancient poem where each line contains exactly five characters exemplifies this type of schemata. Integrating the meaning, sound, and shape of characters (words) with the contents of specific experiences fully extends the potential of word composition (*yüci*), often developing ordinary words, grammar, and logic into a new form that adds appeal and beauty. In rhetoric (*xiuci*), two schemata result in such appeal. One closely reflects the contents for a far-reaching profound appeal. It is called figures of speech (*cige* 辭格) or elaborate words (*cizao* 辭藻). The other is relatively distanced from the contents for light and simple enchantment. It is called word play (*ciqu* 辭趣). Composers attentive to rhetorical schemata (*xiuci shoufa* 修辭手法) emphasize the first one, which is often employed in the composition of fiction, poetry, epics, and lyrics. What is called flowery deftness refers to this method.

In reality. . ., flowery deftness is not the only purpose of rhetoric. To borrow an ancient saying,[407] besides "eloquence (*wen* 文)," there is "substance (*zhi* 質)." In other words, there are positive rhetorical schemata and passive rhetorical schemata.

Passive schemata aim for accuracy and clarity with attention to the meaning of word composition (*yüci*). It presents a clear-cut meaning without confusion or misconception. It seeks pragmatic function rather than flowery substance (*huazhi* 華質) or unfitting deftness (*zhuoqiao* 拙巧). When substance fits better than a flowery expression, let substance do its work; when deftness is not needed, leave it out. In category A, the clear precise word composition demands this method. In category C, the part requiring clarity and accuracy demands this method. It stands for the so-called "substance" (*zhi*) in ancient terms.

In category B and part of category C, "composition (*wen*)" for artistic effects cannot do much without passive schemata to achieve precise and clear effects, while a composition that aims for plainness also uses passive schemata. It is what the ancients called the mutuality of substance and composition, as in "composition [*wen*] is tied to substance [*zhi*], and vice versa." Liu Xie says in *A Heart for Eloquence and the Invention of Dragons*, "Words tied with flowery clusters purport to explicate principles. Excessive floweriness that mystifies composition manifests an increasingly clouded mind and principle." (Chapter 31.4). . . . This quote explains the method.

I.3. Three Stages of Rhetoric and Word Composition

Our examination of three stages of word composition can further shed light on rhetorical praxis.

The process of word composition (*yüci*), no matter fragmentary or complete, written or oral, constitutes three steps: 1, collecting material, 2, cutting, tailoring, and arranging, and 3, writing, speaking, or publishing. They all are influenced by political standpoints and worldviews. However, some circumstances differ. For example, material collection is conditioned

---

407. Referring to Liu Xie (Chapter 31.1).

by life experience and knowledge of nature and society. Material selection, reduction, and appropriation are related to intellectuality, analytical insight, logic, reasoning, etc. Writing, speaking, and publishing are tightly related to the tradition of language use as well as genre and style. The three stages are scaffolded in order. By the point of writing, speaking, and publishing, they involve all sorts of complex settings stemming from political standpoints, worldviews, social and life experiences, knowledge of nature and society, as well as insight, intellectuality, logic, and analytical reasoning, all of which are tied closely to the convention of language use, genre, and style. The formation of a word composition is never separated from social and life realities. Material collection must meet these needs. So do the selection, reduction, and appropriation of material, and so do writing, speaking, delivery, and publication. In word composition (*yüci*), the needs often transform themselves into an idea or a theme (*benzhi* 本旨) in writing or speech. From the viewpoint of an individual writer or speaker, a writing or speech indeed grows out of an idea or a theme. It is their job to engage word composition (*yüci*) in those complexities.

Writing and speaking are social acts, which represent the emotional and conceptual interactions between the writer and reader or between the speaker and listener in the real social life. From the very beginning, communication with the reader or the listener is the goal, which in turn is the job of writing and speaking. Thus, the comprehension, reaction, and response on the part of the reader or the listener must be taken into consideration from the beginning. The most critical stage, then, is delivery (*fabiao* 发表), because it is at this point that the writer or the speaker meets the reader or the listener. Each constitutes an important element of communication. At this point, even if the writer who wishes to be "a recluse in a famous mountain" cannot be proud of being so.[408] Word composition (*yüci*), as the medium between the writer and reader or between the speaker and listener, naturally gains attention to whether or not it is understandable, resonant, and appealing. . .

After the material is selected, a word composition (*yüci*) often goes through a process of adjustment and appropriation. Sometimes it is an easy change in writing or a minor correction in speech; sometimes it takes days or months of addition and revision. This process is what we call the rhetorical process. What happens in the process is the so-called rhetorical phenomena (*xiuci de xianxiang* 修辭的現象).

The concrete details of the phenomena are extremely complex. As mentioned previously, they involve political standpoints, world views, social experiences, knowledge of nature and society, intellectuality, logical reasoning, as well as the tradition of language use, genre, and style. They are also impacted by the reader's or listener's receptivity and relatability. Textbooks of composition often expound six key terms, or six most effective core questions—why, what, who, where, when, and how. The first—why—refers to the purpose of writing or speech. For example, is it for persuasion, understanding, or debate? The second—what—refers to the subject matter of the writing or speech. Is it a daily matter, an academic discussion, or another

---

408. In ancient China, a recluse who writes famous treatises was often sought after as a potential political and military advisor. Hence the phrase of "a recluse in a famous mountain," a name for rhetorical figures like Guiguzi, who lived seclusively in the famous "Ghost Valley."

topic? The third—who—refers to who speaks to whom. It is about the connection between the writer and reader and between the speaker and listener. For example, is the audience educated young people or general folks? The fourth—where—refers to recognizing the location of the writer and speaker. Is it in an urban or a rural setting? The fifth—when—asks for the time when the writer or the speaker produces the composition. It ranges from a month or a year to an age or an era. The sixth—how—refers to ways a writing or speech is composed. For example, how is the material selected, appropriated, or arranged? In practice, the concrete details are never limited to merely six categories. But there is no need to labor on a seventh or eighth from a rhetorical view.

Rhetorically speaking, we can encapsulate the above complexities in two statements. (1) rhetoric uses inherited conventions, genres, styles, and all available means of the spoken and written language; and (2) rhetoric befits the theme and context. The available means include rhetorical decisions on the material and verification. The theme and context can be considered rhetorical standards or criteria. The six questions are simply divided subjects in a rhetorical context. A context may be predefined and require logical reasoning; a subject matter may be abstract and purely conceptual, such as the narrative mode previously covered in category A, which usually adopts passive schemata. . . In a context calling for free and emotional expressions or on a detailed real-life subject matter, like the cases in categories B and C, it is not unfitting to use active schemata intuitively . . .

I.4. *The Relationship among Rhetoric, the Context, and the Theme*

Passive rhetoric and active rhetoric aim to appropriate word composition (*yüci*), according to the theme and context. This, however, does not mean that they are void of preference. (1) passive schemata attend more to themes, and active schemata more to occasions. (2) passive schemata are for communication, and active schemata for emotional appeal. (3) superficial and deep meanings created with active schemata often differ from those created with passive schemata. When we analyze active rhetorical artifacts, we usually interpret them based on the context, feel them emotionally, and study them in singular sentences or contextualize them within a whole text. It is not accurate to take a word as it is (in a metaphor). For example, it is said that "a day without seeing you is like three autumns." The word "autumn" here refers to "year." It cannot be simply read as the autumn season. . .

As we know, active rhetoric, performative and seamless, is mostly used for emotional appeal and reflects life and social circumstances shared between the writer and reader or between the speaker and listener. These are their common experiences. People in Shangdong Province use Mountain Tai to emphasize an important matter because they often see the mountain. . . Ancients who often saw flying arrows (*feishi* 飛矢) used them for speediness. Sometimes active rhetoric evolves from the mood of the writer and the speaker or from their relationship with their audience, depending on their closeness or remoteness, positions, experiences, and other factors. As a result, ironies, sarcasms, rhetorical questions, hyperboles, innuendos emerge. Sometimes they take the form of question with no intent for an answer;

sometimes they simply express emotional responses and impressions. All these methods are contextualized improvisations.

These schemata, at a brief glance, seem to have little to do with a theme. Yet, they are necessary means in its development. When we speak to or write for an audience, we are communicating. To achieve effectiveness, we must study how to utilize word composition (*yüci*): sometimes acute and straightforward, sometimes euphemistic and gentle, sometimes stimulating and invigorating, and sometimes calm and smooth. Applying all possible means to make a speech (*ha yü* 話語) or written composition (*wen zhang* 文章) persuasive and appealing. In other words, depending on the specific situation of writing and speech, it takes all sorts of creative performative methods to communicate one's standpoint and idea vividly, excitingly, and forcefully to the target audience. It can be said that language is an instrument or a weapon in communication. Metaphorically as a weapon here, rhetoric (*xiuci*) activates radiation and explosion. It is appropriated with power to move humans. It cannot be said that rhetoric (*xiuci*) has nothing to do with the theme of composition.

In short, the primary goal of rhetoric (*xiuci*) is to fit the thematic context. It is not embellishing word composition (*yüci*), nor is it separated from expressing emotions and ideas. Occasionally when it shows flowery deftness, it nonetheless results from contextualization, and not merely from the intent of decoration. It is not a decorative piece on a dinner plate to show off ornamented extravagance. When its practice is unusually abnormal, it is still an effort of adjustment, and not a purposely eccentric deviation from the rules. Pragmatic effortless rhetoric is a direct or an indirect representation of society; it is a necessary means to meet real-life needs. Successful rhetoric fits all sorts of complex themes and contexts by exhausting all possible means of the language and written word to such a degree that seems to leave no room for betterment, at least on the part of the writer or the speaker. For example, Flaubert taught *le mot juste (the right word)* to his disciple, Guy de Maupassant. Regardless of the form of composition, if there is only a single suitable word, this is the word the writer or the speaker should choose. Put differently, it (method) is similar to a remark by Anatoly Vasilyevich Lunacharsky (1875–1933 CE), "The contents follow a pattern to work out naturally on their own."

I.5. Rhetorical Techniques and Rhetorical Schemata

Rhetorical techniques come from two sources. The first is the thorough understanding of the theme and context grounded in rich life experiences. The second is the profound knowledge of language and word use, knowledge that is accumulated daily through constant observations of rhetorical practices. Techniques are improvisation changeable in situations. What to adopt for a theme and situation does not follow, or is limited by, any rules. Only being fully prepared with the two (sources) can one improvise effortlessly on all occasions.

Of the two sources, one involves more than just language and word use, and the other is all about language and word use. Both emphasize improvisation with an awareness of the theme and situation. In daily practice, both must be stressed. In enriching one's life, one cannot stop studying or observing how the language and word are used. Only after careful examinations and studies can one use them effortlessly or advance the uses to embody creativity, ingenuity, and uniqueness.

Therefore, it is a daily practice to examine closely and study systematically rhetorical devices (*xiuci fangshi*). Attentive observations prevent cloudy understanding, while systematic studies prevent confusion and disorganization.

1. Close examinations occur on two levels. (A) the individual level. As I have pointed out previously, each specific rhetorical artifact fits a specific theme and situation. In other words, the individual features of each (rhetorical) device can only be observed in the theme and context where they are used. This way we can see that language and word uses are rooted in the real life of varied specificities. They are not clichés to be plagiarized or bended to fit other themes and situations. Furthermore, independent examinations of each different case should be conducted to reveal varied unique features of its language and word use. As we know, in classical spoken Chinese, even though similar rhetorical devices (*xiuci fangshi*) are applied to both written and oral forms, oral expressions are often more understandable and more natural. There must be differences and similarities in varied degrees that are worth exploration. In the case of cover word (*cang ci* 藏词), most proverbs in the classical language come from *Book of Poetry*, *Book of History/Shang*, and other ancient books familiar to the educated. The spoken form of the classical language narrows them down to idioms familiar to ordinary people, making them more friendly and interesting. Our observations need to pay attention to these linguistic extensions. Moreover, different genres and styles result in small differences among similar features. For example, in comparison with poetry, folklores are plainer, repeating the same devices throughout. This feature also requires special attention. (B) Examination of purpose. Taking the cover word as an example again. Its meaning is hidden intentionally behind borrowed classical terms. The allegorical device, however, must combine an unfamiliar term with a familiar one to unfold the intended meaning. Otherwise, nobody can understand it. . . Of course, it conveys an indirect meaning that requires more than a brief glance. Anyone who stops on the surface will not understand the purpose. Furthermore, attention must be paid to historical and social influences on word use. General speaking, most cover words are playful for fun and humor. Similar to lantern riddles, they are suited for festival occasions.

2. Systematic studies. There are also two levels. (A) patterns of a device. A cover word that uses a classical allegory at the end of a phrase for an indirect meaning is called pause-end word (*xiehouyu* 歇後語). Those that use a classical allegory at the beginning of a phrase are called head-cover (*cang tou* 藏头). For example, the age of fifteen is called "the age of the will for learning." The age of thirty is called "the age of establishment." The first allegory is borrowed from the saying that "At fifteen years of age, one develops the will to learn." The second comes from the proverb that "At thirty years of age, one establishes oneself." In these cases, the beginning part, as the head-cover, is left out. . . (B) Systemic features across devices. Take the example of the cover word again. We need to know not only the interconnection of a cover word but also its connection with and reference to other devices, such as metaphors, puns,

palindromes, and others. Doing so helps differentiate all sorts of rhetorical devices in order to recognize their features effectively without confusing puns and allegories with metaphors and word puzzles, which sometimes are mistakenly identified as palindromes. In practice, this (method) can also enable effortless improvisations.

1.6 The Need, Advancement, and Objective of Rhetoric

The examination and study discussed above demand time and tireless daily labor. Everyone cannot do both simultaneously. Careful examinations detect small variations among devices, and systematic studies reveal their general similarities, without overlooking small variations. The generalization shall leave out small variables to foreground patterns of similarities, which lead to the construction of a sizeable system. Thus, studies focus on similarities, and daily observations on differences. Attention to both is possible but requires experience as the foundation, which ensures careful examination and understanding of rhetorical functions and special features for efficacy.

Our ancestors must have known some of the fundamentals. They passed down treatises and books to us; they wrote poetry, dialogues, commentaries on eloquence (*wen*), essays, and various notes to record their experiences, which we use as references in examination. Regrettably, most of them are not specifically about rhetoric (*xiuci*). Using examples mostly from ancient classics, their contents are of different sorts, generally lacking objectivity in illustration. Although their classical examples can serve as references, they do not systematically explain functions of rhetorical artifacts. Thus, some scholars have imitated Western or Eastern[409] rules and methods of inductive reasoning, comparison, and historical study. They classify and collect rhetorical artifacts from the daily use and literary history, all for the purpose of establishing the field of rhetoric. Translated from the West and East, "rhetoric" as a field of study began after the May Fourth Movement.[410] Wang Gou (王構 1245–1310 CE) in the Yuan Dynasty (1279–1368 CE) was actually the first who used "rhetoric" formally in his book, *Rhetorical Assessment and Criteria* (*Xiuci Jiangheng*修辭鑑衡). A fledging work, it is not refined but can be considered the beginner of works specifically on rhetoric. However, they have little to do with the so-call inductive, comparative, and historical methods of rhetorical study.

The job of rhetoric is to inform us of forms and principles of rhetorical artifacts and a system of rhetorical concepts through examining, analyzing, synthesizing, categorizing, describing, and illustrating (1) various rhetorical artifacts of language and word use and (2) treatises on rhetoric. Primary sources from the former and secondary sources in the latter reveal some patterns of a system and can serve as basics for our examinations or as resources for our applications. Rhetoric cannot set up rules, nor can examples do for language and word use. Neither can force us to follow them. Therefore, inductive patterns cannot be considered rules. But pragmatic examples are important, for they are proofs for deduction, arguments,

---

409. "Eastern" here refers mainly to Japanese. See Wu (2009, 150–54).

410. Also called the New Cultural Movement, it grew out of the student protest on May 4, 1919, and was transformed into cultural, social, and educational reforms.

or counterarguments. We often hear the demand, "show me the proof." Examples are proofs. The book, *Figures of Speech* (*Xiucige* 修辭格), by Tang Yue (Yueh Tang) is recognized for its accomplished rhetorical studies because he pays close attention to pragmatic examples.[411] Although old treatises were not written primarily on rhetoric, . . . they made contributions to studies of rhetoric by paying attention to pragmatic examples, which can demonstrate how rhetoric befits the theme and situation, as well as their inductive functions. For this reason, inferences must categorize and document sources for future reference and conceptual exploration. As for scholarly works, regardless whether they are written by Chinese or foreigners and whether they are written in the past or today, they can serve as references in comparative or historical studies and as reminders or proofs in illustration and illumination. . . . Rhetoric sheds light on the following matters:

I.   Components of a rhetorical device. Use analogy as an example. Its illustration should be defined by three factors: (1) what is compared, (2) words used, and (3) other matters that affect its composition.

II. Transformation of a rhetorical device. For example, an analogy may take three forms.

   (1) Simile—the words in an analogy refer to a category, as in that "the virtue of a gentleman is like the wind." But sometimes the word "like" is omitted.

   (2) Metaphor—the words point to obvious comparisons, as in that "the virtue of a gentleman is the wind."

   (3) Metonymy—the comparable is substituted with another word, as in that "the wind of the teacher is as high as a mountain and as long as a river." The word "wind" substitutes "virtue (*de*)." It is recorded that the original sentence in *An Ode to Mr. Yan* by Fan Zhongyan (範仲淹) was that "the virtue of the teacher is as high as a mountain and as long as a river." When Fan sought the input from Li Taibo (李泰伯), Li suggested to replace "virtue" with "wind." Now we can induce "wind" as a metonymy from the phrase of "a gentleman's virtue."

III. The distribution of rhetorical devices. Simile is used everywhere in ancient and current writings as well as in classical and today's spoken languages. The classical language uses "*ru*" (如) and "*you*" (猶) in an analogy, while the spoken language transforms them to "*haoxiang*" (好像), "*rulong*" (如同), "*yiyang*" (一样), "*jiushi*" (就是), etc.[412]

IV. The relationship of a rhetorical device with the theme and situation.

---

411. See more on Tang Yue's work in Wu (2009, 157–58).

412. These words, regardless in classical or modern Chinese, could all be translated into "as" or "like," except for the last one which means "to be."

V. Interconnections among different devices. For example, an analogy shares some similarities with a metonymy but is very different from a cover word.

Of these five matters, the first three are explained in detail by many books on rhetoric, and last two are often briefly generalized sometimes in a survey or mentioned in passing, because doing so may improve categorization and avoid bias or inadvertent omissions.

I.7 The Purpose of Rhetorical Studies

Rhetoric thus defined can be said to be a report of the test results of how language and words are used. Its basic function is in the flexible accurate understanding of language and word use, particularly in reading and listening. We can make three points about it.

Determine meanings. In the past, rhetorical artifacts were thought to be only implicitly understood but not explicitly expressed in words. In fact, most rhetorical artifacts can be explained in words. Our knowledge of their components and purposes, to a large degree, allows for determining their meanings to expand the boundaries of word expressions. . . If we know the metonymic interconnections (among related words), we do not need to cite the original contexts to validate the explanation.

Clarify problematics. It provides solutions to uncertainties and difficulties in rhetorical studies. For example, in his essay "Travel to the Mountains and Rivers in Liu Zhou," Liu Zongyuan (柳宗元 773–819 CE) writes, "The heavenly mountains in the west . . . have caves atop them . . . Most birds there are cuckoos. The Stony Fish Mountain is full of pure rocks, yet devoid of tall trees and grass. The small mountain looks like fish, known for being a home for the cuckoos. The caves are grand fairyland." Many readers are mystified by "home for the cuckoos." Some think that "the home" refers to "caves." But if they understand the metonymic associations by reading the Classic of Mountains and Seas (Shanhaijing 山海經),[413] they would have known for certain that "the home" is the "heavenly mountains."

Defy bias. It is believed that the classical language befits aesthetic (literary) composition (*meiwen* 美文), while the spoken word befits practical composition (*yingyongwen* 應用文). The belletristic writing refers mostly to elaborate uses of ornate beautiful words. In fact, colorful words in the classical language are applicable to the spoken language. For example, "spring and autumn" in the classical phrase of "the most prosperous Spring and Autumn" (*chun qiu ding sheng* 春秋鼎盛) are considered beautiful. But their rhetorical functions are similar to those of "East and West" (*dong xi* 东西) in the spoken language. If their metonymic interconnections are understood, we could be impartial to the classical language or its spoken counterpart.

---

413. A book on geology containing 18 short passages allegedly composed before 200 BCE by unknown authors (*Chinese Encyclopedia* 785).

Step-by-step systematic practices should be in place. Rhetorical treatises have categorized examples of word use. They provide conveniences for exercises. Next is writing and speech, which must target the theme and situation. They differ from reading and listening that do not require target audience to see the effect; they also differ from exercises purported for practice. Another point is that effective devices tried in the past do not always remain the same to serve as prescribed remedies. Neither can they be borrowed for the sake of convenience. But they are not irrelevant to practices of writing and speech and positively speaking, can prevent the following malpractices.

> Literal imitation. In the past, those who did not know rhetorical principles (*xiuci tiaoli* 修辭條理) often literally copied what ancients had written. Now clear rhetorical principles offer room of creation. It seems that literal imitations have been reduced to half as before. We now know what should not be copied again and again. For example, the flying arrow is not seen anymore. Why should it be used to indicate speediness? We also know that Mountain Tai is not an unusually giant mountain. Why should we still use it to symbolize importance or height?

> Overelaborate imitation. It refers to those who overlook the relationship between language use and the theme and situation. They make this mistake by taking beautiful words out of the context and saving them for future use in a different context. Yet, the theme and context decide the beauty and ugliness of word use. Words themselves are not beautiful or ugly. Their beauty depends on where and how they are used. Proper use makes them beautiful; improper use makes them ugly. Recently, some critics call ornate flowery words that were once considered beautiful "misplaced clichés" because they are improperly used.

Put positively, these ill practices can be remedied, depending on how the listener and reader respond and how the writer and speaker adjust their method. General speaking, the method must be carefully developed. The illustration must be clear. The example must be purposeful and suitable. To reach these objectives, the evaluative criteria should not disagree with the progress of modern language and word use or their nature. A good writing or speech is shaped by its contents, which determine its form. The contents in turn are often impacted by the standpoint, worldview, and social experience. Without the correct political standpoint, without the proletarian worldview, and without the revolutionary social practice, there is no wholesome content or form. Rhetoric itself can be said as such.

COMPREHENSIVE BIBLIOGRAPHY

Ames, Roger, and David Hall, trans. and eds. 2001. *Focusing the Familiar.* Honolulu, HI: University of Hawaii Press.

The Analects of Confucius. 1999. Translated by Roger Ames and Henry Rosemont Jr. New York: Ballantine Books.

Aristotle. *Rhetoric.* 2001. In *The Complete Works of Aristotle*, edited by Jonathan Barns, Princeton: Princeton University Press.

—. *On Rhetoric.* 2007. 2nd ed. Translated by George Kennedy. New York: Oxford University Press.

Bacabac, Florence E. 2018. "Reviewing Conduct Books as Feminist Rhetorical Devices for Agency Reforms." *Peitho Journal* 21 (1): 158–67.

Barnstone, Tony, and Chou Ping. 1996. *The Art of Writing: Teaching of the Chinese Masters.* Boston, MA: Shambhala Publications.

Barwarshi, Anis, and Mary Jo Reiff. 2010. *Genre: An Introduction to History, Theory, Research, and Pedagogy.* Fort Collins, CO, and Anderson, SC: The WAC Clearinghouse and Parlor Press.

Bazerman, Charles. 1994. "Systems of Genres and the Enactment of Social Intentions." In *Genre and the New Rhetoric,* edited by Aviva Freedman and Peter Medway. 67–84. New York: Taylor and Francis.

Bloch, J., and Chi, I. 1995. "A Comparison of the Use of Citations in Chinese and English Academic Discourse." In *Academic Writing in a Second Language: Essays on Research and Pedagogy,* edited by Diane Belcher and George Braine, 231–74. Norwood, NJ: Ablex.

Bol, Peter K. 1992. *This Culture of Ours: Intellectual Transitions in T'ang and Song China.* Stanford: Stanford University Press.

Chaffee, John. 1985. *The Thorny Gates of Learning in Song China.* Cambridge: Cambridge University Press.

Chan-Kuo Tse. 1970. Translated by J. I. Crump Jr. New York: Oxford University Press.

Chen, Shi-Hsiang, trans. 1952. *Essay on Literature Written by the Third-Century Chinese Poet Lu Chi.* Revised ed. Portland, ME: Anthoensen Press.

Chen, Guanglei, and Wang Junheng. 1998. *The History of Chinese Rhetoric Studies: Pre-Qing, Two Han, and Wei Ji South North Dynasties.* [In Chinese.] Shenyang, Jilin: Jilin Education Press.

Chen, Wangdao. 1976. "Preface to the 1975 Reprinted Edition." In *Xiucixue fafan* [An introduction to rhetoric], by Chen, Wangdao, 1–2. Shanghai: Shanghai Education Press.

—. 1999. *Xiucixue fafan* [An introduction to rhetoric]. Reprint. Shanghai: Shanghai Education Press.

Cheng, Yu-Yu. 2011. "The Origins of *Wen* in the Chinese Tradition." Translated by Emily Sun. *The Yearbook of Comparative Literature* 57: 189–212.

—. 2017. "Text and Commentary in the Medieval Period." In *The Oxford Handbook of Classical Chinese Literature,* edited by Wiebke Denecke, Li Wai-Yee, and Xiaofei Tian. 123–32. London: Oxford University Press.

Cherniack, Susan. 1994. "Book Culture and Textual Transmission in Sung China." *Harvard Journal of Asiatic Studies* 54 (1): 5–125.

Chinese Encyclopedia. 1979. [In Chinese.] Shanghai, China: Shanghai Cishu Chubanshe [Shanghai Reference Press].

Confucius. 2003. *Analects: With Selections from Traditional Commentaries.* Translated by Edward Slingerland. Indianapolis: Hackett Publishing.

Confucius. 1971. *Confucian Analects, the Great Learning, & The Doctrine of the Mean.* Translated by James Legge. New York: Dover Publications.

de Bary, William Theodore. 1960. *Sources of Chinese Tradition.* New York: Columbia University Press.

de Bary, William Theodore, and Irene Bloom, eds. 1999. *Sources of Chinese Tradition: from Earliest Times to 1600.* New York: Columbia University Press.

Dieter, Otto Alvin Loeb. 1950. "Stasis." *Communication Monographs* 17 (4): 345–69.

Dong, Zhongshu. 2016. *Luxuriant Gems of the Spring and Autumn.* Translated by John Major and Sarah Queen. Columbia University Press.

Doran, Rebecca. 2017. "Education and Examination System." In *The Oxford Handbook of Classical Chinese Literature,* edited by Wiebke Denecke, Li Wai-Yee, and Xiaofei Tian, 95–111. London: Oxford University Press.

Fang, Yong, and Li, Bo, eds. 2011. *Xunzi.* Beijing: Zhonghua Shuju [China Press].

Feng, Xinming, trans. 2008. *The Classic of Xiao.*

Forke, Alfred. 1901–1902. "The Chinese Sophists." *Journal of the North China Branch of the Royal Asiantic Society* 34: 1–100.

Galambos, Imre. 2017. "The Chinese Writing System." In *The Oxford Handbook of Classical Chinese Literature,* edited by Wiebke Denecke, Li Wai-Yee, and Xiaofei Tian, 31–45. London: Oxford University Press.

Gao, Huaping, et al., eds. 2015. *Hanfeizi* [in Chinese]. Beijing: Zhonghua Shuju [China Press].

Gao, Linguang. 2016. *Wenxin diaolong: A Critical Study of Literature in Pre-Qin and Two Han Periods* [in Chinese]. Beijing: China Press.

Garrett, Mary. 1991. "Asian Challenge." In *Contemporary Perspectives on Rhetoric,* 2nd ed., edited by Sonja K. Foss, Karen A. Foss, and Robert Trapp, 295–306. Prospect Heights, IL: Waveland.

—. 1993a. "Pathos Reconsidered from the Perspective of Classical Chinese Rhetorical Theories." *Quarterly Journal of Speech* 79 (1): 13–39.

—. 1993b. "Classical Chinese Rhetorical Conceptualization of Argumentation and Persuasion." *Argumentation and Advocacy* 29 (3): 105–15.

Guiguzi, China's First Treatise on Rhetoric. 2016. Translated by Hui Wu with commentaries by Hui Wu and C. Jan. Swearingen. Carbondale, IL: Southern Illinois University Press.

Guo, Shaoyu, and Wensheng Wang, eds. 2001. *Zhongguo lidai wenlun xuan* [Selected Chinese historical treatises on writing]. 4 vols. Shanghai: Shangahi Guji Chubanshe [Shanghai Classics Press].

Hall, David, and Roger Ames. 1998. *Thinking from the Han.* Albany, NY: State University of New York Press, 1998.

Hamill, Sam, trans. 2000. *Lu Ji's Wen Fu: The Art of Writing.* Minneapolis, MN: Milkweed Editions.

Hanfeizi [in Chinese]. 2016. Edited by Jue Zhang. Shanghai: Shanghai Guji Chubanshe [Shanghai Classics Press].

Hu, Huanshen. 1930. *On Rhetorical Schemata.* [In Chinese.] Shanghai, China: World Press.

Hu, Shi. 1917. *A Collection of Hu Shi's Works.* [In Chinese.] Taipei: Yuandong Tushu Gongsi.

Hughes, E. R. 1951. *The Art of Letters: Lu Chi's "Wen Fu," A.D 302. A Translation and Comparative Study.* New York: Pantheon Books.

Hutton, Eric, trans. 2014. *Xunzi: The Complete Text.* Princeton, NJ: Princeton University Press.

Jia Yuxin and Cheng Cheng. 2002. "Indirectness in Chinese English Writing." *Asian Englishes* 5 (1): 64–74.

Jin, Zhaozi. 1934. *Pragmatic Chinese Rhetoric.* [In Chinese.] Shanghai, China: China Press.

Jullien, Francois. 2004. *Detour and Access*: Strategies of Meaning in China and Greece. Translated by Sophie Hawkes. New York: Zone Books.

Kaplan, Robert. B. 1966. "Cultural Thought Patterns in Intercultural Education. *Language Learning* 16: 1–20

—. 1972. *The Anatomy of Rhetoric: A Prolegomena to a Functional Theory of Rhetoric.* Philadelphia: Centre for Curriculum Studies.

Kennedy, George. 1980. *Classical Rhetoric and Its Christian and Secular Tradition from Ancient to Modern Times.* London: Croom Helm.

Kennedy, George. 2001. *Comparative Rhetoric.* New York: Oxford University Press.

Kern, Martin. 2003. "Western Han Aesthetics and the Fenesis of the 'Fu'." *Harvard Journal of Asiatic Studies* 53 (2): 383–437.

Kirkpatrick, Andy. 1995. "Chinese Rhetoric: Methods of Argument." *Multilingua: Journal of Cross-Cultural and Interlanguage Communication* 14 (3): 271–95.

— 2004. "Medieval Chinese Rules of Writing and their Relevance Today." *Australian Review of Applied Linguistics* 27 (1): 1–14.

—. 2005. "China's First Systematic Account of Rhetoric: An Introduction to Chen Kui's (陈骙) Wen Ze (文则). *Rhetorica* 23 (2): 103–52.

Kirkpatrick, Andy, and Zhichang Xu. 2012. *Chinese Rhetoric and Writing: An Introduction for Language Teachers.* Fort Collins, CO, and Anderson, SC: The WAC Clearinghouse and Parlor Press. Kirkpatrick, Andy, and Yan Yonglin. 2002. "The Use of Citation Conventions and Authorial Voice in a Genre of Chinese Academic Discourse." In *Discourses in Search of Members: A Festschrift for Ron Scollon,* edited by David C.S. Li, 483–508. University Press of America.

Knoblock, John. 1988. *Xunzi: A Translation and Study of the Complete Works.* Vols. 1–3. Stanford, CA: Stanford University Press.

Kracke, E. A. 1953. *Civil Service in the Early Song China.* Cambridge Mass: Harvard University Press.

Kroll, Paul W. 2017. "Anthologies in the Tang." In *The Oxford Handbook of Classical Chinese Literature,* edited by Wiebke Denecke, Wai-Yee Li, and Xiaofei Tian. 303–15. London: Oxford University Press.

Lan, Haixia. 2017. *Aristotle and Confucius on Rhetoric and Truth.* New York: Routledge.

Lanham, Carol. 2001. "Writing Instruction from Late Antiquity to the Twelfth Century." In *A Short History of Writing Instruction,* edited by James J. Murphy, 79–121. Mahwah, NJ: Lawrence Erlbaum,.

Latourette, Kenneth Scott. 1946. *The Chinese: Their History and Culture.* New York: Macmillan.

Lavagnino, Alessandra. 2017. "A Chinese Regard Oblique." *De Gruyter. Asia.* 71 (3): 1003–13.

Li, Feng. 2013. *Early China: A Social and Cultural History.* Cambridge: Cambridge University Press.

Li, Xueqin. 2003. *Guwenzi xue chujie.* [Beginning steps toward learning ancient characters]. Reprint. Beijing: China Press.

Liao, W. K., trans. 1939. *The Complete Works of Han Fei Tzu.* Vol. 1. London: Arthur Probsthain.

Liao, W. K., trans. 1959. *The Complete Works of Han Fei Tzu.* Vol. 2. London: Arthur Probsthain.

Liu, Dabai. 1999. "Preface to the First Edition." [In Chinese.] In *Xiucixue fafan* [An introduction to rhetoric] by Chen Wangdao, Reprint. 288–91. Shanghai, Shanghai Education Press.

Liu Xie. 2016. *Wenxin diaolong.* [A Heart for Eloquence and the Invention of Dragons], edited by Wang Yunxi and Zhou Feng. Shanghai: Shanghai Guji Chubanshe [Shanghai Classics Press].

Liu, Xuqing. *Zhongguo xiezuo lilun jiping* [Anthology and commentary on Chinese theories on writing]. Hohhot, Inner Mongolia: Inner Mongolia Education Press [in Chinese], 1992.

Lu, Xing. *Rhetoric in Ancient China Fifth to Third Century B.C. E.: A Comparison with Classical Greek Rhetoric.* Columbia, SC: University of South Carolina Press, 1998.

Lu, Xing, and David Frank. 1993. "On the Study of Ancient Chinese Rhetoric/Bian 辩." *Western Journal of Communication* 57 (Fall): 445–63.

Liu, Yameng. 1991. "Aristotle and the Stasis Theory: A Reexamination." *Rhetoric Society Quarterly* 21 (1): 53–59.

—. 1996. "To Capture the Essence of Chinese Rhetoric: An Anatomy of a Paradigm in Comparative Rhetoric," *Rhetoric Review* 14 (2): 318–35.

Liu, Yancheng. 1988. *Wen ze zhuyi* [in Chinese] [Commentary and modern Chinese translation of the *Wen Ze.*] Beijing: Shumu Wenxian Chubanshe.

Lyon, Arabella. 2010. "Writing an Empire: Cross-Talk on Authority, Act, and Relationships with the Other in the *Analects, Daodejing,* and *HanFeizi.*" *College English* 72 (4): 350–66.

—. 2013. *Deliberative Acts: Democracy, Rhetoric, and Rights.* University Park, PA: The Pennsylvania State University Press.

Ma, Shinian. 2011. *Hanfeizi de chengshu jiqi wenxue yanjiu* [A study of the background and literary significance of *Hanfeizi*]. Shanghai: Shanghai Guji Chubanshe (Shanghai Classics Press).

Mao, LuMing. 2007. "Studying the Chinese Rhetorical Tradition in the Present: Representing the Native's Point of View." *College English* 69 (3): 216–37.

Matalene, Carolyn. 1985. "Contrastive Rhetoric: an American Writing Teacher in China." *College English* 47 (8): 789–808.

McMullen, David. 1988. *State and Scholars in Tang China.* Cambridge: Cambridge University Press.

Miller, Carolyn. 1984. "Genre as Social Action." *Quarterly Journal of Speech* 70 (2): 151–67.

Miller, Carolyn, Amy J, Devitt, and Victoria J. Gallagher. 2018. "Genre: Permanence and Change." *Rhetoric Society Quarterly* 48 (3): 269–77.

Moloughney, Brian. 2002. "Derivation, Intertextuality and Authority: Narrative and the Problem of Historical Coherence." *East Asian History* 23: 129–48.

Mou, Zongsan. 1970. *Li shi zhe xue* [The philosophy of history]. Hong Kong: Ren sheng chubanshe [Life Press].

Nadeau, Ray. 1964. "Hermogene's *On Stases,*" *Speech Monographs* 31 (4): 361–424.

Nü Si Shu [Four women's books]. 2016. Beijing, China: Tuanjie Shubanshe [Unity Press].

Owen, Stephen. 1992. *Readings in Chinese Literary Thought.* Cambridge, MA: Harvard University Press.

—. 1996. *The End of the Chinese Middle Ages. Essays in mid Tang Literary Culture.* Stanford: Stanford University Press.

Pang-White, Ann A., trans. 2018. *The Confucian Four Books for Women: A New Translation of the Nü Sishu and the Commentary of Wang Xiang.* New York: Oxford University Press.

Qi, Liangde. ed. 2008. *Wenxin diaolong jiaozhu tongyi* [Wen Xin Diao Long: commentary and translation]. Shanghai: Shanghai guji shubanshe [Shanghai Classics Press].

Qian, Mu. 1994. *Lun yu xin jie* [New interpretation of the analects]. Taibei: Lianjing.

Queen, Sarah. 1996. *From Chronicle to Canon: The Hermeneutics of the Spring and Autumn According to Tung Chung-shu.* Cambridge, England: Cambridge University Press.

Raphals, Lisa. 1998. *Sharing the Light: Representations of Women and Virtue in Early China.* New York: State University of New York Press.

Rapp, Christof. 2010. "Aristotle's Rhetoric." In *The Sanford Encyclopedia of Philosophy,* edited by Edward N. Zalta.

Rouzer, Paul. 2017. "Chinese Poetry." In *The Oxford Handbook of Classical Chinese Literature,* edited by Wiebke Denecke, Wai-Yee Li, and Xiaofei Tian, 241–57. London: Oxford University Press.

Schaberg, David. 2002. "The Logic of Signs in Early Chinese Rhetoric." In *Early China/Ancient Greece: Thinking through Comparison,* edited by Steven Shankman and Stephen W. Durrant, 155–86. Albany, NY: State University of New York Press.

Scollon, Ron. B. 1995. "Plagiarism and Ideology," *Language in Society* 24 (1): 1–28.

Shen, Changyun, et al. 2000. *Zhaoguo shigao* [A historical account of the state of Zhao]. Beijing: Zhonghua Shuju [China Press].

Shen, Zhukun. 2012. *Tuhui nusishu baihua Ji* [Four women's books with illustrations and commentaries]. 2nd ed. Beijing: Zhongguo Huaqiao Chubanshe [China Overseas Press].

Shih, Vincent Yu-chung, trans. 1969. *The Literary Mind and the Carving of Dragons by Liu Hsieh.* Taibei, Taiwan: Tunhuang Press.

Swearingen, C. Jan. 2009. "Ren, Wen, and Baguwen: The Eight-Legged Essays in Rhetorical Perspective." In "Symposium: Comparative Rhetorical Studies in the new Contact Zone—Chinese rhetoric Reimagined," edited by C. Jan Swearingen and LuMing Mao. *College Composition and Communication* 60 (4): W106-W114.

Sima, Guang. N.d. *Jia Fan* [Family rules]. https://ctext.org/wiki.pl?if=gb&chapter=759218.

Sima, Qian. 2004. *Shi Ji* [The Grand scribe's records]. With Commentary by Zhaoqi Han. Volume I. Changsha, Hunan: Yuelu shushe [Yuelu Press].

Song, Dachuan, and Wang Jianju. 1999. *Zhongguo jiaoyuzhidu tongshi* [The history of Chinese educational systems]. Vol. 2. Jinan, China: Shandong Jiaoyu Chubanshe [Shandong Education Press].

Ssu-Ma, Ch'ien. 1994. *The Grand Scriber's Records.* Vol. 7, edited by William H. Nienhauser, translated by Tsai-fa Cheng et al. Bloomington, IN: Indiana University Press.

Tan Quanji. 1978. *Wen ze yanjiu* [A study of the *Wen Ze*]. Hong Kong: Wenxue Chubanshe.

Tang, Junyi. 2017. "Kongzi yu ren ge shi jie" [Confucius and human dignity]. *360DOC.*.

—. 1974. *Zhongguo zhe xue yuan lun* [An Original Treatise on Chinese Philosophy]. Hong Kong: Dong fang ren wen xue hui [Eastern Association of the Humanities].

Tang, Yue. 1923. *Xiucige* [Figures of speech]. Shanghai: Shanghai: shangwu yinshuguan [Commercial Press].

Taylor, G., and T. G. Chen. 1991. "Linguistic, Cultural and Subcultural Issues in Contrastive Discourse Analysis: Anglo-American and Chinese Scientific Texts. *Applied Linguistics* 12 (3): 313–36.

Tian, Xiaofei. 2017. "Literary Learning: Encyclopedias and Epitomes." In *The Oxford Handbook of Classical Chinese Literature,* edited by Wiebke Denecke, Wai-Yee Li, and Xiaofei Tian, 132–46. London: Oxford University Press.Thompson, Wayne N. 1972. "Stasis in Aristotle's *Rhetoric." Quarterly Journal of Speech* 58 (2): 134–41.

Wang, Gou. 1937. *Xiuci jianheng* [Rhetorical assessment and criteria], edited by Wang, Yunwu. Beijing: Shangwu Yinshuguan [Commercial Press].

Wang, Robin. 2015. "Dong Zhongshu's Transformation of Yin-Yang Theory and Contesting of Gender Identity. *Philosophy East and West* 55 (2): 209–31.

—. ed. 2003. *Images of Women in Chinese Thought and Culture.* Indianapolis, IN: Hackett.

Wang Songmao. 1988. *Wen Ze zhuyi bayu* [A postcript to Liu Yancheng's commentary and modern Chinese translation of the Wen Ze]. Beijing: Classic Press.

Wang, Xianshen, ed. 2016. *Hanfeizi Ji Jie* [A collection of editorial notes and commentaries on Hanfeizi]. 1896. Beijing: Zhonghua Shuju [China Press], 1998, Reprinted in 2016.

Wang, Xiang. 2011. *Nü si shu nu xiaojing* [Four Women's Books and Doctrine on Women's Filial Piety]. Fujiang, China Zhongguo Huaqiao Chubanshe [China Overseas Press].

Wang, Yuanhua. 2004. *Wenxin diaolong jiangsu* [Lectures on wenxin diaolong]. Guilin, China: Guangxi Normal University Press.

Wang, Yunxi, and Zhou Feng, eds. 2016. *Commentary on wenxin diaolong by Liu Xie.* Shanghai: Shanghai guji chubanshe [Shanghai Classics Press].

Wardy, Robert. 2000. *Aristotle in China: Language, Categories and Translation.* Cambridge: Cambridge University Press.

Watson, Burton, trans. 1964. *Han Fei Tzu: Basic Writings.* New York: Columbia University Press.

—, trans. 2003. *Xunzi: Basic Writings.* New York: Columbia University Press.

Wen, Xinzi, ed. 2013. *Nusishu pindu quanji.* [Commentaries on four women's classics]. Beijing: Central Broadcasting and TV Education Press.

Wu, Hui. 2005. "The Paradigm of Margaret Cavendish: Reading Women's Alternative Rhetorics in a Global Context." In *Calling Cards: Theory and Practice in the Study of Race, Gender, and Culture,* edited by Jacqueline Jones Royster and Ann Marie Mann Simpkins. 171–86. Albany, NY: State University of New York Press.

—. 2009. "Lost and Found in Transnation: Modern Conceptualization of Chinese Rhetoric." *Rhetoric Review* 28 (2): 148–66.

—. 2016. "Redrawing the Map of Rhetoric." In *Guiguzi, China's First Treatise on Rhetoric,* 1–31. Carbondale, IL: Southern Illinois University Press.

—. 2018. "*Yin-Yang* as the Philosophical Foundation of Chinese Rhetoric." *China Media Research* 14, no. 4 (Oct.): 46–55.

—. 2020. "From Oratory to Writing: An Overview of Classical Chinese Rhetoric (500 BCE-220 CE). In *The Routledge Handbook of Comparative World Rhetorics,* edited by Keith Lloyd, 86–95. New York: Routledge.

Wu, Hui, and C. Jan Swearingen. 2016. "Interality as a Key to Deciphering *Guiguzi:* A Challenge to Critics." *Canadian Journal of Communication* 41 (3): 503–19.

Wu, Xuande. 2000. *Zhongguo jiaoyu zhidu tongshi*: *mingdai* [The History of chinese educational system: the Ming dynasty]. Vol. 4. Jinan, Shangdong.

Xi, Shunnian. 2002. *Zhongguo shuyuanliu* [The origin of the Chinese book]. Jiangsu Guji Chubanshe [Jiangsu Classics Press].

Xiao, Tong, ed. 2002. *Wenxuan* [Selected treatises on writing]. With commentaries by Li Shan. Reprint. Changsha, Hunan: Yuelu chubanshe [Yuelu Press].

Xie, Dan, and Shu Tian, eds. 2007. *Xunzi* [in Chinese], Hohhot, China: Yuangfang Chubanshe [Distant Land Press].

Xu, Gengsheng. 1933. *The Course in Rhetoric.* [In Chinese.] Shanghai, China: Broad Interests Press [in Chinese].

Xu, Shen, ed. 2005. *Shuowen jiezi* [Illustrating writing and decoding characters]. Modern Edition. Beijing: Social Sciences Academic Press [in Chinese].

Yang, Bojun. 1958. *Lun yu yi zhu* [The Analects: a translation and commentary]. Beijing: Zhonghua shuju [China Press].

Yang, Ming. 2016. *Notes on the Full Collection of Lu Ji.* [In Chinese.] Shanghai: Shanghai Classics Press.

Yang, Shuda. 1969. *A Study of Chinese Rhetoric.* [In Chinese.] 3rd expanded ed. Taiwan: World Press.

Yu, Qiding, and Shi Keshan. 1999. *Zhongguo jiaoyuzhidu tongshi* [The history of Chinese educational systems]. Vol. 1. Jinan, China: Shandong Jiaoyu Chubanshe [Shandong Education Press].

Zhan, Heying Jenny, and Roger Bradshaw. 1996. "Book of Analects for Women: Consort Song (Tang)." *Journal of Historical Sociology* 9, no. 3 (Sept.): 262–68.

Zhang, Cangshou, and Jonathan Pease. 1999. "Roots of the Han Rhapsody in Philosophical Prose." *Monumenta Serica* 41: 1–27.

Zhang, Dainian. 1995. *Zhang Dainian wen ji* 6. Beijing: Qinghuan University Press.

Zhang, Fuxiang, ed. 1998. *Nan song guan ge lu* [Official Records of the Southern Song] by Chen Kui and others. Beijing: Zhonghua Shuju Chubanshe.

Zhang, Yiping. 1934. *Lectures on Rhetoric.* [In Chinese.] Shanghai, China: Sky Horse Press [in Chinese].

Zhao, Heping. 1990. "'*Wen Xin Diao Long*': An Early Chinese Rhetoric of Writing Discourse." Diss. Purdue University.

—. 1994. "Rhetorical Invention in *Wen Xin Diao Long.*" *Rhetoric Society Quarterly* 24 (3–4): 1–15.

Zhao, Kuifu. 2008. "Foreword." In *Guiguzi yanjiu* [A study of Guiguzi] by Xu Fuhong. 1–12. Shanghai: Shanghai guji chubanshe [Shanghai Classics Press].

Zheng, Ziyu. 1984. *Zhongguo xiucixue shigao* [A historical overview of Chinese rhetorical studies]. Reprint. Shanghai, China: Shanghai Education Press.

Zheng Ziyu (郑子瑜). 1979. *Zhongguo xiucixue shigao* [A historical overview of Chinese rhetorical studies]. Shanghai: Shanghai Education Press.

Zhou Zhenfu. 1999. *Zhongguo xiucixue shi.* [*A History of Chinese Rhetoric*]. Beijing: Shangwuyin Shuguan.

Zong, Tinghu, and Li Jinling. 1998. *Zhongguo xiucixue tongshi. Vol 2.* Sui Tang Wu Dai Song Jin Yuan juan [*A Complete History of Chinese Rhetoric*: The *Sui, Tang, 5 Dynasties, Song, Jin and Yuan Dynasties*]. Jilin: Jilin Jiaoyu Chubanshe. [The complete 5 volume series is edited by Zheng Ziyu and Zong Tinghu] [in Chinese].

Zuo Qiuming. 2013. *Zuo Zhuan* [in Chinese], edited by Wang Longyan. Shanghai: Sanlian shudian [Shanghai Trinity Press].

Zhu, Hua. 2019. "Rhetorical Listening: Guiguzi and Feminists in Dialogue." *China Media Research* 15, no.1 (Jan.): 3–12.

GLOSSARY OF TERMS

Term	Translation	Textual Reference (in alphabetical order)
bian 辯	disputation, debate, argument, argumentation	Hanfeizi I.3.1, IV.12.4, XVII.41; Liu Xie 31.3; Xunzi 5
ban kou 辯口	eloquent mouth	Ban Zhao 4
buzuo 不怍	boastful [talk]	Confucius 14.20
caochuang 草創	draft, brainstorming	Confucius 14.8; Liu Xie 32.2
ci 辭	spoken word, speech, word, eloquence	Ban Zhao 4; Chen Wangdao 1; Hanfeizi I.3.1, IV.12.4, XVII.41, Lu Ji 1, 3, 5, 9, 10, 15, 18; Liu Xie 2.1, 3.10, 18.7, 28.1, 31.1, 32.1, 32.2; Xunzi 22.6, 22.7, 22.9
ci 詞	phrase, word	Ban Zhao 4; Chen Wangdao; Hanfeizi XVII.41; Liu Xue 18.15, 32.1
cige 辭格	figures of speech	Chen Wangdao 1.2
ciqu 辭趣	word play	Chen Wangdao 1.2
cizao 辭藻	ornate word	Chen Wangdao 1.1, 1.2
da wen 大文	grand composition	Xunzi 22.7
Dao 道	the Way	Confucius 1.14, 1.15, 14.3, 15.37; Hanfeizi XVIII.48.6 Liu Xie 1; Queen Xu 2, 3; Xunzi 22.7
De 德	virtue, ethic	Ban Zhao; Chen Wangdao 1.5; Liu Xie 50.1; Queen Xu 2, 3; Wang Jiefu 1.3, 1.7, 1.10, 9.1, 12
fabiao 发表	delivery	Chen Wangdao 1.3
hayü 話語	speech, discourse	Chen Wangdao 1.4
jian 諫	to persuade, proposition, admonition, critical remarks	Confucius 4.18, 19.10; Hanfeizi IV.12.7, XVIII.48.6; Wang Jiefu 10.18
jian yan 奸言	treacherous speech, speech without morality	Xunzi 5.9

ju 句	sentence	Liu Xie 32.3
junzi 君子	deferential person, exemplary person, ethical rhetor	Confucius 1.14, 2.13, 4.10, 4.24, 15.23, 16.6, 20.3; Liu Xie 2.1, 49.6, 50.1; Xunzi 5.12, 5.13, 22.7, 22.8, 22.9; Wang Jiefu 12.9
li 礼	propriety, rite	Confucius 1.13, 1.15, 11.26
li 理	principle, reasoning	Liu Xie 18.15, 31.3, 32.1, 43.1; Lu Ji 4, 8, 9, 20; Song Ruozhao 1
lishen 立身	to establish herself, [women's] self-establishment	Song Ruozhao 1
lun 論	argument, argumentation, treatise	Hanfeizi IV.12.7; Liu Xie 3.10, 18.7, 32.3, 50.1; Lu Ji 6,7
meiwen 美文	aesthetic, belletristic, literary composition	Chen Wangdao 1.7
yanne 言訥	to speak slowly	Confucius 13.27
ning yan 佞[言]	glib-talk, obsequious or glib speech	Confucius 5.5, 14.32
qi 氣	energy	Queen Xu 3
qiaoyan 巧言	crafty word/speech	Confucius 5.25
quan 權	weighing, appropriateness [*kairos*]	Confucius 9.30
yanrang [言]讓	discourse in yielding words	Confucius 11.26
yanren [言]訒	discourse in slow words, unintelligible speech	Confucius 12.3; Xunzi 22.9
ren 仁	equitable-attributes, benevolence, ethics of rhetoric	Confucius 1.3, 5.5; Ban Zhao 4; Queen Xu 3; Xunzi 5.12
ren 人	recognized human, sage of rhetoric	Song Ruozhao 1.1
runse 潤色	polish	Confucius 14.8
shenming 神明	omniscient intellectual conscience	Ban Zhao 4; Liu Xie 31.4.
shi 仕	state-official	Confucius 2.18, 13.20
shu 術	[rhetorical] strategy, art of rhetoric	Hanfeizi XVII.41; Liu Xie 43.1
shui 說	persuasion, to persuade, a persuader	Hanfeizi IV.12; Lu Ji 7; Liu Xue 3.10; 18.10; Xunzi 5.10
shui zhe 說者	persuader	Hanfeizi IV.12.8
shuo 說	persuasion, speech, talk, to speak	Hanfeizi IV.12.7, XVII.41; Lu Ji 17; Xunzi 22.7

song 訟	counterargument	Hanfeizi XVII.41
tan 談	discussion, talk	Hanfeizi IV.12.7
taolun 討論	to confer, discuss	Confucius 14.8
ti 體	genre, style	Liu Xie 32.1, 32.2, 32.3, 50.1
ting dao 听道	way/method of listening	Hanfeizi XVIII.48.6
wen 文	eloquence, speech, writing, rhetorical knowledge and skills, word composition, composition	Chen Wangdao 1.2, 1.5; Hanfeizi XVII.41; Liu Xie 1.1, 1.2, 2.1, 3.12, 31.1, 31.3, 32.1, 49.6, 50.1; Lu Ji 1, 2, 4, 7, 18, 20; Xunzi 5.9, 22.7
wen 問	inquire	Confucius 11.22; Hanfeizi XVII.41
wenci 文辭	written composition	Chen Wangdao 1.1
wen zhang 文章	eloquent composition, written composition	Chen Wangdao 1.4; Liu Xie 2.1, 31.1, 50.1; Lu Ji 2
xie shuo 邪說	vicious speech	Hanfeizi XVIII.48.6
xin 信	credibility	Confucius 2.22, 19.10
xin yan 信言	sincere/creditable speech	Hanfeizi I.3.1
xin 心	heart, mind, mindset, mentality	Liu Xie 1.2, 50.1; Lu Ji 4; Queen Xu 3; Wang Jiefu 12.8
xiu ci 修辭	to polish the speech or word, rhetorical study, rhetoric	Chen Wangdao 1.1, 1.4, 1.5, 1.7; Liu Xie 3.12
xiuci fangshi 修辭方式	rhetorical devices	Chen Wangdao 1.1, 1.5
xiuci shoufa 修辭手法	rhetorical schemata	Chen Wangdao 1.2, 1.5
xiuci tiaoli 修辭條理	rhetorical principles/criteria	Chen Wangdao 1.7
xiuci xianxiang 修辭現象	rhetorical artifacts/phenomena	Chen Wangdao 1.1, 2.1, 1.3, 1.5
xiushi 修飾	to edit, polish	Confucius 14.8
xiushen 修身	self-development	Liu Xie 2.1; Queen X 2; Wang Jiefu 1.5

yan 言	the *Dao*/ways of discourse, speech, persuasion, eloquence, language, to speak	Ban Zhao 4; Confucius 4.22, 10.1, 10.2 11.26, 12.3, 13.3, 14.1, 14.3, 14.4, 14.27, 15.8, 15.17, 15.41, 16.6, 16.8, 16.13, 17.19, 20.3; Hanfeizi I.3.1, IV.12.4, IV.12.5, XVII.41, XVIII.48.6; Liu Xie 2.1, 3.12, 18.15, 27.1, 31.2, 31.3, 50.1; Lu Ji 1, 4, 5, 9, 19; Queen Xu 2, 3; Xunzi 5.9; Wang Jiefu 9.2, 10.19, 12.7, 12.24
yi 義	appropriateness [*kairos*]	Confucius 4.10, 4.16, 7.3, 14.12, 15.17, 17.23
yin-yang or yin and yang 阴阳	interactive corresponding energies	Liu Xie 43.1; Wang Jiefu 1.1
yingyongwen 應用文	practical/professional composition	Chen Wangdao 1.7
yüyu 語	discussion, talk, language, remark, to speak	Confucius 6.21, Hanfeizi IV.12.3, XVIII.48.6; Liu Xie 32.3, Queen Xu 3; Song Rouzhao 1
yüci 語辭	the word of speech, speech composition, language and word use	Chen Wangdao 1.1, 1.2, 1.3, 1.4
zheng 爭	argument, dispute	Hanfeizi IV.12.5, XVII.41
zhengming 正名	rectification of names, correct naming	Confucius 13.3; Xunzi 22
zi 字	character, word	Liu Xie 32.3
zuo wen 作文	to compose writing; writing composition	Lu Ji 1

3 East African Rhetorics

Prefatory Introduction

Leonora Anyango

The Art of Translating Orature in Eastern Africa

The East African region of Africa is vibrant. On the political and economic front, immediately after independence from British rule, the region consisted of the countries of Kenya, Uganda, and Tanzania. These countries formed the East African Community that worked together to promote the region. The community began in 1967 but was later disbanded in 1977, before being revived in 2000. In the new East African community, there are the countries of Kenya, Uganda, Tanzania, Rwanda, Burundi, and South Sudan.

On the linguistic front, the region boasts approximately three hundred ethnic languages. During and after the fight for independence, the first three countries in the bloc (Kenya, Uganda and Tanzania) struggled with how to unify their people through a regional language. Kiswahili quickly grew as the lingua franca of the region, and both Kenya and Tanzania made it an official language. Kenya, meanwhile, also had English as the other official language. East African rhetorics have been largely influenced by the major languages spoken. At the center of this battle have been the literary giants of the region, some of whom have been in favor of vernacular languages for writing, while others have been in favor of English and Kiswahili. East African rhetorics have been characterized by issues concerning the preservation and promotion of indigenous languages, especially whether there is a need to do so. People have also debated the use of English and the desire to preserve oral cultures. Should the style of English language needed for oral culture preservation be closer to the African languages represented in the literary modes? Those who debate these issues includes novelist Chinua Achebe, who is not East African but has a strong voice on orature.

African cultures and traditions have long embraced oral forms of knowing. The pervading presence of orality in African cultures cannot be camouflaged. In fact, it is a source of pride for the African people, inasmuch as it also provides a wealthy repertoire used by contemporary African writers in their narrative writing, poetry, and songs, as a way of enriching their own writing. The move by African writers to embrace orality emanates from the deeply rooted quest to not only keep this tradition alive due to its rich heritage but also to create a form of literature that is uniquely African, albeit rendered in Western languages like English and French.

The fight for a right to recognition and visibility among African writers using the unique language of orality is nothing new. It dates to the days before the colonization of African states when European narratives "rendered these African stories primitive and barbaric."[1] It is still argued whether African orality can and should be considered literature. In her seminal work, *Oral Literature in Africa*, Ruth Finnegan wishes that these arguments could be put to rest since "it is misleading as well as unfruitful to attempt to draw a strict line between the verbal art of literate and of non-literate cultural traditions."[2] Kermit Campbell articulates this thought by chastising the categorization of human culture into two groups: "Societies Without Writing" and "Ancient Literate Societies." Campbell contends that this arbitrary divide "assumes that societies are categorically one or the other, literate or oral, and that literacy is non-transferrable."[3] He identifies the Nubia, Axium and Mali cultures of Africa that were both traditionally oral and literate.

A famous saying from *Things Fall Apart* by Chinua Achebe is "proverbs are the palm-oil with which words are eaten."[4] Here, Achebe's proverb carries rhetoricity within it on certain levels. First, he is not only pointing to the importance of proverbs in his community as a means of delivering and enjoying conversations, but he is also pointing to the agricultural nature of this community and the presence of palm tree and its importance. Secondly, considering the allusion of proverbs as food, there is an implication that while palm oil nourishes the body, proverbs nourish the mind and entertain the audience as the speaker employs them. The proverb, as it were, not only transports language, but it also transports culture, geography, and all that brings meaning and clarity, into the other language. In strong support of African orature, Achebe, without mincing words, opines:

---

1. Imbo 2002, 2. The irony of this is that, on the contrary, Greek orality has been long celebrated as an anchor of rhetorical thought. Most comprehensive histories of Greek rhetoric indicate that there was a time when "the entirety of Hellenic culture, dating back to the Bronze Age and beyond, could only be transmitted by constant repetition and memorization by every citizen. Prose preservation of this tradition was not practicable" (1). Over time, the Greek oral traditions gradually gave way to written literacies, raising rhetorical practices that relied less on an oral mindset.

2. Finnegan 2012, 9.

3. Campbell 2006, 258.

4. Achebe 1958, 7.

> What I do see is a new voice coming out of Africa, speaking of African experience in a worldwide language. So my answer to the question Can an African ever learn English well enough to be able to use it effectively in creative writing? is certainly yes. If on the other hand you ask, Can he ever learn to use it like a native speaker? I should say, I hope not. It is neither necessary nor desirable for him to be able to do so. The price a world language must be prepared to pay is submission to many different kinds of use.[5]

This "submission to many different kinds of use" is the subject and object of orature. It is the meaning of orature that writers seek as they negotiate the use of two culturally and linguistically separate languages. It is the place and space where orature curves out its domain and finds the freedom to express itself as an art with its own character and stance, emanating from a culture and identity that prides itself in the excellence of this very art.

An example of translating orature into English is exhibited below by Ngugi wa Thiong'o's *Matigari*. When Ngugi wa Thiong'o departed from writing in English at a certain point in his writing career and decided to write in Gikuyu, he made the point that his own language was self-sufficient, elevated, and capable of delivering literature in its original authenticity. He did not get enough support from his writing community as he had hoped, mainly because other African writers felt "abandoned" since they did not understand, and therefore could not read his books. In *Decolonising the Mind* he laments thus:

> It was almost as if, in choosing to write in Gikuyu, I was doing something abnormal. But Gikuyu is my mother tongue! The very fact that what common sense dictates in the literary practice of other cultures is being questioned in an African writer is a measure of how far imperialism has distorted the view of *African realities*. [emphasis added][6]

Part of what Ngugi saw as *African realities* here is the capability of African writers to express themselves as Africans, in languages that they deem fit for their purposes and contexts as African nations. Chinua Achebe purports that this expression does not have to be in the multiple hundreds of African languages, which other Africans will not understand, and the rest of the world will never know about. While he sees African languages as important tools for writing, he feels that English has helped in bridging the gap between authors because they can see, talk about, and read one another's works even though they do not understand one another's languages. He tells a story of meeting Shaaban Robert, an African poet, who only wrote in Swahili, limiting their contacts as writers. His present of two books from the author, "which I treasure but cannot read-until I have learned Swahili,"[7] illustrates the need of using a language

---

5. Achebe 1997, 347.
6. Thiong'o 1986a, 27–28.
7. Achebe 1997, 345.

that is more universal. Achebe strongly feels that English can be *made* to serve the African writer. He eloquently summarizes his thoughts here:

> I have been given this language and I intend to use it. . . . I feel that the English language will be able to carry the weight of my African experience. But it will have to be a new English, still in full communion with its ancestral home, but altered to suit its new African surroundings.[8]

This "altering" is what Kwaku Gyasi (1999) laboriously discusses as the translation act of the African writer.

In his work *Writing as Translation*, Gyasi sees the very act of the African writer owning English and using it for his own purposes as a translation act. To him, translation for African writers is a multi-pronged process that has them going beyond "transportation or transmission or transposition" to the domain of "transformation and transmutation, for all these activities take place when an African writer sets out to write in a European language."[9] In choosing to write in their own English, or "Africanize" their writing, Gyasi posits, the African writers are performing "both linguistic and political acts."[10] The linguistic acts manifest themselves in the language and creativity therein, while the political acts are evident in the contestations of the spaces of struggle for the representation of African languages as capable and in a position to defy being subdued by imperialism as it was during colonialism. Thus, the very act of thinking in vernacular and writing in English is in itself an act of translation.

When works written in African languages are translated into English or other European languages, a power struggle ensues and the effort to resolve it becomes a ground for rhetorical discussions of meaning. Simon Gikandi[11] illustrates this with his discussion of the translation of Ngugi's *Matigari* into English. While he applauds the work of Wangui wa Goro in translating this work, he sees a problem when it comes to comparing the translated work with the original Gikuyu novel. Beginning with the title, the original work is *Matigari ma Njiruungi*, while the translated work is simply entitled *Matigari*. This, Gikandi says, comes from a place of caution by Wangui who eliminates the second part of the title, which has strong political connotations as a language that had been used by the Mau Mau freedom fighters. Njiruungi, with the meaning of "bullets," is a word that Wangui wa Goro chooses to leave out altogether for her audiences reading in English. Therefore, rather than the title of Ngugi's work translating as "The remnants of the bullet," it ends up translating only as "The remnants." Gikandi sees this as a departure that has nothing to do with linguistics but everything to do with politics. This, in turn, affects the novel's trajectory in English. It becomes one that follows Eurocentric conventions, thus "posing no threat to the rhetoric or exercise of state power" with

---

8. Ibid., 348–49.
9. Gyasi 1999, 80.
10. Ibid., 85.
11. Gikandi 1991, 161–67.

the title adhering to the "common European convention of naming a novel after its hero."[12] Gikandi further analyzes this move as one that waters down the original novel in Gikuyu, rendering the relationship between the Gikuyu version and the English one that of inequality. The English version becomes more elevated and more "powerful than Gikuyu."[13] Through translation, therefore, Ngugi's novel is bound to survive, but as a novel in English.[14] This, unfortunately, becomes the ultimate antithesis for Ngugi's original purpose; that of discarding a foreign language that personifies imperialism.

The translation of *Matigari*, however, does not only pose a political struggle for power. Within the text itself, there are instances where proverbs are not translated fully as they were represented in Gikuyu. On the surface, this might be considered a linguistic issue, but, it still enhances the political struggle between the two versions. Gikandi's take on this matter creates a lens with which we can further dissect how proverbs are represented in other translated works:

> . . . the first paragraph of the original ends with two powerful Gikuyu sayings: "Kwigita ti guoya. Kwihuuga ti Gukiiga." A literal translation of these sayings would be: "Protecting oneself is not cowardice. Being careful is not foolishness." In the English edition, however, these sayings are effaced, possibly for the sake of fluency, and replaced by a simpler alternative: "It was all over now, but he knew he still had to be careful." This translation captures the spirit of the original, but fluency is only attained by effacing the linguistic difficulties that give the Gikuyu language its power and identity. Such effacement makes the English translation of the novel into a simplistic, sanitized version of the original.[15]

Here, we cannot fail but see two things occurring. First, it is possible to confirm that the direct translations of the Gikuyu proverbs would still work in English, even though they would be presenting something that English language may not be used to. The translator, however, decides not to use them. Secondly, our curiosity is piqued as to why the translator, herself of Gikuyu origin, decides to avoid the proverbs altogether. These are the questions that point to the rhetoric of meaning and representation. On the one hand, choosing a certain way of translation while preserving meaning, and on the other hand, trying to represent the language and culture of a people, become the rhetorical stance and choice that matters. The gaps and spaces between this choice are what causes the "effacement" that eventually results in the "simplistic, sanitized version of the original." Not fulfilling the core purposes of the novel, in this case the cultural, linguistic, and political, brings to the fore what makes translation rhetorical. It is

---

12. Ibid., 165
13. Ibid.
14. Ibid.
15. Ibid., 166.

worth noting, though, that Wambui wa Goro (1989),[16] in the process of translating *Matigari*, transforms into an author in her own right, adapting her own rhetorical stance to the original text, as if to say, "I am making it my own." This idea is described eloquently by Valentino et al. (2017), who argue that:

> . . . one can simply observe the degree to which such notions about communion with the source are discarded the more visible the translator becomes, especially when the translator's own inventions are highlighted. The rhetorical positioning of the translator shifts, and she or he becomes an author, discarding the translator's cloak, and voilà, visibility and invention are joined in the authorial persona. The entire implied argument pivots on the fulcrum of the translator's authority (*ethos*).[17]

In the case of *Matigari* and the example of the proverbs, we see Wambui wa Goro putting the burden of the source aside and, as she writes her way into the translation, her own "inventions are highlighted." These inventions, however, do not occur *tabula rasa*. They are informed by her thoughts and assessment about her audience (more urban, educated, mixed ethnic groups) and the themes they would be more interested in, as opposed to Ngugi's audience (rural peasants mainly of Gikuyu origin). This "authorial persona" in translation is something Taban lo Liyong takes ownership of in his re-translation of *Wer pa Lawino (Song of Lawino),* after Okot P' Bitek, the author, translated it. These are the conflicts that will be addressed in this chapter.

---

16. Thiong'o 1989.
17. Valentino, et. al. 2017, 4.

3.1 Nilotic, 20th Century, Kenya, Uganda

"My Other Heart Is Telling Me . . .": Translating Orature as a Rhetoric of Meaning

Leonora Anyango

INTRODUCTION

In *The African Origins of Rhetoric*, Cecil Blake traces the beginnings of rhetoric and a culture in ancient Egypt that was strongly rooted in both written and oral cultures.[18] Blake, working with what is believed to be the oldest book that ever existed, lays out the importance of both the spoken and the written in these ancient communities. The oldest book, *The Instruction of Ptah Hotep and the Instruction of Ke'gemni* is recorded as dating back to "about four thousand years before Christ."[19] Carol Lipson, in "Ancient Egyptian Rhetoric: It All Comes Down to Maat," concurs by capturing both the orality and literacy of early Egyptian life to show that these harmoniously coexisted. She states that the letters, which were "common among the administrators of the country," often began with quotes from and references to the previous elements in a dialogue[20] It is this very form of African orality that Ptah Hotep utilizes in instructing his son on governance. He begins with the words, "Here begin the proverbs of fair speech. . . ."[21] That this ancient book contains proverbs in the same way that African culture has always celebrated them, is a paradox that shows the preservation of African culture in writing, amidst the orality that has always been shown to be the center and mainstay of this culture.[22]

It is such knowledge regarding orality and literacy in African communities that is a precursor for the present discussion. There is a silence somewhere in the history of Africa that does not seem to acknowledge the presence of written cultures. On the other hand, there is the magnified presence of an oral culture that, although rich and celebrated every day by her people as the primary source of knowing and education for her communities, African orality has often found itself on the back bench, having been forced to sit as a not-so-important legacy worth embracing and celebrating in the face of literacy and all the reasons that literacy is placed on a pedestal. Prominent African scholars and writers like Grace Ogot, Ngugi wa Thiong'o, Chinua Achebe, Okot p'Bitek, Taban lo Liyong, and others, have tapped orality as a source of strength for their excellence in writing, and stood for the integrity of African orality

---

18. Blake 2009.
19. Ibid., 45.
20. Lipson 2004, 85.
21. Ibid., 42.
22. Anyango-Kivuva 2021, 218.

as authentic literature. It was in the face of this struggle for authenticity and representation that African scholars coined and began using the word "orature" to present and describe orality as authentic literature and to demonstrate how that literature had morphed into a unique and now much celebrated kind of writing.

In the title of this chapter on orature, there is the phrase "My other heart is telling me . . ." This is a Luo idiomatic phrase that means "I am also thinking that . . ." or "I have a different thought on. . . ." It seemed befitting as part of the title for this chapter in the sense that the translation of orature is multipronged. It is not linear, and it comes with cultural, historical, and linguistic stories that, instead of being viewed as a burden or nuisance, should be embraced as grounds for rhetorical analysis. The challenge lies in how the future of translating orature may look. As new and emerging African writers take on other forms of writing that do not necessarily reflect forms of African orature, translation of their works, if ever needed, may also take different forms as "the oral, African language, and European language writings, co-exist today and struggle for their space"[23]

DEFINING ORATURE: A RHETORIC OF MEANING

What is the meaning of "oral literature"? Is there any such thing? Ruth Finnegan sees no reason to deny the characterization of oral forms like songs, narratives, poems, etc. as "literature."[24] In her book, *Oral Literature in Africa*, Finnegan unequivocally announces her sentiments when she firmly states that

> . . . we would hardly suggest that works written and, in part, orally transmitted before the advent of printing were therefore not literature, any more than we would be prepared to state dogmatically that the Homeric epics—or an African poem—only became literature on the day they were first written down. Even in a society apparently dominated by the printed word the oral aspect is not entirely lost. Perhaps because of the common idea that written literature is somehow the highest.[25]

East African writers have continuously sought ways to harmonize their world of writing without leaving their oral culture behind. This situation ushers in the discussion on 'orature' as a terminology of importance for African writers who choose to write from the oral culture that they grew up in and with. Ngugi wa Thiong'o states that "nearly all African writers have returned to African languages. What they write in whatever language derives its stamina, stature, identity from African languages."[26] wa Thiong'o looks closely at the tradition of orality by stating that in these works "the production line runs from orality to aurality: the

23. Thiong'o 1998, 1.
24. Blake 2009.
25. Ibid., 21.
26. Thiong'o 1998, 102.

mouth produces, the ear consumes directly. . . . This verbal artistic production carries the name orature."[27] Ngugi wa Thiong'o credits the coinage of the term "orature" rightfully to the Ugandan linguist Pio Zirimu, who coined the term due to "the difficulties of containing the world of the oral text within that of the literary."[28] Micere Mugo also credits the term orature to Pio Zirimu and adds that "the spoken tradition should be simply known as Orature—the creative imaginative art of composition that relies on verbal art for communication and that culminates in performance."[29]

Orature therefore is a term embraced by heavyweights of African literature who draw from their own oral culture to write their works. While working with orature or the memories of it, African writers richly employ the beauty of their heritage into their writing and incorporate songs, proverbs, story within a story, and other devices that are typical of this oral heritage into the writing. While doing this, they also work with African languages and English to negotiate the best meaning that would bring forth clear understanding in English. Ultimately, it is the rhetoric of meaning that is peddled within and between two languages as writers seek ground in the production of literature. The rhetoricity of this process lies in the fact that the negotiation of meaning becomes important for the author as s/he persuades their readers to understand his culture and the beauty of it, and/or bring out meanings that are most important. This importance lies in the perception of the author as s/he works between and within languages to discern what meanings would be clear and well received by the audience.

TRANSLATIONS AND COMMENTARIES OF LUO AND ACHOLI TEXTS

From the name, Nilotic languages are a cluster of languages of the people who migrated from the North of Africa along the River Nile to their present habitation.[30] Both Luo and Acholi are Nilotic languages. The Luo inhabit the area along Lake Victoria in Kenya, Uganda, and Tanzania, while the Acholi inhabit Northern Uganda and South Sudan. As seen above, the rendering of orature in English or other languages requires a conscious effort to represent meaning in the best way possible for the understanding of the reader. In both orature rendered directly in English and that translated from Luo or Acholi, it is evident that meaning is important to the writer and/or translator, and it is key to the authorial and translational moves that are made. Thus, orature and the language of transmission become rhetorical tools as the speaker moves to render content and meaning.

---

27. Ibid.
28. Ibid., 111.
29. Mugo 1991, 40.
30. Nilotic languages are mostly similar as a cluster, but very different from English.

Grace Ogot's Work: Preserving Orature through *Princess Nyilaak* and *Simbi Nyaima*

Achebe warned African writers in their use of orature not to use the English language "as a native speaker." In the case of orature, African writers employ songs, proverbs, idioms and narrative styles like a story within a story, to their advantage while writing in English. These choices are often "informed by an epistemological and sociological need, to recuperate the past to appropriate the inherent dignity grounded in African cultural values for the sake of transacting the past with the present."[31] Thus, this *transacting* becomes about both the past and the present. It reaches into the territories of textual presentations to provide a platform for uniqueness of language presentation and style. Most important in this *transacting* is the ability to transform the all-important element of performance into the text narration domain while being aware of the role of "an African oral tradition critic," which is "to be an entertainer, a historian, and an orator, because criticism and creativity are intertwined."[32] This is a noble duty whose fulfillment moves the African writer into an equally noble action—the writing of works that will live up to these standards and purposes.

How, then, does the African writer, writing in English, fulfill the goals of an entertainer, a historian and an orator? The work of East African author Grace Ogot offers an illustration to this noble duty. In her historical account of *Princess Nyilaak,* she gives us a clear glimpse that is satisfactory to the mind as a fulfillment of her raconteur role. Rich with loaded prose, song, and performance language that invites imagery to the mind, the novel has instances of vivid sceneries that take the reader to the place of action and give testimony to the prowess of the writer. In the example below, Ogot praises the beauty of Amula, the mother of *Ruoth* Kwanga, the King:

> Amula had smooth and beautiful black skin that never grew old. She had no wrinkles on her forehead or around her neck. She was heavily built with proud shoulders that she carried well as she walked. She had a well-rounded face and she always walked with her head raised, and hated women who walked quickly barely touching the ground as if their spouses did not pay legible dowry![33]

Here, Ogot shares the standard of beauty in the Luo community that she is writing about and that she belongs to. The Luo historically had Kings who ruled different groups of clans. *Princess Nyilaak* is a historical (non)fiction about the daughter of a King of the Luo who was slated to become King (not queen as there never had been a female ruler and therefore no name for it) after the Ruoth King, her father, never bore a son. In the book, as in the Luo culture, the "proud shoulders that she carried well" are a desirable quality for a woman of Amula's stature,

---

31. Akingbe, et al. 2012, 361.
32. Akingbe 2012, 362.
33. Ogot 2018, 51.

the first wife of the King, who is also mother and grandmother of the heirs of the throne. A "raised head" is a sign of confidence that also radiates through her gait. The culture of paying dowry is also revealed here as a source of pride for a woman, a gesture from her husband's family that shows how valuable she is, thus a source of inner pride and confidence. While this inner pride cannot be seen, it is embodied in a woman's person, which can be seen when someone beholds her demeanor. It is worth noting also that this pride is not from "I," the individual who possesses it. It is gained through communal effort, a value that is tapped from others, living in harmony with the community that has nodded in unison with her through the bride price and an enduring marriage to royalty.

Ogot further shows her custodianship of oral culture in her use of song in *Princess Nyilaak* Through the communal act of weeding to produce food, she shows how, to boost the morale of the workers, a village drummer would be a part of this exercise. "The weeding song" is inviting to the ears, and one can almost imagine how it went with the rhythm of the sound of the hoes meeting the ground as people worked on the farm. Ogot sets the stage by introducing the song and the drummer, then she showcases Luo traditional singing and its components:

> Soon the weeding song greeted their ears, with the drummer soloist belting out:
> "Gone is the bounty season
> Bounty season of sorghum and beans
> Gone is the season of the drum headed millet
> And the busting beans."
> And the chorus replied in a booming, earth shattering chorus:
> Erooo![34]
> Erooo!
> Erooo!
> Erooo!
> The drummer sang again:
> "And who gives in the bounty harvest?"
> And the chorus replied in unison:
> "Who else gives? But Jok Rubanga!
> He who nourishes
> The land with rain and dew
> Eroo!
> Eroo!"
> And then the drummer joined the chorus all with one voice;
> "If Rubanga wishes
> This season be greater
> Than the season past
> Only if Rubanga wishes.[35]

---

34. A word in the Luo language, which can be translated as "That is it!" or "That is so."
35. Ogot 2018, 72, 73.

This song is laden with cultural overtones. For an oral artist and performer, it brings in the rhythmic sounds of a lead soloist who is also the drummer, and the group of people who uphold his leadership in music for a harmonious flow. The song is also a celebration of the past bountiful season. It culminates with a prayer to Rubanga, the God, the deity of this community, for the next harvest. This is a prayer for better harvest than the last, one that requires all voices in unison, to agree for Rubanga's action. The drummer joins in with the rest of the chorus to affirm unity in expressing this fundamental wish.

Many are the instances where in *Princess Nyilaak*, Grace Ogot exemplifies her role as the entertainer, orator, and historian. However, worth noting is how the author taps into oral language to enrich her writing. She uses phrases like "soon the weeding song *greeted their ears*," when she would have simply said, "Soon they heard the sound of the weeding song." The sounds that cannot be translated are left to "greet the reader's ears" as well and provide a cushion that helps in the transfer of some original language aspects into the next. While this is not a translated work *per se*, the author is using skills from one language to transfer it to another, making it an act of translation.[36] Giving this delivery a form of "stability" while delivering thoughts from two distinctly different languages is the challenge African authors must surmount.

Grace Ogot also wrote *Simbi Nyaima* in Luo, which she later translated as *Simbi Nyaima: The Village That Sank*.[37] Right from the translation of the title, the negotiation of meaning with a reader from another language has already started. Being that *Simbi Nyaima* is not English, Ogot must have felt that its presence in the title would be a hindrance to readers who would want to buy the book. She, therefore, made the choice to include "the village that sank" as part of the title to give the non-Luo speakers a hint as to what the story is about. It is important to note here that "the village that sank" is what happened in the story as this village got engulfed and became a part of the lake that was by its side. In the Luo version, the title *Simbi Nyaima* is left as is because the community of readers do not need an explanation since this is a popular etiological narrative in the language. Grace Ogot recreates and retells this long-held myth among the Luo that community members of the village near the lake refused to accommodate an elderly woman who was traveling through it and could not continue her journey after nightfall. The sinking of the village was a punishment for those who decided to disobey the moral regulations of the society.

As in the example of the title, Ogot makes similar moves in the book as she self-translates. While translation is not verbatim, there are some places where she decides to leave out certain phrases or add to them. She uses songs in this book in a way that shows the art of storytelling. For example, the following song is sung during a celebration of a marriage that has just taken place,[38] in praise of the groom:

---

36. Gyasi 1999, 75–87.
37. Ogot 1983.
38. Refer to the Appendix at the end of this chapter for the Luo version.

> Solo: Who is freeing the grasshoppers from under the ground?
> Chorus: Ochieng Yogo is doing it
> Solo: Who is freeing the grasshoppers from under the ground?
> Chorus: The brown one, the son of Oracha's mother is doing it. [39]

In this English translation, Ogot adds certain things that were not in the Luo version. First, she marks the places where the soloist sings and that where the entire group (chorus) sings. In the Luo version, the assumption is that the singers already might know where to come in, but she now wants to add the privilege to the English reader for clarity. The other reason may be to show how culturally the songs are sung. Secondly, she adds the phrase "from under the ground" which is not in the Luo version. In the Luo version, there would be no need because the verb "to free" a grasshopper also may mean "from under the ground" or the Luo people know that this is where it is released. Because the phrase "to free the grasshopper" is an idiom (because they are really referring to the bride here), Ogot deemed it necessary to further explain the song.

In the next song, Awino the bride has joined the musicians and she is praising herself and her beauty. Here, Ogot adds even more into the English translation, including an introductory line:

> Musician, do you know me?
> I am Awino Rapel, the slim-waisted wasp
> The daughter of the father of Oyoo "The Dark Jungle"
> I am the slender one whose beautiful teeth
> Should not be used for eating *Obambo*, tilapia that is dried in the open sun.[40]

Here, Ogot makes several moves to render meaning in her translation. As noted above, the introductory line, "Musician, do you know me?" is not in the Luo version. It might be that the singer was addressing the solo singer of the larger group that had arrived to sing praises for her marriage.

Ogot also chooses cultural aspects that would be easy to understand like "daughter of the father of Oyoo" to maintain the flavor of orality in English, when she could have said "sister of Oyoo. Eventually, she explains the word *obambo* in the last line, which is not necessary in Luo as the speakers are assumed to already know the meaning.

It is, therefore, evident that while making choices of what to translate from one language to another, Ogot is conscious of whether the meaning is coming through in the language of translation. Her thought processes while making these choices are rhetorical in nature as they constitute careful thought and questioning as to what counts in terms of meaning for the readers of her work in English. What is obvious for Luo readers is not belabored in the Luo version. However, when it comes to English, it becomes paramount that the meaning be

---

39. Ogot 1983, 25.
40. Ogot 1983, 26.

conveyed as clearly as possible. This is not the same with when Ogot writes orature directly in English. When she writes in English, she translates first in her mind and then renders directly into English, a process that leaves her with what brings the flavor that is carried by orature. The process in English, therefore, already brings with it a cleaned-out document that has the extras in mother tongue taken care of. Seeing both the English and Dholuo versions together helps us appreciate the process and the work that even a self-translating author of An African language goes through to bring work in English.

The Defence of Lawino: Re-Translation of Orature as Rhetoric

Okot p'Bitek was a famous Ugandan literary mogul.[41] He wrote *Wer pa Lawino*, a poem (song) in Acholi, his mother tongue, and published it in 1969 at a time when African literature was being redefined using postcolonial theories. By this time, he had already published *Song of Lawino*, the translation of *Wer pa Lawino*, into English, and it was already acclaimed as an African literary classic. *Song of Lawino* is acclaimed in African literature as a song to protest the encroachment of Western culture into African lives. It not only speaks of the imprisonment through culture alone, it also "appears to articulate the idea of African literary freedom," one that frees the poet from the shackles of "form" and "welcomes considerable flexibility that often reflects the cultural and linguistic values of a people."[42] p'Bitek "crafts his poem along the lines of Acholi oral tradition" using it to showcase a society that is grappling with continuing to embrace its own culture amidst the encroaching Western culture that is threatening to engulf it. In the song, Lawino is a true cultural ambassador of her people. She is not ashamed of her culture, and she is bold enough to demand the respect she deserves as Ocol's (first) wife. She abhors, and does not admire even remotely, the ways of Clementine, her husband's second wife. She openly sneers and jeers at Clementine's concept of beauty and style of living as a Westernized woman:

> She dusts the ash-dirt all over her face
> And when little sweat
> Begins to appear on her body
> She looks like the guinea fowl!
> The smell of carbolic soap
> Makes me sick,
> And the smell of powder
> Provokes the ghosts in my head;
> It is then necessary to fetch a goat

---

41. Okot p'Bitek is mainly known for his epic poem *Song of Lawino* (1966). It was first written in Acholi as *Wer pa Lawino* (1969). It has been translated into numerous languages, including numerous African languages. He also wrote *Song of Ocol* as Ocol's (Lawino's Husband) response to *Song of Lawino*. *Song of Lawino and Song of Ocol* were published in one volume in 1985. His other works include *Horn of my Love* (1974), and *Hare and Hornbill* (1978), among others.

42. Usongo 2011, 179.

> From my mother's brother.
> The sacrifice over
> The ghost-dance drum must sound
> The ghost be laid
> And my peace restored.[43]

Lawino does not admire the use of powder or any other make-up, and she claims to get sick to the point that she needs to exorcise the "ghosts." Being the author's mouthpiece and cultural ambassador, she addresses everyone in the clan by using phrases such as "my clansmen"[44] or "brother."[45] She calls their attention to the atrocities committed to her community when culture is abandoned and ignored. Her husband's insults are directed not only to her, but to the entire community:

> My clansmen, I cry
> Listen to my voice:
> The insults of my man
> Are painful beyond bearing,[46]

She then uses orature (proverbs) to report to the community what Ocol is doing.

> My husband pours scorn
> On Black People,
> He behaves like a hen
> That eats its own eggs
> A hen that should be imprisoned under a basket,[47]

Lawino, by talking of "imprisonment," feels that Ocol should suffer the consequences from the community for deserting it. He should be 'imprisoned' for abandoning the culture of his people.

Taban lo Liyong took it upon himself to critique and re-translate *Song of Lawino*. lo Liyong and Okot p'Bitek were born in the same culture of the Acholi people of Northern Uganda, and they grew up speaking Acholi language. Their lives were intertwined as authors and scholars from the same ethnic group who shared a lot together and could be described as friends.[48]

---

43. p'Bitek 1985, 38.

44. Ibid., 35.

45. Ibid., 37.

46. Ibid., 36.

47. Ibid.

48. In "On Translating the Untranslated," Taban Lo Liyong gives stories of how they visited each other with p'Bitek while living in Kenya, "I was often Okot's guest in Kisumu, and he was often mine in Nairobi." (1993, 87). p'Bitek passed away in 1982, around two decades before Taban lo Liyong debuted his own translation, *The Defence of Lawino* (2002)

On reading the original in Acholi, lo Liyong decided to re-translate for many reasons, the main one being that "word for word, line by line, even chapter by chapter, *Song of Lawino* is a watered down, lighter, elaborated, extended version of *Wer pa Lawino*."[49] In the preface of his version, *The Defence of Lawino*, he writes:

> *Song of Lawino* (the English Language version), is not strictly a faithful translation of *Wer pa Lawino*. It is a version, if you like, of *Wer pa Lawino* in which, whatever was topical, striking, graphic and easily renderable into English received due prominence. But the darker, more ponderous, more intricate parts, or those nuances that only the best *nanga* (harp) players know how to reproduce, suffered summarising or mutilation. Or new recasting.[50]

lo Liyong did several things differently with his translation. First, he gave it a totally different title and called it *The Defence of Lawino*. Therefore, all the titles are presented as "submissions" to the elders. This was Lawino's "defence of indigenous African ways," and she needed to submit it straight to the elders.[51] Secondly, lo Liyong translated chapter fourteen, the final chapter, and included it in his translated volume. p'Bitek had not included chapter fourteen, one that lo Liyong sees as the cornerstone of the song, saying,

> Whatever was striking, dramatic, and sarcastic was highlighted. And, by the same token, whatever was more philosophical and deeper was suppressed or left out. And Chapter 14, which included a restatement of his arguments but had no Clementine to laugh and no foibles of Ocol[52] to hold up for criticism, therefore became a casualty. By not translating Chapter 14, Okot left the major theme of the song unresolved.[53]

The major theme of the song, a proverb in Acholi, was translated by Lo Liyong in "submission fourteen" as

> Pumpkin boles in abandoned homesteads are never uprooted.
> Pumpkins in homesteads are never uprooted.
> Pumpkins are not for uprooting! That's all![54]

---

49. p'Bitek 2001.
50. Ibid., xi.
51. Ibid.
52. Notice the spelling here for Ocol. In *Song of Lawino*, p'Bitek writes it as "Ocol." However, lo Liyong in *The Defence of Lawino* writes it as "Ochol." This can be accounted for due to the pronunciation of the word, as in Acholi, the sound "c" is pronounced as "ch." In this work, both spellings are used depending on the author being referenced. However, in general commentary in the work, "Ocol" is used.
53. lo Liyong 1993, 88.
54. p'Bitek 2001, 106.

Restated, it is a call to always embrace one's own culture and not abandon it in pursuit of other cultures. Thirdly, since lo Liyong sees every chapter as a submission to the elders, his chapter titles change and are different from how p'Bitek translated them. Rather, lo Liyong sees his *Defence* as the correct and closest translation to *Wer pa Lawino*, not to mention the fact that he also knows *Wer pa Lawino* has an unmatched linguistic and thematic superiority and that no one would "do the original work justice."[55] His chapter titles begin with the words, "My husband . . ." followed by whatever point Lawino wants to make. Only the last two chapters (thirteen and fourteen) begin differently. For example, chapter one in *Defence*, in this case "Submission One," is entitled "My husband calls me names and abuses my parents too because we uphold African ways."[56] In p'Bitek's *Song of Lawino*, Chapter one's title is "My Husband's Tongue Is Bitter." Submission seven is entitled "My husband rejects me because I do not know how to reckon or keep European time."[57] In p'Bitek's *Song of Lawino*, Chapter seven's title is "There Is No Fixed Time for Breastfeeding."

Taban lo Liyong's re-translation emerges as its own work of art, almost like a story and not a poem. It renders itself to more of a narrative genre than a poetic one. He is full of praise for *Wer pa Lawino* and states that it is a powerful treatise that comes with deep language and borrows from other African languages to make it even richer. The rhythm and rhyme in the Acholi version give it its linguistic luster that outshines *Song of Lawino*. Examples from both works show that p'Bitek, the author and translator of the work, looked more for ways to present his work as song or poetry. On the other hand, lo Liyong, in retranslating, was more focused on the closeness of meaning to the Acholi version, almost in the verbatim sense, and the loss that he observed as having happened in *Song of Lawino*. In *From Wer pa Lawino to Song of Lawino with Loss,* lo Liyong enumerates many instances that makes him believe *Wer pa Lawino* is fuller, richer, and more thematically complete than *Song of Lawino*. Some of these reasons include

- *v.* There are parts of Wer pa Lawino that are omitted in Song of Lawino completely. It is as if they were lost or different versions of Wer pa Lawino or Song of Lawino existed and some versions were preferred.
- *vi.* Sometimes, in the place of the omitted parts of Wer pa Lawino new materials are substituted in Song of Lawino.
- *vii.* Parts of the material in Wer pa Lawino seem chopped up and rearranged (or dis-arranged) in Song of Lawino.[58]

Side by side examples from both works would help to illustrate these points. From titles to verses, only a glance would reveal structural differences. This is how p'Bitek's *Song of Lawino* begins:

---

55. Ibid., xvi.
56. Ibid., 1.
57. Ibid., 39.
58. lo Liyong 1997, 97.

> Husband, now you despise me
> Now you treat me with spite
> And say I have inherited the stupidity of my aunt;
> Son of the Chief,
> Now you compare me
> With the rubbish in the rubbish pit,
> You say you no longer want me
> Because I am like the things left behind
> In the deserted homestead.
> You insult me
> You laugh at me
> You say I do not know the letter A
> Because I have not been to school
> And I have not been baptized.[59]

And this is how *The Defence of Lawino* begins:

> My husband, though you still despise me
> My man, though you still abuse me
> Claiming that I have inherited the clumsiness of my aunt;
> Beloved prince, though you reduce me
> Comparing me to the rubbish in the refuse heap;
> Though you cheapen me, broadcasting that you like me no more
> Claiming that I am equal to debris left in the deserted home;
> Though you abuse me, and do it shamelessly,
> Claiming it is because I don't even know 'a'
> And that I have not got school education
> And that I have not even got a baptism name;
> You compare me to pups, making senseless noise;

The last line in this stanza, "You compare me to pups, making senseless noise," is one that p'Bitek, in his original translation, had as a new stanza altogether:

> You compare me with a little dog,
> A puppy.[60]

Notably, the phrase "making senseless noise," is not in p'Bitek's translation, while we know from *Defence* that it was in the original Acholi version. It is such "omissions" that make lo Liyong posit that "chapter for chapter, on the whole, each line in *Wer pa Lawino* has more syllables, *more dense meanings* than in *Song of Lawino*" (emphasis added). In these beginning

---

59. p'Bitek 1985, 35.
60. p'Bitek 2001, 35.

lines, though, line by line, there is little deviation of meaning from the first translation, *Song of Lawino*, as lo Liyong claims. For example, the line "claiming it is because I don't even know 'a'" has very little difference, if any, with p'Bitek's "you say I do not know the letter A." We would say, then, that while these stanzas may seem different, most of these differences are on the periphery, not so much at the center or crux of the message. In other words, these differences may be, for the most part, attributed to form rather than content.

In chapter eight of *Song of Lawino*, Lawino showcases the importance of the names of her people, as opposed to the interest that Ocol, her husband, shows when it comes to European and Christian names. As the cultural ambassador of her people, Lawino stands firm and proudly praises the names of her people, while Ocol claims Lawino "is not enough." p'Bitek's presentation is as follows:

> My husband rejects me
> Because, he says
> I have no Christian name.
> He says
> Lawino is not enough.
> He says
> Acoli names are *Jok* names
> And they do not sound good.
> They are primitive, he insists,
> And he is a progressive man
> Ocol wanted me
> To be baptized 'Benedeta'. [61]

On the other hand, lo Liyong re-translates this as follows:

> Ochol hates me claiming I've not received my name
> He claims my name "Lawino" is not enough;
> That Lawino is a useless name, for ignorant people
> Hence I have no name that would please his heart
> Ochol would like me to be called Benedeta.[62]

Here, we see the difference in the choice of words. lo Liyong, for example, does not use the word "baptize" while p'Bitek does. Also, we see an addition rather than a deletion when p'Bitek seems to have added the idea of Acholi names being *Jok*[63] names. Otherwise, the

---

61. p'Bitek 1985, 82.

62. p'Bitek 2001, 59.

63. The Jok are a group of people in East Africa who share cultural, linguistic and historical affiliation. They share a history of the Nile Valley economy and culture. The names of their clans and/or sub-groups begin with the root word "Jok," for example, the Jok-Ajok and the Jok-Omolo and the Jok-Owiny. The Acholi also belong to this group, thus Lawino's reference to Jok.

differences in these translations, as noted before, may be nested in structure, and especially length of lines and deletions or additions, rather than at meaning level.

In his critique of *The Defence of Lawino*, Mark Lilleleht notes that Taban lo Liyong is more concerned with the literal comparisons than those of meaning, "of translation than poetry."[64] He sees in p'Bitek's *Song* the work of an accomplished poet, while in lo Liyong's *Defence* this poetry is lost, giving way to a laborious verbosity. Thus, *Defence* becomes a "(poetic) failure" with a "clunky literalness over which so many of lo Liyong's lines stumble."[65] He then quotes Lawino's thoughts about Clementine's so-called beauty that derails her husband:

> And when she walks
> You hear her bones rattling,
> Her waist resembles that of the hornet.
> The beautiful one is dead dry
> Like a stump,
> She is meatless
> Like a shell
> On a dry river bed.[66]

In comparison, lo Liyong's rendition is a far cry from any semblance of poetry:

> My husband-sharer walks like a person whose life-force is detained
> Like a ghost, she walks without audible steps!
> There is no enthusiasm in anything Tina does;
> All said, she is incapable of feast-cooking for a crowd.
> She looks sickly, but it is actually hunger!
> She doesn't eat, claiming food makes her fat!
> She claims the doctor's order is for her not to eat
> She's now twiggy, her bones rattle as she walks.[67]

Lilleleht sees in the *Song* a richness through poetry and few words that p'Bitek captures in his self-translation. As for lo Liyong, he says that the Clementine in *Defence* does not come through with the same "irony of p'Bitek's meatless beautiful one."[68]

Being a speaker of Acholi, the dedication of lo Liyong in re-translating *Song of Lawino*, a highly acclaimed classic, could not have been without proper cause. In various works related to the issue of this re-translation, lo Liyong justifies this move and undertakes a project that took him over two decades to complete. If this project was at best a laborious one, lo Liyong may have given up on it. However, as elaborated in "From Wer pa Lawino to Song of Lawino

---

64. Lilleleht 2008, 158.
65. Ibid.
66. Ibid.
67. p' Bitek 2001, 7.
68. Lilleleht 2008, 158.

with Loss," lo Liyong felt a higher duty to his own people to fill the gaps that he saw glaring at him in *Song of Lawino*. He taps into his own conscience to set things right by offering his people, who he says, now have a wider population reading in English than Acholi, a chance to get *Wer pa Lawino* in the best form he deems fit. This way, he contends, readers are not cheated into accepting the version where "all proverbs, wise sayings, and puns, were rendered into sarcastic English."[69] Most importantly, he sees chapter fourteen, the crux of Lawino's song, and the theme of the book, as one that readers needed to see, read and experience. To this end, he would be vindicated. To poets who still cherish p'Bitek's song, he still falls short. The rhetorical fulfilment of all this, however, lies in the one-sidedness of lo Liyong's victory in vindicating the Acholi version. It is in the hollowness and vacuum of his claims that are not tested by the waters of the author's thoughts and input. The absence of p'Bitek in this conversation numbs the capabilities of the architectural foundations that would expand these conversations in more exciting directions that would bring to the fore a fundamental rhetorical question: how would Okot p'Bitek respond?

CONCLUSION

Translation of African orature is not a straightforward, uncomplicated matter, owing to the fact that African languages and European languages (including English), are different linguistically and culturally. The differences become problematic when these languages come into contact through the complex decision-making required by translation. In this case, two African scholars—one the author of the original work, and the other a person that speaks the same language—ended up on two different paths with the same work in translation. However, there may be reasons beyond the original work that call for the valuation of difference. Garuba and Okot see these differences as emanating from "lateral texts and circuits of value." Of importance to them is the fact that *Song* preceded *Wer* in publication and therefore *Wer* "existed . . . only as a notional text, an intangible ghostly presence said to be the source of translation."[70] On the other hand, *Wer* was mainly for the Acholi community in the sense that:

> . . . what makes *Wer pa Lawino* an Acholi classic is different from what makes *Song of Lawino* an African classic. For instance, *Wer pa Lawino* is not so much valued for "Africanisation" through borrowing from Acholi oral literary tradition. This was (and still is) a non-issue for a people with a predominantly oral culture. *Wer pa Lawino* is to a large extent valued in the Acholi community for its linguistic dexterity, the creative manipulation of the Acholi language, the humourous rendition of ordinary actions and situations, and the entertainment qualities therein.[71]

---

69. lo Liyong 1997, 89.
70. Garuba and Okot 2017, 314.
71. Garuba and Okot 2017, 324.

The two lateral texts, therefore, have different circuits of value, and for this reason, their translations would not escape the riddles of nuance. This is not in itself negative in comparative rhetoric as these nuances are a part of the expansion of rhetorical knowhow.

Mao and Wang state that "the one and only game for us comparative rhetoricians is how we broaden our vision to promote different ways of doing and knowing, and how we develop different terms of engagement. . . ."[72] In this work, examining the translation of orature has provided the fertile ground for promoting indigenous ways of knowing as well as the connection it offers with other forms of written oral literature. Having Taban lo Liyong question Okot p'Bitek's translation, and further providing translation for p'Bitek's untranslated work is a work of rhetoric that promotes "other ways of being, seeing and making knowledge." Being that the two are authors from the same culture, their work provides a lens with which the art of translation becomes "dialectical—through which both self and other will inevitably be changed and transformed."[73] In this case, questioning meaning in one's own culture as presented by another of the same culture in two different languages is indeed questioning the self. In questioning the self, there emerges a space of questioning the other. Both translators agree on taking on a foreign culture that is encroaching on theirs—the Western culture being embraced by Clementine. However, *how* they take it on linguistically becomes the bone of contention.

Wang's phrase "transrhetorical practice" aptly captures this exercise. She defines it as a "meaning-making process of translation (including both interpretation and articulation) that takes place in the interstices of two or more different worlds caught in highly asymmetric power relations."[74] The linguistic power relations between African languages and English have been showcased here in multiple works, with the in-depth analysis of Taban lo Liyong's retranslation. The rhetorical space of meaning making between the Acholi and English worlds is what led lo Liyong into his transrhetorical practice of retranslation. That is why, as Davila-Montes argues, "the dealings of translation with meaning cannot ignore the deep impingements that both translation and meaning have on rhetoric."[75]

---

72. Mao and Wang 2015, 242.
73. Ibid.
74. Wang 2015, 248.
75. Davila-Montes 2017, 1.

APPENDIX: LUO VERSION OF SIMBI NYAIMA SONGS IN THIS WORK

Song 1

"To ng'ano maelo dedeno?"
To jowadgi nene odoko matek niya:
Ochieng' Yogo ema oele.
To nene onwoyo niya:
"Ng'a ma oelo dedeno?
To nene gimedo niya:
"Silwal wuod min Oracha ema oele!"

Song 2

"An Awino pino iye odwer, nya wuon Oyoo Thim
Rapenda ma lake tar thirri ka pe
Lak ma ok chamgo obambla!"

Comprehensive Bibliography

Achebe, Chinua. 1958. *Things Fall Apart.* London: Heinemann.

—. 1997. "English and the African Writer." *Transition*, 75/76: 342–49.

Adeeko, Adeleke. 1999. "Theory and Practice in African Orature." *Research in African Literatures* 30 (2): 222.

Akingbe, Niyi, et al. 2012. "Sustaining the Heritage: Assessing the Aesthetics of Verbal Symbolisation and Signification in Idanre Orature." *Venets: The Belogradchik Journal for Local History, Cultural Heritage and Folk Studies* 3 (3): 360–75.

Anyango-Kivuva, Leonora. 2014. "Inspirations from Mama's Two Wisdoms." *Writing on the Edge* 24 (2): 75–88.

—. 2015. *Stories of Living and Learning, Survival and Resilience.* PhD diss., Indiana University of Pennsylvania.

—. 2021. "Ubuntu: A Closer Look at An African Rhetoric of Community and Life." In *The Routledge Handbook on Comparative World Rhetorics*, edited by Keith Lloyd, 216–25. London: Routledge.

Blake, Cecil. 2009. *The African Origins of Rhetoric.* London: Routledge.

Campbell, Kermit. 2006. "Rhetoric from the Ruins of African Antiquity." *Rhetorica: A Journal of the History of Rhetoric* 24 (3): 255–74.

Carlos, Claudia. 2009. "Translation as Rhetoric: Edward Jerningham's 'Impenitence' (1800)." *Rhetoric Review* 28 (4): 335–51.

Connors, Robert. 1986. "Greek Rhetoric and the Transition from Orality." *Philosophy and Rhetoric* 19 (1): 38–65.

Davila-Montes, Jose. 2017. "Translation as a Rhetoric of Meaning" *Poroi* 13, no. 1 (May): 1–28.

Finnegan, Ruth. 2012. *Oral Literature in Africa.* Cambridge, UK: Open Book Publishers.

Garuba, Harry, and Okot, Benge. 2017. "Lateral Texts and Circuits of Value: Okot p'Bitek's Song of Lawino and Wer pa Lawino." *Social Dynamics* 43, no. 2 (July): 312–27. https://doi.org/10.1080/02533952.2017.1372054.

Gikandi, Simon. 1991. "The Epistemology of Translation: Ngũgĩ, Matigari, and the Politics of Language." *Research in African Literatures* 22, no. 4 (Winter): 161–67.

—. 2011. "Contested Grammars: Comparative Literature, Translation and the Challenge of Locality." In *A Companion to Comparative Literature,* edited by A. Behdad and D. Thomas, 254–72. West Sussex: Wiley-Blackwell.

Gyasi, Kwaku. 1999. "Writing as Translation: African Literature and the Challenges of Translation." *Research in African Literatures* 30, no. 2 (Summer): 75–87.

Habila, Helon. 2019. "The Future of African Literature." *Journal of the African Literature Association* 13 (1): 153–62. https://doi.org/10.1080/21674736.2019.1594898.

Ige, Segun, Gilbert Motsaathebe, and Omedi Ochieng, eds. 2022. *A Companion to African Rhetorics.* Lanham, MD: Lexington/Rowman & Littlefield.

Imbo, Samuel. 2002. *Oral Traditions as Philosophy: Okot p'Bitek's Legacy for African philosophy.* Lanham, MD: Rowman and Littlefield.

Legg, Emily. 2011. "Writing Orality: Claiming Rhetorical Sovereignty within Ecologies of Rhetorics." PhD diss., Purdue University.

Lilleleht, Mark. 2008. Review of *The Defence of Lawino (Wer pa Lawino),* by Okot p'Bitek. Translated by Taban lo Liyong. *Research in African Literatures* 39 (2): 156–58.

Lipson, Carol. 2004. "Ancient Egyptian Rhetoric: It All Comes Down to Maat." In *Rhetoric Before and Beyond the Greeks,* edited by Carol S. Lipson and Roberta A. Binkley, 79–98. State University of New York Press.

Lipson, Carol, and Roberta Binkley. 2004. *Rhetoric Before and Beyond the Greeks.* Albany, New York: SUNY Press.

lo Liyong, Taban. 1993. "On Translating the 'Untranslated': Chapter 14 of Wer Pa Lawino by Okot P'Bitek." *Research in African Literatures* 24 (3): 87–92.

—. 1997. "From Wer pa Lawino to Song of Lawino with Loss." *Journal of Postcolonial Writing,* 36 (1): 93–109. doi:10.1080/17449859708589265.

—. 2018. "Indigenous African Literary Forms May Determine the Future Course of World Literature." *English in Africa* 45 (2): 17–28. https://doi.org/10.4314/eia.v45i2.2.

Mao, Luming, et al. 2015. "Manifesting a Future for Comparative Rhetoric." *Rhetoric Review* 34 (3): 239–74. doi:10.1080/07350198.2015.1040105.

Mucina, Devi Dee. 2011. *Ubuntu: A Regenerative Philosophy for Rupturing Racist Colonial Stories of Dispossession.* PhD diss., University of Toronto.

Mugo, Micere. 1991. *African Orature and Human Rights.* Lesotho: Lesotho Institute of Southern African Studies. National University of Lesotho.

Nunziata, Daniele. 2017. "The Scramble for African Orature: The Transcription, Compilation, and Marketing of African Oral Narratives in the Oxford Library of African Literature, 1964 to 1979." *Journal of Postcolonial Writing* 53 (4): 469–81. doi:10.1080/17449855.2017.1307258.

Ogot, Bethwell. 2004. *A Political and Cultural History of the Jii-Speaking Peoples of Eastern Africa.* Kisumu, Kenya: Anyange Press.

Ogot, Grace. 1983. *Simbi Nyaima: The Village that Sank.* Translated by Grace Ogot. Kisumu: Anyange Press.

—. 2012. *Days of my Life.* Kisumu, Kenya: Anyange Press.

—. 2018. *Princess Nyilaak.* Kisumu, Kenya: Anyange Press.

Okumu, Charles. 1992. "The Form of Okot P'Bitek's Poetry: Literary Borrowing from Acoli Oral Traditions." *Research in African Literatures* 23 (3): 53–66.

Ong, Walter. 1982. *Orality and Literacy: The Technologizing of the Word.* London: Methuen.

p'Bitek, Okot. 1969. *Wer Pa Lawino.* Nairobi: East African Publishing House.

—. 1985. *Song of Lawino and Song of Ocol.* Oxford. Heinemann.

—. 2001. *The Defence of Lawino.* Translated by Taban lo Liyong. Kampala: Fountain.

Usongo, Kenneth. 2001. "Cultural Identity and Literature: A Study of Okot p'Bitek's *Song of Lawino. Matatu*" 39 (1): 179–90.

Valentino, et. al. 2017. "Rhetoric, Translation, and the Rhetoric of Translation: An Introduction." *Poroi* 13 (1): 1–12.

Wang, Bo. 2015. "Transrhetorical Practice." *Rhetoric Review* 34 (3): 246–49.

wa Thiong'o, Ngugi. 1986a. *Decolonising The Mind: The Politics of Language in African Literature.* London: Heinemann.

—. 1986b. *Matigari Ma Njiruungi.* Nairobi: Heinemann.

—. 1989. *Matigari.* Translated by Wangui wa Goro. London: Heinemann.

—. 1998. *Penpoints, Gunpoints, and Dreams: Toward a Critical Theory of the Arts and the State in Africa.* Oxford: Oxford University Press.

Williams, Jenny. 2013. *Theories of Translation.* Palgrave Macmillan Limited.

GLOSSARY OF TERMS

Term	Translation
Acholi	language spoken in Northern Uganda and parts pf Sudan. It is a Nilotic language that shares its origins with the Luo people of Kenya, Uganda and Tanzania. The culture of the Acholi, rooted in the language, is the subject of discussion in Okot p'Bitek's long poem/song, *Song of Lawino*.
eroo	word (exclamation) in Luo language that means "That is so!" or "It is so!"
Gikuyu/Kikuyu	language spoken mainly in Kenya. It is the largest ethnic language and group in Kenya. It belongs to the Bantu Ngugi wa Thiong'o, the literary mogul, writes in this language. While Gikuyu is the indigenous word for this language, it is also known as Kikuyu.
Jok	group of people in Eastern Africa who share cultural, linguistic and historical affiliation. They share a history of the Nile Valley economy and culture. The names for their clans and/or sub-groups begin with the root word "Jok," for example the Jok-Ajok and the Jok-Omolo and the Jok-Owiny.
Kwigita ti guoya. Kwihuuga ti Gukiiga.	Gikuyu proverb meaning "protecting oneself is not cowardice." Being careful is not foolishness. It is used by Ngugi wa Thiong'o in his Gikuyu version of the novel *Matigari*.
Luo/Dholuo	Nilotic group of people living mainly in present day Kenya, Uganda and Tanzania. Author Grace Ogot belongs to this ethnic group and has written in the language. The indigenous name for this language is Dholuo, where "Dho" means language. Therefore, *Dholuo* is the language of the Luo people.
matigari	word that means "remnants" in Gikuyu and is the title given to Ngugi wa Thiong'o's English translation of his Gikuyu book Matigari ma Njiruungi.
Matigari ma njiruungi	Gikuyu phrase meaning "remnants of a bullet." In the translated version, only the first word appears.
Nyilaak	Nyilaak was born a Luo princess. She was later slated to be "King," being the only child of the first wife. This is a historical narrative that was re-narrated by Grace Ogot to be the novel entitled *Princess Nyilaak*. She ends up being King of her people chosen by *Rubanga* (See below).

obambo/obambla	tilapia dried in the sun. During this process, the food hardens. Grace Ogot refers to it in her book *Simbi Nyaima* as a food that beautiful beautiful Awino cannot eat with her beautiful white teeth.
Rubanga	Deity/God of the Luo people. Grace Ogot uses this name to refer to the deity that the Luo people turn to in times of need.
ruoth	king. This title was preserved for the leader of the Luo Kingdoms, who were generally men. When Princess Nyilaak was being installed, there was no feminine version of this title.
Simbi Nyaima	area named in Grace Ogot's novel in Dholuo that sank. Lake Simbi is said to have been partly land before. The people of the village were punished for their lack of fulfilling the moral obligation of kindness. They refused to shelter an elderly woman who was passing through their village at night. The area was named Simbi Nyaima after the village that sank.
Te Okono Obur Bong Luputu: Wer pa Lawino	title that Okot p'Bitek first gave is Acholi song/poem. It is translated as *Lawino's Thesis. The Culture of Your People You Don't Abandon*. The first part of the title is an Acholi proverb. Later, this song was published as *Wer pa Lawino* (see below).
Wer pa Lawino	*Song of Lawino*. The English version does not include the proverb that was part of the original Acholi version. This famous song is now known in Acholi in the short form "Wer Pa Lawino."

4 Indian and Nepali Rhetorics

Prefatory Introduction

Uma S. Krishnan

Before providing a brief overview of Indian and Nepali rhetorics, I offer an explanation of why the rhetorical traditions of these two countries have been placed together in this collection. Both countries have shared religious beliefs, scriptures, philosophical ideas, communicative practices, and linguistic and cultural heritages throughout history. The Embassy of Nepal, for example, posts that Nepal and India share such a special closeness that "culture sees no borders."[1] Generally speaking, both cultures can locate or celebrate origins in the ancient religious scriptures of the world and of the Hindus, *The Vedas*—hymns which, as Sri Aurobindo writes, reflect "living conscious Art forming its creation in the puissant but well-governed movement of a self-observing inspiration."[2]

According to most Vedic scholars, *The Vedas*—knowledge of anything and everything—have always existed, without a beginning or an end, and have been considered as "cosmic knowledge"[3] imparted from the Gods. Sri Aurobindo writes,

> *Veda,* then, is the creation of an age anterior to our intellectual philosophies. In that original epoch, thought proceeded by other methods than those of our logical reasoning and speech accepted by modes of expression which in our modern habits would be inadmissible.

---

1. Government of Nepal, Embassy of Nepal, New Delhi, India. https://in.nepalembassy.gov.np/.
2. Aurobindo 1998b, 9-11.
3. Krishnan 2021.

The hymns were transmitted to mankind through *rishis*, enlightened gurus or teachers who "depended on inner experience and the suggestions of the intuitive mind for all knowledge that ranged beyond mankind's ordinary perceptions and daily activities" to adhere and capture this knowledge and pass it on to humanity forever.[4]

In many ways, the *Vedas* and the *rishis* can be considered the beginning points of Indian and Nepali rhetorics. Just as ancient rhetoricians hoped to convey cosmic knowledge to their audiences through various classifications and forms, the *rishis* wanted to illuminate and share the divine utterances with others, leading to the development of strategies or methods that could be used to organize and impart them. The first method was to compose texts in such a way as to preserve their purity of form. The second method was to transmit the texts in such a way that they could be effectively passed on from one generation to another for posterity. The third method was to showcase and implement the divine knowledge through commentaries, so that it could be understood, incorporated and implemented in everyday life; usually, they are in the form of the four *Purusharthas*, or four basic objectives to develop a noble character: (1) *dharma* (virtue or righteousness); (2) *artha* (means or material prosperity); (3) *kaama* (desire or pleasure); and (4) *moksha* (liberation or release from desire).[5] The *rishis'* main purpose for creating these complex rhetorical structures was to make humans aspire to reach superior or divine consciousness, to provide them an opportunity to see what the veil of life (*maya*) hides from us and the revelation behind it. Raimundo Panikkar refers to the *Veda* as a "process of discovery."[6]

To achieve their first goal, the *rishis* created an enormous and systematic methodology for classifying and sub-classifying texts and subtexts that leaves modern-day rhetoricians perplexed by their complexity and inter-connectivity. The first level of classification presents the *Vedas* as a unified collection of hymns, or *Samhitas,* in four parts—*Rig, Yajur, Sama,* and *Athrava Veda*—with the principal intention of preserving and protecting the *Vedic* content in its core form. One of the contributors in this chapter, Anne Melfi, limns this particular aspect of the *Rig Veda*, demonstrating the complexity and uniqueness of its utterances by explaining how just two words can provide audiences with a gamut of possibilities for interpreting and comprehending the nature of the Supreme Godhead. Melfi also reveals how these two words from this entire body of work are enough to reveal the powers of speech and of lexicon to create a transcendental connection between the human and the divine.

The *rishis* achieved their second rhetorical goal by creating an oral methodology to impart knowledge from the teacher, *guru*, to the student, *shishya*. This was done through a process of listening, repetitive chanting (*śrutis*), and memorization (*smritis*), passing in this precise way from one generation to the next. Given how knowledge was acquired through *śrutis* and *smritis*, the resulting *Vedas* were considered absolutely authoritative texts—non-debatable, non-alterable and difficult to understand. Interestingly, Shreelina Ghosh addresses the importance

---

4. Aurobindo 1998b, 9–11.
5. Ramaswamy 2015, 55–56.
6. Panikkar 1977, 13.

of chanting, memorizing and repeating the *Vedic* verses in their purest form—the *Natya-Shastra*, a form of dance—and Trey Conner and Richard Doyle elaborate on the importance of repetitive chanting. Only by implicitly following, chanting, and repeating the teacher's guidelines were the students able to discern the mysteries surrounding the human body and the divine soul. Conner and Doyle write about the common musical (*kriti*), dance (*kummi*), and ludic (*ammanai*) forms of rhythmic turn-taking actions or beats (repetitions), that were followed by people of *Sengottai*, to reveal the *Advaita* philosophy—a non-duality that exists between the self and the supreme, as revealed in the *Chandyoga Upanishad*. Only through the repetitive usage of sound utterances of *Omkara* (the primordial sound of the universe, *OM*), and through musical and poetic chanting experiences, can one reach higher yogic realization leading to *moksha* or liberation.

To achieve their third goal, the *rishis* created a subgroup of classification that could allow for the four *Vedas* to be comprehended and utilized in ways more adjacent to daily living: *Brahmanas* (commentaries or chants); *Aranyakas* (mystic meaning); *Upanishads* (relation between physical, metaphysical and supra-physical); *Vedangas* (limbs of Vedas); and *Upavedas* (applied knowledge). The *Vedangas*, or limbs of the *Vedas*, were again sub-classified into six disciplines by associating them with parts of the body: *Chandas* (the meter created by beats using the legs); *Kalpa* (a ritual performed by the hand); *Vyakarana* (grammar spoken through the mouth); *Shiksha* (phonetics created through the nose); *Nirukta* (understood through listening by the ears); and *Jyotisha* (seeing the celestial through the eyes).

The *Vedas* were taught in *Sanskrit*, also known as the language of Gods, having a unique grammatical structure closely tied to its principles of classification. Sanskrit scholars like Samapadananda Mishra believe that the language has four distinctive aspects that separate it from other languages: (1) it facilitates and establishes continuity based on how it is structured and used; (2) it demands exact repetition and precision, like a mathematical formula; (3) it allows for maintenance and preservation of the ancient wisdom and knowledge; and (4) it fosters discussions on the relationship of man to his body parts, their movements, his existence in this universe, relation to other members of the society, community obligations and conduct, and overall purpose in life.[7]

The Vedic period was also instrumental in developing additional rhetorical approaches, or *Upangas*, which were key to understanding one's relationship to earth and to the universe. True to form, the *Upangas* were subclassified into eight groups as *Puranas* (epics and stories), *Nyāya* (the science of logic/argument, whereby one learns about the nature of objects and their relationship), *Mimamsa* (analysis of the *Vedas*), *Dharma Shastras* (one's conduct and behavior), *Ayurveda* (the science of body and healing), *Dhanurveda* (archery or military science), *Gandharva Veda* (the science of the celestial arts, such as music and dance), *and Sthapatyaveda* (the science of architecture). Some scholars also include the *Artha Shastras* (the science of wealth) in this group.

---

7. Coudry 2006, 100.

What is important to observe here is that these subclassifications served to structure a wealth of concepts in such a logical manner as would appeal to diverse listeners. Keith Lloyd describes how *Nyāya* arguments were used in antiquity to develop higher-order thinking through a methodical step-by-step process that could also address metaphysical concepts. Lloyd further advocates for teaching *Nyāya* logic in contemporary classrooms as a way of acquiring many Aristotelian concepts through new eyes. Shuv Raj Rana Bhat uncovers the rhetorical strategies used in the *Garuda Purāṇa*, a text that deals with the journey of the soul after death. Rana Bhat does not look comparatively at the differences between the *Vedas* and the *Purāṇas*, but he does describe how the priestly Brahmin class—using certain rhetorical tactics of fear and guilt—maintained their power (hegemony) and social order in a caste-based Hindu society.

With this brief background in mind, we might approach Indian and Nepali rhetorics as a series of living aspects, emerging from the *Vedas* and/or spanning forward from the Vedic period,[8] reflecting rhetorical activities from roughly the sixteenth century BCE to the eighteenth century CE. Together, these contributions make a compelling argument for how rhetorical strategies have been used in oral and written texts, in different ways, to reveal the relationship between mind, body, and soul. They also make a compelling demonstration of how such rhetorical strategies can be effectively used to heighten self-consciousness of our action, our duties in life, and our obligation toward others. Indeed, the selections in this chapter reflect the vastness of Indian and Nepali rhetorics, ranging from ancient to modern.

Given this complexity that characterizes these ancient texts, I once questioned a Vedic scholar about the length, width, and depth of the *Vedas*. He said in reply, "Understanding the Vedic tradition is like entering an ocean of knowledge. Many decades will pass by before the rhetorician recognizes that he/she has covered only a mile of this space, as it is limitless and can be approached in so many ways. Sometimes, I feel one lifetime will not be enough to explore this Vedic Universe."

---

8. Scholarly sources date the beginning of the Vedic period as 2000 BCE and the culmination of the period sometime between 400 and 1100 CE, with earlier or later estimates depending upon textual clues. Some of those differences are reflected in this chapter.

4.1 Indian-Poetic, c. 1750–400 BCE, Ancient India

Winning Eloquence: A Tip from Two Hymns of the Rig Veda, the *Richo Akshare* Verse (1.164.39) and the Hymn of Knowledge (10.71)

Anne Melfi

INTRODUCTION: CONTEXT AND ORIGIN

In ancient India, sages developed a theory of speech and its power based on seed concepts proclaimed in a particular hymn of the Rig Veda, concepts which form the basis of a rich and varied rhetorical culture that grew and flourished for millennia and is still influential today.[9]

The Vedic Period of Indian antiquity is thought to fall around 1750–400 BCE with the Vedas completed by 1750 BCE, according to current scholarly estimates;[10] however, clues in the text suggest a much earlier origin, and some scholars even place the origin of the Vedas prior to 3100 BCE.[11] Vedic civilization is thought to have spanned from the Hindu Kush in what is now Afghanistan,[12] thrived in the teeming metropolises of the Indus Valley around the Sindhu (Indus) and Saraswati Rivers, which carried robust international trade, and extended eastward across what is now northern India, since the Saraswati River ran dry by 1750 BCE.[13] Vedic civilization had a formative and lasting influence on the cultural matrix throughout China, Japan, and Southeast Asia.[14]

Historical details, however, are still the subject of speculation and debate,[15] and they shift with new archeological discoveries and textual evidence toward ever more distant pre-history.[16] Fortunately, more telling than a people's dates and records of migration is their inner journey, where their core values unfold; these values can better reveal their motives for speaking and the forces that drive their rhetorical culture. All of these the voluminous Vedic texts contain. This discussion presents two primary texts: the most salient and much referenced verse of the Rig Veda, hymn 1.164, verse 39, better known as the *Richo Akshare* verse of the

---

9. Berger and Herstein 2014, 1074. "Understanding the . . . Indian (Vedantic) context is crucial to the success of foreign business . . . in India."

10. Proferes 2009.

11. Feuerstein, Kak, and Frawley 2001, 18.

12. Prasad 2015, Map 1.

13. Feuerstein, Kak, and Frawley 2001.

14. See Malhotra (2011); Goldman and Goldman (2009); Meyer-Dinkgräfe (2005, 109).

15. See Bryant and Patton 2005.

16. Feuerstein, Kak, and Frawley 2001.

Rig Veda;[17] and hymn 10.71, known as the Hymn of Knowledge,[18] or in Sanskrit, the *Jnanam Sukta,* which elaborates on the practical effects of the central principle that the *Richo Akshare* verse proclaims.

These hymns tell how one can tap the power of speech to accomplish the goals of speech, both personal and cosmic, by opening one's awareness to the transcendental source of speech. The verses presented below and the theory developed from them serve as keys to understanding the Vedic rhetorical paradigm and its myriad practices—how they work, their motives for speaking, and their ultimate goal.[19] Awareness of the principles and cosmology that define the paradigm makes visible the common connections and shared motives and purposes among the highly diverse rhetorical modes and methods of India that flowered from Vedic civilization, thus simplifying the otherwise daunting task of teaching them as part of the coherent rhetorical tradition from which they spring.

The verses below, translations from the Vedic Sanskrit source texts, suggest that the primary purpose that drives this paradigm is not to persuade, as in the Western rhetorical tradition, but rather to become established in truth, wholeness, and harmony with cosmic law, that is, to live in *dharma,* and thus attain *moksha,* liberation.[20] Maharishi Mahesh Yogi[21] posits that this approach "is not negotiation. It's not persuasion. It's reality of life and living."[22] The practical value of these abstract concepts should become evident with the briefing that follows. It is designed to prepare the reader to better appreciate these influential texts that have come down to us from antiquity.

THE VEDAS: CONTENT AND FORM

The *Richo Akshare* verse and the Hymn of Knowledge are part of a body of an "enormously long text . . . , 1,028 hymns with an average length of ten stanzas per hymn" organized into ten books (*mandalas*) that comprise the Vedas.[23] All were composed orally and orally preserved in perfect linguistic condition to the present day through prodigious acts of memorization by

---

17. Maharishi 1981, 3.

18. Rig Veda 1888. Unless otherwise noted, Rig Veda hymns cited in this chapter are referenced from this translation. Because H. H. Wilson's numbering system for the hymns differs from that generally used, this chapter follows the common standard to identify the verses discussed, rather than that used in Wilson's translation.

19. These practices range from drama and the arts (as set forth in the *Natyashastra*) to logic and debate. Some great debaters of the Vedic tradition are Yagyavalkya and Gargi seen in the Brihadaranyaka Upanishad 1884; and Buchta. Another great debater is Shankara (b. 686 CE). See Stroud (2009). The traditional analogical approach to dialogic argument is codified in the *Nyaya-Sutra*. See Keith Lloyd's article on the *Nyaya-Sutra* in this volume.

20. For a discussion of this subtle concept of dharma, see Adhikary (2009); Maharishi (2016, 26-27).

21. Founder of the Transcendental Meditation Program.

22. Maharishi 2006.

23. Elizarenkova 1995, 1.

pundits who employed exacting mnemonic heuristics so that the practical value of the knowledge that the verses contain would not be lost, for Veda means knowledge in its holistic value.

After countless millennia of oral transmission of the equivalent of two thousand printed pages, "only one uncertain reading of a single word can be found in the entire Rig-Veda," in hymn 7.44.3.[24] The verses of the Veda are the work of a host of poet sages who are called "*rishis*," seers, for their ability to perceive and express the laws of nature in holistic form. The Vedic hymns contain all fields of knowledge. Among the topics found there, Bhattacharyya lists, for example, "incisive, intrepid logic and metaphysics; science of government; the practical arts of agriculture, commerce, [and] medicine; knowledge of self or spiritual truth."[25] They also consider language, poetics and rhetorical concerns.[26] Maharishi Mahesh Yogi writes, "The Vedas are the lighthouse of eternal wisdom leading . . . to supreme accomplishment."[27] But the wisdom encoded in the Vedas is generally not easy to decipher.[28]

Sanskrit scholars concur that the language and style of the Vedas, since they are encoded in metaphor and symbol, pose a challenging puzzle for interpreters of the Vedic Sanskrit texts, even for those steeped in the Vedic legacy.[29] Multi-dimensionally resonant, a Vedic word (*mantra*) or image can elicit a universe of associations and meanings. With spare, compact, elliptically efficient style, the Vedic poets "often rely on shared knowledge to allow their contemporary audience to 'fill in the blanks' of allusive expressions."[30] Such allusive language and style creates the possibility for the hymns to contain the most holistic and full meaning of the *rishis'* cosmic cognitions.[31] But this approach poses a challenge for translators and modern readers.[32]

A cow is not always a cow in the Vedic milieu. Such familiar words can easily be misunderstood. The Sanskrit word for cow, *go,* also means Mother Earth, so the image of a cow can stand for the Earth; both nourish and support life. Thus, myths are made.[33] A cow can stand in for several different concepts which can be pivotal for grasping the meaning of a passage.[34] Cow can stand for "speech" and is one of many synonyms for *Akshara,* the second word of the *Richo Akshare* verse presented below; it means both pure transcendental consciousness, as

24. Feuerstein, Kak, and Frawley 2001, 17.

25. Bhattacharyya 2010, xxviii.

26. Elizarenkova 1995.

27. Maharishi 1981, 9.

28. Feuerstein, Kak, and Frawley 2001, 24.

29. Prahladachar 2006, 24n2.

30. Jamison and Brereton 2014, 80.

31. This is quite likely one reason why Indian scholars define rhetoric in terms of figuration. See Metzger (1996, 346); Chakraborty (2008); Krishnaswamy (2001, 385). N. Krishnaswamy aptly summarizes that rhetorical approach as "the art of giving effectiveness to truth."

32. Gonda 1984; Smith 2016.

33. Bronkhorst 2001; Smith notes that homophony, relating like-sounding words as meaning-maker was cross-culturally omnipresent in the pre-modern world.

34. Bronkhorst 2001, 159.

indestructible and eternal, and also "word" or "syllable."[35] By association, it can mean a poet/singer, poetry, and poetic inspiration and the deep insight and wisdom that come with it.[36]

The young Krishna is known as "chief cowherd" (*Govinda*), who eternally plays with his friends in a field of "cows," an image that invokes all of the above meanings; thus, Krishna plays in the field of transcendental bliss consciousness, the field of speech. In Rig Veda hymn 10.19,[37] *rishi* Brigu, author of the hymn, wants to find his lost "cows," singing, "I invoke the knowledge of the place, of their going, of their coming, of their departure, of their wandering, of their returning (I invoke) him who is their keeper.[38] . . . reward us with riches."[39]

In the lines above, "cow" can mean poetic inspiration and eloquence and/or opulence. If the *rishi* invokes the source of eloquence to overcome writer's block and find the wellspring of verses, he indeed finishes with a fine hymn in hand. "Cows" can also mean wealth, so harnessing the fountainhead of wealth would be an equally fitting and concurrent point of the hymn. The hymn has also been interpreted as an allegory for how to attain *moksha* (liberation) and so enjoy all manner of fulfillment in life.[40] Layers of meaning coexist in the hymn, where speech and wealth and transcendental consciousness are connected in *go*, the cow metaphor.

Hymn 164, the home of the first source text presented here, is such a richly-woven tapestry of metaphors, so full of abstract concepts presented in bursts of imagery that jump cut from one verse to another, that it has been called "the riddle hymn."[41] So, although every verse proclaims some facet of the Vedic view of speech and communication and how they work, it will be more feasible to focus on verse 39 here—for it is much less metaphorical in expression, and then offer the Hymn of Knowledge, which elaborates on the salient points that the *Richo Akshare* verse proclaims. The concepts presented in these hymns, which we will explore, are lively throughout the Vedic literature and their ancillary texts, implicitly or explicitly. Indeed, the *Richo Akshare* verse appears verbatim in the "Svetashvatara Upanishad," 4.9.[42] While this verse is less metaphorical than others in hymn 1.164 of *rishi* Dirgatamas, readers who are new to the Vedic paradigm may benefit from a briefing on key terms and concepts to better mine its meanings.

---

35. Elizarenkova 1995, 111.

36. Monier-Williams, Leumann, and Cappeller 2005; "go," devotes four pages of fine print to the Sanskrit word *go*.

37. This hymn by *rishi* Bhrigu is numbered 10.2.3 in the numbering system used in Wilson's translation of the Rig Veda, *Rig-Veda Sanhita—A Collection*.

38. Rig Veda 2013, 10.19.4.

39. Ibid., 10.19.7.

40. Maharishi 2010, 99.

41. Houben 2000.

42. Egenes and Katz 2015.

THEORETICAL CONTEXT

A simple glossary of unfamiliar terms would be of only marginal help. Rather, new terms and concepts will come to life in the context of Bhartrihari's contribution to Vedic speech, communication, and rhetorical theory. His dates are uncertain, but current consensus among scholars places this renowned Sanskrit author and philosopher well after the Vedic Period, ca. 450–500 CE.[43] His treatise on speech and grammar, the *Vakyapadiya*, reflects long-standing prevailing thought and practice in accord with such works as the *Yoga Sutra*,[44] which in turn reflects long-standing theory and practice in accord with the Vedas,[45] so dates of appearance in print do not necessarily serve as good markers for the origin of ideas.

Bhartrihari's treatise makes the first extant mention of the names of the levels of speech, though it is Rig Veda 1.164 verse 45 that is the first text known to proclaim that four levels exist, but that just one level is commonly known and discussed. The three other levels are hidden and known only to the wise.[46] These three are not found in Western theories of speech and rhetoric; they are, however, central to the Vedic worldview, and "correlative quadripartitions of speech and the universe occurred even in the Upanishads.[47] So the concept of levels of speech must be grasped if one is to make sense of the Vedic literature on its own terms.

Fathoming the Deep Levels of Speech

In the Vedic view, beyond audible speech and the written word, deep within the mind lies the foundation of eloquence and fulfillment in life; for speech has its source in transcendental consciousness, *Para*, the silent source of speech which creates the universe.[48] From *Para*, an idea arises in its wholeness, and if one's conscious mind is open to that almost unbounded level of awareness, one sees an idea as a gestalt, as if glimpsing an entire text or work of art in all its nuanced conceptual detail in a dimensionless point, nearly free of space-time, more felt than articulated. Bhartrihari calls this level of speech *Pashyanti*, "the seeing one"[49] and

---

43. Coward 1976, 11.
44. Desmarais 2008, 16-17; the date of the *Yoga Sutra* is still a matter of debate. Proposed dates range from the fifth century BCE to the third century CE, and even as late as the fifth century CE; Bryant 2009, 510n43-44; Bryant argues that an early date appears more likely, pointing out that arguments for a later date "have all been challenged" and are "problematic." The enduring continuity of the culture tends to confound the search for origin dates in its history of ideas.
45. Kothari and Om 2014.
46. Padoux 1990, 166–67.
47. Padoux 1971; Maharishi 2010.
48. Maharishi 2010, 209; Coward and Goa 2004, 36–37; Rig Veda, 1.164.39 and 45; Andersen 2010, 123. Padoux 1990, 166, 192; Bhartrihari does not count *Para* as a level of speech, but does recognize it as the source from which speech bubbles up into expression. Others, such as Abhinavagupta, do count *Para* as a level of speech, albeit in its unmanifest form, but also agree with Bhartrihari "on the actual content of each stage" of speech.
49. Coward and Goa 2004, 38.

"visionary speech."[50] From there the idea takes form in the linear flow of language or spatial arrangement of art on the *Madhyama* level, or silent speech-in-thought, where one might plan a letter or remember a poem. From there emerges speech one can hear or read, the *Vaikhari* level of speech,[51] the success of which in achieving its purposes depends upon the connectedness of the speaker to the source.[52] Therefore, development of this connectedness, a state of consciousness called *yoga*, (unity or union) is considered essential, according to the Vedic verses presented herein.

Maharishi illustrates the principle with a diagram that compares the mind to an ocean, in Figure 4.1, with waves of activity at the surface but silent at the depth. I have adapted his diagram, adding the names of the levels of speech, which correspond to the levels of mind.[53] He explains that, "a thought impulse arises from the silent creative centre within [at point A], as a bubble starts from the bottom of the sea. As it rises, it becomes larger; arriving at the conscious level of the mind, it becomes large enough to be appreciated as a thought, and from there it develops into speech and action" at point B.[54]

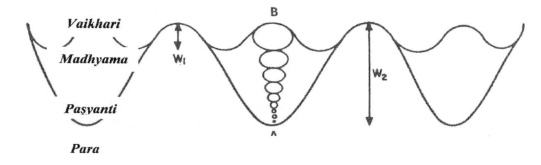

Figure 4.1: The Vedic Levels of Speech. Adapted from Maharishi's diagram (*Bhagavad-Gita*, 470), with permission from Maharishi International University and Maharishi Vedic University. I have added the names of the levels of speech.

The arrow at W_1 shows the range of conscious awareness commonly experienced, while W_2 shows the full potential range of consciousness awareness, which can be attained, Maharishi writes, by a simple technique for "turning the attention inwards, [which] takes the mind from the experience of a thought at the conscious level (B) to the finer states of the thought until the mind arrives at the source of thought (A). This inward march of the mind results in the expan-

---

50. Padoux 1990, 166.
51. Coward and Goa 2004, 38.
52. Rig Veda 1888, 211; Andersen 2010, 123.
53. Andersen 2010, 120-124.
54. Maharishi 1990, 470.

sion of the conscious mind (from W$_1$ to W$_2$),"[55] an ideal condition for successful eloquence.[56] Methods for achieving this state of *yoga*, which are also referred to as *yoga*, can be quite arduous, and many believe that the goal is difficult to achieve, and then only by a fortunate few. However, Maharishi points out that this is a mistaken belief, owing to misinterpretation of the venerable texts on *yoga*,[57] and he notes that his Transcendental Meditation allows the mind to transcend without effort[58] and has been used successfully by individuals from every walk of life and virtually every culture around the world.[59] This suggests that the *Richo Akshare* verse and the Hymn of Knowledge set realistic expectations when they require one to open his/her awareness to the transcendental source of thought, which is also the source of speech, and creation as a prerequisite for optimal rhetorical efficacy.

This principle could hardly be considered integral to rhetorical theory in the Western paradigm,[60] yet some contemporary scholars have referred to a source of eloquence which issues from deep within. Kristie Fleckenstein has described how in the Italian Renaissance St. Catherine of Siena wrote of a transcendental source from which her eloquence issued forth and moved both populace and Pope, a divine silence as the source of meaning, of words, and of life, an ineffable infinity which finite words could not express,[61] a vision similar in many ways to the Vedic view. Still, this area has remained uninvestigated in the field of rhetorical studies, even though James Berlin introduced the ideas of American transcendentalist Ralph Waldo Emerson into the history of nineteenth century rhetorical theory as a revolutionary alternative perspective.[62] Berlin includes Roberta K. Ray's view of Emersonian rhetoric, a vision of Platonic transcendence as "the basis of reality . . . that underlies all material existence" and which "embodies truth, beauty, and goodness," in turn inspiring intuitive eloquence in the speaker, who could then compellingly inspire others to apprehend "higher truths."[63] Berlin reasons, however, that this Platonic vision "denies the possibility of a rhetoric of public discourse" as it

---

55. Maharishi 1990, 470.

56. Maharishi 2010, 155.

57. Maharishi 1990, 160; in his commentary on chapter 2, verse 59, Maharishi writes that, "It is wrong to assume that unless the senses are controlled one cannot realize the Truth. As a matter of fact, the converse is true. . . . Wrong interpretations of this and other verses have led many genuine seekers of Truth to undertake rigorous and unnatural practices to control the senses, thus wasting their lives and benefiting neither themselves nor others." See also 377.

58. Maharishi 1990, 118–20.

59. Maharishi 1986, 43, 84.

60. Orme-Johnson 1987, 341–42; the Vedic levels of speech should not be confused with, for example, structuralism founder Ferdinand de Saussure's three levels of linguistic activity nor should his concept of *language* as the human potential for speech, for such a notion as *Para*, a transcendental source of speech has no place in Saussure's theory.

61. Fleckenstein 2011, 44.

62. Berlin 1984, 11.

63. Ibid.

is based on "a private vision of a realm that transcends the material";[64] therefore, Berlin does not make transcendence the basis of his Emersonian rhetoric,[65] which he instead aligns with the views of Susanne Langer.[66] Conversely, Roger Thompson argues that when "Berlin aligns Emerson with social constructivist understandings . . . he mischaracterizes Emerson's project, the reconciliation of Plato . . . with social action";[67] Plato inspired Emerson to unambiguously assert that the deeper one dives into inner transcendental truth, the more acceptable by the audience (and therefore the more compelling) and the more true is one's speech.[68]

The Rhetorical Tradition does not include discussion of a transcendental source of eloquence,[69] aside from Plato's *Phaedrus*. Thus, these considerations raised in the rhetorical studies literature leave many open questions yet to be pursued in depth in the West. Yet rigorous attention to the source of speech and systematic application of methods for tapping its power is the specialty of the Vedic paradigm and integral to the Vedic worldview in which speech and language are embedded in the fabric of consciousness.[70] Maharishi Mahesh Yogi explains that successful communication depends upon having awareness open to the full range of speech, the full range of the mind, which proceeds from the transcendental source of creation,[71] echoing the message of the *Richo Akshare* verse: If one is "well connected to the source of speech, which is unbounded, infinite, eternal, all comprehensive, then speech will always be flowering into those values of unboundedness and widest comprehension and greatest focus, which will accomplish the maximum value of communication."[72] Bhartrihari similarly explains that when awareness is awake to the deep, expanded level of mind/speech (*Pashyanti*), "then the full meaning of *mantras* [Vedic words] stands revealed"; comprehension is complete.[73] According to Patanjali, awareness that is open to this deep level, the state of *yoga*, knows only the truth.[74] Conversely, when awareness is limited to the surface, shallow levels of speech, then comprehension is limited to a superficial, perhaps literal, understanding, or even a completely mistaken one, so that communication fails,[75] as the Hymn of Knowledge proclaims. Fullness of comprehension and knowledge comes with fullness of consciousness, that by which one is capable of being conscious *of* anything.

---

64. Ibid., 43–44.
65. Ibid., 46–47.
66. Ibid., 46.
67. Thompson 2015, 126.
68. Thompson 2017, 81–82, 17–24.
69. Bizzell and Herzberg 2001.
70. See Coward and Goa (2007) and (2013, 1–4); Choudhuri (2006, 56); Desai (2009, 00:09:30); Padoux (1990); Maharishi "Enlivening" (2010); Maharishi "Phonology" (2010); Maharishi "Root" (2010).
71. Maharishi 2010.
72. Maharishi 2010, 155.
73. Coward and Goa 2004, 40.
74. Patanjali 2010; see also Maharishi (2010, 194–95).
75. Orme-Johnson 1987, 344–48.

Bhartrihari writes in *Vakyapadiya* 2.332 that absent-mindedness obscures the meaning that is inherently present in words.[76] Meaning and comprehension are structured in the very nature of consciousness, which is accessible at the source of thought/speech,[77] even before audible speech or writing arises. In other words, "Knowledge is structured in consciousness."[78] This maxim, coined by Maharishi Mahesh Yogi, is the most concise of his several translations of the start of the *Richo Akshare* verse. It highlights the salient point that the fabric of consciousness is the fabric of knowledge, the fabric of speech. Limited conscious awareness hinders the ability to achieve one's purpose, analogous to posting a sign for an audience who cannot read.

Thus, Vedic culture places great emphasis on cultivating *yoga*, union with the transcendental source.[79] *Yoga* pertains to both the state of *yoga* and also the means for attaining it. According to the *Yoga Sutra* of Patanjali, "Yoga is the complete settling of the activity of the mind. Then the observer is established in the Self."[80] In other words, transcending the surface levels of speech and opening awareness to the source of thought/speech, one attains *yoga*. One of the ways the *Bhagavad-Gita* describes the state of *yoga* is in terms of its effect: "Yoga is skill in action."[81] It is an essential component of training in the arts so that the performer may fulfill the rhetorical purpose.[82] Thus *yoga* is highly rhetorical in its consequences. Why that would be so is embedded in the nature of *Para*.

The Cosmology of Speech in the Richo Akshare *Verse*

Although *Para* is known as the field of infinite silence, nevertheless, according to the *Richo Akshare* verse, the silence is also lively with impulses of creative intelligence called the *devas*, generally translated as "gods." These impulses are *mantra* (words), virtual sounds, whose various vibratory frequencies are also known as the laws of nature; taken together, they are the fabric of consciousness, the aggregate of all the laws of nature, which comprises *Brahman*, the unitary wholeness of everything, manifest and unmanifest, which, vibrating in different frequencies, structures and governs the universe, both manifest and unmanifest. The *Richo Akshare* verse proclaims that the *richas*, the verses of the Veda (knowledge), are composed of this field and that one must therefore open conscious awareness to this field of creative intelligence to benefit from the knowledge contained in the expressions of the Veda. Otherwise, what can speech/knowledge, the *mantras* of the Veda, do for you?

---

76. Coward 1989, 167.
77. See figure v.2.1.
78. Maharishi "Nature" 2010, 40–41.
79. Maharishi "Relation" 2010, 00:55:59.
80. Patanjali 2010, 1.2–3.
81. Maharishi 1990, 2.50.
82. Kothari and Om 1996, 73.

Implicit in the verse is a call to action, the duty to attain direct knowledge/experience of the Reality so the full value of life may be known and lived.[83] Sage Bhartrihari similarly describes the ultimate Truth of how the universe works at the start of the *Vakyapadiya*, where he affirms: "Brahman . . . whose very essence is the Word, who is the cause of the manifested phonemes, . . . from whom the creation of the world proceeds":[84] speech is *Brahman*.[85] Similarly in Indian music theory, the universe is nothing but pulsations of the sonic absolute: He is the *rasa* (essence, taste or savor) that the artist strives to convey to inspire in the audience, a taste of and for *Brahman*.[86]

For some, the Vedic view of the universe may sound fanciful; however, recent advances in physics suggest otherwise. Though not established in Western rhetorical theory, this unitary vision bears a striking resemblance to the way that string theory of quantum physics describes the universe.[87] Columbia University professor of mathematics and physics Brian Greene explains that the universe according to string theory consists of "a huge number of . . . filaments of vibrating energy, vibrating in different frequencies. Different frequencies produce different particles. The different particles are responsible for all the richness in the world around us. And there you see unification." Greene asserts that all of this virtual vibration—virtual sound, in effect— which appears as the universe occurs within an unmanifest unified field of all the laws of nature.[88] In figure 1, one could print "unified field" next to *Para*. Thus, as the Katha Upanishad proclaims, "Manifest diversity is unmanifest—there is nothing else."[89] That is *Brahman*, the whole.

Greene's universe according to string theory seems a close paraphrase of the *Richo Akshare* verse, suggesting that Vedic cosmology presents not just a literary conceit or cryptic philosophy, but a science that probes the truth about the universe, a science of consciousness, *Ved vigyan*. Greene, however, seems to speak from a Western scientific view of reality when he

---

83. Maharishi "Relation" 2010, 190–200.

84. Bhartrihari 1971.

85. Muktika Upanishad 1914, 1; Brihadaranyaka Upanishad 1884 and 1962, 4.1.2; "speech is indeed *Brahman*," Choudhuri, 2006, 63n28; the Vedic literature repeatedly equates Speech with *Brahman*. Choudhuri (2006) finds examples in "*Vagbrahma – Gopatha Brahmana* 1, 2, 10; *Vagvai Brahma – Aitareya Brahmana* 6, 3; *Prajapatirhivak – Taittiriya Brahmana* 1, 3, 4, 5; *Vagvai Prajapatiḥ – Shatapatha Brahmana* 5, 1, 5, 6; *ya sa vagbrahmaiva tat – Jaiminiyopanishad Brahmana* 2, 13, 2.

86. Desai 2009, 00:09:30 and 01:56; see also Kirkwood (1990, 93, 101).

87. As pointed out in Melfi (2020, 135).

88. Greene 2005, 18:55; superstring theory is a mathematical model such as Einstein used to formulate theories like relativity, which was later validated by empirical evidence. The elegant mathematical calculations of string theory make sense of the universe but do not work in a three-dimensional universe, or a four- or five-dimensional one. In an eleven-dimensional universe, the math works perfectly, Greene points out here. Since then, the discovery of the Higgs boson, announced on March 14, 2014, suggests that these dimensions exist, thus lending validation to string theory.

89. Katha Upanishad 2015, 2.1.11.

excludes consciousness, arguing that the purview of physics is the physical universe alone,[90] which he has nevertheless described as nonphysical virtual vibrations. His logic begs the question: When this unified field underlies and governs the whole universe, can anything at all be excluded, much less one so consequential as consciousness? String theorist John Hagelin thinks not. Winner of the prestigious Kilby award for physics and president of Maharishi International University, he argues in favor of a conscious universe, which he describes as a symphony of creative intelligence, and, he asserts, "That's what we're made of." His assertion echoes the Upanishads, which proclaim: "I am *Brahman*," [91] and so are you, "Thou art that,"[92] and "All this is that,"[93] and "that totality, wholeness, is consciousness."[94] Thus the unitary vision of the Upanishads also exists in the Vedic hymns, though the hymns present a multitude of laws of nature, or gods (*devas, mantras*). As the Muktika Upanishad proclaims, "Like the oil in the sesamum seeds, Vedanta is well established (or latent) in the Vedas."[95]

Vedic science is within the purview of the Vedic grammarians, philosophers of speech and language, revered sages whose numbers include Maharishi Patanjali, author of the *Yoga Sutra* and the *Mahabhashya* (great commentary) on grammar, Abhinavagupta the aesthetics philosopher (c. 950–1020 CE), and Bhartrihari. Chaitanya writes that "according to Patañjali, the grammarian is a Yogi whose inward vision enables him to look within to see the eternal flow of pure consciousness."[96] The philosophy of speech and communication are integral to the Vedic worldview,[97] for speech has its basis in the transcendental powerhouse of the universe.

The imperative is to open one's awareness to this field as the *Richo Akshare* verse, in effect, enjoins so that one may gain benefit from the total potential of natural law available deep within, because cultivating that abstract *Brahman* brings practical side-benefits that are essential to living the full value of life and making the most of speech, as the Hymn of Knowledge illustrates. Life in harmony with all the laws of nature is life in *dharma*, attuned to the whole, a leading principle of Vedic culture.[98] The *Richo Akshare* verse establishes the main imperative, and the Hymn of Knowledge compellingly presents, in vivid metaphor and example, its consequences for life in society.

---

90. Greene 2017.

91. Brihadaranyaka Upanishad 1884 and 1962, 1.4.10.

92. Chandogya Upanishad 1884 and 1962, 6.11.

93. Ibid., 3.14.1.

94. Aitareya Upanishad 2015, 3.1.3.

95. Muktika Upanishad 1914, 1.

96. Chaitanya 1962, 53.

97. Coward and Goa 2004, 272; Choudhuri 2006, 56; Desai 2009, 00:09:30; Padoux 1990; Maharishi "Enlivening" 2010; Maharishi "Phonology" 2010; Maharishi "Root" 2010.

98. Adhikary 2010, 7.

TRANSLATIONS AND COMMENTARIES

Reading the Richo Akshare Verse and the Hymn of Knowledge[99]

In the translations below, wherever masculine-gendered language is used, it undoubtedly applies to all people, male and female, and "he" could just as well be rendered more accurately, if more awkwardly, as "he or she." Many great Vedic women are renowned as *rishis, gurus,* and debaters of powerful eloquence, such as Gargi Vachanavi, known for her incisive logic and tireless dialectical inquiry, *guru,* and great master of debate.[100] Also revered is *rishi* Vagambhrini, author of the *Hymn of Speech (Vak)*, Rig Veda 10.125, which proclaims the power and purview of the source of speech as substance and governor of the universe and that attention to the source of speech, personified in the goddess *Vak,* if neglected, will block wisdom, understanding, and fulfillment in all of life's joys—status, wealth, and so forth.[101] *Rishi* Vagambhrini's hymn is very much aligned with the theme of the *Richo Akshare* verse.

In the "Hymn of Knowledge," specifically, figurative language that might well puzzle the reader calls for some explanation. In this hymn, speech in its transcendental state (*Para-Brahman*) is represented by Brihaspati, the lord of speech and the *guru* of the gods, who is also associated with *Brahman,* for Speech is *Brahman.* Another flavor of Speech in verse one, who whispers eloquence to the listener on the fine feeling level, "by means of affection," is personified as Saraswati, the goddess of wisdom and the arts and sciences, also known as personified Speech (*Vak*). "Affection" in this passage corresponds to the intuitive *Pashyanti* level.

Think of "*soma*" (line 10) in terms of the flow of consciousness. An herbal drink called "*soma*" is part of some rites, which symbolically enact cosmic processes using various paraphernalia and substances to represent cosmic events and concepts.[102] Line 11 refers to such a rite or *yagya,* one of the means for establishing attunement with the laws of nature.[103]

The word "*brahmans*" appears in this context to reference those whose awareness is open to the full range of speech/consciousness. The metaphors suggest the need to cultivate friendship with the transcendental field of speech, and to refine speech "as (men winnow) barley with a sieve,"[104] so that one may enjoy all glories, earthly and divine. The hymn also lists some consequences for neglecting "the duty of a friend."[105] In this context, it would be a mistake to po-

---

99. The reader should bear in mind that each Sanskrit word has multiple meanings, several of which may be relevant in the context, giving a holistic and resonant meaning in concise form. Variants are listed in the glossary at the end of this chapter.

100. She appears, for example, in the Brihadaranyaka Upanishad 1884 and 1962, 3.1.1. See Buchta (2010) for a discussion of her status.

101. Singh 2006, 48.

102. Patton 2005, 44-58, 80.

103. See Dange (2006, 89).

104. Rig Veda 1888 and 2013, 10.71.2.

105. Rig Veda 1888 and 2013, 10.71.6.

liticize "*brahmans*" in terms of caste politics,[106] an anachronistic reading contrary to the point of the hymn, which proclaims that proper orientation to the source creates one's quality of life. With proper attention to the transcendental field of speech, the hymn suggests, enlightenment and fulfillment in life may be attained, along with fruitful eloquence.

Rig Veda Hymn 1.164, verse 39 of the Rig Veda[107] *by rishi Dirgatamas*

The *richa*—the expression of the Veda—is situated in *Akshara*, the imperishable transcendental field in which reside all the impulses of creative intelligence, responsible for the whole manifest universe.

He whose awareness is not open to this field, what can the *richas* [[108]] accomplish for him? Those who know this level of reality are established in evenness, wholeness of life.

Rig Veda 10.71, the Hymn of Knowledge of rishi Brihaspati

That, Brihaspati, is the best (part) of speech which those giving a name (to objects) first utter; [[109]] that which was the best of those (words) and free from defect, (*Saraswati*) reveals it though secretly implanted, by means of affection.

When the wise create Speech [[110]] through wisdom winnowing (it) as (men winnow) barley with a sieve, then friends know friendship; good fortune is placed upon their word.

(The wise) reached the path of Speech by sacrifice, they found it centered in the *Rishis*; having acquired it they dispersed it in many places; the seven noisy (birds) meet together.

One (man) indeed seeing Speech has not seen her; another (man) hearing her has not heard her; but to another she delivers her person as a loving wife well-attired presents herself to her husband.

They call one man firmly established in the friendship (of Speech), they do not exclude him from (the society of) the powerful (in knowledge); another wanders with an illusion that is barren, bearing Speech that is without fruit, without flowers.

---

106. See Feuerstein, Kak, and Frawley (2001, 22).

107. Translation by Maharishi 1981, 3.

108. The verses of the Veda.

109. Coward, 1989, 170; word, because it is structured in the fabric of consciousness, is held to be eternal; Bronkhorst 2001, 169; writes that "the idea of words being made by anyone, human or superhuman, was totally unacceptable in India"; Patanjali observed that the grammarian does not make words the way a potter makes a pot. The sense in verse one is that the wise utter the names but do not fabricate them. "For Plato, by contrast, there were more-than-human original name-givers."

110. I preserve the capitalization, spellings, and punctuation used by the translator.

He who has abandoned the friend who knows the duty of a friend, in his speech there is not a particle (of sense); what he hears, he hears amiss; for he knows not the path of righteousness.

Friends possessing eyes, possessing ears, were (yet) unequal in mental apprehension; some seemed like pools reaching to the mouth, others reaching to the loins, others like pools in which one can bathe.

Although *Brahmans* who are friends concur in the mental apprehensions which are conceived by the heart (of the wise), yet in this (assembly) they abandon one man (to ignorance of the sciences) that are to be known, others again who are reckoned as *Brahmans* (wander at will in the meanings of the Veda).

Those who do not walk (with the *Brahmans*) in this lower world nor (with the gods) in the upper world—they are neither *Brahmans* nor offerers of libations; they, devoid of wisdom, attain Speech, having sin-producing (Speech), becoming ploughmen pursue agriculture.

All friends rejoice when the friendly (libation), the support of the assembly (of the priests), has arrived (at the sacrifice); for (*Soma*), the remover of iniquity, the giver of sustenance, being placed (in the vessels), is sufficient for their invigoration.

One (the *Hotri*) is diligent in the repetition of the verses (of the *Rich*[111]); another (the *Udgatri*) chants the *Gayatra* (the *Saman*) in the *Shakvari* metre; another the *Brahma* declares the knowledge of what is to be done; another (the *Adhwaryu*) measures the materials of the sacrifice.

---

111. The hymns of the Rig Veda.

4.2 Indian-Poetic, c. 4th–5th century BCE, Ancient India

Śruti and *Smriti*: Role of Listening, Chanting, and Memorization in Rhetorical and Pedagogical Practices of Indian Classical Dance

Shreelina Ghosh

INTRODUCTION

The thousand-year-old stone temple walls in eastern and southern India bear evidence of the presence of temple dance practices in various parts of India. Although the dances were meant to be performed inside the temples as offerings to the presiding deity of these Hindu temples, they were sometimes performed outside the temples for entertainment. The seven or eight classical dances that developed from the roots of these ancient temple dances adhere to the strictly codified Sanskrit treatise of dramaturgy. The two major texts are *Natyashastra* and *Abhinaya Darpana*.[112] An ancient practice that managed to retain most of the foundational codes while adding layers of innovation with each passing generation depends much on an organized and strictly regulated but adaptable pedagogic system. Yet, despite the meticulous detail with which each aspect of the dance is portrayed in the *Abhinaya Darpana* and the importance of transmitting this knowledge through generations, there is no mention of any systematized way in which the dance was taught. Interestingly, although *Natyashatra* or other texts of the performance of the dance do not have any guidelines on teaching methods, the master-disciple or *guru-shishya* tradition of teaching has helped the dance retain its basic values and performance style. The *guru-shishya* tradition,[113] a vital essence of Indian classical art, helped the dances preserve their foundational values and form through the pedagogical processes of *śruti* (listening/chanting, "that which is heard") and *smriti* (memorization, "that which is remembered") with carefully structured and controlled adaptability.

Śruti and *smriti* facilitated transmission of knowledge from the guru to the disciple before the ancient scriptures of Hindu philosophy, the *Vedas*, were written down. Some of the interpretation of the *Vedas* differed from one guru to the other. In his explanation of the prosody of the Vedic chants, Rahul Das argues that *śruti* or listening/chanting is "a mode of expression which allows a very wide interpretation."[114] This enrichment of the *Vedas* could be a result of

---

112. Nandikeshvara wrote *Abhinaya Darpana* between the fifth and fourth centuries BCE. It is used by the practitioners of Indian classical dance till date.

113. The *guru-shishya* tradition of learning traditionally involves the practice of the disciple staying at the guru's house during the course of study. They would be responsible for the household chores for the guru and his (rarely her in ancient times) family and in return receive the knowledge of the art. This relationship has the expectation of extreme respect and reverence for the guru.

114. Das 1996, 26.

the delicate balance between strict adherence to the scripture and openness to multiple inter-pretations. The *Vedas* are the *śruti* texts because they are believed to have been revealed by God to man. *Vedas* do not have a human author. *Smriti* are elaborations of the original *śruti* texts. Vedic scholars interpreted the Vedic knowledge from their memory and wrote the *sm-riti* texts like the *Itihasas* (the great narrative epics *Ramayana* and *Mahabharata*), the *Puranas*, the *Agamas*, and the *Darsanas*.[115] Receiving knowledge, chanting it repetitively, memorizing, and re-interpreting this knowledge is foundational to traditional learning in ancient Indi-an culture.

In the rhetorical pedagogy of several South Asian artistic practices (including Indian clas-sical dance), chanting is an essential part of training. In this chapter, I argue that chanting is a form of education for students of Indian classical dance, specifically that it teaches them how to embody the thousand-year-old memory of the dance and how to pass down the memory in its purest form to the next generation. I focus on the composition of verses and argue that the rhetorical practices of chanting and memorization are pivotal in learning this dance form.

Origins and Context

Indian classical dance was in practice long before recorded history, and its resonance in the postures of India's present-day dance practices is indicative of its prototypical nature. The figurine of the dancing girl from the pre-historic ruins of Mohenjodaro (Figure 4.2L) reflects a bent knee and torso posture that is similar to the three-bend style of the classical dance form of Odissi (Figure 4.2M and 4.2R),[116] a dance originating in the eastern coastal state of Orissa. The earliest practices of this dance were likely for entertainment, conducted as a court room practice, or performed for rituals, such as harvest. Its depictions on the walls of caves and tem-ples dating back to the first century BCE reveal that the dance was practiced in the temples, offered to the deity alongside cooked food, flowers, incense, and sandalwood paste.[117] The inscriptions on the natural caverns of Udaygiri (in Orissa) depict the form of women playing the flute, drums and cymbals.[118] Similar figures of dancing girls are etched on the walls of hundreds of temples in Orissa, like Konark, Puri Jagannath, Rajarani, Khajuraho, and Bhu-baneshwar. There are poses of the dancer engaged in *aharya* or decorating herself by looking at a mirror. The poses often depict ritualistic offerings of flowers and playing of musical in-struments, and appear alongside several other spiritual, erotic, and martial arts poses etched on the walls. These same dance postures occur in modern renditions of this dance to this day.

---

115. Singh 2008, 2.

116. A typical posture of Odissi dance is the *tribhangi* or the three-bend posture, a graceful feminine style of the body. The three bends occur at the neck, the waist, and the knee.

117. y Royo 2007, 155.

118. Patnaik 1971, 74.

Figure 4.2: Three dancing figures in Tribhanga, or the three-bend posture. L: "Dancing girl of Mohenjodaro," Gary Todd licensed under Creative Commons; M: "Sculpture of Alasa Kanya at Vaital Deul, Feb 2008" by Sujit kumar licensed under Creative Commons; R: modern-day Odissi dancer, used with permission by Kaustav Mukherjee.

For some practitioners, Odissi is not only an artistic expression, but also a way of living, shaping the perception of the world and the way in which the dancer communicates. It is a demanding art that takes years of training and focuses on precise and meaningful movements in which the body, presence, and aesthetic are central to its performance and learning. The knowledge of the art is handed down from generation to generation by the guru, derived from the Sanskrit root [gṛ], which means, "to praise or invoke." In the term "*guru*," *gu* signifies darkness, and *ru* signifies "the one who destroys." Guru is not only the one who instills knowledge, but also the one who destroys darkness and provides the student with light to unfold truth, knowledge, and wisdom. Guru is considered to be the human form of abstract divinity that helps one realize God is the guru himself. Odissi dance has survived through many generations of the *guru-shishya parampara*, or master-student tradition.

As a result, chanting became the principal rhetorical pedagogical tool for training students how to embody the thousand-year-old memory of the dance and how to convey its memory in the most unchanged form. At the same time, preserving the dance form became important to learning Vedic texts,[119] as repetition of the dance connecting the movements with the verses from *Natyashastra* became crucial in preserving the meanings of the gestures.[120] Indologist Michio Yano writes, "the Vedas were not written compositions but they were 'what is heard'

119. The *Vedas* are the most ancient example of rhetorical practices of the Indian subcontinent.

120. *Paash mudra* describes the interlocking of two index fingers in a slightly bent manner. It is used to denote enmity or fight, whereas *keelak mudra* describes the interlocking of two little fingers in a slightly bent manner. It is used to denote love and affection. While the mudras look very similar, if the wrong fingers interlock, the meanings change significantly.

(*Śruti*) by the inspired sages and they were transmitted exclusively by oral method in the first millennium after its formation."[121] Like the tradition of Odissa, the *Vedas* were handed down through the *guru-shishya* tradition. Chanting, repetition, and memorization of the thousands of verses of the ancient *Vedas*[122]—including the *Upanishads, Brahmanas, Aranyakas,* and *Samhitas*—preserved these works before they were written down.[123]

Verses from *Natyashastra* provided detailed information on the methods of performing rituals and their significance, as rhetorical movements of the palm and fingers denoted the tonal details that contribute significantly to the meaning-making process of Vedic utterances.[124] To learn them, students would memorize the masters' hand movements indicating rising and falling intonations, pitch, and length of each syllable, which can significantly alter the meaning of a word. Young dancers are taught to depict various things with the *pataka* hand gesture (Figure 4.3),[125] where all fingers are together and palm is flat with no bent fingers. By the time young dancers learn the *Natyashastra* verses and are taught to demonstrate each word in the verse using *pataka,* the actual performance of the dance usually comes naturally to them.

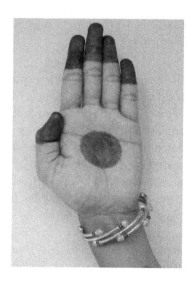

Figure 4.3: The *pataka* single-hand gesture, *Natyarambhe,* which signals the beginning of the dance; courtesy of "Hastamudra" Sreejithk, 2000. Licensed under Creative Commons.

---

121. Yano 2006, 145.

122. Natyavidushi 2011, 103.

123. Ibid., 112.

124. The four ancient Indian collections of hymns composed between 2000 and 1100 BCE consist of *Rig, Sama, Yajur,* and *Atharva.* Interestingly, pupils of the *Vedas* practiced a rhythmic movement of the hand to denote the rise and fall of the tunes of the chant. While *Vedas* are central to the Hindu philosophy, *Upanishads, Brahmanas, Aranyaka,* and *Samhitas* were later texts composed to unpack and reveal the various aspects of the philosophically impenetrable *Vedas.*

125. *Pataka* literally means "a flag." The hand held flat with no bent fingers is the basic hand posture that a student learns at the beginning of dance instruction.

There are some mythical beliefs regarding the codification of the dance that should also be discussed here. First, at around 400 BCE, Bharatmuni wrote *Natyashastra*,[126] apparently under the guidance of the mythical dancers and Hindu deity, Lord Shiva,[127] as a way of textualizing the oral knowledge of dance. The classical dances adhered to the theories of movement, expression, and performance that Bharatmuni prescribed. Ancient scriptures on performance and dramaturgy explained how the dance was to be performed with meticulous detail. The dances were like manuals explaining the movements of various parts of the body, decoration of the body, dancing space, and so on. The meaning of each pose and movement was explained in Sanskrit verse, although the art of performance was and remains founded on the relationship of the student with the instructor. Second, according to the Sangeet Natak Academy (Academy of Performing Arts of the Government of India), the Indian classical dances were associated with various regions, including Bharatanatyam, Kuchipudi, Kathakali, and Mohiniattam from the southern peninsular part of India; Odissi from the eastern coast of India; Manipuri and Shattriya from the Himalayan northeast region; and Kathak from the Gangetic planes of North India. Regardless of their origins, the traditional way of learning these traditional dances, was through *śruti* and *smriti*, where students were expected to retain the traditional teachings in their mind through repetition and practice.

The Role of the Guru

Practitioners of Odissi believe that simply following the grammatical structure is not enough for learning the art of Odissi. Although thorough, meticulous, and explicit in its description of how the dance should be performed, the *Abhinaya Darpana* is rarely used as a manual. Students do not typically learn directly from primary source texts; the traditional pedagogy of Indian classical dance depends upon the accuracy with which each guru can demonstrate it to a learner. Learning in the *guru-shishya* tradition involves complete surrendering to the guru and absorbing the knowledge of the guru in one's self. The role of the guru is vital in the learning of this dance because of the rhetorical interpretation of the dance that the guru provides to the disciple. The guru would sit in front of the class and sing the *bols* (or the counts) chant on the time cycle and sometimes play on the *mardala* or the drums. The guru would then demonstrate one piece of a composition several times and ask disciples to repeat the same piece closely more than fifty times. Here, the teacher interprets and enacts the meaning-making imagery in the verses; eventually, students are able to perform the entire dance from memory. Thus, repetition is key to teaching and learning.

There have been some adaptations in the pedagogical process and one major adaptation is the inclusion of digital tools as way to learning. Using digital tools has reduced the need for

---

126. In Sanskrit, "Natya" means drama and "Shastra" means scriptures. The idea of writing under the guidance of mythical Gods and demi-gods might means that Bharatmuni was invoking them as he wrote this text.

127. Vatsyayan 1996, 2.

students to chant for memorization, allowing students to record the dance piece they wish to learn instead of undergoing the traditional demands of repeating a piece several times in order to etch the movements into one's muscle memory. This new method makes adaptation possible, although it is met with resistance. Traditional practitioners want to ensure that adaptation does not spoil the authenticity of the art. In a conversation with Gangadhar Pradhan, one of India's most renowned Odissi teachers until his death in 2010,[128] I asked guru Pradhan whether a student could learn a dance by following the steps in a video or reading from a textbook.[129] Pradhan was skeptical of any tool (whether ancient sculptures or verses or digital recordings) replacing the centrality of the guru. According to Pradhan, the guru is an artist who needs to be "awake" at all times when interacting with students. They are responsible for transmitting traditions from one generation to the next, and therefore must advise, teach, and remember what is traditional. Only in the last fifty years or so have gurus seen the sculptures on the thousand-year-old stone temple walls, researched them, and used them to perfect the poses. In fact, most veteran practitioners and gurus made no conscious effort to research or link their practice with the *Shastras* (Sanskrit verses), arguing instead that the dance originated from nature.

To illustrate his point, Pradhan demonstrated an *abhinaya*, or expressional dance piece, depicting a series of *bhavas* (moods of the heroine). Then he connected the natural movements of the *alasa* (the languorous stretching of the body when the heroine is tired of waiting in her bed chambers) to the sculptural depictions of the same pose, to show that Odissi was a body language already imbibed in verses, sculptures, and natural body movements—it already communicated a complex storyline. In that same conversation he argued the importance of studying Odissi's grammatical system guided by the guru: "You cannot learn Odissi without thorough practice under a guru. It is not the same as learning dance pieces. That is not Odissi learning." To Pradhan, dancing a series of poses was not the true meaning of imbibing the art of Odissi oneself. Maguni Das, a veteran guru of *gotipua* (an acrobatic limb of Odissi dance style), shared Pradhan's opinions about the relevance and importance of the guru when interpreting the texts in the treatise.[130] He stated in a 2008 interview that "the Guru needs to help students understand not only the dance but also the rich tradition that comes with it that determines what is proper and what is not." The guru must reveal its metaphorical significance. After that, the essence of this esoteric art form takes years to fully master.

Prickett has critiqued this process, using terms such as "serfdom," which could imply that, in such a relationship, the *shishya* (disciple) is expected to replicate the learning without doubting the guru.[131] I argue that this is not an accurate representation of this tradition. Indeed,

---

128. To understand how Odissi was being taught and to learn more about the role of the guru in the teaching and learning, I surveyed and interviewed thirty novice and seasoned practitioners of the art. Documenting and analyzing those conversations richly informed the process for my inquiry into the pedagogic methods actually followed by several dancers across the world.

129. Pradhan 2008.

130. Das 2008.

131. Prickett 2007, 29.

in the relationship between the guru and the student, there is space for questioning, as the critical and choreographic abilities of the student are developed throughout the process of learning. By creating embodied meaning out of the classical rhetorical canons provided by the treatise of dramaturgy and performance, gurus reveal in the disciples the awareness of the rhetorical capacity of the body. The gurus not only encourage disciples to explore and to develop expertise in the rhetorical and performative functions of the static and moving body but also to create more meaningful interpretations out of these functions delineated in the texts. Students are first expected to learn the traditions before exploring and adding to them. As well, light modifications and re-interpretations add richness to the art with every passing generation. Every student is a future guru; thus, the act of learning, chanting, embodying, repeating, and memorizing is very important. Once the teacher has instilled the understanding of the verses in the student, the student enacts a personal response to the verses. However, to make innovative interpretations, the practitioner is expected to accrue enough learning of the traditional standard interpretation of the verses. A classical Indian artist (dancer or musician) is known by his or her intellectual lineage or *gharana*. That knowledge in turn determines the stylistic nuances of their artistic performance. The teacher, in all cases, is at the center of the pedagogic act in the Indian rhetorical tradition of classical dance.

In describing her experience of learning Odissi as a foreigner and newcomer to Indian culture, Schnepel argues that it is more important to internalize the meanings of the verses that describe the gestures and style of the dance than to memorize them.[132] This is an important perspective coming from an adult learner who was making conscious decisions of the method of learning and reflecting upon them. This is different from the pedagogic tradition of younger students who spend years and years repeating the movements until they are naturally internalized. In this context, Archana Kanungo makes an interesting connection of the imbibing of the body movements of the dance to tantric mapping of the movements on a body. She writes, "For the dancer using Odissi as a long-term body discipline, the tantric body map provides a path to an integration of the 'body-mind-consciousness' complex through dance, that is well entrenched in time tested systems of yoga."[133]

Furthermore, in "Contestations: Constructing a Historical Narrative for Odissi," dance scholar Ananya Chatterjea bases her study on a similar interview and conversations, acknowledging Odissi gurus and scholars, such as Kelucharan Mahapatra, Sanjukta Panigrahi, Raghunath Panigrahi, Kapila Vatsyana, Bhagirathi Das (an Odissi dress maker) and "other dancers and students of Odissi."[134] These conversations reveal the history of dance from a variety of perspectives, transmitted as they are to these interviewees by generations prior. To me, the historical accuracy of these stories is less important in this context than the traditional memory that shapes the value system of the present generation of artists. The sense of trust that the learner has when they accept the interpretation of the grammatical texts channelized through the guru is foundational in the continuity of this tradition.

---

132. Schnepel 2009, 190.
133. Kanungo 2013.
134. Chatterjea 2007, 154.

TRANSLATION AND COMMENTARY

In this next section, I use my findings from these conversations to translate several verses from the *Natyashastra*. Specifically, I perform a critical and interpretative translation of extracts from the second- and third-century CE dramaturgical work *Abhinaya Darpana* by Nadikesvara. *"Abhinaya Darpana"* literally means "Mirror of Expressions" in Sanskrit, and it was written in the form of Sanskrit verses to help students repeat, memorize, and learn. It is a treatise of Indian dramatic art that explains how meanings are made through the movement or combinations of movements of the eyes, hands, feet, mouth, and torso (Figure 4.4).

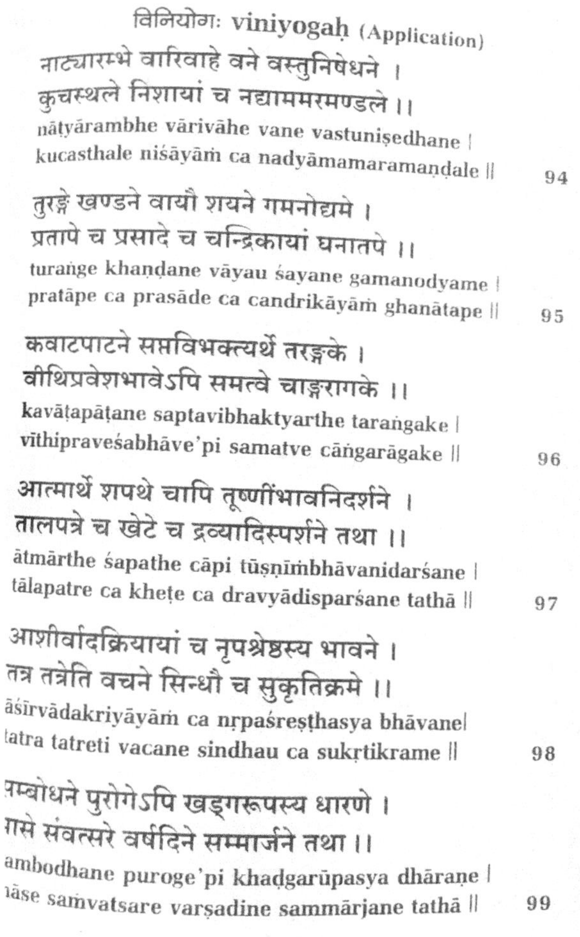

विनियोगः viniyogaḥ (Application)

नाट्यारम्भे वारिवाहे वने वस्तुनिषेधने ।
कुचस्थले निशायां च नद्याममरमण्डले ॥
nātyārambhe vārivāhe vane vastuniṣedhane |
kucasthale niśāyāṁ ca nadyāmamaramaṇḍale || 94

तुरङ्गे खण्डने वायौ शयने गमनोद्यमे ।
प्रतापे च प्रसादे च चन्द्रिकायां घनातपे ॥
turaṅge khaṇḍane vāyau śayane gamanodyame |
pratāpe ca prasāde ca candrikāyāṁ ghanātape || 95

कवाटपाटने सप्तविभक्त्यर्थे तरङ्गके ।
वीथिप्रवेशभावेऽपि समत्वे चाङ्गरागके ॥
kavāṭapāṭane saptavibhaktyarthe taraṅgake |
vīthipraveśabhāve'pi samatve cāṅgarāgake || 96

आत्मार्थे शपथे चापि तूष्णींभावनिदर्शने ।
तालपत्रे च खेटे च द्रव्यादिस्पर्शने तथा ॥
ātmārthe śapathe cāpi tūṣṇīṁbhāvanidarśane |
tālapatre ca kheṭe ca dravyādisparśane tathā || 97

आशीर्वादक्रियायां च नृपश्रेष्ठस्य भावने ।
तत्र तत्रेति वचने सिन्धौ च सुकृतिक्रमे ॥
āśīrvādakriyāyāṁ ca nṛpaśreṣṭhasya bhāvane|
tatra tatreti vacane sindhau ca sukṛtikrame || 98

सम्बोधने पुरोगेऽपि खड्गरूपस्य धारणे ।
गासे संवत्सरे वर्षदिने सम्मार्जने तथा ॥
ambodhane puroge'pi khaḍgarūpasya dhāraṇe |
āse saṁvatsare varṣadine sammārjane tathā || 99

Figure 4.4: This is the original Sanskrit verses describing the uses of the hand gesture, *pataka*. This is from *Abhinaya Darpanam*, translated by Manmohan Ghosh. Photograph by Shreelina Ghosh.[135]

135. Ghosh 1957, 88.

The passage I have chosen in Figure 4.4 describes the various uses of the *hasta mudra* (hand gesture) *pataka*. *Pataka* is the first and simplest of the twenty-eight *asamyuta hastas* (one-hand) and twenty-four *samyuta hastas* (two-hand gestures) in classical dance. Each hand gesture has verses to explain its several meanings and uses. In addition to the *hasta mudras*, verses also depict the use of the *drishti bhedas* (eyes), the *pada bheda* (feet), and *griva bheda* (neck). The texts also explain how the dancer should conduct herself or himself, describe the space of performance, or depict different deities, castes, and planets.

Figure 4.5: Uses of the *pataka* single-hand gesture; L: *Natyarambhe*, which signals the beginning of the dance; M: *Nishedhane* (to say no); R: *Khandane* (act of cutting forcefully). All photographs courtesy of Shreelina Ghosh.

The Sanskrit verses are a series of words or concepts that the *pataka* can depict. In the traditional way of Vedic teaching and learning, these verses are interpreted by the teacher and repeated several times by the students until they are memorized. In short, the students chant and interpret the meanings enacted by the teacher. I attempt to translate the meanings from the original Sanskrit so that students of my generation may better understand how the traditional memory of the practice is inscribed and preserved through text:

> Beginning of the dance, cloud, forest, to dissuade,
> Chest, night, river, and the heaven.
> Horse, cutting forcibly, the wind, sleep, prepare to go,
> Power and compassion, moonlight and sunlight.
> Open doors, make seven divisions of something, waves,
> To enter, to level a surface, apply color on the body.
> Self, take an oath, silence,

Palm leaf and shield, to touch things.
To bless, the greatest king,
To say here and there, the sea, good deeds.
To address, to follow, to hold a sword,
Month and year, a rainy day, to massage.
These are various uses of the Pataka gesture.

Here is the breakdown of the gestures as they appear chronologically in this verse:

- *Natyarambha* signals the beginning of the dance. Here, the Odissi begins with the basic posture of *Chowka* (square posture) (Figure 4.5L). This is followed by *Varivahe*, the Cloud or bearer of water. Here the guru explains how the *pataka* denotes the rising movement of the water vapor and then settling in the sky as cloud. Then follows the *Vane* (forest). At this point, the *pataka* shows the shapes of tall and pointed trees. *Vastunishedhane* means "to say no," thus the oscillating movement of the hand is accompanied by the nodding of one's head as if to say "no" (Figure 4.5M). Finally, *Kuchasthale* is a posture shown to depict two breasts. Here, the *pataka* can either be placed on the chest or can show a curved movement in front of the chest to denote the shape of the breast. This posture represents both the sensuality of the dancer and the maternal image of the Mother Goddess.
- Additional verses contain insight into other postures. *Nisha* means "the night." For that posture, the palm faces outwards as the darker side of the hand is towards the dancer depicting night.
- For *nadi* (the river), the shape of the meandering river is depicted with both hands. The *pataka* can also be used to show the waves of the river.
- The *amaramandale* refers to the celestial abode. For this posture, the *pataka* hand is held upwards, and the wrists are rotated outwards to show the heavens.
- *Turange* is a horse, and its *pataka* is accompanied by the eye movement denoting speed.
- In *Khandane*, the *pataka hasta* strikes and cuts something with a forceful movement (Figure 4.5R). This rule of the *pataka hasta* makes it the ideal gesture to denote swordplay during combat scenes in story reenactments.
- To depict *Vayu* (or wind), the *pataka hasta* vibrates subtly and moves diagonally to depict the slow movement of the breeze.
- In *Shayane*, the dancer shows the sleeping pose with their head resting on the *pataka hasta*.
- In *Gamanodyame*, the *pataka hasta* shows the direction where the dancer is intending to move.
- The next two gestures make sense only when they are accompanied by facial expressions. In *pratapa*, the facial expression of valor is accompanied by the *pataka* hand movement showing an upward heightening of status. Sometimes the tremor of the hand with dramatic and exaggerated eye movement can be used to show ex-

treme valor. And in *prasada*, a compassionate expression with the *pataka* hand depicts benediction.

- *Chandhrika* means moon and its light, and it is depicted with the left *pataka* hand shows the moon and the right moves diagonally while trembling slightly to depict the gentle moonlight. The same gesture of *pataka* moves from the serene moonlight to the depiction of scorching heat on *ghanathape*, where the expression of discomfort is also accompanied by the act of shying away from the strong sunlight.
- In *kavatapatane*, the *pataka* hands are shown to close or open a door.
- *Saptavibhaktyarthe* means seven divisions are being made with the act of chopping with a *pataka hasta*.
- In *taranga*, the hand moves in such a way as to depict the motion of the waves. *Pravesha* is entering somewhere with the hand depicting the path of the movement.
- *Samatva* is the act of leveling of something with the two *pataka* hands.
- *Angaragake* is applying something on one's body using the *pataka* hand. In dance, we may use it to depict the act of applying sandalwood on one's own body.
- *Atmarthe* is putting the *pataka* hand on one's chest as if to say "I." There is a subtle variation in expression where the *pataka* hand is placed on one's chest to depict the act of making a promise for *shapate*. Or the *pataka* can also be held out palm facing toward the person to whom the promise is being made.
- *Tushnebhava* is when the *pataka* hand is placed on one's lips to depict silence or asking someone to be quiet.
- *Ashirvada* is when the *pataka* hand gestures the act of blessing.
- *Nripashreshta* is denoted by the hand placed over the head, palm facing outward to depict a crown. The gesture is that of the greatest king.
- *Talapatra* is depicted by placing the *pataka* hand in front of the dancer to show the palm leaf. The dancer can write on the leaf or read from it to make its significance clearer.
- *Khete* also is shown with the hand in front of the dancer but this time the palm faces outward to depict a shield.
- In *dravyadisparshane*, *pataka* is shown as being used to touch different things. *Tatra Tatrapi Vachane* means "this and that" or "here and there." The *pataka* hand is accompanied by eye movements to make this meaning.
- *Sindhou* is an extensive body of water (sea or ocean) that can be shown using the *pataka* gesture.
- *Sukriti krame* is when the *pataka* hasta depicts the dancer's approval of someone's good work.
- In *sambodhane*, the *pataka* is pointed to someone to depict the act of addressing or calling that person.
- *Purogepi* is the *pataka hasta* held in a way to show the way when the dancer is entering a city.

- In *kharga rupasya dharane*, the *pataka gesture* with an extended hand diagonally held up depicts a sword ready to engage in combat.
- Both hands held in *pataka* gesture are maneuvered to depict the rise and setting of the sun to show the length of time in *mase, samvathsare*. The two tremoring *pataka* hands further move downwards from above to show the rain falling from the sky. The movement is repeated several times to depict a rainy day, or *varshadine*. In *samarajane*, the *pataka* hand depicts the act of sweeping. For instance, the heroine awaiting the arrival of her beloved sweeps the floor before spreading petals.

These are some of the various ways in which *pataka* is used. Usually, Odissi dancers do not change the way these gestures are performed when copying their gurus, as the rules of the hand movements, the neck movements, and so on, constitute the basic grammar that is recognized by all classical Indian dancers. However, although the foundational grammar is the same, the verses are interpreted differently in different classical dance forms of India. For instance, the *pataka* hand gesture is used both in Odissi and in Bharatanatyam (another classical dance style) to show waves or *tarangake*. Yet in Odissi, the wave is shown with both hands moving up and down in a wave-like motion from left to right, while in Bharatanatyam, the hands tremble and move in a circular downward rotating movement of the hand showing the waves. The grammar of the dance is fundamental to all classical dances, but each dance-style is unique in how it applies the grammar differently.

As well, if these ancient meaning-making practices are being used to convey a contemporary theme, then the established grammar may be adapted to reflect the contemporary theme in an acceptable way. For instance, *pataka* can depict a laptop computer as a contemporary writing device, in place of the traditional palm leaf. Or *pataka* can depict an airplane if the script of the dance requires that representation. The verses in the treatise remain unchanged and the foundational grammar does not deviate from what was traditionally taught and learned, yet this thousand-year-old classical art is often imbibed with modern representations to remain relevant in every age.

ROOTEDNESS AND BRANCHING OUT

For about two thousand years, the *guru-shishya* method kept the tradition alive. Gurus adapted their teaching method following the way they learned. Prominent dancer and teacher of the current generation, Rahul Acharya, opined in an interview, "the treaties on dance talk about the grammar and performance . . . none of them focuses [sic] on the teaching methodology. The idea is, this is the book of instructions; develop your own method of teaching."[136] The basis of the learning method was the unquestioned reverence of the guru. Yet, times have changed, and the dance is no longer a sacred esoteric practice conducted at the residence of the guru. The dance is often taught through technology, and often collaboratively. Stu-

---

136. Acharya 2018.

dents are more exposed to the practices and styles of the art across the world. The traditional practitioners of the dance support and encourage the adaptations of the dance as long as the traditional values like sacredness and the reverence for the guru remain fundamental and un-spoiled in these practices. It is expected that traditions will be preserved when these learnings are subsequently presented in front of people. Any changes are expected to be thoroughly vetted and guided by the guru in order to maintain authenticity.[137]

Critical re-interpretation of the traditions and innovation are encouraged once a level of expertise achieved by the practitioners of the art. An understanding of where to stretch to boundaries and where to stop comes from the sense of responsibility that is passed down by the guru along with the knowledge of the art itself. Indeed, it is the balanced negotiation of tradition and adaptation that helps Indian classical dance to survive—repetition of the origi-nal etches the traditional meaning of practice, while modifications of the sacred are meant to improve respectfully upon the traditions without diminishing their significance.

As a cornerstone of Eastern rhetorical pedagogy, the *guru-shishya* tradition of teaching offers insight into the values of respect, sacredness, and responsible adaptation of art forms beyond dance. Practitioners of Odissa dance protect it intently, not because they want it to remain an esoteric practice for a privileged few but because they understand that each minute gesture of the dancer, each slight movement of the eyelid or the twitching of the cheek mus-cle, is a powerful signifier in the historical tradition. In turn, I offer this rhetorical discussion of *patakas* not as a doctrine of how things ought to be but as a reference for understanding this pedagogical tradition rhetorically. Although there is no primary text that carries explicit instruction in how to teach this art, the pedagogy of the dance, like the dance itself, can be transmitted from one generation to the next.

---

137. Kumar 2013, 18.

4.3 Indian-Logical, c. 200 CE, Ancient India

Rhetorical Commentary on Book 1, Chapter 1 of the *Nyāya Sūtra,* Trans. S. S. Vidyabhusana

Keith Lloyd

INTRODUCTION

The ancient Indian philosophy, *Nyāya,* one of six recognized orthodox Hindu schools of thought, finds full expression in the *Nyāya Sūtra* (न्याय सूत्र). Its influential methods were adopted by Buddhists, Jains, and Muslims. Nyāya-like arguments appear in Indian literature from the Ancient *Upaniṣads*[138] to the modern activist Ambedkar. Translator S. S. Vidyabhusana suggests that the philosophy began with *Medhātithi* Gotama in the sixth century BCE and was codified by Akṣapāda Gotama in the second century CE.[139] Its methods were adopted by other schools of Hindu thought such as *Vaiśeṣika, Mīmāṃsā,* and *Sāṃkhya.*

Nyāya allied itself to the Hindu Vaiśeṣika epistemological and metaphysical system, tying logic and reasoning to liberation, *mokṣa,* from the cycles of death and rebirth. The *Nyāya Sūtra* contains 528 brief aphoristic *sūtra* (सूत्र "threads") in five books of two chapters each, and covers epistemology, reason, logic, debate, and metaphysics. The first book introduces sixteen "categories" of knowledge, pathways leading interlocutors to liberation from false knowledge and cycles of rebirth.

Nyāya philosophy developed as a Brahminical logical and philosophical tradition, but due to European curiosity and Colonialism, beginning in the nineteenth century its principles have become more widely known, especially among philosophers interested in "Eastern" philosophies.[140] Unlike Aristotle's *Rhetoric,* which identifies rhetoric as an art rather than a science,[141] it grounds rhetorical theory in epistemology; the *Sūtra* describes both *Tarka-Vidya,* the science of debate, and *Vada-Vidya,* the science of discussion. Though still predominantly studied by comparative philosophers, it also potentially expands rhetorical studies well beyond Greco-Roman traditions.[142]

Since Nyāya and Aristotelian philosophy emerged somewhat in tandem, this chapter references Aristotle's *Rhetoric* for contrast. In Aristotle's view, rhetoric concerns modes of per-

---

138. The diacritical ṣ and ś are both "sh" sounds. A line over the vowel indicates lengthening. ṃ nasalizes the preceding vowel. To pronounce ṇ roll the tongue back, as in the word *noun.* The ṛ sounds like the r in occur.

139. Vidyabhusana 1920 and 1988, 27.

140. Ganeri 1996, 4.

141. Aristotle 2004, 9.

142. Lloyd 2013, 285–299; Lloyd 2007b, 19–42; Lloyd 2007a, 365–384.

suasion.[143] Many arguments today exhibit Aristotelian patterns, and "Aristotle [remains] a highly influential source of modern argumentation theory."[144] Similarly, Nyāya-type arguments appear in all sorts of Indian arguments.[145] Though rooted in practical argumentation, Nyāya became the domain of select scholars and keepers of Indian traditions. Commentaries over the centuries, including those by Vātsyāyana (c. 450–500 CE), traditionally published in parallel with the sūtras, Uddyotakāra's *Nyāyavārttika* (c. sixth through seventh centuries CE), Vācaspati Miśra's *Tātparyatīkā* (ninth century CE), Udayana's *Tātparyapariśuddhi* (tenth century CE), and Jayanta's *Nyāyamañjarī* (tenth century), made the philosophy ever more exacting and refined.

In his book *Uses of Argument*, philosopher Stephen Toulmin pointed out that, at the time of his writing, "formal logic has indeed lost touch with its application."[146] Similarly, though elements of the sixteen categories are related to medical diagnosis in the second century CE *Caraka-Saṃhitā*, Nyāya philosophy dislodged from practical reasoning. Vidyabhusana regrets that instead of reaching "perfection," it became a "parasite" of "religious dogma" and "alaṅkāra"[147] ("rhetoric;" lit. "decoration"). Taking rhetoric to mean *how we frame what we say* rather than *ornamentation*, this commentary suggests that Nyāya is best understood as emerging from practical reasoning within a Hindu context. Respectful of this deep tradition, I extend Nyāya's relevance as sensitively to its origins as possible by approaching the text in a Hindu manner, through an explication of the Sūtras and an exposition of its etymologies.

The Indian terminologies, as will be illustrated below, provide rich insights into fresh ways to interpret rhetoric, audience, the role of the rhetor—virtually every aspect of the "rhetorical situation." The field of rhetoric, too often locked into Greek and Latin terms and concepts, cannot help but benefit from these alternate terminologies and perspectives.

SOURCES

The following commentaries are based upon *The Nyāya Sūtras of Gotama*, translated by Mahamahopadhyaya Satista Chandra Vidyabhusana.[148] This is the most authoritative translation to date, and I know of no author who refers to the Sūtras who does not use this translation, referencing Vidyabhusana's translation exactly. The book includes the original Sanskrit text

---

143. Aristotle 2004, 5.
144. Rapp and Wagner 2013, 7–30.
145. Lloyd 2018, 18–21; Lloyd 2013, 295–298.
146. Toulmin 2003, 8.
147. Vidyabhusana 1920 and 1988, xix.
148. Published by the Panini Office, Bhuvane & Wari Asrama, Bahadurganj, Kishanganj district, Bihar, India. The book was originally printed by Apurya Krishna Boss at the Indian press in 1913, and it is available for free use online at archive.org. Some of the text may need to be reformatted, depending on the program used to open it.

with individual translations of all terms[149] in Alphabetic Diacritics, English translations of the Sūtras, and commentaries from Vātsyāyana (c. 450–500 CE), considered the first and most significant commentator of the Sūtras. Because the Sūtras are difficult to understand without commentary, readers will notice that Vātsyāyana's remarks are interspersed in all modern translations. Thus, Nyāya scholars commonly reference him as something like a second author.

TRANSLATION AND COMMENTARIES

Commentary on Vātsyāyana's Translation of Book I, Chapter 1

Nyāya (न्याय) basically means "justice" or right reasoning. The Sūtras in this chapter, identified in full except where noted, explain how to reason in a just manner. However, in this context debate, and even justice, differ from the usual English terms. The Sūtra tells us that most human beings live in a state of sleep—*saṁśaya* (*samaiti* "same" and *śaya* "sleep"). Debate and reasoning, rightly conducted, create a state of wakefulness in the interlocutors, almost as if Aristotle, instead of defining rhetoric as "the art of finding the best available means of persuasion," had defined it as "the art of finding the best available means of *enlightenment*." It is a *philosophical rhetoric*.

Through the study and application of the sixteen categories, persons living in a state of illusion and *doṣa* (meaning both "doubt" and "sleep"), can use its methods to accurately perceive the world, accurately make inferences and comparisons, and stop embodying the actions of sleeping person—getting caught up in fear, desire, and ignorance. While Aristotle calls justice one of several "excellences of the soul,"[150] he notes that "Justice is the virtue through which everybody enjoys his own possessions in accordance with the law."[151] On this point, in contrast, Nyāya philosophy differentiates itself with an alternate sense of "justice," which is neither about possession nor an abstract legal construct but rather an accurate method for interpreting reality that can benefit all humanity. As Amartya Sen remarks in his book, *The Idea of Justice*, the term Nyāya refers to "realized justice,"[152] which differs from *niti*, "dreaming about achieving—some perfectly just society or social arrangements." Nyāya, in contrast, is "about preventing manifestly severe injustice."[153]

---

149. Definitions for Sanskrit terms are based in the text and checked through the website *spokensanskrit.de*. A secondary base of comparison is *Vedabase.net*.

150. Aristotle 2004, 26.

151. Aristotle 2004, 38.

152. Sen 2009, 20.

153. Sen 2009. See for instance, "Rhetoric and Social Justice" 2016.

Book I, Chapter 1, Sūtras One through Forty-One

Sūtras One and Two

1. Supreme felicity is attained by the knowledge about the true nature of sixteen categories, viz., means of right knowledge (*pramāṇa*), object of right knowledge (*prameya*), doubt (*saṁśaya*), purpose (*prayojana*), familiar instance (*dṛṣṭānta*), established tenet (*siddhānta*), members (*avayava*), confutation (*tarka*), ascertainment (*nirṇaya*), discussion (*vāda*), wrangling (*jalpa*), cavil (*vitanda*), fallacy (*hetvābhāsa*), quibble (*chala*), futility (*jati*), and occasion for rebuke (*nigrahasthana*).

2. Pain, birth, activity, faults and misapprehension — on the successive annihilation of these in the reverse order, there follows release.

The first Sūtra outlines the sixteen "categories," which not only define terms but progressively explain how to use the five-part method of reasoning, the *avayava* (identified in Sūtra 32), to liberate oneself from ignorance, fear, and fruitless desires. The "categories," *padārthas* (literally पद् pad "foot" + artas अर्थ "sense"), would be better translated as "correct pathways." The list begins with how we know, the *pramana* (pra परा "before" + mana मन "mind"), then offers what we should think about, the *prameya* (अर्थ experiential "knowledge").

The beginning of reasoning is doubt, *saṁśaya* (संशय "same sleep"), which provokes the rhetor to seek potential answers through similar instances, *dṛṣṭānta* (दृष्टान्त lit. "seeing stance") and through what is already known, *siddhānta*, "tenets" (सिद्धान्त lit. "point of instruction" (i.e., "doctrines, rules, theories, axioms").

The first six terms lead to the seventh category, the *avayava* (अवयव), "members" (literally "of a body") or the five-part method of reasoning central to Nyāya described in Sūtra 32. The rest of the terms contextualize debate using the five-part method. It proceeds through argumentation or speculation, *tarka* (तर्क), if-then reasoning which results in ascertainment, *nirnaya* (निर्णय "create a proper fit"). Reasoned dialogue can take three forms: *vada* (वद) or fruitful "discussion;" "wrangling," *jalpa* (जल्प lit. "chatter"), arguing only to win; "cavil," *vitanda* (वितण्डा "frivolous"), arguing only against. The rhetor should understand them all, but *vada* is preferred because the most fruitful.

The rest of the terms are related to logical "fallacies," a misleading Latin term. While formal logic allows valid arguments that are not necessarily true, Nyāya rhetoric defines failed arguments as those that lack real-world application. *Hetvabhasa* (हेत्वाभास) is rooted in *hetu* (हेतु) "reason," and literally means "appearance of reason." "Quibble (*chala* छल) "shaking") is arguing just to argue. "Futility" (*jati* जाति "self-refuting reply"), arguing when one clearly has no basis for their reasoning, is often mistranslated as "sophisticated reasoning," aligning Nyāya with Plato's negative critique of the Sophists.

Hetvabhasa, what is untrue, unjust, leads to "occasion for rebuke," *nigrahasthana* (निग्रहस्थान) (i.e., being told one has lost the argument and interlocutors have failed to come to agreement).

Sthana (सूतन) is related to the English word *stand* and *nigraha* (निग्रह) means something like "weak" or "defeated."

Though the debate may be framed in traditional for and against positions, the goal here is *vada*, finding fruitful solutions agreeable to all (see notes below on contents of Chapter 2). Nyāya rhetoric is disciplined dialogic focusing, inferencing, and comparing, aligned with sifting of motives and testing, intent on just and fruitful outcomes. Rhetoric, from this perspective, is deeply reflective and highly engaged in discovering equitable and sharable perspectives and solutions.

As the second Sūtra indicates, though the five-part Nyāya method can be used on its own, the Sūtra aligns the rhetor's motive in with Hindu/Vedic belief in reincarnation. Nyāya holds that the world exists (is not an illusion, *maya*, as in Buddhists and some Hindu schools). We can nonetheless be blind to reality because of desire, fear, or ignorance, "misapprehension"—a state of darkness or *doṣa* (दोषा), often translated as "fault." Nyāya's sixteen pathways open the door to *mokṣa* (मोक्ष), a state of liberation from desire, fear, and ignorance, which leads to liberation from death and rebirth.

Sūtras Three through Eight

3. Perception, inference, comparison and word (verbal testimony) — these are the means of knowledge.

4. Perception [prātyakṣa प्रत्यक्ष "manifest"] is that knowledge which arises from the contact of a sense with its object and which is determinate, unnameable and non-erratic.

5. Inference [anumāna अनुमान] is knowledge which is preceded by perception, and is of three kinds, viz., *a priori*, *a posteriori* and commonly seen.

6. Comparison [upamāna उपमान] is the knowledge of a thing through its similarity to another thing previously well known.

7. Word [*śabda* शब्द-] is the instructive assertion of a reliable person.

8. It is of two kinds, viz., that which refers to matter which is seen and that which refers to matter which is not seen.

In the third Sūtra, Nyāya begins with the ultimate epistemological question: how do we know anything? Obviously, our primary knowledge comes from perception, *prātyakṣa* (प्रत्यक्ष). Beyond immediate sensory input, we make inferences, *anumāna* (अनुमान), like when we conclude it is raining outside when we see wet tracks on the floor by a doorway, and comparisons, *upamāna* (उपमान), like when we conclude that a strange animal in front of us is similar enough to a known animal to be of the same species. Since much of what we know comes through the words of others, Nyāya encourages us to follow "authoritative" words, *śabda* (शब्द

literally "sound"), words of the learned and insightful, those who used Nyāya processes to settle previous inquiries.

Interestingly, the root of both inference and comparison is the word *māna*, or "mind." As illustrated in Table 4.1, while perception enlightens the whole being, inference and comparison are products of the mind.

Table 4.1: Perception, Inference, and Comparison

Derivation	Root	Derivation	Derivation	Root
perception		*inference*	*comparison*	
prātyakṣa		anumāna	upamāna	
prāt	yakṣa	anu	upa	māna
give light	spirit/being	below	above	mind

According to the fourth Sūtra, perception, *pratyakṣa* is generally reliable because it is testable, identifying Nyāya as a practical philosophy. Knowledge, rightly perceived, is "determinate," "unnamable," and "consistent." In noting that perception should be "unnamable," Nyāya acknowledges that humans may use words unproductively, or as tools of liberation, but ultimately, the world itself remains "nameless."

Vātsyāyana describes "indeterminate knowledge," like when one "from a distance cannot ascertain whether there is smoke or dust," and "non-erratic perception" such as a mirage when "the sun's rays" react with "earthly heat" as illusions rather than perceptions, which must be "non-erratic." The implication here is important rhetorically. From its beginnings, rhetoric has been about what Fairbanks and others call "fact, value, or policy." [154] For Nyāya, valid perceptions are based in evidence, and readily apply to all modes of reasoning.

Sūtra five identifies inference as "knowledge which is preceded by perception," whether *pūrvavat* (पूर्ववत्, cause to effect), *śeṣavat* (शेषवत्, effect to cause), or "commonly seen" (root: nana नाना many dṛṣṭa दृष्ट seen." Vātsyāyana redundantly adds the Latin *"a priori,"* like when "one seeing clouds infers that there will be rain;" *"a posteriori,"* as when "one seeing a river swollen infers that there was rain;" *"commonly seen"* he likens to when "one seeing a beast possessing horns, infers that it possesses also a tail, or one seeing smoke on a hill infers that there is fire on it." The exemplar of the smoke/fire/hearth used to teach the five-part Nyāya method is of the third type. Rhetors use these kinds of inference to create arguments from fact and for analogical arguments. Rhetors also use inference to fill in what may be missing in arguments, as in Aristotle's enthymeme.

Anyone trying to explain new ideas ultimately relies on comparison, the sixth Sūtra. Teachers apply new material to previous material; effective paragraphs and sentences move from what is established to what is proposed. Comparison is also the basis of metaphor,

---

154. Fairbanks 1994.

which Lakoff and Johnson, in their book *Metaphors We Live By*,[155] suggest is the basis of all human conceptualization.

Sūtra seven identifies the fourth and last means of knowledge, the words of a "reliable person," whom Vātsyāyana notes "may be a *risi*, Arya or *mleccha*, who as an expert in a certain matter is willing to communicate his experiences of it." A *ṛṣi* (ऋषि) is a "seer," sage," "ascetic." An *Arya* (आर्य) is a "wise and honorable person," and also the root of "Aryan." Surprising is his inclusion of "*mleccha*," (म्लेच्छ), Non-Aryan, outcast, foreigner, etc. Though formally taught only to Brahmin caste, Nyāya is inherently egalitarian in this respect. For rhetors, this Sūtra emphasizes that valid perspectives may come from all types of people.

Sūtra eight identifies two types of *śabda*, reliable testimony, seen and unseen (i.e., through our own observations, or through tested inferences). Though Nyāya values *siddhānta* (सिद्धान्त), established "tenets," it also recognizes that such teachings must be based in shareable perceptions and inferences, whether from *risi*, *Arya*, or *mleccha*.

These Sūtras lay the groundwork for the Nyāya method, the seventh category (Sūtra 32). Through perceptions, inferences, comparisons and the tested words of others, we create statements, reasons, and analogical examples in support of particular interpretations. This equates rhetorical reasoning with all human reasoning; rhetoric is essential to human life.

Sūtras Nine through Sixteen

9. Soul, body, senses, objects of sense, intellect, mind, activity, fault, transmigration, fruit, pain and release — are the objects of right knowledge.

10. Desire, aversion, volition, pleasure, pain and intelligence are the marks of the soul.

11. Body is the site of gesture, senses and sentiments.

12. Nose, tongue, eye, skin and ear are the senses produced from elements.

13. Earth, water, light, air and ether — these are the elements.

14. Smell, taste, colour, touch and sound are objects of the senses and qualities of the earth, etc.

15. Intellect, apprehension and knowledge — these are not different from one another.

16. The mark of the mind is that there do not arise (in the soul) more acts of knowledge than one at a time.

Since the list of objects of right knowledge in the ninth Sūtra includes the senses, intellect and mind, valid perceptions may be external or internal. In line with Vaiśeṣika philosophy, "soul," *atman* (आत्मन्), is the individual form of the universal all-soul Brahman. The feminine root of the word translated "intellect" *buddhi* (बुद्धि), *budh* (बुध), means to be "awake." Thus, a Buddhi is an awakened one. Mental activities can be purposeful, but without con-

---

155. Lakoff and Johnson 1980 and 2003.

sciousness. Unless our "activities" are those of a person who is awake, they are fruitless. That is why fruit, *phala* (फल), activity, *pravritti* (फल), and transmigration, *pretyabhāva* (प्रेत्यभाव literally "rebirth"), are categories for reflection foundational to Nyāya's purpose, to become liberated from "doubt," *duḥkha* (दु:ख literally "pain"), create karmic fruit, and find "release," *mokṣa* (मोक्ष). From this perspective, rhetors are called upon to rise above their minds, to have a greater awareness of the world, to reason from *atman* (आत्मन्), from a state of being awake, connected with the Self, in a way that sparks awake-ness in our interlocutors.

In the tenth Sūtra, "marks," *liṅgam*, means "origin," or "source," and is used here to mean "sign." While Descartes notably said, "I think, therefore I am," this Sūtra implies that we desire, therefore we exist, we feel pain, therefore we exist, etc.

Sūtras eleven through fourteen align Nyāya with the ancient view that the world is made up of five elements: earth, water, light, air and ether. Vatsyāyana associates the senses and elements: "Smell is the object of nose and the prominent quality of earth, taste is the object of tongue and quality of water, color is the object of eye and quality of light, touch is the object of skin and quality of air, and sound is the object of ear and quality of ether."[156] "Sound" *śabda* (शब्द), translated as "reliable testimony" above, is associated with the divine element (resonating with the Latin *quintessence*), marking the divine nature of language itself.

Sūtras fifteen and sixteen express in brief an argument for some aspect of us beyond the mind. We cannot think about more than one thing at a time, so how do we change thoughts? Nyāya responds that we can do this because of *buddhi*, the ability to understand, interpret, infer, and atman, the universal soul that animates us.

Sūtras Seventeen through Twenty-Two

17. Activity [pravṛtti प्रवृत्ति] is that which makes the voice, mind and body begin their action.

18. Faults [doṣa दोषा] have the characteristic of causing activity.

19. Transmigration [punar पुनर् utpatti उत्पत्ति "again resurrect"] means re-births.

20. Fruit [phala फल] is the thing produced by activity and faults.

21. Pain [duḥkha दु:ख] has the characteristic of causing uneasiness.

22. Release [mokṣa मोक्ष] is the absolute deliverance from pain.

These verses identify the human condition—an endless cycles of desire and aversion and rebirth—in Nyāya/Hindu terms. Vātsyāyana identifies "three kinds of action" . . . "vocal, mental and bodily, which he can be "good or bad":

Bodily actions which are bad are: —(1) killing, (2) stealing, and (3) committing adultery. Bodily actions which are good are: — (1) giving, (2) pro-

---

156. Vatsyāyana 1996, 7.

tecting, and (3) serving. Vocal actions which are bad are: — (1) telling a lie, (2) using harsh language, (3) slandering, and (4) indulging in frivolous talk. Vocal actions which are good are:—(1) speaking the truth, (2) speaking what is useful, (3) speaking what is pleasant, and (4) reading sacred books. Mental actions which are bad are: —(1) malice, (2) covetousness, and (3) skepticism. Mental actions which are good are:—(1) compassion, (2) refraining from covetousness, and (3) devotion.

Though this commentary reads like a list of positive and negative commandments, in this context, the positive ones describe the ideal rhetor. Vedic perspectives stress living to produce the most fruitful consequences.

Sūtras eighteen through twenty explain why people continue to die and be reborn. "Faults" (doṣa), which Vātsyāyana identifies as "affection, aversion, and stupidity," lead to the "fruit" of transmigration (*punar* पुनर् + *utpatti* उत्पत्ति): births, "the connection of soul with body, sense-organs, mind, intellect, and sentiments," and deaths, "the soul's separation from them." No matter what we do, our activity leads to some kind of fruit. Seeking pleasure and avoiding pain leads to transmigration; living for and promoting true knowledge of the world bears the fruit of *mokṣa*.

As I have noted elsewhere,[157] according to Arindam Chakrabarti, Naiyayikas (followers of Nyāya) developed the idea that even pleasure is a type of suffering, since we always anticipate losing it even as we have it. After centuries of debate, they concluded that *mokṣa* must be sought not as an object of pleasure but rather as a cessation of pain, as one removes a thorn from one's foot.[158] One can trace the outline of that point of view in these Sūtras.

Sūtras eighteen through twenty-four lead us toward the Avayava, the five-part approach to reasoning that the Nyāya Sūtra promotes in Sūtra thirty-two. In Sūtra eighteen, we learn that most of the things we do are driven by three motives, "affection," "aversion," and "stupidity"—always running from something, to something, or acting destructively out of ignorance, a very apt description of the human condition. Though not all rhetors believe in reincarnation, sifting our motives of fear, desire, and stupidity invites rhetoric sensitive to social and political justice.[159]

Sūtras Twenty-Three through Thirty-One

23. Doubt, [saṃśaya संशय], which is a conflicting judgment about the precise character of an object, arises from the recognition of properties common to many objects [see the list of "objects" in Sūtra nine], or of properties not common to

---

157. Lloyd 2019, 6.

158. Chakrabarti 1983, 180-81.

159. When I once asked my students what is left when we eliminate desire, fear, and stupidity from an issue, one student immediately and wisely responded, "justice," the actual meaning of the word Nyāya.

any of the objects, from conflicting testimony, and from irregularity of perception and non-perception.

24. Purpose [prayojana प्रयोजन] is that with an eye to which one proceeds to act.

25. A familiar instance [dṛṣṭānta दृष्टान्त] is the thing about which an ordinary person and an expert entertain the same opinion.

26. A established tenet is a dogma resting on the authority of a certain school, hypothesis, or implication.

27. The tenet [siddhānta सिद्धान्त] is of four kinds . . . *a dogma of all the schools, peculiar to some school, a hypothetical dogma, and an implied dogma.*

These Sūtras confirm Nyāya's emphasis on beginning with the outcome. What do we wish to attain? The rhetor who wishes to be released from this world of pain and rebirth interprets "conflicting" interpretations purposefully to find fruitful interpretations, not just win or convince. The pain (21) of experience and desire for more (22) leads us to saṃśaya, "doubt (23), which leads us to our prayojana (24), our rhetorical purpose, which, according to Vātsyāyana, is "the thing which one endeavours to attain or to avoid."

I have omitted sutras twenty-eight through thirty-one because they only describe contemporary examples of the four kinds of tenets. Generally speaking, however, sūtras twenty-five through thirty-one outline the rhetor's resources. Given that the Nyāya method places analogy, dṛṣṭānta, at the center of argument, the Sūtra indicates that successful rhetors must search for a suitable analogical and familiar instance, the dṛṣṭānta, shared by both expert and layperson alike. For Naiyayikas, the need for common ground is built into the argumentative method itself.

The Naiyayika then, like today's rhetor, researches sources—applicable "tenets" of various schools. Not all tenets are the same, and skilled rhetors need to differentiate tenets shared by all schools, some schools, hypothetical tenets, and tenets that have not yet been articulated but are implied. Many of us fail to make such distinctions and assume that our point of view is the only valid point of view. These distinctions provide a handy rubric for interpreting sources. What is relatively universally accepted and what is seen as opposite? How could we hypothetically reframe an issue? What do we infer is the position of the speaker or writer?

Sūtras Thirty-Two through Forty-One: The Avayava—The Nyāya Method of Reasoning

32. The members (of a syllogism) are proposition, reason, example, application, and conclusion.

Proposition [pratijñā प्रतिज्ञा] — This hill is fiery,

Reason [hetu हेतु] — Because it is smoky,

Example [dṛṣṭānta दृष्टान्त] — Whatever is smoky is fiery, as a kitchen,

Application [upamana उपमान] — So is this hill (smoky),

Conclusion. [nigamana नगिमन] — Therefore this hill is fiery.

33. A proposition is the declaration of what is to be established

34. The reason is the means for establishing what is to be established through the homogenous or affirmative character of the example.

35. Likewise through the heterogenous or negative character.

36. A homogeneous (or affirmative) example is a familiar instance which is known to possess the property to be established and which implies that this property is invariably contained in the reason given.

37. A heterogeneous (or negative) example is a familiar instance which is known to be devoid of the property to be established and which implies that the absence of this property is invariably rejected in the reason given.

38. Application is a winding up, with reference to the example, of what is to be established as being so or not so.

39. Conclusion is the re-stating of the proposition after the reason has been mentioned.

40. Confutation [tarka तर्क], which is carried on for ascertaining the real character of a thing of which the character is not known, is reasoning which reveals the character by showing the absurdity of all contrary characters.

41. Ascertainment [nirṇaya नर्णिय] is the removal of doubt, and the determination of a question, by hearing two opposite sides.

These Sūtras describe and contextualize the five-part Nyāya method of reasoning. The diagram of the *avayava* (32), is rather Westernized by the translator. Table 4.2 shows the Sanskrit terms:

Table 4.2: Sanskrit Terms in the Five-Part Nyāya Method of Reasoning

Transliteration	Sanskrit	Translation
pratijñā	परतज्ञिआ	promise, vow, proposal
hetu	हेतु	reason, motivation
dṛṣṭānta	दृष्टानृत	instance, paragon, example
upamāna	उपमान	comparison, resemblance
nigamana	नगिमन	summing up, going in or into

The speaker offers a proposal based in an expressed reason and offers a connective shared analogy—agreeable to both sides—that supports the relation between the proposal and the reason. Discussion ensues, and if the interlocutors agree that the comparison is valid, they establish the conclusion as binding. Rather than the rhetor making a case *to* an audience, the rhetor is making a case *with* the audience.

As the "(of a syllogism)" indicates in Sūtra thirty-two, the Nyāya method was dubbed the "the Indian syllogism" by both European and Indian scholars in the nineteenth and early twentieth century. However, the Nyāya method differs from the Aristotelian approach enough that the phrase is more a hindrance than a help. European scholars mostly found it lacking.[160] Recent scholars such as J. N. Mohanty, Bimal Matilal, and Jonardon Ganeri[161] emphasize Nyāya's uniqueness, framed and suited to an Indian environment. The traditional textbook logical syllogism derived from Aristotelian roots has three parts, a major premise, a minor premise, and a conclusion. The Nyāya method has five parts, *avayava* (अवयव), "limbs" as in members of a body. Since the "conclusion" comes first, the method literally reverses Aristotle's ordering of the syllogism. The second "premise" provides a supportive reason for the opening hypothesis. The approach is more scientific than "logical."[162] We are testing a proposition, not setting up logical consequences from established propositions.

Rather than connected premises, the first three elements are one argument. The proposal and reason are established in the analogical example: "Fire and smoke occur in the hearth, and I see smoke on the hill, therefore, the hill must be on fire." In the last two steps, interlocutors reaffirm that all the elements of the proposed argument are applicable (the "application"—a "winding up," such as in Sūtra Thirty-Eight), and restate in agreement the conclusion, called a *nigamana* (निगमन) or "binding" of the minds.[163]

To clarify how the method works, consider a different example:

> Pratijna (proposal): Human beings are all one.
>
> Hetu (supportive reason): Because they are all made of the same substances.
>
> Drṣtānta (supportive analogy): Like a glass of ocean dipped from the ocean.

Things made up of the same substance are one, much like a glass of ocean dipped from the ocean. Humans are all made up of the same substances, so they are most likely one.

Over time, Naiyayikas, at first influenced by Buddhist antagonists, and later, European philosophers, added something like a major premise:

> The hill is on fire
>
> Because it is smoky. [And where there is smoke there is fire.]
>
> As in the kitchen.

---

160. Ganeri 1996, 6–7; Lloyd 2007, 369.

161. Mohanty 2000. Matilal 1998. Ganeri 2001b. Ganeri 2001a.

162. Rogers 1993.

163. "That the hill is on fire is probable, but not proven, compares to Aristotle's statement that "the theory of rhetoric is concerned . . . with what seems probable." Aristotle 2004, 10.

They called this relation *vyapti* (व्याप्ति), the inherent presence of one thing in another (i.e., smoke inheres in fire). Distrustful of general statements because no one has experienced every possible scenario, the *vyapti* needed only to be acceptable to the interlocutors as established enough to be called a concomitance ("commonly seen" above). For rhetors, this method offers a rich approach to argumentation.[164]

Sūtras thirty-three through forty define the terms above, but only Sūtras thirty-six and thirty-seven add new information. Arguments here are not so much proven, as all other "contrary characters" are shown to be absurd. In doing so, doubt is removed. The door is open to future reinterpretation. This is the end of Book I, Chapter 1.

The first Sūtra in the second chapter of book one describes procedures for Nyāya debate. Speakers take opposing positions, offer arguments following the five-part method, and discussion ensues.

> NS 1.2 Discussion [*vada*] is the adoption of one of two opposing sides. What is adopted is analyzed in the form of five members, and defended by the aid of any of the means of right knowledge, while its opposite is assailed by confutation, without deviation from the established tenets.

These procedures have been explained above. Otherwise, the second chapter in Book 1 details the terminologies in the first chapter, and almost all the remaining Sūtras feature technical descriptions of fallacies (i.e., descriptions of all the ways the five-part method could be misaligned) or feature arguments against contrary views from other Hindu schools and Buddhists. They are not necessary for this basic description of Nyāya rhetoric.

Conclusions and Implications

For the student of rhetoric, these sūtras bear multiple significances. First, they provide insight into an approach to human reasoning based in a rich cultural context virtually untouched by Greek notions of rhetoric. For those versed in Hindu traditions, Nyāya provides a concrete methodology for reasoning and dialogue leading to *mokṣa*, usually seen as attainable only through renunciation and meditation. The Nyāya Sūtra in the first chapter emphasizes that rhetorical training primarily involves practicing the sixteen categories. In the fourth chapter,

---

164. For instance, in 2020 when white police officers in the US killed Jacob Blake, a black man, by shooting him in the back, protests broke out in Kenosha, Wisconsin. During one protest, a seventeen-year-old white "vigilante" shot three people, killing two. Blake's father, when asked about systemic racism in the US, pointed to how police shot his unarmed son but drove past the white vigilante, though protesters identified him as an active shooter.

Blake's father framed the argument in a very Nyāya-like manner:

Pratijna (proposal): We have two justice systems in America

Hetu (supportive reason): Because black and white people meet opposite treatments.

Dṛṣṭānta (connective analogy): Like the treatment of Jacob Blake and the white vigilante.

it details that rhetorical training involves: "purifying of our soul by abstinence from evil;" and "following the spiritual injunctions gleaned from the Yoga institute" (NS IV.2.456); and practicing Nyāya dialogue (NS IV.2.458). Regardless of background and beliefs, however, rhetors can easily adopt its methods of reflection, research, and sifting of motives before and during our interactions.

For those schooled in Greco-Roman rhetoric, Nyāya offers fresh perspectives on a number of Aristotle's concepts. First, while Aristotle begins his rhetoric with the statement that "Rhetoric is the counterpart of Dialectic,"[165] he is using one to understand the other, to identify their differences, not to establish a unified understanding of philosophy and rhetoric. In contrast, Nyāya scholars never separated philosophy from "rhetorical" practices like argumentation or debate, and because of this, *its theory of debate flows from its epistemology.*

Second, the five-part Nyāya method operates distinctly from the three-part Aristotelian approach, even though they developed in a similar time period, and these distinctions may offer insight into both *Rhetoric*'s circulation and recirculation.[166]

Third, Aristotle identifies two types of persuasive proof, enthymemes or examples,[167] the enthymeme being "a syllogism dealing with . . . practical subjects"[168] and enthymemic argument consisting of two premises and a conclusion, one of which may be left out if commonly understood.[169] He defined examples as "subsequent supplementary evidence,"[170] and analogies as "illustrative parallels"—historical parallels or similar fables.[171] The Nyāya method combines claim and reasons with an exemplary analogy, combining the power of enthymeme and example in one method.

Fourth, at various points throughout his lectures, Aristotle defines rhetoric's purposes: to "discuss," "maintain," and "defend" some statements, and to "attack" others.[172] Today, "discuss" and "maintain" are often lost to "attacking" and "defending." Deborah Tannen, in her book *Argument Culture*, observes, "The argument culture urges us to approach the world— and the people in it—in an adversarial frame of mind." It assumes that "The best way to discuss an idea is to set up a debate; the best way to cover news is to find spokespeople who express the most extreme, polarized views and present them as both sides."[173] Nyāya, in defining arguing to win as "jalpa," "speaking nonsense," refocuses us on the more positive realms of discussion and maintenance.

Fifth, Aristotle, in his *Rhetoric*, says that speaker's *ethos*, the ethical stance toward an audience, affects their openness to the speaker: "rhetorical persuasion is effected not only by

---

165. Aristotle 1924, 1.
166. Lloyd 2013, 285; Lloyd 2011, 78–81.
167. Aristotle 2004, 9.
168. Ibid., 112.
169. Ibid., 11.
170. Ibid., 111.
171. Ibid.
172. Ibid., 3.
173. Tannen 2012, Chapter 1. Rpt. in the *Washington Post*, 1998.

demonstrative but by ethical argument; it helps a speaker to convince us, if we believe that he has certain qualities himself, namely, goodness, or goodwill towards us, or both together."[174] A Nyāya perspective encourages a second look at the rhetor's ethical stance by encouraging self-reflection and vada dialogue, a sifting of one's motives of fear and desire to focus on just and fruitful truth. Nyāya Sūtra NS IV, 2.456 states, "there should be a purifying of our soul by abstinence from evil and observances of certain duties as was by spiritual injunctions gleaned from the Yoga institute." As the Sūtra notes in NS 1.1.7, we can rely on a person's testimony only if those words are "the instructive assertion of a reliable person."

Sixth, Aristotle, in his *Rhetoric*, defines desire as "the craving for pleasure," one of several "emotions"[175] from which rhetors may appeal to audiences: "the more a thing is desired, the better it is."[176] Fear may also be utilized: "when it is advisable that the audience should be frightened, the orator must make them feel that they really are in danger of something."[177] Nyāya reminds us that fear may also be a destructive impulse; reasoners need to look past their own fears and the fears of their interlocutors for solutions, and practice learning rhetoric through "discussions [*vada*] with unenvious persons" (NS IV. 2. 458).[178]

Knowledge of Nyāya can expand views of rhetoric itself. In 2010, Joseph Henrich, Steven J. Heine, and Ara Norenzayan published "The Weirdest People in the World?" in the journal *Behavioral and Brain Sciences* in which they questioned the source of authoritative methodologies. They write,

> Behavioral scientists routinely publish broad claims about human psychology and behavior in the world's top journals based on samples drawn entirely from Western, Educated, Industrialized, Rich, and Democratic (WEIRD) societies. Researchers—often implicitly—assume that either there is little variation across human populations, or that these "standard subjects" are as

---

174. Aristotle 2004, 37. An article on "branding" oneself on social media sounds very much like Aristotle might today: "A personal brand statement works best when it embodies the interests of the people you are trying to reach." Such branding might be effective whether one was a thief or a saint. "A Guide to Branding Yourself on Social Media" 2020.

175. Aristotle 2004, 48, 70.

176. Ibid., 33.

177. Ibid., 83.

178. Nyāya rhetoric has pedagogical implications. After reading Paulo Freire's "The 'Banking' Concept of Education," in which he compares education to the cultural depositing of information into student's minds, I invite students to apply their own educational analogies (e.g., students as robots, schools as prisons or factories) to help create connections between students in discussions, and often, with claims and reasons, foster thoughtful and researched essays and fresh perspectives on alternatives. Class discussions sift through motives and promote egalitarian perspectives, lessening the chance students will create simplistic arguments. Active use of Nyāya reasoning can promote creative thinking about pressing issues.

representative of the species as any other population. Are these assumptions justified? [179]

Their answer is, unsurprisingly, "no." Their exhaustive study from a "comparative database from across the behavioral sciences" revealed that "WEIRD subjects are particularly unusual compared with the rest of the species—they are frequent outliers rather than representative of widespread norms. The domains they reviewed include "visual perception, fairness, cooperation, spatial reasoning, categorization and inferential induction, moral reasoning, reasoning styles, self-concepts and related motivations, and the heritability of IQ."[180] Other than "inheritability of IQ," every category they list in their discussion could also describe Nyāya rhetoric. They continue, "we need to be less cavalier in addressing questions of human nature on the basis of data drawn from this particularly thin, and rather unusual, slice of humanity."[181] As the field's understanding of "Non-Western" continues to expand beyond even our recent conversations, it is possible that the present "rhetorical tradition" may eventually prove to be an outlier. This movement already seems evident in rhetorical studies of normative practices in India, China, the Middle East, Africa, the Americas, and even understudied European environments.

These examples illustrate that rhetoric that promotes dialogic thinking focused beyond ignorance, fear, and misplaced desires is much needed in today's fragmented sociopolitical environment. Knowledge of Nyāya reasoning opens a door to such possibilities.

---

179. Henrich 2010, 61.
180. Ibid.
181. Ibid.

4.4 Hindu, between 850 and 1000 CE, Nepal

Rhetoric as a Vehicle of Social Order in the *Garuda Purāṇa*[182]

Shuv Raj Rana Bhat

INTRODUCTION

Challenges in the Historiographic Study of the Garuda Purāṇa

Widely "recited in Nepal on the occasion of funeral and ancestral ceremonies (*srāddha*),"[183] the *Garuda Purāṇa* is one of the great eighteen canonical *Purāṇas* that involves a dialogic communication between the Lord Vishnu and Garuda, the King of birds. Like other *Purāṇas*, the *Garuda Purāṇa* survived in the transferred form from one generation to another before it was written and "compiled between 850 and 1000 CE."[184] Generally regarded as a sacred treatise of the Hindus, it deals with diverse issues pertaining to grammar, astrology, medicine, death, funeral rites, reincarnation, hell, heaven, torments of the Yama,[185] yoga, and liberation. According to Varma, the *Garuda Purāṇa* "depicts the condition of the soul on its perilous journey after death. It also discusses the religious ceremonies which are to be performed for the salvation of the soul."[186] When a member of a Hindu family passes away, relatives, particularly sons, gather to observe the funeral rites for thirteen days. The presence of sons is considered to be indispensable because they are the only people who can light the funeral pyres of their parents.[187] One of the major observances is the recitation of the *Garuda Purāṇa* by a pandit, a Brāhmiṇ Hindu priest, learned in Sanskrit and Hindu philosophy. As a deliberative

---

182. The *Garuda Purāṇa* is a Hindu scripture. Originally written in Sanskrit, this text has two parts: Purva-khanda (first part) and Uttara-khanda (second part). The focus of this research is on the second part that basically deals with heaven, hell, death, funeral rites, yoga and liberation. This text still has an enormous influence on the Nepali Hindus, and is commonly recited during funeral rites.

183. Höfer and Shrestha 1973, 52–53.

184. Hazra 1940, 144.

185. Yama is the Lord of death.

186. Varma 1978, 283.

187. When we lost our beloved father sixteen years ago, for instance, two of my brothers were out of my home country Nepal. No sooner had they received the message than they went back to Nepal and joined the funeral rites. During this period, the mourners, dressed in white as opposed to black clothes worn as an expression of lamentation in some western cultures, live in an isolated space or room, not to be touched by anybody, including animals and birds. One of the few things they are allowed to eat is rice cooked in ghee without any spices, curries or pickles. Salt is totally avoided during these thirteen days. In fact, my own personal experience has inspired me to write about the *Garuda Purāṇa* tradition as a rhetorical practice.

rhetoric, the *Garuda Purāṇa* or, more specifically, the pandit, as a deliberative orator, exhorts the mourners to fulfil all ritualistic rites as mentioned in the *Garuda Purāṇa*, including fasting, donating money or land or gold or flowers to relatives and the pandit. While Aristotle's deliberative rhetoric has political resonance,[188] the *Garuda Purāṇa* as a deliberative rhetoric has religious overtones, exhorting the mourners to do all they can to secure the heavenly abode for the deceased or departed soul.

With a view to giving readers new insights into broadly practiced Hindu rhetorical traditions, this section primarily seeks to make a historiographic study of the translated text of the *Garuda Purāṇa*. However, in the context of Nepal, historical study of the *Purāṇas*, particularly the *Garuda Purāṇa*, remains a subject of considerable complexity for several reasons. First, as stated by Lipson and Binkley, "little attention to date has been given to one type of needed addition to the history of rhetoric: examination of non-Western rhetorics and particularly of ancient non-Western rhetorics prior to and contemporary with the development of classical rhetoric."[189] At the same time, rhetorical study of texts, particularly Hindu scriptures, has received little or no attention in Nepal. Even if there is an extant literature on Nepal or South Asia, it seeks to eliminate the history of the eastern people. Gerald James Larson's Orientalist representation of the East as having no history offers an excellent example of deterritorialization, to use Mary Louise Pratt's terminology,[190] which refers to a process of removing time, history, and context from a culture. To quote Larson, historical interpretation is "a category which has no demonstrable place within any South Asian "indigenous conceptual system" (at least prior to the middle of the nineteenth century) . . . historical interpretation is *ours*, not *theirs*! In a South Asian environment, historical interpretation is *no* interpretation. It is a zero-category.[191]

Second, unlike Greco-Roman rhetoric, the ancient/medieval Nepali scriptures, particularly the *Purāṇas*, do not explicitly deal with the issue of rhetoric as contents of texts like in *On Rhetoric* by Aristotle,[192] *Gorgias*[193] or *Phaedrus*[194] by Plato and *On the Ideal Orator*[195] by Cicero. Third, there is no consensus among the scholars on the genesis, authorship and the content of the *Purāṇas*. The final challenge stems from the mythical nature of the text itself, as the word *Purāṇa* means sacred texts pertaining to Hindu folklore, legends and mythology, a sharp contrast with history. As a result, one has to largely rely on the literature produced by Indian

---

188. Aristotle 2007, 52-55.
189. Lipson and Binkley 2004, 2.
190. Pratt 1992, 63.
191. Larson 1980, 305.
192. Aristotle 2007, 52-55.
193. Plato 2008.
194. Plato 2002.
195. Cicero 2001.

and western scholars to make a historiographic study of Nepali Hindu rhetorics as elaborated in the *Garuda Purāṇa*.

"Historiography," according to Walzer and Beard, "is the critical study of the assumptions, principles, and purposes that have informed a historical account—in our case here, of rhetoric."[196] Viewed along this line, the "assumptions," beliefs and "principles" that have informed the *Garuda Purāṇa* encompass "the doctrine of reincarnation: the dogma that each human self (*atman*) is reborn after one lifetime into another body,"[197] religious scriptures as "the sources of regulatory norms and socially-relevant maxims and precepts,"[198] religious practices such as *vrata*[199] and *dana,*[200] the concept of hell and heaven and the *Purāṇas* as "an instrument for the propagation of Brahmanical ideals of social reconstruction and sectarian interests, a medium for the absorption of local cults and associated practices, and a vehicle for popular instruction on norms governing everyday existence."[201] Partly building on the existing research by Chakrabarti, Varma, Nath, Hazra, and Walzer and Beard and partly drawing on a divergent line, I argue that the *Purāṇas* in general and the *Garuda Purāṇa* in particular rely on rhetorical strategies—*dana* as a mode of salvation, instillation of fear, yoga as a path to liberation and aestheticization of heaven—to persuade people to live and see the world in accordance with the doctrines of the Purāṇic philosophy. I further contend that this religious rhetoric basically entails Brāhmiṇic cultural values and ideologies that helped them to maintain social order in the ancient/medieval caste-based Hindu society particularly in Nepal and India.

Meaning, History and Genesis of the Purāṇas

The term "Purāṇas" elicits diverse responses from various scholars from both sides of the Atlantic. Two eminent scholars—Ravi M. Gupta and Kenneth R. Valpey—discuss the *Purāṇas* in terms of "a genre of sacred literature that began as oral histories recited by bards in public assemblies, even as they are recited today. At nearly four hundred thousand verses in Sanskrit, the bulk of the material found therein reached stable form during the reign of the Guptas in the fourth and fifth centuries CE."[202] The Gupta period aforementioned is considered to be the Golden Age of India that made great advancements in various fields including the Hindu religion. Similarly, in his attempt to trace the meaning and roots of the *Purāṇas*, P. L. Bharga-

---

196. Walzer and Beard 2011, 2.

197. Kennedy 1998, 175.

198. Varma 1978, 284.

199. A religious act of devotion and austerity undertaken for the fulfillment of specific desires. Chakrabarti 2008, 34.

200. Ritualistic gift-offerings to religious beneficiaries especially to Brahmana priests, mendicants and other religious institutions. Nath 1987, 13.

201. Chakrabarti 2008, 52.

202. Gupta and Valpey 2013, 1.

va contends that "The material handed down by the *sutas*[203] from very early times came to be called Purāṇa, a name which appears to be the abridged form of some such words as *Purāṇam akhyanam* (i.e., old narrative)."[204] Well versed in the *Purāṇas* and Hinduism, Vettam Mani, however, takes resort to Sanskrit stanzaic verse form to discuss the features of the *Purāṇas*:·

> Sargasca pratisargasca
> > *Vamso manvantarani ca /*
> *Vamsanucaritam capi*
> > *Purāṇam pancalaksanam //*[205]

In the aforementioned verse, the author highlights the five characteristics that constitute the *Purāṇas*: *Sarga*, *Pratisarga*, *Vamsa*, *Manvantara* and *Vamsanucarita* in which the first two qualities, *Sarga* and *Pratisarga*, pertain to natural creation and renovation whereas the last three—*Vamsa*, *Manvantara* and *Varmsanucarita*—have to do with the history of sages and patriarchs, the period of different Manus and the genealogy of kings respectively.[206]

That the *Purāṇas* are fundamentally concerned with the genealogy, creation, and regeneration of the universe, and various descriptions and glorification of the great Hindu gods and goddesses is further substantiated by Ronald B. Inden, Jonathan S. Walters, and Daud Ali in *Querying the Medieval: Texts and the History of Practices in South Asia*. According to them, the five distinguishing features (*panchalaksana*) that constitute the *Purāṇas* pertain to the "divine origin and ordering of the world."[207] The first three characteristics include "cosmogony (*sarga*), the "emission" of the cosmos at the beginning of a grand cosmic formation (*mahakalpa*) from the body of a cosmic overlord," "regeneration (*pratisarga*) of the cosmos at the beginning of the present cosmic formation (*kalpa*)" and "the successive generation and population (*vamsa*) of the world." The last two refer to the "accounts of the epochs of Manu (*manvantarani*) and "the genealogical succession of kings (*vamsanucarita*)."[208] The reiteration of five distinguishing features may appear to give homogenous accounts of the *Purāṇas*. However, there are authors, such as Wendy Doniger (also known as Wendy Doniger O'Flaherty), who find the *Purāṇas* replete with contradictions and confusions. Doniger's main contention is that "The *Purāṇas* are not about what they say they are about. They *say* they are about the "Five Signs," which are listed at the start of most *Purāṇas*: creation (*sarga*, "emission"), secondary creation (*prati-*

---

203. The *suta* is a person "of probably mixed caste [the son of a Brahmana mother and a Ksatriya father], but of high rank in the court and a speaker of Sanskrit, who combined in himself the office of charioteer and equerry as well as that of chronicler and bard" (Maurer 1988).

204. Bhargava 1977, 490.

205. Mani 1975, 617.

206. Mani 1975, 617.

207. Inden et al. 2000, 31.

208. Ibid., 31-32.

sarga), the genealogy of gods and kings, the reigns of the Manus . . . and the history of solar and lunar dynasties."[209]

Similar to the contentious contents of the *Purāṇas*, tracing the roots of the *Purāṇas* poses challenges and controversies for today's researchers, owing to their survival in the oral form from one generation to another in ancient and medieval times. According to Cheever Mackenzie Brown, "Purāṇas were publicly sung and recited, and in the process underwent constant revision and recreation or elaboration."[210] "The fluid nature of this oral literature," Brown further states, "was by no means halted when it was committed to written form, so that several versions and recensions of these texts have arisen."[211] The original date of their inception in fact remains a topic of speculation. P. L. Bhargava argues that while the *Purāṇas* tell the tales of ancient kings and heroes, "how these tales originated, who were responsible for preserving and handing them down from generation to generation, and when they came to be collected and edited are questions which have exercised the minds of scholars for a long time."[212] Vettam Mani's references to *Mahabharata, Upanisads* and *Smirti,* which deployed the word "Purāṇa" to respectively denote "stories about devas and siddhas,[213]" "itihasas" (epics) and "commentaries on Vedas" reveal that the *Purāṇas* "existed even before historic times" and "have a hoary past."[214] Referring to the uncertainty about the origin of the *Purāṇas,* Walter Harding Maurer explains, "The fluidity of the Purāṇaic tradition is in larger measure due also to its being essentially an oral tradition, even to this day, far more subject to change and embellishment than were it a bookish tradition."[215] Likewise, the scholars are at variance with each other when it comes to the authorship, contents and the number of the *Purāṇas.* Vettam Mani and Cheever Mackenzie Brown refer to Vyasa as the person who blazed the trail of all the *Purāṇas.* Brown writes that "in general, authorship of the Purāṇas is ascribed to him [Vyasa]."[216] As to the number of the *Purāṇas,* even though many agree on the great eighteen *Purāṇas,* the translators of the *Garuda Purāṇa*, Ernest Wood and S. V. Subrahmanyam refer to "17 or 18 canonical Purāṇas, divided into three categories, each named after a deity: Brahma, Vishnu and Shiva."[217] One of these eighteen *Purāṇas* is the *Garuda Purāṇa*, the focus of the current research. What follows is a brief review of it, including its history, origin, authorship, and content.

---

209. Doniger 2009, 279–80.

210. Brown 1974, 10.

211. Ibid.

212. Bhargava 1977, 489.

213. The group of devas called Siddhas lived on the Himalayas near the hermitage of Kanva.

214. Mani 1975,17.

215. Maurer 1988.

216. Brown 1974, 11.

217. *The Garuḍa Purâṇa* 1911.

A Bird's-eye View of the Garuda Purāṇa

Generally recited "while cremating the bodies of the dead,"[218] the *Garuda Purāṇa* is considered to be one of the *Vishnu Purāṇas*. Like the indefinite dates of the composition of other *Purāṇas*, it is an uphill task to exactly pinpoint the date and the genesis of the *Garuda Purāṇa* owing to historians' skepticism. According to Kunal Chakrabarti, "it was only after the publication of R. C. Hazra's study of the Purāṇaic records on Hindu rites and customs in 1940, in which he delineated with meticulous care the period of composition of the *Purāṇas* . . . that historians began to feel comfortable with these texts as important and authentic."[219] Nevertheless, attempts have been made to mark the beginning of the *Garuda Purāṇa*. For example, according to Ludwik Sternbach, "it was already known in the eleventh century CE"[220] Despite Alberuni's visit to India in the same century, adds Sternbach, "it is impossible to establish in what form the Garuda Purāṇa was known to Alberuni and, in particular, whether it then contained the three *Samhitas*[221] forming now an integral part of the Garuda Purāṇa."[222] R. C. Hazra's meticulous and extensive study of the *Garuda Purāṇa*, especially with his references to Rupa Gosvamin and Goplalabhatta's quotations and spurious 'Tarksya,'[223] helps him to trace the date of composition. Through his examination of the extant treatises, Hazra concludes, "It is, therefore, highly probable that the extant Garuda was compiled between 850 and 1000 CE."[224]

Additionally, "a comparison between the Garuda and the extant Agni tends to show that the former was modeled on the latter. So the Garuda [*Purāṇa*] should be dated in the tenth century CE. This date is not, however, applicable to all the chapters of the Garuda."[225] In "Some Minor Purāṇas," the same author claims that the treatise cannot have been composed "earlier than about the middle of the ninth century."[226] As to the voluminous nature of the work, Hazra further states that the *Garuda Purāṇa* is an encyclopedic work that consists of two parts: Purva-khanda (first part) and Uttara-khanda (second part).[227] According to Hazra, the chapters in the Purva-khanda invoke all five characteristic themes of a Purāṇa and "astronomy, astrology, testing of gems (ratna Pariksa), omina and portenta, chiromancy, medicine, metrics, grammar, politics . . . knowledge of the supreme Brahma, and the stories of Ramayana, Mahabharata and Harivamsa."[228] Pertaining to death and funeral rites, the second half known as Uttara-khanda is not only unsystematic but also immense. "In motley confu-

---

218. Mani 1975, 617.
219. Chakrabarti 2001, 6.
220. Sternbach 1957, 186.
221. Vedic collections
222. Sternbach 1957, 186.
223. Garuda, the King of birds
224. Hazra 1940, 144.
225. Ibid., 144.
226. Hazra, 1938, 73.
227. Ibid., 141.
228. Ibid.

sion and with many repetitions," states Hazra, "we find doctrines on the fate of the soul after death, *karman*[229], rebirth and release from birth, on desire as the cause of samsara, on omens of death, the path of Yama, the fate of the pretas[230] as causing evil omens and dreams."[231]

Rhetorical Strategies in the Garuda Purāṇa

In this study, I use "a translation of an abridged version of the *Garuda Purāṇa*."[232] Translated from Sanskrit to English, this text can be publicly accessed among the Hindu offerings on *The Internet Sacred Text Archive*.[233] Of the two parts that constitute the *Garuda Purāṇa*, only the second part is presented in the website. While sixteen chapters pertaining to hell, heaven, *dana*, yoga and liberation constitute the second section, the translated text presented hereafter is only the first chapter of the *Garuda Purāṇa* entitled "An Account of the Miseries of the Sinful in this World and the Other." The translated text provides readers with footnotes that enable them to understand and interpret certain Hindu rhetorical terms and religious terminologies. My commentary encompasses the analysis of major rhetorical tactics deployed in the selected sections of the second part of the *Garuda Purāṇa* in order to probe into the rhetorical traditions practiced in the caste-based Hindu society of the medieval age. The principal rhetorical strategies—*dana* as a pathway to redemption, instillation of fear, construction of heaven and practice of yoga—used by Brahmins to influence the common mass and maintain social order provide important insights into historical, cultural, political and religious aspects of lives led by Hindus.

Brahmins (*Brāhmaṇas* in Sanskrit) were the members of Hindu caste that allowed them "the highest place" in their society. According to Julius Lipner,

> the Brahmins had the most exalted status and were set up as the unattainable model of society in many respects. This is because, by hereditary occupation, they presided over the most important form of available power: that of the sacrificial ritual which was the source of temporal and spiritual wellbeing. The Veda itself attests to the pre-eminence of Brahmins.[234]

Being the privileged and intellectual class of the Aryan society, their duties involved performing sacrifices, serving the Vedas by "reciting, practising and teaching it," performing domestic rituals, and "living an exemplary life, receiving donations so that the donor can acquire merit."[235] As a result of performing their duties on various occasions, these Brahmins would enjoy greater privileges: "allowances," "preferences even in the courts of justice" and

---

229. Deed or action
230. Ghosts.
231. Hazra 1940, 141.
232. *The Garuḍa Purâna* 1911.
233. Ibid.
234. Lipner 1994, 72.
235. Ibid., 73.

"inheritance" in marriage. In addition to these, they "have to be satisfied with money or food or both . . . visits to holy places are to be attended with gifts and feasts to Brahmans; in almost all religious ceremonies, the Brahmans are to be sumptuously fed; gifts are to be made to them after noticing an evil omen, dreaming bad dreams, and listening to the Purāṇas."[236]

As the Brahmins considered themselves to have possessed the "knowledge of the *Brahman*"[237] and therefore had "the right to decide the rules of conduct (*dharma*), they maintain[ed] the "order in which each entity occupie[d] a necessary and logical place in a hierarchical structure."[238] In their attempts to propagate their beliefs, intentions, motivations and values in the society, they started devising rhetorical tactics that would ultimately prolong their hegemony. One of the strategies subsumed the setting up of *varnasramadharma*[239] and "the authority of the Vedas" because this had a direct connection with "that of their own supremacy, and that if they would succeed in the former, the latter would follow as a direct consequence. This consciousness is most probably one of the causes why in the Purāṇas they strain every nerve to establish the *varnasramadharma* and the authority of the Vedas."[240] Their literacy with the Sanskrit language (as opposed to the common mass who were ignorant of it), their knowledge of the *Brahman*, the authority of the Vedas and the *Purāṇas* and their privileged position in the society lent them greater ethos or credibility to establish Brahminical religious system or ideology that would be known as Hinduism. Consequently, they started constructing their worldviews that percolated to the local people through the religious scriptures such as the *Garuda Purāṇa*. In what follows is a translation of the *Garuda Purāṇa* and a discussion of rhetorical tactics deployed by the Brahmins to maintain their hegemony in the society.

Translation of the *Garuda Purāṇa* by Ernest Wood and S.V. Subrahmanyam

Garuda Purāṇa: *Homage to the Blessed Ganeṣa*

Chapter 1: An Account of the Miseries of the Sinful in this World and the Other

1. The tree Madhusūdana,—whose firm root is Law, whose trunk is the Vedas, whose abundant branches are the Purāṇas, whose flowers are sacrifices, and whose fruit is liberation—excels.

2. In Naimiṣa, the field of the sleepless Ones,[241] the sages, Saunaka and others, performed sacrifices for thousands of years to attain the Heaven-world.

---

236. Hazra 1940, 257.
237. *Brahman* is the sole underlying reality of all diversity (Lipner 1994, 73).
238. Chakrabarti 2001, 15.
239. A social and moral order predicated on caste. Kasturi 2018, 105.
240. Hazra 1940, 257.
241. The superphysical beings, who do not sleep.

3-5. Those sages once, in the morning, having offered oblations to the sacrificial fire respectfully asked this of the revered Sūta sitting there:—The sages said: The happiness-giving path of the Shining Ones has been described by you. We now wish to hear about the fear-inspiring Way of Yama;[242] Also of the miseries of the World of Change,[243] and the means of destroying its pains. Please tell us correctly about the afflictions of this world and the other.

6. Suta said: Listen then. I am willing to describe the way of Yama, very difficult to tread, happiness-giving, to the virtuously inclined, misery-giving to the sinful.

7. As it was declared to Vainateya[244] by the Blessed Viṣṇu, when asked; just so will I relate it, to remove your difficulties.

8-9. Once, when the Blessed Hari, the Teacher, was sitting at ease in Vaikuṇṭha, the son of Vinatā, having bowed reverently, inquired:—Garuḍa said: The Path of Devotion, of many forms, has been described to me by you, and also, O Shining One, has been told the highest goal of the devotees.

10. Now I wish to hear about the fearsome Way of Yama, along which is the travelling, it is revealed, of those who turn away from devotion to Thee.

11. The name of the Lord is easily pronounced, and the tongue is under control. Fie, fie upon the wretched men who nevertheless go to hell!

12. Tell me, then, O Lord, to what condition the sinful come, and in what way they obtain the miseries of the Way of Yama.

13. The Blessed Lord said: Listen, O Lord of Birds, and I will describe the Way of Yama, terrible even to hear about, by which those who are sinful go in hell.

14-16. O Tārkṣya, those who delight in sin, destitute of compassion and righteousness, attached to the wicked, averse from the true scriptures and the company of the good, Self-satisfied, unbending, intoxicated with the pride of wealth, having the ungodly qualities, lacking the divine attributes, Bewildered by many thoughts, enveloped in the net of delusion, revelling in the enjoyments of the desire-nature,—fall into a foul hell.

17. Those men who are intent upon wisdom go to the highest goal; the sinfully-inclined go miserably to the torments of Yama.

18. Listen how the misery of this world accrues to the sinful, then how they, having passed through death, meet with torments.

---

242. Yama is the Lord of death.
243. Saṁsāra: The three worlds in which men circle through births and deaths.
244. A name of Garuḍa, Vinatā was the mother of Garuḍa.

19. Having experienced the good or the bad actions, in accordance with his former earning—then, as the result of his actions, some disease arises.

20. Powerful death, unexpectedly, like a serpent, approaches him stricken with bodily and mental pain, yet anxiously hoping to live.

21-24. Not yet tired of life, being cared for by his dependents, with his body deformed through old age, nearing death, in the house, He remains, like a house-dog, eating what is ungraciously placed before him, diseased, with failing digestion, eating little, moving little, With eyes turned up through loss of vitality, with tubes obstructed by phlegm, exhausted by coughing and difficult breathing, with the death rattle in his throat, Lying encircled by his sorrowing relatives; though being spoken to he does not answer, being caught in the noose of death.

25. In this condition, with mind busy with the support of his family, with senses unconquered, swooning with intense pain he dies amidst his weeping relatives.

26. In this last moment, O Tārkṣya, a divine vision arises,—all the worlds appear as one—and he does not attempt to say anything.

27. Then, at the destruction of the decayed senses and the numbing of the intelligence, the messengers of Yama come near and life departs.

28. When the breath is leaving its place, the moment of dying seems an age, and pain like the stinging of hundred scorpions is experienced.

29. Now he emits foam; his mouth becomes filled with saliva. The vital breaths of the sinful depart by the lower gateway.

30-31. Then, two terrifying messengers of Yama are come, of fierce aspect, bearing nooses and rods, naked, with grinding teeth, As black as crows, with hair erect, with ugly faces, with nails like weapons; seeing whom his heart palpitates and he releases excrements.

32. The man of the size of a thumb, crying out 'oh, oh,' is dragged from the body by the servants of Yama, looking the while at his own body.

33. Having put round him a body of torment, and bound the noose about his neck, they forcibly lead him a long way, like the king's officers a convict.

34-35. While thus leading him the messengers menace him, and recount over and over again the awful terrors of the hells,—"Hurry up, you wicked man. You shall go to the abode of Yama. We will lead you now, without delay, to Kumbhīpāka and the other hells."

36. Then hearing these words, and the weeping of his relatives; crying loudly "Oh, oh," he is beaten by the servants of Yama.

37-38. With failing heart and shuddering at their threats, bitten by clogs upon the way, afflicted, remembering his misdeeds, Hungry and thirsty, roasting in the sun, forest-fires and hot winds, struck upon the back with whips, painfully he walks, almost powerless, along a road of burning sand, shelterless and waterless.

39-40. Here and there falling exhausted and insensible, and rising again,—in this way, very miserably led through the darkness to the abode of Yama, The man is brought there in a short time and the messengers show him the terrible torments of hell.

41. Having seen the fearful Yama, the man, after a time, by command of Yama, swiftly comes back through the air, with the messengers.

42. Having returned, bound by his past tendencies, desiring the body but held back with a noose by the followers of Yama, tortured by hunger and thirst, he weeps.

43. He obtains the rice-balls given by his offspring, and the gifts made during the time of his illness. Nevertheless, O Tārkṣya, the sinful Denier does not obtain gratification.

44. The Śrāddha,[245] the gifts, and the handsful of water, for the sinful, do not uplift. Although they eat the rice-ball offering, still they are tortured with hunger.

45. Those who are in the departed condition, deprived of the rice-ball offering, wander about in great misery, in an uninhabited forest, until the end of the age.

46. Karma not experienced does not die away even in thousands of millions of ages; the being who has not experienced the torment certainly does not obtain the human form.

47. Hence, O Twice-born,[246] for ten days the son should offer rice-balls. Every day these are divided into four portions, O Best of Birds.

48. Two portions give nourishment to the five elements of the body; the third goes to the messengers of Yama; he lives upon the fourth.

49. For nine days and nights the departed obtains rice-balls, and on the tenth day the being, with fully formed body, acquires strength.

50. The old body being cremated, a new one is formed by these offerings, O Bird; the man, the size of a hand (cubit), by this experiences good and evil on the way.

51-53. By the rice-ball of the first day the head is-formed; the neck and shoulders by the second; by the third the heart forms: By the fourth the back forms; and by the fifth the navel;

---

245. Ceremony for the dead
246. Members of the three higher castes take a "second birth" when invested with the sacred thread; all birds are twice-born, in and from the egg.

by the sixth the hips and secret parts; by the seventh the thigh forms; Likewise next the knees and feet by two; on the tenth day hunger and thirst.

54. Dwelling in the body formed by the rice-balls, very hungry and pained with thirst, on both the eleventh and twelfth days the departed eats.

55. On the thirteenth day the departed, bound by the servants of Yama, walks alone along the road like a captured monkey.

56. The extent of the way of Yama measures eighty-six thousand Yojanas,[247] without Vaitaraṇī, O Bird.

57. Two hundred and forty-seven Yojanas each day the departed travels, going by day and night.

58-59. Having passed successively through these sixteen cities on the way, the sinful man goes to the place of the King of Righteousness[248]:—Saumya,[249] Sauripura,[250] Nāgendrabhavana,[251] Gāndharva,[252] Shailāgama,[253] Krauncha,[254] Krūrapura,[255] Vichitrabhavana,[256] Bahwāpada,[257] Duḥkhada,[258] Nānākrandapura,[259] Sutaptabhawana,[260] Raudra,[261] Payovarshana,[262] Shītādhya,[263] Bahubhīti[264]:—before the city of Yama, the abode of righteousness.

60. Held by the nooses of Yama, the sinful, crying out "Oh, oh," having left his own house, goes on the way to the city of Yama.

---

247. A Yojana is between eight and nine miles.
248. Another form of Yama
249. Calm place
250. Town of Saturn
251. Residence of the Lord of Serpents
252. Place of Singers
253. Inaccessible mountain
254. Name of a mountain
255. Town of cruelty
256. A wonderful place
257. Many calamities
258. Misery-giving
259. Town of varied cries
260. Very hot place
261. Savage
262. Rains
263. Very cold
264. Many horrors

DANA AS A MEANS OF ATONEMENT

While English terminologies such as *gift*, *donation* and *grant* are generally deployed to refer to the concept of *dana*, they cannot pragmatically capture the religious overtones associated with the word notwithstanding semantic sameness or proximity. In Hinduism, the notion of *dana* is considered to be a highly benevolent and noble act. In the past, "no religious ceremony was deemed complete without it; no act of religious devotion was considered fruitful unless accompanied by it."[265] Defined with highly positive terms, such as generosity, sacrifice, spiritual blessing, altruism, charity, giving and alms, *dana* is said to bring about a number of advantages to the giver: greater prosperity, befriending strangers, getting rid of evils and vices and expiating sins. According to C. Mackenzie Brown, "Dana, or giving, is a major topic in many of the Purāṇas and is extolled as a highly meritorious act, as well as an act of bhakti or devotion. The giving of books of the Purāṇas is an act pleasing to God (Visnu, or whomever) similar to other acts of piety such as reciting or listening to the names or stories of God."[266]

Even though the practice of *dana* seems to be altruistic, it is never a purely neutral act. Like every action in the world, the act of giving is triggered by certain ambitions, interests and intentions of the actors involved in it. The very concept of *dana* is motivated by various factors such as desires to secure a space in the abode of the God after one's death, absolve sins, erase superstitious fears and fulfill self-interests.[267] The notion of *dana* presupposes at least two participants who get involved in the act of giving and receiving. One may wonder who the receiver and the giver are, what factors motivate the giver to give *dana* to the receiver and whether this altruistic act is a one-way act or a reciprocal one. Vijay Nath argues that "at the beginning of sixth century BCE brahmanas stand out as the chief and the most dominant category of donees receiving spontaneous veneration and gifts."[268] As the *Garuda Purāṇa* shows, dying persons are usually the donors who get motivated to make offers or *dana* in order to ensure heavenly abode after their death. This extract bears witness to the tradition: "A righteous son is honored even by the shining ones. He should cause his ailing father to make gifts on earth."[269]

Dana is one of the forms of *vrata*, "a religious act of devotion and austerity undertaken for the fulfillment of specific desires."[270] The other forms of *vrata* include fasting, bathing, *Tapas*, morning prayer, worship of goddess, feeding brahmanas and srāddha. The giver's unshakable faith on *dana*—the conviction that *dana* ensures the heaven for the departed soul to rest peacefully until eternity—can never be overlooked or undermined in Hinduism. This faith was inculcated in the minds of people by Brahmins who considered religious rites such as *Vrata* to be the kairos or the opportune time, to use a classical rhetorical term, for the "dis-

265. Nath 1987, 1.
266. Brown 1986, 77.
267. Nath 1987, 84–85.
268. Ibid., 82.
269. *The Garuḍa Purâṇa* 1911, Chapter VIII, lines 113–14.
270. Chakrabarti 2001, 34.

semination of the brahmanical message. Brahminism transformed the character of the indigenous *vrata*, drew upon its potential to arrange a gathering, widened its scope, and inflated its number to make it as pervasive and frequent as possible."[271] In his discussion of Brahmanical ideology in medieval Bengal, Chakrabarti discusses different strategies used by Brahmins: "the goddesses and the *vartas*" were "two important elements adopted by the *brahmanas* from religious practices of the local population, and these were invested with a significance that transcended local boundaries."[272] "The *brahmanas*," continues Chakrabarti, "did not disturb most of the prevailing normative goals, such as those sought through the performance of indigenous *vratas*, but they made it appear as if these goals would be best realized if the *vratas* were performed in the brahmanical way."[273] With extracts from the translated texts embedded in it, the following discussion shows various practices of *dana* in a greater detail.

Chapter VIII entitled "An Account of the Gifts for the Dying" narrates various kinds of *danas* (gifts) to be given by the dying person on the deathbed to the deserving persons so as to make the following argument: "All the gifts made by human beings in this world clear the way for them on the path of the world of Yama."[274] In response to the questions posed by Garuda, the King of birds, the Lord Vishnu replies that the good person nearing death, afflicted by the diseases "should make reparation for any sins committed knowingly or in ignorance."[275] Then when he knows that he is going to die "he must perform his ablutions, and worship Viṣṇu in the form of Śālagrāma,"[276] a representation of Vishnu made out of stone. The rite of the worship demands that the worship has to be performed "with fragrant substances, with flowers, with red saffron, with leaves of the holy basil, with incense, with lamps, with offerings of food and many sweetmeats, and other things."[277] This is followed by presenting *danas* or gifts to Brāhmiṇs, feeding them with the offerings, and reciting "the eight and the twelve syllabled mantras."[278]

While it is stated in the scripture that gifts of various kinds can be offered, certain gifts are considered to be superior to other gifts due to additional and uplifting value attached to them. For instance, the gift of gold to Brahma and other sages gratifies them, enabling them to become granters of boons, which in turn, uplifts the departed soul who reaches the heaven without going to the world of Yama. The persons enjoying prosperity in the upper strata of society, such as the king, are denied access to heaven and are reborn many times as beggars if they deny offering the gifts of land to the God who is considered to be "the twice-born." Burjor Avari mentions the Gupta Dynasty who "actively gave away much land in the form of land grants. This practice was prevalent in its nascent form even during the early centuries of the post-Vedic era, when the kings were enjoined to give gifts to their brahman priests or royal

---

271. Chakrabarti 2001, 34.
272. Ibid., 16.
273. Ibid., 16.
274. *The Garuḍa Purâṇa* 1911, Chapter VIII, line 94.
275. Ibid., Chapter VIII, line 4.
276. Ibid., Chapter VIII, line 5.
277. Ibid., Chapter VIII, line 6.
278. Ibid., Chapter VIII, line 7.

officials."[279] Avari's reference to gift-making to Brahmin priests in the ancient time attests to the fact that the *Purāṇas* were the instruments of Brahminic hegemony, a rhetorical tactic used to dominate by consent.

Among the various kinds of gifts accompanied by rites, the reference to the *dana* of Vaitarani[280] cow is intriguing in the Hindu culture. The soul of the deceased has to undergo many ordeals, such as "holding onto a cow's tail to cross the Vaitarani, a horrible river of blood and filth that marks the boundary of Yama's kingdom."[281] The construction of the Vaitarani, the filthy river, reminds me of David Spurr who, in his book *The Rhetoric of Empire*, discusses the rhetoric of debasement. Associated with filth and defilement, debasement pertains to the text's reproduction of myths about the non-West that creates an image of a foreign place that is somehow abhorrent or dangerous to Europeans.[282] While the imperialistic context in which Spurr speaks of the rhetoric of debasement is different, European imperialists and Brahmin priests share a commonality: both present the myth as though it is a true story (the text's reproduction of myth and the myth of the departed soul).

While the soul is on its way, relatives on earth perform religious rites such as "śrāddhas, during which friends on earth seek to provide it with shoes, umbrellas, clothing, and money"[283] as offerings. Similarly, as almost all the *danas* offered during religious rites are given to Brahmans,[284] Hindus of the highest caste traditionally assigned to the priesthood, these offerings are also given to a Brahman with an anticipation that the departed soul will benefit from it. Among many verses in the *Garuda Purāṇa*, the following is interesting:

> Having given even once a tawny cow, milkgiving, with the calf and other necessary things, to a well-conducted and austere Brāhmiṇ, learned in the Vedas—one is absolved of all these sins. The giver is released by her at the end from the accumulated sins . . .

---

279. Avari 2007, 163–64.

280. Vaitarna or Vaitarani river, as mentioned in the *Garuḍa Purâna* and various other Hindu religious texts, lies between the earth and the infernal Naraka, the realm of Yama, Hindu god of death and is believed to purify one's sins. (Wikipedia)

281. *Encyclopedia Britannica* 2018.

282. Spurr 1993, 76.

283. *Encyclopedia Britannica* 2018.

284. Brahmans are members of the highest-ranked of the four varnas or classes of Hindu society. The other three are Kshatriyas, Vaishyas and Shudras. The word "Brahmans" has been variously spelled and pronounced as Bahuns (in Nepali colloquial expression), Brahmins without diacritics (in *The Bhagavad-Gita*, the holy book of the Hindus), Brāhmiṇs with diacritics (in *The Garuda Purāṇa*), Brāhmanas with diacritics (in Sanskrit), Brahmans (by Hazra) and brahmanas with a small letter b (by Vijay Nath). In this study, the word "Brahmans" is also used interchangeably with all other terms aforementioned. *The Bhagavad-Gita* defines Brahmins as being innately rational, knowledgeable, honest, patient, clean, austere, calm and faithful.

> Sons, grandsons, brothers, kinsmen and friends who do not make gifts on
> behalf of a dying man are without doubt slayers of Brāhmaṇ.[285]

What is so intriguing here is the way that Brahmins and Brāhmaṇ are represented and valo-
rized. Brahmins are put on a pedestal for being learned in the Vedas, arguably the most sacred
religious scripture of the Hindus. Brahmins, who have been performing religious rituals and
rites for ages, have also been in the ruling position a long time. These are the people who
perform the words of Brāhmaṇ, the ultimate reality underlying all phenomena in the Hindu scriptures.

Because of their affinity and scholarship in the Hindu treatises, such as the *Purāṇas*, Brahmins have been using the Purāṇic philosophy as an instrument to rule the common people.
The rhetoric of allegation and admonition—the ones who do not make gifts "on behalf of a
dying man are without doubt slayers of Brāhmaṇ"—clearly suggests that religious scriptures
were turned to the advantage of the ruling elite class. Even the way language is used in the title
of this chapter is revealing. The title reads "An Account of the Gifts for the Dying" as if the
receiver of the gifts is the dying person, but in fact it is the dying person and his/her relatives
who have to make *danas* that ultimately go to the Brahmans who perform the religious rites.
Even though the *dana* promises the heavenly abode for the deceased soul, the way valuable
danas—such as gold, iron, land, milk-giving cows—are honored posits that the religious per-
formers (Brahmans) are more interested in gratifying their material desire than solacing the
bereaved souls.

Instillation of Fear

The *Garuda Purāṇa* seeks to instill fear into the minds of the common people through the
creation of a horrendous *narak* (hell), a place for the sinners who have committed *pāpa* i. e. "offences against the moral and ritual law, which require penances (*prayaỹcittas*)."[286] Hindu scriptures, including the *Garuda Purāṇa*, refer to two types of *pāpa* or offences or sins: "*upapātaka*
('lesser sins'), such as teaching the Veda for money, adultery, killing a woman or a man from
a low caste, and MAHĀPĀTAKA ('capital sins') which were difficult to atone for."[287] Capital
sins include killing a Brahmin, stealing gold from a Brahmin, incestuous relationships, and
intoxication. Some sins are pardonable while others are unpardonable. The sins that cannot
be expiated by any means lead to one's downfall, including the "loss of CASTE in this life and
punishment in the next."[288]

The references to two kinds of sins draw one's attention to the kind of hierarchy and discrimination existing in Hindu society that is based on a caste system. According to Jones and
Ryan, "a BRAHMIN committing a crime, for instance, will not be punished in any way as

---

285. *The Garuḍa Purâṇa* 1911, Chapter VIII, lines 60-61, 118.
286. Klostermaier 1998, 171.
287. Ibid., 172.
288. Ibid., 172.

strictly as a SHUDRA (person of the servant class) would be for the same crime."[289] As the most learned scholars and enjoying the highest level of privileges in the society, Brahmins devised the concept of *pāpa* as a rhetorical strategy, directly leading people to *narak* or hell. This very concept of *pāpa* has a rhetorical effect on the people, psychologically deterring them from doing the evil for the fear of going to hell. Various kinds of sins are mentioned in the first six chapters of the *Garuda Purāṇa* to create fear in people, one of the strategies for disciplining them. At the very outset of the first chapter, entitled "An Account of the Miseries of the Sinful in this World and the Other," one finds the Lord Vishnu and the Garuda, the King of birds, engaged in a conversation about the consequences of sins and the terrible way of Yama. In response to the Garuda's inquiry, the Lord Vishnu replies, "those who delight in sin, destitute of compassion and righteousness, attached to the wicked, averse from the true scriptures and the company of the good . . . unbending . . . having the ungodly qualities, lacking the divine attributes . . . reveling in the enjoyments of the desire-nature—fall into a foul hell."[290]

One interesting thing to notice in this conversation is the interlocutors who, unlike in Plato's dialogue that deploys human characters, are the divine figures: the supreme Hindu God Vishnu and the Garuda, the Kings of birds. As opposed to Socrates, who often poses in the guise of a curious persona in the dialogue despite his knowledge, Garuda in the scripture is represented as an ignorant character in constant need of divine guidance, instruction, and education from Vishnu. One could question why Hindu Gods are used in the conversation on human life and death. The divine figure, such as the Lord Vishnu, is highly respected and even revered in many parts of South Asia where Hinduism is the main religion. From childhood, the Hindus have been taught that the truest knowledge is Brāhma and that God is never wrong.

In many myths, legends and folklores, gods and goddesses have been depicted as the saviors of the humankind. Thus, the presence of God as one of the participants in the dialogue is certainly to build ethos or credibility. Therefore, God is the ultimate, the unquestionable. The Lord Vishnu describes the way of Yama (the ruler of hell) as a dreadful trajectory that the sinners follow to hell. The God as the narrator uses various metaphors and similes to create a grotesque and harrowing description of the insurmountable death that approaches the dying person. The person on the deathbed is described as being "encircled by his sorrowing relatives" who, at the sight of the body, "deformed through old age, nearing death" and "exhausted by coughing and difficult breathing,"[291] weep bitterly. Having experienced the pain like stinging of the hundred scorpions at his death, the man is welcomed by two terrifying messengers of Yama, the ruler of hell, with "grinding teeth," "ugly faces" and "nails like weapons."[292] As the Hindus believe in life hereafter, the messengers bind the noose around his neck and forcibly drag the body along the way where he is menaced by the awful terrors of hells. The hungry

---

289. Jones and Ryan 2007, 323.
290. *The Garuḍa Purâna* 1911, Chapter I, lines 14–16.
291. Ibid., Chapter I, lines 21–24.
292. Ibid., Chapter I, lines 30–31.

and thirsty body (because he is leading another life in the other world), roasting in the sun, shuffles through a road of burning sand and then "through the darkness to the abode of Yama."[293] As can be noticed, the account of the journey to the other world is replete with high voltage descriptive rhetoric accompanied by occasional metaphors and imagery that inflict agonizing pain on the sinner.

By creating horrific images of the dying person, Yama, and hell in the minds of the faithful, the scripture aims to instill a positive attitude toward life as "everything attracts its opposite."[294] The very construction of the concept named hell is a rhetorical move on the part of the Brahmins to create fear among the common mass so that they will sensibly refrain from doing evil deeds. According to Yumiko Onozawa, narratives about hell "tend to serve as moral guidelines for discipline mandated for an individual in order to avoid attaining hell in his or her afterlife. A code of moral conduct serves as the guideline for proper conduct in this world, and one's conduct in this world determines one's future existence in other worlds . . . according to the moral code."[295] Onozawa further states that "Accounts of hell . . . are sometimes utilized by a religious tradition as a mechanism of social control. Hell-narratives serve, in this case, to establish and maintain the structure of the society."[296] The *Garuda Purāṇa* holds that one's life after death—either in hell or heaven—is determined by the *karma* (deed or action) one performs in this life. Good *karma* in this life ensures one's place in heaven, whereas bad *karma* directly leads one to hell. Nevertheless, a closer look at the extant literature posits that "the karma theory is turned inside out against itself: by acquiring merit in certain ways, one abolishes rebirth."[297] To illustrate this, O'Flaherty narrates the "hair-raising description of the torments of hell," in which "the Brahmin author of the text is asked by a desperately worried listener if this is, really and truly, inevitable; the Brahmin then proceeds to narrate several chapters laying out the types of gifts to Brahmins that are certain to protect the generous sinner from the slightest danger of going to hell."[298]

Aestheticization of Sworga (Heaven)

Contrary to *pāpa* or sin that leads one to hell, *punya* or "the result of good karma" or good deed is a necessary condition for securing heavenly abode after one's death.[299] If the rhetoric of *pāpa* dissuades one from committing evil things, the rhetoric of *punya* persuades one to do good deeds. According to Klostermaier, one can attain *punya* from certain religious performances, such as dipping "in a sacred river at a particular time, or the giving of a gift to a brah-

---

293. Ibid., Chapter I, lines 38–39.
294. Paz 1998, 45.
295. Onozawa 2002, 2.
296. Ibid., 6.
297. O'Flaherty 1980, 27.
298. Ibid.
299. Klostermaier 1998, 117.

min."[300] Klostermaier's reference to "the giving of a gift to a brahmin" attests to the fact that the notion of *punya* is a rhetorical tactic devised by Brahmins in order to benefit themselves.

The *Garuda Purāṇa* aestheticizes *sworga* or heaven, a place secured only for the few selected Hindus who have gained *punya*. Chapter XIV "An Account of the City of the King of Justice" is reminiscent of the rhetoric of empire devised and developed by Mary Louise Pratt in her seminal book *Imperial Eyes: Travel Writing and Transculturation*. Pratt develops a trope that goes by the name of monarch-of-all-I-survey, which is constituted by aestheticization, density of meaning and mastery.[301] Aestheticization is a rhetorical trope that is deployed to portray the landscapes as paintings. While the context in which Pratt wrote was colonial, unlike the present religious context, the way the trope is used is similar. The *Garuda Purāṇa* certainly draws the readers' attention to the aestheticization of the Heaven. Its value has been enriched by the idea that it is accessible only by the few meritorious. Heaven is the reward for ethical rhetorical performances. Ornamented with gold, the magnificent mansion of the King of Justice is described as being "Pleasing to the mind with cupolas of the splendour of the autumnal sky; with beautiful crystal stairways and walls beautified with diamonds, and with windows of strings of pearls, decorated with flags and banners; rich with the sounds of bells and drums; and embellished with golden fringes."[302] On such a pure heavenly throne is shown the Lord of Justice sitting:

> There the Lord of Justice, on a throne pure and incomparable, ten yojanas[303] in extent, bedecked with all kinds of jewels—
>
> Sits, the Best of the Good, his head dignified with the regal umbrella, ornamented with earrings, prosperous, made splendid with a large crown.
>
> Adorned with all ornaments, splendid as a blue cloud, and fanned by celestial damsels bearing in their hands fans of hair.
>
> Multitudes of celestial choristers and numerous groups of celestial damsels, round about, serve him with songs, music and dances.[304]

The description of the Lord's sitting on the throne through the profuse use of adjectives is followed by the construction and classification of four kinds of trajectories leading to the abode. Similar to Spurr's rhetoric of classification in which the colonizer classifies colonized people in accordance with how modernized they are, the classification of four gateways into the city of the King of Justice is based on the types of deeds human beings do on earth. Those who go into the mansion of righteousness by the three gateways—eastern, northern and west-

---

300. Ibid.
301. Pratt 1992, 197.
302. *The Garuḍa Purâna* 1911, Chapter XIV, lines 20-21.
303. A Yojana is between eight and nine miles.
304. *The Garuḍa Purâna* 1911, Chapter XIV, lines 31-34.

ern—are those of good deeds. The eastern way decorated with the shade of trees, jewels, chariots, swans, gardens and nectar is reserved for the holy Brahmin-sages, stainless royal sages, worshippers of deities, devotees of Shiva and those who make gifts of land, cows and houses and listen to the *Purāṇas.*[305] Likewise, the northern way is meant for those who are learned in the Vedas, who are worshippers of Dūrgā and Bhanu, who die for the sake of Brāhmiṇs, in the service of the master, at the sacred waters and on holy ground and those who delight in making great gifts. The western way is separated for those "who contemplate the good scriptures, those entirely devoted to Viṣṇu, those who repeat the Gāyatrī-mantra."[306] That there exist different types of heavens is substantiated by Julius Lipner's assertion that "good karma can propel one into the appropriate heaven (there are numerous grades of heaven or svarga) where suitable reward is experienced in the form of heightened earthly pleasures in the company of the gods."[307]

As this classification of pathways into the city of the King of Justice shows, access to the heavenly abode is allowed only to those people who are directly influenced by the ideology of the powerful Brahmins, those who offer expensive gifts, have great reverence for the holy scriptures, gods and goddesses, and die for the sake of the Brahmans. I find Velcheru Narayana Rao's argument about the *Purāṇas* worth quoting in this context: "purāṇas act as 'vehicles of Brahmanic ideology.'"[308] Likewise, basing his idea on the works of Chakrabarti, Adheesh Sathaye regards purāṇic texts as "elite cultural practices that naturalize a particularly 'religious' *ecumene.*"[309]

Yoga as a Rhetorical Tactic for Liberation

The final rhetorical tactic discussed here is that of yoga, which turned out to be "a means of deliverance" once "the doctrines of Yoga entered the Puranic mainstream."[310] Just like the practice of religious rites, such as *dana,* and reading of the religious scriptures, such as the Vedas and the *Purāṇas* in a Brahminical way would enable people to go to heaven after their death, adherence to yoga ensured people "the rewards of the other world."[311] The last two chapters, XV and XVI, in the *Garuda Purāṇa* deal with the issue of yoga, the path to salvation. Lipner contends that "in the Sanskritic tradition, and often in modern works on Hinduism, three basic forms of religious path or yoga are distinguished: Jñāna-yoga, Karma-yoga, and Bhakti-yoga, namely the disciplines of knowledge, works, and devotion respectively."[312] Similar connotations of yoga are presented in the *Garuda Purāṇa* which vehemently asserts

---

305. Ibid., Chapter XIV, lines 51–54.
306. Ibid., Chapter XIV, line 67.
307. Lipner 1994, 193.
308. Sathaye 2009, 139.
309. Ibid., 140.
310. O'Flaherty 1980, 27.
311. Ibid., 51.
312. Lipner 1994, 250.

that "[t]hose who die for the sake of Brāhmiṇs . . . those who die in the practice of Yoga . . . and those who delight in making great gifts—these, entering by the northern gate, reach the Assembly of Righteousness."[313] Furthermore, "Knowers of Truth attain liberation; righteous men go to heaven; sinners go to an evil condition; birds and others transmigrate."[314]

CONCLUSION

This study has aimed to explore the rhetoric of Hinduism as reflected in the translated text of the *Garuda Purāṇa*, although the medieval Hindus did not use the word "rhetoric." Such an investigation of the selected sections of the second part of the scripture has revealed how the lives of the medieval Hindus were influenced by the doctrines of religious scriptures, particularly their profound beliefs in *dana*, yoga, heaven, and hell. The kind of rhetorical strategies the Brahmins devised—*dana* as a pathway to redemption, instillation of fear, construction of heaven and practice of yoga—further unveils a shrewdness that enabled them to earn the most exalted status in their society. In other words, they aimed to convince people to live their lives along the lines laid down by the *Purāṇas* "without compromising" [the Brahmins'] "principal objective of establishing the Brahmanical social order."[315] This clearly demonstrates that the treatises like the *Garuda Purāṇa* were not merely faithful narrations of the accounts of funeral rites, death, hell, heaven, yoga, myths, and traditional folklore but also acted as rhetorical instruments in the hands of the Brahmins who were, in a way, the backseat drivers of innumerable gods and goddesses of Hinduism. The rhetoric of the *Garuda Purāṇa* was imbued with values, ideologies, and motivations of the highest class of Hindus, who used the rhetorical tactics to maintain the social order in the caste-based Hindu society. It is true that the present study is limited to some selected chapters of the *Garuda Purāṇa*. The implication and limitations of this research point to the importance of future research on the first part and all sixteen chapters from the second part of the *Garuda Purāṇa*.

---

313. *The Garuḍa Purâṇa*,1911, Chapter XIV, lines 63–64.
314. Ibid., Chapter XVI, line 116.
315. Chakrabarti 2001, 52.

4.5 Hindu, c. 18th Century CE, India

I Say "Cat," You Say "Cradle": Ecstatic Signification and the Kitchen Songs of Avudai Akkal of Sengottai

Trey Conner and Richard Doyle

INTRODUCTION

Avudai Akkal of Sengottai was an eighteenth-century Tamil child-widow composer of songs of awakening addressed specifically to women circumscribed by oppressive social restrictions.[316] Taking classical Brahminical *topoi* directly into the realm of domestic routine and practical life, Akkal leveraged popular musical (*kriti*), dance *(kummi)*, and ludic *(ammanai)* forms of rhythmic turn-taking to encode and deliver otherwise inaccessible esoteric rhetorical instructions in the practice of Advaita Vedanta, which trains practitioners in the experience of "not-twoness" identified as *moksha* or liberation. Singers paradoxically connect in their experience of difference. In the experience of this nonduality, neither the subject nor the object assumes a separate existence as both can be known and perceived to emerge out of a higher order of abstraction, termed variously God, Self, Universe.

To practice encountering this nondual state, Akkal's songs of freedom contained explicit classic instructions in *viveka* (discernment between real and unreal), *vairagya* (withdrawal from all familiar attachments), *neti-neti* (analysis by negation), *pranayama* (breath control), *atma vichara* (self-inquiry), and *adhyaropa-apavada* (superimposition/negation), all of which enable a transformation of the mind and body that enables the experience of *Advaita*. The communities of women who safeguarded Akkal's songs and who continue to evolve them according to developments in the performance and transmission of Carnatic music (*kriti* techniques of composition, performance, and improvisatory play) also took on these Advaitic instructions, which Akkal integrates with descriptions of and recipes for self-care, kitchen work, and housekeeping.[317] Akkal artfully combined pedagogical, poetic, and musical elements to create an embodied performance-rhetoric for right-conduct—how to live—and right-view—proper understanding of who you are—for a demographic otherwise often excluded from such elevated instruction. By necessity, these instructions needed to be concise, effective, and easily repeated. So concise were these recipes that we might put them in the tradition of "pith instructions."

---

316. Natarajan 2016, 315–16. Natarajan renders the first English translations (from Tamil) of Akkal's songs.

317. Ibid., 320. Not only has Natarajan graciously rendered the first and only English translations of Akkal's songs, she also continues to conduct interviews with present-day singer-safeguardians of Akkal's songs in Tamil Nadu, India.

While pith instructions are mostly associated with the Tibetan Buddhist traditions, such as Dzogchen and Mahamudra, The New Testament's Sermon on the Mount, particularly the Beatitudes's refrain of "blessed," offers similarly direct instruction that requires participation and practice in the nondual state where, uncannily, the "meek inherit the earth." Pith instructions are like memory crystals; as a genre, they offer distillations and compressions of otherwise elaborate, heavily coded, and institutionally protected techniques for the alteration of consciousness—an experience of unity—akin to the recipes that would have circulated through Akkal's kitchens.

Pith instructions are often transmitted orally,[318] incorporating call and response refrains (e.g., mantra), whose repetition can exceed any "meaning" beyond words and concepts, *anirvachaniya*.[319] Because these instructions move beyond the sayable or the unsayable, the said or unsaid, the pith genre takes us into what the Sanskrit rhetorical tradition of *alamkarashastra* codes as *dhvani*, the power of suggestion.

Because pith works through this register of suggestion in Akkal's songs, we have to sing and play along to receive the teaching. Just as Jesus taught through parables and poetics that require individual effort in order to awaken to "the kingdom within you" (Luke 17:21), Akkal's songs are essentially and not accidentally multi-player games for *moksha*. To best transmit the syncretic and practical nature of these teachings, we as scholars/practitioners offer these songs within a "cat's cradle" of interconnections and interweavings that anyone can play even when, especially when, they do not understand.

THE GOLDEN RECORD: "HOW DO YOU WORK THIS THING?"

In a time-robbing *rondeau* of redundancy, Akkal's *Vedanta Vandu* ("Vedanta Bee") drones *dhvanic* pith instructions as it focuses on the dissolving final intoning bee-sound of the Advaitic Mandukya Upanishad's A-U-M structure[320] and invites singers to play that reminder inwardly, simply by repetitiously singing it: *ommmmm*. *Dhvani* (continuous *ommmmm* singing) is said to ring the inner *prajna* (wisdom) doorbell and open up beyond past, present, and future: *turiya*. Chanting this sound, says the song, tunes the singer beyond space and time. Such "essential meditation instructions are called pith instructions," explains Dzogchen master Tulku Urgyen Rinpoche, "and they are both profound and direct."[321] Such *Dhvani* offers the practitioner a way to directly investigate the vast realms of inner space or "primordial wakefulness."

---

318. Sometimes taking the form of a whisper. "As lineage-holder in Ear-whispered Kagyu transmission of Tibetan Buddhist practice of Wakefulness, Chogyam Trungpa is 'Rinpoche' or 'Precious Jewel' of millennial practical information on attitudes and practices of mind speech, and body that Western Poets over the same millenia have explored, individually, fitfully, as far as they were able—searching thru cities, scenes, seasons, manuscripts, libraries, back alleys, whorehouses, churches, drawing rooms, revolutionary cells, opium dens, merchant's rooms in Harrar, salons in Lissadell." (Ginsberg 2001, xi).

319. Neither existent nor nonexistent; indescribable.

320. "M corresponds to Prajna. Those who know this, by *stilling the mind*, find their true stature and inspire everyone around to grow" (Eswaran 1987, 61, emphasis added).

321. Rinpoche 2009, 186.

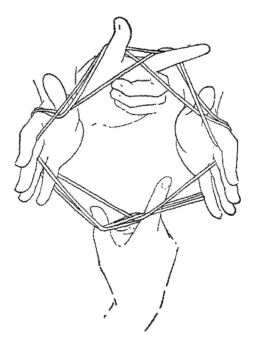

Figure 4.6: Cat's Cradle. Figure 743 sampled from C. F. Jayne's 1906 *String Figures*[322]

Meanwhile, after at least 1.76 million years of hurling objects into outer space,[323] human beings were on the cusp of being able to hit it out of the park: the Voyager spacecraft hurtled past Uranus, looking back at that pale blue dot, snapping a cosmic selfie. It was, of course, festooned with an LP record ready to be transduced at 33 ⅓ RPM, spindled as a whirling disk over which a stylus electromagnet might, in some extraterrestrial future, drag. This jewel was the Golden Record: a 12-inch gold plated copper disk grooving the analog differentials of pit and valley upon which that alien stylus would gently bob. While a good deal of worthy attention has been focused on the content of this golden disk—what was on it, what wasn't—less attention has been paid to the question of the LP's genre. Into what taxonomical file in the 1974 Sam Goody's Records should that slabby be filed?

322. Jayne 1906. An accessible excerpt can be found at http://www.stringfigures.info/cfj/real-cats-cradle.html
323. Calvin 1991, 173–96.

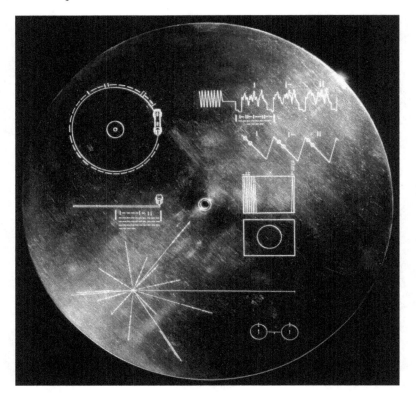

Figure 4.7. Detailed diagram of the cover of the Golden Record, shown with its extraterrestrial instructional sleeve.[324]

While this question of classification might seem unimportant, the challenge of placing the Voyager's instructions into a category may indeed augur a larger difficulty with Voyager as a technology of extraterrestrial communication: Even the category of the LP raises the question of the missing instructions for the instructions. In other words, the instructions presuppose the possibility of understanding the instructions. Instructions were included, but no workable instructions for *how* to follow those instructions will be found by any future ET who happens to be *sans* turntable.[325]

---

324. Jet Propulsion Laboratory, California Institute of Technology. "The Golden Record Cover." Accessed August 1, 2020. voyager.jpl.nasa.gov/golden-record/golden-record-cover/.

325. "Allied pilots, during World War II, who had to fly over certain remote and exotic areas such as Borneo (now called Kalimantan), were encouraged to carry a loop of string up to six feet long, the ends of which were tied together to make a single loop about three feet long. The idea was that if they crash landed their plane in an area where non-English-speaking natives were likely to be present, the pilot should (when someone approached through the jungle), casually take the loop of string from his pocket and begin to make a 'cat's cradle' string figure, and as many other string figures as he knew. It

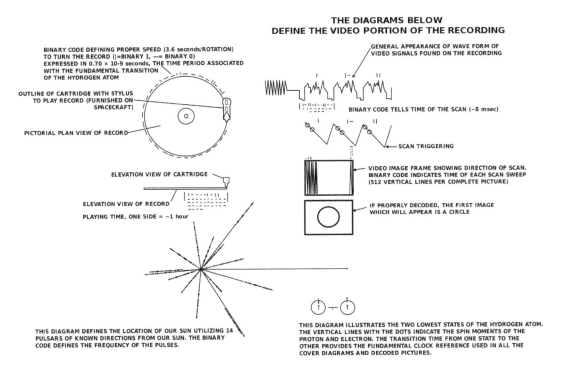

EXPLANATION OF RECORDING COVER DIAGRAM

Figure 4.8: The explanatory diagram is of little help in the matter.

It is this endogenous inclusion of the instructions in Advaita, the method for following the instructions themselves, that may instruct us in the extraordinary efficacy of Akkal's songs for transforming two singers or dancers into not-two, *Advaita*. Just as the string figure game of cat's cradle essentially and not accidentally requires two players who take turns weaving the whole, the songs require subtle turn taking to discover the not-two. Poet and playwright William Butler Yeats, whose experience translating the classic Sanskrit Upanishads with Shree Purohit Swamy would have acquainted him with key Vedanta texts, wondered over this very distinction, or lack thereof, in his "Among Schoolchildren":

---

is said that, on more than one occasion, this was actually tried. In each case, the story goes, the native watched with increasingly friendly interest, and then *politely borrowed* the loop to demonstrate some string figures popular in his own tribe" (Post 2020, emphasis added).

Are you the leaf, the blossom or the bole?
O body swayed to music, O brightening glance,
How can we know the dancer from the dance?[326]

Across time both Akkal and Cat's Cradle remind us to look where this poet points: How can we distinguish, dear reader, the reader from their reading?

SOUND AND ATTENTION, ATTENTION TO SOUND

Although we know, from the interview efforts and scholarship of Kanchana Natarajan, that Avudai Akkal was born in Sengottai, a town in the Tenkasi district of Tamil Nadu, India, we have no precise dates for Akkal, and "no personal details of her life are invoked in any song, except the central event of her dramatic encounter with her guru and her subsequent initiation by him into the path of Advaita."[327] Natarajan's interview sources—the singers and living oral tradition of Akkal's songs—suggest that after her excommunication from her own *agraharam* for defying oppressive gender-codes, Akkal went with her teacher Tiruvisainallour Shridhara Venkatesa Ayyawal to study with Brahmin scholars in the king's court: Akkal's guru Ayyawal lived from 1655? to 1740, and was in 1693 given land and a scholarly post (by Sahaji I of the Travancore Royal Family) in an *agraharam* ("tax-free residential colony") in Truvisainallur along the Kaveri river.[328]

Here, sometime in the early eighteenth century, Ayyal "insisted that Akkal was a *jnani*," or an adept of self-knowledge, and here Akkal studied with Ayyal and the other male scholars commissioned by the king. She learned the complex and often scholastic arguments of the logicians, "the fundamentals of Mimamsa, Samkhya, Nyaya, Buddhist and Charvaka philosophies," and she also "began singing songs about this mode of sublimity . . . advaitic truth," sitting in stillness at the Kaveri river's edge, and at times earning the reputation of "an *unmattha* (one who wanders like a madwoman)" who composed songs "while in this state of spiritual intoxication."[329] For a modern reader, Akkal may perhaps be best compared to a martial artist of the inner realms with mad poetry skills and a total devotion to God.

That devotion is illuminated when Natarajan tells "the legend of her disappearance": on a walk down by the river to Shenbaga falls with three devotees, Akkal "signalled to them not to follow her further. She walked on alone, never to return . . . thus, the only evidence of Akkal's person is the legacy of her songs."[330] In some sense both literal and figurative, Akkal is said to have disappeared into her songs. The songs lived on in colloquial Tamil language sung and transcribed in personal notebooks by women throughout the eighteenth and nineteenth centuries in Tamil Nadu. An unknown scholar published Akkal's *Vedanta Pallu* in Tamil, in

---

326. Yeats 1933.
327. Natarajan 2016, 50.
328. Ibid., 53, 29, 32.
329. Ibid., 53–54.
330. Ibid., 54.

1896 (a copy of this text resides at the University of Köln, Germany), and "in 1910 one N. Vaitiyanatha Bharati of Thanjavur published a book that included at least fourteen of Akkal's songs" in Tamil.[331] Today, in Tamil Nadu, Natarajan interviews Tamil-speaking singers of Akkal's songs to prepare her own translations and analyses in English, cited herein.

The songs comprising Akkal's *padagal* are vehicles for rhetorical instruction in Advaitic practices of self-care and self-inquiry—and in *Vedanta Vandu* ("Vedanta Bee"), the Carnatic *kriti* song template functions as a precise "acetate" or substrate by which Akkal "records" her instructions in and as song. Songs are to be sung, performances are "recordings," played: the sounding and resounding itself, not the form, carries the instructions. The way we hear it, Akkal's kitchen songs sing of the power of the sung and heard word, enjoining and amplifying the pith emphasis on first-hand experience and knowledge. *Vedanta Vandu*'s repeating *pallavi* "O bee! Become my messenger and visit the great master! Worship his feet; bee acquainted with his glories and come back to me!"[332] threads the pattern by repeating between each verse of the *charanam* (root of the song, the verses in total) and thereby sets the tonic[333] in *Vedanta Vandu*, cradling—knotting and distributing[334]—the pollination process as the enactment and transmission of pith instructions for the discovery, mapping, and sharing of interior states that can't be named as they are not quite there, suggestions that are neither subject nor object: *dhvani*. Like all Akkal's kitchen songs, *Vedanta Vandu* forms a common collective: turn-taking continues apace as we turn within. Akkal teaches: let go. Let go of *kriti* and *kummi* forms, let go of turn-taking, just give up, let your love flow. Don't prove or improve, don't surmise or even improvise. Akkal's formulas, mnemonics, sampled classical Upanishadic imagery and apothegms point within, and the suggestion is crystal clear while never really uttered and only perhaps rarely heard.

---

331. Ibid., 35.

332. Ibid., 346–51.

333. "Regarding the apparent duality of Homeward vs. Outward, many years later I discovered a musical analogy, which has turned out to be inspiring and helpful for my own process of integration: in tonal (i.e., traditional) music of all cultures, the tonic is the fundamental note that informs the entire development of a melody. Very often, a song will even begin and end on this tonic note. In Indian music it is played as a drone throughout the performance of the piece. If we liken this tonic drone to Home, and the notes of a sublime melody to episodes of Outward-bound adventure, then it is possible to leave Home, yet in a deeper sense, never leave Home. And the melody is all the more beautiful for its moments of divergence, even dissonance, provided that the tonic is not forgotten" (Rowe 2012, 13).

334. "Cat's cradle is about patterns and knots; the game takes great skill and can result in some serious surprises. One person can build up a large repertoire of string *figures* on a single pair of hands; but the cat's cradle figures can be passed back and forth on the hands of several players, who add new moves in the building of complex patterns. Cat's cradle invites a sense of collective work, of one person not being able to make all the patterns alone. One does not 'win' at cat's cradle; the goal is more interesting and more open-ended than that. It is not always possible to repeat interesting patterns, and figuring out what happened to result in intriguing patterns is an embodied analytical skill. The game is played around the world and can have considerable cultural significance. Cat's cradle is both local and global, distributed and knotted together" (Haraway 1994, 59-71).

But lest this emphasis on "ecstatic signification"[335] risks orientalizing Akkal's work and privileging the court language of Sanskrit for its interpretation, we will weave a brief derive back through ancient Greece,[336] where the sound of speech—the non-semantic but pragmatic unspeakable work of sound itself in the utterance—was also of great importance. This thread is part of a larger project of weaving together diverse rhetorical traditions in a manner worthy of cat's cradle, perhaps the world's oldest game or art form—an alternative rhetorical source rooted neither in speech nor writing but capable of weaving together both.

The grammarian Dionysios Thrax and the Epicurean Philodemus of Gadara were among those who emphasized the supreme importance of *orthoëpy*, or "correct reading according to intonation, timbre-quality, and quantity," for any eloquence training, and they did so because reading meant *reading aloud*.[337] Early euphonist Lasus of Hermione began to focus on *sound itself*, apart from pronunciation, when he, following the Pythagoreans, studied the strings of lyres and how they vibrated, how they felt. His far-reaching conception of *mousike* cradled literature and music together in one knotted sonic loop, perhaps in response to writing's disruptive effects on the practice of the spoken word, the low rumble of "tumble" described by Socrates in *Phaedrus*.[338] So when Lasus and his student Pindar admonish speakers and singers who favor that roughest and toughest of sibilants, sigma, (Cat's cradle) W. B. Stanford believes there is "an objective acoustic basis for the prejudice: the rougher sibilants emit in pronunciation a larger proportion of higher partials (or "overtones," or "harmonics"),"[339] the resonant

---

335. Munn 1973, 177–78.

336. We can also look to Africa. For example, Dereje Birbirso details "the Oromo Gada System unique principle and ritual of "móggassa, 'name-giving, sawing maxims' also called Makk'á/Luba Bása Gadaa, literally, 'the social-linguistic actions of freeing/unveiling of names/rites' or 'the name-giving praxis' in accordance to Gada System . . . móggassa is a causative from mógga/mak'a '(to) name, mock, curve, altercate; to give way, get out of the way to the boundary, to mix, confound, doze; branch (road), namesake, abundance, gruel, wilderness, weft, woof'. Oromo concepts of making rhetorics, literary figures/metaphors and proverbs/folklores (mógmógsa/mak'mak'sa) rest down in this proto-concept . . . interweaving genre varieties, the Oromo wiseman speaks and sings in rhythmatic verses styled by "the usual" and "artful sound parallelism" and connected "forming a kind of parallelism of sounds or images" (Cerulli 1922, 21, 87, 67, 69, 96) or, as another scholar expresses it, forming "parallelism of sounds" and "image" in "vocalic harmony" (Bartels, 1975, 898). It is the reflection of that old tradition that even the contemporary time elderly Oromo skilled in Oromo wisdom speaks "in ritual language, as it was used in old times at the proclamation of the law" (Bartels 1983, 309) . . . in "the long string of rhyme, which consists of repeating the same verse at the end of each couplet" or a "series of short sententious phrases" that are "disposed to help memory" (de Salviac 2005 [1901], 285). " Birbirso 2014, 12–15. See also Dingemanse 2019, 13–33.

337 Stanford 1967, 7, emphasis added.

338. "And when they have been once written down they are tumbled about anywhere among those who may or may not understand them, and know not to whom they should reply, to whom not: and, if they are maltreated or abused, they have no parent to protect them; and they cannot protect or defend themselves" (Plato 1892).

339. Stanford 1967, 8.

self-triggering fractal feedback aspect of thusly tuned and heard sounds which unfold as larger resonant patterns beyond meaning. Cat's cradle.

Vedanta Vandu resounds with this global tradition of emphasizing the transporting effects of sound itself, delivering pith instructions for loosening the knot in the heart with sound and finding the Source of all cat's cradling, in song. "O bee! Become my messenger!" is the repeated refrain, the *pallavi*. "O bee! Become my messenger!" After some sounding and resounding out loud, we notice Akkal's song is perfectly pithed to the tune of the often inaccessible Upanishads: if you hear them, you will drop your outward wandering senses and lose the clinging clinch of desire and become free: Moksa. "O bee! Become my messenger!" In the sixth verse of *Vedanta Bee*, specific instructions on how to hear a great saying (the *mahavakya* "Aham Brahman")—itself an instruction in how to listen—and how to train in that view, are encoded: inquire upon the "I-thought." Look into your mind to find the source of your feeling of being separate, and sing along: "O bee! Become my messenger!"

> Hearing the exposition *Aham Brahman*,
> the persistent illusion 'I am a jiva' disintegrated.
> Blessed by the enquiry into *aham padartha*,
> I am sleepless day and night...
> Tell him this, O bee...![340]

We can begin to inquire into (take turns with) the very idea of "I" (aham padartha) by singing songs—which are essentially sequences of sound and silence—and becoming aware of the one doing the singing. The Mandukya Upanishad, rendered in Eknath Earswaran's translation, translates it this way:

> There is no mind in Prajna, there is no
> Separateness; but the sleeper is not
> Conscious of this. Let him become conscious
> In Prajna and it will open the door
> To the state of abiding joy[341]

When the sweet sound of "I am Brahman" is heard and the sleeper awakens to the bliss of nonseparation and no-mind in prajna, the instruction is to not attach, but rather let go into self-inquiry: Who am I? "O bee! Become my messenger!" Akkal's Vedanta bee has become a mind that does not exist delivering a message where there is no distinction between receiver and sender. Buzz buzz. Who hears? Who intones this "empty sound"?[342] When ninth-century author and theorist of Sanksrit poetics, Anandavardhana, and his eleventh-century Kashmi-

---

340. Natarajan 2016, 350.
341. Easwaran 1987, 60.
342. *dhvani*, "sound, echo, noise, voice, tone, tune, thunder . . . the sound of a drum . . . empty sound . . . a word, allusion, hint, implied meaning, poetical style. . . . delighting by it's sound, a bee" (Monier-Williams 2005).

ri polymath commentator, Abhinavagupta, insist on the crucial subconscious dimension of *santa-rasa*,[343] and the equipoise of perfect rhythm in sound,[344] we must agree to simply let it go and, along with Akkal and those other songsters Lennon-McCartney, let it be. "O bee! Become my messenger!"

Hearing the buzz of the bee, and letting it be, is hearing the Upanishads. Akkal's song is pith-ware for the Mandukya, already one of the most compressed Upanishads: "In its succinctness the Mandukya distills essentials of mystical insight . . . thus is was always treated as almost a sutra . . . with great mnemonic value"[345] A tight script for transcending time and opening the inner door to Turiya, the transcendental fourth state of consciousness that is neither waking, dreaming, nor dreamless sleep, the Mandukya traces the indivisible *omkara*[346] seed syllable phonetically as an A U M triplet that begins in overlong nasalized close-mid back rounded vowel outward pronunciations (a, u) and converges in a humming bilabial closure (m), buzzing inward towards that which cannot be heard, the unstruck sound, Brahman.

In *Vedanta Bee*, cat's cradle is the gesture that also weaves the Chandogya Upanishad's mahavakya (great saying) and essential trope of any practice of nondual listening: *Tat tvam asi.* The student, seeking truth, finds that they are that which they seek: thou art that, or "you are woven through that."

Cat's cradle, viewed as a sequence of gestures, enacts this essential trope of immanence where what is apparently external can be seen to be internal, and vice versa. In the Gospel of Thomas, which is not a narrative account of a person but rather a set of pith instruc-

---

343. "By the use of examples Ananda builds up a typology of *dhvani* (suggestion)," Ingalls explains in his introduction to the primary texts. The first type, *avivaksitavacya*, is suggestive language with unintended denotation, wherein the denoted sense is either left aside (*atyantatiraskrta*), or not left aside but instead shifted elsewhere—that is to say, troped (*arthantarasankramita*). Anandavardhana's second type of suggestion literally goes further. In *vivaksitanyaparavacya* suggestion, "the literal sense is intended but only as leading on to something further" (Ingalls 14). This second type of suggestion also parses into "two varieties, depending on whether or not we are conscious of the succession from the literal to the 'something further'" or not, and for Anandavardhana and his commentators the "much more important of the two varieties is that where we are not conscious of any interval between the two senses (*asamlaksitakrama*), for in this variety the 'something other' is a rasa. . . the ultimate aim of literature" (Ānandavardhana and Abhinavagupta 1990, 14-15).

344. "Some images represent hierarchy of time and relations between musical levels: in the Upanishads, time is sometimes likened to Brahman sitting the centre of a spider web, as the cosmic spider; one musical inference that may be drawn is perhaps that the time of Indian music, like time in general, is a condition of balance, of "zerogravity," poised in the midst of an interlocking set of components at various levels and an equilibrium of opposing tensions. This is testified to by Abhinavagupta,who defined the sole purpose of *tala* as the achieving of *samya* (equipoise)" (Rowell 1979, 99).

345. Easwaran 1987, 59.

346. *omkara* is the word or even recipe for *making the sound* of the seed syllable OM. Nityananda Misra explains that *omkara/onkara* signifies "the *exclamation* or the *sound* OM . . . the suffix *kara* also explains words like *humkara omkara* ("grunting sound") and *chitkara* ("shouting sound") . . . the word *omkara* literally means "the sound OM" . . . the saguna aspect of OM" (Misra 2018, 29, emphasis added).

tions, Jesus describes the way to the Kingdom as precisely such a recipe of folding subjectivity through itself: "When you make the inside the outside and the outside the inside . . . then you have entered the kingdom."[347] Here, we again pass the string to Avudai Akkal, and look to the seventeenth and eighteenth verses of *Vedanta Vandu*, for pith instructions in listening and turn-taking.

In Natarajan's translation of the seventeenth verse of *Vedanta Vandu*, all roads lead to the Self, the honeycombed hideout at the heart of that most epic of songs, the *Chandogya Upanishad*. In this translation, Akkal's instructions are clear: to properly sing *omkara* (the making of Om, sounding Om), you must abandon all *upadhis*. *Upadhis* are disguises, vehicles, body, mind, memory. Set to suggestive (dhvanic) song, *upadhis* are recognized as metonymy, as "that which places its own attributes to something nearby" and "conditionings."[348] In Hindu logic (Nyaya), *upadhis* are the conditions that accompany the major term, which is supplied to limit the general middle term.[349] In rhetorical terms, *Vedanta Vandu* prescribes the proleptic *practice* of dispassionate non-attachment (*abhyasa-vairagyabhyam*) when it urges us to abandon all conditionings, misplaced identifications, and premises, thereby surrendering the surrenderer into the resonance. *Dhvani* is the resonant register of redundancy in language and sound that takes us beyond conditioned associations and identifications, the vibration that "heals" metonymy.[350] Hear this entire verse by saying it aloud:

> Just as the nectar imbibed from different flowers
> Merges into one stream of honey in the honeycomb,
> So too, with all upadhis abandoned
> The Self alone exists as one and indivisible.
> This great awareness penetrates
> To the inmost depth of my being.[351]

Beyond metonymy, the Vedanta Vandu *dhvani* is the means by which the *rasa* is renounced. That *rasa* "is communicated by a semantic capacity of language other than and complementary to the generally recognized capacities of literal denotation and metonymy. This novel capacity [Anandavardhana] calls *dhvani* , which means literally 'noise' or 'sound,' *but by re-*

---

347. "They said to him, 'Shall we then, as children, enter the kingdom?' Jesus said to them, 'When you make the two one, and when you make the inside like the outside and the outside like the inside, and the above like the below, and when you make the male and the female one and the same, so that the male not be male nor the female female; and when you fashion eyes in the place of an eye, and a hand in place of a hand, and a foot in place of a foot, and a likeness in place of a likeness; then will you enter the kingdom.'" "The Gospel of Thomas" (1990, 129).

348. www.theosophy.world/encyclopedia/upadhi

349. For a comparative treatment of Nyaya and Aristotle's enthymeme, see Lloyd (2011) .

350. See also the "enthymeme of our suffering" discussion in Doyle and Conner (2021).

351. Natarajan 2016, 350.

cursion *(an instance of itself)*, 'overtone,' 'suggestion'."[352] Thus, such high (buzzing) frequency renunciations of *rasa*, which itself is a "relishing," brings recognition of *dhvani-rasa* unity.

Akkal flows with, and sings pith instructions for enacting, the essential *mahavakya*[353] honeycombed as a looping refrain into the Chandogya Upanishad VI. 9. 1-4, *Tat Tvam Asi*, you are that:

> As bees suck nectar from many a flower
> And make there honey one, so that no drop
> Can say, 'I am from this flower or that,'
> All creatures, though one, know not that they are
> that One.
> There is nothing that does not come from
> him.
> Of everything he is the inmost Self.
> He is the truth; he is the Self supreme.
> You are that, Svetakatu; you are that.[354]

Akkal's Upanisadic bee song may also bring tantric Mahavidya imagery into view, as it does in the eighteenth verse:

> the compassion of the Satguru
> Who rests on the mattress called Sadashiva
> On the cot that has the four quarters of Brahman
> As its supporting legs,
> Has granted me the fruit of all the Vedas.
> Tell him this, O bee![355]

But this image, and its seeming association with one's body, must dissolve in the din, as all *uphadhis* are dropped, forgotten in a melting honeyed flow, *santa-rasa*. "I may be a practitioner of wordy indulgences, Or may have detached from the sensuous realm."[356]No matter, pitter patter, attached or no, worry not and boast not—just don't forget the sacred resonant words. How to do this?

Vibrate with them. This vibrational "thinking" of the sacred nonsignifying bee buzzing *omkara* phonemes, takes you past remembering and forgetting into *rasa*, the process of perception perceiving *itself*, or Trika tantric Abhinavagupta's *pratiyamana eva hi rasa*.[357] In the tradition of Advaita master Avudai Akkal: "thinking [of the sacred resonant words given by

---

352. Gerow 1965, emphasis added.
353. Upanisadic "great saying," of which there are four.
354. Chandogya 1962, 184.
355. Natarajan 2016, 350
356. Ibid., 350
357. Cited in Deutsch 1975, 2.

the guru] at all times, like a wasp, I have become *tadakaram*." [358] In the tradition of Dzogchen master Tulku Urgyen Rinpoche: at all times you are going to *rigpa*. Like a bee's pollination, "training is simply short moments of recognition repeated many times and supported by devotion and compassion." [359] The "moments of recognition" cradled by these diverse traditions are nonconceptual and nonsignifying. Vibrational. A wasp alights upon this flower:

> Wasp and orchid, as heterogeneous elements, form a rhizome. It could be said that the orchid imitates the wasp, reproducing its image in a signifying fashion (mimesis, mimicry, lure, etc.). But this is true only on the level of the strata—a parallelism between two strata such that a plant organization on one imitates an animal organization on the other. . . [360]

This is cat's cradle in a mirror. Deleuze and Guattari's treatment of the wasp/orchid dyad echoes through anthropologist Natasha Myers's description of "getting involved with each other" as others, the experimental and reciprocal capture of humming and omming along in song and therefore echoing together across time. [361] But the *Vedanta Vandu* song points even further inward, past your disappearance, amplifying the resonance until this reciprocal capture becomes a squandering, [362] a release, a letting go; a letting be: Vairagya. [363]

In discontinuity and silence, there is for Akkal no grasping, only letting go. Taking turns with "other" singers and dancers is one and the same as turning within, letting go into the silence after the *omkara*, letting go into the resounding recursive ongoing instance of buzzing heard in repetitive visitations to the lotus-feet of the guru, a *dhvani* of life, and eloquence, beyond individual organisms—beyond yourself: Cat's cradle.

---

358. Natarajan leaves the Sanskrit term *tadakaram* in her English translation, but unpacks this term in a footnote as "the *process* whereby . . . Self is assumed" (Natarajan 2016 355, emphasis added).

359. Rinpoche 2009, 82.

360. Deleuze and Guattari 1987, 10.

361. Myers 2017.

362. "The sun gives without ever receiving" (Bataille 1991, 28).

363. Ramana equates "thought of God" with *abhyasa-vairagyabhyam*, the "practice of dispassion" in Munagala (226, 525-26, 540).

Comprehensive Bibliography

Acharya, Rahul. 2018. Personal Interview, (October 18).

Adhikary, Nirmala Mani. 2009. "An Introduction to Sadharanikaran Model of Communication." *Bodhi: An Interdisciplinary Journal* 3 (1): 69–91. doi:10.3126/bodhi.v3i1.2814.

—. 2010. "Sancharyoga: Approaching Communication as a Vidya in Hindu Orthodoxy." *China Media Research* 6 (3): 76+.

—. 2014. "Re-orientation, Ferment and Prospects of Communication Theory in South Asia." *China Media Research* 10 (2): 24–28.

Aitareya Upanishad. 2015. In *The Upanishads, a New Translation*. Translated and edited by Thomas Egenes and Vernon Katz. New York: Tarcher/Penguin.

Ānandavardhana and Abhinavagupta. 1990. *The Dhvanyāloka of Ānandavardhana with the Locana of Abhinavagupta*. Translated by Daniel H. H. Ingalls, Jeffrey Moussaieff Masson, and M. V. Patwardhan; edited by Daniel H. H. Ingalls. Cambridge: Harvard University Press.

Andersen, Susan K. "Language, Expressing the Full Range of Life." In *The Flow of Consciousness: Maharishi Mahesh Yogi on Literature and Language 1971 to 1976*, Part 2, edited by Rhoda F. Orme-Johnson and Susan K. Andersen, 119–36. Fairfield, IA: Consciousness-Based Books-Maharishi University of Management Press.

Aristotle. 1924. *Rhetoric*. In *The Works of Aristotle*, vol. 11, translated by W. Rhys Roberts. Oxford: Oxford UP

—. 2007. *On Rhetoric*: *A Theory of Civil Discourse,* 2nd ed., translated by George A. Kennedy. New York: Oxford University Press.

Aurobindo, Sri (Aurobindo Ghose). 1998b. *The Secret of the Veda*. In *Complete works of Sri Aurobindo* (Vol. 15). Pondicherry, India: Sri Aurobindo Ashram Publication Department.

Avari, Burjor. 2007. *India: The Ancient Past: A History of the Indian Sub-Continent from c.7000 BC to AD 1200*. New York: Routledge.

Bataille, George. 1991. *The Accursed Share,* vol. 1, translated by R. Hurley. New York: Zone Books.

Bateson, Gregory. 2002. *Mind and Nature: A Necessary Unity*. Cresskill, NJ: Hampton Press.

Beatles. 1970. *Let It Be*. Apple Records AR 34001 (JS 1750), 1970, 33⅓ rpm.

Berger, Ron, and Ram Herstein, 2014. "The Evolution of Business Ethics in India." *International Journal of Social Economics* 41 (11): 1073–86. doi:012910.1108/ijse-05-2013.

Berlin, James 1984. A. *Writing Instruction in Nineteenth-Century American Colleges*. Carbondale, IL: Southern Illinois University Press.

Bharata. 1967. *The Natyasastra*. Translated by Manmohan Ghosh. Calcutta: Manisha Granthalaya.

Bhargava, Purushottam Lal. 1977. "The Origin and Development of Purāṇas and Their Relation with Vedic Literature." *Annals of the Bhandarkar Oriental Research Institute* 58: 489–98.

Bhartrihari. 1971. *The Vākyapadīya: Studies in the Vākyapadīya,* vol. 1. Translated and edited by K. Raghavan Pillai. New Delhi: Motilal Banarsidass.

Bhattacharyya, Sibajiban. 2010 *Development of Nyaya Philosophy and its Social Context*, vol. 3 part 3 of *History of Science, Philosophy and Culture in Indian Civilization,* edited by D. P. Chattopadhyaya. New Delhi: Centre for Studies in Civilizations.

Birbirso, Dereje Tadesse. 2014. "Plato's *Cratylus*: A Comparative Historical Linguistic and Social Semiotic Analysis from Ancient African Perspective." Paper presented in *Haramaya University School of Foreign Language Studies 3rd Annual Critical Reflection Session* (March): 12–15.

Bizzell, Patricia, and Bruce Herzberg, eds. 2001. *The Rhetorical Tradition: Readings from Classical Times to the Present.* 2nd ed. New York: Bedford/St. Martins.

Brewer, Judsin A., et al. 2011. "Meditation Experience Is Associated with Differences in Default Mode Network Activity and Connectivity." *Proceedings of the National Academy of Sciences* 108 (50): 20254–59.

Brihadaranyaka Upanishad. 1884, 1962. In *The Upaniṣads, Part 2*, translated by F. Max Müller, 73–227. *The Sacred Books of the East*, vol. 15, edited by F. Max Müller. New York: Dover.

Bronkhorst, Johannes. 2001. "Etymology and Magic: Yāska's Nirukta. Plato's Cratylus, and the Riddle of Semantic Etymologies." *Numen* 48 (2): 147–203.

Brown, Cheever Mackenzie. 1974. *God as Mother: A Feminine Theology in India: An Historical and Theological Study of the Brahmavaivarta Purāṇa.* Vermont: Stark (Claude) & Co..

—. 1986. "Purāṇa as Scripture: From Sound to Image of the Holy Word in the Hindu Tradition." *History of Religions* 26 (1): 68–86.

Bryant, Edwin F., trans. and ed. 2009. *The Yoga Sūtras of Patañjali: A New Edition, Translation, and Commentary with Insights from the Traditional Commentators.* New York: New Point Press.

Bryant, Edwin F., and Laurie L. Patton, eds. 2005. *The Indo-Aryan Controversy: Evidence and Inference in Indian History.* New York: Routledge.

Buchta, David. 2010. "Gārgī Vākaknavī as an Honorary Male: An Eighteenth Century Reception of an Upaniṣadic Female Sage." *The Journal of Hindu Studies* 3: 354–70.

Calvin, William. 1991. *Ascent of Mind.* New York: Bantom Books.

Captain Beefheart and His Magic Band. 1969. *Trout Mask Replica.* Reprise Records STS-1053, 33⅓ rpm.

Chaitanya, Krishna. 1962. *A New History of Sanskrit Literature.* Bombay: Asia Publishing House.

Chari, V. K. 1977. "The Indian theory of suggestion (dhvani)." *Philosophy East and West* 27 (4): 391–99.

Chakrabarti, Arinda, 1983. "Is Liberation (mokṣa) Pleasant?," *Philosophy East and West* 33 (2): 167–82.

Chakrabarti, Kunal. 2001. *Religious Process: The Purāṇas and the Making of a Regional Tradition.* New Delhi: Oxford University Press.

Chakraborty, Amitava. 2008. "Rhetoric in South Asia." In *The International Encyclopedia of Communication.* Edited by Wolfgang Donsbach. Blackwell Publishing.

Chandogya Upanishad. 1884, rpt. 1962. In *The Upaniṣads,* Part 1. Translated by F. Max Müller. *The Sacred Books of the East.* Vol. 15, edited by F. Max Müller. New York: Dover.

Chatterjea, Ananya. 1996. "Training in Indian Classical Dance: A Case Study." *Asian Theatre Journal* 13 (1): 68–91.

Chatterjea, Ananya. 2007. "Contestations: Constructing a Historical Narrative for Odissi." *Nordic Theatre Studies* 19: 19–34.

Chernoff, John Miller. 1981. *African rhythm and African sensibility.* Chicago: University of Chicago Press.

Chinese Buddhist Encyclopedia. 2020. "Pith Instructions." chinabuddhismencyclopedia. com.

Choudhuri, Usha. 2006. "Vāg Vai Saraswatī." In *Veda as Word,* edited by Shashiprabha Kumar, 55–63. New Delhi: Special Center for Sanskrit Studies, Jawaharlal Nehru University-D.K. Printworld.

Cicero. 2001. *On the Ideal Orator.* Translated by James M. May and Jakob Wisse. Oxford: Oxford University Press.

Collier, John, and Burch, Mark. 1998. "Order from Rhythmic Entrainment and the Origin of Levels through Dissipation." *Symmetry: Culture and Science, Order / Disorder Proceedings of the Haifa Congress* 9 (2–4): 165–78.

Coudry, Anuradha. 20016. "Sanskrit and Evolution of Human Speech, Based on Sri Aurobindo's Linguistic Theory." *International Journal of Humanities and Peace* 22 (1): 100. *Gale Academic OneFile.* link.gale.com.

Coward, Harold G. 1976. *Bhartṛhari.* Boston: Twayne Publishers-G.K. Hall & Co.

Coward, Harold G. 1989. "The Meaning and Power of Mantras in Bhartṛhari's *Vākyapadīya.*" In *Mantra,* edited by Harvey P. Alper, 165–76. Albany, NY: State University of New York Press.

Coward, Harold G., and David J. Goa. 2004. *Mantra: Hearing the Divine in India and America.* 2nd ed. New York: Columbia University Press.

Cush, Denise, Catherine Robinson, and Michael York, eds. 2008. *Encyclopedia of Hinduism.* London: Routledge.

Cushman, Ellen, and Shreelina Ghosh. 2012. "The mediation of cultural memory: digital preservation in the cases of classical Indian dance and the Cherokee stomp dance." *Journal of Popular Culture (Boston)* 45(2): 264–83.

Cushman, Ellen, Guiseppe Getto, and Shreelina Ghosh. 2012. "Learning with Communities in a Praxis of New Media." *Texts of Consequence: Composing Rhetorics of Social Activism for the Writing Classroom.*

Dange, Sindhu S. 2006. "From 'Mortal' to 'Divine' Through Vāk." In *Veda as Word,* edited by Shashiprabha Kumar, 49–97. New Delhi: Special Center for Sanskrit Studies, Jawaharlal Nehru University-D.K. Printworld.

Das, Maguni C. 2008. Personal Interview. July 23.

Das, Rahul Peter. 1996. "'Vedic' in the Terminology of Prabhupada and His Followers." *ISK-CON Communications Journal* 4 (2): 23–38.

Derrida, Jacques. 1978. *Writing and Difference.* Translated by Alan Bass. Chicago: University of Chicago Press.

Desmarais, Michele. 2008. *Changing Minds: Mind, Consciousness and Identity in Patanjali's Yoga Sutra.* Delhi, India: Motilal Banarsidass.

Deleuze, Gilles, and Felix Guattari. 1987. *A Thousand Plateaus: Capitalism and Schizophrenia.* Minneapolis: University of Minnesota Press.

Desai, Gita, dir., auth. 2009. *Raga Unveiled: The History and Essence of North Indian Classical Music.* [no place]: Produced by Gita Desai and Mukesh Desai, DVD.

Deutsch, Eliot. 1975. *Monographs of the Society for Asian and Comparative Philosophy, no. 2. Studies in Comparative Aesthetics.* Honolulu, HI: The University Press of Hawaii.

Dick, Philip K. 1995. "Man, Android, and Machine." In *The Shifting Realities of Philip K. Dick: Selected Literary and Philosophical Writings* edited by Lawerence Sutin, 211–32. New York: Vintage Book.

Dingemanse, Mark. 2019. "'Ideophone' as a Comparative Concept." In *Ideophones, Mimetics, Expressives,* edited by Kimi Akita and Prashant Pardeshi, 13–33. Amsterdam: John Benjamins, 2019.

Doniger, Wendy, ed. 1993. *Purāṇaa Perennis: Reciprocity and Transformation in Hindu and Jaina Texts.* New York: State University of New York Press.

Doniger, Wendy. 2009. *The Hindus: An Alternative History.* New York: The Penguin Press.

Doyle, Richard, and Trey Conner. 2020. "Chanting the Supreme Word of Information: Sacred!? Redundant?!" In *Responding to the Sacred,* edited by Michael Bernard-Donals and Kyle Jensen, 119–40. University Park: Penn State University Press, 2020.

Easwaran, Eknath. 1987. *The Upanishads.* Tomales: Nilgiri Press.

Egenes, Thomas. 2015. Introduction to *The Upanishads, a New Translation,* translated and edited by Thomas Egenes and Vernon Katz, 1–28. New York: Tarcher/Penguin.

Elizarenkova, Tatyana J. 1995. *Language and Style of the Vedic Rsis,* edited by Wendy Doniger. SUNY Series in Hindu Studies. Albany, NY: State University of New York Press, 1995.

Encyclopedia Britannica. 2018. "The Fate of the Soul." www.britannica.com.

Feuerstein, Georg, Subhash Kak, and David Frawley. 2001. *In Search of the Cradle of Civilization.* 2nd ed. Wheaton, IL: Theosophical Publishing House-Quest Books.

Fleckenstein, Kristie. 2011. "Out of 'Wonderful Silence' Come 'Sweet Words': The Rhetorical Authority of St. Catherine of Siena." In *Silence and Listening as Rhetorical Arts,* edited by Krista Ratcliffe and Cheryl Glenn, 37–55. Carbondale: Southern Illinois University Press.

Ganeri, Jonardon, 1996. "The Hindu Syllogism; Nineteenth-Century Perceptions of Indian Logical Thought," *Philosophy of East and West* 46 (1): 1–16.

—. 2001a. "Indian Logic and the Colonization of Reason." In *Indian Logic: A Reader,* edited by Jonardon Ganeri, 1–25. Richmond, Surry UK: Routlege/Curzon.

—. 2001b. *Philosophy in Classical India.* New York: Routledge.

The Garuda Purāṇa. 1911. Translated by Ernest Wood and S. V. Subrahmanyam.

Gerow, Edwin. 1965. "Indian Poetics." In *The New Princeton Encyclopedia of Poetry and Poetics.* Princeton: Princeton University Press.

Getto, Guiseppe, Ellen Cushman, and Shreelina Ghosh. 2011. "Community Mediation: Writing in Communities and Enabling Connections through New Media." *Computers and Composition* 28 (2): 160–74.

Ghosh, Manomohan. 1957. *Abhinayadarpanam: A Manual of Gesture and Posture Used in Hindu Dance and Drama.* Firma KL: Mukhopadhyay.

Ghosh, Shreelina. 2013. "Modern Rendition of Ancient Arts: Negotiating Values in Traditional Odissi Dance." *On Interdisciplinary Studies in Humanities* 5 (2): 76–88.

—. 2015. "Technological Mediation in Odissi Dance: A Transnational Perspective of Digitized Practice and Pedagogy in a Traditional Artistic Community." In *Business Law and Ethics: Concepts, Methodologies, Tools, and Applications,* 474–91. IGI Global.

Ginsberg, Allen. 2001. Introduction to *First Thought Best Thought: 108 Poems,* by Chogyam Trungpa. Boulder: Shambhala Press.

Givan, Benjamin. 2007. "Apart Playing: McCoy Tyner and 'Bessie's Blues.'" *Journal of the Society for American Music* 1 (2): 257–80.

Goldman, Robert, and Sally Sutherland Goldman. 2009. "*Rāmāyaṇa.*" *Saccred Texts, Ritual Traditions, Arts, Concepts.* Vol. 2 of *Brill's Encyclopedia of Hinduism.* Handbook of Oriental Studies, Sect. 2, edited by Knut A. Jacobsen, et al., 111–26. Boston: Brill, 2009.

Gonda, J. 1984. *The Vision of the Vedic Poets.* New Delhi: Munshiram Manoharlal Publishers.

"The Gospel of Thomas. II, 2." 1990. *The Nag Hammadi Library in English,* translated by Thomas O. Lambdin and edited by James M. Robinson and Richard D. Smith. Rev. Ed. New York: HarperCollins.

Greene, Brian. 2005. *Brian Greene: Making Sense of String Theory.* TED Talk, www.ted.com.

—. "Reimagining the Cosmos." 2014. Interview by Krista Tippett. *On Being.* National Public Radio. Transcript.

Griswold, H. D. 1999. *Religion of the Ṛigveda.* Rpt. Delhi, India: Matilal Banarsidass.

"A Guide to Branding Yourself on Social Media." 2020. *Grin.* grin.co.

Gupt, Bharat. 1994. *Dramatic Concepts Greek and Indian: A Study of the Poetics and the Natyasastra.* New Delhi: Jawaharlal Nehru University-D.K. Printworld, 1994.

Gupta, Ravi M. and Kenneth R. Valpey. 2013. "Introduction: Churning the Ocean of Lila Themes for Bhagavata Study." In *The Bhagavata Purāṇa: Sacred Text and Living Tradition,* edited by Ravi M. Gupta and Kenneth R. Valpey, 1–20. New York: Columbia University Press.

Hagelin, John S. 2007. *John Hagelin Ph.D. on Consciousness and Superstring Unified Field Theory.* Part 1. *YouTube.* www.youtube.com/watch?v=OrcWntw9juM.

Haraway, Donna Jeanne. 1994. "A Game of Cat's Cradle: Science Studies, Feminist Theory, Cultural Studies." *Configurations* 2 (1): 59–71.

Hazra, Rajendra Chandra. 1938. "Some Minor Purāṇas." *Annals of the Bhandarkar Oriental Research Institute* 19 (1): 69–79.

—. 1940. *Studies in the Purāṇaic Records on Hindu Rites and Customs.* Calcutta: The University of Dacca.

Heimann, Betty. *Indian and Western Philosophy: A Study in Contrasts.* London: George Allen & Unwin, 1937.

Henrich, Joseph, Steven J. Heine, and Ara Norenzayan. 2010. "The Weirdest People in the World?" *Behavioral and Brain Sciences* 33: 61–135.

Höfer, András, and Bishnu P. Shrestha. 1973. "Ghost Exorcism among the Brahmans of Central Nepal." *Central Asiatic Journal* 17 (1): 51–77.

Houben, Jan E. M. 2000. "The Ritual Pragmatics of a Vedic Hymn: The 'Riddle Hymn' and the Parvargya Ritual." *Journal of the American Oriental Society* 120 (4): 499–501.

Inden, Ronald B., Jonathan S. Walters and Daud Ali. 2000. *Querying the Medieval: Texts and the History of Practices in South Asia.* Oxford: Oxford University Press.

Ingalls, Daniel H. H. 2001. "Logic in India (1955)." In *Indian Logic: A Reader,* edited by Jonardon Ganeri, 110–16. Richmond, Surry UK: Routledge/Curzon.

Iyer, A.K. Subramania, ed. and trans. 1965. *The Vākyapadīya of Bhartṛhari with the Vṛtti: Chapter 1, English Translation.* Poona, India: Deccan College.

Jacobsen, Knut A., Helene Basu, Angelika Malinar, and Vasudha Narayanan, eds. *Brill's Encyclopedia of Hinduism.* 6 vols. Handbook of Oriental Studies Sect 2. India. Edited by Johannes Bronkhorst and Angelika Malinar. Boston: Brill, 2009.

Jamison, Stephanie W., and Joel P. Brereton, eds. and trans. 2014. Introduction to *The Rigveda.* 3 vols. New York: Oxford University Press.

Jayne, C. F. 1906. *String Figures and How to Make Them.* New York: Charles Scribner's Sons.

Jet Propulsion Laboratory, California Institute of Technology. N.d. "The Golden Record Cover." voyager.jpl.nasa.gov/golden-record/golden-record-cover/

Jones, Constance A., and James D. Ryan. 2007. *Encyclopedia of Hinduism.* New York: Infobase Publishing.

Joshi, Kireet. 2006. "Veda as Word." In *Veda as Word,* edited by Shashiprabha Kumar, 13–20. New Delhi: D.K. Printworld.

Kanungo, Archana. 2013. "The Role of Odissi Dance and Music in Indian Society: A Case Study of Odisha." *Kanungo Archana,* International Research Journal for Social Science and Corporate Excellence.

Kasturi, Malavika. 2018. "Gurus and Gifting: Dana, the Math Reform Campaign, and Competing Visions of Hindu Sangathan in Twentieth-century India." *Modern Asian Studies* 52 (1): 99–131.

Katha Upanishad. 2015. In *The Upanishads, a New Translation,* translated and edited by Thomas Egenes and Vernon Katz. New York: Tarcher/Penguin.

Katz, Vernon. 2011. *Conversations with Maharishi: Maharishi Mahesh Yogi Speaks about the Full Development of Human Consciousness.* 2 vols. Fairfield, IA: Maharishi University of Management Press.

Kazanas, Nicholas. 2007. Review of *Veda as Word*, edited by Shashiprabha Kumar. *The Adyar Library Bulletin* 71: 272–78.

Kennedy, George Alexander. 1998. *Comparative Rhetoric: An Historical and Cross-cultural Introduction*. New York: Oxford University Press.

Kirkwood, William G. 1990. "Shiva's Dance at Sundown: Implications of Indian Aesthetics for Poetics and Rhetoric." *Text and Performance Quarterly* 10: 93–110.

Kirkwood, William G. 1989. "Truthfulness as a Standard for Speech in Ancient India." *The Southern Communication Journal* 54 (Spring): 213–34.

Klostermaier, Klaus K. 2014. *A Concise Encyclopedia of Hinduism*. Oxford: Oneworld Publications.

Kothari, Deepika, dir., and Ramji Om, dir. and auth. 2014. *History of Yoga*. Mumbai: Vishuddhi . DVD.

Krishnaswamy, N. 2001. "Indian Rhetoric." In *Encyclopedia of Rhetoric,* edited by Thomas O. Sloan, 384–87. New York: Oxford University Press.

Kumar, Aastha. 2013. "Constructing and Performing the Odissi Body: Ideologies, Influences And Interjections." *Journal of Emerging Dance Scholarship* 1: n.p.

Kumar, Shashiprabha, ed. 2006. *Veda as Word*. New Delhi: D.K. Printworld.

Larson, Gerald James. 1980. "Karma as a 'Sociology of Knowledge' or 'Social Psychology' of Process/Praxis." In *Karma and Rebirth in Classical Indian Traditions*, edited by Wendy Doniger O'Flaherty, 303–16. Berkeley: University of California Press.

Lipner, Julius. 1994. *Hindus: Their Religious Beliefs and Practices*. London: Routledge.

Lipson, Carol S., and Roberta A. Binkley. 2004. "Introduction." In *Rhetoric Before and Beyond the Greeks*, edited by Carol S. Lipson and Roberta A. Binkley, 1–24. Albany, NY: State University of New York Press.

Lloyd, Keith. 2007a. "Rethinking Rhetoric from an Indian Perspective: Implications in the Nyaya Sutra." *Rhetoric Review* 26 (4): 365–84.

—. 2007b. "A Rhetorical Tradition Lost in Translation: Implications for Rhetoric in the Ancient Indian Nyāya Sūtras." *Advances in the History of Rhetoric* 10 (1): 19–42.

—. 2011. "Culture and Rhetorical Patterns: Mining the Rich Relations Between Aristotle's Enthymeme and Example and India's Nyāya Method." *Rhetorica* 29 (1): 76–105.

—. 2013. "Learning from India's Nyāya Rhetoric: Debating Analogically through Vāda's Fruitful Dialogue." *Rhetoric Society Quarterly* 43 (3): 285–99.

—. 2015. "The Rhetoric of Performance in India: The Confluence of Nyaya Vada [Logic] and Sadharanikaran [Performance] in Past and Present Discourses." *Foreign Language and Literature Research* 1 (2): 88–99.

—. 2018. "The Impulse to Rhetoric in India: Rhetorical and Deliberative Practices and Their Relation to the Histories of Rhetoric and Democracy." *Advances in the History of Rhetoric* 21 (3): 223–46.

—. 2019. "Logic and Religion Working Together: Implications within India's Nyāya Reasoning." *International Journal of Hinduism and Philosophy*. A Journal of the Bhagavad Gita Research Foundation (BGRF) www.bgrfuk (November): 1–12.

Maharishi Mahesh Yogi. 1971. "The Relation between Name and Form in the Veda." Arcata, CA. Videotaped lecture. Available at Maharishi International University. Transcription available in Orme-Johnson and Andersen, 189–203.

——. 1972a. "Literature: Poetry and the Veda." Parts I and II. December 22, 1972. La Antilla, Spain. Available at Maharishi International University. Audiotaped lecture. Transcription available in Orme-Johnson and Andersen, 89–116.

——. 1972b. "The Phonology of Creation." December 28, 1972. La Antilla, Spain. Available at Maharishi International University. Audiotaped lecture. Available at Maharishi International University. Transcription available in Orme-Johnson and Andersen, 208–33.

——. 1972c. "The Root *Bhū* and Vedic Grammar." Lake Tahoe, CA. Audiotaped lecture. Available at Maharishi International University. Transcription available in Orme-Johnson and Andersen, 235–45.

——. 1974. "The Nature of Learning and the Progress of Knowledge." August 22, 1974. Arosa, Switzerland. Audiotaped lecture. available at Maharishi International University. Transcription available in Orme-Johnson and Andersen, 29–43.

——. 1975. "Enlivening Consciousness, the Common Basis of All Languages: The Ground for Perfect Communication" (January 17). Vitznau, Switzerland. Videotaped lecture. Transcription available in Orme-Johnson and Andersen, 149–55.

——. 1981. *Education for Enlightenment: Introduction to Maharishi International University 1981.* Fairfield, IA: Maharishi International University Press.

——. 1986. *Thirty Years Around the World: Dawn of the Age of Enlightenment.* Vol. 1, 1957–64. Stichting Drukkerij en Uitgeverij, Netherlands: Maharishi Vedic University Press.

——. 1990. *Maharishi Mahesh Yogi on the Bhagavad-Gita: A New Translation and Commentary, Chapters 1 to 6.* Reprint. New York: Penguin.

——. 2001. *The Science of Being and Art of Living: Transcendental Meditation.* New York: Plume.

——. 2006. "Fortune Creating Homes and Misfortune Creating Homes." Videotaped lecture. Call number: MSAE3452. [Vlodrop, Netherlands]: [Maharishi Vedic University].

——. 2009. *From Where the Speech Returns, Natural Law Administers Creation.* Videotaped lecture. Maharishi Foundation International-Maharishi Vedic University: Netherlands.

——. 2010. *The Flow of Consciousness: Maharishi Mahesh Yogi on Literature and Language 1971 to 1976.* Edited by Rhoda F. Orme-Johnson and Susan K. Andersen. Fairfield, IA: Maharishi University of Management Press.

Maharishi Patañjali Yoga Sutra. 2010. Translated by Thomas Egenes. Fairfield, IA: First World Library.

Malhotra, Rajiv. 2011. *Being Different: An Indian Challenge to Western Universalism.* New Delhi: HarperCollins/India Today.

Mani, Vettam. 1975. *Purāṇaic Encyclopaedia: A Comprehensive Dictionary with Special Reference to the Epic and Purāṇaic Literature.* Delhi: Motilal Banarsidass.

Matilal, Bimal Krishna. 1997. *Logic, Language, and Reality.* Delhi: Motilal Banarsidass.

——. 1998. *The Character of Logic in India,* edited by Jonardon Ganeri and Heeraman Tiwari. New York: State: University of New York Press.

Maurer, Walter Harding. 1988. "Review of *The Purāṇas*" by Ludo Rocher. *Journal of the American Oriental Society* 108 (4): 633–36.

Melfi, Anne. 2020. "Foundations in Vedic Rhetorical Culture: Approaching Moksha Analogically." In *The Routledge Handbook of Comparative World Rhetorics,* edited by Keith Lloyd, 135. New York: Routledge.

Metzger, David. 1996. "Indian Rhetoric (Sanskrit)." In *Encyclopedia of Rhetoric and Composition: Communication from Ancient Times to the Information Age,* edited by Theresa Enos, 346–47. New York: Routledge.

Meyer-Dinkgräfe, Daniel. 2005. *Theatre and Consciousness: Explanatory Scope and Future Potential.* Chicago: University of Chicago Press.

Misra, Nityananda. 2018. *The Om Mala: Meanings of the Mystic Sound.* New Delhi: Bloomsbury Publishing.

Misra, Vidya Niwas. 1971. "Sanskrit Rhetoric and Poetic" *Mahfil* 7 (3/4), Sanskrit Issue: 1–18.

Mohanty, J. N. 2000. *Classical Indian Philosophy.* Lanham, MD: Rowman and Littlefield.

Monier-Williams, Monier. 1851. *A Dictionary, English and Sanskrit.* London: W.H. Allen and Co.

Monier-Williams, Monier, Ernst Leumann, and Carl Cappeller. 2005. *Sanskrit-English Dictionary: Etymologically and Philologically Arranged with Special Reference to Cognate Indo-European Languages.* 2nd ed. Delhi: Motilal Banarsidass; [Columbia, Mo.: Distr. South Asia Books].

Moore, Evelyn K. 2012. "The Conflict between Philosophy, Rhetoric and Theology." In *The Passions of Rhetoric: Lessing's Theory of Argument and the German Enlightenment,* 1–18. New York: Springer.

Muktika Upanishad. 1914. In *Thirty Minor Upanishads,* translated by K. Narayanasvami Aiyar. Madras: Printed by Annie Besant at the Vasanta Press.

Natarajan, Kanchana. 2016. *Transgressing Boundaries: The Songs of Shenkottai Avudai Akkal.* New Delhi: Zubaan Press.

Nath, Vijay. 1987. *Dana: Gift System in Ancient India: A Socio-Economic Perspective.* New Delhi: Munshiram Manoharlal Publishers.

Natyavidushi, Jaya. 2011. "Importance of Body Language in Effective Multicultural Communication." *Annals of the University of Craiova. Series Geography/Analele Universitatii din Craiova. Seria Geografie* 14: 102–27.

The Nātyaśāstra of Bharata. 1926. "Chapter six, Rasadhyayah (On the Sentiments), with the Abhinavabharati, a commentary by Abhinavagupta," edited with an English translation of Rasadhyayah by Subodhchandra Mukerjee, Sastri, 1926.

The Nyaya Sutras of Gotama. 1913. Translated by Mahamahopadyhyaya Satista Chandra Vidyabhusana. Bihar, India: The Panini Office Bhuvane & 'Wari Ashrama.

O'Flaherty, Wendy Doniger. 1980. "Karma and Rebirth in the Vedas and Purāṇas." In *Karma and Rebirth in Classical Indian Traditions,* edited by Wendy Doniger O'Flaherty, 3–37. Berkeley: University of California Press.

Oliver, Robert T. 1971. *Communication and Culture in Ancient India and China*. Syracuse, NY: Syracuse University Press.

Ong, Walter J. 2013. *Orality and Literacy*. Routledge.

Onozawa, Yumiko. 2002. "An Analysis of Hell-narratives in Early Hinduism and Theravada Buddhism." Master diss., University of Saskatchewan.

Orme-Johnson, Rhoda F. 1987. "A Unified Field Theory of Literature." *Modern Science and Vedic Science* 1 (3): 323–73.

Orme-Johnson Rhoda F., and Susan K. Andersen, eds. 2010. *The Flow of Consciousness: Maharishi Mahesh Yogi on Literature and Language 1971 to 1976*. Fairfield, IA: Maharishi University of Management Press.

Padmasambhava. *Treasures from Juniper Ridge: The Profound Treasure Instructions of Padmasambhava to the Dakini Yeshe Tsogyal, Recorded and Sealed by Yeshe Tsogyal*. Translated and edited by Erik Pema Kunsang and Marcia Binder Schmidt. Hong Kong: Rangjung Yeshe Publications, 2008.

Padoux, Andre. 1990. *Vāk: The Concept of the Word in Selected Hindu Tantras*. Translated by Jacques Gontier. Albany, NY: State University of New York Press.

Panikkar, Raimundo. 1977. "The Vedic Epiphany." In *The Vedic Experience*: *Mantramanjari,* edited by Raimundo Panikkar, 3–29. Berkeley: University of California Press.

Patnaik, D. 1971. *Odissi Dance*. Bhubaneshwar: Orissa Sangeeta Natak Akademi.

Patanjali. 2010. *Maharishi Patañjali Yoga Sutra*. Translated by Thomas Egenes. Fairfield, IA: First World Library.

Patton, Laurie L. 2005. *Bringing the Gods to Mind*. Berkeley, CA: University of California Press.

Paz, Octavio. 1998. "The Day of the Dead." In *Encounters,* edited by Shreedhar Lohani and Rameshwor Adhikari, 45–50. Kathmandu: Ekta.

Pillai, K. Raghavan, trans. and ed. 1971. *The Vākyapadīya: Studies in the Vākyapadīya,* Vol. I. Delhi, India: Motilal Banarsidass.

Plato. *Gorgias*. 2008. Translated by Robin Waterfield. Oxford: Oxford University Press.

—. 1892. *Phaedrus*. Translated by Benjamin Jowett.

—. 1921. *Cratylus*. Translated by Harold M. Fowler.

—. 2002. *Phaedrus*. Translated by Robin Waterfield. Oxford: Oxford University Press.

Prabhavananda, Swami. 1992. *The Sermon on the Mount According to Vedanta*. Hollywood: Vedanta Press.

Pradhan, Gangadhar. 25 July 2008. Interview by Shreelina Ghosh. In Person. Konark, Odissa, India.

Prahladachar, D. 2006. "Vedāpauruṣeyatva," In *Veda as Word,* edited by Shashiprabha Kumar, 21–30. New Delhi: D.K. Printworld, 2006.

Prasad, R. U. S. 2015. *The Rig-Vedic and Post-Rig-Vedic Polity (1500–500 BCE)*. Wilmington, DE: Vernon Press, 2015.

Pratt, Mary Louise. 1992. *Imperial Eyes: Travel Writing and Transculturation*. 2nd ed. London: Routledge.

Prickett, Stacey. 2007. "Guru or teacher? Shishya or student? Pedagogic shifts in South Asian dance training in India and Britain." *South Asia Research* 27 (1): 25–41.

Proferes, Theodore. 2009. "Vedic Period (1750–400 BCE)." *Historical Perspectives, Poets, Teachers, and Saints, Relation to Other Religions and Traditions, Hinduism and Contemporary Issues.* Vol. 4 of *Brill's Encyclopedia of Hinduism.* Handbook of Oriental Studies, Sect. 2. India. Ed. Johannes Bronkhorst and Angelika Malinar. Leiden, Netherlands: Brill.

Purohit Swamy, Shree, and William Butler Yeats. 2003. *The Ten Principal Upanishads.* New Delhi: Rupa Publications, 2003.

Rabjam, Longchen. 2006. *The Precious Treasury of Pith Instructions.* Translated by Richard Barron and Llama Chokyi Nyima. Junction City: Padma Publishing.

Ramaswamy, Anbil. 2015. *A Critical Study of Hinduism with Major World Religions: Comparisons and Contrasts.* Chennai: RNR Printers and Publishers.

"Rhetorical Patterns: Persuasion and Argument." 2020. Lincoln University. 2020. www.lincoln.edu/departments/languages-and-literature-department/rhetorical-patterns/rhetorical-patterns-persuasion.

"Rhetoric and Social Justice." 2016. *Present Tense: A Journal of Rhetoric in Society* 5, no. 3 (May). www.presenttensejournal.org/category/volume-5/issue-3/.

The Rig Veda. 1888. *Rig-Veda Sanhita—A Collection of Ancient Hindu Hymns, Constituting Part of the Seventh and Eighth Ashtaka of the Rig-Veda.* Translated by H. H. Wilson and edited by W. F. Webster. London: Trübner & Co., 1888.

Rogers, Joseph M., and Mahendra Kumar Jain. 1993. "Inference and Successful Behavior." *The Quarterly Review of Biology* 68 (3): 367–97.

Rotman, Brian. 2008. *Becoming Beside Ourselves: The Alphabet, Ghosts, and Distributed Human Being.* Durham: Duke University Press.

Rotman, Brian. 2009. "Gesture and the 'I' Fold." *Parallax* 15 (4): 68–82.

Rowe, Joseph. 2012. "The Gnostic of Mount Whitney: A Personal and Philosophical Memoir of Franklin Merrell-Wolff." *The Franklin Merrell-Wolff Fellowship.* www.merrell-wolff.org/fellow_contributions/remembrances_memoirs

Rowell, Lewis. 1979. "The Subconscious Language of Music and Time," *Music Theory Spectrum* 1 (Spring): 96–106.

Roy, Suvratadev Sharmana Vandyopadhyay. "Translation of Texts on Music." Unpublished paper. www.academia.edu/1886886/Translation_of_Texts_on_Music.

Royster, Francesca. 2020. "Valerie June, Ghost Catcher." *Journal of Popular Music Studies* 32 (2): 18–27.

Rustomji, Roshni. 1981. "Rasa and Dhvani in Indian and Western Poetics and Poetry" *Journal of South Asian Literature* 16, no. 1, Part I: East-West Literary Relations (Winter/Spring): 75–91.

Sarkar, Kaustavi. 2020. "Indian Classical Dance Education in Diaspora." *Dance Education in Practice* 6 (3): 6–14.

Sathaye, Adheesh. 2009. "Why Did Hariścandra Matter in Early Medieval India? Truth, Fact, and Folk Narrative in the Sanskrit Purāṇas." *The Journal of Hindu Studies* 2: 131–59.

Schnepel, Cornelia. 2009. "Bodies Filled with Divine Energy: The Indian Dance Odissi." *Paragrana* 18 (1): 188–99.

Shankar, Bindu S. 2004. "Dance imagery in South Indian Temples: Study of the 108-Karana Sculptures." PhD diss., The Ohio State University.

Sen, Amartya. 2009. *The Idea of Justice.* Cambridge, Ma: Harvard University Press.

Singh, Ajay Pratap. 2008. "Designing of Cultural Knowledge Portal: A South Asian Experiment." In 74 IFLA General Conference and Council (August): 10–14. Quebec, Canada.

Singh, Praveen. 2020. "Shruti and Smriti (Śruti and Smrti)." In *Keywords for India: A Conceptual Lexicon for the 21st Century*, edited by Rukmini Bhaya Nair and Pter Rondal deSouza, 332. London: Bloomsbury.

Singh, S. P. 2006. "Vāgāmbhṛṇi." In *Veda as Word,* edited by Shashiprabha Kumar, 45–54. New Delhi: D.K. Printworld, 2006.

Smith, Frederick M. 2016. Review of *The Rigveda* (3 volume set), edited and translated by Stephanie W. Jamison and Joel P. Brereton. *Asian Ethnology* 75 (1): 249–54. doi:10.18874/ae.75.1.22.

Spurr, David. 1993. *The Rhetoric of Empire: Colonial Discourse in Journalism, Travel Writing, and Imperial Administration.* Durham: Duke University Press.

Schrodinger, Erwin. 1980. "The Present Situation in Quantum Mechanics: A Translation of Schrödinger's 'Cat Paradox' Paper." Translated by John D. Trimmer. *Proceedings of the American Philosophical Society* 124 (5): 323–38.

Stanford, W. B. 1967. *The Sound of Greek: Studies in the Greek Theory and Practice of Euphony.* Berkeley: University of California Press.

Sternbach, Ludwik. 1957. "An Unknown Cänakya MS. and The Garuda-Purāṇa." *Indo-Iranian Journal* 1 (3): 181–200.

Strange, Allen. 1973. *Electronic music: Systems, techniques, and controls.* Dubuque: Wm. C. Brown Company Publisher.

Stroud, Scott R. 2009. "Argument in Classical Indian Philosophy: The Case of Śankara's Advaita Vedānta." In *Ancient Non-Greek Rhetorics*, edited by Carol S. Lipson and Roberta A. Binkley, 240–64. West Lafayette, IN: Parlor Press, 2009.

Suzuki, D. T. 1963. *Outlines of Mahayana Buddhism.* New York: Schocken Books.

Svetashvatara Upanishad. 2015. In *The Upanishads, a New Translation,* translated and edited by Thomas Egenes and Vernon Katz. New York: Tarcher/Penguin.

Tannen, Deborah, 1998. *The Argument Culture: Moving from Debate to Dialogue.* New York: Ballantine Books.

Theologia Germanica: Which Setteth Forth Many Fair Lineaments of Divine Truth, and Saith Very Lofty and Lovely Things Touching a Perfect Life. 1857. Translated by Susanna Winkworth. Andover: John P Jewett & Co.

Thompson, Roger. 2015. "Emerson and the Democratization of Plato's 'True Rhetoric'." *Philosophy and Rhetoric* 48 (2): 117–38.

Timalsina, Sthaneshwar. 2007. "Metaphor, Rasa, and Dhvani: Suggested Meaning in Tantric Esotericism" *Method and Theory in the Study of Religion* 19: 134–62.

Toulmin, Stephen E. 2003. *The Uses of Argument.* 2nd ed. Cambridge: Cambridge University Press.

Tulku Urgyen Rinpoche. 2009. *Rainbow Painting: a Collection of Miscellaneous Aspects of Development and Completion.* Hong Kong: Rangjung Yeshe Publications.

Van Halen. 1980. "And the Cradle Will Rock. . . " *Women and Children First.* Warner Brothers HS3415, 33⅓ rpm.

Varma, Vishwanath Prasad. 1978. "Ethics and Sociology of Politics in Some of the Purāṇas." *The Indian Journal of Political Science* 39 (2): 270–98.

Vātsyāyana, Kapila. 1996. *Bharata: The Nāṭyaśāstra.* Sahitya Akademi.

Venkataramiah, Sri Munagala. 1955. *Talks with Sri Ramana Maharshi.* Tiruvannamalai: Sri Ramanashram.

Vidyabhusana, Satish Chandra. 1920 and 1988. *A History of Indian Logic.* Delhi: Motilal Bandaridass.

Viswanathan, Tanjore. 1969. "Etijanmamidi kriti in Raga Varali, Tala Misra Capu." *South Indian Flute.* World Pacific (WPS-21451), 33⅓ rpm.

—. 1977. "The Analysis of Raga Alapana in Indian Music." *Asian Music* 9 (1): 13–71.

Vos Post, Jonathan. 2020. "Me Human, You Alien: How to Talk to an Extraterrestrial." *Magicdragon.com.*

Waldman, Anne. 1996. "Poetry as Siddhi." In *Buddhist Women on the Edge: Contemporary Perspectives from the Western Frontier,* edited by Marianne Dresser, 264. North Atlantic Books.

Walker, Jeffrey. 2011. *The Genuine Teachers of This Art*: Rhetorical Education in Antiquity, Columbia: University of South Carolina Press.

Walzer, Arthur E., and David Beard. 2011. "Historiography and the Study of Rhetoric." In *The SAGE Handbook of Rhetorical Studies,* edited by Andrea A. Lunsford, Kirt H. Wilson and Rosa A. Eberly, 13–33. Thousand Oaks: SAGE Publications.

Widdison, L. 2019. "The Power of Suggestion: Rasa, Dhvani, and the Ineffable." *Journal of Dharma Studies* 2: 1–14.

Yano, Michio. 2006. "Oral and written transmission of the exact sciences in Sanskrit." *Journal of Indian philosophy* 34 (1–2): 143–160.

Yeats, W. B. 1933. "Among Schoolchildren." In *The Poems of W. B. Yeats: A New Edition,* edited by Richard J. Finneran. New York: Macmillan. www.poetryfoundation.org/poems/43293/among-school-children

y Royo, Alessandra Lopez. 2007. "The Reinvention of Odissi Classical Dance as a Temple Ritual." *The Archaeology of Ritual* 3: 155.

Zimmer, Heinrich. 1992. *Myths and Symbols in Indian Art and Civilization.* Edited by Joseph Campbell. Princeton: Princeton University Press.

Glossary of Terms

Term	Translation
abhinaya (अभिनय)	gesture
abhyāsa (अभ्यास)	practice
adhyāropa-apavāda (अध्यारोप)	superimposition/negation
akṣāra (अपवाद)	word or syllable; speech/language; by association, poet/singer, poetry; poetic inspiration and the attendant deep insight and wisdom; transcendental pure consciousness (*Para*); indestructible, eternal; second word of the *Richo Akshare* verse by which the verse is known.
ālakṣyakrama (आलक्ष्यक्रम)	marlinspike (*alaksyakrama-dhvani*)
alankāraśastra (अलङ्कार शास्त्र)	trope and ornament driven tradition of rhetoric in Sanskrit poetics
ammanai (in Tamil, அம்மானை)	game and genre of poetry
anāhata (अनाहत)	unstruck
anirvachanīya (अनिर्वचनीय)	neither existent nor non-existent; indescribable
apart-playing	simultaneous turn-taking
ātmā vichāra (आत्मा विचार)	self-inquiry
Brahman	The totality; one conscious wholeness encompassing both the unmanifest, transcendental and relative manifest aspects of the universe; the cosmic Self; the inexpressible. Speech is *Brahman* and *Para-Brahman*, the source of speech, collectedness of all the *mantras* or all the laws of nature; the goal of all evolution; state of consciousness experientially open to that ultimate reality: "Having attained it, a man is not deluded … He attains eternal freedom" (*Bhagavad-Gita* 2.72).
chanda (छन्द)	study of meter and rhythm in poetry, verse, and music
deva (देव)	from *div*, to shine; literally, shining one(s), god(s), laws of nature, impulses of creative intelligence that comprise and govern the universe; the fabric of one unitary transcendental wholeness, according to the *Richo Akshare* verse.
dharma (धर्म)	right action; justice; harmony or attunement with natural law, which governs the universe. A defining principle of Vedic civilization and the dharmic religions.
dharmakāyā (धर्मकाय)	sunyata, empty essence

Dhvani (ध्वनी)	poetic theory of suggestion, the means of finding rasa; resonance, thunder, as a verb: to sound, roar, make a noise, echo, reverberate," and "to cause sound, to make resound" and as a noun describes "an empty sound," "the sound of a drum," and simply "a word." And also "delighting by its sound, a bee." Acoustic element of speech.
ḍṛśyam (दृश्यम्)	distortion
d -- (दृष्टान्त)	instance, paragon, example
duru (गुरु)	teacher; honorific appellation of a preceptor (Monier-Williams), with the connotation of a teacher of holistic knowledge, including the spiritual, *dharmic* component of any field of knowledge, whether dance, architecture, mathematics, or metallurgy.
hetu (हेतु)	reason, motivation
kṛtī (कृती)	Carnatic song form
kummi (in Tamil, கும்மி)	Carnatic dance form
levels of speech	speech emerges from silence toward audible expression, through four stages or levels of development, from its silent transcendental source, *Para*, to the first flash of cognition of an idea, *Pashyanti*, to the linear flow of silent speech in thought, *Madhyama*, and finally to its audible expression, *Vaikahari*. There are, of course, many gradations in between.
mādhyama (माध्यम)	One of the levels of speech; the silent thinking level of the sequential flow of language not perceptible as audible speech, as when one thinks of a poem or plans one's day.
mantra (मन्त्र)	Vedic work(s), expressions of the laws of nature, the *devas*. From *man*, mind, and *tra*, instrument, tool; literally, mind tool; word; word(s) of the Veda, Vedic Sanskrit vocabulary; each *mantra* is the name-form or vibrational quality of the *deva*(s)/laws of nature/impulses of creative intelligence; verse(s) of the Veda.
mokṣa (मोक्ष)	relinquishment, abandonment, liberation, enlightenment.
mora	musical technique of turn-taking, whereby a complex pattern is repeated three times, in cross-rhythmic tension with the fundamental tala (rhythm) of a performance
nigamana (निगमन)	summing up, going in or into

para (पर)	One of the levels of speech; the transcendental, silent source of the other levels; pure consciousness, the home of all the laws of nature, which govern the whole creation; the source of the entire universe.
paśyati (पश्यती)	*Lit.* "to see." One of the levels of speech; *lit.* "the seeing one," the first flash of cognition of an idea as a gestalt, subtler than the linear flow of language.
pratyabhijñā (प्रत्याअभिज्ञ)	self-recognition
prāṇāyāma (पुराणायाम)	the practice of attending to one's own breath
prājña (पुरज्ञा)	wisdom, state of dreamless sleep
prātibhā (पुरातभि)	inspiration of the poets
pratijñā (पुरतिज्ञा)	promise, vow, proposal
pratīyamāna eva hi rasa (पुरतयिमन एव ह रस)	the process of perception perceiving itself
rasa (रस)	The goal of all poetry according to Abhinvagupta. *Lit.* "juice" or "flavor"; essence; telos. Without *rasa*, it is not art, and its purpose is to inspire a taste of and for *Brahman*, the ultimate *rasa*, and catalyze *moksha*, according to the *Natyashastra*.
richa/ṛcā (ऋचा)	verse(s) of the Veda
Rig Veda / ṛgveda (ऋग्वेद)	From *rik*, luster, splendor, hymn, and *vid*, knowing, knowledge; knowledge in its holistic value available in the structure of pure consciousness; the seminal text of the Vedic civilization, which consists of 1,028 hymns cognized by enlightened sages called *rishis* (seers) and orally transmitted and preserved for millennia prior to written language, dating from 1750 BCE at the latest; root source of all the arts and sciences of life and living.
rigpa (in Tibetan རིག་པ་)	direct knowledge of primordial state
rishi/ṛṣi (ऋषी)	Vedic seer(s) who heard/cognized the Vedic hymns within pure consciousness, sang them out, and taught them to their descendants for posterity.
śānta-rasa (शान्त रस)	peaceful rasa
śravaṇaṃ (शरवण)	hearing
tonic	tonal center of a piece of music

upadiś (उपदिश्)	disguises, vehicles, body, mind, memory; conditionings, identifications; also, a premise
upamāna (उपमान)	comparison, resemblance
upāya (उपाय)	In his *Outlines of Mahayana Buddhism*, D.T. Suzuki takes time, in a lengthy footnote, to explain the Sanskrit term *upaya*: "From the standpoint of pure intelligence," or *prajna*, "Bodhisattvas do not see any particular suffering existences … but when they see the universe from the standpoint of their love-essence," or *karuna*, "they recognize everywhere the conditions of misery and sing that arise from clinging to the forms of particularity. To remove these, they devise all possible means that are directed towards the attainment of the final aim of existence" (Suzuki 298). Suzuki goes on to say that the technical Sanskrit term *upaya*, whether translated as "expedient," "stratagem," "device," or "craft," simply does not translate well.
vaikhari (वैखरी)	one of the levels of speech; the perceptible level, where speech bursts forth into communication that can be heard and/or read.
vairāgya (वैराग्य)	withdrawal from all familiar attachments, withdrawal of the senses.
Veda (वेद)	from *vid*, knowing, knowledge; see *Rig Veda*. In antiquity, sage Vyasa divided the Veda into four: *Rig Veda, Sama Veda, Yajur Veda,* and *Atharva Veda*.
viveka (विवेक)	discernment between real and unreal
Vritti/vṛttī (वृत्ती)	commentary or gloss, sometimes with interpretation and analysis, of an ancient text
yoga (योग)	rom *yuj*, "to yoke," "to join," "to unite." *Lit.* unity; state of enlightenment when one is established in unity with the cosmic Self, *Para*; state of attunement with that; unbounded awareness, which is open to the full range of the mind/speech; that state which is the basis of fulfilling all the goals of life; "skill in action" (Bhagavad-Gita, 2.50). The methods of attaining that state of fullness of life, which in India are primarily associated with meditation but in the West are popularly known as the practice of physical postures, *yoga asanas*; body of knowledge on the theory and practice of attaining the state of *yoga*; proper name of one of the six systems of Indian philosophy.

5 INDONESIAN RHETORICS

PREFATORY INTRODUCTION
Gregory Coles

When we speak of "Indonesian rhetorics," we invoke a category that did not exist prior to the twentieth century. More than seventeen thousand ethnically and linguistically diverse islands that comprise modern-day Indonesia had no reasons for a shared identity as "Indonesian" except their relative proximity and their shared colonization by the Dutch. Yet claiming collective national identity proved crucial in these islands' efforts to gain independence from the Dutch in the 1940s. The nascent *Republik Indonesia Serikat* (United Indonesian Republic) asserted its linguistic unity by adopting a Malay trade dialect as its national language and renaming the dialect *Bahasa Indonesia* ("the language of Indonesia"). Remarkably, this dialect was the native language of only five percent of Indonesia's newly declared citizenry, whereas forty-two percent of Indonesians were native Javanese speakers, and another fifteen percent were native Sundanese speakers. The choice of *Bahasa Indonesia* as national language was highly strategic for uniting an otherwise disparate group because it "avoided the factionalism that would have resulted had the choice been one of the majority languages."[1]

Although the Indonesian national language is a relative newcomer to the islands that now comprise Indonesia, the rhetorical practices that have formed and flourished beneath the banner of Indonesian identity did not emerge *ex nihilo*. Javanese, Sundanese, and over seven hundred other languages spoken in the Indonesian islands were already home to rich traditions of written and oral rhetorics. In addition to prose and poetry, these traditions also include communal arts like *wayang* shadow-puppet performances, often accompanied by hours-long recitations of local myth and legend. Contemporary Indonesian rhetorics are not reducible

---

1. Kratz 2006, 641.

to these pre-Indonesian rhetorical forms, but neither can the two be fully distinguished. The amalgam of Indonesian rhetorics both includes and exceeds the rhetorics of the hundreds of languages and more than one thousand ethnic groups that were united (whether by choice or by force) into *Republik Indonesia Serikat* in the late 1940s.

Indonesian rhetorics today thus take on an astoundingly diverse number of forms. Many of these rhetorics, especially in public and political settings, take as their core ethical value the national doctrine of *Pancasila*, the ideological brainchild of Indonesia's founding president, Sukarno. *Pancasila* places a high value on consensus and unity, meaning that harmony is a necessary goal of most formal Indonesian rhetorics. However, Indonesia also enjoys a robust tradition of rhetorics of change and resistance. Even Sukarno's own rhetorical practices during Indonesia's founding negotiated a seemingly impossible tension between demanding reform and insisting on collective harmony. The unique progressivism of Sukarno's rhetoric has been mirrored by countless other key Indonesian rhetorical figures in subsequent generations (including, as we will see in the coming pages, his daughter Megawati).

In short, locating a uniquely Indonesian rhetorical tradition cannot be accomplished through tidy delineation, drawing from an already robust corpus of theorizing by rhetorical insiders. The contemporary rhetorical practices of widely known Indonesian voices are themselves the ongoing codification of a still-emerging tradition. This tradition enjoys "traditional" longevity insofar as it continues to evoke the centuries-old linguistic and rhetorical practices of the Indonesian islands. However, it also partakes in a kind of rhetorical iconoclasm by coalescing these once-distinct practices within a new framework of national unity. As scholars continue to sketch the ever-shifting parameters and trajectory of the Indonesian rhetorical tradition in coming years, at least three considerations deserve specific attention in helping to locate likely sources of this tradition.

First, it is important to consider the ways in which religious practice shapes the direction and scope of Indonesian rhetorics. Islamic influence was one of the few common ties shared between many of the Indonesian islands before they were collectively occupied by the Dutch. As of this writing, approximately eighty-seven percent of Indonesians identify themselves as Muslim.[2] Islam has thus served as a natural locus of postcolonial identity, not least by informing the rhetorical practices of many prominent Indonesian rhetors. Islamic practice in many Indonesian communities differs from Islamic practice in other parts of the world; some Indonesian Muslims blend traditional animism and spirituality into their religious observance. Nonetheless, historic and global Islamic rhetorical traditions continue to inform the practice of Indonesian rhetoric. Indonesians of other faiths (or without any faith affiliation) who negotiate their own religious and linguistic identities within the Indonesian rhetorical tradition may thus do so with a complex awareness of their own nonnormativity, as Amber Engelson's work thoughtfully illustrates.[3] Thus, religious texts (and texts that self-consciously engage

---

2. US Department of State 2016.

3. Engelson 2020.

with religious identity) are likely to be generative sources of rhetorical tradition for the Indonesian context.

Second, we must remember that *Bahasa Indonesia* is Indonesia's lingua franca but is not a first language for the majority of its speakers.[4] Although it is taught in schools and functions as the language of nationwide public and popular discourse, most Indonesians grow up speaking languages like Javanese, Sundanese, Madurese, or any of about seven hundred other local languages in their homes and neighborhoods. In addition to these local languages that coexist alongside *Bahasa Indonesia*, other languages like Arabic and English also play a substantial role in various sectors of Indonesian society (with the influence of Arabic felt especially in religion and the influence of English felt especially in the academy). The boundaries between these many languages often bend and blur, leading to combinatory dialects called by nicknames like *gado-gado* (the name of a local mixed salad). Language scholar Subhan Zein refers to this linguistic situation in Indonesia as *superdiversity* or *superglossia*.[5] Any capacious understanding of the linguistic terrain in Indonesia, Zein rightly argues, cannot be understood apart from these dynamics. Thus, national Indonesian rhetorics are marked by the opportunities and constraints of a linguistic meeting ground upon which only a minority of speakers hold a home field advantage. How does this frequent second-language status inform Indonesian rhetoric in terms of its constitutive cultural power, its standard range of topics, its preferred strategies for ornamentation, and so forth? On this count, future scholars might wish to compare the formulation of Indonesian rhetorics to the formulation of English-speaking rhetorics in nations where English is not predominantly a first language—drawing, for instance, from the work of Suresh Canagarajah and others on World Englishes. The best sources of rhetorical texts in *Bahasa Indonesia* are likely to be those realms of society where this language most predominates: commerce, administration, education, and media.[6]

Finally, rhetorical traditions in Indonesia are undeniably shaped by the distinctive relationship that exists between orality and written literacy for many Indonesian citizens. On the one hand, Indonesia boasts an impressive literacy rate of 95.7 percent for those age fifteen and older as of 2018, with the rate at 99.7 percent for those fifteen to twenty-four years old.[7] Yet this high literacy rate does not mean that written literacy holds as much cultural importance in Indonesia as it does in some nations with comparable literacy rates. On the contrary, as Ariel Heryanto observes, "Compared to their counterparts in more literacy-dependent societies, people in Indonesia, including the literati and graduates of higher education, prefer to share important information and messages through face-to-face communication."[8] Despite their high capacity for using and understanding the written word, many Indonesians seem to privilege the oral in their rhetorical practices, leading Heryanto to classify Indonesia as "a pri-

---

4. "Sensus Penduduk" 2010.
5. Zein 2020.
6. Ibid.
7. UNESCO Institute for Statistics 2022.
8. Heryanto 2010, 183.

marily orality-oriented society."[9] The sources of the ever-emerging Indonesian rhetorical tradition are thus inflected by orality in ways that may violate the expectations of cultures more reliant on written literacy. For this reason, it is likely that the Indonesian rhetorical tradition will draw with special emphasis on texts that exhibit secondary orality, including televised speeches, film, popular music, and other digital media, as well as on primary oral texts such as aphorisms, traditional music, and narrative arts.

---

9. Ibid.

5.1 Post-National, c. 2014 CE, Indonesia

Address at the *Rakernas Partai Nasdem* (National Democratic Parties Convention), by Megawati Sukarnoputri

Gregory Coles

The aura of the woman is full of motherliness, of love and affection, and she often speaks from her heart. So if the women here want to become members of the party, don't think that by wandering aimlessly, you'll become someone influential. Not a chance. I guarantee it. But if you, with conviction, speak what is in your thoughts and in [your heart], with unity between your words and your actions, then you will become like me.

—Megawati Sukarnoputri

CRITICAL INTRODUCTION

This chapter excerpts a political speech delivered by Indonesia's first female president, Megawati Sukarnoputri, at the *Rakernas Partai Nasdem* (National Democratic Parties Convention) on May 27, 2014.[10] The convention was held in Indonesia's capital city, Jakarta, and televised nationwide. Since Megawati's address lasted approximately fifty-four minutes, a full transcription and translation would be unwieldy. Instead, I have selected excerpts that show the shape of the whole address while exemplifying Megawati's articulation of three Indonesian rhetorical ideals: *hormat* ("honor"), *persaudaraan* ("camaraderie" or "brotherhood"), and the tension between *jalan terus* ("keep moving forward") and *tinggal disini* ("stay here"), a tension I call *historicized progressivism*.

Unlike many of the rhetorical source materials included in this collection, Megawati's speech is not ostensibly a work of rhetorical theory. Nonetheless, Megawati's rhetorical self-consciousness is highly illuminating. As well as being a former president and a political party chair, Megawati is also the daughter of Indonesia's founding president, Sukarno, and as such she represents for many Indonesians a continuation of the rhetorical legacy that founded the nation. She never offers a clear articulation of her nation's rhetorical tradition, yet she gives an evocative window into the character of that tradition—a tradition rooted in and inseparable from the politics, linguistics, and lineage of her father Sukarno.

---

10. I have translated these excerpts from their original Indonesian into English; all excised text between excerpts is marked by an ellipsis: "[. . .]." As far as I am aware, no extensive transcription or English translation of the address has been created prior to mine. During translation, I consulted with two Indonesian language translators, Ni Luh Carniti and Dave Coles, who deserve credit for many of the translation's successes and none of its remaining errors.

POLITICAL AND RHETORICAL BACKGROUND

Both the nation of Indonesia and its official language, *Bahasa Indonesia*, are relatively young in the scheme of recorded human history. The rhetorical traditions at play in Indonesia, then, are correspondingly youthful in many ways. This is not to say that influences from antiquity are entirely absent; the strongest influences, however, are those rooted in the tradition articulated during the twentieth century at the birth of the Indonesian nation and *Bahasa Indonesia*. Perhaps more than many rhetorical traditions, the Indonesian rhetorical tradition is synonymous with the nation's short political history. Thus, Megawati Sukarnoputri is a particularly compelling figure for the study of Indonesian rhetoric because the legacy of her political influence can be traced from the earliest days of Indonesia to the present day.

More than a decade after finishing her term as Indonesia's first and only female president in 2004, Megawati[11] remains one of the most influential political and rhetorical figures in the world's largest Muslim nation.[12] As the daughter of Indonesia's founding president, Sukarno,[13] Megawati carries the authority of her father's name and invokes this authority to wield rhetorical power in a Muslim nation that is often suspicious of female leadership. She chairs the political party *Partai Demokrasi Indonesia Perjuangan* (the Indonesian Democratic Party of Struggle, "PDI-P"), and her endorsement was largely responsible for the election of Indonesia's current president, Joko Widodo, in 2014. Jokowi, as he is popularly known, emerged from relative obscurity to become PDI-P's presidential candidate; although he was not a newcomer to politics,[14] his popularity was primarily regional prior to Megawati's endorsement. As PDI-P's chair and a figure with a substantial following, Megawati voiced her support of Jokowi to leverage the support of her entire party: one party official anonymously observed, "Whatever Ibu Mega[15] decides, so goes the party."[16]

To construct a notion of Indonesian rhetoric and Megawati's place within it, it is first necessary to consider what is meant by the category of "Indonesia." The modern-day nation of Indonesia, made up of thousands of islands spread across an area approximately the size of the contiguous United States, has only been in existence since 1945, when a small group of

---

11. Most Javanese women have only one name, their given name. Megawati's second name, *Sukarnoputri* (also spelled *Soekarnoputri*) is a patronym meaning "daughter of Sukarno." When Indonesians refer to her, they typically use only her given name and would never use her patronym alone.

12. As of 2020, Indonesia's population of 263 million people is estimated to be 87.2 percent Muslim. Based on this estimate, thirteen percent of the global population of Muslims resides in Indonesia. See World Population Review (2020).

13. Also spelled *Soekarno*.

14. Jokowi served as the mayor of the central Javanese city of Solo (also called Surakarta) and governor of the Indonesian capital, Jakarta, before running for president.

15. *Ibu* is an Indonesian term of respect for married women and means either *mother* or *Mrs.* depending on the context in which it is spoken. *Mega* is a common affectionate shortening of Megawati's full name.

16. Quoted in Kapoor 2014.

nationalists declared their independence from both Dutch colonizers and Japanese occupiers at the close of the Second World War. Prior to this period, as historians M. C. Ricklefs and R. E. Elson have observed, the very idea of "Indonesia" did not exist.[17] The Indonesian islands were simply a collection of independent ethnic groups, comprised of over seven hundred languages and cultures.[18] There could be no common thread of Indonesian rhetoric where there was no Indonesia.

The unifying figure who brought together these disparate forces into a collective notion of "Indonesia" was Indonesia's first president and Megawati's father, Sukarno. Both a political figure and a military leader, Sukarno led the resistance against the Dutch, who fought from 1945 to 1949 to reclaim their former colony. Sukarno's early years as president were volatile; even after defeating the Dutch, he and other nationalists struggled to unify the Indonesian islands and instill a sense of collective identity. Indonesia's early parliamentary democracy, modeled largely after Western democratic models,[19] failed to produce the necessary momentum to consolidate the floundering young nation, and so in 1957 Sukarno proposed what he called a *Demokrasi Terpimpin* (Guided Democracy), a more centrally authoritative system in which he declared himself president for life. Sukarno's new system was based on the doctrine of *Pancasila* (Five Principles): commitment to God, democracy by consensus, humanitarianism, prosperity, and national unity. The notion of democracy by consensus in particular was a reaction against models of Western democracy that called for polemical disagreement and rule by the majority. Instead, Sukarno argued that harmonious Indonesian democracy would best be achieved by the wisdom of consensus, a process inevitably guided by a single strong leader.

This move to draw in some measure from colonial Western models, while also rejecting and distancing himself from these models in favor of traditional values held by Indonesia's native groups, typified Sukarno's approach both politically and rhetorically. Just as Sukarno himself had been educated in Dutch schools but rejected a colonized Dutch identity, so his speech and political ideals were framed as informed improvements upon European norms. Meanwhile, in drawing from traditional values of the ethnic groups comprising Indonesia, Sukarno needed to take care not to draw too heavily from a single ethnic and linguistic tradition, lest he risk fracturing the myriad identities contained within the idea of "Indonesia." The rhetoric of Sukarno's Indonesia claimed roots everywhere and nowhere, at once syncretistic and *ex nihilo*. Rather than binding itself to concrete cultural traditions of major Indonesian

---

17. Ricklefs 2001; Elson 2008.

18. The precise number of languages represented in Indonesia is disputed, with interpretations varying based on definitional differences in what constitutes an independent language and what is merely a difference in dialect. Linguists place the total number of languages at 719, with 707 of these languages still living; see Lewis, Simons, and Fennig (2015).

19. Of course, as political scholars like David Held have evinced, there is no singular Western model of democracy, since societies that claim the name "democracy" differ substantially in their understanding of how best to grant power (*kratos*) to the people (*demos*). Scholars like Jacques Ranciere and Wendy Brown have even argued that what is nominally known as "democracy" in many Western societies is in fact antithetical to the true practice of democratic rule by the people.

ethnic groups like the Javanese and Sundanese, Sukarno's Indonesia was loosely constructed around a mixture of anti-colonial rhetoric and strategically vague generalizations about the newly defined Indonesian citizens—as people who value harmony, for example. In the sense that *Pancasila* rejected pure democracy in favor of controlled consensus, Sukarno defended this form of government as an explicitly anti-Western and therefore uniquely Indonesian and harmonious mode of thought, though his suspicion of majority rule also bears a resemblance to the cautions against "the tyranny of the majority" that have been central to Western disputes over the nature of democracy.[20] For Sukarno, the danger of centralizing power within a single democratic leader was less formidable than the dangers of mob rule or chaos.

Though the English language might vilify Sukarno's conclusion as "authoritarian," many Indonesian nationalists did not regard Sukarno's move in this way; instead, his willingness to redefine democracy in uniquely Indonesian terms and to do what was necessary in service of Indonesian unification was seen by supporters as a sign of effective leadership.[21] Sukarno's *Pancasila* became part and parcel of the Indonesian identity, a rhetorical move without which Indonesia itself could not be conceived. As time went on, however, an increasing number of Indonesians became uncomfortable with Sukarno's power, and Sukarno's sympathy towards Communism and hostility toward other world powers earned him the enmity of much of the Western world. In 1965–1967, Sukarno was overthrown by military general Suharto[22] following a bloody anti-communist purge endorsed by Western democracies. Suharto instituted what he called an *Orde Baru* (New Order), still claiming the doctrine of *Pancasila*, and served as Indonesia's president from 1967 to 1998. Although Indonesia's political party system continued to exist, Suharto's regime carefully controlled the parties and elections to keep Suharto in power.

In 1987, after years of obscurity, Sukarno's daughter Megawati reentered the political scene, running for a seat in the *Dewan Perwakilan Rakyat* (the People's Representative Council, "DPR"). Threatened by Megawati's quickly rising popularity, Suharto's regime attempted to remove her from her leadership position in *Partai Demokrasi Indonesia* (the Indonesian Democratic Party, "PDI"). On July 27, 1996, the Indonesian military attacked PDI headquarters to remove Megawati and her supporters forcibly. During the bloody attack later known as *Sabtu Kelabu* (Grey Saturday), five of Megawati's supporters were killed, more than twenty others were declared missing, and over one hundred were injured. This incident, as journalist Gary LaMoshi argues, became a "blood-stained unifier for opponents of Suharto, catapulting

---

20. Concerns about the "tyranny of the majority" damaging the integrity of democratic governance have of course been raised by well-known Western thinkers such as John Adams, Alexis de Tocqueville, and John Stuart Mill. For a discussion of how these concerns continue to be salient in contemporary Western discourse, see McAfee (2008). However, the way these concerns are expressed in the context of Western governance differs from Sukarno's vision of consensus.

21. Vickers 2005, 117–50; Ricklefs 2001, 289–365.

22. Also spelled *Soeharto*.

Megawati to national stature as a symbol of opposition to a regime that had reiterated its nakedly oppressive side by attacking unarmed foes over a purely political matter."[23]

Instead of yielding to Suharto's attack, Megawati declared herself the leader of a new political party, the PDI-P, so named because of Megawati's ongoing struggle against Suharto's regime. As the popularity of "Ibu Mega" and her newly established party rose, Suharto's popularity dwindled. Disapproval of Suharto was exacerbated by Indonesia's 1997–1998 *krismon* (monetary crisis), in which the value of Indonesia's currency, the rupiah, against the US dollar plummeted from Rp. 2,700 per $1 in mid-1997[24] to Rp. 17,000 per $1 in early 1998,[25] a depreciation of over six hundred percent. Suharto was forced to resign in May of 1998 and was replaced by his vice president, Bacharuddin Jusuf Habibie. Widely considered a mere extension of Suharto's regime, Habibie was even more unpopular than his predecessor. In fact, the most common theory for Suharto's choice of Habibie as a vice president was that Suharto felt he was less likely to be ousted if his opponents knew that Habibie might assume his position.[26]

Within this context, as the 1999 election approached, Megawati was in many ways the natural choice for president. Not only did she represent opposition to the current unpopular regime, but her campaign shunned the elitism so common to Indonesian politics by claiming that she would fight for the *wong cilik* (a Javanese phrase often translated "grassroots" that literally means "little people").[27] Since the 1999 election was the first fully democratic presidential race in Indonesian history,[28] Megawati's alignment with the *wong cilik* marked her as the embodiment of the election. Yet the challenges faced by Megawati—as a non-military leader, as a symbolic representative of her father's politics and rhetoric, and most of all as a woman— were still substantial. Although Megawati's party won more votes than any other party in the general election, it still fell short of the fifty percent necessary to immediately declare Megawati president. As a result, the presidency was determined by the *Majelis Permusyawaratan Rakyat* (the People's Deliberative Assembly, "MPR"), a parliamentary body whose votes reflected political alliances and grudges more often than they did the interests of the people they represented. Because of Habibie's ever-plummeting popularity, his party offered to support Megawati's ally Abdurrahman Wahid, better known as Gus Dur, as a presidential candidate before the MPR. Gus Dur accepted, withdrawing his support from Megawati's campaign and seizing an unexpected eleventh-hour victory over her.

Megawati's defeat sparked a string of riots, and to mollify the rioters, Gus Dur was forced to select Megawati as his vice president.[29] Despite this gesture of peace, unrest continued until 2001, when Gus Dur was impeached and replaced by Megawati, the candidate whom many Indonesians had seen as the rightful president all along. As was her initial triumph over Su-

---

23. LaMoshi 2004.

24. "Indonesia Floats the Rupiah, and It Drops More Than 6%" 1997.

25. "Meltdown in Asia – Part 4: Chronology of a Crisis" (1998).

26. Bird 1999, 28.

27. Torchia and Djuhari 2011, 92.

28. Liddle 2000, 32.

29. Mietzner 2000, 46–48.

harto and Habibie, Megawati's eventual triumph over Gus Dur when she succeeded him in 2001 came by way of attrition, with Megawati managing to maintain her popularity as her opponents' popularity dwindled. In both contexts, it was her opponents' speech and actions that made them increasingly unpopular, while Megawati maintained her goodwill by remaining notoriously silent.[30] Because her very position as the leader of an opposition party (and as her father's daughter) made her a figure of resistance to Suharto, her silence became an uncensorable protest against the censorship of Suharto's New Order. News coverage of Megawati during her periods of silence often used the word *bertahan* ("to endure"), framing her silence as evidence of strength. These moves enhanced Megawati's image as "an embattled figure," an image that Daniel Ziv argues "cannot be overestimated" in evaluating her popular success.[31]

In addition, Megawati's combination of speech and silence enabled her to enter the political realm while appearing to remain aloof from the corrupt Indonesian political system. Bolstered by the unpopularity of the Suharto regime and particularly the unpopularity of Habibie, Megawati's primary concern was with demonstrating that she was not like her predecessors and opponents. While this claim needed to be asserted verbally (and often was), the true evidence of Megawati's distinction from Suharto and Habibie was her refusal to enter the political fray in the way they had. Again, Ziv's commentary proves enlightening: "To a point, at least, Megawati's silence has indeed seemed golden. The less exposed, the more revered. She has come to represent something Utopian, something beyond the realm of the political."[32] Particularly because she was participating in Indonesia's first fully democratic election, Megawati represented the promise of a whole new Indonesian system, one that escaped the excesses of Suharto politics and hearkened back to the days of her father's leadership.

Though silence would serve Megawati well prior to 2001, it would prove to be a handicap once she finally assumed the office of president. During her presidency, Megawati's silence was criticized as indecisive and ineffective, and her popularity dwindled in much the same way as her predecessors. Unlike the decline of her predecessors, however, Megawati's decline in popularity was less severe, and she still retained substantial influence in Indonesian politics. Even among those who disagreed with her policies or considered her an ineffective president, Megawati remained a symbol of her father Sukarno and of the Indonesian unity and rhetorical identity he had made possible.

Following the end of her presidential term in 2004, Megawati remained the chair of the PDI-P. She ran two moderately successful presidential campaigns in 2004 and 2009 but lost both races to former military general Susilo Bambang Yudhoyono. In 2012, polls showed Megawati as the leading prospective presidential candidate for the 2014 election.[33] However, Megawati distanced herself from these poll numbers, ultimately choosing to endorse Jokowi instead of leveraging her popularity for another presidential race of her own. Although it is

---

30. Megawati's use of silence is a crucial feature of her own rhetorical tactics, a dynamic I examine more fully elsewhere. See Coles (2018, 58–91).

31. Ziv 2001, 76.

32. Ibid., 86.

33. "Dihembuskan 'Angin Surga' Megawati Tak Mau Terlena" 2012.

impossible to say whether or not Megawati could have won the 2014 election if she had chosen to run, the influence of her rhetoric on the outcome of the race between Jokowi and his rival Prabowo Subianto is undeniable. Without affiliation to such a well-known party, it is almost certain that Jokowi could not have mustered the political clout necessary to win the election. Even with the support of Megawati and PDI-P, Jokowi defeated Prabowo by only a slim margin, earning fifty-three percent of the popular vote while Prabowo earned forty-seven percent.[34]

In short, Megawati is not merely a participant in the Indonesian rhetorical context. She is, both by virtue of her father Sukarno and through her own involvement, one of the defining figures in Indonesian political rhetoric. As *Sukarnoputri*, the daughter of Sukarno, Megawati is in a sense inseparable from the very idea of "Indonesia." Her father's doctrine of *Pancasila* has endured as the central philosophy of the Indonesian political system even during the reign of his archrival Suharto. Moreover, as the candidate of the *wong cilik*, the "little people," during the first truly democratic presidential election her nation had seen, Megawati became both the emblem and the enactment of modern-day Indonesian political discourse. Even as she lost three consecutive elections, Megawati's name and identity became irrevocably fixed to the notion of a uniquely Indonesian democracy. As her instrumental role in Jokowi's 2014 election illustrates, Megawati remains a significant rhetorical figure in Indonesia.

Translation and Commentary

Megawati's Address at the Rakernas Partai Nasdem

Megawati's strategies of leveraging rhetorical power are exemplified by her May 27, 2014, address at the *Rakernas Partai Nasdem* (National Democratic Parties Convention). The convention brought together a coalition of five major political parties[35] in support of Jokowi and his running mate Jusuf Kalla for the 2014 election: Megawati's PDI-P, *Partai Nasional Demokrat* (National Democratic Party, "Nasdem"), *Partai Kebangkitan Bangsa* (National Awakening Party, "PKB"), *Partai Hati Nurani Rakyat* (People's Conscience Party, "Hanura"), and *Partai Keadilan dan Persatuan Indonesia* (Indonesian Justice and Unity Party, "PKPI"). The event was hosted by Nasdem, a political party run by media tycoon Surya Paloh; Paloh used his influence to give this event in particular and Jokowi's candidacy in general extensive newspaper and television coverage. Though Paloh was in this sense the primary figure of the event, Megawati exercised a unique place of authority as the chair of PDI-P, the party on whose ticket Jokowi officially ran for the presidency. Equally, she exercised authority as a symbolic

---

34. Marszal 2014.

35. Unlike many Western democracies that tend to be dominated by two powerful political parties, the Indonesian political system includes dozens of parties, many of which form conditional alliances with one another to elect mutually agreeable candidates.

representation of her father, the embodiment of the very idea of Indonesian rhetoric. These dynamics are plainly exhibited in Megawati's own words.

Address

Mr. Surya Paloh, chair of the National Democratic Party. I whispered earlier, "This isn't good—if we keep introducing ourselves with abbreviations, in the end we'll forget what our names are."[36] Mr. Kiyai Nuhaimin Iskandar, chair of the National Awakening Party. Next, Mr. General Purnawirawan Wiranto, chair of the People's Conscience Party. Mr. General Purnawirawan Sutioso, chair of the Indonesian Justice and Unity Party. May the peace, mercy, and blessings of Allah be with you. Greetings to you all, and may God give you health.

If you happen to be coming after that,[37] you certainly need to be creative. Because before me, orators were speaking, and people talking about friendship. So I thought, certainly each of these generals is usually ready to be honored, but on the personal level they're very close in camaraderie and friendship.

[. . .]

I'm a person who considers my role in this republic strange. Why is it strange? From the past until now there have been no female party chairs. [Her listeners laugh and cheer.] Yes, praise Allah. The men here want to applaud me. Before I was the party chair I seemed impoverished—didn't I?—when I was trembling in my seat as a party member. (Because all this I'm telling you now happened before, when I was in Surabaya.) I was asked to become the party chair, and people responded, "Oh, you're not like brother Surya.[38] He organized masses of people."[39] And then he invited me to eat. So I said to him, "Um, brother? You're being shy. If you want to make a party, just make it. Why are you shy to think about profits and losses? You should be like me!"[40]

In 1986 I became a member of the Indonesian Democratic Party. At that time I had to fight with my husband, the late Mr. Taufiq. If he were here, he would laugh. Because I said, "Where are there ever two captains of one ship?"

---

36. Indonesian political parties are known almost exclusively by their abbreviations. For instance, Megawati's party, *Partai Democracy Indonesia Perjuangan* (Indonesian Democratic Party of Struggle), is popularly referred to as *PDI Perjuangan* or PDI-P. Megawati breaks from this tradition of using acronyms (to which the speakers preceding her would have adhered) to use the full name of each party gathered at the convention.

37. That is, if you happen to be speaking after such excellent speakers. This is the beginning of Megawati's complimentary assessment of the powerful generals who have spoken before her.

38. Surya Paloh, chair of the National Democratic Party, the party that hosted the event.

39. The implication is that Megawati didn't have the influence to be a party chair, whereas Paloh did have that influence.

40 Paloh formed a political party and became its chair more than a decade after Megawati began chairing her party. Megawati is thus pointing out with a hint of irony that Paloh had consulted her for advice, since she had become the veteran party chair, even though her detractors had said years ago that he should be a party chair and she should not.

Then he said, "What are you talking about?"

"I'm sure that one day I'll become the party chair."

Then my husband said, "How could you become the party chair? You're a woman." Just look at what kind of woman I am. See, you're laughing. It's true.

About my husband, back in those days, Najwa[41] asked me, "What was Mr. Taufiq to you?" He was, if we were boxing, my sparring partner.[42] Yes, if he said, "Punch punch punch," like that, I went "Block!" just like that. My children already know what kind of person their mother is. If I wear this formal clothing [she touches her shirt], I'll behave differently than I do in my everyday clothes.

Around that time, there was a person who joined PDI Perjuangan, who had previously been a minister in my government. When he came in and saw my style, wow, he started sweating. He said, "Why is it, Ibu, that when you were President you were so sweet? Why is it that now you've become the party chair, you're like that?" That's a secret.

Friends, if I tell too many stories, brother Surya, later your followers can join PDI-P.[43] Of course, a lot of the people here already came as part of PDI-P. So what is the point of all my stories?

Do we want to win or lose? ["Win!" the crowd shouts.] Do we want to win or lose? ["Win!" the crowd shouts.] Do we want to win or lose? ["Win!" the crowd shouts. Megawati laughs.] If it's true that we want to win, then let's win and have no talk of losing. All we still need to think about is how much we'll win by, how big our margin of victory will be. Why is this? I'm constantly saying this until I get bored. Then my kids tell me, "Mom, we know, Mom, let it be."

[. . .]

What is it that we've accomplished, when we accomplish "reformation"? What kind of reformation is it really? Of course we want to create a particular situation, a condition right in the moment. This is what we felt to be so repressive: that which made the children[44] of this nation unable to speak to one another with openness. It was in 1986 when I took the leap (actually, I just signed my name) and joined this party. There was no such thing as good manners in politics back then. Back then the party chair just said, "Ibu, you need to go to Central Java. Consolidate Central Java." Back then I hadn't been active in politics for such a long time. After all, in 1965, my whole family was forbidden from taking part in politics.[45]

My father talked to me at that time, when I returned home and told him, "I'm not allowed to continue my college education, Dad." I wanted to cry. It feels so good, right, to cry in the

---

41. A popular talk show host on whose show Megawati had recently given an interview.

42. Here she uses the English phrase "sparring partner," adding humor for those who understand English and also evincing her cosmopolitan education as an English speaker.

43. In other words, she is joking that her speech might go on so long that people have time to change their political party affiliations.

44. That is, the people; Megawati is emphasizing her rhetorically parental relationship to the Indonesian people.

45. 1965 marked the beginning of Suharto's overthrow of Sukarno, an overthrow that implicated not just Sukarno himself but also his entire family.

embrace of your father? To have him feel the pain deep in your heart—because every Indonesian citizen wants to become more intelligent. And then to be told by my own nation, "You're not allowed to go to college." This is true. I'm not joking.

And then, what did my father say? "Whose child are you?"

Woah. Right in the middle of my crying, I stopped. My tears that were already falling, they went right back into my eyes! They went right back in! Because when I heard my father's question, I immediately answered, "I am the child of Sukarno."

Then he patted my hand like this. "Good. That's my child. Do you know your task?" (He was already giving me a task, which is why I'm such a strange woman.) "Your first task is that you must look after this nation called the Republic of Indonesia."

"Okay," I said, just like that.

[She returns to mimicking Sukarno:] "If you want to be intelligent, just search for knowledge everywhere." This is called being an autodidact,[46] meaning that you learn something here and something else there. This is why when I see today's youth, oh, they have this degree and that degree and that degree, but when I ask, "What are you capable of? What can you offer to your country?" Nothing! Nothing![47] What they're thinking about is that they want to get rich quickly, to get nice positions. Is that what we'll do?[48]

Now, this is why I said we fasted for ten years. PDI Perjuangan was not in the circles of power.[49] Because for me, I said, "That's not my primary task." My primary task is to liberate the nation of Indonesia, to make it as free as possible. Have you gained an understanding of what that word freedom really means?

All this my father said to me. He ordered me to sit down: "You will sit. You will listen. This moment[50] will be my downfall, so you must sit and listen. Look after the Republic of Indonesia."

"Okay," that was all I said.

[Her impression of Sukarno continues:] "Second, always carry out my teachings and my ideas." Now a lot of people are wondering,[51] "Why is Ibu Mega not tired of talking like this?" Because I am not the biological child of Bung[52] Karno, no. I am the ideological child of Bung Karno.

This nation, this country, cannot move forward—

And this has already been demonstrated, and this will move us forward, this will move us forward, because this is the twenty-first century, a century that's so different, when Bung

---

46. She uses the English word *autodidact*.

47. She uses the English word *nothing*.

48. The implied response is, "Of course not; we'll work hard."

49. The ten-year "fast" from power she is referring to is the span between the end of her presidential term in 2004 and the present day in 2014.

50. Sukarno's unseating by Suharto in 1967.

51. The word I have translated "wondering" is *melongok*, literally *looking* or *staring*; thus, by implication, "staring in wonder, wondering."

52. A nickname for *older brother*; Sukarno was commonly called "Bung Karno" by his followers.

Karno poured out his writings, when he fought against colonialists, when he freed many nations around the world by his inspiration. But at that time there were many people who didn't believe what he said would happen. I answered, when my father said all this to me, "Okay, Dad, I will see it through. I will see it through, with all my thoughts and all my heart. God willing, you will see it. You will see it."

You can talk with Bung Karno up there,[53] if you don't believe me. Just pray, and later you'll be able to see him in heaven. This is our culture.

[. . .]

Imagine it. Imagine it. As for a man like Surya Paloh, he can play around, he can zigzag back and forth.[54] Not like me, I'm straightforward, because I think how funny it would be if a woman who became a politician was always zigzagging back and forth. How could that be?

The aura of a woman— the aura of the woman is full of motherliness, of love and affection, and she often speaks from her heart. So if the women here want to become members of the party,[55] don't think that by wandering aimlessly, you'll become someone influential. Not a chance. I guarantee it. But if you, with conviction, speak what is in your thoughts and in here [she points to her heart], with unity between your words and your actions, then you will become like me. It's not that I'm arrogant, no. Not at all. In the past I was attacked, with people saying, "It's not possible for a woman to become president. This Republic of Indonesia has always refused to make a woman president." I just, I said, "That's just human talk. That's just people." But if your name is Allah (may He be glorified in the highest), you say, "What I say shall be, it shall be." And so it happens.

Now, why am I saying this? I always call Mr. Jokowi by the nickname "Mr. Skinny." I try to make him eat, it's so hard to do. Oh. So if I order him to eat a lot, he has to sit in front of me.

I say, "It's good, right, little brother?"

"Yes, Ibu, it's good."

"Yes, have some more rice, little brother."

If he tries to answer by saying, "I'm all done, I'm totally full," [I answer,] "But you're not fattened up yet."

"Yes, my belly's already sticking out like this, Ibu." Later on, when he becomes president, he'll get fatter, right? He'll gain ten kilos.

So a lot of people ask me, "Why is it that you don't want to become president again?" Ah, I'm tired. I'm already full of experience.

[. . .]

---

53. That is, in heaven.

54. This sentence begins with the word *kalau*, which usually means *if* and signals a conditional clause: "If a man like Surya Paloh. . . ." However, since Megawati never completes the sentence by adding an apodosis to resolve the protasis, I have chosen to translate *kalau* as a colloquial preposition: "As for a man like Surya Paloh. . . ."

55. That is, active in politics.

What do I lack as a woman? I was seized by the police, I was brought to that circular building[56] to be interrogated and all that. What do I lack? Now, I've been the daughter of a president, and I've been fallen from that place; I've become an ordinary citizen. I can understand the heartbeat of the people because I myself have been an ordinary person. I've met with farmers, like this and like that, like this and like that.

Now, eventually I was given an opportunity in Surabaya—all shaken up again, just to try to get rid of me—as the party chair of PDI at that time. It's not because I was trying to get glory from a high status, no. Imagine it. In those days it was an era of struggle, and all the people were like little children. At that time they just asked me, "Ibu, we want you to become the party chair. Do you want to help us, Ibu?"

"What kind of help do you want?"

"Help in order that, with conviction, we would not depart from this realm.[57] I will stay here. Until the end."

Those children[58] were extraordinary.

[. . .]

But if there are a lot of people now who don't want to know, young people who don't want to know—"It's done, if I'm already free, enough, stop, I am free"—they don't care how other people are doing, don't care about their living conditions. That's what we have to reawaken. That is nation and character building.[59] When we examine our minds and ourselves first, what do we truly find inside ourselves? Is it true that we as members of the People's Representative Council are only interested in connecting with our colleagues, and so we only make an effort to win the projects that can be gotten? That's the game being played right up to today. Is that what's going to be done?

That's why I continually think about what my father said: "Can you join in and continue the struggle, someday after I am gone?"

"Okay, I promise. I will do it and you will see."

All this is where it comes from, this passion of mine, because I always tell myself, "Don't look to the left or right, don't look with those things called lies. We must keep moving forward."

[. . .]

Try, as Allah wills it, if you want to know what real struggle is, if we are to let out a voice from our mouths, because Bung Karno said, "Look first to see who has a voice. Look first whose throat can make a sound."

We can't be sure yet. If a criminal is going to claim to be righteous and such, there's no way people would say, "Oh, what an angel!" No way. So people are going to investigate and con-

---

56. The police headquarters in Jakarta.

57. By "this realm," Megawati means an ideological commitment to Sukarno's vision of nationhood.

58. That is, those people who wanted to continue following Sukarno. Again, the characterization of Indonesia's people as children is significant to the familial style of Indonesian rhetoric.

59. She uses the English phrase "nation and character building," a phrase that her father Sukarno also discussed in English.

clude[60]: "The people are intelligent. The people have hearts. What they don't have is a voice. Their voices have been silenced, their throats frozen."

Just come and see. Because you've said before, "Oh, I'm tired, most of the legislators go down to the people, and so forth . . . [she mumbles in mimicry of a person making complaints]." Okay, then don't be a legislator, and don't appoint them. It should go that way.[61]

Descend lower, descend lower, meet people, shake hands. This is the Jokowi I have seen, because the people want to know, what does the hand of the president feel like, what does his hand feel like and what does he feel towards us? [She raises her hand.] This hand has shaken thousands, maybe millions of hands. Not only the hands that are clean. Also the hands of the people who are dirty, who have HIV AIDS, who have leprosy, who have tuberculosis—I have shaken those hands. Everywhere I have shaken hands. Everywhere I have shaken hands.

And if you're thinking, "But, Ibu, you lost." [She laughs.] That's a different matter. Because what I say is, "Democracy can't move forward well if the General Election Committee isn't neutral."[62]

[. . .]

Praise be to Allah, all of this happened. We're done, yes? That's enough. And with that, thank you to the National Democratic Party, and to Mr. Surya Paloh, who opened this stage to me and not just my own party's stage. And once more I say, let us within these thirty days, I count thirty effective days,[63] let us not have more meetings just for show, but let us plunge into the field, let us all plunge into the field and take back our constituents if Allah wills it. By the grace of Allah (may He be glorified in the highest), we will win the victory. And so, thank you. May the peace, mercy, and blessings of Allah be with you, and may God give you health. [She raises her fist in the air and leads the audience in a closing chant:] Freedom! Freedom! Freedom!

CRITICAL COMMENTARY

Megawati's address at the *Rakernas Partai Nasdem* illustrates a range of Indonesian rhetorical practices. This is not to reductively suggest that Megawati's approach represents all Indonesian rhetoric, nor that Megawati's rhetorical methods are always unique to the Indonesian

---

60. Megawati uses only the word for *investigate*, but the notion that the investigation will lead to a conclusion is implied.

61. In other words, legislators should indeed go down to the common people and consult with them in lawmaking.

62. This is a veiled reference to the political machinations that caused Megawati to lose the presidential election in 1999. Since she won a plurality but not a majority of the popular vote, the election was decided by the General Election Committee, which formed a number of ad hoc alliances to keep Megawati from assuming power.

63. That is, the time until the election. In total, there were forty-one days between her speech and Jokowi's election, but Megawati implies that only about thirty of those will be effective campaigning days.

rhetorical situation.[64] Nonetheless, Megawati models—and at times, even directs attention to—an important set of Indonesian rhetorical practices. In this critical commentary and glossary, I briefly call attention to just three of the rhetorical ideals exhibited by Megawati's address: *hormat* ("honor"), *persaudaraan* ("camaraderie" or "brotherhood"), and the tension between *jalan terus* ("keep moving forward") and *tinggal disini* ("stay here"), a tension I call *historicized progressivism*.

First, Megawati's *Rakernas Partai Nasdem* address exhibits the practice of public oratory as a performance of *hormat* ("honor"). Megawati's fifty-four-minute speech, full of inside jokes and unexplained allusions, is not given primarily for the listeners' benefit. Her untranslated English words, especially obscure words like "autodidact," would have been understood only by a portion of her audience at the convention and an even smaller fraction of the Indonesian public, many of whom never advance beyond a sixth grade level of public education. Yet this feature does not in itself make the speech an ineffective one. It is common for the speeches of influential Indonesian leaders to be confusing at points to their listeners. Such speeches' primary rhetorical function is to foster confidence in the speaker, and audience understanding is necessary only insofar as it is a means to this end. To use the nomenclature of the ancient Greeks, *ethos* far outweighs *logos* in Indonesian political rhetoric. In Indonesian, this rhetorical ideal is called *hormat*, "honor." Most often, *hormat* is enjoyed by male speakers with a history of military or political leadership speaking in a formal tone that proves their authority. In a very real sense, such an approach cannot simply be acquired through rhetorical learning, because the roots of its effectiveness lie in having a form of culturally approved power to flaunt to accrue *hormat*.

Megawati draws attention to this rhetorical dynamic near the beginning of her speech. The generals who have preceded her are *siap hormat*, "ready to be honored," and the *hormat* they enjoy inspires her to assess them as *orator* ("orators"). That is, their position in society determines the range of their rhetorical possibility. Megawati jokes that she must be creative (*kreatif*) to follow them—and she certainly does manifest some of this creativity in her casual and story-telling (*cerita*) approach. Her speech is full of informal grammatical constructions that are common to everyday conversation, a stark contrast from the usual formalism of Indonesian political speeches. However, her rhetorical moves also emphasize her own *hormat* in comparison with her male colleagues. She observes almost immediately that the men who preceded her are "very close in camaraderie and friendship." She goes on to discuss her own qualifications, including her years of political experience and the charge she received from Sukarno himself to carry on his work. She recounts bits of her political résumé with the provocation, "What do I lack as a woman?" To the degree that these features of the address make a kind of political argument, they make an argument grounded in *hormat*.

---

64. Indeed, many features of Megawati's rhetorical style, not least her navigation of paradoxical identities, are reminiscent of other politically powerful women, including Pakistan's Benazir Bhutto (see Akhund 2000; Weiss 1990, 433–45; Zakaria 1989), Germany's Angela Merkel (see Sheeler and Anderson 2014, 474–95), and even England's Queen Elizabeth I (see Heisch 1975, 31–55; Montrose 2006; Suzuki 2002, 231–53).

When Megawati speaks of the "camaraderie" of the generals who spoke before her, she uses the word *persaudaraan*: the second rhetorical ideal demonstrated in this address. The term *persaudaraan* is derived from the root word *saudara*, meaning "sibling" or "relative," and it thus implies a familial kind of camaraderie, a gender-neutral "brotherhood." Such familial camaraderie is rife in Megawati's address. She adopts the name *Ibu* ("mother" or "Mrs.") for herself, calls her followers her *anak* ("children"), and describes her older sisterly role trying to fatten up future president Jokowi, as well as briefly mentioning her own biological children. In addition, she places great emphasis on her own role as Sukarno's *anak*—not only his biological child, but also his ideological child. All these familial bonds indicate the strength of each person and each group's dedication to the others. Sukarno is the father of Indonesia, and Megawati, by being a dutiful daughter and carrying out his mission for her, has become Indonesia's mother. To be rhetorically persuasive along these lines, Megawati needs not so much to prove the wisdom of particular policies as to tap into the logic of filial obedience that has underwritten Indonesian political rhetoric.

The ideal of *persuadaraan*, after all, is not unique to Megawati. Indonesian friends who are not biologically related often call one another *adik* ("younger sister" or "younger brother"), *kakak* ("older sister" or "older brother"), or *abang / bung* ("older brother") to imply a near-familial sense of closeness. Sukarno made this linguistic practice politically valuable by encouraging Indonesians to call him *Bung Karno*, "older brother Karno." As Indonesia's self-declared president for life, Sukarno defined his plan of "democracy by consensus" in terms of family harmony, making himself a benevolent older brother maintaining family harmony rather than a dictator maintaining national homogeneity. The strength of family bonds makes *persaudaraan* a powerful rhetorical idea whether or not biological family is at play, meaning that it has potential to become part of a teachable rhetorical tradition in Indonesia. Megawati's familial connection to Sukarno is important because she is his biological daughter, to be sure, but it is likewise rhetorically important because it gives her an obvious occasion to continue the metaphor of national family that arrived alongside the very idea of Indonesia. Those who wish to follow in Megawati's rhetorical footsteps can be taught to emphasize the *persaudaraan* of their message even if they are not part of the biological Sukarno family.

Finally, Megawati's address illustrates the power of historicized progressivism in Indonesian rhetoric. That is, Indonesian political speech tends to be characterized by a paradoxical conjoining of progressive values and reminders that such values are rooted in Indonesian tradition. On the one hand, faithfulness to an "Indonesian" rhetoric means faithfulness to the original unifying vision that brought Indonesia together, and that vision is embodied by the historic (and therefore static) person of Sukarno. Then again, Sukarno's *Pancasila* ideals, at the time he presents them while still under Dutch colonial rule, are progressively postcolonial and framed in progressive terms. Indonesian "traditionalism" thus becomes rhetorically progressive. Megawati demonstrates this paradox by praising Indonesians who both *jalan terus* ("keep moving forward") in advancing Indonesian progressivism and *tinggal disini* ("stay here") by remaining faithful to the vision of Sukarno. These seemingly conflicting images are rhetorically congruous because they are both aligned with the person of Sukarno: the faithful Indonesian stays in place within Sukarno's *Pancasila* ideology, an ideology that invites constant forward motion. Megawati likewise depicts herself repeatedly in her *cerita* ("stories") as a person historically rooted in Sukarno's progressivism.

Like *persaudaraan*, historicized progressivism—the paradoxical tension between *jalan terus* and *tinggal disini*—has the capacity to become part of a teachable rhetorical tradition in Indonesia. Indeed, fealty to the Sukarno doctrine of *Pancasila* has always been a central feature of Indonesian public education, enduring through the otherwise starkly dissimilar presidencies of Sukarno and Suharto. During Suharto's tenure, however, censorship of radical ideals became common practice, and "historical studies [were] a leading target of the censors."[65] The original progressivism of Sukarno was sanitized so as to better accord with the status quo of the Suharto regime. While Megawati's return to politics signaled the return of a greater measure of progressivism, certain parts of Indonesian history[66] remain heavily censored because wealthy and still-powerful figures benefit from their censorship. Jokowi's presidential victory in 2014 served as yet another signpost of Indonesia's post-Suharto shift towards progressivism, a sign that historicized progressivism may yet become a commonplace of Indonesian rhetorical education, just as it is already a feature of Indonesian rhetorical action.

---

65. Saunders 1998, 49.
66. Most notably the mass killings motivated by anti-communist sentiment in 1965-1966.

COMPREHENSIVE BIBLIOGRAPHY

Akhund, Iqbal. 2000. *Trial and Error: The Advent and Eclipse of Benazir Bhutto.* Oxford: Oxford University Press.

Arsyad, Safnil. 1999. "The Indonesian and English Argument Structure: A Cross-Cultural Rhetoric of Argumentative Texts." *Australian Review of Applied Linguistics* 22 (2): 85–102.

Becker, A. L. 1980. "Text-Building, Epistemology, and Aesthetics in Javanese Shadow Theatre." *Dispositio* 5(13/14): 137–68.

Bird, Judith. 1999. "Indonesia in 1998: The Pot Boils Over." *Asian Survey* 39 (1): 27–37.

Coles, Gregory. 2018. "'What Do I Lack as a Woman?': The Rhetoric of Megawati Sukarnoputri." *Rhetorica: A Journal of the History of Rhetoric* 36 (1): 58–91.

"Dihembuskan 'Angin Surga' Megawati Tak Mau Terlena." 24 Feb. 2012. *SuaraPembaruan.*sp.beritasatu.com/home/dihembuskan-angin-surga-megawati-tak-mau-terlena/17507.

Elson, R. E. 2008. *The Idea of Indonesia.* Cambridge: Cambridge University Press.

Engelson, Amber. 2014. "The 'Hands of God' at Work: Negotiating between Western and Religious Sponsorship in Indonesia." *College English* 76 (4): 292–314.

—. 2021. "'I Have No Mother Tongue': (Re)Conceptualizing Rhetorical Voice in Indonesia." In *The Routledge Handbook of Comparative World Rhetorics,* edited by Keith Lloyd, 195–205. London: Routledge.

Gouda, Frances. 1993. "The Gendered Rhetoric of Colonialism and Anti-Colonialism in Twentieth-Century Indonesia." *Indonesia* 55: 1–22.

Heisch, Allison. 1975. "Queen Elizabeth I: Parliamentary Rhetoric and the Exercise of Power." *Signs* 1 (1): 31–55.

Heryanto, Ariel. 2010. "Entertainment, Domestication and Dispersal: Street Politics as Popular Culture." In *Problems of Democratisation in Indonesia: Elections, Institutions and Society,* edited by Edward Aspinall and Marcus Mietzner, 181–98. Singapore: Institute of Southeast Asian Studies.

"Indonesia Floats the Rupiah, And It Drops More Than 6%." 14 Aug. 1997. *The New York Times.* www.nytimes.com/1997/08/15/business/indonesia-floats-the-rupiah-and-it-drops-more-than-6.html.

Kapoor, Kanupriya. 4 Mar. 2014. "Three Times a Loser, Indonesia's Megawati is Pivotal in Elections." *Reuter.* uk.reuters.com/article/indonesia-election-megawati/three-times-a-loser-indonesias-megawati-is-pivotal-in-elections-idINDEEA230H320140304.

Kratz, Ulrich. 2006. "Indonesia: Language Situation." In *Encyclopedia of Language and Linguistics,* edited by Keith Brown, 639–41. Amsterdam: Elsevier.

LaMoshi, Gary. 2004. "Blood-Stained Ladder to Indonesia's Presidency." *Online Asia Times* (July 27).

Lewis, M. Paul, Gary F. Simons, and Charles D. Fennig. 2015. *Ethnologue: Languages of the World, Eighteenth edition.* Dallas: SIL International.

Liddle, R. William. 2000. "Indonesia in 1999: Democracy Restored." *Asian Survey* 40 (1): 32–42.

Marszal, Andrew. 22 July 2014. "Indonesia Elections: Jakarta Governor 'Jokowi' Wins but Rival Rejects Final Results." *The Telegraph*. www.telegraph.co.uk.

McAfee, Noëlle. 2008. *Democracy and the Political Unconscious*. New York: Columbia University Press.

"Meltdown in Asia – Part 4: Chronology of a Crisis." 1 July 1998. *BBC News*. news.bbc.co.uk/2/hi/business/122546.stm.

Mietzner, Marcus. 2000. "The 1999 General Session: Wahid, Megawati and the Fight for the Presidency." In *Indonesia in Transition: Social Aspects of Reformasi and Crisis,* edited by Chris Manning and Peter van der Veer, 39–57. Singapore: Institute of Southeast Asian Studies, 2000.

Montrose, Louis. 2006. *The Subject of Elizabeth: Authority, Gender, and Representation*. Chicago: University of Chicago Press.

Rahmita, Frida. 2017. "The New Order Nationalist Rhetoric: The Articulation of Javanese Identity in Post-Colonial Indonesia." *International Academic Forum Journal of Cultural Studies* 21 (1): 34–43.

Ricklefs, M. C. 2001. *A History of Modern Indonesia since c. 1200*. Stanford: Stanford University Press.

Saunders, Joseph. 1998. *Academic Freedom in Indonesia: Dismantling Soeharto-Era Barriers*. New York: Human Rights Watch.

"Sensus Penduduk 2010." 2010. *Badan Pusat Statistik* https://sp2010.bps.go.id/.

Sheeler, Kristina Horn, and Karrin Vasby Anderson. 2014. "Gender, Rhetoric, and International Political Systems: Angela Merkel's Rhetorical Negotiation of Proportional Representation and Party Politics." *Communication Quarterly* 62 (4): 474–95.

Suwarno, Peter. 2013. "Depiction of Common Enemies in Religious Speech: The Role of the Rhetoric of Identification and Purification in Indonesian Religious Conflicts." *Walisongo* 21 (1): 1–17.

Suzuki, Mihoko. 2002. "Elizabeth, Gender, and the Political Imaginary of Seventeenth-Century England." In *Debating Gender in Early Modern England, 1500-1700,* edited by Cristina Malcolmson and Mihoko Suzuki, 231–53. London: Palgrave Macmillan.

Torchia, Christopher, and Lely Djuhari. 2011. *Indonesian Slang: Colloquial Indonesian at Work*. Clarendon, VT: Tuttle Publishing.

UNESCO Institute for Statistics. 2022. "Indonesia: Education and Literacy." uis.unesco.org/en/country/id.

US Department of State. 2020. "International Religious Freedom Report for 2016: Indonesia." www.state.gov/j/drl/rls/irf/religiousfreedom.

Vickers, Adrian. 2005. *A History of Modern Indonesia*. Cambridge: Cambridge University Press.

Weiss, Anita M. 1990. "Benazir Bhutto and the Future of Women in Pakistan." *Asian Survey* 30 (5): 433–45.

World Population Review. 2020. "Muslim Population by Country 2020." worldpopulationreview.com/country-rankings/muslim-population-by-country.

Zakaria, Rafiq. 1989. *Women and Politics in Islam: The Trial of Benazir Bhutto.* Far Hills, NJ: New Horizons.

Zein, Subhan. 2020. *Language Policy in Superdiverse Indonesia.* New York: Routledge.

Ziv, Daniel. 2001. "Populist Perceptions and Perceptions of Populism in Indonesia: The Case of Megawati Soekarnoputri." *South East Asia Research* 9 (1): 73–88.

Glossary of Terms

Term	Translation
anak	"child, children." Megawati calls attention to the importance of *persaudaraan* in Indonesian rhetoric both by highlighting her role as Sukarno's *anak* and by regarding her political party and the whole Indonesian populace as her own *anak*.
bertahan	"to endure." This word was often used to praise Megawati's rhetorically powerful silence under the Suharto administration.
bung	"older brother." A title used for Sukarno by his followers.
cerita	"story, story-telling." This serves as an important part of Megawati's more relaxed rhetorical style, as well as giving her many occasions to mention her familial relationship with Sukarno and demonstrate her commitment to historicized progressivism.
hormat	"honor." One of the rhetorical ideals demonstrated in Megawati's address.
Ibu	"Mother, Mrs." Megawati's followers often call her *Ibu Mega*, and her rhetoric embraces this maternal role.
jalan terus	"Keep moving forward." One of the paradoxical admonitions given by Megawati that demonstrates the rhetorical ideal of historicized progressivism.
kreatif	"creative." The more relaxed rhetorical style that Megawati attributes to herself, as contrasted with the formal oratory of other dignified speakers.
orator	"orators"; especially, highly honored individuals who speak with a formality befitting their status.
pancasila	"Five Principles"; the doctrine that serves as the foundation for Indonesian national values. These five principles are commitment to God, democracy by consensus, humanitarianism, prosperity, and national unity.
persaudaraan	"brotherhood, camaraderie." One of the rhetorical ideals demonstrated in Megawati's address.
tinggal disini	"Stay here." One of the paradoxical admonitions given by Megawati that demonstrates the rhetorical ideal of historicized progressivism.

6 IRISH RHETORICS

PREFATORY INTRODUCTION
Brian J. Stone

THE RHETORICAL ARTS IN LATE ANTIQUE AND MEDIEVAL IRELAND

Early medieval Ireland offers a wealth of primary materials to the historian of rhetoric, materials nearly entirely neglected by students of rhetoric.[1] Though the tradition begins with the fifth-century writings of St Patrick, from the seventh century forward there are extant grammatical tracts, letters, law texts, learned handbooks and colloquies, (pseudo) histories, poetry, hagiography, and liturgical texts in both Latin and the vernacular. It is my hope that this brief introduction and translation of two fascinating texts concerned with law, examples of verbal art composed about the verbal arts, will inspire students of rhetoric to further investigate the rich tapestry of the learning and literature of medieval Ireland. Though the social and historical context in which the rhetorical arts thrived can only be treated briefly here, I will start at the beginning and provide a brief overview of the history of learning in early Ireland. This is necessary to dispel some myths that have been perpetuated in the few studies on rhetoric in early Ireland, namely the notion that Ireland, never having been colonized by the Romans, and due to its location beyond the Roman Empire's *limes* ("frontiers"), remained isolated from outside influence.[2] This unique position in western Europe, this narrative would

---

1. For three case studies and an extensive review of the literature on classical and secular learning in early Ireland, see Stone (2022).
2. This belief is at the heart of the only study of rhetoric in medieval Ireland by those working in rhetorical studies, esp. Johnson-Sheehan and Lynch (2007). This study was important to rhetorical studies as it drew the attention of rhetorical studies scholars to early Ireland and inspired a number of

claim, left Ireland shrouded in Celtic mists, preserving the ancient arts of the druid and the pagan mystic. As we will see, this is far from the truth.

The evidence for the period before the seventh century CE in Ireland is scant consisting in large part of material evidence, including ogam stones, but this evidence does indicate transmarine trade with Britain and the Continent from as early as the fourth century CE.[3] The ogam alphabet is the earliest form of literacy in Ireland, and the dates of ogam stones may date to as early as the third century CE, although the fifth century CE is more commonly accepted. The alphabet consists of a series of vertical lines with horizontal notches representing letters of the Roman alphabet, but the inscriptions are written in the Old Irish vernacular, rather than Latin. Ogam stones are stone slabs with inscriptions, often marking territorial boundaries or burial sites, and they are dispersed around Ireland, especially in the southeast, but are also found in southwestern England and Scotland.

It is likely that the first Romanized Christians to arrive to Ireland in the mid-fifth century, Palladius, a Gallo-Roman, and Patrick, a Romano-Briton, established schools, or at the very least trained several converts in reading and writing. After all, literacy was essential to Christianity, a religion of the book. It is clear from the writings of Patrick and seventh-century British and Irish scholars that communication with Britain, Gaul, and likely the Mediterranean world remained consistent from the fifth century CE on, and long-established trade routes would have provided access to books. Early accounts of Irish monastic communities include names of several British students, and in the sixth century CE Irish monks established important centers of learning in Scotland and, by the seventh century, in northern England.[4]

The Irish were famous for their study of grammar and exegesis, as well as computistics, the astronomical art of calculating the date of the passion and of Easter.[5] The trivium and the quadrivium of the liberal arts were taught in early Ireland, though in a form that suited the purposes of the monastic schools. Schools in the north of Ireland, specifically Bangor, provided the education for two of the most famous early Irish clerics, Colum Cille (521–597 CE) and Columbanus (c. 543–615 CE), and in the writings of Columbanus we see the fruits of intense and wide-ranging study, especially in grammar and rhetoric. By the seventh century CE, such wandering Irish monks, known as *"peregrini,"*[6] had established monasteries in the north of England, including Lindisfarne, and in western Scotland, including Colum Cille's famous monastic community at Iona. Several more were founded throughout western Europe,

---

researchers to take up the call, including the present author. However, it lacked the depth of research in the rather complex and obscure world of medieval Irish literature and history necessary to successfully carry the field forward.

3. For a summary of the material evidence, see Loveluck and O'Sullivan (2016), and the sources cited there. See also Swift (2008); McManus (1997); On the symbolic function of ogam, see Johnston (2013, 13). For images of ogam stones and other resources, see www.ucl.ac.uk/archaeology/cisp/index.htm.

4. See Stone (2022, 45–92).

5. On the advanced study of astronomy in early Ireland, see Bisagni (2020) and the sources cited there; See also the contributions to Kelly and Doherty (2013).

6. On the Irish practice of *peregrinatio*, self-exile for God, see Johnston (2016).

and among the most important were the schools established by Columbanus at Bobbio and Luxeuil and the Abbey of St Gall, established by Columbanus's disciple Gallus.[7]

From our earliest evidence, we see an Ireland that was multicultural (in contact with Romans and Roman Britons from as early as the third century CE), multilingual, and in continuous contact with the European world. A letter from an early eighth-century CE Irish cleric, Cummian, shows that the Irish were even capable of sending a delegation to Rome to settle a dispute over the calculation of the date of Easter.[8] At the Carolingian Court, Irish scholars would make significant contributions to secular learning.[9] By the eleventh century CE, the Irish developed an interest in world history that resulted in the translation of Roman epic and the vernacular composition of Irish pseudo-history inspired by this Latinate tradition, a practice in vogue throughout Europe during this period.[10] From the extant manuscript evidence we get a glimpse of the Irish reverence for oratory and verbal art, including a rich rhetorical vocabulary in the vernacular.[11] In short, Ireland was not an isolated out-post, shrouded in "Celtic mists," but was a part of the western intellectual world.[12] It is in this context that a vast body of Latin and the largest body of vernacular literature in the medieval west was produced, literature of great interest to the student of rhetoric.

---

7. See O'Hara (2018).

8. An edition, translation, and introduction to the letter is given in Walsh and Ó Cróinín (1988). This letter is ripe for rhetorical study as it provides evidence of an early form of rhetorical letter writing, as well as evidence for rhetorical debate in early church synods.

9. See Meeder (2016); Contreni (1992); Contreni (1982); Contreni (1977).

10. See Miles (2011).

11. See Clarke and Ní Mhaonaigh (2020).

12. For an overview of the rhetorical arts in late antique and early medieval Ireland and a discussion of the socio-cultural and historical context, see Stone (2022).

6.1 Medieval Irish-Gaelic (Non-European), c. 700 CE, Ireland

Selected Texts in Early Medieval Irish Rhetoric

Brian J. Stone

LATIN AND VERNACULAR GRAMMAR IN MEDIEVAL IRELAND

In the *Chronicle* of Prosper of Aquitaine, there is an entry for 431 CE that tells us Pope Celestine, inspired by successes in eradicating the so-called "Pelagian heresy" in Britain, sent a learned, Gallic bishop, Palladius, to Ireland.[13] Around the same time, Ireland's patron saint, Patrick, arrived in Ireland from Britain. Though evidence of Palladius's mission does not survive, two of Patrick's writings, his *Confession* and *Letter to the Soldiers of Coroticus* reveal something of the nature of rhetorical learning in sub-Roman Britain.[14] Patrick's writings, along with those of the sixth-century CE monk, Gildas, provide scholars with a rare glimpse into the rhetorical education and rhetorical practice of Roman Britons after Roman legions had fled the western frontiers.[15] Christian communities in early Ireland were under the leadership of the British Church from the very beginning, so this also tells us something of the dawning of Latin learning in Ireland.

This scholarly intercourse with Britain continued throughout the early medieval period. Bede (c. 673–735 CE), writing in the eighth century CE, tells us of numerous Saxon students who traveled to Irish monasteries between 651 and 664 CE due to their reputation for advanced learning.[16] In a pointed but humorous letter to a student, the English scholar, Aldhelm of Malmesbury (639–709 CE), who was himself educated at Malmesbury under the tutelage of the Irish monk, Máeldub, warns of the Irish proclivity for the study of mythology and the secular arts, including ". . . not only the grammatical and geometrical arts to say nothing of the thrice-three scaffolds of the art of physics—but also, the fourfold honeyed oracles of allegorical or rather tropological disputation of opaque problems in aetherial mysteries."[17] Aldhelm's letter reveals more about the competition between the revered Irish schools and scholars at Canterbury than any actual concerns, but it also suggests that secular learning was not taboo in Ireland. Contact with Spain was also consistent throughout the seventh century CE, and many of Isidore of Seville's (c. 560–636 CE) writings—writings that would be foun-

---

13. Charles-Edwards 1993, 7–10.

14. For rhetorical translation and analyses of Patrick's writings, as well as a review of the scholarship and complete historical context, see Stone (2022); Stone (2014).

15. On Gildas's rhetorical learning, see Lapidge (1984).

16. See Ó Cróinín (2004, 6).

17. Howlett 1994, 43; On Aldhelm's Irish education, see Dempsey (1999).

dational to medieval learning—came to Ireland prior to their British and continental neighbors.[18] Indeed, many of the computistical tracts used by Bede came to his desk from Ireland.[19]

The early Irish wrote in both Latin and the vernacular, Old and Middle Irish, and there is a vast body of extant literature in both. [20] In general, compositions in Latin were of an ecclesiastical nature and were intended for a wide audience. One learned in Latin (*légend*, "Latin learning") is referred to in Irish law-texts and annals as *ecnaid* ("wise man" or "ecclesiastic scholar") and *sapiens*, and the leader of monastic school was referred to as *fer léiginn*.[21] Latin was the *lingua franca* of Christian communities throughout western Europe. The Latin of early Ireland, as well as its British neighbors, is known as Hiberno-Latin, and it is a unique form of Latin, a regional variation used by a people for whom Latin was a second language, and there is a rich body of Hiberno-Latin literature composed in Ireland.[22] In Ireland and Britain, we see the development of "*hisperic*" Latin, an archaizing and intentionally elevated style that developed in the insular world. Among the finest gems of Hiberno-Latin literature are the *Hisperica famina* ("Western Orations"), an early rhetorical text written in *hisperic* Latin and of Irish provenance, either of the seventh or eighth century CE, modeled on late antique scholastic colloquies, and largely secular in content.[23] There are also numerous Latin grammars, many composed in the seventh century.[24] These grammars are, in large part, based on those of Donatus and Priscian, though they also reveal knowledge, at a very early date, of Isidore, Martianus Capella, and a number of late antique grammarians.[25]

Priscian and Donatus were known to the Irish by the early seventh century CE.[26] A ninth-century copy of Priscian's complete grammar, likely composed in Ireland, and containing around 3,000 Old Irish glosses, has resided at the Irish monastic foundation, St Gall Stiftsbibliothek, since the late ninth century CE.[27] One of the earliest Latin grammars, *Ars*

---

18. See Hillgarth (1984).

19. See Ó Cróinín (1983); see also the arguments in Walsh and Ó Cróinín (1984).

20. For an overview of early Irish literature, see Ní Bhrolcháin (2009); see also Ó Cathasaigh (2008); Ó Cathasaigh (2006); Ní Mhaonaigh (2006); see also the relevant chapters in Ó Cróinín (2005).

21. For a discussion of terminology for learned individuals in early Ireland, see Johnston 2013, 98–110; see also Richter (1996) for a quantitative analysis of the occurrence of terms for ecclesiastical and secular learned personnel.

22. See Ó Cróinín (2005, 371–405).

23. For an edition and translation, see Herren (1974); On rhetoric and the *Hisperica famina*, see Knappe (1994); see also Stone (2022).

24. For an overview of the grammatical tradition in Ireland, see Ahlqvist (1983); for close studies, see the work of Law included in the bibliography; For editions and a more comprehensive discussion, see relevant chapters in Stone (2022), and the sources cited there.

25. See Ó Cróinín (1993).

26. See Hofman (1996); Hofman (2000).

27. See Bauer, Hofman, and Moran (2017), who provide digital access to the over 3,000 Old Irish glosses on the most famous Priscian manuscript, the St Gall Priscian, St Gall Stiftsbibliothek MS 904. The manuscript totals 240 pages and was written by Irish scribes circa 850–851 CE, most likely in

Asporii (Asper's Grammar"), which Ó Cróinín dates to the early seventh century CE, adapts Donatus to early seventh-century CE monastic contexts, leading Louis Holtz to comment "Donatus has undergone a conversion to asceticism."[28] Donatus had been fully Christianized. This stands in stark contrast to later grammars, including the *Anonymus ad Cuimnanum* and the *Epitomae* and *Epistolae* of Virgilius Maro Grammaticus, both of which are of significant interest to students of rhetoric.[29] Since Latin was a second language to Irish scholars, the grammar of Donatus did not serve their purposes.[30] Therefore, the Irish innovated, creating grammars intended for second language learners. In addition to the grammars, the Irish metrical and exegetical tracts also reveal something of rhetorical learning and practice.[31]

Irish scholars, such as Columbanus and Colum Cille (Latin, Columba), were well-known throughout western Europe, and the monasteries they established were essential to the development of the Carolingian Renaissance.[32] Columbanus's Latin writings have been subject to a number of studies, and his rhetorical dexterity is without question.[33] He was schooled in Ireland in the late sixth century CE, and this is our best evidence of rhetorical education in early Ireland, though a detailed rhetorical study is wanting. In addition to the extant writings of Columbanus, there are a number of Latin letters, grammar handbooks, sermons, poems, and hymns that are of great interest to the historian of medieval rhetoric.[34]

In addition to the Latin grammars, there is also an extant vernacular grammar, *Auraicept na nÉces* ("The Scholar's Primer"; hereafter *Auraicept*), the oldest (canonical) part of which has been dated to the 'Old Irish' period, specifically c. 700–900 CE. The *Auraicept* draws on Priscian and Donatus, as well as Martianus Capella and Isidore, among others, but it is most significant for its insight into the linguistic training of the poet in early Ireland.[35] In addition to grammatical instruction, the *Auraicept* was clearly part of a wider educational program. As Deborah Hayden has noted, the *Auraicept* "was composed in an intellectual milieu similar to that which produced numerous other Hiberno-Latin grammars, biblical exegeses, and vernacular legal texts."[36] Literary and legal sources serve as examples in elucidation of grammatical precepts, and medical metaphors abound. This suggests a learned milieu in which the foundations of the *trivium* were essential to more advanced specialization in one or more areas,

---

Ireland, though it was brought to the continent between 855 and 863 CE, arriving at St Gall later in the ninth century CE. These glosses are one of the earliest sources for the Old Irish language.

28. Holtz 1981, 144.

29. See n. 137 below; for an edition of the *Anonymus*, see Bischoff and Löfstedt (1992); for a translated excerpt of Virgilius Maro Grammaticus, see Copeland and Sluiter (2012).

30. Ó Cróinín 1995, 174–76.

31. For an overview of Irish metrics, see Stifter (2016), and the primary sources cited there; for a overview of the exegetical texts, see Stone (2022, 89–91).

32. See Riché (1977, 256–57, 273–74, 297).

33. See Lapidge (1997); O'Hara (2018).

34. For a detailed discussion in the context of a history of rhetoric, see Stone (2022).

35. For a critical edition, see Ahlqvist (1983); see also Hayden (2014); Hayden (2011).

36. Hayden 2011, 3.

and learning was not as specialized as modern academics might imagine.[37] Grammar and rhetoric were already merging at the time of Quintilian's composition of his famous *Institutes of Oratory* (c. 95 CE), and Hayden surveys the various manifestations of peripatetic ideals of epideictic rhetoric, likely drawn from Isidore, in the Irish grammatical and legal tradition.[38] The *Auraicept* includes material that was added to the canonical section over the centuries, and in some of these additions Hayden sees the influence of rhetorical concerns with style. Recent studies of Celtic grammatical tracts have shed light on linguistic study in the insular world, though much work remains to be done.[39]

As noted above, ecclesiastical texts were mostly composed in Latin by ecclesiastic scholars, or *ecnai*. Secular texts, on the other hand, composed by the secular *filid* ('poet-jurists,') and, perhaps, clerics, were composed in Old Irish. The early Irish created the largest body of vernacular literature in all of western Europe, and many of these texts have only been edited and translated in the last few decades. Therefore, there is a wealth of material awaiting historians of medieval rhetoric.

VERNACULAR LEARNING, LAW, AND LITERATURE

The vernacular of early Ireland is known to scholars today as Old Irish, *Sengoídelc*. It is an Indo-European language of the Goidelic Celtic family.[40] For this reason, Irish culture is often identified as a Celtic culture; however, it is important to note that the early Irish were not aware of a shared linguistic cultural heritage among themselves and their "Celtic" neighbors.[41] Vernacular Irish is divided into three distinct periods. The Old Irish period includes texts composed between 600–900 CE. The Middle Irish period ranges from 900–1200 CE, and Early Modern Irish from 1200–1600 CE. Most evidence for the language and literature of the Old Irish period comes from later manuscripts, many dating between 1100–1500 CE, though the texts they contain have been dated linguistically and based on text–internal evidence to as early as the seventh century CE. The ninth-century CE *Book of Armagh* is the oldest manuscript containing continuous Irish prose, but the late eleventh-century CE *Lebor na hUidre* ("Book of the Dun Cow") is the oldest manuscript containing complete secular material in prose and verse.[42] By the eighth century CE, Irish began to replace Latin as the chosen medium in Irish monastic *scriptoria*.

---

37. Ó Cróinín (1988, 240) has remarked, "Irish computists, exegetes, hagiographers and even grammarians drew on a common body of materials; the separation of these disciplines is a modern departure from medieval practice."

38. Hayden 2011, 4–9.

39. See Hayden and Russell (2016).

40. For an overview of the Celtic languages, see Russell (1995); For resources for learning Old and Middle Irish, see de Vries (2013); Stifter (2006).

41. For a discussion of the problems and purposes of the designation "Celtic," see Sims-Williams (1998); Ahlqvist (2008).

42. In Byrne's 'Introduction' in O Neill and Byrne (1984, xv).

The survival of manuscripts in an Irish environment was unlikely, and what was not lost to the ravages of time and the Viking Wars of the ninth century CE may have been destroyed by monastic in-fighting and English colonizers.[43] However, a large number of manuscripts have survived in Irish monastic communities on the continent. These manuscripts can be identified as Irish due to the distinct orthography and script employed by Irish scribes.[44] Often referred to as the "Irish hand," the insular script used in Ireland and by Irish schools on the Continent and in Britain was developed from a variety of scripts available in early Ireland. The Irish script was basically a half-uncial, also known as Irish majuscule. This script was used in major manuscripts, mainly composed in Latin, meant for circulation or reverence, such as *Book of Kells*. The Irish miniscule, or "small hand," was used in vernacular texts and for smaller books often meant for "in-house" use.[45] The Irish also introduced a system of punctuation and page layout that we still use to this day.[46] For students whose native language was not Latin, *scriptio continua* was not practical and, as with so much of the early Irish learned tradition, scholars and scribes innovated. It is likely that students and masters alike practiced writing on wax tablets, as evidenced in the discovery in 1914 of the late seventh- or early eighth-century CE 'Springmount Bog Tablets' in a bog in County Antrim.

In addition to a distinctive orthography the Irish are famous for manuscript illuminations, the most famous examples including the *Book of Kells, Book of Durrow, Book of the Dun Cow, Stowe Missal*, and *Book of Armagh*.[47] As far as I am aware, these illuminated manuscripts have yet to be studied by scholars of visual and material rhetoric and exegesis, which is surprising given the artistic mastery they exhibit and the syncretic cultural context from which they emerged.

Of particular interest here are the law texts, which tell us much about the organization of early Irish society and the centrality of verbal art to social and political life. The growth of the church in the fifth and sixth centuries CE certainly had a profound impact on pre-Christian social organization. Pre-Christian Ireland consisted of a vast number of *túatha* ("petty kingdoms") with no central hierarchical authority. It was in large part an agrarian, dynastic society, though transmarine trade was common in coastal communities. The *túath* was the basic jurisdictional and political unit of early Ireland, presided over in secular matters by a *rí túath* ("king of a *túath*").[48] Tomas Ó Cathasaigh explains the social function of the *rí* ('king') in the context of Indo-European ideology, arguing that "the king comprises three functions: the sacred, including sovereignty; physical force; and a third function, fertility, that includes food production."[49] The "truth" of the king (*fír flathemon*) and the justice of his pronouncements

---

43. See Ó Corráin (2011, 2012, 2013).
44. For an overview, see O'Neill and Byrne (1984).
45. Byrne 1984, xii.
46. Ó Cróinín 2004 provides an accessible and comprehensive overview.
47. See "Illuminated Manuscripts" and Cornel and Schnoor (2018).
48. Etchingham 1999, 141.
49. Ó Cathasaigh 2005, 15.

certify his rule, and this is related to his sovereignty and the flourishing of his *túath*.[50] If a king were to utter a false judgment, famine and plague may strike the community and a blight on his reign would result.[51] Similar responsibilities lie with the *fili* (poet–jurist) and bishop, for as the church developed, the bishop took on a more authoritative role.

The (pseudo)historical texts are also of interest to the student of rhetoric, and I cannot treat them adequately here. However, the most significant include Middle Irish translations of Roman epic, the Old and Middle Irish (pseudo)histories—especially moments of direct speech—and learned and legal texts.[52] Most important to this chapter are the legal texts, to which I will now turn.

Below, I include translations of a poem and a learned handbook associated with an important legal school known as the *Nemed* School, a scholarly circle located in Munster. The *Bretha Nemed* textual tradition consists of two primary legal-texts, *Bretha Nemed Déidenach*[53] ("The Last *Bretha Nemed*"), which delineates the privileges of the poets, with a specific interest in satire, and *Bretha Nemed Toísech*[54] ("The First *Bretha Nemed*"), which delineates the privileges of the church. There are also two primers intended as an introduction to the study of the *Bretha Nemed*, *Uraicecht Becc* ("Small Primer"), and *Uraicecht na Ríar* ("The Primer of Stipulations").[55]

In the Irish tradition, attribution of a text to a legendary figure is commonplace, and the *Bretha Nemed* is no exception. *Roscada* and maxims, as will be discussed below, are often attributed to, or promulgated by, such figures. Liam Breatnach notes that in the legal tradition many of these take the form of dialogue that should be regarded as a stylistic feature.[56] However, the extant manuscripts were composed in *scriptoria*, and Breatnach argues that *Bretha Nemed Toísech*, tripartite in structure, was actually written in Munster by three kinsmen called

---

50. Ó Cathasaigh 1978, 37.

51. See Wiley (2005). Examples are given from the *Senchas Már* in Lea (2017, 217n2): "Sancha Mac Col Cluin was not wont to pass judgment until he had pondered upon it in his breast the night before. When Fachtna, his son, had passed a false judgment, if in the time of fruit, all the fruit in the territory in which it happened fell off in one night [. . .] if in time of milk, the cows refused their calves; but if he passed a true judgment, the fruit was perfect on the trees; hence he received the name of Fachtna Tulbrethach [Tulbrethach, lit. "swift to judgment"]. Sencha Mac Aillila never pronounced a false judgment without getting three permanent blotches on his face for each judgment. Fithel had the truth of nature, so that he pronounced no false judgment. Morann never pronounced a judgment without having a chain around his neck. When he pronounced a false judgment, the chain tightened around his neck. If he pronounced a true one, it expanded down upon him."

52. For an analysis of Latin learning in Middle Irish saga, see Clarke and Ní Mhaonaigh (2020), and the sources cited there; see also Ní Mhaonaigh (2015, 2017); Miles (2011); Poppe and Schlüter (2011); O'Connor (2013, 2014); Clarke (2006, 2009, 2014).

53. Trinity College, Dublin MS 1317 H.2. 15B.

54. British Library MS Nero A 7.

55. Edition and translation in Breatnach (1987).

56. Breatnach 2005, 371–74.

Ui Búirechain: Forannán, a bishop, Máel Tuili, a poet, and Báethgalach, a judge.[57] Like other significant law texts, the *Bretha Nemed* relates the seven grades of the *filid*, the seven grades of the church, other relevant legal materials, as well as poetry about the verbal arts and a handbook on the nature of higher learning.

The *filid* were an elite group. Though there was significant regional variation in their makeup, and though their function changed over time, several legal texts tell us that they consisted of a hierarchical, hereditary caste with a series of seven grades, the *ollamh* being the highest in rank, and *ánroth* the second highest in rank. One of the primary things distinguishing one's grade was honor–price, the amount one received for rendering one's services. To achieve the rank of *ollamh*, one's father and grandfather must have been a *fili*. In addition, one was required to memorize 350 compositions, be "knowledgeable in all historical science (genealogy/tales, etc.)," and be "knowledgeable in the jurisprudence of Irish law."[58] The poetic ranks are successive stages in an educational progression that an individual may achieve in their lifetime. Though they depend in some cases on one's lineage, they are based primarily on the extent of the poet's learning.[59] The *filid* were essential to early Irish society, as a passage from the *Corpus iuris Hibernici* makes clear: "A *túath* is not a túath without an ecclesiastical scholar, a churchman, a poet, a king by whom contracts and treaties are extended to (other) *túath*'s."[60]

All judgments were given in authoritative speech through persons of the *nemed* ("privileged") classes, including poets, judges, highly ranked clerics, and rulers. In addition to the *fili*, there was the *brithem* ("judge") and *aigne* ("lawyer").[61] The juridical class coexisted with that of the *filid*, and they in large part shared a learned tradition. In some instances, *filid* are portrayed as rendering judgments on legal matters, as are kings. This had to do with the nature of native Irish law. As noted above, in the early period there was not a clear distinction between disciplines, and legendary figures and the tales they abound in were the basis of judgments. Therefore, to be qualified to practice law in early Ireland, one needed to be familiar with the corpus of tales. The judgments of clerics, on the other hand, were to be based on the truth and precedent of scripture. Rulers, however, had at their disposal all sources of authority.[62]

The *filid*, sometimes translated as "poet–jurist," but also containing the archaizing meaning "poet–seer," practiced *filidecht*, which covered the entire field of poetry, praise–poetry, satire, history, genealogy, *dinnsenchas* ("lore of place–names"), grammar, *senchas* ("ancient lore"), and the law, though their function changed over time. They were primarily concerned with secular learning, though some were associated with ecclesiastical communities, perhaps even taking cleric's robes, and they were certainly not isolated from Latin learning. As Liam Breat-

---

57. Breatnach 1984, 439–59.

58. Breatnach 1987, 103.

59. Ibid., 87.

60. Ibid., 90.

61. On different types of judges and lawyers, see Breatnach (1990, 7–13).

62. See Stacey (2007, 167–71).

nach puts it, "the *fili* was much more than a versifier—he was a learned academic who had undergone a rigorous education in all branches of secular knowledge; furthermore, he wrote in prose as well as verse."[63] The relationship of the legal and poetic aspect is the most significant to the texts translated below. The *brithem* was a judge who could not travel widely like the *fili* but was required to stay with the king of a *túath* at all times. This ability to travel freely among *túatha* distinguished both *filid* and clerical learned classes from other noble classes. Despite this freedom, there was a strict ritual associated with such circuits witnessed in both law-texts and (pseudo)history.[64] The promise of protection allowed for continued interaction and the exchange of books and knowledge which resulted in a degree of standardization of the Old Irish language.

The *filid* gave judgments based on the "three rocks," *roscada* (sg. *roscad/rosc*), a type of ar-chaizing which Stacey defines as "legal principles or precedents couched in rhetorical poetic language,"[65] *fásaige* ("maxims"), and *tesdemuin* ("testimony").[66] The language of *rosc* is ob-scure, alliterative, highly stylistic, performative, and rhetorical, and it often consists of max-ims or aphorisms. While the nature and origin of such discourse is debated, Johan Corthals argues that though there may have been a native verse prior to the arrival of Latin learning, it developed in textual form from late antique rhetorical traditions.[67] It is most likely that *roscada* were intentionally obscure (*dorcha*, "darkened") and archaic, as this may have given it an air of authenticity, and it may have also served to protect the coveted knowledge of this elite, learned class.[68] In a section of the "Pseudo-Historical Introduction the *Senchas Már*," the narrator explains how the poets lost sole authority over rendering judicial verdicts: "Dark was the speech that the poets spoke in that case, and the judgment they gave was not clear to the princes."[69] Due to the obscurity of their specialized discourse that only they could understand, this legendary account continues, kings and clerics won the right to render verdicts. This "dark speech," also referred to as *bérla féne* ("legal language") and *bérla na filid* ("language of the poets"), is in contrast to *bélrae bán*, the "fair language" of the Scripture, though both types

---

63. Breatnach 1990, 4.

64. See Breatnach (2004).

65. Stacey 2007, 169.

66. See discussion in Stone (2022, 199–200) and the texts cited there.

67. See Corthals (1996).

68. Hayden (2011, 11–16) brings together some of the most salient examples of the desire for obscure language among the poets intended to preserve their authority and prestige and protect their knowl-edge from the uninitiated. A prime example comes from an Old Irish poem *Amra Choluim Chille*: "*Culu*: here the poet has an obscuration, i.e., specifically, a *dechned*. For *cul* is the usual word, but the poet add u here to fill up the poetry, or to make its track hard to be known. For *fortched* is the same as darkening. For *fortched* consists in this, the obscuration and disguising of words by making in them diminution and augmentation and mutation. And there are four kinds of it, namely *dichned* and *dechned* and *formolad filed* and *cennarchos*" (12). See also Stacey (2007) for an extensive study of performance and "dark speech."

69. Carey 1994, 19.

of discourse were authoritative in specific judicial contexts, and both were distinguished from *gnáthbérla* ("plain language").[70] In addition to *roscada*, law-texts such as the *Bretha Nemed* are also composed in rhetorical prose that is highly stylistic.[71]

There is another verbal art the *filid* practiced that is central to the verse translated below: satire ("áer") and praise ("*molad*").[72] Satire was an incredibly powerful social tool, and the purpose and place of lawful satire is discussed in the law-texts. If one refused to pay a fee rendered by a just judgment, the *fili* had the lawful right to satirize the individual.[73] Satire was deeply feared, and on the *fili*'s words hung one's reputation and status in society. Indeed, status was not static, and it could be stripped. In his edition of the law-text *Críth Gablach*, the influential Irish scholar D. A. Binchy wrote of satire as "the formidable weapon with which members of the poetic orders (*grád filed*) enforced claims either on their own behalf or on behalf of other persons who employed them."[74]

There were certain legal contexts in which satire was lawful, both inside and outside the *fili*'s own *túath*, and to satirize outside of the law carried serious repercussions for the *fili* who strayed. As for the subject of the satire, they were to be given ample warning and the opportunity to settle the dispute. Such a warning included the composition of a *trefocal*, which was a metrically perfect mixture of praise and blame, as well as a statement of the offense.[75] According to the *Corpus iuris Hibernici* (hereafter, *CIH*), the event of a potential satire could last up to thirty days and consisted of a ritualistic performance: "the ten-day period of notice, and the ten-day period of *trefocal*, and the ten-day period of submitting pledges."[76] There were also Christian adaptations of satire, as well, in the form of maledictory psalms.[77] The psalms of malediction consisted of the singing of specific psalms in a ritualistic manner, including the ringing of bells and the presentation of relics, to persuade the target to repent.

The counterpart to satire was praise, and if one atoned for one's transgressions, the *fili*'s praise was capable of washing away the stain of satire. The *CIH*, as well as other texts, describe this verbal art according to colors: "'These are the three colours of poetry, i.e. white and bland and speckled. White by which one praises, black by which on satirises, speckled by which one gives notice.'"[78] The *trefocal* was spotted as it contained both praise and blame. Praise poetry was not composed only for secular patrons but was also presented to clerics, and elements of

---

70. See discussion in Stacey (2007, 91–99 and 164–165).

71. A straight-forward but thorough overview of Irish law, including terminology and a review of relevant literature, is given in Charles-Edwards (2005); see also Breatnach (1990).

72. See Breatnach 2006; McCana 2004.

73. For an introduction to the sources, as well as edition and translations of satire, see McLaughlin (2008).

74. Binchy 1941, 69.

75. Breatnach 2004, 25.

76. Ibid., 26.

77. See Bitel (2006/s007); Wiley (2006).

78. Ibid., 25.

praise poetry came to influence Irish hagiography.[79] Praise poetry here should not be considered in the same light as praise poetry that survives in Norse, Anglo-Saxon, and Welsh sources, namely court poetry. As Alex Woolf has argued, the "court poet" parallel to those from other regions, such as the *scop*, did not emerge in Ireland until the Middle Irish period. Woolf reviews archeological evidence and argues that an appropriate venue, such as the royal residences, or royal feasting halls, of the Norse and Anglo-Saxons did not exist in early Ireland, and Irish kings did not retain war-bands. Therefore, the social context in which a court poet would perform was absent from early Ireland. However, early Irish royal gatherings were largely open-air activities, known as the óenaig, so it could be that poets did perform such a function despite the lack of material evidence. Praise was just as powerful as satire, and a poet was entitled to a predetermined payment dependent on the type of poem presented to the patron and the grade of the poet.

Like satire and praise, the performance of law was at times a largely public matter. For everyday matters regarding everyday people, the matters were likely handled privately in the company of the proper authorities. However, some cases were heard in open-air courts, called *airecht*, perhaps at an óenach (annual fairs, subject to regional variation, and held at ritualistically important times, including the Irish holidays, *Imbolc, Bealtaine, Lughnasadh*, and *Samhain*), likely performed and received in a manner akin to oratorical performances of other cultures, and presided over by kings, bishops, and *filid* or *britha*.[80] Whether public or private, Irish law was a performative event that required individuals specialized in the verbal art appropriate to the context.[81]

*Ros*c is common to a variety of genres in early Ireland, including law-texts, sagas, and narratives associated with law texts. Such speech is always put in the mouth of someone important, be it a legendary *fili*, such as Amairgen or Cenn Faelad, a king, such as Cormac mac Airt or Conchobar mac Nessa, a hero, such as Cú Chulainn, or druids or supernatural entities, such as the Morrígan. This marked discourse was the province of the learned and the royal class. For *roscada* to possess force, it was necessary that one uttering such verse possess *fír flathemon* "ruler's truth" or *fír filid* "poet's truth." In short, one had to be a good, pure, and just individual of high status (*nemed*) for *roscada* to be forceful. One may think here of the idea in rhetoric handbooks from Hellenic, Hellenistic, and late antique authors that the orator must be *vir bonus*, "just" and "good." However, whether these concepts of the ruler's and poet's justice derive from pre-Christian Irish tradition or from the influence of Latin scholars, such as Isidore, is still a point of debate, but it is most likely a syncretic development.[82]

---

79. There is a notable absence of extant praise poetry from the early Irish period. See Woolf (2013).

80. Charles-Edwards 2005, 341–42; In *The Triads of Ireland*, Meyer (1906), a collection of triads from several manuscripts, three fairs are named: Teltown, Croghan, and Colman Elo.

81. Stacey (2007) provides a study of the performative element of Irish law essential to the student of early Irish rhetoric.

82. Watson (2018) argues that *fír flathemon* and *fír filid* derive from Isidore's *Etymologies*. Watson's case is strong, as even though there may have been such a concept in pre-Christian Ireland, the evidence

The "Pseudo-Historical Prologue to the *Senchas Már*" is an important early Irish law-text that is the product of a collaboration of secular and ecclesiastical learned classes. In it we are told of the importance of speech to the rendering of just verdicts and the individuals who may render them:

> In what is judgment bound in Irish legal tradition? Not difficult.[83] In truth and entitlement and nature. Trust is established on the basis of *roscada* and maxims and true testimonies. Entitlement is established on the basis of oral contracts and acknowledgment. Nature is established on the basis of [the] remission [of obligations] and proper arrangements. Truth and entitlement together are established through dignitaries (*nemed*). Any judgment that is not grounded in one of these is not valid at all. Any judgment of the church that exists is established on the basis of truth and entitlement and Scripture. [The] judgment of a poet, moreover, is established on the basis of *roscada*. The judgment of a ruler, moreover, is established on the basis of them all: on *roscada*, and precedents, and true testimonies.[84]

The term for maxim in Irish is *fásach*, and along with *roscada* and the testimony of witnesses or authorities, it formed the foundation of Irish law, the "three rocks" mentioned above.[85] The distinctions made here are between divine law and secular law, and the theories of both are likely culled from the writings of Isidore and the Latin Church Fathers.[86] The "Pseudo-Historical Introduction" accounts for both secular law and canon law and the proper authority and position of each. A concern of several law texts is the grades of the *filid*, but there are also grades established for the church, with the bishop taking a position of great authority. However, the *rí* "king" is often superior to all. However, in the early eighth-century *Críth Gablach*, a law–tract on social classification, the question is posed "who is nobler, the king or the bishop?" and the cleric is granted the highest nobility as "the king rises up before him on account of the Faith."[87]

It is clear that verbal art and ritualized speech were essential to social and political life in early Ireland. "The Cauldron" and "The Primer" are examples of such verbal art. At the same time, these texts describe and celebrate the learning that make it possible, and in this they both function as *encomia*. The "Cauldron" is dated to the early eighth century CE by Liam

---

that remains is written, and Latin learning influenced the presentation of such concepts both in terms of style and content.

83. This is a typical, catechetical formula in early Irish learned texts. *Ceist? Ní hansae* ('Question? Not difficult.')

84. Trans., Stacey (2007, 168).

85. In a summary of the evidence from a variety of law-texts, Stacey (2007, 169) writes that the king is "the master of all languages: poetic, evidentiary, and scriptural—even if this mastery consists largely of his listening to the 'speakers' under his authority."

86. For a discussion, see Watson (2018).

87. See Charles-Edwards (1999, 41).

Breatnach, whereas Corthals dates the "Handbook" to the eighth or ninth century.[88] These are both prime examples of the Irish tendency to fuse native secular learning with Latin ecclesiastical learning. Rather than create systematic handbooks, the Irish favored enigmatic narrative and verse ripe with symbolic meaning; the reader is asked to participate in the process the texts delineate.

COMMENTARY ON "THE CAULDRON OF POETRY AND LEARNING"[89]

"The Cauldron of Poetry and Learning" is a reiteration of the primary themes and contents of the *Bretha Nemed* law texts in prosimetric form. The title "The Cauldron of Poesy" was originally given by Liam Breatnach (1981) in his edited edition of the manuscript. However, Johan Corthals (2013) suggests "The Cauldron of Poesy and Learning" may be a more apt title given that our text deals with more than just the poetic arts. [90] The text is preserved in Trinity College in Dublin[91] and in the British Library in London.[92] It is representative of the art of the *filid* and relates the student's succession to higher levels of learning and associated status. It begins with a section in *rosc* attributed to the legendary poet Amairgen. The text then moves on to a prose section that begins with a question on the origins of poetic and oratorical inspiration within a person before moving on to a discussion of the nature and source of ability in poetry and learning. The metaphor of the cauldron is employed here, an important symbol in early Irish literature, as well as a central feature of everyday life in medieval Ireland. Three types are elucidated: *Coire Goiriath*, *Coire Érmai*, and *Coire Sofis*. The three cauldrons are formed in a person at birth, though in different positions in different individuals, and all three cauldrons contain and distribute knowledge of the verbal arts. Here, we may see a reproduction of the notion of natural talent discussed by several Roman rhetoricians, and Corthals argues the poem may represent an Irish version of Apuleius's three wine bowls.[93] The metaphor consists of the turning of the cauldron to three positions, upside down, on its side, and upright, by way of learning.

The first cauldron, *Coire Goiriath*, is associated with learning in youth and may be a cognate to the first stage of the Roman education system, time spent with the grammarian, as it involves knowledge of masculine, feminine, and neuter, as well as letters and vowels. Since the middle cauldron is arguably the most important because it gets the most extensive treatment in our text, we will next turn to the third cauldron, *Coire Sofis*. This third cauldron is representative of the third and highest stage of learning and concerns knowledge of all the arts. It is upright in those who have mastered all branches of learning.

---

88. Breatnach 1981, 55; Corthals, 2007.
89. Breatnach's edition, normalization, and textual emendations are used in this translation.
90. On prosimetrum in Celtic literature, see MacCana (1997).
91. MS 1337 (H 3. 18, 1337).
92. MS Egerton 152 f 41.
93. Corthals 2013.

The second and most significant cauldron, the one that occupies a middle stage of learning between the other two, is the *Coire Érmai*. As Liam Breatnach points out, unlike the other two cauldrons "there is no mention of knowledge (*soas*) being distributed from it."[94] Rather, this cauldron is said to amplify and is filled by way of various types of joy and sorrow, both internal and external. Breatnach says that these four types of joy refer to the four stages in a student's career: "reaching adolescence, a successful apprenticeship to a teacher, the acquisition of the prerogatives of poetry after study, and finally the acquisition of *imbas*."[95] While this metaphor applies to all students of the arts, it is also true that some students have more natural ability than others. For these students the third cauldron is either upside down in the ignorant, on its side in the bards (who are deemed to be of lower status than the *filid* in legal texts[96]), and upright at birth in the ánroth (the second highest level of learned person within the order of the *filid*) and in the *ollam* (the highest of the learned class).

The cauldrons are metaphors for sources of various types of knowledge and inspiration. That associated with the third and highest of the cauldrons, the *Coire Sofis*, is *imbas forosnai*, a magical inspiration or divine seeing that arises from a ritualistic practice elaborated in several early Irish literary texts. The origins of this "seeing," this poetic inspiration, is the Well of Seagis, a legendary and enchanted well that lies in the *síd*, an Irish word for "Otherworld." The nine hazel trees of the *síd* drop their mast into the well where it is carried down the Boyne River into the mortal world. These hazel nuts possess in their core the divinatory power of *imbas*. This association invokes the secular tradition that is the provenance of the *filid*. Elizabeth Boyle has argued that in the early Irish poem "Finn and the Man in the Tree" the recurrence of this trope indicates the possibility that the cracking of the outer shell of the nut to eat the meat inside is an allegory for exegesis, which was an important rhetorical practice in this era.[97] We must entertain the possibility, therefore, that even though there is likely an oral tradition from which this trope derives, it is used figuratively here to elucidate the relationship of secular and Latin learning, or to explain Latin learning by way of secular tropes and motifs. In short, it is evidence of syncretism, rather than ancient knowledge.

Imbas Forosnai was one requirement of the *filid* according to the law texts. As so many other facets of early Irish culture, the verbal art of the *filid* is triadic. *Uracecht Becc*, an Old Irish tract on status, states there are three things required of a master *fili*: "*teinm laedo* and *imbas forosnai* and *díchetal do chennaib*."[98] This triad is also represented in the beginning of the *Bretha Nemed*. John Carey argues that the terms likely originally had a straight forward association, *teinm laedo* (sometimes rendered *anamain*) meaning "technical expertise," *díchetal*

---

94. Breatnach 1981, 49.

95. Ibid., 50.

96. Such texts include the *Bretha Nemed, Corus Breatha Neimead, Uraicect Becc, Uraicecht na Ríar, Coic Conara fugill, Críth Gablach,* and *Immacallam in dá Thuarad*. For editions and translations, see relevant citations in Stacey (2007); see also the extensive editions and translations by Breatnach.

97. See Boyle (2016, 32–33).

98. Carey 1997, 42.

di chennaib meaning "improvisational facility" and *imbas* meaning "inspiration."[99] Over time, however, the usage was romanticized, as so many archaic features of early Irish culture and learning were in the later Middle Ages, and they took on a supernatural aura, being associated with magical techniques and prophetic powers of the *filid*. Though the origins for this terminology used to describe verbal art may be found in pre-Christian religions, those associations were diluted by the eighth century, and as Mark Scowcroft writes, they should instead be seen as providing the learned class with "a corpus of hidden learning and 'implicit metaphor' as compelling and useful as classical mythology for the rest of medieval Christendom."[100]

The cauldron provides a potent image and metaphor for learning and rhetorical practice as the cauldron was not only a common trope in early medieval Irish and Welsh literature[101] but it was also an important cultural symbol, the size of one's cauldron representing one's social status. In the law-text *Críth Gablach*, commoners of *mruigfer* rank must possess "a bronze cauldron in which a boar can fit," whereas someone who is "lord of precedence" must have a "a cauldron which fits a cow along with a flitch of bacon."[102] In the *Bretha Nemed Toísech*, the status of a hospitaller comes from three attributes: "have a never-dry cauldron, a dwelling on a public road, a welcome for every face."[103]

"The Cauldron" is an encomium on the verbal arts and their practitioners. In prosimetric form, the text lays out the learned order of the *filid*, the prestige associated with their status and rank, as well as the learning necessary to achieve that status and rank. One function of the text was likely mnemonic, as the complexity of both ecclesiastical and secular learning are treated in prosimetrum and with *brevitas*. The catechetical structure, or question-and-answer format, of several sections marks the text as pedagogical. But it is also a display of the verbal arts it praises, and in this it is an example of verbal art.

"The Cauldron" provides a glimpse of the form the trivium of the liberal arts took in early Irish learning. The first cauldron, the cauldron of *Goiriath*, is associated with *grammatica*, as from it "fine speech" pours in "similes" and "colors," along with "many great spells" in "masculine, feminine, and neuter." The foundation of fine speech, and thus of the verbal arts of the *filid*, is mastery of the grammatical arts. This mirrors the trivium of the Roman curriculum in which the student moves from study of grammar to the heights of rhetorical learning. The cauldron of *Goiriath* "distributes knowledge to people in their adolescence," and grammatical learning is then amplified in the next stage of learning, represented by the cauldron of Érmae.

It is in this cauldron that the rhetorical arts are most prevalent, as from it come praise, satire, legal pronouncements, all that oratory encompassed in early Ireland. It is at this stage that knowledge is "united," referring to both ecclesiastical and secular traditions, and as one gains experience, represented by the various emotions, some clearly of a secular nature, the

---

99. Ibid., 47.

100. Scowcroft 1995, 156–67.

101. Examples of this include stories of the Dagda's magical cauldron and the magical cauldron that revives the dead in the Welsh tale *Mabinogi*; See Williams (2016, 10).

102. See Kelly (2010, 33.)

103. Ibid.

cauldron turns to an upright position. But the pinnacle of learning is achieved only at the arrival of "divine joy," or "divine grace," which reveals the extent of Christian influence. Since the hierarchy of the *filid* is based on lineage and academic achievement, not all will achieve the heights of learning, and not all will have their cauldron visited by divine grace. However, mythological figures from the legendary past relate this doctrine, as Amarigen describes the cauldron of *Goiriath*, and Néde describes the cauldron of Érmae. It was mentioned above that it is a common feature of early Irish literature, especially the law texts, for doctrine to be promulgated or pronounced by, put in the mouth of, legendary figures, and these individuals are portrayed elsewhere as having insight into divine, Christian knowledge through their prophetic abilities and thus as akin to the Old Testament prophets. Therefore, their words are as authoritative as those of scripture. This mythopoesis grants credibility to secular traditions and practitioners and places them on par with ecclesiastical learning. However, the heights of learning can only be achieved by those whose cauldrons are visited by divine grace.[104]

"The Cauldron" is a demonstration of learning that accounts for the complexity of early Irish learned communities. While many scholars think of this text as one dealing with poetic inspiration, it is my intention in this translation to make it clear that poetry was only one of the verbal arts its authors were concerned with, and an early Irish form of oratorical practice is evident. Though it is likely that western rhetorical traditions influenced the authors, and while there is much research left to be done in this regard, it is also representative of a learned order and verbal arts that lie outside the western tradition.

Translation of "The Cauldron of Poetry and Learning" [105]

The fine Cauldron of *Goiriath* is mine,

> That God has lovingly given to me from out of the mysterious elements,[106]
> A noble privilege which makes the breast noble
> Out of which fine speech pours forth
>
> (V)
> I am grey-bearded Amairgen, blue-haired and white-kneed

---

104. For further discussion, see Stone (2022, 214–15).

105. The language of this text is notoriously difficult. Breatnach's essential work in editing the texts of the *Bretha Nemed* school require a level of expertise and knowledge that few possess. In many instances, I defer to Breatnach's (1981) translation of the text. It is my hope that my translation offers a contribution to our understanding of the tradition of eloquence in early Ireland and makes this fascinating text available to a wider audience.

106. The "mysterious elements" appear again in "The Primer," and though the verse form does not allow for elaboration, these allusions do seem reminiscent of neo-Platonic, Christian philosophy, particularly that of the pseudo-Dionysius, but also witnessed in Macrobius, Martianus Capella, and Isidore.

I tell of the work of my *cauldron*, its similes and comparisons,[107] which

(X)
God does not provide equally for all,
inclined, upside down, upright
no knowledge, partial knowledge, full knowledge
to make poetry for Éber[108] and Donn

(XV)
With many great spells,
in masculine, feminine, and neuter,
in the signs for double letters, long vowels, and short vowels,
I relate, in this way, the nature of my cauldron

(XX)
I praise the Cauldron of Knowledge
Where the law of every art is ordained
Where prosperity increases
Which amplifies every artistic craft
Which exhorts one through poetic craft

(I)
Is the source of poetic art in a person's body or in the soul?
Some say in the soul since the body does nothing without the soul.
Others say in the body since it is inherent in one's heritage i.e. from one's father
or grandfather, but it is better to say that the source of poetic art and knowledge
is present
in every person, though in every other person it does not
appear, while in another it does.

(V)
What does the source of poetic art and every other knowledge consist
of? Not difficult; three cauldrons are born in every person,
i.e. the Cauldron of *Goiriath* and the Cauldron of *Érmae* and the Cauldron
of Knowledge.
The Cauldron of *Goiriath* is that which is born upright in a
person and distributes knowledge to people in

---

107. *Condelgib*, according to the *Electronic Dictionary of the Irish Language* (eDIL), appears under the heading *coindelg*, and refers to the comparative degree in grammar in the *Auraicept* §668.
108. Sons of Míl, ancestor of the southern Gaels-Éber-name of several persons in the legendary accounts of the origin of the Gaelic race.

their adolescence.[109]
After it has been turned, the cauldron of *Érmae* amplifies;
It is that which is born on its side in a person.
The Cauldron of Knowledge, it is that which is born upside down
and out of it is dispensed [like beer or mead] the knowledge of all the arts.

(X)
The Cauldron of Érmae, then, is upside down in every other person, i.e., in ignorant men. It is on its side in bards[110] and those who practice verse (*raind*).[111] It is upright in the ánroth[112] of poetic knowledge, law, and satire. And the reason why every student does not possess the same poetic skill at that stage of learning is because the Cauldron of *Érmae* is upside down in him until sorrow or joy turns it.[113]

How many divisions are there of the sadness which turns it? Not
Difficult; four: desire, grief, the sadness of jealousy, and exile for
God's sake, and it is from within the student that these four sorrows make the cauldron upright, although they are induced from outside the student.

There are then two divisions of joy by which the cauldron is transformed into the Cauldron of Knowledge, divine joy (*fáilte deodha*)[114] and human joy (*fáilte dóendae*).

Of human joy, it has four divisions: (I) the power of sexual desire,
and (II) the joy of safety and freedom from everyday worries, such as an abundance of food,
clothing, and shelter until one begins bardic practice (*bairdne*), and (III) joy at the prerogatives of poetry after diligent study and (IV) joy at the arrival of *imbas* born of the nine hazels of fine mast that gathers at the well of *Segais* in the *síd*.[115] The fine mast of the nine hazels is sent upstream along the surface of the Boyne River, as thick as a lamb's fleece, swifter than a racehorse, in the middle of June once every seven years.

Divine joy, however, is the shedding of divine grace on the Cauldron of Érmae, so that it turns it upright, and so that there are people who are both divine and secular

---

109. This could be a reference to grammar, the first in the three-part Greco-Roman education.
110. According to the *Electronic Dictionary of the Irish Language* (eDIL), bardic craft, or bardic composition, is less highly regarded than *filidecht*.
111. A type of verse, perhaps associated with legal disputes and dividing things up, such as property
112. Second highest order of poet to *ollam*, the top ranking.
113. This cauldron is associated with poetic art, but it is not the highest cauldron, or level of learned classes.
114. Godly/divine.
115. Otherworld/fairy world.

prophets and commentators both on divine grace and on (secular) learning, and after the turning of the cauldron they utter divine utterances and perform divine miracles, and their words become maxims and judgments, and they become a model for all speech. But it is from outside the student that divine joy makes the cauldron upright, although it is produced internally.

(I)
I praise the Cauldron of Érmae
With knowledge of grace
With currents of knowledge
With strewings of *imbas*,

(V)
the chanting of wisdom
the uniting of learning[116]
the stream of splendor[117]
the exalting of the ignoble[118]
the mastering of language[119]

(X)
swift thinking
the darkening of speech[120]
the craftsman of historical knowledge
the cherishing of pupils,
where laws are observed

(XV)
where senses are divided
where one excels in melodious expression
where knowledge is disseminated

---

116. Like the prose section above, this refers to the unity of secular and ecclesiastical learning, a subject of intense debate throughout late antiquity and into the Middle Ages, but one realized in early Ireland.
117. "*Sruth*," "stream," is commonly used in early Irish legal texts to describe eloquence, whether gently, sweetly flowing, or a rushing torrent.
118. This seems to suggest that through verbal art a *fili* might make noble one who is ignoble, perhaps as praise washes away the stain of satire.
119. Grammar.
120. As noted above, the obscurity of the *roscada* was a virtue as it was not only a social indicator of status, but the learned language was to be the possession of an elite group of scholars. "Darkening" of speech was a sign of one's advanced learning and membership to such an elite group. In the simplest sense, this could refer to metaphor, but it also likely refers to complexity of style and advanced figuration.

where the nobles are exhorted
where the ignoble is ennobled[121]

(XX)
where names are restored[122]
where songs of praise are sung
in a lawful manner
with distinctions of grades
with pure measures of nobility

(XV)
with the fair oratory of sages
with streams of learning,
a noble brew in which is brewed
the basis of all learning
which is set out according to law

(XXX)
which is advanced to through study
which *imbas* sets in motion
which joy turns
which is revealed through sorrow,
its power enduring

(XXXV)
whose protection does not diminish
I acclaim the Cauldron of Érmae.
What is the Érmae? Not difficult; an artistic "noble training" or an
artistic "after-turning" or an artistic course, i.e. it confers
knowledge and status and honour after being converted.

(I)
The Cauldron of Érmae
It grants, it is granted
It amplifies, it is amplified
It nourishes, it is nourished

---

121. It is unclear whether epideictic rhetoric in early Ireland, in the form of praise poetry and satire, was a native craft, a witness to an Indo-European inheritance, or an adaptation of epideictic from Roman Latin learning.

122. In the art of the *filid*, praise poetry was deemed a cure for satire. Therefore, this is likely an allusion to the restoration of one's name following a lawful or unlawful satire.

(V)
It exalts, it is exalted
It requests, it is requested
It praises, it is praised
It preserves, it is preserved
It arranges, it is arranged
It supports, it is supported.
Good is the well of measure,
Good is the acquisition of speech,
Good is the confluence of power[123]
which builds up strength.[124]

(XV)
It is greater than any domain,
It is better than any heritage,
It brings one to the grade of scholar,
It separates one from fools.

COMMENTARY ON "ORDER OF HIGHER KNOWLEDGE FROM THE PRIMER FOR THE STUDENTS OF HIGHER KNOWLEDGE" ("*DLÍGED SÉSA A HURAICEPT NA MAC SÉSA*")[125]

"The Primer" reflects many of the same themes of the "The Cauldron," and it is clear that both texts are associated with the same tradition. It is preserved in a seventeenth–century CE manuscript in the hand of Dubhaltach Mac Firbhisigh, Trinity College MS 1317 (H 2. 15 B), identified by Breatnach as *Bretha Nemed Dédenach*.[126] A glossary known as *O Davoren's Glossary* contains numerous references and citations from this text, and a fragment containing

---

123. This metaphor of flowing like a stream—or liquids meeting in the cauldron, poured into and out of it, just as broth, beer, or mead, works together with the mythological origins of *imbas* and is distinctively Irish, but Corthals (2013) argues it also relates to Apuleius's metaphor of the three wine bowls. While this is distinctively and culturally Irish, it may be another example of syncretism.

124. The metaphor of flowing liquid, either sweet and potent like flowing liquor, or powerful like a river, is witnessed in other Irish texts. For example, in the seventh-century *Hisperica famina* one of the rhetors compares his oratory to a torrent when he says "My eloquence flows along like a mighty torrent, carrying all before it" (Herren, 1974-1987, ll. 87-102). A section of The Book of Ballymote, edited by Breatnach (2004, 31) reads "'The expedition of a poet for a fair stream of words, for a poetic occasion, without previous notice to the dwelling of the lord . . . a flood of words . . . according to entitlement or he goes away in ignorance without…entitlement.'" Other examples of this metaphor in the *Bretha Nemed* texts include Breatnach (1989, 18-19), "a torrent of mighty oceans can be established" and "The law of the church is a sea obliterating small streams" and Binchy (1955, 44), "Cerball of the red-sworded Curragh whom hosts used to proclaim, like a sea obliterating small streams."

125. Edited in Corthals (2007).

126. See Breatnach, (1987, 42–57) for edition and translations of parts of the text.

a section on voice is preserved in Trinity College E 3.3. What makes this text unique is the apparent allusion to the "woman of poetry" witnessed in the works of Martianus Capella's (c. fifth century CE) *De nuptiis philologiae et mercurii* ("The Marriage of Philology and Mercury") and Boethius's *De consolatione philosophiae* ("Consolation of Philosophy") along with what appears to be an adaptation of the rhetorical doctrine of the five canons of rhetoric. "The Primer" offers an explanation of the nature of voice, its importance in composition, the source of poetic inspiration, the significance of poetry in society, as well as the just rewards of the student who achieves the heights of learning. The text is not composed in verse but in highly rhetorical prose. The structure is that of a diptych in that it treats corporeal and social aspects of verbal art, respectively, couched in admonition at the beginning and end and a prayer in the middle. The text is not introductory, but is rather an introduction to final stages of study in the Irish curriculum, the acquisition of higher knowledge found in the Donat commentaries and in the works of the seventh-century CE Irish grammarian, Virgilius Maro Grammaticus.[127]

Martianus Capella's text is an allegory in which Philology and Mercury are to be married through the efforts of Apollo, and, at the wedding feast, Apollo brings forth seven women who are the personification of the liberal arts. The seven liberal arts consist of the trivium—grammar, logic, and rhetoric—and the quadrivium—music, geometry, arithmetic, and astronomy. It is an encyclopedic text that attempts to capture the full extent of antique learning in textbook form. The section on rhetoric is in large part based on Cicero's *De inventione*, but in the manner of other late antique *compendia*, such as Fortunatianus's (fourth century CE) *Ars rhetorica* and Julius Victor's (fourth century CE) *Ars rhetorica*.[128]

In Boethius, philosophy is personified as a beautiful woman, his "sovereign comfort," with whom he converses about the nature of philosophy and the comfort of knowing the one true God through contemplation. Though Boethius does not treat specifically of rhetoric in this work, the personification of philosophy provides a creative framework for delineating philosophical concepts through dialogue.

The woman in "The Primer" is portrayed as the source of the verbal art of the *filid*. The text veers in different directions, but there is discussion of the nature of grammar, the source of language and of grammar, the nature of a word, and the role of *filidecht* in society.[129] In this way, it reflects the concerns of the *Bretha Nemed Dedanách, Bretha Nemed Taoísech,* and "The Cauldron."

"The Primer" is written in rhetorical prose, and elements of verse appear throughout. The student of Latin learning will recall that, in general, verse was the province of the grammarian, whereas prose was the province of the rhetor. In the original Irish text, there is *chiasmus, anaphora, paranomasia,* and *polyptoton,* showing the influence of Latin grammar on the ver-

---

127. See Corthals (2013, 127).
128. See Copeland and Sluiter (2009, 148–66).
129. See discussion in Poppe (2016).

nacular. There are clear reminiscences of grammar handbooks, especially the (likely) seventh-century handbook of the Irishman Virgilius Maro Grammaticus.[130]

The authority figure invoked in this text is Ai mac Ollamain meic Delbaith. He is a god of poetry of the mythological race of the Tuatha Dé Danann, whose exploits are most famously related in the *Lebor Gabála Érenn* ("The Book of the Invasions of Ireland"). Also invoked in allusion to a law-case is Fiachna mac Delbaíth, a legendary king also of the Tuatha Dé Danann, who had three daughters: Banba, Fódla, and Ériu. This last daughter, Ériu, is the Gaelic name for Ireland, Ériu in Old Irish, modern Irish, Éire. These authorities serve to situate the origins of poetry and its societal role in legal contexts in the distant past, thus granting it antiquity and credibility.

In the section on voice, which comprises a majority of the text, pseudo-Cicero is cited in Latin (III xi. 19-20). This is significant for a number of reasons. For one, it demonstrates that in the eighth century CE, Irish scholars had access to the *Rhetorica ad Herennium*, though the quotation may have been contained in a grammatical miscellany. The influence of Donatus's grammar is also clear, as there is a distinction between *vox articulata* and *vox inarticulata*, an "educated voice" and "uneducated voice." However, the text is not only indicative of *grammatica*, but of multiple disciplines, steeped in medical theory of the day. The text poses a series of questions: Where does the voice come from and what inspires it? What types of voice are there? What accents and tones of the voice? The breath finds its origin in the wind, and from there it finds its way to the liver, where there is an inner fire. The voice is brought out as "the fiery smoke of the soul," the "spirit whipped by breath," most likely allusions to Isidore's *Etymologies*. In short, the voice is a manifestation of the soul.

The nature of breath and the voice was central to antique and late antique rhetorical theory, and in "The Primer" several texts are syncretized with native learning. There is also a section on memory, another one of the five canons of rhetoric discussed in pseudo-Cicero, and a section on "arrangement of the beautiful art," which provides evidence that the scholars of the *Bretha Nemed* may have possessed a full copy of the *Rhetorica ad Herennium*, or an adaptation thereof, rather than a few quotations in a grammatical miscellany. In our text, the canons are related to poetic craft, which, given the discussion above, one could take to be an adaptation of rhetorical doctrines to the purposes of Irish scholars. It also could lead us to conceive of *filidecht* as verbal art, rather than poetry, and all of the connotations it brings to mind.

In the final sections of the text, we see the manifestation of poetry as a splendid woman surrounded by scholars in the form of young maidens. Her role is "triumphing over the restlessness, over the cries of the masses," which is a clear allusion to the purpose of rhetoric throughout antiquity in an allegory common to Late Antiquity. Earlier in the text, the author writes that the goal of higher poetic learning is "victories over the unrest, over the cries of the crowd, mastery in the rough knowledge." As noted above, the Irish were unlikely to copy an external text verbatim. Rather, the Irish tended to take secular and ecclesiastical Latin texts

---

130. On Virgilius, see Law (1995), and, especially, the review by Ó Cróinín (1998); See also Naismith (2009) and references therein.

and use them in innovative and creative ways, including grammar handbooks. In "The Primer," we see discussion of the role of voice (with direct allusion to delivery in the *Rhetorica ad Herennium*), arrangement, and memory, and the personification of the poetic arts as a beautiful woman quieting the crowds and rendering judgments.

Of course, one also sees the influence of native beliefs about the nature of learning and the role of the *fili* in society. We hear of the importance of payment for a composition, the hierarchy of the *filid*, and the origins of the legal craft in the distant Irish past, yet this is placed side-by-side with Latin learning. It is not that one tradition is greater than the other, but one tradition may be understood by way of another, and they exist in parallel.

At the end of our text, we see the rewards of successful composition, as the poet who has achieved the highest degrees of composition "sings his song in the joyful festival hall to surpass the lower degrees and to be honored by the higher grades." The successful student enjoys a festive drinking hall, cups full of ale, and the praise of his superiors.[131] The primer is complete, and the student understands the rewards that await beyond his hard labors.

Translation of "Order of higher knowledge from the primer for the students of higher knowledge" ("*Dlíged sésa a huraicept na mac sésa*")

I. Here follows the doctrine of knowledge from the textbook of the disciples of knowledge

Scattered, student of knowledge, you should sit in the knowledge of the scholars. What is the art? What is the knowledge in whose secrets the special knowledge of the scholars could be? You shall command proper memory. Rehearse, student. Come to the reserved art, best you should spread clear streams.[132] Rest in the mouth, victories over unrest, over the cries of the crowd, mastery of difficult knowledge, arrangement of the beautiful art. With many difficult cases, a variety of houses should deal with the realization. Come to the compensated art. The right ear–the wheel of erudition–arrangement of the doctrine, augmentation of listening. The left ear hears unconcealed scholarship. The call of my tongue is an advantage for both of your ears. I claim the voice by which poetry is proclaimed.

II. The doctrine of obedience

The right ear—wheel of erudition—arrangement of the doctrine, augmentation of listening.

---

131. See Corthals (2010), for further examples of poetry celebrating a student's completion of a course of study with festive drinking and poetic performance.

132. "Stream" here could refer to streams of knowledge, streams of oratory, or both. See n. 102 and n. 109.

Unconcealed scholarship in the left ear. The call from my tongue is an advantage for your two ears.

III and IV. On the system of voice[133]

I praise the voice by which poetry is proclaimed

   No poetry shall you proclaim until you know what the firm voice is;

      the correct arrangement of speech

   What the fine voice is;

      secret counsel

   What the educated voice is

      storytelling and chanting

   What the confused voice is

      the bellowing of cattle, bleeting of sheep etc.

   What the heavy voice is

      the sound of the sea crashing over rocks

   What the light voice is

      the whistling of humans and the voices of birds

   Where in the human being does the voice reside?

      in the furnace of the side, and the recess of the liver

   What it pursues in the human? How many itineraries it knows?

      in the spaces of the diaphragm through the liver, in the spaces of the diaphragm to the cavity of the chest, the second way to the throat, the third way to the mouth, the fourth from the mouth, and from the hearth of the side

   How many seats does it have?

      These are the five thresholds of the voice and the breath: in the side, in the back, in the chest, in the throat, in the mouth.

   What sets them in motion? What sharpens them? What lies behind them?

      These are their four ways: from the hearth to the back, from the back to the chest, from the chest to the throat, from the throat to the mouth.

   What is older than the voice?

      A sound in the throat

---

133. Here I follow Carey (1990) and Poppe (2016), in their treatment of selections from this section and combine sections III and IV to aid the reader. Section III consists of a series of questions, and section IV a series of answers to those questions.

What is younger than the voice?

    A word outside the mouth

What calls the voice to life?

    the mind

At which time is it voice?

    in the mouth

At what time is it word?

    outside the mouth

At what time is it sound?

    when it is in the throat; for sound is in the throat, voice in the mouth

What is a sound without word?

    when it is in the throat

What is a word without sound?

    a written word

What is word without voice or sound?

    finger reckoning[134]

What is the mother of a word?

    voice

What is the mother of voice?

    sound

What is the mother of a sound?

    breath

When is she a message? When is she a statement? When is she a satire? When is she a word? When is she poetry? When is she recitation? Until I get (the answer), until I know it, until it has been solved out right, you shall not have any poetry proclaimed.

A breath, a wind, on the basis of both categories. Or if a sense is complete, if it names something, or if the sense is complete when it names something, and one or two syllables become a denomination without it. Something distinguishes a lasting desire in a stanza. The word outside, if it distinguishes something, it is a bard's art or *filidecht*. That is the metric recitation of the *fili*.

These are the three parts of the voice: volume, strength, and flexibility. As Cicero said, "the voice is divided into three categories, according to its volume, strength, and flexibility."

---

134. A reference to counting on the fingers.

V. On the purity of the breath

I describe the breath with beautiful desires, daughter of the wind, revelation of the soul, child of life. Flow water, collect the noble stream, which wandered through the abdominal winds, foster mother, which lifts up the bodies of the people, whip (*Ail*),[135] which jumps around the tendons of the body, which is bitter, which is tasty, which is cold, which is hot, which is tight, which is fine, which is heavy, which is light. She is seen, she is not seen. She touches, she does not touch. She bypasses the bridle of the joints. She creates the voice in the hearths of the page. It moves through the liver, into the space of the diaphragm, then through the atmosphere.

Daughter of the Túairgnithe, whose seat is the mother of the voice, the dull one, which is clear, the pure one; the smoke of the fire is from the world of invisible elements. Noble river, which mysteriously flows the way back to the source of the spring to the place where it begins its journey. Solid and fluid at the same time, she should not break out tearfully, nor should she arrive asleep. Shrine of life, from which I examine every limb, every height (or joint), through the sinew of the tendons. Ever-living revelation of life, fiery smoke of the soul in the lightless elements. I describe, etc.

VI. This is the creed of poetry

> In the time of need
>
> May I take a safe path,
>
> And let my tongue guide me,
>
> So that God help me in the fields of concord.[136] Amen.

VII. Be grateful when greeted by a multiform, colorfully designed poem, a noble woman with firm rules, because she deserves rewards. Because without pay she will not communicate. Because every message is entitled to payment. She provides assistance; she is assisted. In the face of her beauty serenity arises. Because it means delivery of joy in all ears. Every outstanding juridical person, every outstanding one, every stately jurist, distinguished and ingrained in the secrets of scholarship received with joy, knows her. She learns; she is learned; she protects; she is protected; she entertains; she is entertained. In its place, a woman full of treasures and desires is beckoned. For she deserves to be heard, to be thanked by the *túatha* for the rewards of the noble woman.

---

135. Satire.

136. This is a common rhetorical trope in both the Roman and late antique Christian literature. For an overview of its use in *pax Romana* and writers such as Gregory the Great, who was well known in Ireland, and an argument of its continued significance in the writings of Columbanus, see Bracken (2018); however, in medieval philosophy, the marriage of secular and divine learning was often referred to as *concordia,* though this is seen predominantly among scholastic philosophers, giving the theory that this refers to concord in the Roman sense more weight.

VIII. The reward of the poem follows

How was the poem? How was she sung? How was she sung before? In what form did she appear? Who was given the gift of poetry for the first time? Was it a deep sleep or a story? Was it knowledge? Was it watching without hearing? Was it hearing without watching? Was it an invention of mind? Was it an appearance of moral obligation? In which age of the world was poetry invented? What was first proclaimed in the performance of the poem? Which king first proclaimed the poem after its invention? What honorary prize was then acquired by the king? How was the poem invented? In one piece or in parts? How many lyres does she have? How many appearances does she have? How many colors (figures?) does she have?[137] How many divisions does she have? How many faces does she have? How many branches does she have?[138] What is their relationship?

Ancient knowledge of the exalted woman with a crowd of scholars, provision of joy, removal of sorrow, inspiration for the mouth, feast for the ears, entertainment of the mind, reward of poetry. Be grateful, poem.[139]

IX. The Answers

In the darkness of Ai mac Ollomain of Fiachna mac Delbaith, in the form of a young girl, to the Ai mac Ollomain, in sleep, in the mind, with the eye, through the listening ear. It is a court settlement in the fifth century, or at the beginning of the fourth era, by means of the *laíd arachuir*[140] of Fiachna mac Delbaeth, thirty cows, in stories or even in a single mass,[141] *filid* and bardic art, reputation, a royal heir, and homeland, white, black, and colorful,[142] the seven classes of the *fili's* art and the seven classes of

---

137. "*Colores*" is a rhetorical concept discussed in many late antique rhetorical writings, including Martianus Capella and Fortunatianus. See Carruthers (2010, 254–57); This could also refer to the colors of satire, praise, and trefocal, namely, black, white, and speckled.

138. "*Cenel*" is used in the sense of the division of Roman rhetoric in the Old Irish miscellany called *Hibernica minora*: *hisin cethramad ceniul na sulbaire romanta* "in the fourth kind of Roman rhetoric" (13.440).

139. One will recall here Cicero's claim that rhetoric is to teach, delight, and persuade: "Now there are three things in my opinion which the orator should effect: to teach, delight, and to persuade his listener. By what virtues in the orator each one of these is effected, or from what faults the orator fails to attain the desired effect,…a master of the art will be able to judge" (Hendrickson 1971, 187–89). This is reiterated in the pseudo-Cicero *Rhetorica ad Herennium*.

140. This is a type of meter discussed also in the c. tenth-century metrical tract *Mittelirische Verslehren* II §16; see Thurneysen (1891).

141. Recall that judicial verdicts were rendered in verbal art, and there is a close connection between the Irish legal tradition and *filidecht*.

142. This is an allusion to the colors of satire, praise, and trifocal, black, white, and speckled.

the bardic art, or twelve parts, as he says above, five faces of protective poetry and cursing poetry, that is, satire and praise.

X. Be grateful, poetry, daughter of erudition, sister of the intellect, daughter of the spirit, full, proud, exalted, rich, who lifts up the thread of art, with fine, correct art.

It proclaims legal judgments, it brings abundance, it stifles ignorance, it communicates every truth, every law, every rank, every judgment, everything that is free, all wisdom,[143] every settlement, every order, everything noble, every calculation (reckoning), every place of honor in the joyful festival hall.[144] It promises everything that is fair, every beauty, every ornament. In the midst of treasures, it proclaims the authority of kings and queens.

Noble poetry is her customary name, the poetry which came to Ai mac Ollamain meic Delbaith, of nobility, of good legal bond, already in form, of good origin. For it deserves to be communicated from the lofty places of honor. Because after her message she is entitled to juicy drops of wheat (ale). The first time she asks the thirst of four people. Later, with the drink of nine persons, it proceeds with all that is right due to the excellence (?) of the law in the tenth part, to the honorable communications.

XI. Pour and pour, make entry and unify her name in one breath. Already smooth, of good legal bond, a stream of treasures, if it is on the tongue. To listen and to be silent, to be attentive when her name is in the ear. Highly honored, radiant yellow, always blessed, her name is tranquil, if she is enjoyed. Great sunshine with the light of the nobility, through which the joyful festive hall shines, is her name among the minstrels.

Everlasting beautiful woman is her well-known name, the poetry, which Ai mac Ollamain meic Delbaith has given his name, which awards each according to his right, the disbursed sum (?) of his honour-price, in which the festive times were enjoyed. Place where everyone excels before he reaches his rightful place. For wisdom is concealed (darkened) in the secrets of learning.[145] It is not negligent people, led by their own desires, who reap the truth. For true, beautiful art, you should strive for the *Bretha Nemed*

---

143. This is taken to be a form of *soifist*. It appears in the *Electronic Dictionary of the Irish Language* (eDIL) under the heading *soifist ind* (a Latin loan-word). It is also glossed as *sophissma* in the *Irish Glosses* line 842.

144. As part of legal proceedings, individuals were seated throughout the hall or open-air court based on their rank. See Kelly (1988, 193–96).

145. That is, the obscurity of *roscada* and rhetorical prose keeps the ignorant from obtaining the learning of the specialized *filid* caste, but darkening of speech also refers to figurative language. This conception of knowledge as incompatible with wealth and desire is also reminiscent of the riddling, sapiential Hiberno-Latin literary tradition in which Virgillius Maro Grammaticus can be placed, and of which there are plentiful other examples from early Ireland. See Bracken (2006); on obscure styles, see Carey (1996).

Comprehensive Bibliography

Ahlqvist, Anders. 1982. *The Early Irish Linguist: An Edition of the Canonical Part of the Auraicept na n-éces.* Helsinki: Societas Scientiarum Fennica.

—. 2008. "Celtic!" *Arts: The Journal of the Sydney University Arts Association* 30: 74–94.

Bauer, Bernhard, Rijcklof Hofman, and Pádraic Mauer. 2017. *St Gall Priscian Glosses.* www.stgallpriscian.ie/.

Bieler, Ludwig . 1979. *The Patrician Texts in the Book of Armagh.* Dublin: The Dublin Institute for Advanced Studies.

—. 1987. "The Humanism of St. Columbanus." *Ireland and the Culture of Early Medieval Europe.* Dublin: Valorum Collected Studies Series.

—. 1993. *Libri Epistolarum Sancti Patricii Episcopi: Introduction and Commentary.* Dublin: Royal Irish Academy Dictionary of Medieval Latin from Celtic Sources.

Binchy, D. A. 1941. *Críth Gablach.* Dublin: Dublin Institute for Advanced Studies.

—. 1955. "Bretha Nemed." *Ériu* 17: 4–6.

—. 1975–1976. "The Pseudo-historical Prologue to the *Senchus Már.*" *Studia Celtica* 10–11: 1528.

Bisagni, Jacopo. 2020. *From Atoms to the Cosmos: The Irish Tradition of the Divisions of Time in the Early Middle Ages.* Kathleen Hughes Memorial Lectures 18. Department of Anglo-Saxon, Norse, and Celtic, University of Cambridge.

Bischoff, Bernhard, and Bengt Löfstedt, eds. 1992. *Anonymus Ad Cuimnanum.* Brepols: Typographi Brepols Editores Pontifichi.

Bitel, Lisa M. 2006–2007. "Tools and scripts for cursing in medieval Ireland." *Memoirs of the American Academy in Rome* 51-52: 5–27.

Boyle, Elizabeth, and Deborah Hayden. 2014. *Authorities and Adaptations: The Reworking and Transmission of Textual Sources in Medieval Ireland.* Dublin: Dublin Institute for Advanced Studies.

Boyle, Elizabeth. 2016. Allegory, the áes dána and the liberal arts in Medieval Irish literature." In *Grammatica, Grammadach and Gramadeg: Vernacular Grammar and Grammarians in Medieval Ireland and Wales,* edited by Deborah Hayden and Paul Russell, 11–34. Amsterdam: Amsterdam Studies in the Theory and History of Linguistic Science–Series 3.

Bracken, Damien, and Alexander O'Hara, eds. 2006. "Virgil the Grammarian and Bede: A Preliminary Study." *Anglo-Saxon England* 35: 7–21.

—. 2018. "Columbanus and the Language of Concord." In *Columbanus and the Peoples of Post–Roman Europe.* Oxford: Oxford University Press.

Breatnach, Liam. 1981. "The Cauldron of Poesy." *Eriu*: 41–73.

—. 1984. "Canon Law and Secular Law in Early Ireland: The Significance of *Bretha Nemed.*" *Peritia* 3: 439–59.

—. 1987. *Uraicecht Na Ríar: The Poetic Grades in Early Irish Law.* Dublin: Dublin Institute for Advanced Studies.

—. 1990. "Lawyers in Early Ireland." In *Brehons, serjeants and attorneys. Studies in the History of the Irish Legal Profession*, edited by Daire Hogan and W. N. Osborough, 1–13. Dublin: Irish Academic Press.

—. 1996. "Poets and Poetry." In *Progress in Medieval Irish Studies.*, K. McCone and Katharine Simms, 65–77. Maynooth: An Sagart.

—. 2004. "On Satire and the Poet's Circuit." In *Unity in Diversity: Studies in Irish and Scottish Gaelic Language, Literature and History,* edited by Cathal G. Ó hÁinle and Donald E. Meek, 25–35. Dublin: School of Irish, Trinity College.

—. 2005. *A Companion to the* Corpus iuris Hibernici. Dublin: Dublin Institute for Advanced Studies.

—. 2006. "Satire, Praise, and the Early Irish Poet." Ériu 56: 63–84.

Calder, George. 1995. Auraicept na n-éces: *The Scholars' Primer*. Dublin: Four Courts Press.

Carey, John. 1990. "Vernacular Irish Learning: Three Notes [1. *Nathair imchenn*; 2. *Compóit mérda*; 3. *Brisiud cend for mac fri cloche*]." Éigse 24: 37–44.

—. 1996. "Obscure Styles in Medieval Ireland." *Mediaevalia* 19: 23–39.

—. 1997. "The Three Things Required of a Poet." Ériu XLVIII (1997): 41–58.

—. 2011. *A Single Ray of the Sun: Religious Speculation in Early Ireland*. Aberstwyth: Celtic Studies Publications.

Carruthers, Mary. 2010. *Rhetoric beyond Words: Delight and Persuasion in the Arts of the Middle Ages*. Cambridge: Cambridge University Press.

Chadwick, Nora K. 1935. "*Imbas Forosnai.*" *Scottish Gaelic Studies* 4 (2): 97–135.

Chapman-Stacey, Robin. 2007. *Dark Speech: The Performance of Law in Early Ireland*. University of Pennsylvania Press.

Charles-Edwards, T. M. 1999. 1993. "Palladius, Prosper, and Leo the Great: Mission and Primatial Authority." In *Saint Patrick, AD 493–1993*, edited by David N. Dumville and Lesley Abrams, 1–12. Woodbridge: Boydell.

—. 1998. "The Context and uses of literacy in early Christian Ireland." In *Literacy in Medieval Celtic Societies*, edited by Huw Pryce, 62–82. Cambridge: Cambridge University Press.

—. 1999. *The Medieval Gaelic Lawyer*. Quiggin Pamphlets on the Sources of Mediaeval Gaelic History 3. Cambridge: Department of Anglo-Saxon, Norse and Celtic, University of Cambridge.

—. 2000. *Early Christian Ireland*. Cambridge: Cambridge University Press.

—. 2005. "Early Irish Law." In *A New History of Ireland: Prehistoric and Early Ireland,* edited by Dáibhí Ó Cróinín, 331–71. Oxford: Oxford University Press.

Clarke, Michael. 2006. "Achilles, Byrhtnoth, and Cú Chulainn: from Homer to the Medieval North." In E*pic Interactions: Perspectives on Homer, Virgil and the Epic Tradition Presented to Jasper Griffin by his Pupils*, edited by Michael Clarke, Bruno Currie, and Oliver Lyne, 243-72. Oxford: Oxford University Press.

—. 2009. "An Irish Achilles and a Greek Cú Chulainn." In *Ulidia 2: Proceedings of the Second International Conference on the Ulster Cycle of Tales*, Maynooth 24–27 July 2005, edited by Ruairí Ó hUiginn and Brian Ó Catháin, 238-51. Maynooth: An Sagart.

—. 2013. "Linguistic Education and Literary Creativity in Medieval Ireland." *Cahiers de l'ILSL, N* 38: 39–71.

—. 2014. "Demonology, Allegory and Translation: The Furies and the Morrígan." In *Classical Literature and Learning in Medieval Irish Narrative,* edited by Ralph O'Connor, 101–22. Cambridge: D. S. Brewer.

—. 2016. "International Influences on the Later Medieval Development of *Togail Troi.*" In *Adapting Texts and Styles in a Celtic Context. Interdisciplinary Perspectives on Processes of Literary Transfer in the Middle Ages. Studies in Honour of Erich Poppe,* edited by Axel Harlos and Neele Harlos, 75–102. Münster: Nodus.

Clarke, Michael, and Máire Ní Mhaonaigh. 2020. "The Ages of the World and the Ages of Man: Irish and European Learning in the Twelfth Century." *Speculum* 95 (2): 1–35.

Copeland, Rite ,and Ineke Sluiter, eds. 2009. *Medieval Grammar and Rhetoric: Language Arts and Literary Theory, AD 300–1475.* Oxford: Oxford University Press.

Cornel, Dora, and Franziska Schnoor. 2018. *The Cradle of European Culture: Early Medieval Irish Book Art.* Schwabe Verlasgsgruppe.

Corthals, Johan. 1996. "Early Irish Retoirics and Their Late Antique Background." *Cambrian Medieval Celtic Studies* 31: 18–37.

—. 2007. "Stimme, Atem und Dichtung: Aus einem Lehrbuch für die Dichterschüler (*Uraicept na Mac Sésa*)." Helmut Birkhan Ed. *Kelten-Einfälle an der Donau. Akten des Vierten Symposiums deutschsprachiger Keltologinnen und Keltologen…Linz/Donau* 17 (21): 127–48.

—. 2010. "The Áiliu Poems in *Bretha Nemed Dédenach.*" Éigse 37: 59–91.

—. 2013. "Decoding the Caldron of Poesy." *Peritia* 24–25: 74–89.

Davies, Oliver. 2000. *Celtic Spirituality.* Paulist Publishing.

Dempsey, G. T. 1999. "Aldhelm of Malmesbury and the Irish." *Proceedings of the Royal Irish Academy: Archaeology, Culture, History, Literature* 99 (1): 1–22.

Etchingham, Colmán. 1999. *Church Organization in Ireland, AD 650–1000.* Maynooth: Laigin Publications.

Harlos, Axel, and Neele Harlos, eds. 2016. *Adapting Texts and Styles in a Celtic Context: Interdisciplinary Perspetives on Processes of Literary Transfer in the Middle Ages. Studies in Honour of Erich Poppe.* Münster: Nodus Publikationem.

Hayden, Deborah, and Paul Russell eds. 2016. *Grammatica, Grammadach and Gramadeg: Vernacular Grammar and Grammarians in Medieval Ireland and Wales.* Amsterdam Studies in the Theory and History of Linguistic Science–Series 3. Amsterdam: John Benjamins.

Hayden, Deborah. 2011. "Poetic Law and the Medieval Irish Linguist: Contextualising the Vices and Virtues of Verse Composition in *Auraicept na nÉces.*" Ériu 64: 1–21.

—. 2014. "Some Notes on the Transmission of *Auraicept na nÉces.*" *Proceedings of the Harvard Celtic Colloquium* 32: 134–79.

Herren, Michael W. 1974. *Hisperica famina.* Toronto: Pontifical Institute of Mediaeval Studies.

—. 1981. "Classical and Secular Learning among the Irish before the Carolingian Renaissance." *Florilegium* 3: 118–57.

—. 1987. *The Hisperica Famina II: Related Poems.* Toronto: Pontifical Institute of Mediaeval Studies.

—. 1996. *Latin Letters in Early Christian Ireland.* Brookfield: Ashgate.

—. 1998. "Scholarly Contacts Between the Irish and the Southern English in the Seventh Century." *Peritia* 12: 24–53.

Hillgarth, J. N. 1984. "Ireland and Spain in the Seventh Century." *Peritia* 3: 1–16

Hofman, Rijcklof. 1996. *The Sankt Gall Priscian Commentaries Vol. 1 and 2.* Münster: Nodus Publishing.

—. 2000. "The Irish Tradition of Priscian." In *Manuscripts and Tradition of Grammatical Texts from Antiquity to the Renaissance: Proceedings of a Conference Held at Eirce, 16-23 October 1997, at the 11th Course of International School for the Study of Written Records,* edited by Mario De Nonno et al., 257–87. Cassino: Edizioni Dell Universita Degli Studi Di Cassino.

Holtz, Louis. 1981. *Donat Et La Tradition De L'Enseignement Grammatical.* Paris: Centre National De La Recherche Scientifique.

Howlett, D. R. 1994a. *Liber Epistolarum Sancti Patricii Episcopi.* Dublin: Four Courts Press.

—. 1994b. "The Earliest Irish Writers at Home and Abroad." *Peritia* 8: 1–17.

—. 1995. *The Celtic Latin Tradition of Biblical Style.* Dublin: Four Courts.

—. 2000. "*A Brittonic Curriculum: A British Child's ABC 123.*" *Cambridge Medieval Celtic Studies 40*: 21–26.

Hughes, Kathleen. 1953. "The Distribution of Irish Scriptoria and Centres of Learning from 730 to 1111." In *Studies in the Early British Church,* edited by Nora K. Chadwick, et al., 243–72. Cambridge: Cambridge University Press.

—. 1963. "Irish Monks and Learning." In *Los monjes y los estudios. IV semana de estudiosmonásticos, Poblet 1961,* edited by Nora K. Chadwick, et al., 61–86. Poblet: Abadía de Poblet, 1963.

—. 1972. *Early Christian Ireland: Introduction to the Sources.* London: The Sources of History Ltd.

"Illuminated Manuscripts." *Encyclopedia or Irish and Celtic Art.* www.visual-arts-cork.com/cultural-history-of-ireland/illuminated-manuscripts.htm#context.

Irish Script on Screen. Royal Irish Academy. www.isos.dias.ie/.

Johnson-Sheehan, Richard, and Paul Lynch. 2007. "Rhetoric of Myth, Magic, and Conversion: A Prolegomena to Ancient Irish Rhetoric." *Rhetoric Review* 26 (3): 233–52.

Johnston, Elva. 2013. *Literacy and Identity in Early Medieval Ireland.* Suffolk: Boydell Press.

—. 2016. "Exiles from the Edge? The Irish Contexts of *Peregrinatio.*" In *The Irish in Early Medieval Europe: Identity, Culture, and Religion,* edited by Roy Flechner and Sven Meeder, 38–52. New York: Palgrave Macmillan.

Kelly, Fergus. 2005. *A Guide to Early Irish Law.* Dublin: Dublin Institute for Advanced Studies.

—. 2010. "Cauldron Imagery in a Legal Passage on Judge (CIH 1307.38-1308.7)." *Celtica* 26: 31–43.

Kelly, Mary, and Charles Doherty, eds. 2013. *Music and the Stars: Mathematics in Medieval Ireland*. Dublin: Four Courts Press.

Kenney, James F., ed. 1966. *Sources for the Early History of Ireland: Ecclesiastical*. New York: Columbia University Press.

Knappe, Gabrielle. 1994. "On Rhetoric and Grammar in the *Hisperica famina*." *Journal of Medieval Latin* 4 (4): 130–62.

Koch, John T., and John Carey, eds. 2003. *The Celtic Heroic Age: Literary Sources for Ancient Celtic Europe and Early Ireland and Wales*. Aberystwyth, Wales. Celtic Studies Publications.

Laing, Lloyd. 1985. "The Romanization of Ireland in the Fifth Century." *Peritia* 4: 261–78.

Lapidge, Michael, ed. 1997. *Columbanus: Studies on the Latin Writings*. Woodbridge: Boydell Press.

Lapidge, Michael, and Richard Sharpe, eds. 1985. *A Bibliography of Celtic Latin Literature 400–1200*. Dublin: Royal Irish Academy.

Law, Vivien. 1981. "Malsachanus Reconsidered; A Fresh Look at a Hiberno-Latin Grammarian." *Cambridge Medieval Celtic Studies* 1: 83–93.

—. 1982. *The Insular Latin Grammarians*. Suffolk: The Boydell Press.

—. 1995. *Wisdom, Authority, and Grammar in the Seventh Century: Decoding Virgilius Maro Grammaticus*. Cambridge: Cambridge University Press.

—. 1997. *Grammar and Grammarians in the Early Middle Ages*. London: Longman Publishing.

Lea, Henry Charles. 1892, 2017. *Superstition and Force*. Project Gutenberg. www.gutenberg.org/ebooks/58750.

Löfstedt, Bengt, ed. 1977. *Sedulius Scottus: In Donati Artem Minorem in Priscianum in Evtychem*. Brepols: Typograph Brepols Editores Pontifich.

—. 1965. *Der Hibernolateinische Grammatiker Malsachanus*. Uppsala: Studia Latina Upsaliensia.

—. 1977. *Ars Lavreshamensis: Exposition in Donatum Maiorem*. Brepols: Typographi Brepols Editores Pontifichi.

—. 1982. *Ars Ambrosiana: Commentum Anonymum in Donati Partes Maiores*. Brepols: Turnhout.

Loveluck, Christopher, and Aidan O'Sullivan. 2016. "Travel, Transport and Communication to and from Ireland, c. 400-1100: an Archaeological Perspective." In *The Irish in Early Medieval Europe: Identity, Culture, and Religion*, edited by Roy Flechner and Sven Meeder, 19–37. New York: Palgrave Macmillan.

MacCana, Proinsias. 1974. "The Rise of the Later Schools of the Filidheacht." *Ériu* 25: 126–46.

—. 1979. "*Regnum* and *Sacerdotium*: Notes on Irish Tradition." *Proceedings of the British Academy* 65: 443–79.

—. 1997. "Prosimetrum in Insular Celtic literature." In *Prosimetrum: crosscultural perspectives on narrative in prose and verse*, edited by Joseph Harris and Karl Reichl, 99–130. Cambridge: Brewer.

—. 2004. "Praise Poetry in Ireland before the Normans." Ériu 54: 11–40

McCone, Kim. 1990. *Pagan Past and Christian Present in Early Irish Literature.* Naas: An Sagart.

McLaughlin, Roisin. 2008. *Early Irish Satire.* Dublin: Dublin Institute for Advanced Studies.

McManus, Damian. 1997. *A Guide to Ogam.* Maynooth: An Sagart,.

Meeder, Sven. 2016. "Irish Scholars and Carolingian Learning." In *The Irish in Early Medieval Europe: Identity, Culture, and Religion,* edited by Roy Flechner and Sven Meeder, 179–94. New York: Palgrave Macmillan.

Melia, Daniel F. 2008. "The Rhetoric of Patrick's Letter to the Soldiers of Coroticus." *Proceeding of the Annual CSANA Meeting 2008: CSANA Yearbook* 10: 96–104.

Miles, Brent. 2011. *Heroic Saga and Classical Epic in Medieval Ireland.* Woodbridge: Boydell and Brewer.

Moran, Pádraic. 2012. "Greek in Early Medieval Ireland." In *Multilingualism in the Graeco-Roman World,* edited by Alex Mullen, James Patrick, 172–200. Cambridge: Cambridge University Press.

Naismith, Rory. 2009. "Real and Metaphorical Libraries in Virgil the Grammarian's '*Epitomae*' and '*Epistolae*.'" *The Journal of Medieval Latin* 19, 2009. 148–72.

Ní Bhrolcháin, Muireann. *An Introduction to Early Irish Literature.* Dublin: Four Courts Press, 2009.

Ní Mhaonaigh, Máire. 2006. "The Literature of Medieval Ireland: from the Vikings to the Normans." In *The Cambridge History of Irish Literature,* edited by Margaret Kelleher and Philip O'Leary, 32–73. Cambridge: Cambridge University Press.

—. 2015. "The Hectors of Ireland and the Western World." In *Sacred histories: a Festschrift for Máire Herbert,* edited by John Carey, Kevin Murray, and Caitríona Ó Dochartaigh, 258–68. Dublin: Four Courts Press.

—. 2016. "*Légend hÉrenn* 'The Learning of Ireland' in the Early Medieval Period." In *"Books Most Needful to Know": Contexts for the Study of Anglo-Saxon England,* edited by Paul E. Szarmach, 1–46. Old English Newsletter Subsidia 36. Kalamazoo MI: Western Michigan University Press.

—. 2017. "The Peripheral Centre: Writing History on the Western "Fringe"". *Interfaces: A Journal of Medieval European Literatures* 4: 59–84.

Ó Cathasaigh, Tomás. 1977. *The Heroic Biography of Cormac mac Airt.* Dublin: Dublin Institute for Advanced Studies.

—. 1986. "Curse and Satire." *Éigse* 21: 10–15.

—. 2005. "The First Anders Ahlqvist Lecture—Irish myths and Legends." *Studia Celtica Fennica: Essays in Honour of Anders Ahlqvist* 2: 11–26.

—. 2006. "The Literature of Medieval Ireland to c. 800: St. Patrick to the Vikings." In *The Cambridge History of Irish Literature,* edited by Margaret Kelleher, 6–31. Cambridge: Cambridge University Press.

—. 2012. "Early Irish *Bairdne* 'Eulogy, Panegyric.'" *Studia Celtica Fennica* 9: 54–61.

O'Connor, Ralph. 2013. *The Destruction of Da Derga's Hostel: Kingship and Narrative Artistry in a Mediaeval Irish Saga.* Oxford: Oxford University Press.

—. 2014. *Classical Literature and Learning in Medieval Irish Narrative.* Woodbridge: D. S. Brewer.

Ó Corráin, Donnchadh. 2011–2013. "What Happened to Ireland's Medieval Manuscripts?" *Peritia* 22-23: 191–223.

O'Hara, Frank. 2018. *Columbanus and the Peoples of Post-Roman Europe.* Oxford: Oxford University Press.

O Cróinín, Dáibhí. 1983. "The Irish Provenance of Bede's Computus." *Peritia* 2: 229–47.

—. 1993. "The Irish as Mediators of Antique Culture on the Continent." In *Science in Western and Eastern Civilization in Carolingian Times*, edited by Paul Leo Butzzer and Dietrich Lohrmann, 41–52. Berlin: Birkhauser Verlag.

—. 1995. *Early Medieval Ireland: 400-1200.* New York: Longman.

—. 1998. "Vivien Law. Wisdom, Authority and Grammar in the Seventh Century. Decoding Virgilius Maro Grammaticus." *The Journal of Medieval Latin* 8: 231–34.

—. 2004. *The First Century of Anglo-Irish Relations, AD 600-700.* Dublin: National University of Ireland.

—. 2005. "Hiberno-Latin Literature to 1169." In *A New History of Ireland: Prehistoric and Early Ireland*, edited by Dáibhí Ó Cróinín, 371–403. Oxford: Oxford University Press.

—, ed. 2005. *A New History of Ireland: Prehistoric and Early Ireland.* Oxford: Oxford University Press.

O'Neill, Timothy, and F. J. Byrne. 1984. *The Irish Hand: Scribes and their Manuscripts from the Earliest Times to the Seventeenth Century.* Dolmen Press.

Poppe, Erich. 2004. "*Imtheachta Aeniasa*: Virgil's *Aeneid* in Medieval Ireland." *Classical Ireland* 11: 74–94.

—. 2016. "*Caide máthair bréithre* 'what is the mother of a word,'". In *Grammatica, Grammadach and Gramadeg: Vernacular Grammar and Grammarians in Medieval ireland and Wales,* edited by Deborah Hayden and Paul Russell, 65–84. Amsterdam Studies in the Theory and History of Linguistic Science–Series 3. Amsterdam: John Benjamins.

Poppe, Erich, and Dagmar Schlüter. 2011. "Greece, Ireland, Ulster, and Troy: Of Hybrid Origins and Heroes". In *Other Nations: The Hybridization of Insular Mythology and Identity,* edited by Wendy Marie Hoofnagle and Wolfram R. Keller, 127–44. Heidelberg: Universitätsverlag Winter.

Riché, Pierre. 1976. *Education and Culture in the Barbarian West Sixth Through Eighth Centuries.* Translated by John J. Contreni. Columbia: University of South Carolina Press.

—. 1981. "Columbanus, His Followers and the Merovingian Church." In *Columbanus and Merovingian Monasticism,* edited by H. B. Clarke and Mary Brennan, 59–72. Oxford: British Archaeological Reports.

Richter, Michael. 1996. "The Personnel of Learning in Early Medieval Ireland." In *Ireland und Europa im früheren Mittelalter: Learning and Literature,* edited by Próinséas Ní Chatháin, 275–309. Klett-Cotta.

—. 2008. *Bobbio in the Early Middle Ages: The Abiding Legacy of Columbanus.* Dublin: Four Courts Press.

Russell, Paul. 1995. *An Introduction to the Celtic Languages.* Boston: Routledge.

—. 1996. "Gwr gwynn y law': Figures of Speech in 'Gramadegau'r Penceirddiaid' and Latin Grammarians."*Cambridge Medieval Celtic Studies* 32: 95–104.

—. 2005. "What Was Best of Every Language: The Early History of the Irish Language." In *A New History of Ireland: Prehistoric and Early Ireland*, edited by Dáibhí Ó Cróinín, 405–50. Oxford: Oxford University Press.

Sharpe, Richard, ed. 1987. *Ireland and the Culture of Early Medieval Europe.* London: Vaiorum Reprints.

—. 1997. *Handlist of the Latin Writers of Great Britain and Ireland Before 1540.* Brepols: Brepols.

—. 2010. "Books from Ireland, Fifth to Ninth Centuries." *Peritia* 21: 1–55.

Sims-Williams, Patrick. 1998. "Celtomania and Celtoscepticism." *Cambrian Medieval Celtic Studies* 36: 1–36.

Stifter, David. 2006. *Sengoídelc: Old Irish for Beginners.* Syracuse: Syracuse University Press.

—. 2016. "Metrical Systems of Celtic Traditions." *North-Western European Language Evolution* 69 (1): 38–94.

Stone, Brian James. 2014. "Scriptural Ethos and Imitation: The Pauline Epistles and St. Patrick's 'Confessio.'" *Proceedings of the Harvard Celtic Colloquium* 34: 240–68.

—. 2022. *The Rhetorical Arts in Late Antique and Early Medieval Ireland.* Nieuwe Prinsengracht: Amsterdam University Press.

Swift, Catherine. 2008. "Commentary: The Knowth Oghams in Context." In *Excavations at Knowth: Historical Knowth and Its Hinterland*, edited by F. J. Byrne, et al., 120–27. Dublin: Royal Irish Academy.

Thurneysen, Rudolf. 1891. "*Mittelirische Verslehren.*" In *Irische Text emit Wörterbuch* 3, edited by Ernst Windisch and Whitley Stokes, 1–182. Leipzig.

Vries, Ranke de. 2013. *A Student's Companion to Old Irish grammar.* San Bernadino: Forgotten Scholar Press.

Walsh, Maura, and Dáibhí Ó Cróinín. 1988. *Cummian's Letter De Controversia Paschali: Together with a Related Irish Computistical Tract De Ratione Conputandi.* Toronto: Pontifical Institute of Medieval Studies.

Watson, Daniel. 2018. *Philosophy in Early Medieval Ireland: Nature, Hierarchy and Inspiration.* Unpublished PhD Thesis, National University of Ireland, Maynooth.

Wiley, Dan M. 2001. "The Maledictory Psalms." *Peritia* 15 : 261–78.

—. 2005. "Niall Frossach's True Judgement." Ériu 55: 19–36.

Woolf, Alex. 2013. "The Court Poet in Early Ireland." In *Princes, Prelates and Poets in Medieval Ireland: Essays in Honour of Katherine Simms*, edited by Seán Duffy, 377–88. Dublin: Four Courts Press.

GLOSSARY OF TERMS

Term	Translation
áer	satire
áes dána	people of arts
aí	law case
aigne	legal advocate (*glasaigne* "fettering advocate"; *aigne airechta* "court advocate"; *aigne fris-n-innle breith* "advocate whom judgment encounters")
airecht	court
árach	giving of security (in court); one of the steps given in court procedure, others including: *tacrae* "pleading," *fecrae* "rejoinder," *breth* "judgment," *forus* "promulgation," and conclusion
ar-cain	sings, chants, recites, applied to poetry, charms, and magical formulas, but also to legal pronouncements and maxims
bairdne	bardic craft
bán bérla	white language (language of scripture)
bérla féne	language of the jurists
bérla na filed	language of the poets
briathrach	sweet-worded
brithem	judge/jurist
dorcha	darkened (with obscure style and/or metaphor)
ecnaid	ecclesiastical scholar (also, *sapiens*)
ecne	canon law
éices	scholar, sage
enach	literally "face," but meaning honor
filid	poetic caste endowed with social power; *ollam*, the highest ranked among the *filid*, whose father and grandfather were also a *fili*, and who has memorized 350 compositions; ánroth, second ranked. For a complete account of rank, see Breatnach, 1987.
filidecht	craft of the *filid*
five paths to judgment (in legal contexts)	*fír*, "truth," *dliged*, "entitlement," *cert*, "justice," *téchtae*, "propriety," and *coir n-athchomairc*, "proper enquiry"
fír filid	"truth of poets"; a requirement of any legitimate judgment rendered by a poet that it be true and just
fír flathemon	"truth of princes"; a requirement of a legitimate judgment rendered by a king that it be true and just

gnáthbérla	everyday language
goídelg	eloquence, good Irish
imbas forosnai	poetic inspiration; one of the three requirements of the poet. The other two include *díchtal do chennaib*, "chanting from heads" to mean extempore recitation, and *tenm laeda*, relating to technical expertise.
insce	eloquence
labra	gift of speech; *deg-labarthach*, "well-spoken"; *labairt*, "good speech"; *labarthae*, "eloquence"
léignid	learned man, scholar; also, *scolaige*
mac léginn	literally "son of learning," but meaning student
milbel	"honey-mouthed" (i.e., eloquent)
nemed	dignitary, privileged class
roscada	obscure, unrhymed, alliterative style associated with legal contexts. One of the "three rocks of judgment," the other two being *fásaige*, "maxims" and *tesdemuin*, "testimony."
retoiric	rhetoric
rí	king of a túath
saí litre	ecclesiastical scholar
scéla	traditional Irish tales, associated with oral tradition
serc léigind	"a love of learning"
salim escaine	"psalms of malediction"
séistech	house of advanced learning (i.e., a classroom)
scélaigecht	traditional lore
scol fénechais	school of native law
scol filed	school of verbal art/poetry
scol léiginn	school of Latin learning
sofis	"knowledge, science, learning"; also *sous*, *sós*
sruth	stream, river, torrent; often used to describe eloquence, as in *sulbaire ind labartha*, "a stream of eloquence of speaking," *Milan Glosses on the Psalms*, 89d3
suithnge	eloquent; *suithengthaid*, one who is skilled in speech and is hired by a plaintiff in court
trifocal	a combination of satire and praise ritually performed over a period of 10 days as a warning to give a defendant an opportunity to give restitution before the actual satire began
túath	territorial, dynastic unit

7 MEDITERRANEAN RHETORICS

PREFATORY INTRODUCTION
Steven B. Katz

A BRIEF OVERVIEW OF THE LONG HISTORY AND SHORT DEVELOPMENT OF JEWISH RHETORIC AND BEYOND, TO BYZANTINE AND MEDITERRANEAN RHETORICS

The inclusion in *Global Rhetorical Traditions* of this section[1] that includes Jewish rhetorics is a significant event. Like the other sections in this collection, what is presented here is not necessarily to be found in the Greco-Roman tradition we are all heir to. Not to misconstrue: the Greco-Roman rhetorical tradition (or sets of traditions) is monumental, powerful, and probably provides most of the primary ideas and concepts that still shape thinking and inform discourse. But the Greco-Roman tradition also has been so persuasive and pervasive that it has had the effect of occluding—but not obliterating, and in many later cases interfacing and intermingling in unexpected ways with—other, alternate rhetorical traditions.

My focus has been on the long history of Judaism and sacred writings all the way back to the Hebrew Bible (or *Tanakh*), and the short history of the field of Jewish rhetorics. For Jewish rhetorics is a fairly new field of study. While scholars may have heard of Biblical or Jewish or Holocaust Studies, very few have ever heard of "Jewish rhetorics." In this, Jewish rhetorics perhaps share with other alternate rhetorical traditions represented in this volume a geo-glob-

---

1. See the rationale for including both Byzantine and Hebraic rhetorics under the umbrella of "Mediterranean Rhetorics," in the section titled *"Global Rhetorical Traditions* in Brief," in Graban's introduction to this volume.

al space of historical concealment and philosophical neglect.[2] In addition, many if not most alternative rhetorical traditions, including Jewish rhetorics, may not have been understood *as rhetoric* in their own time and place, possibly not until the Greco-Roman discipline of rhetoric had been reinvigorated and made robust enough in the twentieth century "in the West" to awaken the sleeping rhetorical consciousness of other cultures as well. But outside very small "esoteric" circles of hidden scholars laboring in magical academic temples or shouting into deserts of research from oases of the vast fertile lands of extant unexplored material, the field of Jewish rhetorics did not exist. "In the beginning" there was classical rhetoric. And there was Jewish Studies. "It was morning. It was evening." Day and night. And that was that.

Certainly, in more literary circles, a handful of noted scholars had been drawn to Jewish texts and sources—usually in relation to the Greco-Roman tradition but also in relation to deconstruction and other modern and postmodern movements hyper-focused on language and text. For example, Susan Handelman brilliantly examined the philosophy of language underlying the writings of the Rabbinic period in Judaism (circa 200 BCE–600 CE) in relation to Platonic and Aristotelian ideas concerning the nature of thought and reality, as well as in relation to deconstruction and other twentieth-century schools and movements in which language is central. J. Hillis Miller, with others at Yale, also had become not only an importer and proponent of the Continental School of literary philosophy, particularly deconstruction in which every word in a text contains its opposite and there is no final signified; but Miller was also attracted to Midrash, in which he found kindred approaches to deconstruction. Crossing over academic fences and fields if not faiths (for he too is Jewish, and at Yale, but not a rhetorician), Harold Bloom had declared and then demonstrated that the Kabbalah, from the *Zohar* to *Etz Chaim*—with their mystical stories of the creation of the universe out of Hebrew letters, broken vessels, Sefirot or supernal lights, and eternal sparks—was a theory of "*rhetoric*" in which these divine complex contradictory linguistic elements constituted another way of reading and interpreting poetry and reality.

During the last decade of the twentieth century and now in the twenty-first, an increasing number of scholars in the discipline of rhetoric and composition began studying Jewish rhetorics as well. In these contemporary postmodern but still "esoteric" circles, one major question was whether there is such a thing as Jewish rhetoric, and if there is, how should it be defined? How is it similar to and distinct from other rhetorics? Is Jewish rhetoric even possible to define? These were the questions that focused and propelled several years of all-day pre-conference seminars at the National Communication Association, led by Yehoshua Gitay and Samuel Edelman in the 1990s. Gitay had been studying the application of Aristotle to the *Tanakh* (Hebrew Bible) for years, and Edelman had been focusing on figures of speech in Hebrew texts, directly addressing the need to develop a historical theory of, as well as programs in, Jewish rhetorics. Out of these seminal NCA pre-conference seminal seminars was born a special issue of the *Journal of Communication and Religion* on Jewish rhetoric, edited by

---

2. One is tempted to say "Western" or "non-Western traditions," but as Jim Ridolfo demonstrates in his segment on Hebraic rhetoric in this section, these and other geographical terms may be misleading if not inaccurate, for the Judeo rhetorical tradition is "Western." And "Eastern."

David Frank. It was from these questions and intellectual context that my own, subsequent work emerged retrogressively: on the Kabbalah as a suppressed rhetorical philosophy; on the rhetoric of the Hebrew alphabet; on the Baraita of the 32 Rules as Hebrew "topoi," the latter of which focused on the permutation of letters; on the temporality of aleftbet as sonic cosmic events; and on the *Tanakh* or Torah itself as a rhetorical theory in which G/d, the Master Rhetorician—beyond Cicero's search for the Ideal Orator, or Kenneth Burke's dream of (con)substantiality—delivered the first lesson in rhetoric by speaking the universe into existence.

In the early decades of the twenty-first century, other scholars moved the diasporic boundaries of Jewish rhetoric further, with analyses of Jewish texts, relations, influences, and ostensible origins of modern rhetoric and composition. David Frank had analyzed and argued for an understanding of Chaim Perelman's theory of juridical argument in the "New Rhetoric" in relation to the legalistic Talmud. Greenbaum and Holdstein edited and published *Judaic Perspectives in Rhetoric and Composition*. Mainstream presentations on Jewish rhetoric at Rhetoric Society of America and College Composition and Communication conferences were contained in global rhetoric sessions, and two collections of comparative rhetorical essays edited by Lipson and Binkley grew from these fruitful interactions. But as I explore in "What Is Jewish Rhetoric?" published in *The Routledge Handbook of Comparative World Rhetorics*, this earlier work in Jewish rhetorics also revealed lists of questions, issues, problems, and the difficulties in *defining* Jewish rhetoric, and perhaps any cultural rhetoric, by similarity and difference, by essence and/or exclusion, which can serve as a case study—a very mini "guide for the perplexed," if you will—of comparative and world rhetorics in general. It may well be that new approaches to studying Jewish and other cultural rhetorics, like the ones suggested by Ridolfo or Fernheimer, are necessary for the field to continue to move forward.

At the beginning of the third decade of the twenty-first century, the discipline of rhetoric now includes Jewish rhetorics, and at least some scholars in the field of Jewish Studies. This is in no small measure due to the work of Janice Fernheimer, who for many years has been studying African American Jewry as well as Jewish feminism. In 2007, Fernheimer, along with David Metzger and me, organized a three-day Rhetoric Society of America Summer Institute seminar at Rensselaer Polytechnic Institute on Jewish rhetoric that brought rhetoricians (including Patricia Bizzell) and Jewish studies scholars together to *drash* and *kibbutz*, and eventually form *Klal Rhetorica* (rhetorical community). Fernheimer also edited a special issue of *College English* on Jewish rhetoric, and later with Michael Bernard-Donals a comprehensive volume on *Jewish Rhetoric: History, Theory, Practice*.

"Jewish rhetorics," at least in this section of *Alternative Sources for Rhetorical Traditions*, is now taking a different and thought-provoking turn.

The following essays, on Byzantine and Mediterranean rhetorics, expand the notion of the way writers and scholars and works inside and outside Judaism remixed and/or referenced the Hebrew *Tanakh*. For me, the hallmark of these studies is the way the Bible is historically, socially, culturally, philologically, and philosophically reconstructed (including by other religions!) with other sources—and not only as a local response but in ways that transcend geographical time and space. This would seem to represent a next step in examining Jewish rhetorics, and generally what has been dubbed "comparative" or alternative rhetorics by focusing on multi-dimensional methods of studying texts as much as, if not in place of, traditional definition. The rhetorics that are so discussed, such as Byzantine and the Mediterranean rhetorics in this section, are thus intersectional rather than geographically limited—a historical cross-section of social, cultural, philological, philosophical themes in trends and threads on space and time in which Jewish rhetoric is both "locally" and broadly defined and is not locked into any geographical place. Indeed, while Byzantine and other rhetorics will not be regarded as Jewish rhetorics *per se* in the same way that the *Nofet Zuphim* (*Book of the Honeycomb's Flow*) is, those rhetorics too may make use of Jewish texts and sources.

The "three" works in this section of this volume are therefore not all Jewish rhetorics as conventionally defined, but they all can be considered Mediterranean Rhetorics, with the implications that entails. A number of noteworthy methodological issues arise, many of them related to questions I raised in *The Routledge Handbook of Comparative Rhetoric*. Some of these are at least partly answered here, such as the question of how to continue to define Jewish rhetorics in the Diaspora. One of the new issues that arises is this: Does a rhetoric, like Jewish, or Byzantine, or Mediterranean, have to first define itself, even methodologically, beyond the "dialogic" as Maha Baddar proposes, before it can "join" a larger community? In cultural terms to which Fernheimer might relate, does the rhetoric want to become part of a larger, more diverse community in which it finds itself?[3] Does the assimilation of text dilatorily dilute or beneficially expand identity? Of course, the answer will not be monolithic: some (people or texts) within a community like the Jewish one, or even within a country, will want assimilation; others will resist. But does cultural resistance mean that texts cannot or will not be reintegrated and used anyway? Obviously not. How that happens is of great scholarly significance. Further, another question might be whether we would be able to *see* a rhetorical peoples/traditions/texts/scholars in later communities of work where they had been absorbed without earlier evolutionary work on the nature and origins prior to dispersal. Could we study the Bible in "transmission" and "translation" as Ridolfo expertly does, without first studying/knowing the Hebrew Bible/Jewish tradition "itself"? Yes, and no.

Of course, one response, harkening back to deconstruction and postmodernism generally, but also hinting at contemporary "posthumanistic" approaches, is that we never study anything in isolation. Texts are "already written."[4] And texts, like other entities and objects, are *emergent*, bodies through which other, multiple and almost unpredictable sources and destinies are discovered and "flow." This section on Mediterranean Rhetorics, then, avoids "colonization" by transcending attempts at essentialist definitions and exclusionary differences, as I and other scholars perhaps tended to do in early work in the field of Jewish rhetoric. In this sense and others, these "new" approaches are an advance, although they may not answer

---

3. Ridolfo might say that it happens, whether it wants to or not, to integrate, to survive and thrive, and we will see the "traces" of this in studying the rhetorical composition of any book.

4. Even texts by G_d? Freud and Miles would say absolutely yes, and in my poem "In the Beginning" I have implied as much by the fact that G_d is using a mainframe (and thus there are other "users") to create the world!

all questions, even about sources or methods. But it doesn't attempt to. Rather, the new approaches proceed slowly and carefully by "*pilpul*" applied beyond Talmud to pick and pull and pluck with acute but wide-ranging logic, texts in which Hebrew as well as other localized strands of spatial and temporal rhetorics, religions, histories, and cultures are a woven like "a coat of many colors." And nevertheless, it is a start—and a globally hopeful and more inclusive one at that. In the *Pirkei Avot* (*Ethics of our Fathers,* a tractate of the *Mishnah*), we are told that "you will not finish the work, but you are not free to desist from it."[5] This section on Mediterranean Rhetoric thus represents not only a next step in the growing field of "comparative" rhetorics (and within that, Jewish rhetorics in the context of other local and global rhetorics, cultures, traditions, and conditions) but also a continuation of the work of "*tikkun olam*"—"the repair of the world." It cannot come soon enough.

---

5. See the Scherman and Zlotowitz (1984) translation, *Pirkei Avos*. The section/tract quoted here is 2:21.

7.1 Byzantine, Non-European Crusades, c. 1061–1067 CE, Byzantium

Michael Psellos's *"Synopsis of Rhetoric in Verses,* Based on the Hermogenian Corpus": Translated with Introduction and Notes

Jeffrey Walker

With "An Introduction to Psellos" by Hui Wu and Tarez Samra Graban[6]

AN INTRODUCTION TO PSELLOS

Michael Psellos is recognized as a "towering figure in the history of Byzantine letters" whose works include 500 letters and 160 works among which the best-known is *Chronographia*, a historical account of eleventh-century CE Byzantine rulership.[7] Besides being studied as a philosopher, theologist, and a political figure, Psellos's theoretical and critical reflections have drawn increasing attention from scholars in literature and art, including the studies and translations in *Michael Psellos on Literature and Art*. However, before Jeffrey Walker's study and translation of Psellos's encomium of his mother, Psellos "almost never has been approached as a rhetorician per se, although that is what he most fundamentally was, and almost none of his writings have ever been subjected to sustained rhetorical analysis and criticism."[8] To further bridge the gap, Walker completed the commentary and translation of Psellos's "Synopsis of Rhetoric in Verses" in 2017, part of which is presented in this chapter.[9]

Historical records show that Psellos was born in Constantinople to a middle-class family, though his father claimed some aristocratic forebears.[10] At five years old, he started learning grammar, orthography, and Homeric poetry. At eleven, he began studies in rhetoric and philosophy. This classical education provided him with entry to local administration and imperial service. At twenty-three, he became secretary in the imperial court. Two years later in 1043 CE, his writing drew the attention of emperor Konstantinos Monomachos (1042–1055 CE), whose patronage helped advance Psellos's career with increasing wealth and social network. But by the 1050s CE, Psellos fell out of Monomachos's favor. It seemed that he had no choice but to become a monk at a monastery in Bithynia, where he changed his name from Konstantinos to Michael. Soon after, in 1055 CE, Psellos returned to Constantinople, where he

---

6. We thank the University of Notre Dame Press and Professor Jeffery Walker for granting their permission to reprint these excerpts. The excerpted chapter was edited and reformatted to fit the scope and style of this book.

7. Papaionannou 2017, 1–3.

8. Walker 2004, 50.

9. Walker 2017, 31–65.

10. Papaionannou 2017, 3; Hussey 1953.

remained until his death, to resume his work as a teacher, speaker, and advisor and to continue writing. It is said that "Psellos taught everything from basic grammar, Homeric poetry, and Aristotelian logic to Hermogenian rhetoric and Neoplatonic philosophy" and wrote almost all subjects "from medicine to law and from vernacular expressions to occult sciences,"[11] and from speeches and letters to verses on rhetoric for teaching purposes, such as *Synopsis of the Rhetorical Forms*" and "*Synopsis of Rhetoric in Verses.*" The latter's English translation by Walker includes the verses of "On Issus," "On Invention," "On Forms," and "On the Method of Force" and is accompanied by detailed synopses and copious notes. For this book, "On Issues," we have selected "Invention 1" and "Invention 3" to demonstrate Psellos's writing on rhetorical instruction. Readers who wish to read Walker's complete translation of "*Synopsis of Rhetoric in Verses*" can find it in *Michael Psellos on Literature and Art.*[12]

CONTEXT

Michael Psellos's poem *Synopsis of Rhetoric in Verses* (Σύνοψις τῆς ῥητορικῆς διὰ στίχων) was probably composed sometime between 1060 and 1067 CE for the young emperor-to-be Michael VII Doukas. The manuscripts say that its companion-poem, a synopsis of "grammar" (literacy and literature: *Poem.* 6), was written "to the most pious Emperor, lord Michael Doukas, at the command of his father and Emperor, so that with sweetness and contentment he would bear his lessons"; and the *Synopsis* is billed as written "to the same Emperor." Within the poem itself, the recipient is repeatedly addressed as crown bearer, lord, or master (στεφηφόρε, δέσποτα, and ἄναξ), but no name appears.

It is possible that Psellos has reworked material composed much earlier for Constantine IX Monomachos, the emperor who first raised him from obscurity and made him "Consul of the Philosophers."[13] As he says in the *Chronographia,*[14] during the 1040s CE he entertained Constantine with lessons in philosophy and metaphysics, and when the imperial patron grew fatigued with such abstruse matters, "I took up the rhetorical lyre, charmed him with its word-harmonies and rhythms, and led him toward another kind of excellence" with lessons in the rhetorical resources for both style and argument.[15] Psellos concludes the *Synopsis of Rhetoric in Verses* by declaring it "full of sweetness, full of charm, / sweet-speaking, sweet-voiced, and unusually sweet-singing" (ll. 543–44). If this poem is not a reworking of the earlier material presented to Constantine IX, it seems to have been written in the same (or a similar) "charming" and entertaining style.

---

11. Papaionannou 2017, 5.

12. Walker 2017, 31–65.

13. See Westerink (1948, 80).

14. References to oft-read classics in Walker's original chapter, including those by Psellos and Aristotle, use only the title and the passage number without indicating a specific edition. This chapter follows suit.

15. Sewter 1953, Verse 6. 197.

Psellos's synopses of both grammar and rhetoric, as well as a third didactic poem apparently also for Michael Doukas, *Synopsis of the Laws* (*Poem.* 8), are composed in *politikoi stichoi*, a Byzantine term that scholars normally translate as "political verse," though "public verse" might be better. (The adjective *politikos* can be translated as political, civic, public, communal, common, of the city.) Political verse was the basic medium of popular (or "folk") Greek poetry from medieval to modern times; it was recited and sung in taverns, and scrawled as graffiti in the streets of Constantinople; it was used in popular religious poetry, notably the hymns of Symeon the New Theologian at the turn of the eleventh century CE; and, in Byzantine high society from the eleventh century CE on, it became an important medium as well for poetry presented to imperial audiences, especially didactic and civic-ceremonial poetry. The rules of political verse were fairly simple: each line consisted of fifteen syllables, broken into two half-lines of eight and seven syllables respectively, usually with a caesura (a brief pause) between them. Within this two-part line, the rhythm of stressed and unstressed syllables was fairly flexible, though there generally was a major stress on the next to last syllable of the line (perhaps with a rising tone). There was no rhyme, and no set stanzaic structure: the poet composed line-by-line. Political verse was so different from the ancient, classical forms of Greek poetry, and seemingly so loose, that Byzantine scholars were sometimes undecided whether it was really "poetry" at all, or subliterary poetry, or a kind of rhythmic prose. It was the "modern poetry" of Psellos's day.[16]

The "sweet" and charming qualities of Byzantine political verse often do not come through in English translation (without making the English sound bizarre), so it may be helpful to provide a brief snippet, in transliteration, from the *Synopsis* in its original Greek. Here are the poem's first three lines (try reading them aloud, with emphasis on the stress-accents):

> Εἰ μάθοις τῆς ῥητορικῆς / τὴν τέχνην, στεφηφόρε, ἕξεις
> καὶ λόγου δύναμιν, / ἕξεις καὶ γλώττης χάριν, ἕξεις καὶ
> πιθανότητα / τῶν ἐπιχειρημάτων.

In the translation presented in the following pages, this comes out as:

> If you learn the art of rhetoric, crownbearer,
> you'll be an able speaker, and you'll have a graceful tongue,
> and you'll have the most persuasive epicheiremes (arguments).

The translation here partially (if imperfectly) reflects the rhythmic and figural texture of the original, but even a partial reflection frequently is not possible in reasonably "natural"-sounding English. It will help to keep in mind, as you read, that Psellos is in fact writing *verse* with a lively, rhythmic, richly figured style. (In the Greek lines quoted here, one can find anaphora, polysyndeton, isocolon, and perhaps chiasmus.) At its worst, political verse

---

16. For further discussion, see Lauxtermann (1999); Jeffreys (1974); and Beaton (1980); see also Bernard (2014, 243–51) with a discussion of Psellos' poems in political verse.

could take on the hippity-hoppity, repetitive feel of greeting-card doggerel. At its best, it could clip along with the verve, variety, expressiveness, and charm of (say) the best poetry of an Alexander Pope (or even good hip-hop lyrics). Psellos handles it fairly well. It is not difficult to imagine that young Michael Doukas would have been "charmed" enough to "bear his lessons" with "sweetness and contentment," and would have enjoyed listening to, and perhaps reciting, the verses of Psellos's poems on grammar, on rhetoric, and on the laws.

One should not assume, however, that Psellos is writing the same kind of poem as Pope's famous *Essay on Criticism*—though the *Synopsis* is indeed an "essay" of sorts in verse. As the title indicates, Psellos is writing a *synopsis*, an overview, of the material that Michael was supposed to be cheerfully learning in his "lessons" in rhetoric. In essence, the *Synopsis* is a rapid, compressed summary of the contents of the so-called Hermogenian corpus, a collection of rhetorical treatises attributed to the second-century CE rhetorician Hermogenes of Tarsos.[17]

Psellos surveys four of the five treatises attributed to Hermogenes, in the standard order: *On Issues* (1 volume), *On Invention* (4 volumes), *On Forms* (2 volumes), and *On the Method of Force* (1 volume). *On Issues* is concerned with the identification and analysis of the question at issue in a dispute (the στάσις, the precise point of disagreement), and the use of selected "headings" or topics appropriate to the different kinds of issues to generate relevant arguments; *On Invention* is concerned with methods for handling the standard parts of an oration (preface, narration, and proofs), with the fourth volume devoted to figures of speech; *On Forms* is an "advanced" treatise concerned with the detailed analysis of particular stylistic qualities (such as clarity, dignity, vehemence, rapidity); and *On the Method of Force* is, perhaps, a "capstone" treatise (or it was understood as such) on various methods for speaking "forcefully"—that is, with δεινότητα, a hard-to-translate term that basically means "awesomeness" (or "terrifying-ness"), and in late-classical rhetoric generally means something like stunning skillfulness, impressiveness, and virtuosity. In Byzantine rhetorical terminology, moreover, δεινότης is identified with disguised, double, or allusive meaning, or what Psellos calls "paradoxes and profundities" (l. 507).[18]

Of these four Hermogenian treatises, only two are recognized by modern scholars as actually written by Hermogenes: *On Issues* and *On Forms*. The others were added at some point in late antiquity or the early middle ages, perhaps to substitute for actual Hermogenian treatises that had been lost, or perhaps by simple misidentification, or both.[19] Whatever the facts of authorship may be, in Psellos's day all four treatises were believed to have been written by Hermogenes and to comprise the complete, basic course of rhetorical instruction. In the notes to the following translation of the *Synopsis*, the unknown author (or authors) of *On Invention* and *On the Method of Force* is referred to as "Hermogenes"

---

17. See also Papaioannou (2017, 21).

18. Kustas 1973.

19. Kennedy 2005, xiii–xv, 201–03.

(with quotation marks), while the author of the genuine treatises is referred to as Hermogenes (without quotation marks).

The Hermogenian corpus, from *On Issues* through *On the Method of Force*, amounts to 429 pages in the standard earlier modern edition.[20] Psellos reduces it all to 545 lines of verse, which run a mere twenty pages in Westerink's 1992 edition (the text on which this translation is based) —equivalent to perhaps ten pages of prose. So the *Synopsis* is very compressed indeed. This raises a question about how it was meant to be used. In fact, Psellos's rendition of the Hermogenian lore is at times so compressed, so elliptical, that one can scarcely grasp what he is talking about unless one is familiar *already* with the Hermogenian source. This observation suggests that the "synopsis" is meant as a "reminder" (ὑπόμνημα), a set of review-notes set to verse for ease of memorization and review: a pleasant way for young Michael Doukas to recall his lessons. One might infer, then, that the lessons would have been first presented in duller and more detailed form. But that idea does not square so well with a notion that Psellos composed his verse synopses of grammar, rhetoric, and law to beguile the imperial student into "bearing his lessons" with good cheer.

It seems unlikely that Michael Doukas would have read the Hermogenian texts themselves, or would have patiently sat through a "reading" or even a detailed exposition of their contents. Psellos's "portrait" of Michael, at the end of the *Chronographia*, presents him as a shallow dilettante and moral weakling (while pretending to praise him; see the discussion of "figured problems" at ll. 345–47). Aside from Michael's weakness as a student, moreover, the Hermogenian texts are notoriously reader-unfriendly, even for professional scholars (although, apparently, ancient rhetoricians found Hermogenes more serviceable for teaching than his competitors).[21] It is arguable that the Hermogenian texts were never meant, in the first place, to be read by students, and that they were meant, rather, as a technical resource for the rhetoric-teacher. There are, for example, passages where it is quite clear that Hermogenes is addressing himself to professional teachers, and talking *about* but not *to* the student. The Hermogenian texts provided an exposition of terms and concepts to be used in guiding students through their declamation exercises—practice-orations composed in response to the fictive scenarios or "cases" (ὑποθέσεις) given in set "problems" (προβλήματα) —as well as rhetorical-critical study of the canonical orators and writers students were encouraged to take as models for imitation. But declamation was the central, crucial activity: in declamation, the student would put all of his rhetorical knowledge together and actualize it in discourse-creation and performance. (The Greek word for declamation, μελέτη, means "practice, exercise, rehearsal.") Ultimately, the student's ability to declaim, and beyond that to perform in actual public discourse, was more important than his ability to recite rhetorical precepts—though he could, of course, use the precepts to reflect on his own (and others') performances.

---

20. Patillon 2008–2012.
21. Heath 2004, 44.

Psellos closes the *Synopsis* (l. 545) with a reference to "profiting" from "speaking play-fully," παίζων λογικῶς, which could also be rendered (more literally) as "playing discur-sively, rationally, argumentatively"—in other words, playing "games" of speechmaking and debate. He also says the "profit" in this "play" will be aided by (or even derive from) the τεχνύδριον he has provided (l. 541): a "mini-art," an "art in miniature." This suggests that the *Synopsis* is a brief version and "reminder" of the things that Psellos has been saying to Michael in conjunction with his "playful" speaking exercises.

He also says, in mid-synopsis, "Take the overview from me, and then forthrightly ask your questions, / and I will tell you the solution of the problem: / then you will not wonder, lord, at the writer's art, / if you have a quick survey of the whole" (ll. 287–90; presumably the "writer" is Hermogenes). Here the "overview" (σύνοψις) stands forth as an "abbreviat-ed" version of, and replacement for, the whole "art" (τέχνη) embodied in the Hermogenian corpus; and where the "abbreviated" mini-art needs filling out, Michael must ask his ques-tions, "wonder" about things, and receive more detailed explanations. If Michael was at-tentive, there must have been many questions; but if he was not, perhaps he was entertained anyway by the sprightly music of a sometimes-incomprehensible (for him) piece of poetry.

However the text was originally meant to be used, modern readers who are not familiar with the Hermogenian treatises—and few are—may frequently find Psellos's brief ren-ditions too elliptical, too obscure for comfort, and may wish to "ask [their] questions," too. For this reason the translation has been annotated fairly copiously with additional explana-tions. There are also notes that indicate which Hermogenian book and chapter Psellos is re-ferring to, and some that address problems of translation. Readers who wish to undertake a more detailed comparison of Psellos's treatments with the Hermogenian originals now have a full set of English translations available.[22]

This is not the place for a detailed comparison of Psellos with Hermogenes, but the notes do indicate what seem to be occasional divergences, exclusions, modifications, addi-tions, or confusions. A careful examination of what Psellos includes, leaves out, changes, or expands will show that the *Synopsis* is not a mere summary, but an interpretation and adaptation of its source. On one hand, for example, in his treatment of *On Issues* Psellos more or less omits Hermogenes's sometimes-maniacally detailed discussions of the "divi-sion" of each issue into "heads" of argument (which comprises about two-thirds of the text), while focusing more on the general outline of the theory (the subject of the opening two chapters). On the other hand, he omits mention of virtually any chapter from *On In-vention*, which at four volumes is by far the longest Hermogenian treatise, and he adds some non-Hermogenian examples from patristic sources (Basil the Great, Gregory of Nazianzos, and John Chrysostom)—which either are his own additions or a reflection of Byzan-tine teaching practice in his day. His treatment of *On Forms* is accurate and fairly detailed, though he adds no new examples; at one point (l. 475), he finds Hermogenes's treatment of

---

22. Heath 1995; Wooten 1987; Kennedy 2005; see also Patillon, *Corpus Rhetoricum* (French transla-tion with detailed commentary of the entire corpus).

one variant of the "subtle" style dubious. He treats *On the Method of Force* very sketchily. And so forth. One can derive a picture from such details of what Psellos and his contemporaries found more or less useful and more or less intelligible in Hermogenian rhetorical theory. He seems interested in the general idea of στάσις, but not so much the details of Hermogenes's system; he is very much engaged with teaching how to handle the parts of an oration; he is interested in advanced stylistic criticism (something that shows up elsewhere, in his critical essays); and he passes along a few pointers for speaking deftly, selecting about half of what the Hermogenian text discusses.

EDITIONS AND TRANSLATIONS

The translation that follows uses the Greek text of Westerink (1992), based on all eight available manuscripts;[23] numbers in square brackets indicate verse numbers in that edition. I have tried to render it line-by-line as much as possible, so that the line numbers of the translation generally correspond to the line numbers in Westerink. (Psellos does, in fact, generally treat the political-verse line as a unit of meaning, and as a unit of composition.) In addition, I have generally followed Westerink's "paragraph" divisions, again for ease of matching the translation to the Greek original. I have added, as "signposts" in the right-hand margin, the titles of the Hermogenian books where Psellos begins to take them up as well as the Greek term of the Hermogenian "forms." I have generally rendered technical terms in English equivalents, while preserving the Greek term in brackets (e.g., [ὑπολήψεις] for "prejudgments"); the exceptions are terms that have already been absorbed into the English technical vocabulary of rhetoric and are fairly familiar (e.g., metaphor, enthymeme, epicheireme). In the notes, all citations of the Hermogenian source are to the edition of Patillon.

Synopsis of Rhetoric in Similar [i.e., Political] Verses to the Same Emperor

If you learn the art of rhetoric,[24] crownbearer,
you'll be an able speaker,[25] and you'll have a graceful tongue,

---

23. Including Paris, BNF, gr. 1182; Moore 2005, 482.

24. τῆς ῥητορικῆς τὴν τέχνην: *technê*, "art," signifies either a body of techniques/ principles for methodically accomplishing a goal (as in the "arts" of sculpture, music, navigation, engineering, politics, etc.), or—particularly in the case of rhetoric—a *handbook* that offers a systematic exposition of the art's principles (cf. Latin *ars*). In what follows I will generally render *technê* as "art." "Art of rhetoric" here also indicates specifically the Hermogenian corpus.

25. ἕξεις καὶ λόγου δύναμιν: literally "you will have power of speech"; reading δύναμιν here as "power, capacity, ability, faculty." The "power" of discourse is a commonplace in earlier rhetoric; see, e.g., the introductory statements in Dionysios of Halikarnassos' *Roman Antiquities* 1.1.3, Diodoros of Sicily's *Library of History* 1.2.5, and, especially, Hermogenes' *On Forms* 1.1. Cf. also Aristotle, *Rhetoric* 1.2.1.

and you'll have the most persuasive epicheiremes.[26]

On Issues [I.4]

The art surveys political questions,[27]
and a political question, according to the technographer,[28]
is a doubtful matter that is arguable and divisible[29] on both sides,
according to the customs and laws of cities,
concerning the just, the good, and the advantageous.
Indeed the kinds [εἴδη] of rhetoric are just these three—
judicial [δικανικὸν], advisory [συμβουλή], and panegyrical [πανήγυρις] —
for the end of judicial rhetoric is the just,
of panegyrical [πανηγυρικοῦ] the good, and of advisory the advantageous.[30]

A disputable question, my lord, is given
no limit by the art (for that is a matter of law);
but the art establishes the point in question at any time.[31]

Questions differ in their potential,

---

26. ἐπιχείρημα: in rhetorical theory, an argumentative movement composed of linked subarguments and amplifications (compare the *sorites* in logic, composed of linked syllogisms). See note 60, below.

27. Literally, "it is a *theôros* of political *zêtêmata*." Θεωρός seems to echo the Aristotelian definition of rhetoric as "a faculty of observing (δύναμις τοῦ θεωρεῖν) in any given case the available means of persuasion" (*Rhetoric* 1.2.1); thus θεωρός can be understood here as "observer" in the sense of a "surveyor" of the rhetorical resources available for any given "question." Ζήτημα is a technical term in Hermogenes, signifying the political or civic "question" (or "inquiry") with which the rhetor is concerned in a particular case.

28. "the writer of the τέχνη" (i.e., Hermogenes).

29. Μερική: "divisible" into parts, i.e., the particular "headings" of invention that Hermogenes prescribes for different stases (types of issues, such as fact, definition, or quality).

30. These are, of course, the standard three "species"/genres of classical rhetoric. Aristotle's *Rhetoric* calls them δικανικόν ("judicial" discourse); συμβουλευτικόν or δημηγορικόν ("advisory" or "public" discourse, i.e., on questions of policy or action); and ἐπιδεικτικόν ("display"); later rhetorical handbooks tend to prefer the term πανηγυρικόν to ἐπιδεικτικόν (cf. Lauxtermann 1998; also Papaioannou 2013a: 103–13). Modern English translations of these terms (reflecting Latin influence) frequently render them as forensic, deliberative, and epideictic; I have tried to stay closer to the original sense of the Greek and to Byzantine usage.

31. The point here is that the art of rhetoric itself prescribes no predetermined end (or outcome) to the process of disputation, but it identifies the precise point in dispute, the στάσις, and supplies a series of positions for the arguers on opposing sides; the process of disputation can in principle go on indefinitely, but in a trial the ending is set by trial procedure.

for they bear greater and lesser persons [πρόσωπα] and actions [πράγματα].[32]
Often they are inconclusive in either respect,
and then the power of the rhetor is revealed,[33]
when he takes up a case that is weak in either way
and by the power of reasoning strengthens it and prevails.[34]
There are also many ill-formed problems,
which are ill-balanced or even prejudiced in nature;[35]
and there are, moreover, those that are by nature wholly invalid,
as they are one-sided or ultimately insoluble.[36]
Questions are valid,[37] are brought to trial, and are declaimed on
when they involve both a person and an action that admits of judgment,
and that gives rise to persuasive arguments on either side.

Altogether, lord, there are thirteen
issues [στάσεις], as they are called, from the disputation
of rhetors using persuasive epicheiremes.[38]

---

32. Technical terms in *On Issues*, denoting the "persons" (historical figures, such as "Demosthenes," stock characters such as "rich man," etc.) and the "actions" (or "facts") laid down in the set problems for declamation exercises.

33. I am rendering ῥήτωρ "untranslated" as rhetor, since it can mean either "orator" (or "speaker" or "writer") or "rhetorician" (a teacher of rhetoric).

34. I.e., the given facts in a well-formed declamation problem (persons, actions, circumstances) are normally insufficient in themselves to determine the outcome of the case, so that success will depend on the inventional and argumentational powers of the rhetor. A very similar notion is expressed by an anonymous scholar preserved in mss. from the tenth c. and later: rhetorical training consists, he says, of "disputable and evenly balanced problems for the reason that whenever one side of the case is argued with greater strength, the power of the speaker is revealed, and not of the problem itself, which furnishes either side of the case with equal strength" (Walz 1834, 49). This idea is not found in Hermogenes, though one might argue that it is implicit.

35. Hermogenes recognizes three kinds of faulty (yet arguable) declamation problems: the "ill-balanced" (ἑτερορρεπής), the "ill-formed" (κακόπλαστα, e.g., proposing a historical scenario that is contrary to fact), and the "prejudiced" (προειλημμένη, cf. *On Issues* 1.24). Psellos, however, seems to consider the ill-balanced and the prejudiced as types of the ill-formed.

36. Ἀσύστατα: literally "without cohesion, indeterminate, unformed"; Hermogenes deploys this term to mean "invalid" declamation problems that are not capable of producing a determinate issue, and thus are of no use for declamation exercises. Hermogenes identifies eight types of "invalid" issues (*On Issues* 1.14–21), of which Psellos mentions two. (The "one-sided" differs from the "ill-balanced" and "prejudiced," above, as it has no arguments at all on one side.) In the next three lines Psellos paraphrases Hermogenes' criteria for distinguishing coherent or "valid" problems (1.13). It is worth noting that he is here moving through the Hermogenian material in backwards order.

37. I.e., forming a coherent or determinate issue to be argued.

38. Introducing a review of Hermogenes' synopsis-chapter (*On Issues* 2). This etymology from "disputation [τὸ στασιάζειν]" is not Hermogenian. The thirteen *issues* that follow are: (1) conjec-

The first of these is conjecture: this is, master,
an examination that substantiates what is the case from a clear sign,
or from particular suspicions about a person.[39]

The second is definition, as it is called:
an examination of the name for an action.[40]

The third is practical deliberation: it investigates what should be done,
from which it receives its name, crownbearer.[41]

The fourth is counterplea, on grounds of non-liability,
when a forceful accusation demands accountability for some act.[42]

The fifth, in turn, is counterstance: here the defendant
grants the charge that has been brought against him,
and sets against it some good outcome from the very thing that he has done.

If [sixth] someone admits to having committed murder,
he shows that the victim himself deserved it:
he frames a countercharge, and countercharges justly.

If [seventh] he can aptly place the blame on someone else
(if something is to be punished), it is a shift of issue;
but [eighth] if he is without defense, the issue is forgiveness.

---

ture [στοχασμός], (2) definition [ὅρος], (3) practical deliberation [πραγματική], (4) counterplea [ἀντίληψις], (5) counterstance [ἀντίστασις], (6) countercharge [ἀντέγκλημα], (7) shift of issue [μετάστασις], (8) forgiveness [συγγνώμη], (9) letter [ῥητόν] and intent [διάνοια], (10) rhetorical syllogism [συλλογισμὸν ῥητορικόν], (11) conflict of law [ἀντινομία], (12) ambiguity [ἀμφιβολία], and (13) objection [μετάληψις].

39. This line (34) is an exact quote from Hermogenes (*On Issues* 2.1.5 ap. crit.; Patillon treats it as an interpolation); it seems to suggest the headings of "motive and capacity" in developing arguments about the likelihood that a person committed an alleged act. What Psellos makes less than clear is that "conjecture" involves questions of fact, and inquiry into the kinds of proof by which claims about fact can be substantiated—an ἔλεγχος οὐσιοποιός, a process of "examination establishing what is."

40. For example, if it is established that someone killed someone (the question of fact), one may dispute whether the killing was murder, justifiable homicide, an accident, etc. (the question of definition). Psellos (like Hermogenes) is thinking of the defendant, who will seek to put a favorable name on the act he is charged with.

41. I.e., the name of this issue, πραγματική, derives from τὸ πρακτέον, "what should be done"—cf. πρᾶγμα, "action, business" (the main concern of political deliberation).

42. That is, "counterplea" arises when a defendant admits to an action but denies that it was wrong or that he has any legal liability. This is the first of a set of issues (4–8) discussed by Hermogenes under the general heading of "judicial discourse" (δικαιολογία), all of which arise from the position taken by the defendant.

If [ninth] a punishable act is connected with law,[43]
and one side puts forth the letter of the law
while the other sagely takes the law by its intentions, the issue is letter and intent.

If [tenth] some act resists assimilation to the letter of the law,
then one works up a rhetorical syllogism:
this is a comparison of the uncodified to the codified.[44]

If [eleventh] there is a controversy involving two or more laws
and it is a question of selecting not many but one of them,
naturally the issue is conflict of law.

But [twelfth] ambiguity is an issue that proceeds
from the prosody of accent or the parsing of words.[45]

If [thirteenth] there is controversy whether any judgment should be made,[46]
the issue is objection, which you divide as follows,
for codified and uncodified kinds of this occur:
call the codified kind [ἔγγραφον] a complete legal exclusion,
possessing the strength and power of argument from law;
and call the uncodified kind [ἄγραφον] non-legal, for it does not cite law,
but is more rational.[47] In fact two issues,

---

43. Psellos here transitions to the "legal" issues (9–12), which are concerned with the interpretation of laws.

44. This issue deals with extension of a law to novel situations that it was not originally written for (or that it does not directly mention), by "inference" (συλλογισμὸν) from certain features of the act in question to analogous acts explicitly covered by the law (see Hermogenes *On Issues*, 2.11; and Heath (1995, 34), who renders this issue as "assimilation"). Psellos' "rhetorical syllogism" may echo Aristotle's definition of the enthymeme (*Rhetoric* 1.2.8).

45. Psellos has in mind ambiguities in the meanings of written laws, arising from differences in meaning determined by pitch-accent (in words otherwise spelled or pronounced the same) or from different possible ways of parsing a word or phrase.

46. This thirteenth issue constitutes a fourth main type of position, alongside conjecture (στοχασμός), definition (ὅρος), and quality (ποιότης, with its "rational" and "legal" subdivisions); it has to do, in essence, with whether the matter in question can reasonably be brought to trial at all or should simply be dismissed (or, perhaps, transferred to a different venue).

47. The distinction here is between "objection" founded on the charge of παραγραφὴ ("outside/against what is written")—an argument that the case falls outside of written law, or that the charge itself or the procedure is illegal—and "objection" founded on appeals to principles not explicitly encoded in written law, such as notions of appropriate venue or whether there is a prima facie basis for a trial (or a debate). This distinction further corresponds to the division (in Hermogenes) between the "rational" and "legal" subdivisions of the "qualitative" issues—the "rational" issues (3–8) involving the qualitative

practical deliberation and objection, as the art says,48
in a certain way lie between the rational issues and the legal ones,
not as unified wholes, but as composed of elements from both.49

Each of the abovementioned issues
is called by both special [ἰδικοῖς] and generic [γενικοῖς] names:
each is split up into both special and common [κοινοῖς] heads, in a certain way,
of which some belong particularly to the prosecution,
and some to the defense, while the common topics belong to both.

Again, according to another division, the subject-matter of the issues
is in a certain way divided into types, since a speech has genre,
and it is minutely subdivided, with no gap permitted.50
That is the theory of issues, lord.

On Invention 1 [l. 81]

Next you should be told as well about prefaces,
and the invention of the rest of the speech, and figures.51

A speech composed with art, master,
has both body and soul, both head and feet:
the thought is its soul, the diction is its body,
the introductory matter is its head, and the epilogue is its feet.

Indeed there are many topics of prefaces,

---

judgment of an act (in terms of considerations of justice, moral defensibility, mitigating circumstances, etc.), and the "legal" issues (9–12) involving the interpretation of written laws.

48. The remark that follows does not explicitly appear in the Hermogenian text (as we now have it), though it is inferrable from it (see the following note).

49. That is, they may draw on both "rational" and "legal" topics. As Heath's (1995) analysis of Hermogenes' *On Issues* shows, Hermogenes treats the different issues as drawing on overlapping sets of "heads" and topics. Psellos seems here to be recognizing that point, if only glancingly.

50. This short, highly general segment on the subdivision of each issue into headings and topics (ll. 72–79) represents the latter two thirds of Hermogenes' *On Issues* (chapters 3–12), in which the "division" and handling of each issue is discussed in detail; Psellos has explicitly "covered" only Hermogenes' introductory discussion (chaps. 1–2). Psellos's mention of an "other division" appears to invoke the Aristotelian notion of ἴδια and κοινὰ from the *Rhetoric*, especially Aristotle's treatment of the ἴδια belonging to the advisory, epideictic, and judicial species/genres in book 1—though this account does not really square well with the treatment of topics in Hermogenian issue-theory.

51. Psellos here begins his overview of the four books of the Pseudo-Hermogenian treatise *On Invention*; Book 1 is concerned primarily with the "invention" of prefaces; the other books are concerned with "the rest of the speech, and figures."

but Hermogenes writes in his treatise of just four kinds.

[First, the topic] from prejudgment of persons and actions: one should, with respect to prejudgment of the matter at hand, compose prefaces that give thanks or express regret.[52]

[Second,] from division:[53] this is such,
master, that when two crimes have been committed,
and each of them is to be judged and punished,
we divide and compose a preface such as this:
if this person is to be punished even for one of these crimes,
how much should he be chastised on account of both?
And likewise for the second and third types,
master, of this topic of the preface:
division from prejudgment and from considerations of time.[54]

Again, the art establishes a third topic of prefaces,
which it designates as "from abundance,"[55]
as when accusing someone of murder I add
that I could accuse him of sacrilege as well—
a greater and worse crime than the first.

The fourth topic of prefaces is from the occasion [τοῦ καιροῦ],
as when one claims in public proceedings that what is sought
has come to pass already in events that have transpired.[56]

A whole preface consists of these four parts:
opening, elaboration, proposition,

---

52. The topic of ὑπόληψις, "prejudgment" (*On Invention* 1.1; "supposition," Kennedy 2005, 5; "préjugé," Patillon), involves opening with a *response* to existing attitudes toward "the matter at hand," or in other words the givens of the case: insofar as they can be regarded as good or bad, the speaker can open with expressions of thanks or grieving.

53. In *On Invention* 1.2 "division (ἐκ διαιρέσεως)" appears as "subdivision (ἐξ ὑποδιαιρέσεως) ("subordination," Kennedy 2005, 17)," of which "Hermogenes" recognizes the three types mentioned here. The idea is to amplify the seriousness of the matter in question by invoking "subdivisions" or subsidiary considerations.

54. All three types of "division" involve cases with multiple misdeeds; the second involves repeat malefactors whose known bad past can be discussed, and the third looks to "time" as it involves repeat malefactors who should be dealt with "once and for all," so that their crimes will no longer be repeated.

55. ἐκ περιουσίας: *On Invention* 1.3 (Patillon: "*a fortiori*"; Kennedy 2005, 23: "superfluity"). The idea is that the speaker *could* indict the accused for an even greater crime than he actually is charged with.

56. *On Invention* 1.4.

and finally the closing, which completes the preface.[57]

A preface is adequately amplified
by doubling a word, or doubling a colon.[58]

The four parts may be illustrated with an example, thus:[59]
"What memorial of martyrs would be satisfactory, for one who loves martyrs?"
This is the opening of the speech. Next observe the other parts:
"For the honoring of martyrdom is an act of goodwill to the Lord."[60] This clearly is an
elaboration of the opening.
"With speech, therefore, honor him who has been martyred."[61]
This clearly is the proposition. Next see the closing:
". . . so that you yourself would willingly become a martyr."[62]
It is called a closing, since it is a final part
in which the whole preface seems to come to rest,[63]
and also an elaboration of the proposition,
which we do to venture an additional remark as we embark—
concerning which, I shall teach you the progression of the speech.[64]

---

57. πρότασις, κατασκευή, ἀξίωσις, βάσεως: On Invention 1.5. "Hermogenes'" third term is ἀπόδοσις, "which is an ἀξίωσις." Ἀξίωσις seems to signify an evaluative statement, or an announcement of the speaker's central claim. "Hermogenes" says that the "more political" (as opposed to "panegyrical") kind of preface may consist of a "plain ἀξίωσις," i.e., a simple announcement of the proposition the speaker intends to argue for (106–07). Κατασκευή, which (as a rhetorical term) usually signifies "confirmation" or "proof," here seems to signify any sort of supporting statement, development, or elaboration. See Kennedy (2005: 9n9; 27nn40, 44).

58. On the definition of a colon, see above, n5.

59. The example that follows is not, of course, from "Hermogenes": Psellos quotes from Basil the Great's very popular On the Forty Martyrs of Sebasteia, though not with complete accuracy (see below). For the original see *Homily* 19 (PG 31, 508–25 [508b1–4 and 6–7]), read on the martyrs' feast day, March 9 of the Byzantine calendar.

60. Psellos compresses Basil's statement, which in its full form is (roughly), "for the honor paid by fellow-servants to the good bears proof of our goodwill to our common Lord" (PG 31, 508b2–4).

61. Again, Psellos loosely paraphrases Basil's language: "With sincerity call blessed him who has borne martyrdom" (PG 31, 508b6–7).

62. Here Psellos actually expands Basil's briefer phrase, "so that you would voluntarily die a martyr" (PG 31, 508b7), which is a continuation of the preceding line. The only locution in common to both Psellos' and Basil's versions is τῇ προαιρέσει, "voluntarily" ("by choice").

63. βαίνειν ἔοικε, literally "seems to walk on," with a notion of the preface coming to rest sententiously (with "panegyrical" flourishes) in its βάσις. Cf. the perfective senses of βαίνειν as "stand" (or "stand on a base"); and the senses of βάσις as a "step, measured movement, rhythmical close," and also "base" or "pedestal."

64. According to "Hermogenes" (106–07), the βάσις takes on a panegyrical or "epiphonematic" function when it gives a reason for the proposition (ἀξίωσις). An ἐπιφώνημα, in rhetoric, is a sententious

And that is a brief art of prefaces for you.

On Invention 3 [l. 175]

The preconfirmation (for this must be mentioned too)
is called the preliminary part of confirmation;[65]
and this also should be taught to you with examples,
not from the Demosthenic writings, but from those of the Theologian.
For this masterful philosopher and rhetor,
when impelled to confirm God's monarchy,
set forth all three heads of his argument:
"There are," he said, "three ancient doctrines concerning God:
anarchy, polyarchy, and finally monarchy."[66]
The presentation of these three headings, then,
is a preconfirmation artistically set forth.

There is, too, a kind of rebuttal called "forcible,"[67]
when we take up our opponents' strongest argument
and turn it against them, as though demonstrated by themselves,
as Chrysostom did in his *Philogonios*.[68]
When he was introducing his argument on the mysteries,
He barred the unrepentant from coming to communion,
as some maintained that they would not

"added remark" used to finish off a passage with a flourish. Psellos conceives this as a flourish performed as a speaker completes his preface and "embarks on" or "goes into" the body of the speech.

65. Psellos is now moving to the subject-matter of *On Invention* 3, which deals with methods of κατασκευή, "confirmation/proof " of one's case; προκατασκευή, "preconfirmation," is the subject-matter of 3.2. Preconfirmation, like the "preliminary statement" (προκατάστασις) of a narrative, is in essence what modern handbooks call a "forecast" statement of what is to come in a particular section of a discourse.

66. Gregory Nazianzos, *On the Son* = *Or.* 29.2.

67. Βίαιον: *On Invention* 3.5 (though it is the third chapter, according to the text of "Hermogenes" and followed here by Psellos). It seems odd, to the modern mind, to move directly to "rebuttal" from "preconfirmation" without taking up "confirmation" itself. However, since the Hermogenian *On Issues* generally treats the actual arguments in a case as arising from the *denial* of an accusation, and generally organizes its issuesystem around the positions of *defense*, it may in fact be logical to think of the "confirmation" (or "proof") of a case as starting from λύσις, "rebuttal" (or, more literally, "release, loosening, undoing" of the charge). It is also possible that Psellos is taking λύσις in the more general sense of a "solution" to a problem (i.e., "loosening" or "untying" a knot).

68. In what follows, Psellos "quotes" very loosely from John Chrysostom's *On the Blessed Philogonios* (PG 48 755.21–23). For an English translation of the passage, see Harkins (1982, 180–81) (*Homily* 6.35).

submit to communion every day, but only once a year.
The masterful teacher, he of the tongue called golden,
forcefully replied, "this itself is a grievous error,
since you neither purify yourself nor make progress toward complete purification
when you partake of the holy mysteries just one time."

    In a speech, the heading [κεφάλαιον] of the case
is introduced either by us or our opponents,
the latter of which requires a wholly artistic and embellished rebuttal.[69]
It is introduced artistically in "four-wheeled" fashion,
with the proposition and support, a counterproposition,
and an oppositional rebuttal from the counterproposition.
The proposition introduces the support,
and the support is the opponent's argument,
while the counterproposition is a promise of rebuttal,
after which the rebuttal arises from epicheiremes.

    The epicheireme confirms the rebuttal,
and elaboration [ἐργασία] is a function of epicheiremes,
just as the enthymeme is, in turn, [a function] of elaboration, and the epenthymemes
of proenthymemes.[70]
From manner, person, time, place, and cause—
but primarily from the facts themselves, for in them lies the subject-matter,[71]
the elaboration gathers the preliminary arguments

---

69. *On Invention* 3.4. Here Psellos (with "Hermogenes") continues the theme of refutative (or defensive) strategies as the starting-points of "confirmation"; what follows is a technique for developing "headings" of argument introduced by the opponent.

70. Psellos is jumping around in the Hermogenian chapters on epicheiremes, enthymemes, and ἐργασία (*On Invention* 3.5–9). "Hermogenes," having taught that λύσις is "confirmed" by epicheiremes, says that ἐργασία "confirms" (or "elaborates," κατασκευάζει) the epicheireme, and that the enthymeme "confirms" (κατασκευάζει again) the ἐργασία (3.8.151). The epicheireme, in the loosest sense an "argument," is commonly conceived in rhetorical treatises as a five-step movement consisting of "a proposition, supporting reason, proof of the reason, embellishment, and conclusion" (Kennedy 2005, 85). An enthymeme is a stylistically pointed summing-up of a claim and its proof, often functioning as a "cap" to a passage of discussion (such as an ἐργασία consisting of examples, or, even, a bundle of subordinate enthymemes), and is often stated in antithetical form (see below); thus the supporting-reason-plus-proof part of an epicheireme can be understood as an enthymeme in itself, and an ἐργασία can be understood to be summed up, "confirmed," or *completed* by an enthymeme also, so that the epicheireme can be understood as being composed of enthymematic parts. An "epenthymeme" is an additional enthymeme added as a supplement (or embellishment) to a preceding ("pro") enthymeme (3.9.152).

71. Ὕλη, "wood," or raw material, i.e., to be carved or worked upon (*On Invention* 3.6.2). Psellos seems to differ from "Hermogenes," who seems to have in mind something like the Aristotelian notion of "material cause."

and is fortified with illustration and examples,
and comparisons of lessers, greaters, equals, and opposites.
The natural form of enthymemes is drawn
from every circumstance by means of comparisons;
the epenthymeme is a doubled enthymeme.[72]

You must use objections [ἐνστάσει] and counter-rejoinders [ἀντιπαραστάσει]
in all cases,[73] for they are serviceable in their way,
but the objection is more confrontational,
and introduces denial and rebuttal of the act in question, while the counter-rejoinder
is more subtle.

Thus, if someone should say, "You were not required to kill,"
he has taken up a counterstance [ἀντίστασιν] that rejects the act;[74]
but if someone says, "It may have been necessary, but not in such a manner,"
he has spoken a counter-rejoinder, a more moderate rebuttal.
But what should be brought first to questions in dispute
is impossible to say; judge this according to your reason.
However, a counter-rejoinder smooths the way.[75]

The so-called "from a beginning until its end"
is the most essential heading of them all,[76]
and it is elaborated in different ways—

---

72. See n. 60. The "epenthymeme" is an enthymeme "added onto" ("epi") an enthymeme.

73. *On Invention* 3.4. The "objection" or ἔνστασις is in essence a denial of some proposition, thereby putting it ἐν στάσει (in dispute); the "counter-rejoinder" or ἀντιπαράστασις answers the opponent's counterstatement to the objection, at which point the issue becomes more precise.

74. This is, apparently, counterstance functioning as an ἔνστασις, "objecting" to a claim that the defendant had acted in self-defense.

75. The interesting points here—which seem to be Psellos' additions—are that ἀντιπαράστασις is preferable to flat ἔνστασις and that one does not begin a process of argumentation by flatfootedly declaring one's thesis (the sort of thing commonly recommended in modern textbooks). Rather, one first engages with an opponent's position, establishing the precise issue to be resolved through ἀντιπαράστασις, and then unfolding a *lusis* by means of epicheiremes, each elaborated with ἐργασία and enthymemes.

76. Τὰ δ' ἀπ' ἀρχῆς λεγόμενα μέχρις αὐτοῦ τοῦ τέλους: *On Invention* 3.10.154–58. "Hermogenes" calls it ἀπ' ἀρχῆς ἄχρι τέλους, "from beginning to end." Psellos' version of the name suggests that this topic has to do with a sequence of events treated as an entelechial unfolding from an originating event [ἀρχή] to its logical or necessary outcome [αὐτὸ τὸ τέλος]. It has relevance for practical deliberation, which tries to project the probable results of a proposed action, as well as for any discourse, including the narration of a judicial discourse, or history, where one would need to narrate a rationally coherent sequence of events and represent characters, very much in the manner of an Aristotelian plot; thus a discussion of style and prosôpopoïïa comes into play.

not with circumstantial details, but with various partitions, extended periods
delivered in a single breath [πνεύμασι], and tightly-woven periods.[77]
Each subdivision accomplishes a characterization,
and finishes artistically with a supposition.[78]
In a practical deliberation, this so-called heading
of "from a beginning until its end" is difficult to refute;
use the headings of objection mainly.[79]

    The arrangement of epicheiremes, lord,
is of two kinds: demonstrative [ἀποδεικτική] and panegyrical [πανηγυρικωτέρα].[80]
The former is judicial, and requires
an especially contestatory style of civic discourse;
the latter is altogether beautiful and brilliant, and colors the discourse.
If, then, a speech includes both kinds of arrangement,
save the more brilliant kind for last.
"Definition, counterdefinition, ratiocination and rebuttal
are four names, but with two functions,"[81]
for ratiocination and definition derive their power from the same things,
as do counterdefinition and rebuttal of ratiocination.
When the speech is setting forth the subject-matter,
the ratiocination itself and its rebuttal
follow from the matter and come after it,

---

77. I.e., one does not elaborate this heading by adding more circumstantial details, but by breaking it into numerous small parts, which can be done (says "Hermogenes") with various figures, and by using complex sentence-structures. In rhetorical terms, a "period delivered in a single breath" (πνεῦμα) is a unit of oratorical prose rhythm. Composition by πνεῦμα lends itself to a paratactic, "additive" style. A period (περίοδος) is, of course, a "periodic" (hypotactic/cumulative as opposed to paratactic/additive) sentence. Both πνεῦμα and περίοδος are discussed as "figures" in *On Invention* 4.3, 4.4.

78. Πλαστόν: a fictive epicheireme added at the end of a "beginning-to-end" sequence, as a striking way of rounding out the facts (*On Invention* 3.11). "Hermogenes" does not suggest, as Psellos seems to, that a πλαστόν should be added to *every* subdivision. Psellos seems to be thinking of the uses of "beginning-to-end" in history-writing or poetry, and of the "cuttings" as scenes with characters making speeches.

79. *On Invention* 3.12. "Objection," μετάληψις, is not a topic of invention but the general *issue* of arguing for dismissal or transference of a proceeding; it functions here as a means of dismissing an opponent's version of the facts (his story "from beginning to end") as prima facie improbable or inadmissible or otherwise defective (e.g., there are no witnesses or other evidence to confirm the story).

80. *On Invention* 3.13.

81. *On Invention* 3.14. This is a quotation of the opening sentence of the chapter, slightly rearranged to fit the meter of "political verse."

while definition and counterdefinition come first.[82]
Learn, as well, the embellishment [διασκευὴν] of the problem,[83]
for vivid representation of the action is subtle,
as I said before concerning narrative.
Here the rhetor must aim at probability.
Even if embellishment is possible twice, or often,
it should not be used indiscriminately, but should be managed economically,
so that you won't be thought vulgar for using it all the time.
But if you wish to bring it into a speech at a certain point,
you can derive a pretext for discussion from a single word:
for example, if you say "find me so great a number,"
it is available to your argument, lord, from history.[84]

On Invention 4 [l. 269]

The first figure of speech is opposition [ἀντίθετον],
which provides you with a twofold line of thought:[85]
from a question of fact in its natural form
it takes the opposite thought to its completion.
For example, "it is day, for if it were not day . . .

---

82. Psellos's compression makes the point here somewhat murky. The idea is that counterdefinition [ἀνθορισμὸς] follows from definition [ὅρος], and rebuttal from ratiocination; that definition/counterdefinition (of the established facts, actions) necessarily precedes rebuttal/ratiocination [λύσις/συλλογισμός]; and that all of this requires a prior narration of the facts. "Hermogenes" suggests that definition and ratiocination, on one hand, can be confirmed by "the same epicheiremes," while, on the other, counterdefinition and rebuttal can likewise be confirmed by "the same epicheiremes" appropriate to them (3.14; Kennedy 2005, 124–25).
83. *On Invention* 3.15. The "problem" [πρόβλημα] is the set-problem for a declamation exercise. What Psellos and "Hermogenes" have in mind are quasi-digressive amplifications on particular points, chiefly in the form of narratives drawn from history (when they are relevant), and that "embellish" the bare facts with vivid, emotive, poetic, or exaggerated (but still credible) description. This was typically treated in ancient handbooks as a function of epilogues, though the epilogue proper is not treated (or even mentioned) by "Hermogenes" (Kennedy 2005: 127).
84. A very elliptical rendition of an example from "Hermogenes" (3.15), where discussion (in a declamation) of the sacrifice of 300 prisoners calls up a further discussion of the 300 Spartans who died at Thermopylae, which is then employed as a "commonplace" to embellish the vivid description of the sacrifice and to heighten the sense of outrage. The "single word" that provides the pretext is "300."
85. *On Invention* 4.1–2. Psellos now turns to the subject-matter of book 4, which is concerned with figures of speech.

then it is day."[86] That is the figure of opposition.

The period [περίοδος] is a key to epicheiremes,[87]
bundling together copious thoughts and figures,
and their overall conception, with accurate art.
Various declensions make up a period,
but the vocative delivered in a single breath is not the place for one:[88]
[for example,] "O, you—what name could anyone properly call you by?"[89]
He [Demosthenes] has not bundled it, but strung it out, so it's not a period.
There are many types of periods, master.
There is the monocolon, and the double too,
and there's the tricolon as well, and the quadruple.[90]
A period can also take chiasmus,[91] or be inverted in some way.
The examples of all this are clear.[92]
Take the overview from me, and then forthrightly ask your questions,
and I will tell you the solution of the problem:
then you will not wonder, lord, at the writer's art,
if you have a quick survey of the whole.

There is also the figure of the rhetorical period delivered in one breath:[93]
it is a composition of speech completing a whole thought
in cola [κῶλα] and phrases [κόμματα] smaller than cola.
The hexasyllabic or briefer phrase
is counted the same as a poetic measure,
while anything above a trimeter up to a heroic verse
is considered a straight, extended colon.

---

86. Again Psellos gives an elliptical rendition of "Hermogenes'" example. As "Hermogenes" gives it, it is: "*Since it is day, that must be done. This is the action in question. And the opposite of this is, For if it was not day, but night, perhaps it should not be done; but since it is day, it is appropriate to do it*" (4.2). As Kennedy notes (2005, 141n207), this is a standard example in ancient (especially Stoic) logic; Psellos apparently regards it as familiar enough to be merely mentioned in abbreviated form.
87. *On Invention* 4.3.
88. *On Invention* 4.4–5, on "a period delivered in a single breath" (πνεῦμα) and its "extension" (τάσις), are both glancingly alluded to here, and discussed more fully below. Psellos is here echoing "Hermogenes'" language (at 4.3).
89. Demosthenes 18.22 (*On The Crown*), as quoted (accurately) by "Hermogenes" (4.3).
90. That is, periods composed of single, double, triple, and quadruple cola.
91. The figure of "crossover" parallelism (e.g., "fair is foul and foul is fair"); the name derives from the Greek letter χ.
92. I.e., in "Hermogenes."
93. *On Invention* 4.4.

There are two types of artistic periods delivered in a single breath:
either you take one thought and variously ring the changes on it
in cola and phrases; or you take many different thoughts
and elaborate each one in phrases and cola.

Vigor of speech [ἀκμὴ λόγου] (for you must learn this too) is
a quick change of figures within a period delivered in a single breath;
but there is also a vigor of thoughts [ἀκμὴ νοημάτων],
when, having filled out a thought with a period delivered in a single breath,
you slip unnoticed into another, and thence another.[94]

The dilemma [διλήμματον] is a striking figure of speech:[95]
when, having split a question into two alternatives,
each of which is a trap,[96] you ask your opponents to reply,
either you render them unable to speak,
or else they rashly speak and you defeat them.

Echo [παρήχησις] is the figure of similar words
that sound the same, lord, with different meanings,
as when Xenophon said, "He persuades [πείθει] Peithias."[97]

The circle [κύκλος] is rounded off, if someone puts the same pronoun,
or another part of speech, at the beginning and end [of a construction].[98]

There are two types of additional remark [ἐπιφωνήματος].[99]
The first is a statement interjected from outside the subject at hand,
by which you take up a sort of accompaniment,[100]

---

94. Ἀκμὴ, usually translated as "florescence" or "vigor" (as a stylistic term), literally means "zenith" or "culminating point"; "Hermogenes" seems to think of it, in vigor of speech, as a process of varying the figural constructions employed in the "extension" of a single idea in a single *pneuma* (i.e., ringing the changes on a single idea); and, in vigor of thought, as a process of building to a climactic statement by moving "unnoticed" from one idea to another, as one moves from one *pneuma* to another, while seeming to reiterate the same idea. The notion of an "extended *pneuma*" glancingly alludes to *On Invention* 4.5, on τάσις (a "chapter" consisting of a single brief paragraph).

95. *On Invention* 4.6. "Striking" here translates δριμύς, more literally "sharp, piercing, keen, shrewd."

96. Ἀμφίκρημνον, literally "having cliffs all around," or in other words "hemmed in on all sides."

97. *On Invention* 4.7. Πείθει τὸν Πειθίαν is a pun on "the Pythian," an epithet of Apollo. "Figure" in line 312 translates κάλλος, literally "beauty," which Psellos repeats from "Hermogenes," and which Kennedy (2005, 173) renders as "ornament."

98. *On Invention* 4.8.

99. *On Invention* 4.9. As noted above, an ἐπιφώνημα is a sentencious "added remark" used to finish off a passage with a flourish.

100. ἐπᾴδων, literally "sing along to."

and venture cautiously an additional commentary.
A brief Homeric example should be mentioned:
"And together with Euros, Notos roused and rushed headlong,
and stormy Zephyr, and sky-born Boreas,
and they covered with clouds the land and sea alike;
and down from heaven rushed the night."[101] This last item
is an additional remark brought in from outside the subject,
alien yet legitimate (as you may wish to understand),
venturing to derive the night from heaven.[102]
Some recognize a second [type of] additional remark,
when, having extended in varied cola a period delivered in a single breath,
one adds a colon that pulls everything together,
as in Homer's elegant description of Ajax,
which recapitulates everything with a single colon:
"One evil after another was hammered on."[103]
A third [type of] additional remark is quite acceptable if you bring in
metaphorical expressions from what has been said earlier
and properly apply them to make comparisons.

    A metaphor [τροπὴ] is the use of a common word
for both the presented fact and something else that is introduced.[104]

    Dignified language [σεμνὸς λόγος] beautifies a name with a name:[105]
for if you call a prostitute a courtesan,[106] you transform her;
you dignify what she is called by artfully translating it.
But if some wholly artless statement has not been properly prepared for,

---

101. *Odyssey* 5.295–96 (Psellos's ll. 322–23), and 293–94 (ll. 324–25); describing the east, south, west, and north winds respectively, when stirred up by Poseidon. Psellos modifies Homer's lines to fit the meter of political verse—and follows "Hermogenes" in "quoting" them out of order for the sake of illustrating ἐπιφώνημα.

102. "Alien" because "night" is not properly part of a description of the winds; "legitimate" as a supplement because it, like them, is part of a description of the darkening sky. Kennedy (2005, 175n256) considers this example in "Hermogenes" to be unilluminating; Psellos likewise seems to be struggling to explain it.

103. *Iliad* 16.111.

104. *On Invention* 4.10; "Hermogenes'" point is that a "trope" is a word "which can be applied in common to the subject and a subject brought in from elsewhere" (4.10; Kennedy 2005, 179). Psellos' highly compressed rendition of this idea makes it fairly obscure.

105. *On Invention* 4.11.

106. That is, call a πόρνη a ἑταίρα.

call it bad taste [κακόζηλον] for what is fitting in a speech.[107]

There is also a figured kind of problem [πρόβλημα τῶν ἐσχηματισμένων],
either by implication, indirection, or opposition,
and implication is more rhetorical by far.[108]

Comparative problems absolutely must be described for you.
In conjecture, and in motive and capacity, it is easy: what the "I" and
the "you" have ascribed to motive easily produce a comparison for you, crownbearer.[109]

And that is the end of the *Invention* for you.

---

107. *On Invention* 4.12. Κακόζηλον, more literally, means "bad imitation" or tasteless emulation of γενικώτατος λόγος, "most proper speech" or speech most suitable to its kind (or genre).

108. On Invention 4.13. "Figured problems" are cases for declamation exercises in which the ostensible subject of the speech is actually a cover for something else. In the "by implication" type (κατ' ἔμφασιν) the speaker hints at things that cannot be spoken openly (i.e., because they are too shameful or too politically dangerous); in the "by indirection" type (κατὰ πλάγιον) the speaker's arguments lead to different conclusions than those they are ostensibly proving; and in the "by opposite" type (κατ' ἐναντίον) the speaker says the opposite of what he means. Kennedy (2005, 189–93) translates these types as "by implication," "deflected," and "by the opposite"; Patillon renders them as "by allusion" (par allusifs), by indirection" (par indirects), and "by the contrary" (par le contraire).

109. *On Invention* 4.14: προβλήματα συγκριτικά, "comparative problems" (i.e., for declamation exercises) involve the weighing of alternatives, usually at the issue of conjecture or definition; "motive and capacity" are subheads of conjecture.

7.2 Byzantine, c. 12th Century CE, Byzantium

The Alexiad of Anna Komnene: Introduction and Commentary

Ellen Quandahl

INTRODUCTION

Anna Komnene (Dec. 2 or 3, 1083–c.1154 CE), a royal princess, rhetorically trained historiographer, and patron of letters, is the author of the *Alexiad*, a multi-volume history of the reign of her father, Byzantine emperor Alexios I Komenos (ruled 1081–1118 CE). The work is an encomiastic account of Alexios coming to power through usurpation and defending and preserving an empire challenged by both external and internal enemies. It builds on an unfinished account, *Materials for History*, undertaken by Anna's husband, Nikephoros Bryennios, which had been requested by her mother, Empress Eirene Doukas. Often writing in the first person, Anna draws attention to her rhetorical training, articulates a theory of history writing, and mourns her imperial parents. Using atticizing Greek diction, with veiled and explicit references to prior texts, the work presents all aspects of civic and religious culture—diplomacy, administering and defending the empire, the making of war and alliances, and the writing of history—as fundamentally performative and rhetorical.

The *Alexiad* is often military in flavor, with a Thucydidean emphasis on battle campaigns, strategies, formations, and individual scenes of combat. These are given an epic, heroic cast, as the echo of *Iliad* in Anna's title suggests, and built out through a layering of references to the texts of Greek paideia and Byzantine culture. Given that pagan literature (*thurathen paideia*, literature from "outside the door") was not widely available to women, one of Anna's achievements, rather obvious but not much commented on, is her use of that literature in an unapologetic way. At the same time, she represents her parents as Orthodox Christians, and in the relatively few passages in which Alexios is not on campaign, Anna depicts him confronting heresies at home. She offers insights into the roles of women, with her grandmother serving as Alexios's co-partner in government and her mother accompanying him on campaign. Battles, heresies, and Anna's first-person observations and mourning—these provide the overall experience of the work.

The locus of Anna's writing is the women's monastery, Kecharitomene, described in its founding document, or *typikon*, written under the signature of Empress Eirene. Anna served as protectress of the monastery, only taking the veil at her death. There she composed the *Alexiad* from the 1130s until perhaps 1148 CE, and, according to her eulogist, gathered a circle of scholars and commissioned commentaries on some works of Aristotle.[110]

---

110. Tornikes 1970, 283.

Anna is also known through a preface to her last will and testament, thought to be written by her;[111] through the long funeral speech for her composed by Georgios Tornikes; and through cameo appearances in two near-contemporary histories, by John Zonaras and Niketas Choniates. The secondary literature, often eliding Zonaras and Choniates, constructs an account of her plotting with her mother after Alexios's death to wrest the crown from her brother John, failing, and living in bitter exile in the convent for the rest of her life. This sexualized account of female anger, forwarded by Gibbon in *The Decline and Fall*, has been frequently repeated, and much scholarship has taken a gendered and psychological cast.[112]

CRITICAL APPROACHES: TRANSLATIONS AND COMMENTARY

Pioneering work on the *Alexiad* appeared in English in 1928, just as the field of Byzantine studies was beginning to coalesce, with a translation by Elizabeth S. Dawes and a magisterial study the following year by Georgina Buckler. E. R. A. Sewter offered a new translation with scholarly apparatus in 1969, updated by Peter Frankopan in 2009. In 1996, James Howard-Johnston attributed much of the *Alexiad* to Nikephoros Bryennios, based on the notion that Anna would not have had knowledge of military history. In 2000, in the volume *Anna Komnene and Her Times*, Ruth Macrides offered a measured response, suggesting that Anna's history is predominantly military because she takes up her late husband's unfinished work, and because she writes a new form of history, as epic, inflected with the Homeric world of arms and men, at a time when epic romance was in vogue. Also in that volume are, among others, Barbara Hill's feminist reading, and Paul Magdolino's contextualizing of competing praises of emperors against which Anna writes. Peter Frankopan's 2012 volume *The First Crusade: the Call from the East* reads the *Alexiad* as the "most important and difficult" of valuable histories of the period and notes its distinctive geographic focus, which, we could add, maps an empire that crosses the boundaries of "east" and "west." In 2014 Penelope Buckley, reading with attention to genre and antecedents, argued that the *Alexiad* is a work of literary artistry that builds a legend of Alexios. In 2016, Leonora Neville made a case for Anna as affecting emotion and writing lamentation (*threnos*), a female genre, to enable her to take on the masculine genre of history writing. Her 2012 book on the *Materials for History* reads Bryennios as using a Roman moral framework to criticize Alexios and Anna rebutting him through archaic Greek rather than Roman cultural imagery. With the exception of this book, several pieces on *ekphrasis* of persons, Stratis Papioannou's translation and commentary on the will, and a rhetorical introduction by Quandahl and Jarratt, little specifically rhetorical work on Anna Komnene has been done, though it is now recognized that in Byzantium "rhetoric was the point at which all other branches of learning met."[113]

---

111. Papioannou 2012, 108.
112. For example, see E.R.A. Sewter (1969, 11, 13–14).
113. Magdolino 1993, 335.

The selections and analysis that follow are anchored in Papioannou's observation that in Byzantium "rhetoric commanded protocols of the self."[114] That is, to compose a self, and generally to author, meant to speak in the voices of others. From their earliest training in the progymnasmata, preliminary exercises, Byzantine students learned to express themselves, their subject matters, and their emotions through the voices of exemplary others, using earlier texts that were culturally significant and that formed "the horizon of expectations" of learned audiences.[115] That insight makes it possible to move out from speculative readings of Anna's motives and emotions and to read the whole history as innovating by using and transforming prior texts.

While we readily note the reminder of *Iliad* in Anna's title, the allusion to Herodotus in her opening lines, and references to Greek tragedy and the Bible, making the work familiar and readable, other references to works not much in evidence in our rhetorical scholarship may go unnoticed. Most important among Anna's predecessors, for example, is rhetor and historian Michael Psellos, to whom attention is paid below. Even where emotion is concerned, in Anna's day, as in ours, the texts of culture inflect their construction. Readers have criticized Anna's expressions of her grief and Alexios's suffering. But Byzantine precedents construct as noble the enduring of sorrow and surmounting of private grief in a public text.[116] Imperial panegyrics of other emperors thematize suffering and toil, against which the *Alexiad* asserts the patriotic suffering of Alexios.[117]

The old notion that Byzantine writing was "Byzantine"—obscurantist—then, may have to do with ways of reading or not reading its astounding hybridity. As Jeffrey Walker has suggested, texts that may be unreadable to us might have produced a polyvalent "semiotic cloud" for their Byzantine readers.[118] To read Anna as constructing her lively and feeling persona and her material out of a cultural past takes us into the heart of Byzantine rhetorical practices.

In its totality, the *Alexiad* presents the reign of Alexios and history itself as rhetorical—kairotic, polytropic, and layered with the past. That global use and view of rhetoric is in evidence in the excerpts here, chosen to illustrate the following distinctively rhetorical and overlapping features of the work: writing in the first person, citationality, rhetorics of gender, geographic location and point of view, figured discourse, a theory of historiography and rhetorical culture, and ekphrasis. Many other rhetorical categories could be adduced. Lamentation (*thrēnos*), imperial praise (*basilikos logos*), comparison (especially of persons) (*synkrisis*), direct speech and quoted documents, for example, warrant scholarly attention. Nearly all of the forms that Byzantine students would have learned through the progymnasmata are in evidence.[119]

---

114. Papioannou 2013, 23.

115. Ibid., 19.

116. Ibid., 213–14.

117 . Magdolino 2000, 23.

118. Walker 2004, 58.

119. For translations of these exercises see Kennedy (2003). On the presence of progymnasmata forms in *Alexiad* see Mullet (2006, 1–28). For overviews of Byzantine rhetorical education, see Valiavitcharska (2013, 237–60), and Whitby (2010, 239–50).

The *Alexiad* is rhetorically significant, then, because it is the work of a historiographer who is trained in Greek rhetoric. She has been called the first female historian and one who writes from a distinctly Byzantine perspective, offering "an interpretation of this period that is very different from those of western chroniclers."[120] She is keenly aware of the designs of Europeans on Constantinople and its territories. A work that crosses borders, the *Alexiad* troubles notions of "western" and "eastern" rhetoric.

Excerpts from the *Alexiad*, translated by E. R. A. Sewter, revised by Peter Frankopan[121]

Prologue, from sections 1 and 4, pages 3–4, 7—First person writing and citationality

Time, which flies irresistibly and perpetually, sweeps up and carries away with it everything that has seen the light of day and plunges it into utter darkness, whether deeds of no significance or those that are mighty and worthy of commemoration; as the playwright says,[122] it brings to light that which had been obscure and shrouds from us what had been visible. Nevertheless, the science of History is a great bulwark against this stream of Time; in a way it checks this irresistible flood, it holds in a tight grasp whatever it can seize floating on the surface and will not allow it to slip away into the depths of oblivion.

I, Anna, daughter of the Emperor Alexios and the Empress Eirene, born and bred in the purple,[123] not without some acquaintance with literature—having devoted the most earnest study to the Greek language, in fact, and being not unpractised in rhetoric and having read thoroughly the works of Aristotle and the dialogues of Plato, and having fortified my mind with the *tetrakus* of sciences (these things must be divulged, and it is not boasting to recall what Nature and my own zeal for knowledge have given me, nor what God has apportioned to me from above and what has been contributed by circumstance); I desire now by means of my writings to give an account of my father's deeds, which do not deserve to be consigned to silence nor to be swept away by the flood of Time into an ocean of obscurity; I wish to recall everything, the achievements before his elevation to the throne and his actions in the service of others before his coronation. . . .

Now that I have decided to write the story of his life, I am fearful of wagging and suspicious tongues: someone might conclude that in composing the history of my father I am glorifying myself; the history, wherever I express admiration for any act of his, may seem wholly false and mere panegyric. On the other hand, if my father should ever lead me, under the compulsion of events, to criticize some action taken by him, not because of what he decided

---

120. Kristeva 2010, 5–6.

121. Komnene 2009. All subsequent references are to this edition.

122. "*playwright says*: Sophocles, *Ajax*, 646–7" [Tr., 480].

123. "*Anna . . . purple*: Anna Komnene was born on 1 December 1083 in the purple chamber (*porphyra)* in the imperial palace where children and reigning emperors were born" [Tr., 480].

but because of the circumstances, here again I fear the jokers: in their all-embracing jealousy and refusal to accept what is right, because they are malicious and full of envy, they may cast me in the story of Noah's son Ham, and, as Homer says, blame the blameless.[124]

Whenever one assumes the role of historian [*historias ēthos*],[125] friendship and enmities have to be forgotten; often one has to bestow on adversaries the highest commendation, where their deeds merit it; often, too, one's nearest relatives have to be censured, as and when their behavior deserves it. The historian, therefore, must shirk neither from remonstrating with their friends, nor from praising [*epainein*] their enemies. For my part, I hope to satisfy both parties, both those who are offended by us and those who accept us, by appealing to the evidence of the actual events and of eyewitnesses. The fathers and grandfathers of some men alive today saw these things. . . .

To put before the public the life history of such an emperor reminds me of his supreme virtue, his marvellous qualities—and the hot tears fall again as I weep with all the world. When I remember him and make known the events of his reign it is for me a theme of lamentation [*thrēnōn*]; others will be reminded of their loss. However, this is where I must begin the history of my father, at the point where it is better to begin, where the narrative will become at once clearer and more accurate.

COMMENTARY ON PROLOGUE

First-person writing was coming into frequent use in the eleventh and twelfth centuries CE, and Anna likewise inserts herself, her relationship to writing, and her emotions into the text. In her Prologue, she offers her credentials, her reasons for writing the history, the difficulty of writing about a beloved father, and the tension of writing history while mourning her husband and imperial parents. The excerpt shows that her ethos also emerges out of much citation and allusion, offering her learned readers the pleasure of recognizing elements of their shared *paideia*. Anna's opening lines, for example, echo those of Herodotus, and refer directly to the playwright Ajax. As Georgina Buckler notes, Anna's Prologue introduces in addition "one quotation from John of Epiphania, one from Polybius, one from Sophocles, two from Euripides, one from Homer, one allusion to the Bible, one to mythology, four to history, [and] seven geographical names."[126] For Byzantine audiences, this citationality is a mark of a learned and successful performance.

---

124. "*Noah's son Ham . . . blame the blameless*: Genesis 9:20–27; *Iliad*, XI.653, XIII.755 and *Odyssey*, XX.135, I.32. Ham came across his father asleep, drunk and naked, and was cursed, when the latter woke up. Anna means the unjustified accusation of lack of filial devotion" [Tr., 480].
125. Interpolated Greek words are from *Anna Comnenae Alexias*, ed. Diether Reinsch and Athanasios Kambylis (Berlin: Walter de Gruyter, 2001). Each is maintained in the grammatical case in which it appears in this edition.
126. Buckler 1929, 11.

Book III.7–8, pages 94-95—Gender; Writing History v. Paneyric

[T]he reader may well censure my father for transferring the government of the empire to the women's quarters, but if one knew this woman's [Anna Dalassene's] spirit, her surpassing virtue, intelligence and energy, one's reproaches would soon turn to admiration. For my grandmother had an exceptional grasp of public affairs, with a genius for organization and government; she was capable in fact, of managing not only the Roman Empire, but every other empire under the sun as well. She had vast experience and knew the nature of things, aware of how each thing starts and how it ends, which things destroy others and which contradict and complement each other. She was intuitive about what needed doing, and clever at getting it done.

Her intellectual ability, moreover, was paralleled by her command of language. She was indeed a most persuasive orator [*rhētōr*], without being verbose or long-winded. Nor did the inspiration of the argument readily desert her, for just as she would begin by hitting just the right note, she would also end up by saying the appropriate thing too. . . .

Such were the events that marked the beginning of the reign. One could barely at that stage call Alexios emperor given that he had entrusted supreme authority to his mother. Another person might yield here to the claims of panegyric and extol the native land of this remarkable woman; he might trace her descent from the Adrianoi, the Dalassenoi and the Kharonoi,[127] while embarking on the ocean of their achievements. But I am writing history and my fitting task is not to describe her through the family and kinsmen, but by reference to her character, her virtue and the events that form the proper subject of history.

COMMENTARY ON BOOK III.7–8

Interest in rhetoric of gender is of course a contemporary, rather than Byzantine, phenomenon. Yet this passage shows the role and rhetorical prowess of an extraordinary woman, Anna Dalassene, while at the same time showing Anna Komnene as a self-conscious writer of history. The circumstances are that Alexios has just taken the throne, but is compelled to ride out from the capital to face his great Norman enemy, Robert Guiscard. Just before the excerpted passage, Anna, noting her duty to report the details of both deeds and decrees, apparently quotes an imperial document in which Alexios hands full power to his mother to rule in the capital. She then details Anna Dalassena's intellect, persuasive oratory, and her powers of legislating and organizing. The portrait is extraordinary as a response to those who may have censured Alexios for handing power to a woman, and it complicates contemporary summations of the ideal Byzantine woman.[128] A little further on, Anna pauses to reflect that while an

127. "*Adrianoi . . . Kharonoi*: Relatively well-known families in this period. Bryennios says that Anna Dalassene's father was named Kharon (after the ferryman at Hades) since whenever he fought someone, he dispatched them directly to the next life. While the Kharon name is not unusual, few of its bearers are well-known or famous in this period" [Tr., 493].
128. For example, Hill 1996, 7–17.

orator could write a panegyric, "such license is not for the writer of history."[129] She references the rules for writing praise, which we can find in rhetorical treatises by Menander Rhetor and Aphthonius, who call for extolling a subject's native land, descent and achievements; instead, she will document those subjects that are proper to history-writing.

Book VI.11, pages 176–77—Geographic Location and Point of View

There was a time when the frontiers of Roman power [*Rōmaiōn hēgemonias*] were the two pillars at the limits of east and west—the so-called Pillars of Herakles in the west and those of Dionysos[130] not far from the Indian border in the east. As far as its extent was concerned, it is impossible to say how great was the power of Rome; it included Egypt, Meröe, all the land of the Troglodytes, the countries near the Torrid Zone;[131] on the other side, the famous Thule and all the peoples who live in the region of the north, over whom is the Pole Star. But at the time we are speaking of, the boundary of Roman power on the east was our neighbour the Bosphorus, and on the west the town of Adrianoupolis. The Emperor Alexios, fighting two-fisted against barbarians who attacked him on either flank, manoeuvred round Byzantion, the centre of his circle as it were, and proceeded to broaden the empire; on the west the frontier became the Adriatic Sea, on the east the Euphrates and Tigris. He would have revived the ancient prosperity of the empire, too, had not a succession of wars and constant dangers and troubles checked his ambitions (for he was always taking risks and playing with high stakes).

COMMENTARY ON BOOK VI.11

The Byzantines, who were Greek speakers, referred to themselves as Romans (*Romaioi*) and to their territories as the Roman Empire, the continuation of the empire whose capital was moved to Byzantion by Constantine in the fourth century CE.[132] In the excerpt, Anna offers a geographic history. She describes a time, distant from her own, when the Roman empire comprised the known civilized world, and a present moment when it is reduced almost to Constantinople itself. Using place-names from antiquity, she links her world to the Greek

---

129. *Alexiad* III.8, 97.

130. "*Pillars of Herakles . . . of Dionysos*: The pillars flanked the Straits of Gibraltar and at an unknown location in India were thought in antiquity to hold up the skies" [Tr., 504].

131. "*Meröe, all the land of the Troglodytes . . . Torrid Zone*: Meröe was a town far up the River Nile, inside modern Ethiopia. The Troglodytes were supposedly a tribe of people living around the southern part of the Red Sea. The Torrid or Tropical Zone refers to lands bounded by the Tropics of Capricorn and Cancer. Anna paints a rosy picture of the Roman Empire at its notional peak, even if this predates Alexios's reign by many centuries. She does not distinguish between the Roman and Eastern (Byzantine) Empire" [Tr., 504–505].

132. "Byzantion" refers to the area's Greek name and "Byzantium" to its Latinization. For an excellent discussion of issues in dating, locating, and identifying Byzantium, see Cameron (2006, 5–19).

hegemony *prior* to the Roman empire anchored in Rome, giving it a doubly illustrious history. So the passage speaks more than it says (see figured discourse, below) for an audience who would have recognized the geography at least in part through knowledge of Greek literature of antiquity. Even as Anna keeps a distinctive biographical and encomiastic focus on Alexios, in this and other passages, she draws on rhetorical traditions of praising empire and adds urgency to Alexios's campaigns. Scholarship on the rhetoric of geography and representations of place and peoples in relation to political interests is needed. For this is a work that offers windows onto resettlements of peoples due to battles and conversions, foundings of towns, shifting alliances, and moments of cosmopolitanism, ethnic diversity, and the challenges of varying languages. Moreover, just as Byzantium has been seen as important because its scholars transmitted classical texts to Europe, the *Alexiad* has been valued as a window onto the European phenomenon of the Crusades. But the work treats Alexios's encounters with armies from the east and north, and internal Byzantine pretenders, as well as with those of the first Crusade. For Anna, the "Kelts," "Normans," and "Latins" "had long coveted the Roman Empire and wished to acquire it for themselves. . . . They sold their lands on the pretense that they were leaving to fight the Turks and liberate the Holy Sepulchre."[133]

Book IX.9, pages 255–257—Figured Discourse

When the sun peeped over the horizon and leapt into the sky in glory, all those members of the imperial retinue not infected with Diogenes's pollution, as well as the soldiers who had long served as the emperor's bodyguard, led the procession to his tent; some wore swords, others carried spears, others had heavy iron axes on their shoulders. At some distance from the throne they arranged themselves in a crescent-shaped formation thereby surrounding the emperor. They were all moved by anger and if their swords were not ready to go to work their souls certainly were. Near the throne on either side stood the emperor's relatives, and to the right and left were grouped the armour-bearers. The emperor, looking formidable, took his seat dressed rather as soldier than an emperor. Because he was not a tall man, he did not tower above the rest. Nevertheless it was an impressive sight, for gold overlaid his throne and there was gold above his head. He was frowning and the ordeal had brought an unusual tinge of red to his cheeks; his eyes, fixed in concentration, gave a hint of the troubles that beset him. . . .

However, composing himself and at last ready for the challenge, he began his address to them. (They meanwhile were as silent as fish, as if their tongues had been cut out.) 'You know,' he said, 'that Diogenes has never suffered ill at my hands. It was not I who deprived his father of this empire, but someone else entirely. Nor have I been the cause of evil or pain of any sort so far as he is concerned. Moreover, when, by the will of God alone, I became ruler of the empire not only did I give my protection equally to him and his brother Leo, but I loved them and treated them as my own children. Every time that I caught Nikephoros plotting against me I forgave him. Even though he never mended his ways, I bore with him and concealed most of his offences, in the knowledge that they would have met with widespread contempt.

---

133. *Alexiad* X.6, 279.

Yet none of my favours has succeeded in altering his perfidy. Indeed, by way of gratitude he sentenced me to death.'

At these words they all shouted that they would not wish to see anyone else in his place on the imperial throne; most of them did not mean it, but they flattered, hoping thereby to escape from immediate danger. The emperor seized on the opportunity [*ton kairon*] and proclaimed a general amnesty for the majority of them.

COMMENTARY BOOK IX.9

This is part of one of the most detailed episodes of the *Alexiad*, and, for contemporary readers, perhaps one of the most illegible. What is the rhetoric of the passage? Following military events in Dalmatia and Mytilene, Anna represents Alexios contending with an internal plot on his life by Nikephoros Diogenes, a son of Emperor Romanos IV Diogenes. This was the emperor who was defeated and captured during a disastrous battle at Manzikert in 1071 CE, which was partly responsible for the diminished state of the empire that Alexios took over. Anna reminds her readers of this without specifically naming the defeat: "The elevation of . . . Romanos to the imperial throne and the manner of his downfall have been described by several historians and anyone who wishes to read about him will find the details in their works."[134] She offers a long backstory of Alexios's pity for the sons of Romanos. One of them, Nikephorus, harbored designs on the throne and makes several attempts to kill Alexios in his tent. For Anna's readers, this story may have been richly resonant. They were likely to recognize that in staging this episode she rewrites, merges, and transforms scenes from the *Chronographia* of rhetor Michael Psellos concerning two previous emperors. Anna's text recalls Psellos's representation of his favorite emperor, Constantine IX, as foolishly careless of similar threats.[135] Alexios, by contrast, is measured, kind, and has God's very protection. In the excerpt, Anna describes a sunrise confrontation in a battleground tent between Alexios and his loyalists and the aristocrats won over by Diogenes. Here, she closely follows Psellos's very sentences in a scene concerning another emperor, Michael VI.[136] Psellos had narrated a usurpation by Isaac Komnenos, Alexios's uncle, of Michael's throne. As Penelope Buckley suggests, "[I]ntertwined in the knowledgeable reader's mind with Alexios's brave show is the spectacle of his uncle as Psellos constructed him. The memory of the first shines through the courage of the second while illuminating the second's finer quality." She goes on: "When Michael VI gave Isaac's rebel army amnesty, he lost his throne. Alexios—facing his own hostile army—grants an amnesty like Michael's, yet keeps power by playing in his own way the part of a successful Isaac."[137] Buckley's project is to show the ways in which Anna creates an Alexios of mythic

---

134. *Alexiad*, IX.6, 248.
135. This episode can be found in Psellus (1966, IX.6, 227).
136. *Fourteen Byzantine Rulers* VII, 287–297. The sunrise setting, the emperor's gold-decorated seat, his facial expression, all come from Psellos. That for Byzantines the creative re-use of earlier texts "was not plagiarism but genius" is suggested by Mullet (2010, 237).
137. Buckley 2014, 186–87.

stature. Rhetoricians must also note that this is an extended example of *eschematismenos logos,* figured discourse. That is, for a learned audience, the Diogenes episode speaks more than it says.[138] It tactfully and without direct assertion recalls the state of the empire that Alexios took over and the weaknesses of previous emperors. It constructs a positive comparison of Alexios with those emperors and shows his generous winning over of those who threaten his rule from within. Alexios, as adept in speech as on the battlefield, addresses the rebels and reminds his audience (and Anna's readers) that the diminished empire that he took over was in part due to Nikephoros's father. When Alexios's hearers approve his words, "he seized on the opportunity" (*ton kairon*) and offered them just what is needed to win their favor. The episode is thus historically layered, rhetorically vivid, and valuable for its picture of ongoing struggles for the throne.

The Diogenes episode has a scenic quality could also be read as an example of *ekphrasis.* This is one of the fundamental exercises that Byzantine writers would have practiced since their childhood training as laid out, for example, by Hermogenes: "Ecphrasis (*ekphrasis*) is descriptive speech, as they say vivid (*enargēs*) and bringing what is being shown before the eyes."[139] Aphthonius's version of this exercise offers examples from "the historian" (Thucydides), showing that this school exercise is one to be learned from and carried forward into complex works. At least one Byzantine rhetor, Sikeliotes, connects *enargeia*, vividness, to indicating [*emphainein*] what ought not be spoken outright, for example because it is infamous.[140] Ekphrasis, then, offers opportunities for figured discourse and subtle argument. The same may be said of *synkrisis*, comparison.

Book XIV.7, pages 420-422—The Rhetoric of Historiography

I am not writing the history of things that happened 10,000 years ago, but there are men still alive today who knew my father and tell me of his deeds. They have in fact made a not inconsiderable contribution to the history, for one reported or recalled to the best of his ability one fact, while another told me something else—but there was no discrepancy in their accounts. Most of the time, moreover, we were ourselves present, for we accompanied our father and mother. My life by no means revolved round the home; we did not live a sheltered, pampered existence. . . .

As I was saying, some of my material is the result of my own observations; some I have gathered in various ways from the emperor's comrades in arms, who sent us information about the progress of the wars by people who crossed the straits. Above all I have often heard the emperor and George Palaiologos discussing these matters in my presence. Most of the evidence I

---

138. For an excellent discussion and history of figured discourse, see Ahl (1984, 174–208). Related rhetorical terms are *amphoteroglossia* and *emphasis*. See the glossary of terms at the end of this chapter.
139. Kennedy 2003, 86.
140. Papioannou 2011, 53. Ahl (1984, 178), notes the term *emphainein* in Demetrios: "The effect is more forceful because it is achieved by letting the facts speak for itself rather than having the speaker make the point for himself."

collected myself, especially in the reign of the third emperor after my father,[141] at a time when all the flattery and lies about his grandfather had disappeared: for all men flatter the current ruler, while no one makes the slightest attempt to over-praise the departed, telling the facts just as they are and describing things just as they happened.

As for myself, apart from the grief caused by my own misfortunes, I now mourn three rulers—my father, the emperor; my mistress and mother, the empress; and to my sorrow, the *kaiser,* my husband. For the most part, therefore, I pass my time in obscurity[142] and devote myself to my books and to the worship of God. . . .

The documents that came into my possession were written in simple language without embellishment; they adhered closely to the truth, were distinguished by no elegance whatever and were composed in a manner lacking style and free from rhetorical flourish. The accounts given by the old veterans were, in language and thought, similar to those commentaries, and I based the truth of my history on them by comparing them with what I had heard, from my father in particular and from my uncles both on my father's and on my mother's side. From all these materials the whole fabric of my history—my true history—has been woven.

COMMENTARY BOOK XIV.7

As we saw in the Anna Dalassene passage, Anna Komnene is a self-conscious historiographer, aware of the demands of historical narrative. Here, she details her methods, stressing her research and use of evidence; like Thucydides and Polyibius, she appeals to actual events, documentary evidence and eyewitnesses, and compares the various materials that she collects. She mentions again the great tension of the work, and issue of genre—writing a clear and accurate history even as the memory of her father is a cause for lamentation. Neville has described this as "crying like a woman and writing like a man," writing in a typically female form to authorize her writing a masculine genre.[143] Another view would be the one mentioned above, that there were precedents for representing the enduring of suffering as noble.

Book XV.3, pages 437–438—Parallel Rhetorics of Empire and of Historiography

For my part, I think that to win a victory by sound planning requires courage [*andreian*]; force of character and energy uninformed by thought are not enough—they end not in cour-

---

141. "*the third emperor after my father*: i.e., Manuel I. Komnenos, successor of Alexios' heir, John II. Anna highlights two points of interest: first that her nephew's reign had spawned ill-warranted and extravagant flattery of him; and secondly, that little attention was paid to the life and times of Alexios I. Manuel took the throne in 1143 CE, which helps date the composition of the *Aleciad*" [Tr., 528].

142. "*I pass my time in obscurity*: Anna appears to have been exiled during or soon after 1118, following a failed attempt to take the throne for herself and her husband, Nikephoros Bryennios. Her seclusion was perhaps not as complete as she implies, to judge from the foundational document of the convent where she is widely thought to have lived. See also introduction, p. xiv" [Tr., 538].

143. Neville 2016, 61–74.

age but in foolhardiness. We are courageous in war against men whom we can beat; against men too strong for us we are foolhardy. Thus when danger hangs over us, being unable to make a frontal assault we change our tactics and seek to conquer the enemy without resorting to warfare. The prime virtue of a general is the ability to win a victory without incurring danger—as Homer says, it is by skill [*technēi*] that one charioteer beats another.[144] Even the famous Cadmean proverb censures a victory fraught with danger. As far as I am concerned, it has always seemed best to devise some crafty strategic manoeuvre in the course of battle, if one's own army cannot match the enemy's strength. Anyone can find examples of this in the pages of history. There is no one method of achieving victory, nor one form of it, but from ancient times up to the present, success has been won in different ways [*tropous*]. Victory means the same thing always, but the means by which generals attain it are varied and of intricate [*poikilous*] patterns. . . .

If ever there was a man who had an extraordinary love of danger, it was he; and when dangers continually arose, he faced them in different ways: by marching into them bareheaded and coming to close grips with the barbarians, or on occasions by pretending to avoid conflict and feigning terror. It depended on circumstances and the situation of the moment [*hōs kairos edidou*] . . . .

At this point I must again beg the reader not to rebuke me for being boastful; this is by no means the first time I have defended myself against such an accusation. It is not love for my father which prompts these reflections, but the course of events. In any case, is there any good reason why being truthful should prevent the simultaneous love of one's father and of truth itself? I chose to write the truth about a good man, and if that man happens to be the historian's father it is right that his name should be added as an appendage. But of course the history must by its very nature be founded on truth. There are other ways in which I have demonstrated my love for him, and because of that my enemies have been inspired to sharpen sword and spear against me, which is something anyone who is not ignorant of my life knows well. Besides, I would never betray the truth under the guise of history. There is a time [*kairos*] for showing love for one's father, which I did courageously [*ēndrisametha*] when appropriate, and another for telling the truth, and now that the opportunity has arrived, I will not neglect it.

COMMENTARY BOOK XV.3

In this passage, Anna comments on her father's battle strategies as not only courageous but as varied and kairotic—rhetorical—like her own writing of history. Alexios has been in Bithynia (northwest Asia minor), and there have been rumors that Alexios's actions against Turkish enemies will fail. In the excerpted passage, Anna offers her own view: a victory requires not only uninformed courage, but sound planning, which itself requires courage. Alexios, ever the rhetorical strategist, moves into battle with attention to occasion and circumstances (*kairos*, *pragmata*). In the parallel passage about her writing, Anna suggests that history is a matter

---

144. "*one charioteer beats another: Iliad*, XXIII.318" [Tr., 529].

of telling the truth when the opportunity arrives.[145] The grammar of gender is also worthy of study. The Greek word for manly courage (*andreia*) also appears in Anna's verb for the courage to have shown love for her father (*ēndrisametha*).[146]

Book XV.7, pages 450–451—Ekphrasis

When he hears of things like formation, ranks, prisoners and spoils of war, general and army commanders, the reader will probably imagine that this is the kind of thing mentioned by every historian and poet. But this particular formation was unprecedented, causing universal astonishment, such as no one had ever seen before, unrecorded by any historian for the benefit of future generations. On the way to Ikonion he marched in a disciplined way, keeping in step to the sound of the flute, so that an eyewitness would have said the whole army, although it was in motion, was standing immobile and when it was halting, was on the march. In fact, the serried ranks of close-locked shields and marching men gave the impression of immovable mountains; and when they changed direction the whole body moved like one huge beast, animated and directed by one single mind. When the emperor reached Philomelion after rescuing prisoners from the Turks, the return journey was made slowly, in a leisurely way and at an ant's pace, so to speak, with the captives, women and children, and all the booty in the center of the column.

Many of the women were pregnant and many men were suffering from disease. When a woman was about to give birth, the emperor ordered a trumpet to sound and everyone halted; the whole army stopped at once wherever it happened to be. After hearing that a child had been born, he gave the general order to advance by another, and unusual, trumpet blast. Again, if someone were on the point of dying, the same thing occurred. The emperor visited the dying man and priests were summoned to sing the appropriate hymns and administer the last sacraments. Thus, when all the customary rites had been performed, and only when the dead had been laid in his tomb and buried, was the column allowed to move on even a short distance. . . . By such means Alexios personally supplied the needs of the marchers.

COMMENTARY BOOK XV.7

This ekphrasis of a military formation is less complex than the Diogenes scene, but more cinematic. Alexios moves not only his own troops but men, women, and children who have been rescued from Turks at Philomelion (modern Akşehir in central Anatolia) and Ikionion, toward Constantinople. Anna has said that these are native inhabitants [*autochthones*], "Romans" who take refuge with Alexios. Placed at the center of the formation, all are moved in perfect safety. She introduces the scene by suggesting that "[a]nyone who had seen it would

---

145. For a more detailed comment with further attention to figured discourse, see Quandahl and Jarratt (2008, 326–28).

146. For comments on manly courage as a descriptor for women, see Quandahl (2012, 200–09).

have said that this new arrangement of the force which I have described was a living organism, a moving, fortified town." Alexios rode at the head "like a huge tower or a pillar of fire, or some divine celestial apparition, encouraging his soldiers."[147] In the excerpted passage, several features are worth noting. One is Anna's comment that readers might expect that this sort of thing is described by "every historian and poet" and her claim that this formation is unlike anything recorded by previous historians. Another is the scope and movement of the picture, which offers something of the sublime. She describes the scene almost as if an eyewitness can see it from above: it looks immobile, like mountains, even while in motion. She then zooms in dramatically to the center, showing a compassionate emperor pausing the whole for a birth or death. Finally, this picture hints at something little dealt with in this elite history: the dislocations of war, with peoples caught up in battles, displaced from their towns, and requiring sanctuary. The whole scene sets up the finale of Alexios's campaigns, his establishing of a sanctuary city inside Constantinople, including an orphanage and grammar school for these dispossessed. There Anna herself has witnessed "a Latin being trained over there; or a Scythian learning Greek; or a Roman handling Greek texts; or an illiterate Greek discovering how to speak his own language correctly." She closes that passage with a comment on her own devotion to rhetoric, philosophy, poets and historians, and claims the importance of general education [*enkyliou paideuseōs*].[148]

---

147. *Alexiad* XV.4, 443–44.
148. *Alexiad* XV.7, 454–55.

7.3 Hebraic Mediterranean, c. 15th Century CE, Italy

An Examination of Judah Messer Leon's Hebraic Treatment of the *Nofet Zuphim* (Book of Honeycomb's Flow)

Jim Ridolfo

INTRODUCTION

Judah Messer Leon (born Judah ben Jehiel) was a fifteenth-century CE Italian physician, philosopher, rabbi, and rhetorician who lived from 1420 or 1425 CE to 1498 CE. Messer Leon is perhaps best known as a scholar able to move between religious and secular culture and as a political figure in the Italian Jewish community that pursued educational and organizational reforms. He is the first published author to recast Greek and Roman rhetorics into a Hebrew context, and additionally was the first living author to see his work published on the Hebrew printing press. As a learned doctor, rabbi, and scholar in religious, secular, medical, and biblical knowledge, he straddled both the religious and political world of fifteenth-century CE Jewish Italy, as well as the larger Christian and secular society of Renaissance Italy.[149]

Fifteenth-century CE Italy was a period that featured great academic and cultural change, and these changes are apparent in the life and work of Messer Leon. The second half of the century ushered in an Italian intellectual resurgence of Maimonides and Aristotle. For Italian Jewish communities there were additional cultural and scholarly shifts underway, set in motion by immigration and demographic changes as well as cultural and religious differences between Sephardic and Ashkenazi communities. Arthur Lesley describes in more detail the decentralized authority of fifteenth-century, Jewish Italy:

At this time, small, new and unorganized Jewish communities were appearing in many places north of Rome. These communities were created by the granting of short-term contracts by towns or princes to small Jewish loan-bankers and their households. The Jews were heterogeneous, immigrants from France, Provence, Germany, Spain, the Levant, and southern Italy. Each group had its distinctive daily language, communal practices, school traditions, religious and legal authorities, and the competition between claimants for communal and intellectual authority called into the question the legitimacy of all leadership.[150]

Fifteenth-century CE Italy also faced an influx of new philosophical texts from the scholastics. While texts such as Aristotle's *Rhetoric* had been studied and preserved by the Islamic scholars al-Farabi and Averroes in the tenth and twelfth century CE, Aristotle's works were not translated into Latin until the fifteenth century CE.[151] Messer Leon is part of the first

---

149. For more background on Messer Leon see Bonfil (1994).
150. Lesley 1983, 101–14.
151. Tirosh-Samuelson 1997, 499–573.

generation of Italian scholars to study and engage with the works of Aristotle and the Islamic commentator Averroes. In what follows, I frame Leon's work as both firmly within Jewish rhetorical traditions but also distinctly informed by and connected to centuries of cross-cultural and geographic exchanges throughout the Mediterranean.

THE WORK OF JUDAH MESSER LEON

Scholars such as Robert Bonfil, Isaac Rabinowitz, Hava Tirosh-Samuelson, and Alfred L. Ivry discuss how the *Nofet Zuphim* is a composite of Greek, Roman, and Islamic rhetorics. For example, Ivry describes the book as "a Hebrew translation of Averroes's Middle Commentary on Aristotle's Rhetoric, together with the Latin writings of Cicero, Quintilian, and others."[152] Bonfil notes that the order of the *Nofet Zufim* is a four-part treatise on the subject of rhetoric:

> In the first part Messer Leon deals with the definition of rhetoric, its purpose, importance, the different kinds of speech as regards the different kinds of publics, and the characteristics of the ideal orator. In the second part he discusses the different types of speeches as regards their content. In the third part the author presents the emotional traits of the orator as these are expressed in the different kinds of speeches, while the past part deals with the rhetorical figures (devices).[153]

In each section Messer Leon recasts these rhetorical discussions as they are in the classical versions, but he significantly recontextualizes them through biblical exegesis and pastiche. James Murphy argues for the significance of Messer Leon's biblical pastiche, especially in its Hebraic context. He argues that the *Nofet Zuphim* symbolizes "a new combination of secular classical learning and scriptural exegesis for the education of Jewish professionals in Italy."[154] In his use of pastiche, Messer Leon is the first known Hebraist to "compose a Hebrew treatise on rhetoric based upon the Bible rather than on Greek and Latin sources."[155] Israel Zinberg discusses how Messer Leon rhetorically draws from the Hebrew Bible because Messer Leon wanted to "show that in the realm of style and oratory the prophets and Biblical historians must be acknowledged as the supreme masters."[156]

While Greek, Roman, and Islamic rhetorical knowledge may be found in classical texts that have already been translated into Latin, Messer Leon argues through his rhetorical project of biblical exegesis that all of this secular rhetorical knowledge may be located in sacred texts. In doing so, Messer Leon makes a complex, culturally situated argument for the study of rhetorical texts. He must convince more conservative religious leaders and communities

---

152. Ivry 1999, 199.
153. Rabinowitz 1983, ix.
154. Murphy 1985, 161.
155. Frank 2000, 229.
156. Zinberg 1974, 40.

that scholastic knowledge belongs in *Yeshivot,* Jewish houses of learning. Without a strong argument for the place of these texts, his peers will continue to view these works as extrinsic to the curricula of the Yeshivot. What Messer Leon accomplishes in his composition of the *Nofet Zuphim* is a complex example of remix and pastiche that's culturally and rhetorically framed to reform fifteenth-century CE Italian Jewish education. Bonfil describes this pastiche of texts from different traditions creates a "rather indeterminate flavor, a mélange of late medievalism and of the ingenuous, almost audacious, freshness of a new age hesitantly feeling its way."[157]

COMMENTARY

In previous work on Messer Leon, I have focused on the significance of the *Nofet Zuphim's* publication on the first Hebrew printing press as it relates to rhetorical delivery.[158] To give readers an understanding of Messer Leon's biblical pastiche, I have selected material from chapter twelve of the *Nofet Zuphim,* focusing specifically on rhetorical delivery. In the next section, I have with permission excerpted passages from Robert Bonfil's 1981 facsimile edition of the 1475 printing of the *Nofet Zuphim,* followed by the translated passages from Isaac Rabinowitz's 1983 critical edition and translation published by Cornell University Press. In the translated passages, Rabinowitz indicates instances of Messer Leon's biblical pastiche in **bold**, along with the corresponding biblical citation in brackets.

While largely summarizing the theories of rhetorical delivery found in Aristotle, Cicero, Averroes, and Quintilian, Messer Leon begins his discussion of rhetorical delivery in chapter twelve by grounding its significance in the text of the Hebrew bible. Messer Leon says that delivery has been awarded [by God] "**the strong rod** and **the beautiful staff** [Jer. 48:17]."[159] Following the lead of Cicero and Quintilian, Messer Leon posits that there are two categories of delivery: "either of physical representations, or of sounds and tones. Of physical representations, some are of the whole body, some are of parts of the body, such as the hands, face, and head, these being the most often used in oratory."[160] Structurally, the chapter begins with Messer Leon discussing Aristotle, whom he refers to as "The Philosopher," and book three of the *Rhetoric.* The chapter is peppered with biblical pastiche, but in the last page and a half Messer Leon does significant work to show how all the knowledge he has henceforth discussed is found, *a priori,* in the Hebrew Bible. For example, Messer Leon's analysis of Isaiah is able to coax out the rules for control of the voice, and from the example of Isaiah one also has an image of the countenance of the body. Messer Leon is thus able to reason Cicero and Quintilian's rules for oral delivery from the story of the prophet.

---

157. Bonfil 1981, v.
158. Ridolfo 2014.
159. Rabinowitz 1983.
160. Ibid., 119.

CRITICAL GLOSS

As a graduate student at Michigan State University, I was especially interested in thinking about Jewish rhetorical history alongside questions of delivery and circulation. For the latter, I drew on the work of Steven B. Katz and especially his 1995 *Rhetoric Society Quarterly* article "The Epistemology of the Kabbalah: Toward a Jewish Philosophy of Rhetoric," Rabinowitz and his critical edition of the *Nofet Zuphim*, Lesley's work on medieval Jewish rhetorics, and many others. I was fixated on Messer Leon's reception of Greek and Roman texts, his rabbinical recontextualization of those texts, his translation and recomposition of that work into Hebrew, and his publication of this work on the first Hebrew printing press. In all of these areas, I was interested in how Messer Leon understood the practice of written rhetorical delivery.

In the years after working on that material, I came to think more about the intersection and divergences of a Hebrew or Jewish rhetorical tradition in relationship to what is commonly referred to as the Western rhetorical tradition. On the one hand, as Katz's 1995 article argues, it is undeniable that Jewish rhetorical traditions have had a role in some of the larger structures of Western rhetorical traditions. In his examination of kabbalah or mystical traditions, Katz argues that "perhaps other sacred Jewish texts therefore can inform our understanding of the rhetorical tradition of the West, and deserves examination by scholars in rhetoric as well as Jewish studies."[161] On the other hand, in Janice Fernheimer's 2010 introduction to the *College English* special issue, Composing Jewish Rhetorics, she argues that one of the problems in defining the place of Jewish rhetorics is finding the appropriate "intellectual spaces in which we place them. For example, the geography question calls attention to the tendency to bifurcate rhetorical traditions into the categories of Western or non-Western. Just as Jewish people disrupt the binary of black and white in the United States, so too Jewish rhetorics disrupt the typical binary of Western and non-Western."[162]

What I appreciate about the Katz and Fernheimer discussion here is how it has not only helped me to think about Messer Leon's work in relationship to classifications, such as Western/Non-Western, place and canon, and Jewish rhetorical traditions. It has also helped me to think about Mediterranean rhetorical traditions not just in terms of comparative rhetorics *per se* but about the reception, translation, and retransmission of texts within a particular region and across time, languages, cultural and religious traditions. In this same thread, I would note Maha Baddar's 2010 "The Arabs Did Not 'Just' Translate Aristotle" and its advocacy of a "dialogic approach to comparative rhetorical study" by showing how in the case of al-Farabi, he "used different parts of Aristotle's Organon to create a unique theory of rhetoric that was appropriate to his context in tenth century monotheistic Baghdad."[163]

In the context of Judah Messer Leon and, I would argue, other Mediterranean rhetoricians, Baddar's dialogic approach is helpful to me and, I think, others. How do we as a field treat and study rhetoricians that translate, build upon, and then make their own previous

---

161. Katz 1995a, 119.

162. Fernheimer 2010, 582.

163. Baddar 2010, 231.

rhetorical traditions? The fifteenth-century CE Messer Leon works with Aristotle through the twelfth-century CE texts of the Islamic Andalusian philosopher Averroes (Ibn Rushd), and receives those texts through Hebrew and Latin translations. In that one exchange of ideas across the Mediterranean, it would be reductive and a missed opportunity to say that this is entirely Aristotelian or scholastic. For even in the case of Messer Leon and his *Nofet Suphim*, these texts are recast and put into conversation in relationship to his project of locating all rhetorical knowledge in the Hebrew Bible. In this way, Messer Leon seeks to argue for these rhetorical approaches to his own community by saying that these dialogues he's having with other rhetorical traditions are located within his own textual traditions.

EXCERPTS OF RABINOWITZ'S TRANSLATION OF DELIVERY

Below I have excerpted the last three pages of Rabinowitz's critical translation of chapter twelve, pages 128 to 131 in the *Nofet Suphim*. Note how Rabinowitz identifies Messer Leon's instaces of biblical phrase in bold, along with corresponding references to brackets:[164]

[25] There can be no doubt that the main rules of delivery are clearly expounded by the Holy Books. As for qualities of voice, the prophet Isaiah, upon whom be peace, says: **Cry aloud, spare not, lift up thy voice like a horn, and declare unto my people their transgression**," etc. [Isa. 58:1]. He here points out that the voice, when expressing reproof, should be loud. By the same token, on the other hand, the voice of the unfortunate and of suppliants ought to be subdued, as was said: **And brought down thou shalt speak out of the ground, and thy speech shall be low out of the dust; and thy voice shall be as of a ghost out of the ground**, etc. [Isa. 29:4] Likewise: "**It is not the voice of them that cry for being overcome, neither is it the voice of them that shout for mastery, but the voice of them that sing do I hear**" [Exod. 32:18]. "**there is a noise of war in the camp**" [32:17]; **the voice of mirth and the voice of gladness, the voice of the bridegroom and the voice of the bride**" [Jer. 7:34; 16;19]; ..all statements of this kind teach that the voice should be varied in the way suited to specific circumstances. On movement of the head, Scripture says: **The virgin daughter of Zion hath despised thee and laughed thee to scorn; the daughter of Jerusalem hath shaken her head at thee** [Isa. 37:22; 2 Kings 19:21]. Again, movement of both hands and head: **All that pass by clap their hands at thee; they hiss and wag their head** [Lam. 2:15]. Also on gesticulation of the hands: **For I have heard a voice as of a woman in travail, the anguish as of her that bringeth forth her first child, the voice of the daughter of Zion, that gaspeth for breath, that spreadeth her hands**, etc. [Jer. 4:31]; and in Eze-kiel: "**I will also smite My hands together, and I will satisfy My fury**," etc [21:22]; "**Behold, therefore, I have smitten my hand at thy dishonest gain which thou hast**

---

164. Rabinowitz's critical translation includes additional commentary in his notes about Messer Leon's intended use of particular biblical phrases.

made," etc. [22:13]. Likewise, **From him also shalt thou go forth, with thy hands upon thy head** [Jer 2:37]. So, too, on movements of both hands and feet in unison, in Ezekiel: **Thus saith the Lord God: "Smite with thy hand, and stamp with thy foot, and say, alas!"** [6:11]. Again, on physical representations: **Why shouldest Thou be as a man overcome, as a mighty man that cannot save?** [Jer 14:19]. So, too: **A haughty look, and a proud heart** [Prov. 21:4], **A merry heart maketh a cheerful countenance** [15:13]. Scripture further says: **He that shutteth his eyes, it is to devise forward things; he that biteth his lips bringeth evil to pass** [16:30]; **A base person, a man of iniquity, is he that walketh with a froward mouth; that winketh with his eyes, that scrapeth with his feet, that pointeth with his fingers** [6:12–13].

[26] Our discussion of delivery in the present chapter has here reached its limit.[165]

In the concluding one-and-a-half pages of chapter twelve, Messer Leon provides over a dozen-and-a-half instances of biblical pastiche to reinforce his argument for the study of voice, gesture, and body. This rhetorical move by Messer Leon to leverage this amount of biblical pastiche may be understood as a strong argument for Aristotelian knowledge. Messer Leon is arguing to his more conservative contemporaries that "The Philosopher" and his knowledge about rhetorical delivery that he henceforth discussed in the chapter—all of this knowledge— may already be found *a priori* in the Hebrew bible. Ergo, the study of Aristotelian knowledge is not entirely secular and is appropriate for the curricula of Yeshivot. Messer Leon's argument here and in the rest of the book is significant as it marks a moment in Italian Jewish life when secular and religious education and knowledge are in greater contact.

CONCLUSION

To return to Fernheimer's discussion about locating Jewish rhetorics, there's no doubt that Messer Leon's Hebraic treatment of scholastic rhetoric is imbued with Jewish textual traditions and contemporary community practice. That said, there's also no doubt that Messer Leon is dialogically connected, drawing on Baddar, to a history of Mediterranean conversations that move between Greek, Roman, Islamic, Jewish, and more. This axis of situating texts in conversation with other texts as reflective of local traditions as well as in conversation with different rhetorical traditions is, I would argue, a way we might think of Messer Leon and similar texts and traditions such as Syriac,[166] Turkish,[167] and more, as Mediterranean: reflective of the local culture, history, geography, and exchanges across time, place, language, land, and sea. In this sense, I propose thinking through Mediterranean rhetorics in two ways: building on Baddar, as often dialogically connected to other rhetorical traditions while also being distinct in each's own language, culture, rhetorical situation; and building on Fernheimer, as enacting disruptive practices that complicate canonical understanding of what a Jewish rhetoric is, and where such a rhetoric might be located or enacted spatially, temporally, geographically, textually.

---

165. Rabinowitz, 129–131.
166. See Watt (2005).
167. See Guler and Goksel (2019).

Comprehensive Bibliography

Byzantine

Ahl, Frederick. 1984. "The Art of Safe Criticism in Greece and Rome." *American Journal of Philology* 105 (2): 174–208.

Anna Comnenae Alexias. 2015. Edited by Diether R. Reinsch and Athanasios Kambylis. Berlin: Walter de Gruyter GmbH & Co..

Beaton, Roderic. 1980. *Folk Poetry of Modern Greece.* Cambridge: Cambridge University Press.

Bernard, Floris. 2014. *Writing and Reading Byzantine Secular Poetry, 1025–1081.* Oxford: Oxford University Press.

Buckler, Georgina. 1929. *Anna Comnena: A Study.* London: Oxford University Press.

Buckley, Penelope. 2014. *The* Alexiad *of Anna Komnene: Artistic Strategy in the Making of a Myth.* Cambridge: Cambridge University Press.

Cameron, Averil. 2006. *The Byzantines.* Malden, MA: Blackwell Publishing.

Choniates, Niketas. 1984. *O City of Byzantium, Annals of Niketas Choniates.* Translated by Harry Magoulias. Detroit: Wayne State University Press.

Comnena, Anna. 1969. *The Alexiad of Anna Comnana.* Translated by E. R. A. Sewter. London: Penguin Press.

—. 1928, 2003. *The Alexiad of the Princess Anna Comnena.* Rpt. Translated by Elizabeth A.S. Dawes. London: Kegan Paul.

Dionysios the Areopagite. 1990. *On Divine Names.* Edited by B. R. Suchla, *Pseudo-Dionysius Areopagita, Corpus Dionysiacum.* Patristische Texte und Studien 33. Berlin: De Gruyter.

Frankopan, Peter. 2012. *The First Crusade: The Call from the East.* London: The Bodley Head.

Gouma-Peterson, Thalia, ed. 2000. *Anna Komnene and Her Times.* New York: Garland Publishing.

Heath, Malcolm. 1995. *Hermogenes, On Issues: Strategies of Argument in Later Greek Rhetoric.* Oxford: Clarendon Press.

—. 2004. *Menander: A Rhetor in Context.* Oxford: Oxford University Press.

Hermogenes. 2012. *On Forms.* Edited by M. Patillon, *Corpus rhetoricum, Tome IV: Prolégomènes au De Ideis—Hermogène, Les catégories stylistiques du discours (De Ideis)—Synopse des exposés sur les Ideai.* Paris: Les Belles Lettres.

Hill, Barbara. 1996. "The Ideal Imperial Komnenian Woman." In *Twentieth Annual Byzantine Studies Conference,* edited by Annemarie Weyl Carr et al., 7–17. Amsterdam: Verlag Adolf M. Hakkert.

—. 2000. "Actions Speak Louder Than Words: Anna Komnene's Attempted Usurpation." In *Anna Komnene and Her Times,* edited by Thalia Gouma-Peterson, 45–61. London: Routledge.

Howard-Johnston, James. 1996. "Anna Komnene and the *Alexiad.*" In *Alexios I Komnenos,* edited by Margaret Mullett and Dion Smythe, 260–302. Belfast: Byzantine Enterprises.

Hunger, Herbert. 1969/1970. "On the Imitation (ΜΙΜΗΣΙΣ) of Antiquity in Byzantine Literature." *Dumbarton Oaks Papers* 23/24: 15–38.

Hussey, J. M. 1953. "Introduction." In *Michael Psellus: Chronographia*, translated by E. R. A Sewter. New Haven: Yale University Press, 1953. sourcebooks.fordham.edu/basis/psellus-chrono-intro.asp.

Jeffreys, M. 1974. "The Nature and Origins of the Political Verse." *Dumbarton Oaks Papers* 28: 143–95.

Jordan, Robert, trans. 2004. "*Kecharitomene: Typikon* of Empress Irene Doukaina Komnene for the Convent of the Mother of God *Kecharitomene in* Constantinople." In *Byzantine Monastic Foundation Documents*, edited by John Thomas and Angela Constantinides Hero, 649–711. Dumbarton Oaks Research Library and Collection.

Kennedy, George A, trans. 2003. *Progymnasmata: Greek Textbooks of Prose Composition and Rhetoric*. Atlanta: Society of Biblical Literature.

—. 2005. *Invention and Method: Two Rhetorical Treatises from the Hermogenic Corpus*. Writings from the Greco-Roman World 15. Atlanta: Society of Biblical Literature, Leiden: Brill.

Komnene, Anna. 2009. *The Alexiad*. Translated by E. R. A. Sewter, revised by Peter Frankopan. London: Penguin Press.

Kristeva, Julia. 2010. "Thinking About Liberty in Dark Times." In *Hatred and Forgiveness*, translated by Jeanine Herman, 1–23. New York: Columbia University Press.

Kustas, G. L. 1973. *Studies in Byzantine Rhetoric*. Thessalonike: Πατριαρχικὸν Ἵδρυμα Πατερικῶν Μελετῶν [Patriarchal Institute for Patristic Studies].

Lauxtermann, M. D. 1999. *The Spring of Rhythm: An Essay on the Political Verse and Other Byzantine Metres*. Vienna: Verlag der Österreichischen Akademie der Wissenschaften.

Macrides, Ruth. 2000. "The Pen and the Sword: Who Wrote the *Alexiad?*" In *Anna Komnene and Her Times*, edited by Thalia Gouma-Peterson, 63–81. New York: Garland Publishing.

Magdolino, Paul, ed. 1993. *The Empire of Manuel I Komnenos 1143–1180*. Cambridge: Cambridge University Press.

_____. 2000. "The Pen of the Aunt: Echoes of the Mid-Twelfth Century in The *Alexiad*. In *Anna Komnene and Her Times*, edited by Thalia Gouma-Peterson, 15–43. New York: Garland Publishing.

Moore, Paul. 2005. *Iter Psellianum: A Detailed Listing of Manuscript Sources for All Works Attributed to Michael Psellos*. Toronto: Pontifical Institute of Mediaeval Studies.

Mullet, Margaret. 2006. "Novelization in Byzantium: Narrative after the Revival of Fiction." In *Byzantine Narrative: Papers in Honor of Roger Scott*, edited by John Burke et al., 1–28. Melbourne: Australian Association for Byzantine Studies.

—. 2010. "No Drama, No Fiction, No Readership, No Literature." In *A Companion to Byzantium*, edited by Liz James, 227–38. Malden, MA: Blackwell.

Neville, Leonora. 2012. *Heroes and Romans in Twelfth-Century Byzantium: The "Materials for History" of Nikephoros Bryennios*. London: Cambridge University Press.

—. 2016. *nna Komnene: The Life and Work of a Medieval Historian.* New York: Oxford University Press.

Papioannou, Stratis. 2011. "Byzantine *Enargeia* and Theories of Representation." *Byzantino-slavica: Revue international des études byzantines,* (3): 48–60.

—. 2012. "Anna Komnene's Will." In *Byzantine Religious Culture: Studies in Honor of Alice-Mary Talbot,* edited by Denis Sullivan, Elizabeth A. Fisher, and Stratis Papaioannou, 99–124. London: Brill.

—. 2013. *Michael Psellos: Rhetoric and Authorship in Byzantium.* Cambridge: Cambridge University Press.

—. 2017. "General Introduction." In *Michael Psellos on Literature and Art,* edited by Charles Barber and Stratis Papaioannou, 1–7. Notre Dame, IL: University of Notre Dame Press.

—, trans. 2017. "Synopsis of the Rhetorical Forms based on Hemogenes' On Forms." In *Michael Psellos on Literature and Art,* edited by Charles Barber and Straits Papaioannou, 20–30. Notre Dame, IL: University of Notre Dame Press.

Patillon, Michel. 1973. *Corpus Rhetoricum.* Paris: Les Belles Lettres, 2008–2012. Patristic Studies.

Psellus, Michael. 1996. *Fourteen Byzantine Rulers: The Chronographia of Michael Psellus.* Translated by E. R. A. Sewter. London: Penguin Books, 1996.

Quandahl, Ellen, and Susan Jarratt. 2008. "'To Recall Him . . . Will be a Subject of Lamentation': Anna Comnena as Rhetorical Historiographer." *Rhetorica* 26 (3): 301–35.

Quandahl, Ellen. 2012. "*Andreia* in the Nunnery: Rhetorical Learnedness in Twelfth-Century Byzantium." In *Rhetoric: Concord and Controversy,* edited by Antonio De Valasco and Melody Lehn, 200–09. Longrove, IL: Waveland Press.

Roilos, Panagiotis. 2005. *Amphoteroglossia: A Poetics of the Twelfth-Century Greek Novel.* Cambridge: Center for Hellenic Studies.

Russell, D. A., and N. G. Wilson. 1981. *Menander Rhetor.* Oxford: Clarendon.

Sewter, E. R. A, trans. 1953. *Michael Psellos' Chronographia.* New Haven: Yale University Press.

Tornikes, Georges. 1970. "Logos epi tōi thanatōi porfurogennētou kuras Annēs tēs Kaisarissēs." In *Lettres et Discours,* by Georges et Demetrios Tornikes, edited by Jean Darrouzès, 221–323. Paris: Èditions De Centre National de la Recherche Scientifique.

Valiavitcharska, Vessela. 2013. "Rhetoric in the Hands of by Byzantine Grammarian." *Rhetorica* 31, (3): 237–60.

Walker, Jeffrey. 2004. "These Things I Have Not Betrayed: Michael Psellos' Encomium of His Mother as a Defense of Rhetoric." *Rhetorica* 22 (1): 49–101.

—. 2017. "Synopsis of Rhetoric in Verses, based on the Hermogenian Corpus." In *Michael Psellos on Literature and Art,* edited by Charles Barber and Stratis Papaioannou, 31–65. Notre Dame, IL: University of Notre Dame Press.

Westerink, L. G., ed. 1948. *Michael Psellus, De omnifaria doctrina.* Utrecht: J. L. Beijers.

—, ed. 1962. *Anonymous Prolegomena to Platonic Philosophy.* Amsterdam: North Holland Publishing.

Whitby, Mary. 2010. "Rhetorical Questions." In *A Companion to Byzantium*, edited by Liz James, 239–50. Chichester, UK: Blackwell Publishing.

Wooten, Cecil W., trans. 1987. *Hermogenes' On Types of Style*. Chapel Hill: University of North Carolina Press.

Zonaras, John. 1987. *Epitome Historiarum*. Edited by Th. Büttner-Wobst, 726–68. Corpus Scriptorum Byzantinae, Vol III. Bonn: Impensis Ed. Weberi.

Jewish and Hebraic

Agamben, Giorgio. 2011. *The Sacrament of Language: An Archeology of the Oath*. Translated by Adam Kotsko. Palo Alto, CA: Stanford University Press.

Ariel, David S. 1988. *The Mystic Quest: An Introduction to Jewish Mysticism*. Northvale, NJ: Aronson.

Amram, David W. 1988. *The Makers of Hebrew Books in Italy*. London: The Holland P Ltd..

Baddar, Maha. 2010. "The Arabs Did Not 'Just' Translate Aristotle: Al-Farabi's Logico-Rhetorical Theory." In *The Responsibilities of Rhetoric,* edited by M. Smith and B. Warnick, 230–42. Long Grove, IL: Waveland Press.

Biale, David, ed. 2002. *The Culture of the Jews*. New York: Random House.

Billig, Michael. 1987. *Arguing and Thinking: A Rhetorical Approach to Social Psychology*. Cambridge: Cambridge University Press.

Bloom, Harold. 1975. *Kabbalah and Criticism*. New York: Seabury Press.

Bernard-Donals, Michael, and Janice Fernheimer, eds. 2014. *Jewish Rhetoric: History, Theory, Practice*. Waltham, MA: Brandeis University Press.

Boman, Thorleif. 1960. *Hebrew Thought Compared with Greek*. New York: Norton.

Bonfil, Robert. 1994. *Jewish Life in Renaissance Italy*. Translated by Anthony Oldcorn. Berkeley, CA: University of California Press.

—. 1981. *Nofet Zufim: On Hebrew Rhetoric*. Jerusalem, Israel: The Magnes Press.

Boyarin, Daniel. 1994. *Intertextuality and the Reading of Midrash*. Bloomington, IN: Indiana University Press.

—. 2012. *Socrates and the Fat Rabbis*. Chicago, IL: University of Chicago Press.

Buber, Martin. 1999. *On Judaism*. Edited by Nathan N. Glazer. New York: Schocken Books.

Burke, Kenneth. 1950. *A Rhetoric of Motives*. New York: Prentice Hall.

Burkert, Walter. 1985. *Greek Religion*. Cambridge, MA: Harvard University Press.

—. 1989. *Ancient Mystery Cults*. Cambridge, MA: Harvard University Press.

—. 1992. *The Orientalizing Revolution: Near East Influence of Greek Culture in the Early Archaic Age*. Cambridge, MA: Harvard University Press.

Charney, Davida H. 2015. *Persuading God: Rhetorical Studies of First-Person Psalms*. Sheffield, UK: Sheffield Phoenix Press Ltd.

Cicero, Marcus Tullius. 1942. *De Oratore* Book III. In *De Oratore III, De Fato, Paradoxa Stoicorum, De Partitiones Oratoriae*. Translated by H. Rackham, 1–185. Cambridge, MA: Harvard University Press.

Collins, John Joseph. 1999. *Between Athens to Jerusalem*. 2nd ed. Grand Rapids, MI: Eerdmans.

Dan, Joseph. 1998. *Jewish Mysticism: Late Antiquity Vol 1*. Northvale, NJ: Aronson Press.

Daniels, Peter T., and William Bright, eds. 1996. *The World's Writing System*s. New York: Oxford University Press.

Daube, David. 1965. *Collaboration with Tyranny in Rabbinic Law*. New York: Oxford University Press.

De Burgh, W. G. 1947. *The Legacy of the Ancient World*. 2 Vols. Middlesex, UK: Penguin Publishing.

Edelman, Samuel. 2007. *Within a Widening Gyre*. Cresskill, NJ: Hampton Press.

Encyclopedia Judaica. 1972. 16 Vols. New York: Macmillan.

Fernheimer, Janice W. 2010. "Talmidae Rhetoricae: Drashing Up Models and Methods for Jewish Rhetorical Studies." *College English* 72, (6): 577–89.

—. 2014. *Stepping into Zion: Hatzaad Harishon, Black Jews, and the Remaking of Jewish Identity*. Tuscaloosa, AL: University of Alabama Press.

Fischel, Henry A. 1997. *Rabbinic Literature and Greco-Roman Philosophy: A Study of Epicurea and Phetorica in Early Midrashic Writings*. Leiden, Netherlands: Brill Academic Publishing.

Frank, David. 2003. "The Jewish Counter-Model: Talmudic Argumentation, the New Rhetoric Project, and the Classical Rhetorical Tradition." *Journal of Communication and Religion* 26 (2): 163–94.

Frank, Daniel. 2000. *The Jewish Philosophy Reader*. New York: Routledge.

Freedman, Rabbi H., and Maurice Simon, trans. 1939. *Midrash Rabbah*. 10 Vols. London: Soncino Press.

Freud, Sigmund. 1955. *Moses and Monotheism*. Visalia, CA: Vintage.

Gellis, Eliza. 2020. "Hadassah, That is Esther: Diasporic Rhetoric in the Book of Esther." In *The Routledge Handbook of Comparative World Rhetorics: Studies in the History, Application, and Teaching of Rhetoric Beyond Traditional Greco-Roman Contexts,* edited by Keith Lloyd, 126–33. New York: Routledge.

Gitay, Yehoshua. 2011. *Methodology, Speech, Society: The Hebrew Bible*. Toronto: Sun Media Corporation.

Greenbaum, Andrea, and Deborah Holdstein, eds. 2008. *Judaic Perspectives in Rhetoric and Composition Studies*. Cresskill, NJ: Hampton.

Guler, Elif, and Iklim Goksel. 2019. "Understanding Turkish Rhetoric in the Intertextuality of Two Seminal Texts: The Orkhon Inscriptions and Atatürk's Nutuk." *Advances in the History of Rhetoric* 22 (2): 194–207.

Handelman, Susan. 1982. *Slayers of Moses: The Emergence of Rabbinic Interpretation in Modern Literary Theory*. Albany, NY: SUNY Press.

Haralick, Robert M. 1995. *The Inner Meaning of the Hebrew Alphabet*. Northvale, NJ: Aronson.

Hidary, Richard. 2017. *Rabbis and Classical Rhetoric: Sophistic Education and Oratory in the Talmud and Midrash*. Cambridge: Cambridge University Press.

Harris, Maurice. 1929. *Medieval Jews: From the Moslem Conquest of Spain to the Discovery of America.* 5th ed. New York: Bloch Co.

Ivry, Alfred L. 1999. "Jewish Averroism." In *The Columbia History of Western Philosophy*, edited by Richard H. Popkin, 196–200. New York: Columbia University Press.

Kaplan, Aryeh. 1980. *The Bahir: Illumination.* Revised ed. San Francisco: Red Wheel/Weiser.

—. 1997. *Sefer Yetsirah: The Book of Creation.* Revised ed. San Francisco: Red Wheel/Weiser.

Katz, Steven B. 1991. "In the Beginning" (poem). *Postmodern Culture* 1 (3). doi.org/10.1353/pmc.1991.0015

—. 1995a. "The Epistemology of the Kabbalah: Toward a Jewish Philosophy of Rhetoric." *Rhetoric Society Quarterly* 25 (1-4): 107–22.

—. 1995b. "The Kabbalah as a Theory of Rhetoric: Another Suppressed Epistemology." In *Rhetoric, Cultural Studies, and Literacy: Selected Papers from the 1994 Conference of the Rhetoric Society of America,* edited by John Frederick Reynolds, 109–17. Mahwah NJ: Erlbaum.

—. 1997. "The Alphabet as Ethics: A Rhetorical Basis for Moral Reality in Hebrew Letters." In *Rhetorical Democracy: Discursive Practices of Civic Engagement,* edited by Gerard Hauser and Amy Grimm, 195–204. Mahwah NJ: Lawrence Erlbaum.

—. 2003. "Letter as Essence: The Rhetorical (Im)pulse of the Hebrew Alefbet." Special issue "On Jewish Rhetoric," edited by David Franks. *Journal of Communication and Religion* 26: 125–60.

—. 2009. "The Hebrew Bible as Another, Jewish Sophistic: A Genesis of Absence and Desire in Ancient Rhetoric." In *Ancient Non-Greek Rhetorics*, edited by Carol Lipson and Roberta A. Binkley, 125–50. Anderson, SC: Parlor Press.

—. 2014. "Socrates as Rabbi: The Story of the Aleph and the Alpha in an Information Age." In *Jewish Rhetorics: History, Theory, Practice,* edited by Janice Fernheimer and Michael Bernard-Donals, 93–111. Waltham MA: Brandeis University Press.

—. 2020. "Sonic Rhetorics as Ethics in Action: Hidden Temporalities of Sound in Language(s)." *Humanities*: Special Issue on Ethics and Literary Practice 9 (13): 1–19.

—. 2021. "What Is Jewish Rhetorics? Issues of Faiths, Philology, Diasporas, Nationalities, Assimilations, Resistance: A Case Study." In *The Routledge Handbook of Comparative World Rhetorics: Studies in the History, Application, and Teaching of Rhetoric Beyond Traditional Greco-Roman Contexts,* edited by Keith Lloyd, 49–57. New York: Routledge.

Katz, Steven T. 1983. *The Conservative Character of Mystical Experience.* New York: Oxford University Press.

Kinneavy, James L. 1987. *Greek Origins of Christian Faith: An Inquiry.* New York: Oxford University Press.

Isaacs, Ronald H. 1996. Mitzvot: *A Sourcebook for the 613 Commandments.* Northvale, NJ: Jason Aronson.

Lieberman, Saul. 1962. *Hellenism in Jewish Palestine: Studies in the Literary Transmission Beliefs and Manners of Palestine in the 1st Century BCE through 4th Century CE.* 2nd ed. Edited by Alexander Marx. New York: Jewish Publication Society of America.

Leon, Judah Messer. 1983. *The Book of the Honeycomb's Flow.* A Critical Edition and Translation by Isaac Rabinowitz. Ithaca, NY: Cornell University Press.

Lesley, Arthur M. 1983a. "Review." *Rhetorica* 1 (2): 101–08

—. 1983b. "Nofet Zufim, on Hebrew Rhetoric." *Rhetorica* 1 (2): 101–14.

—. 1984. "Sefer Nofet Tsufim and the Study of Rhetoric." *Prooftexts* 4: 312–16.

Lipson, Carol, and Roberta A. Binkley, eds. 2004. *Rhetoric Before and Beyond the Greeks.* Albany, New York: SUNY Press.

—. 2009. *Ancient Non-Greek Rhetorics.* Anderson, SC: Parlor Press, 2009.

Maimonides, Moses. 1963. *The Guide of the Perplexed.* Translated by Shlomo Pines. Chicago: University of Chicago Press.

Margolis, Max L., and Alexander Marx. 1927. *A History of the Jewish People.* Philadelphia: The Jewish Publication Society of America.

Metzger, David. 2014. "Maimonides' Contribution to a Theory of Self Persuasion." In *Jewish Rhetorics: History, Theory, Practice*, edited by Michael Bernard-Donals and Janice W. Fernheimer, 112–30. Waltham, MA: Brandeis. University Press.

—, and Steven B. Katz. 2010. "The 'Place' of Rhetoric in Aggadic Midrash." *College English* 72 (6): 638–53.

Miles, Jack. 1996. *God: A Biography.* Visalia, CA: Vintage.

Miletto, Gianfranco. 2004. "The Teaching Program of David Ben Abraham and His Son Abraham Provenzali in Its Historical-Cultural Context." In *Cultural Intermediaries: Jewish Intellectuals in Early Modern Italy,* compiled by David B. Ruderman and Giuseppe Veltri, 127–48. Philadelphia, PA: University of Pennsylvania Press.

Miller, J Hillis. 2009. *For Derrida.* New York: Fordham University Press.

The Mishnah: Translated from the Hebrew with Introduction and Brief Explanatory Notes. 2012. Translated by Hebert Danby. Peabody, MA: Hendrickson Publishing.

Moskow, Michal Anne, and Steven B. Katz. 2008. "Composing Identity and Community in Cyberspace: A 'Rhetorical Ethnography' of Writing on Jewish Discussion Groups in the United States and Germany." *Judaic Perspectives in Rhetoric and Compositional Studies,* edited by Andrea Greenbaum and Deborah Holdstein, 85–108. Cresskill, NJ: Hampton.

Munk, Rabbi Michael L. 1983. *The Wisdom in the Hebrew Alphabet: The Sacred Letters as a Guide to Jewish Deed and Thought.* New York: Mesorah Press.

Murphy, James J. 1985. "The Book of the Honeycomb's Flow (Sēpher Nōpheth Ṣūphīm)." *Speculum* 60 (1): 161–64.

Perelman, Chaim, and Lucie Olbrechts-Tyteca. 1971. *The New Rhetoric: A Treatise on Argumentation.* Translated by John Wilkinson and Purcell Weaver. Notre Dame, IN: University of Notre Dame Press.

Philo. 1991. *The Complete Works of Philo.* Translated by C. D. Yonge. Peabody, MA: Hendrickson Publishers.

Pirkei Avos (Ethics of the Fathers): A New Translation with a Commentary Anthologized from the Classical Rabbinic Sources. 1984. Translated by Rabbi Nosson Scherman and Meir Zlotowitz. Brooklyn: Mesorah Publications.

Plato. 1961. "Cratylus." In *The Collected Dialogues of Plato Including the Letters*, edited by Edith Hamilton and Huntington Cairns, and translated by Benjamin Jowett, 421–74. Princeton, NJ: Princeton University Press.

Rabinowitz, Isaac. 1983. *The Book of Honeycomb's Flow: Sepher Nophet Suphim.* Cornell University Press.

Richardson, Timothy. 2013. *Contingency, Immanence, and the Subject of Rhetoric.* Anderson, SC: Parlor Press.

Ridolfo, Jim. 2004. "Judah Messer Leon and the Sefer Nofet Zuphim." *Jewish Rhetorics: History, Theory, Practice,* edited by Michael Bernard-Donals and Janice W. Fernheimer, 46–57. Waltham, MA: Brandeis University Press.

Scholem, Gershom. 1974. *Major Trends in Jewish Mysticism.* New York: Schocken.

Schwartz, Seth. 2012. *Were the Jews a Mediterranean Society? Reciprocity and Solidarity in Ancient Judaism.* Princeton, New Jersey: Princeton University Press.

Sperling, Harry, and Maurice Simon, trans. 1984. *The Zohar: An English Translation.* 2nd edition. 5 Vols. London: Soncino Press.

Stavroulakis, Nicholas. 1990. *The Jews of Greece: An Essay.* Istanbul: Bosphorus Books.

Strack, Hermann L. 1931. *Introduction to the Talmud and Midrash.* New York: Jewish Publication Society of America.

Strack, Herman L., and Günter Stemberger. 1996. *Introduction to the Talmud and Midrash.* Translated by Markus Bockmuehl. Minneapolis, Minnesota: Fortress.

Steiner, George. 2013. *Grammars of Creation.* London: Faber and Faber.

Steinsaltz, Adin. 2006. *The Essential Talmud.* New York: Basic Books.

Shulvass, Moses A. 1973. *The Jews in the World of the Renaissance.* Translated by Elvin I. Kose. Leiden - E.J. Brill and Spertus College of Judaica Press.

Tirosh-Samuelson, Hava. 1997. "Jewish Philosophy on the Eve of Modernity." In *History of Jewish Philosophy,* edited by Daniel H. Frank, 499–573. Routledge History of World Philosophies, Vol. 2. London: Routledge.

Urbach, E. E., R. J. Zwi Werblowsky, and Ch. Wirszubski, eds. 1967. *Studies in Mysticism and Religion, Presented to Gershom G. Scholem on His Seventieth Birthday by his Pupils, Colleagues, and Friends.* Jerusalem: Magnes Press, Hebrew University.

Van Bekkum, Wout Jac. 2003. "Jewish Intellectual Culture in Renaissance Context." In *Medieval and Renaissance Humanism: Rhetoric, Representation, and Reform,* edited by Stephen Gersh and Bert Roest, 227–41. Boston: Brill.

Verman, Mark. 1996. *The History and Varieties of Jewish Meditation.* Northvale, NJ: Aronson.

Vital, Chayyim. 1999. *The Tree of Life: Chayyim Vital's Introduction to the Kabbalah of Isaac Luria. The Palace of Adam Kadmon*. Translated by Donald Wilder Menzi and Zwe Padeh. Northvale, NJ: Jason Aronson.

Watt, John W. 2005. *Aristotelian Rhetoric in Syriac: Barhebraeus, Butyrum Sapientiae, Book of Rhetoric*. Leiden: Brill.

Zinberg, Israel. 1974. *A History of Jewish Literature: Italian Jewry in the Renaissance Era*. Translated by Bernard Martin. Jersey City, NJ: KTAV House, Inc.

Zonta, Mauro. 2006. *Hebrew Scholasticism in the Fifteenth Century: A History and Source Book*. 1st ed. New York: Springer-Verlag.

Glossary of Terms

Term	Translation
amphoteroglossia	double-tonguedness; ambivalence
asapheia	obscurity (See Kustas 1973, 12, on obscurity as a virtue of style in Byzantine rhetorical theory; and Kustas 1973, 88, not a vice when an author "says one thing while intending another and the reader grasps his true intent.")
basilikos logos	imperial oration; speech in praise of an emperor/ruler; Menander Rhetor describes headings and appropriate uses.
ekphrasis	descriptive language; language that brings what is shown before the eyes; one of the preliminary exercises.
emphasis	speaking by implication when one cannot speak openly (See Kennedy, *Invention*, 189.)
enargeia	vividness
encomion	speech of praise, for example expressing greatness or virtue. One of the preliminary rhetorical exercises (*progymnasmata*).
enkyklios paideia	rounded, or general, education; education in the Greek cultural heritage.
epainos	brief words of praise; Aphthonius and Hermogenes suggest that *epainos* is brief, while *encomion* is more developed (from Kennedy, *Progymnasmata* 81, 108).
eschēmatismenos logos	figured discourse; often, using allusion and imitation to say one thing through another.
ēthos	character; disposition; *ēthopoiia*, ēthos making, or speech in imitation of a character, is one of the preliminary exercises.
kairos	opportunity; the opportune moment.
mimēsis	imitation; it is typical of Byzantine composition to acknowledge history and tradition through imitation of past works. (See Hunger, "On Imitation.")
panegyric	speech or composition of high praise
poikilos	varied, manifold, many-colored, intricate (See Walker, *Rhetoric and Poetics*, 139ff.)
progymnasmata	Preliminary exercises; a sequence of exercises for pre-rhetorical training. Kennedy, *Progymnasmata,* offers translations of extant versions.

rhētōr	orator; rhetor.
synkrisis	a comparison; one of the preliminary exercises.
technē	art, as in the art of rhetoric, the art of the general. The craft of doing a thing artfully, by method or technique.
thrēnos	a lament; speech of lamentation.
tropos	way, manner, fashion; turn (See Webb on ekphrasis of tropos, 69ff.) (See Hermogenes chapter on tropos in Kennedy, *Invention*.)
Yeshiva	a Jewish school, particularly for Talmudic study

8 POLYNESIAN-HAWAIIAN RHETORICS

PREFATORY INTRODUCTION

Georganne Nordstrom and kuʻualoha hoʻomanawanui

There is no one word for *rhetoric* in ʻōlelo Hawaiʻi (Hawaiian) that represents how it is used in the Greco-Roman tradition, but assuming this absence of a nomenclature indicates a lack of attention to the rhetorical in Kanaka ʻŌiwi (Native Hawaiian) culture would be a mistake. Indeed, Kanaka ʻŌiwi have a lengthy tradition of critically engaging with language as a call to action and to codify cultural norms, values, and expected behaviors. But even beyond these categories recognizable to Western rhetorical theorists as persuasion and epistemic, the intimate relationship Kanaka ʻŌiwi have with language also manifests in savvy manipulations of meaning and playfulness that continues to be a part of daily interactions.

The careful and comprehensive recording of rhetorical traditions and practices by Kanaka ʻŌiwi culture and language practitioners across the centuries provide a wealth of insight into the ways rhetoric was wielded with keen precision by Kanaka ʻŌiwi. Hoʻopāpā, for example, is described by language and culture expert and researcher Mary Kawena Pukui[1] as follows:

> It was in hoʻopāpā that ancient Hawaiians expressed most fully the constructive aggression of pitting intellect against intellect. Hoʻopāpā was a battle of wits . . . that called for a debater's logic, quick thinking, good vocabulary, and a store of background knowledge. But the hoʻopāpā also employed Hawaiian subtleties of thought. A contest might proceed from seeing who could name the most places with certain climate or geographical similarities, to the instant composition of chants or riddles that included groupings of words,

---

1. Pukui, Haertig, and Lee 1972.

480

word sounds, puns, or the nuances of hidden meanings or linked historical references.

Striking here are the expectations of copia and ability to perform extemporaneously—attributes nurtured in rhetorical training. Intellectual agility in the form of wordplay that exploits the multiple meanings embedded in Hawaiian words is also highly valued in Hawaiian
culture,[2] and often enacted as a rhetorical strategy. Word play is also fundamental in kaona,
which includes hidden meanings, allusions, and veiled references, and is a tradition both pervasive and complex—so much so it is often enacted so that some meanings are comprehensible
only by particular audiences. Woven into performances of these traditions are meiwi,[3] or po-
etic/literary devices, such as ʻēkoʻa (opposites), helu (listings), hoʻomaoe (allusion), and pīnaʻi
(repetition). These are but a sampling of the abundant examples that demonstrate rhetorical
savvy and illustrate how Kanaka ʻŌiwi traditions can expand understandings of the complex
and culturally grounded ways rhetorical acts are exercised.

This chapter discusses several Kanaka ʻŌiwi traditions, such as moʻokūʻauhau (genealogy)
and the use of meiwi, in the genre of mele inoa (name songs) focusing on three specific examples to trace the continuity in how they were taught, received, and transmitted over time.
Just as there is no rendering of *rhetoric* in ʻōlelo Hawaiʻi, the way rhetorical practices were
taught similarly do not align with Euro-American understandings of teaching. Rather, as
the ōlelo noʻeau (proverb) invoked in the chapter, ma ka hana ka ʻike (in working one learns),
points to, learning happens through a process of observation then imitation and innovation to
adapt practices to the dynamics of a current situation. While proficiency in such interactions
would not have been attained in an institutionalized instructional setting like the ones most
of us are accustomed to, it is easy to imagine a novice experimenting with linguistic strategies
and repertoires in hoʻopāpā, for example, similar to the way progymnasmata were used by
students of classical rhetoric in Greece and Rome. Through our discussion, we illustrate the
elegance and dynamics of a long-standing rhetorical practice, which although not taught as a
subject in and of itself, enriches understandings of how rhetorical training and transmission
can be conceived.

---

2. Silva 2004, 12.
3. hoʻomanawanui 2015; Perreira 2011.

8.1 Post-Colonial Hawaiian (Non-European), c. 20th and 21st Centuries, Hawaii

He Inoa no ke Kanaka (In the Name of the Person): *Mele Inoa* as Rhetorical Continuity

Georganne Nordstrom and kuʻualoha hoʻomanawanui

While in recent decades literature produced by and about Kanaka Maoli (Native Hawaiians)[4] has become a robust field of study, positioning Kanaka Maoli traditional communicative practices as rhetorical acts is an area that remains largely under-examined. In their studies of Kanaka Maoli rhetorical practices, Brandy Nālani McDougall and Georganne Nordstrom[5] have suggested that concepts aligned with Western rhetoric, such as kairos, ethos, logos, and pathos, are effective in understanding rhetorical acts enacted by Kanaka Maoli. At the same time, these same projects have demonstrated that while the terms themselves are useful, how they are realized is culturally grounded. To use one of the Aristotelian appeals as example, while it was essential for an aliʻi nui (high chief) to establish ethos with their people, understanding how that ethos is established and the qualities associated with a strong ethos are dependent on understanding the cultural context of the act. This project builds on this work, moving from analysis of reception of a rhetorical act to that of production by acknowledging that the teaching of rhetorical traditions is similarly transmitted through culturally bound pedagogical practices.

In this chapter, we focus on mele inoa, or name songs/chants, written "to honor and to praise individuals of note"[6] as instructional texts that convey rhetorical practices. As tributes to important cultural figures, mele inoa are often delivered in contexts analogous to the Western classical branch of epideictic and demonstrate how Kanaka Maoli rhetorical strategies are grounded in a long history of traditional practices that continue to be enacted through mele (chant, song, poetry), including mele inoa. We include three mele inoa (in both ʻōlelo Hawaiʻi [Hawaiian language] and English translation) composed in different time periods to demonstrate a continuity in pedagogical transmission: the first, "Mele Inoa no Kaumualiʻi" (Name Chant for Kaumualiʻi), represents the traditional period (pre–1778, the date that signals the onslaught against Hawaiian autonomy); the second, "He Mele Inoa no ka Mōʻī Wahine Liliʻuokalani" (A Name Chant for the Queen Liliʻuokalani), was composed during the political turmoil surrounding Hawaiʻi's forced annexation to the US (1898); and the third, "Ka Niʻo o Maleka Ailana" (The Pinnacle of America), is a contemporary mele inoa honoring US President Barack Obama after he was first elected to the nation's highest office in 2008. We begin

---

4. Unless otherwise noted, all translations are by kuʻualoha hoʻomanawanui. We do not italicize Hawaiian words as foreign, as ʻōlelo Hawaiʻi is a living language native to Hawaiʻi where we live and work.

5. McDougall and Nordstrom 2011, 98–121.

6. Silva 2015, 33.

the chapter with a discussion of teaching and learning in a Kanaka Maoli context to support the assertion that all mele, in addition to being rhetorical acts, are also instructional texts. We then situate mele inoa within both epideictic and deliberative branches of rhetoric to illustrate that a Kanaka Maoli audience would receive and understand such performances as conveying both cultural norms and practices that signal and inform kuleana (rights, responsibilities) to the community, which includes ensuring the continuance of Hawaiian rhetorical traditions through such forms as mele inoa. Finally, drawing from Kanaka Maoli scholars work on mele and other oral traditions,[7] we identify six meiwi (rhetorical/literary strategies) in addition to hoʻonaninani (praise)—kaona (hidden/layered meaning), moʻokūʻauhau (genealogy), pono (balance), ʻēkoʻa (oppositional but complementary diads), helu (to list, recount), and pīnaʻi (repetition)— highlighting how the presence of these tropes and strategies represent the deliberate continuance of rhetorical traditions made possible through indigenous pedagogical practices.

MA KA HANA KA ʻIKE: TEACHING AND LEARNING IN A KANAKA MAOLI CONTEXT

Before more fully introducing the three mele that are the focus of this chapter and articulating how they exemplify a continuity in rhetorical form and content, and thus represent the form itself as instructional, it is first important to identify Kanaka Maoli pedagogical approaches to instruction and knowledge transmission. Transmission of knowledge and practice through demonstration, rather than through what George Kennedy calls "conceptualized theories of rhetoric" more familiar in Western cultures with long histories of writing,[8] is a formalized approach to learning in Kanaka Maoli culture, as is represented in the ʻōlelo noʻeau (proverb), *Ma ka hana ka ʻike*[9] (in working one learns), and *Paʻa ka waha, nānā ka maka, hana me ka lima*[10] (shut the mouth—don't ask questions, observe, then imitate by doing it with the hands). Speaking of "traditional cultures," or those that "do not use writing and have been relatively untouched by western civilization,"[11] articulations that would describe Hawaiian culture prior to the aggressive settlement of the missionaries in the 1820s, Kennedy offers the following to illustrate how rhetorical practices might be conceived:

> Although oral societies generally have words for an "orator," for various speech genres, and sometimes for rhetorical devices, and many accord high honor to eloquence, conceptualized theories of rhetoric are found only in societies that use writing, and even there full conceptualization is slow to

---

7. hoʻomanawanui 2015; Perreira 2011; Silva 2015.

8. Kennedy 1999, 15.

9. Pukui 1983, 227.

10. Ibid., 281.

11. Kennedy 1999, 15.

emerge. Speakers cannot explain well how they do what they do, and skill is learned by imitation, not by rule.[12]

While this absence of texts with conceptualized theories of rhetoric might be largely applicable to Kanaka Maoli traditional culture, the representation of transmission being correlated to a kind of non-critical imitation, wherein "speakers cannot explain well how they do what they do," is arguably an interpretation of an indigenous traditional practice grounded in a Western construct.

As the well-known 'ōlelo no'eau that begins this section points to, Kanaka Maoli expect active interactions to be teaching moments that engender critical engagement. For example, ku'u 'upena (throw net) and ho'opāpā (debate) are two common activities in Kanaka Maoli culture that require skills that go beyond imitation to realize success—one must adjust the approach to casting net to account for the changing and sometimes unpredictable ocean, just as in debate one must anticipate the opponent's tactics several exchanges in advance. While the explanation of *how* to do something might not look like it would in a Western context, for Kanaka Maoli, the demonstrative act itself embodies the *how*, which includes an accounting of contextual fluidity when negotiating enactment. Thus, adoption of a technique or practice demands an intellectual acuity that allows for adaptation as well.

The importance of rhetorical speech acts in Kanaka Maoli culture is evident in the articulation of roles and techniques (as Kennedy also acknowledges is common in traditional cultures). Indeed, an orator in 'ōlelo Hawai'i (Hawaiian language) is kākā'ōlelo (orator), and, as we will discuss more fully in the following sections, scholars have identified a catalogue of meiwi, used in mele and mo'olelo (narrative prose).[13] In terms specific to mele, Noenoe Silva has identified characteristics necessary for a haku mele (composer), drawing from the work of esteemed Kanaka Maoli historian and scholar Samuel Kamakau (1815–1876). She explains that because of the social and political significance of mele, the activity of haku mele required education and skill and highlights the kuleana of the haku mele: "mele contained the memory of the people, so the haku mele had to be trustworthy as well as talented."[14] These characteristics Noenoe Silva notes are reminiscent of those articulated by the ancient Greeks (such as Quintilian and Cicero) as necessary for a "good" rhetorician. While there are clear similarities in terms, functions, and roles across the two cultures, how effective rhetorical practices are conveyed are undoubtedly ingrained in cultural norms, which informs pedagogy.

Although writing was introduced in Hawai'i in the 1820s along with Western styles of learning that largely involve one-way instruction (Freire would later famously call this model of teaching a banking model of education), cultural knowledge of appropriate behaviors and practices, including rhetorical acts such as composing mele, continue to be conveyed from one generation to the next through example, demonstration, and collective practice. And while imitation may play a role in this transmission of knowledge, it is definitely a critically

---

12. Ibid., 15.
13. ho'omanawanui 2015.
14. Silva 2004, 182–83.

engaged imitation. While texts that focus on how rhetorical forms and practices are produced in Western contexts typically involve complex conceptualizations of theories of rhetoric, such as in Aristotle's *Rhetoric* or, more recently Sharon Crowley and Debra Hawhee's *Ancient Rhetorics for Contemporary Students*,[15] in Kanaka Maoli culture, knowledge transmission through demonstration is at the piko (center) of Hawaiian pedagogy.[16]

The first mele we introduce was composed during the pre-settler era (pre–1820),[17] a period that would align with Kennedy's articulation of traditional culture in terms of its orality and autonomy, and, to some extent, in that rhetorical acts were "primarily a means of attaining consensus"[18] (although, the purpose of all rhetorical acts are in some ways a means of attaining consensus). The second mele we discuss is written for Queen Liliʻuokalani and published in the period following the introduction of writing in the early nineteenth century. Kanaka Maoli scholars writing about that time period have identified that demonstration continued to be integral to learning traditional Kanaka practices, such as composing mele. And although the mele we discuss in this chapter is written for the Queen, examinations of the Queen as a haku mele are useful here. In *The Queen's Songbook*, an annotated collection of mele written by Queen Liliʻuokalani, the editors note that it is hard to trace how Liliʻuokalani became such an accomplished haku mele whose work is so notably grounded in ʻōlelo Hawaiʻi and meiwi traditions.[19] Her formal education was in English, and for nine years, beginning at age three, she boarded at school where the predominant mode of interaction was in English and she had "limited contact with adult Hawaiians."[20] The editors go on to say that Liliʻuokalani may have "at least indirectly . . . assimilated some of [her] poetic sense" from Konia (her hānai, or adoptive, mother).[21] While unquestionably the Queen was most accomplished and her rhetorical and literary prowess is not typical in any sense, the understanding that techniques were acquired through exposure and immersion rather than formally taught in the Western sense exemplifies transmission of knowledge in Kanaka Maoli culture.[22]

Even after over 150 years of (attempted) assimilation into a Western-style of education, this traditional method of transmission of cultural knowledge and practice through demonstra-

---

15. Crowley and Hawhee 2011.

16. hoʻomanawanui 2018.

17. We are using this term to refer to the period of time preceding the arrival of the missionaries in 1820. This time is often referred to as pre-contact, but Kanaka Maoli had "contact" with outsiders for centuries before 1820. The arrival of the missionaries goes beyond contact, and signifies an aggressive attack on Kanaka Maoli autonomy in government, education, and cultural and linguistic practices.

18. Crowley and Hawhee 2011, 15.

19. Queen Liliʻuokalani 1999, 4–5.

20. Ibid., 4.

21. Ibid., 5.

22. Much of her innate rhetorical and poetic skill can be attributed to her genealogy, what Pua Kanahele calls ancestral knowledge as the Queen comes from a long line of accomplished composers. This advanced sense of poetics is also part of her ethos as an aliʻi, as it was expected of the royals, and/or those close to them, to be gifted in traditional poetics.

tion is still the dominant form of instruction outside of formal institutions. Kumu (teacher) and haku mele Kalena Silva's 2015 article, "A Contemporary Response to Increasing Mele Performance Contexts," discusses contemporary mele composing practices, and identifies the role collected mele "from antiquity" through the twenty-first-century play as "invaluable examples of traditional poetic language use [that] provide a solid foundation for contemporary Hawaiian language composers."[23] The claim here illustrates that the texts themselves are instructional specifically for haku mele and point to a Kanaka Maoli-informed pedagogical practice that begins with example and leads/demands students to identify patterns and tropes. This practice differs in subtle ways from how one might learn rhetorical techniques and their applications in a Western context, which might begin with terms and definitions followed by examples that show students "how it's done." These subtle differences illicit different expectations on the learner in terms of critical engagement.

Although arguably not specifically written as a pedagogical work, Kalena Silva's article can be examined as an example of instruction through demonstration. Following a discussion of the decline and revitalization of 'ōlelo Hawai'i, Silva notes that the focus of the project is to "describe mele composed within four contemporary contexts, including the traditional and contemporary significance of the events and the intent, meaning and form of the mele"[24] (mele inoa being one of those forms). He provides the context and impetus for the mele he includes, identifies different genres of mele, and names several meiwi and traditional practices, noting the "best" mele are:

> . . . rooted in an intrinsic Hawaiian worldview from which skillfully crafted poetic, rather than vernacular, language conveys meaning. Such mele contain thoughtful use of metaphor and simile; they include phrases from and allusions to older mele that support and elucidate meaning; they are deftly structured using meiwi . . . including linked assonance, enumeration [helu] and paired opposites ['ēko'a] for completion, and restatement for emphasis [pīna'i], among other traditional devices; and, where appropriate, they contain kaona, or hidden meaning, to challenge the listener but also delight him or her when the kaona is understood.[25]

In the article, however, there is no *meta* discussion as to when a meiwi might be most effectively used, as one might find in a western instructional text on rhetoric. Silva (2015) does present the rhetorical situation for each mele, which speaks to audience and motivation for composing but leaves it to the reader to identify common patterns to each situation. Although tropes and devices common across mele are noted, identification of the components of the rhetorical situation that would call for a specific meiwi as well as what to consider when constructing a specific meiwi are not as apparent. Silva (2015) does articulate that "an important part of the

---

23. Silva 2015, 30.
24. Ibid., 25.
25. Ibid., 30.

composing process is the paka, or constructive criticism of the mele, provided by knowledge-able peers,"[26] but does not go so far as to articulate what such a paka exercise might focus on. In several places, he highlights examples in a mele when discussing a strategy, often without naming the strategy—in other words, he explains function through demonstration. For example, he explains a specific rhetorical move in one of the mele, saying, "I have described the mele that follows as a mele noi naʻauao, or a poem requesting knowledge; though naʻauao [enlightenment] appears nowhere in the mele, the Hawaiian speaker hears it implied by the frequent references to the ao [dawn] of the new day in relation to the school."[27] Arguably, the technique he is referring to involves hoʻomaoe (allusion) and kaona, but he does not identify the strategy with a term—he simply points it out, and in so doing identifies the kuleana of a Kanaka Maoli audience to expect and look for such tropes. This practice suggests it is expected the reader will be able to see the patterns, and through example gain practice, and arguably even skill.

Considering this approach to learning, mele in general are both a rhetorical speech act and a mode of instruction. The purpose of this project is to identify how mele inoa represent a theory of rhetoric in a Kanaka Maoli context; however, it is difficult to distinguish the rhetoricity in terms of cultural commentary, reproduction of ideological values, and as an instructional text. After all, how to compose a rhetorical piece is intricately tied to the intended cultural commentary, which relies on a shared understanding of ideological positions. In the next section, we present a mele inoa from the pre-settler period and discuss its relationship to the epideictic and deliberative branches of classical rhetoric to articulate the connection between understanding intent and pono composition practices.

Translation and Analysis of Mele I: Mele Inoa Beyond Epideictic

This section begins with a mele inoa composed by Kamakahelei (c. 1720–1794), an aliʻi nui of the island of Kauaʻi, for her son Kaumualiʻi's illustrious ancestor, Kihaapiʻilani of Maui. Kaumualiʻi was the last independent aliʻi nui of Kauaʻi before it was subsumed into Kamehameha II's rule following Kaumualiʻi's death in 1824. Kaumualiʻi and his father, Kaʻeokūlani, were direct descendants of the esteemed aliʻi nui Kihaapiʻilani. The second son of aliʻi nui Piʻilani and his wife Lāʻielohelohe, Kihaapiʻilani was born c. 1600. Piʻilani was so highly regarded, the epithet for the island of Maui, "Nā Hono aʻo Piʻilani" (the bays of Piʻilani), praises his leadership and is still fondly recalled today.

The specific social event that precipitated Kamakahelei's composition of the mele inoa is not known at this time; however, as an aliʻi nui and mother of the next generation of aliʻi nui via Kaumualiʻi, she was well aware of the social and political importance of mele inoa, which kūpuna (older relatives/ancestors) often began composing around the time of an aliʻi nui's birth. Kamakahelei assumed kuleana for teaching her son Kaumualiʻi his own lengthy

---

26. Ibid., 29.
27. Ibid., 32. Ao with the ʻokina diacritical mark (aʻo) means education.

mele inoa beginning when he was a young child. One can imagine how such memorization was exacting and difficult. In terms of the rhetorical implications of this practice, it is likely Kamakahelei composed the mele inoa for Kaumualiʻi as a way to teach her son and remind the chiefly audience—potential rivals to their family's rule—of his illustrious and godly gene-alogical connections through the remembrance of the deeds of his powerful ancestor, which helped raise his own mana (power) and thus legitimized his right to rule. While the overt rhe-torical intent is to demonstrate illustrious genealogy and provide an example of pono behavior for an aliʻi, through this instruction, Kamakahelei was also passing down the reasons for and ways to represent this information; in other words, in addition to affirming his birthright, Kamakahelei was also instructing her young son on the rhetorical situation and corresponding rhetorical techniques and strategies for composing an effective mele inoa of this kind, so that he may one day do the same for his progeny.

At 295 lines, this mele inoa is significantly longer than the more recent ones composed by Prendergast and Boyd we present in Section III. Yet it is significantly shorter than other mele inoa, and appears incomplete. We present only the first sixty-one lines of section twelve below for illustrative purposes.

Mele I: *"He Mele no Kaumualiʻi" (Name Chant for Kaumualiʻi)*

1. Kiha[a]piʻilani, son of Piʻilani, begat Kamakaalaneo

2. Kiha[a]piʻilani with the piercing eyes;

3. Kiha[a]piʻilani with pale yellow skin,

4. The gentle sea breeze that turns gracefully at the cape

5. Kiha[apiʻilani]'s skin truly transformed.

6. Kiha[apiʻilani]'s dignity that was accorded him

7. Was that Kauhi was unblemished; faultless

8. Kauhi's dignity that was accorded him

9. Was of Kaeokūlani with the unusual skin,

10. Blackened

11. It is like the skin of Kauhikea;

12. He is a descendant of Kauhikea;

13. Nāmakaikaluluokalani [The eyes in the calm of the heavens/chiefs]

14. The pula fish of the deep crags [in the reef]

15. Without the redness of skin,

16. He is the one who crosses the stream,

17. Noisily treading over the forest foliage enroute to the sea;

18. He is the fish who breaks the kīholo [large fishhook or net]

19. The eye delights in its frantic effort;

20. The line runs and jerks in the hand

21. Kawelo, a second father with Kakuhihewa.

22. Kanaloa of Loʻewa was the chief's child

23. Pahia and Kaʻili, those two are known,

24. For Kama was barren, his children are the heavens

25. Both Kalewanuʻu and Kalewalani

26. Kama's child is Laʻaloa [very sacred],

27. The child of Kupaeʻeli, by the drum ennobled

28. The noble offspring; the sacred drum proclaims

29. The tap, tap, tapping of Kīhalalē,

30. Causing Kīhalalē to sound as a bird.

31. The rough sharkskin drum, a rumbling skin

32. The sound of the sacred pahu drum booms in measured cadence,

33. The sound reverberates, echoes

34. Like the voice of a bird

35. It is the voice of Kīwaʻa

36. Kīwaʻa the godly bird,

37. Alight, desire to alight from your flying.

38. The kite of Kīwaʻa

39. Let Kawelo arise, let the chief arise!

40. Let Kiha arise, arise chief Hoʻoneʻenuʻu,

41. The chief of the height that is strong and enduring;

42. Of the very high cliff, guarding the sacred, inaccessible chiefs;

43. Inaccessible indeed, made so by their sacredness

44. Increase, ever increase the sacredness of Kauhikea.

45. Kauhi, son of Kamalālāwalu,

46. Kamalālāwalu, the chief of acknowledged power,

47. Whose sacredness is widely known

48. Numerous are the sacred prohibitions (kapu) , many the prostration kapu

49. The hairdresser of the great chief is a chief indeed

50. He is the chief who will enforce the kapu

51. Of the woman in the axe-pit.

52. The chief is sore and aching

53. Due to the sharpened adze removing lumps, a sharpened adze removing lumps

54. Lāʻielohelohe the—

55. Lāʻielohelohe of Kalamakua

56. Is the dark, incompact precipice that stands on high;

57. Dreadful is the sacredness of the chief.

58. Piʻilani of Kawao and Kaohele the—

59. Kaohele chiefly child of Lono

60. The fruitful source that caused the overthrow,

61. The chief who united the island.

COMMENTARY

As noted in the previous section, Kanaka Maoli culture during the pre-settler period (when this mele was composed) would fall into what Kennedy has described as "traditional" culture, and he goes on to note, "much traditional oral poetry is epideictic,"[28] the branch of rhetoric concerned with "praise or blame of what was honorable or dishonorable."[29] As clear references to his dignity (l.6), strength (l.17), and illustrious genealogy (throughout), this mele inoa exemplifies the primary motivation of such mele "to honor or praise individuals of note."[30] As an example of the traditional form of oral poetry and in its purpose of veneration, mele inoa thus clearly align with the classical understanding of epideictic. While mele inoa are certainly epideictic, we posit that through their work to convey cultural norms and values, they are also deliberative, the branch of rhetoric "concerned with determination of the advantages of some future action."[31]

In many classical treatments, particularly Aristotle's, among the three branches, epideictic has arguably received the least attention in terms of its role in influencing public political discourse in general, and civic action in particular, both of which for Aristotle encompass the primary ends of rhetoric in a democratic society. While an Aristotelian purist might acknowledge, "the final cause of rhetoric as a whole is persuasion to right judgment, action, or belief,"[32] epideictic rhetoric has often been perceived as embodying more modest persuasive appeals and associated more with style than the substance usually articulated with judicial or deliberative branches of rhetoric. It's important to note that this relative disdain for the epideictic neither was nor is universal, but it has had traction, even in some contemporary works that seem to dismiss or underestimate the rhetorical work when it comes to transmission of cultural norms and values. In a discussion of Sāmoan ceremonial oratory, a Pacific Island nation with familial ties to Hawaiʻi in both cultural and political norms, Samuel Johnson asserts that "the Samoan model [of rhetoric] . . . is based on a confirmation of ritual and a transmission of cultural content."[33] Although Johnson is specifically examining speech acts in his work, in that such speech acts confirm and transmit cultural knowledge, they perform rhetorical work similar to that of mele inoa. In his project, and in an interesting ironic turn, Johnson argues that cultural reaffirmation and transmission do not fall into the category of epideictic as Aristotle defines it because he does not see cultural transmission as persuasion—thus taking a position similar to Aristotle's dismissive one in terms of the rhetorical prowess of an epideictic act; however, culturally grounding transmission of cultural knowledge and its discursive implications in a particular society demonstrates that such acts are not only persuasive, they are deliberative.

---

28. Kennedy 1999, 79.

29. Ibid., 18.

30. Silva 2015, 32–31.

31. Kennedy 1999, 18.

32. Ibid., 70.

33. Johnson 1970, 273.

This stance on the persuasiveness of a rhetorical act being attributed to an overt entreaty to act does not consider the epistemic role rhetoric plays, as is more fully articulated by scholars such as Kenneth Burke (1950), Sonja Foss (1987), and Gerard Hauser (1999) in the twentieth century.[34] Through the identification of appropriate behavior, such as honoring ancestors, strength and courage in battle, and cunning, this mele inoa conveys characteristics and attributes an individual should strive for and also seek in an ali'i. In the act of identifying what behaviors and actions are worthy of praise, a rhetorical act is informing individuals of acceptable and appropriate behaviors, which, of course, represent a culture's ideology, ethics, and values, and is thus epistemological. With its epistemological characteristics, mele inoa persuades community members toward these values and behaviors, informing them of appropriate ways of being and doing, and thus their civic interaction. Thus, epideictic in this sense does inform rhetorical actions that shape communal discourse; any disparaging assessment of its rhetoricity seems to stem from the ornate style commonly associated with the epideictic rather than the content. Although discussions of the epistemological nature of rhetorical acts are more fully engaged by twentieth century scholars, even Aristotle "admits that epideictic and deliberative rhetoric overlap and suggests that the difference is often one of style. . . . A great deal of what is commonly called epideictic oratory is deliberative, written in an epideictic style," noting the deliberative nature of an epideictic performance when the effect of the ceremonial encompasses influencing someone's point of view about possible action.[35]

Understanding rhetoric as epistemic and that ideology, values, and societal norms are all transmitted through communicative acts does not necessarily translate to comprehending what a rhetorical act conveys to a specific group or its weight in terms of influence. To fully grasp that, rhetorical acts must be contextualized within the culture that produces it. While Aristotle's relative dismissiveness of the persuasiveness of the epideictic in comparison to the forensic and deliberative has been challenged in recent decades, particularly in terms of its epistemic value, to fully capture the persuasive and epistemic potential of a particular oral performance, the culture within which it is being enacted, in this case Kanaka Maoli culture, must be invoked. The persuasive strategies employed in mele inoa that we would consider deliberative in their appeal are perhaps more implicit than what would be recognized in Aristotle's classical (western) rhetoric model, but those models arguably do not privilege the "show me" rather than "tell me" strategies at the heart of Kanaka Maoli knowledge and practices of transmission as explained in the previous section. When Kamakahelei is telling her young son of Kihaapi'ilani's physical prowess and strength—attributes that would enable him to defend and protect his people—she is also telling him how a pono and revered ali'i behaves, and correspondingly, what is expected of him. She is ultimately persuading him to some future action, and cultural training would dictate that her son would be prepared to read those nuances in the mele.

---

34. Burke 1950; Foss and Gill 1987; Hauser 1999.
35. Kennedy 1999, 78–79.

Kaumualiʻi's interaction with the mele in this way reflects the tremendous importance Kanaka Maoli placed on all speech acts as is represented in two ʻōlelo noʻeau: *aia ke ola i ka waha; aia ka make i ka waha*, interpreted as "life is in the mouth, death is in the mouth," meaning that spoken words can give life, and spoken words can kill[36]; and *i ka ʻōlelo nō ke ola, i ka ʻōlelo nō ka make* (life is in speech, death is in speech).[37] The articulation of the power behind speech acts emphasized in these two ʻōlelo noʻeau clearly indicate Hawaiians understood communicative acts as rhetorical, engendering action on some level, whether epistemological or literal. These articulations of pono ways of being and interacting do inform future actions and interactions, and clearly present the advantages of conducting one's self in a particular way, and thus are aligned with deliberative rhetoric.

In that the overt rhetorical end of mele inoa is to praise and honor an individual, these mele clearly align with the classical rhetorical form of epideictic. Through their transmission of values and ideological norms, they also persuade individuals to certain behaviors and ways of being, and as such mele inoa also perform the work of deliberative rhetoric. Moreover, as is apparent from the instructional role in this mele inoa, performed between Kamakahelei and her son, all mele are instructional. Embedded in these important rhetorical acts are examples of rhetorical forms that become a means of instruction for composers in the future creation of mele in this genre.[38]

TRANSLATION AND ANALYSIS OF MELE II AND III: IDENTIFYING MEIWI ACROSS GENERATIONS

This section begins with two mele inoa and their English translations: the first composed in 1898 by Ellen Kekoʻaohiwaikalani Wright Prendergast (1865–1902) for Queen Liliʻuokalani; and the second written for President Barack Obama in 2009 by Manu Boyd (1962–).

Prendergast, a lady in waiting for the Queen, was a prolific haku mele, often publishing under her middle name, Kekoʻaohiwaikalani. Mele II, "He Mele Inoa no Liliuokalani," is one in a series of three mele inoa she composed for the Queen; the first two in the weeks immediately following the illegal overthrow of the Hawaiian monarchy in 1893, and this one in the weeks following the 1898 signing of the Newlands Resolution that authorized annexation of Hawaiʻi to the United States. This mele inoa appeared in the Hawaiian nationalist newspaper *Ke Aloha Aina* on August 27, 1898. *Ke Aloha Aina* was the organ of the political group Hui Aloha ʻĀina, one of two formidable organizations that actively and tirelessly fought for the return of Hawaiian sovereignty before and after annexation. It is part of a prolific body of mele inoa composed for the Queen by myriad Kanaka Maoli. These mele demonstrate love of, support for, and solidarity with the Queen, and were composed in a traditional way that directly ties praise to moʻokūʻauhau and use specific meiwi to elucidate such points.

---

36. Pukui 1983, 9.

37. Ibid., 129.

38. We take up this argument more fully in the next section.

Mele II: "He Mele Inoa no ka Mōʻī Wahine Liliʻuokalani"
(Name Chant for the Queen Liliʻuokalani)

1. This name chant is for you, Liliʻu,

2. The renowned Queen of this world

3. You are a heavenly offering for the nation,

4. Seeking the well-being of Hawaiʻi

5. You alone have faced, oh royal one

6. The turbulent and stormy seas,

7. The vast expanse of the Pacific Ocean,

8. Two thousand miles wide,

9. Your thoughts are not disturbed in the least,

10. By the endless efforts taken on through love

11. Assuming the tasks, dealing with difficulty,

12. The heart surging,

13. Plucked and fulfilled,

14. The desires of royal Liliʻuikekapu [Liliʻu-of-the-sacred]

15. The works of the enemies are nothing,

16. Because of your love for the sands of your birth,

17. That you face without fear,

18. Obtaining justice for the land,

19. For the beloved flag of your nation,

20. And your people,

21. A lightning bolt secured and sealed,

22. In your sacred heart, your Majesty,

23. Eluding the rain and the wind,

24. Huddled up in the cold and chill,

25. The snow of Washington that chills the bones,

26. Nipping the skin like a lover,

27. The stifling heat of the summer sun,

28. The glowing red of the dainty face,

29. That was relieved by the wave of the fan,

30. The gentle breeze of the fingertips,

31. For over a year,

32. Living in the land of strangers,

33. The research patiently tolerated,

34. To where justice may be served,

35. Before the legislative assembly,

36. And the Senate with its disheveled buttons,

37. Dealing unjustly,

38. With the rights of the Hawaiian people,

39. That they have sought in unity,

40. From the great power of America,

41. That your authority be restored,

42. To reign over the government,

43. Yet the schooling cuttlefish appear,

44. The members of the legislature,

45. Opposing their own constitution,

46. The Hawaiian people are united ,

47. Looking to our Almighty God,

48. With him lies the hope,

49. The salvation of Hawai'i for all time,

50. In the presence of the Holy Trinity,

51. Are our rights and our victory,

52. The story is told through your name.

53. Lili'uolōlokūlaniikekapu [Royal Lili'u-of-the-sacred-noon].

Mele III, "Ka Ni'o o Maleka 'Ailana," was composed by Boyd in 2009 to commemorate President Barack Obama's election. While this mele inoa obviously celebrates his victory, expressing pride in a truly amazing accomplishment, there is also subtle pushback to Obama's detractors who questioned the legitimacy of his US citizenship. The mele praises the President's character and, as we will discuss more fully, although he is not Kanaka Maoli, includes rhetorical references that work to tie him to "his" 'āina hānau (birthplace) in Hawai'i and his kūpuna in the same way that would be done if he were.

Mele III: "Ka Ni'o o Maleka 'Ailana" (The Pinnacle of America)

1. This is a song for you, the esteemed child of this land

2. Protected by the hala trees at Kapunahou

3. Favored one of your grandmother

4. Raised well with good values and insight

5. Hawai'i is honored by the news

6. A child of this land has ascended to the pinnacle

7. Of the "island" of America

8. Dodging the violent storms and chilling northwest winds

9. And the bitter cold of the northern border

10. Warmth is found in loving embrace

11. With the cherished beauties by your side

12. Elegant is the presence of our leader

13. The great chief who speaks well of others

14. You now extend to the far reaches of the world

15. May God always keep and protect you

16. Hawaiʻi is honored by the news

17. A child of this land has ascended to the pinnacle

18. This is an expression of aloha for Barack Obama

19. The famous president of America

COMMENTARY

What is immediately noticeable in these two more recent mele is their accessibility in terms of references and style, and that is the case in both ʻōlelo Hawaiʻi and in translation. Kalena Silva calls mele inoa an evolving form,[39] and accounting for the specific time periods and social and political dynamics that these mele respond to results in meiwi doing different work in terms of the values, social protocols, and appropriate/admired qualities they point to; however, the actual rhetorical constructs and devices themselves are consistent across all three mele. In this section, in addition to hoʻonaninani, we focus on three dominant rhetorical constructs that underpin a kuanaʻike Hawaiʻi, or Hawaiian worldview (that Silva notes as an essential quality of "best" mele), kaona, moʻokūʻauhau, and pono, each of which is used pervasively in Kanaka Maoli literary, oral, and visual texts. We also identify three aligned rhetorical devices, ʻēkoʻa, helu, and pīnaʻi that work to reinforce those constructs. Similar to western rhetorical constructs, such as the Aristotelian appeals, in the best mele inoa, none of these would be enacted in isolation, but rather be used to augment each other. Kaona, for example, is found in recitation of moʻokūʻauhau, which uses helu to present one's lineage. To better capture this interaction among rhetorical constructs and devices, in what follows, we discuss the ways several meiwi are at work in discreet passages. We want to stress, however, that while we focus on these six meiwi and discuss specific examples, they do not encompass the entirety of examples or types of strategies present in the mele.

Kaona is arguably one of the most dominant traditions used in Kanaka Maoli oral, literary, and visual texts, and all meiwi can be subjects of kaona. It is often defined as layered meaning, but, in actuality, kaona is much more complex. Kanaka Maoli scholar Brandy Nālani McDougall, who has written the only full length treatment of kaona, explains "kaona is meaning that can be hidden in plain sight, meaning that, on the surface, may seem casual, trivial, or ornamental to those unfamiliar with what George Kanahele calls 'the language of symbols' with which Hawaiians 'spoke' alongside our 'native tongue and within which meaning could

---

39. Silva 2015.

be concealed.'"[40] It is an approach to communicative strategies that allows for a perspective informed by kuanaʻike Hawaiʻi. Kaona is used pervasively in Kanaka Maoli traditions—indeed, the more kaona, the greater the aesthetic appeal. And, as McDougall and Nordstrom note, Kanaka Maoli were trained to look for and decipher kaona.[41] In the following, we point to how kaona works with different meiwi in the mele, and provide a model to haku mele of appropriate forms for mele inoa.

As the dominant purpose of mele inoa, hoʻonaninani is overtly apparent in all three mele. The following excerpts are representative of the many examples that demonstrate such accolades throughout each mele:

> Mele I: *The chief of the heights who strong and enduring / Of the very high cliff, guarding sacred, inaccessible chiefs / Inaccessible indeed, made so by their sacredness* (lines 41–43).

> Mele II: *This name chant is for you, Liliʻu / The renowned Queen of this world* (lines 1–2).

> Mele III: *This is a song for you, the esteemed child of this land* (line 1).

Although in Mele I undisguised praise does not appear until line 41, in both Mele II and III, accolades are declared in line one. Immediately articulating praise, rather than following a preamble, may be one of the ways mele inoa have evolved. Consistent across all three mele, though, exaltation is articulated with ʻāina (land/earth), albeit to different ends. These connections to land represent kuanaʻike Hawaiʻi that likens human potential/ʻano (character) to land and nature and highlights Kanaka Maoli kuleana to ʻāina. As ʻāina ascribes certain traits and kuleana, alluding to it is a useful and common technique in mele inoa as the practice draws attention to admirable qualities and societal values.

Kaona and pono are also often embedded together in nature references, and this interaction is likely more apparent to a contemporary audience in Mele II and III because of the relevance of the references. While pono is commonly associated with the concepts of "goodness, uprightness, morality . . . correct or proper procedure, excellence, well-being,"[42] it also indicates that such qualities are only attained through balance, which is often represented through complementary pairings of opposites, or ʻēkoʻa. Although nature references are commonly used to articulate positive attributes, they can also be used for other purposes, such as representing challenges presented by outsiders alongside attributes that aid the subject in overcoming such challenges. Particular manipulation of such references in Mele II and III model one way they have been used in more recent compositions. In these mele, nature references, through the use of kaona and pono, allude to the subject's (Liliʻuokalani and Obama respectively) adversaries as well as the characteristics they possess that will enable them to overcome.

The helu of references to weather in line 23–30 in Mele II are an example of listing being used as kaona to represent the strife the Queen was enduring (ll. 23–25), the deceit of sup-

---

40. McDougall 2016, 23.
41. McDougall and Nordstrom 2011.
42. "Nā Puke Wehewehe"

posed allies (l. 26), the signaling of oppression in the heat reference in line 27, and the ultimate recognition of her poise and steadfastness in lines 28–30. At the same time, this listing is also an example of using ʻēkoʻa to achieve pono in the contrasting depictions of weather in lines 23–27 as the mele moves from "wind and rain," "cold and chill" to "stifling heat," and finishes with a temperate "gentle breeze." In Mele III, helu is more abbreviated; however, the allusions to nature work very similarly to Mele II, with oppositional pairings of weather referring to adversaries (ll. 8–9) and sources of solace (ll. 10–11). What signals these instances as instructional is the obvious consistency in the way weather is used in Mele II and III. They point to a form haku mele would realize as part of their traditional repertoire, knowing also that audience members could be counted on to recognize and be prepared to decipher such codes.

Moʻokūʻauhau, another key rhetorical construct prevalent throughout Kanaka Maoli communication, involves the recounting of names and places in an individual's genealogy and is often presented using helu. It is a dominant strategy that a haku mele would know to employ when composing mele inoa so that the subject carries with it the mana that is created through the history and illustrious (or infamous) deeds associated with a specific place. Kanaka Maoli historian Lilikalā Kameʻeleihiwa explains that the recitation of genealogies does go beyond "lists of who begat whom," saying, "They are also mnemonic devices by which the moʻolelo, or exploits of the Aliʻi, are recalled. As the lists of names are chanted, the adventures of each Aliʻi are remembered, and these, in turn, form the body of tradition by which their descendants pattern their Chiefly behavior."[43] The extensive genealogical references in Mele I (68 out of 137 lines in the mele) indicate the imperative to establish chiefly descent and divine authority to rule over lands and people when the archipelago was divided amongst competing chiefdoms. In this mele, this work begins in line 1 with "Kihaapiʻilani, son of Piʻilani, begat [Kamalālāwalu]"—a pattern modeled in many mele inoa. As Kameʻeleihiwa notes,[44] with each moʻokūʻauhau reference, through kaona, chiefly pono exploits/behaviors are presented by different ancestors, and exaltation (or scorn) of specific characteristics can be stressed through pīnaʻi, or repetition. For example, naming Kihaapiʻilani's father in the first and then again in later lines of the mele (i.e., ll. 58, 110) reinforces his ʻano, deeds, and mana and bestows them on Kihaapiʻilani. This strategy manifests a kuanaʻike Hawaiʻi that a person is not an individual but a representation and culmination of those who come before them and solidifies the right to occupy the position one holds (or claim it).

As the third in a series, moʻokūʻauhau in Mele II is not as immediate or overt. The first reference to Liliʻuokalani's moʻokūʻauhau is presented through kaona in line 14, which describes her as "Liliʻulani-i-ke-kapu," or "royal Liliʻu in the sacredness," referring to her high ranking aristocratic—and thus sacred—genealogy. Her royal birthright is actually embedded in her name, as nineteenth century Kanaka Maoli writer Moses Manu explains: "Numerous aliʻi—chiefly men and women—descended from [ancient gods]. They were known as *nā ʻliʻi mai ka pō mai*, divine leaders from antiquity who were addressed as *Kalani*, 'The royal one,'"

---

43. Kameʻeleihiwa 1992, 22.
44. Ibid.

an affectionate title "handed down through the ages to the time of our beloved Queen Liliʻuo-kalani."[45] The three different renderings of the Queen's name in the mele is another example of how pīnaʻi is used as emphasis—in this case, of the Queen's royal position. Recitation of her lineage would not serve the same purpose as it had for Kihaapiʻilani—the Queen's right to rule was not being challenged by others with similar or competing lineages; rather, her situation necessitated an argument that she had the right to rule over her sovereign nation to the American imperialist government. Thus, rather than invoke her ancestors, her royal status is accentuated.

Mele III has several interesting adaptations of moʻokūʻauhau. President Obama is not Kanaka Maoli, and therefore does not have a long and illustrious Kanaka Maoli genealogy; however, Boyd modifies moʻokūʻauhau to accommodate this situation: he ascribes him to a place and references his kupuna in lines 2–4. Boyd refers to Obama as a kamaʻāina, or child of the land. While kamaʻāina can be a controversial term as it is often appropriated by settlers to evoke a connection to place through birth (ʻāina hānau) or residency, in this case Boyd seems to be invoking it as a means to create a moʻokūʻauhau for Obama that includes land as it would for a Kanaka Maoli. "Kapunahou" is a reference to Obama's alma mater, Punahou School. Boyd then invokes Obama's grandmother, grounding his ʻano in her good values and insights. Similar to Mele I and II, Obama was also faced with the eminent need to declare his gene-alogical right to rule in a contemporary colonial context. Moʻokūʻauhau works to highlight Obama's pono character inheritance and validates his claim to Hawaiʻi—a rhetorical move that takes on particular significance amidst the Birther Movement that was in full swing in 2009 and called into question the legitimacy of Obama's US citizenship.

The consistency in terms of presence of moʻokūʻauhau and the similar work it does in all three mele points to an established connection between rhetorical construct and purpose that has transcended generations; yet the way moʻokūʻauhau is subtly adapted to account for differing rhetorical situations also emphasizes malleability, an essential quality for rhetorical constructs to remain relevant in contemporary use. Kamakahelei composes a mele inoa for her son to remind him and their contemporaries of his supreme royal genealogy, affirming his right to rule—a practice handed down for generations within traditional, pre-settler culture. In the changing cultural, social, and political context of the nineteenth century, mele inoa and the use of moʻokūʻauhau as a rhetorical device evoking the sovereign's right to rule the kingdom continued, but also adapted. Mele inoa composed to support Queen Liliʻuokalani similarly allude to her moʻokūʻauhau; however, rather than focus on the ʻano of her ancestors, these references assert her royal status as a means to argue for her right to remain sovereign ruler over her nation. Boyd's mele inoa for Obama in a contemporary, Americanized context demonstrates the evolution and flexibility of mele inoa in that a respected Kanaka Maoli haku mele celebrates Obama as an accomplished leader, in part, through characteristics determined by his moʻokūʻauhau and status as kamaʻāina through his birth and residency in Hawaiʻi.

---

45. Manu 1899, 4.

Conclusion

While what we have presented here is only a small sampling of the myriad ways meiwi are employed in just these three mele, the examples we provide demonstrate consistency in terms of both form and purpose and illustrate continuity across generations of composers. One might argue that versions of the rhetorical strategies we discuss here could be found in any number of texts representing other cultures. And they would be correct. What moves these instances beyond the application of a strategy to instructional form is their obvious codification. Despite traversing several hundred years, not only are the same rhetorical strategies used in each text, they are used in strikingly similar ways. Of course, changing socio-political dynamics have resulted in adaptations, but our discussion here has shown that more remains the same than has changed. We began this article noting that scholars have asserted that traditional cultures rarely produced instructional texts on rhetoric. In Kanaka Maoli society, the savvy protocols in place for transmitting this knowledge illustrate that, unlike in the Western style of education, there is little need for such treatment.

Comprehensive Bibliography

Aristotle. 2001. *Rhetoric.* In *The Rhetorical Tradition: From Ancient Times to the Present,* edited Patricia Bizzell and Bruce Herzberg, 179–240. Boston: Bedford's/St. Martin, 2001.

Boyd, Manu. 2009. "Ka Niʻo o Maleka ʻAilana." *Nani Mau Loa, Everlasting Beauty.* Honolulu: Hoʻomau Inc.

Burke, Kenneth. 1950. *A Rhetoric of Motives.* New York: Prentice-Hall Inc.

Cicero. 2001. From: *De Oratore.* In *The Rhetorical Tradition: From Ancient Times to the Present,* edited Patricia Bizzell and Bruce Herzberg, 289–343. Boston: Bedford's/St. Martin.

Crowley, Sharon, and Debra Hawhee. 2011. *Ancient Rhetorics for Contemporary Students,* 7th ed. Boston: Pearson.

Freire, Paulo. 2000. *Pedagogy of the Oppressed.* Translated by Myra Bergman Ramos. New York: Routledge.

Foss, Sonja, and Ann Gill. 1987. "Michel Foucault's Theory of Rhetoric as Epistemic." *The Western Journal of Speech Communication* 51 (Fall): 384–401.

Hauser, Gerard. 1999. "Aristotle on Epideictic: The Formation of Public Morality." *Rhetoric Society Quarterly* 29 (1): 5–23.

hoʻomanawanui, kuʻualoha. 2008. "ʻIke ʻĀina: Native Hawaiian Culturally Based Literacy." *Hūlili, Multidisciplinary Research on Hawaiian Well-Being* 5: 203–44.

—. 2015. "Ka Liʻu o ka Paʻakai (Well-Seasoned with Salt): Recognizing Literary Devices, Rhetorical Strategies, and Aesthetics in Kanaka Maoli Literature." In *Huihui, Navigating Art and Literature in the Pacific,* edited by Jeffrey Carroll, Brandy Nālani McDougall, and Georganne Nordstrom, 247–65. Honolulu: University of Hawaiʻi Press.

Johnson, Samuel R. 1970. "The Non-Aristotelian Nature of Samoan Ceremonial Oratory." *Western Speech* 34 (4): 262–73.

Kamakahelei. 1868. "He Mele [Inoa] no Kaumualii, ke Alii o Kauai." *Ka Nupepa Kuokoa,* March 27 and April 4.

Kameʻeleihiwa, Lilikalā. 1992. *Native Lands and Foreign Desires, Pehea Lā e Pono ai?* Honolulu: Bishop Museum Press.

Kawaeʻaeʻa, Keiki. 2018. *Nā Honua Mauli Ola: Hawaiian Cultural Pathways for Healthy and Responsive Learning Environments,* 2nd ed. Hilo: Hale Kuamoʻo.

Kekoʻaohiwaikalani [Ellen Kekoʻaohiwaikalani Wright Prendergast]. 1998. "He Mele Inoa no ka Moi Wahine Liliuokalani." *Ke Aloha Aina,* August 27, 1898. Reprinted in *ʻŌiwi: A Native Hawaiian Journal* 1: 103.

Kennedy, George A. 1999. *Classical Rhetoric and Its Christian and Secular Tradition from Ancient to Modern Times.* Chapel Hill: University of North Carolina Press, 1999.

Manu, Moses. 1899. "He Moolelo Kaua Weliweli ma waena o Pelekeahialoa a me Wakakeakaikawai." *Ka Loea Kalaiaina,* May 13, 1899.

McDougall, Brandy Nālani. 2016. *Finding Meaning: Kaona and Contemporary Hawaiian Literature.* Tucson: University of Arizona Press.

McDougall, Brandy Nālani, and Georganne Nordstrom. 2011. "Ma ka Hana ka 'Ike (In the Work is Knowledge), Kaona as Rhetorical Sovereignty." *College Composition and Communication* 63 (1): 98–121.

"Nā Puke Wehewehe 'Ōlelo Hawa'i." *Ulukau Electronic Hawaiian Dictionary*. Wehewehe.org.

Perreira, Hiapo. 2011. "He Ha'i'ōlelo Ku'una: Nā Hi'ohi'ona me nā Ki'ina Ho'āla Hou i ke Kākā'ōlelo." Dissertation, University of Hawai'i at Hilo.

—. 2013. "He Ki'ina Ho'okuana'ike Mauli Hawai'i ma ke Kālailai Mo'okalaleo." *Hūlili, Multidisciplinary Research on Hawaiian Well-being* 9: 53–114.

Pukui, Mary Kawena. 1983. *'Ōlelo No'eau, Hawaiian Proverbs and Poetical Sayings*. Honolulu: Bishop Museum Press.

Queen Lili'uokalani. 1999. *The Queen's Songbook*. Honolulu: Hui Hānai.

Quintilian. 2001. From: *Institutes of Oratory*. In *The Rhetorical Tradition: From Ancient Times to the Present,* edited by Patricia Bizzell and Bruce Herzberg, 364–428. Boston: Bedford's/St. Martin.

Silva, Kalena. 2015. "A Contemporary Response to Increasing Mele Performance Contexts." *Huihui, Navigating Art and Literature in the Pacific*. Edited by Jeffrey Carroll, Brandy Nālani McDougall, and Georganne Nordstrom. Honolulu: University of Hawai'i Press.

Silva, Noenoe. 2004. *Aloha Betrayed, Native Hawaiian Resistance to American Colonialism*. Durham: Duke University Press.

GLOSSARY OF TERMS

Term	Translation
ʻāina	land; *lit.* that which feeds
ʻāina hānau	birthplace, *lit.* land of one's birth
aliʻi (nui)	chief; aliʻi nui, high chief
ʻano	character, characteristics
ao	dawn, day, daylight, light; *fig.* knowledge, enlightenment
aʻo	instruction, education; to teach, learn
ʻēkoʻa	oppositional but complementary dyads
haku mele	composer of song or poetry
hānai	adopted; *lit.* [brought into the family] through the act of feeding (a child) food from one's mouth
helu	to list, recount
hoʻomaoe	allusion
hoʻonaninani	praise
hoʻopāpā	debate; an intellectual contest of wit, memory, and knowledge
kākāʻōlelo	orator, often a chiefly advisor; a person skilled in use of language
kamaʻāina	native born of a place; *lit.* child of the land
Kanaka Maoli	Native Hawaiians, or the Indigenous people of the Hawaiian Islands. In the context of this essay, "Kanaka" is a shortened referent to Kanaka Maoli.
kaona	metaphoric, layered, "hidden" meaning
kapu	sacred, forbidden to touch or access because of sacred prohibitions
kuanaʻike Hawaiʻi	Native Hawaiian worldview, perspective
kīholo	large fishhook or net
kuleana	right(s), responsibilit(ies)
kumu	teacher, source
kupuna	elder, older relative, ancestor; kūpuna (plural)
kuʻu ʻupena	*lit.* to throw or cast a fishing net
lāhui	nation, people
mana	power, often spiritual, inherited or gained/lost through one's actions
meiwi	culturally-derived rhetorical, poetic, and/or literary devices commonly used in speech and writing

mele	chant, song, poetry
mele inoa	honorific name chants/songs
mele noi naʻauao	a chant, song, or poem requesting knowledge
Mōʻī	sovereign, king, queen; modern word from the nineteenth century
moʻokūʻauhau	genealogy, *lit.* continuity of the upright thigh (femur) bone(s)
moʻolelo	narrative; history, literature, storytelling, writing, *lit.* succession of words
naʻauao	intelligence, enlightenment, learned, knowledgeable; *lit.* enlightened innards
naʻau	innards or guts, considered the seat of Hawaiian intelligence (as opposed to the brain)
ʻōlelo Hawaiʻi	Hawaiian language; the language of the Indigenous people of Hawaiʻi
ʻōlelo noʻeau	proverb, poetical saying
paka	constructive criticism of a mele provided by knowledgeable peers
piko	center, navel
pīnaʻi	repetition, of sounds, syllables, words, phrases, themes, ideas
pono	balance, harmony

9 RUSSIAN RHETORICS

PREFATORY INTRODUCTION
Maria Prikhodko

In the *Stylistic Encyclopedic Dictionary of the Russian Language*, the word "rhetoric" is associated with terms like "eloquence" (многоречивость), "nonsense" (пустословие), and "inclination to eloquence" (краснобайство). Other prominent definitions of Russian rhetoric include "a science of eloquence" (Bukharkin et al.) and a science of *pomysly* (помыслы, velleity), or having thoughts or intentions without deeds. The latter two definitions both establish the *slovo* (слово, word)[46] as its own genre of more solemn eloquent texts, where each word may have political or religious connotations, be understood as *nravstvennij* (нравственный, moral), or be understood solely as *pouchitelnij* (поучительный, testamental).

This chapter sheds light on some of the traditions and practices of Kievan Rus' that originate didactic eloquence and that contain clues to Russian rhetoric's epideictic and discursive roots.[47] Kievan Rus' was a powerful medieval state centered in Kiev that impacted the political, religious, and cultural lives of Eastern Europe. It was the East European Plain, where ethnic Slavs (Russians, Ukrainians, and Belarusians) settled down and assimilated ethnically, culturally, politically, and socially with "peripheral" ethnicities like Finno-Ugrians, Balts,

---

46. *Slovo* (слово, word) is a Kievan Rus' genre that included such texts as religiously educational literature. According to the Novosibirskaya Orthodox Church, the exigence for writing such literature often came from a series of prominent historic, civil, or religious events, or from urgent social problems, or from *nravstennij* (нравственный, moral) dilemmas.

47. In Jonathan Clarke's history of Kievan Rus' it "witnessed the official acceptance of Christianity in 988 CE with the baptism of Vladimir Monomakh, an event that drastically changed the ethnoreligious roots of Eastern Slavs. Kievan Rus' ceased to exist after the sacking of Kiev by the Tatars in 1240" (2019, 30).

Khazars, and Turkic-speaking nomads (e.g., Pecehengs, Polovtsians, and Torks)—an area of about fifty thousand people in all. Yet, a small portion of princes their retinues, a mixture of Varangian, Slav, Finno-Ugric, and Turkic communities overpowered the rest.

Characterized by homiletic and celebrational discourse, the Kievan Rus' *vetijstvo* (ветийство, vitality) served one ultimate purpose: to unite/consolidate an audience in spiritual growth, celebrational *pomysly* (помыслы, velleity), and long-term influence. What prevented this didactic rhetorical tradition from canonization and expansion into more contemporary practices was its methodological inconsistency, including a lack of theorized knowledge about it. However, although the Kievan Rus' knowledge base was scarce, Georgij Khazagerov has argued that there are some identifiable and unique Kievan Rusi'eloquent traits: (1) an urgency toward kindness; (2) respect for the written word and for wisdom; (3) elevated emotional stance and imagery; and (4) meekness in speech.[48] Here, "respect," "wisdom," "imagery," and "meekness" all exemplify how Kievan Rus' eloquence values *smislovaja emkost'* (смысловая емкость, thoughtful capacity),[49] centered on *serdchnost'* (сердечность, wholeheartedness) as a symbol of innocence.

One of the essential sacred texts for exploring how this emerged in the Russian rhetorical tradition is Vladmir Monomakh's *Pouchenije* (Поучение Владимира Мономаха, the *Testament of Vladimir Monomakh*). The chosen lines from this *Testament* represent the behavior code of a ruler, which later was expanded to the code of behavior of a good man. The following commentary on Vladimir Monomakh's *Testament* presents an attempt to bring consistency to the rhetorical glossary of didactic eloquence, which, ten centuries later, became engrained in the Russian education system as a foundational *nravstvennij* (нравственный, moral) teaching, but without its religious accents.

---

48. Khazagerov 2002, par. 5

49. *Smislovaja Emkost'* (смысловая емкость, thoughtful capacity) is a language ability to transfer some thoughts or ideas with certain flexibility or sensitivity. See Zenkin 2017, 60.

9.1 Kievan Rus', c. 859–1240 CE, Kiev (Eastern Europe, Rurik Dynasty)

The *Testament of Vladimir Monomakh*: A Rhetoric of Moral and Didactic Eloquence in the Kievan Rus' Traditions

Maria Prikhodko

Lack of logical purism and excessive beauty of speech combined in it [Kievan Rus' eloquence] with a high nravstvennij heat.

—Georgii Khazagerov

INTRODUCTION

In the linguistic and political state of Kievan Rus' (859–1240 CE), what Georgii Khazagerov[1] emphasized as "moral (нравственный, *nravstvennij*) heat" was an essential criterion for building the axiological platform of a higher plane of existence. Like an apple seed in the orchard, it became the essential component of a person's self-development. At the time, the highest level of knowing belonged to the Church and adhered to Scripture, but this axiological concept was the center of a canonical rhetorical[2] culture that was essential to Russia's contemporary system of education. As two eschatological values held by devoted Orthodox Christians, meekness and moral heat have since become standards of the speech culture (культура речи, *kultura rechi*) that defines how united and patriotic the nation and its future generations should be.

This speech culture is a unique discipline formed in Russia in the 1920s as a result of studying literary norms. It evolved from a rhetor's obligation to develop a culture of language identity that would define his image as a highly qualified specialist and interlocutor.[3] This discipline has since expanded to include a culture of organizing public discourse and speech, and a culture of public thought and ideas. One of its key rationales is to revive public or national unanimity (единомыслие, *edinomyslije*). It requires every literate person using Russian to apply language norms, including appropriateness of literary language, logic, expression, richness, and linguistic purism.

In the Kievan Rus' "eloquent" tradition, then, the purpose of written and spoken communication was not primarily to deliberate or to persuade, but to nurture, support, and guide in order to grow morally in some specific genres. In fact, the turbulent historical context of this

---

1. Khazagerov 2002, par. 9.
2. I use "eloquent" instead of "rhetorical," because the latter was not in use in Kievan Rus'. Instead, terms like *vetijstvo* (ветийство, knitting with words) and *blagorechije* (благоречие, a benevolent speech) were more commonly used, and they enacted intimate connections with the Bible, sages of Church homilies, or the Holy Scripture.
3. Annushkin 2009, 14.

linguistic state did not allow the term "rhetoric" to appear because it would have signified the art of public speech, a fundamental principle of any democracy where authorities and citizens were free to express their voice, the existence of which Natalija Orlova[4] and Vladimir Annushkin[5] adamantly questioned in Kievan Rus' times. Instead, the eloquent tradition marked a time when the ultimate aim of communication was to converse (беседовать, *besedovat'*) in the form of written testament (поучение, *pouchenije*), hagiography (житие, *zhitije*), saying words (говорение, *govorenije*), reasoning (рассуждение, *rassuzhnedinje*), and thinking through (размышление, *razmyshlenije*). Rather than promoting the development of citizenship ideals or the maintenance of empire, these genres functioned anthropologically to depict the ideal person who lives one's life as Jesus—"[S]aints [and knyazya (lords) go[ing] through the path of restoring the likeness of God."[6] The process of creating an ideal personality made in the image of God symbolized praying and achieving glorified senses of how to be in the world.

The Kievan Rus' vitality (ветийство, *vetijstvo*) was performed in a homiletic style, intended to teach and preach predominantly with religious texts, rather than to persuade and manipulate.[7] "Designed to be recited,"[8] Kievan Rus' texts had acoustic and rhythmic qualities effective for an oral delivery. The goal was to remind readers of an emergent Christianity, purportedly to help them forget about paganism and create appropriate moral (нравственный, *nravstennij*) ideals. Since there were neither rhetorical schools nor explicit rules to communicate, texts were imitative[9] with infinite thinking through and with exhortations to master humble but well-mannered speech acts, such as the following: "do not be ferocious, do not reprove, do not laugh extensively, do not avoid preaching those enthralled by power" (не свиреповать словом, не хулить в беседе, не смеяться много, не уклоняться учить увлекающихся властью).[10]

One of the essential sacred texts to explore how these genres and rhetorical traditions emerged in the Russian tradition is Vladimir Monomakh's *Pouchenije* (Поучение Владимира Мономаха, the *Testament of Vladimir Monomakh*). The excerpted lines in this chapter represent Monomakh's code of behavior for a Russian ruler, which was later expanded to become the code of behavior of a good man.[11] The text consists of a request to not laugh at *Pouchenije* (Поучение Владимира Мономаха, the *Testament of Vladimir Monomakh*) and its interpretation, for its main purpose was to offer instruction on how to rule the country and live in peace

---

4. Orlova 2019, 5.

5. Annushkin 2009, 59.

6. Dorofeeva 2010, 97–101.

7. Orlova 2010, 166–71.

8. Franklin 2011, xcvi.

9. Ibid., xcvi.

10. Monomakh n.d.

11. "Good man" – here "man" is translated as a human being rather as a gender-charged noun. Russian is a masculine-gendered language based on a gender binary paradigm (Sitnikova) which is embedded into the patriarchy. Historically, since ancient times, including Kievan Rus', men have held power and occupy leading roles in politics and religion. However, in this chapter I consider gender non-binaries when translating and discussing nravstvennost' and blagost' as part of the Russian eloquent tradition.

with other *knyazija* (князья, lords).[12] Deeply religious, Monomakh relied heavily on The Holy Scriptures to provide him with a code of behavior for being a model parent to his heirs.[13]

In the remainder of this chapter, I recount the historical and political context of the rhetoric of the Kievan Rus' in relation to its literacy development. Then I present excerpts from Monomakh's *Pouchenije* that exemplify metaphorical ways of preaching and nurturing about moral norms of communication in the form of *beseda* (a dialogue about superstitious topics). The commentary and translation that follow demonstrate why this style of written communication, its authentic rhetoric with elements of reasoning and hagiography and testament, became embedded within the writing curriculum of the Russian educational tradition.

ADOPTION AND RESISTANCE TO BYZANTINE RHETORICAL TRADITIONS

Vladimir Monomakh (1053–1125 CE) was one of the most prominent lords of Kievan Rus'. As a son of mixed heritage, born to the Kievan knyaz Vsevolod and the Byzant princess Maria, he was able to unite all three sectors of the Old Russian State and to eliminate strife, keeping it politically, militarily, and culturally united.[14] In 1097 CE, Monomakh arranged a meeting with the other Ryurikovich' knyazs, who ruled Kiev, Novgorod, Chernigov to establish rules to live in peace and unite against Cumans, claiming the need to "unite with our hearts and . . . obey our Russian soil."[15] Once the states were united, Monomakh introduced Christianity from the Byzantine Empire, also referred to as the Eastern Roman Empire, to the Kievan Rus'. Christianity in this Russian tradition promoted new norms that centered around the feelings of compassion and love of others [neighbors], although these new norms admittedly reached a limited audience, owing to high rates of illiteracy among Russian peasants and a strong allegiance to their former traditions.[16]

Prior to 999 CE, the Kievan Rus' had been under pagan influence, when the most heeded voices were those of wood and water spirits, together with guardian spirits like *domovoj* (домовой, a household guardian spirit),[17] all of which symbolized their clans' progenitor.[18] In 999 CE, a colossal religious shift from paganism to Christianity[19] occurred under the Monomakh's rule, effectively replacing paganism as the official state religion. However, given

---

12. Knyaz' (close to a lord) is a historical Slavic title, given to a ruler of a land.

13. Nenarokova 2008, 110.

14. Perevezencev n.d.

15. Monomakh n.d.

16. Riazanovsky 2000, 140

17. Dixon-Kennedy 1998, 59. Domovoj (a guardian household) is a Slavic pagan deity who has been known as a household guardian. He has been known as Chur [Чур] who protects a house from robbery and sends any devilry purely by saying his name aloud "Chur me" [Чур меня].

18. Vertsman n.d. *Domovoj* (домовой, a spirit) is a benevolent spirit, "being the guardian of the dwelling, he looks after its occupants, defending them against evil spirits and mischief. His presence feels through unexplained and terrifying noises."

19. Dixon-Kennedy 1998, 60.

paganism's historically strong presence, Kievan Rus' adopted only the ascetic components of Byzantine culture in a catechistic form that materialized mostly in literary genres, rather than in rationalization, scientific analysis, or theological dogmatism. As a result, these literary traditions exposed Russian Christians to hagiographic rhetorical genres, including *govorenje* (говоение, saying words), *beseda* (беседа, a talk), *rassujdenije* (рассуждение, reasoning), and of course *pouchenije* (поучение, testament) aimed to nurture a soul for its moral growth.

While the Byzantine rhetorical tradition taught that rhetors could direct persuasive messages to their audience via informed interaction of ethos, logos, and pathos, in Kievan Rus' the reader was expected to decipher the meaning of a given text. Khazagerov explains that this eloquent tradition emerged from the unique status of the Kievan Rus' rhetor—often a priest or a prince, accustomed to speaking genuine truth or edification that required no analysis or critique. For example, *pomysel* (помысел, valleity) and *smirenije* (смирение, humility) were presented as theological axes indicating how the audience—in this case, Vladimir Monomakh's children or future younger readers—should adhere to the Holy Scriptures to master sufficient literacy, seek compassion and love of others, and thus achieve the next stage of spiritual growth.[20]

Unlike the deliberative rhetorical practices of ancient Greece, in Kievan Rus', sermons and eloquent speeches, mostly created in monasteries, purported to save souls and enlighten rather than to persuade.[21] Their rationale was to be coherent with the Bible and the Scriptures, "to elucidate the signs, . . . through the sense and structure of the rhetoric,[22] the inner harmony beneath the outer diversity.[23] During Kievan Rus' times, the general population was mostly illiterate, so reputable men generally wrote testaments as forms of education for their children and grandchildren. The key didactic element of such testaments was to emulate a good, humble Christian[24] by adhering to three moral standards: *blagost'* (благость, glory), *bezmolvije* (безмолвие, tranquility), and meekness or *smirenije* (смирение, humility). From the available genres, Kievan Rus' authors typically chose a static form of narration, which mostly described how saints achieved the Vault of Heaven, or their personal transformation.[25]

The *Testament's* Influence on Russian Educational Traditions

Since the twelfth century CE, the *Testament of Vladimir Monomakh* has heavily influenced the theological and *vospitatel'nij* (воспитательный, educational) values embedded in the Rus-

---

20. Nenarokova 2008, 110.

21. Khazagerov 2002.

22. Annushkin Brill, 59. Strangely, in the English-medium texts, Kievan Rus' traditions are still named "rhetorical," although there is no evidence that such Greek terms existed back then (Annushkin). Instead, the rationale was not to persuade but rather to save souls (*slovesnost* —"simple way of expressing one's own wisdom by voice").

23. Franklin 2011, xcvi.

24. Khutorskoj 2001, 66.

25. Dorofeeva 2010, 100.

sian educational system and in Russian family traditions. In fact, Monomakh's *Testament* has been reinterpreted as a spiritual will to the nation, especially to the younger generations. In plenty of junior high school programs in contemporary Russia, Monomakh's *Testament* is embedded into the curriculum as a secular moral component. Due to the Post-Soviet Union ban on all religions, the religious accents of his text were diminished in favor of its moral accents, such as seeking the meaning of life, showing compassion to others (including one's enemies), achieving empathy, demonstrating love, honoring family as a principal entity, expressing moral beauty, and taking up a moral shield. Krupinina explains that the *Testament* teaches the new generations to believe that their lives are under the protection of an army of saints, including Monomakh, and according to the spiritual traditions of their fathers, recorded in the *Testament*.[26]

In his seminal work *Letters about Kind and Beautiful*, Dmitrij Likhachev, one of Russia's most prominent twentieth-century philosophers, reinterpreted Monomakh's *Testament* using a plethora of Old Russian artifacts for the modern reader.[27] Ultimately, Likhachev created a list of commandments that became widely adopted in composition topics in Russian schools:

- love close ones and strangers.
- create good not thinking of profit.
- love peace in yourself but not yourself in the world.
- be retentive, for in memories is your strength.
- learn to read with interest and pleasure, without rushing; reading is a way to live wisdom.[28]

Similar and related topics have become traditional *sochinenije* (written forms) for students in high-school composition classes as well.[29] For example, *Edinij Gosudarstvennij Ekzamen* (Единый Государственный Экзамен, the Unified State Exam) in the Russian Language Arts lists the following questions:

- What does the native language mean for a human?
- What would irresponsibility towards the native language lead to?
- What would constitute the wealth of the Russian language?
- How does school impact a child's identity formation?
- Why is it important to remember one's teachers?
- What should a true teacher be?
- How bad is a reluctance to study?

---

26. Krupinina n.d.
27. Lickachev n.d.
28. Orthodox Gimnasium of Sergius Radonezh 2006.
29. *Sochinenije* is a written form of *rassuzhdenije* (рассуждение, reasoning) that is assigned to assess high school graduates' civic and *nravstvennij* (нравственный, moral) values.

As seen in the selected list, *nravestvennij* (нравственный, moral) norms are reflected in how students are taught to reason and to define linguistic and ethical norms—irresponsibility, meaning, truth, identity formation, wealth of a language—through their school literacies. These norms, among others, formulate the normative, communicative, and ethical components of *kultura rechi* (культура речи, speech culture),[30] characterizing how united and patriotic the nation and its future generations should be.

Vladimir Monomakh's Rhetorical Treatise

When reading Monomakh's *Testament* as a rhetorical treatise, we should attend to the nuances in his language use. In the tenth century CE, the prominent written language in Kievan Rus' was Old Church Slavonic, a liturgical language used by the Russian Orthodox Church. According to Pereltsvaig, the language co-existed in a state of diglossia with Old Russian: the former was used in Kievan Rus' liturgies, whereas the latter was used primarily as a vernacular.[31] The resulting phonetic and morphological changes from Old Church Slavonic to Russian Cyrillic to English serve to complicate interpretive work (i.e., the ancient meaning translates as "my children, when heard my speech, do not laugh" [дѣти мои, слышавъ сю грамотицю, не посмѣйтеся], while the contemporary meaning translates to "my children, when heard my speech, do not laugh at me" [дети мои, услышав эту грамотку, не посмейтесь надо мной]).[32]

As a medieval text for spiritual growth, the *Pouchenije* was religiously symbolic, owing to its *nravstvennij* (нравственный, moral) worldview and humble attitude towards the Creator. In this text, the author acts as a doer, so that the way of its composing is a form of life—hagiography and reasoning—could adhere to the Holy Scriptures through a plethora of citations, quotations, or borrowings, connected by numerous conjunctions ("and," "or") as a way of respecting the religion and its sacred texts. Hence, the *Testament's* language and style are infused with theological and *nravstvennij* (нравственный, moral) concepts, such as velleity, meekness,[33] and *dusha* (душа, soul) that constitute the "spiritual will" of ruling a unified nation, as he passed them on to his children in the form of pedagogical recommendations. Rhetorical practices of meekness in the *Testament* often encompass attempts at confession, conveying that "thus our Lord has promised us the victory of our enemies through three means of conquering and overcoming them: tears, repentance, and almsgiving."[34] Or, they signal conscious acceptance in *dusha* (душа, soul) ("have a pure dusha" or "point your dusha up above").[35] According

---

30. Department of Russian 2021.

31. Peteltsvaig 2015, 5.

32. Monomakh n.d.

33. *Smirenije* (meekness), a feeling of oneself as part of someone's world, grands an objective aesthetic contemplation, which leads to acceptance.

34. Monomakh n.d.

35. Ibid.

to Adrianova-Peretz, in Ancient Rus', "a human's image or interpretation of essence takes an enormous place that founded the mechanism of morally rhetorical verbal artwork."[36]

Overall, the *Testament* establishes Monomakh's image as a well-experienced compassionate and meek rhetor, eager to pass on his collected and unified experiences to future generations. In contemporary educational traditions, this rhetoric of edifying the younger generations and passing on prior wisdom informs writing practices as early as middle school. For example, Azman Khazbulaeva,[37] a middle-school teacher of the Russian language and literature, asks students to analyze generic features of *Pouchenije*—such as imperative mood, direct address, conjunctions, enumerations, and hagiographic insertions. Students examine such passages as "[D]o not *svirepovat'* (свиреповать, be furious) with a word, do not *hulit'* in *beseda* (не хулить, а говорить, do not lie in a talk), and do not laugh much . . . hold eyes down but hold the *dusha* (душа, soul) upright." Students are then assigned homework to compose their own *pouchenija* (поучения, treatises) to encourage their younger siblings to be in unanimity with the elder generation (themselves):

> Never charge others; learn to charge on yourself;

> Do not brag. Wait for someone to praise you.[38]

Such treatises were always contextualized with hagiographic insertions to emphasize unobtrusive and authentic tone, for example:

> If you have to kiss a christ, then, checked on your heart, kiss and think of only what you could accomplish, and, when kissing, follow your word, otherwise, if a promise is broken, you will destroy your soul.[39]

Excerpts and Translation from *Pouchenije* (Поучение, the *Testament*)

The following translated excerpts from Monomakh's *Testament* reflect a Romanization of Russian Cyrillic. To make the text more comprehensible to contemporary readers, each word written in Cyrillic was transliterated into Latin and then translated to English. However, some verbs like *svirepstvovat'* (свирепствовать, to be furious) are non-translatable, though they exist in English as adjectives or nouns. As well, some concepts like *nravstvennost'* (нравственность, close to morale) do not have equivalents in English. The interpretive differences mostly occur around abstractions. When contrasting Old Church Slavonic and Russian, Pereltsvaig makes a valuable point about preserving the abstractions, saying,

---

36. Adrianova-Peretz n.d.

37. Khazbulaeva n.d.

38. Khazbulaeva n.d.

39. Monomakh n.d.

When it comes to verbs and deverbal nouns, OCS-derived [Old Church Slavonic-derived] forms typically denote more abstract actions, whereas their East Slavic-derived counterparts are concrete and physical: e.g. *vozvrat* (возврат, 'return') can be *v prošloe* (в прошлое, 'to the past'), whereas *razvorot* (разворот, 'turn') can only apply to physical entities.[40]

Accordingly, in the translation below, I refer frequently to abstract actions like *pomysel* rather than merely using "thought," and I refer to *nravstvennost'* (нравственность, close to morale) rather than simply replacing it with "morale" to raise the complexity of terms that were important to Kievan Rus' eloquence but are less relevant to contemporary secular minds, or to the minds of the "nominal Orthodox."

Translation

1. Learn, as a owning a God in heart,[41] to be a pious performer; learn, according to the Holy Scripture, to "control eyes, to have abstinence of tongue,[42] meekness[43] of mind, obedience of body, suppression of anger, pure *pomysly* (помысли, thoughts), urging one to do good deeds, for the Lord's sake; if you are deprived, do not seek revenge; if you are hated, love; if you are persecuted, be patient; if you are decried, stay silent and kill the sin.

2. Gathered around young men, Vasilij taught them to have a pure and virgin *dusha* (душа, a soul), a meager body, a meek beseda (беседа, a talk) to commit to a word given to God: "Eat and drink without any noise, *pokoritsja* (покориться, knock under, obey without ease) to parents, share love with young, *besedovat'* (беседовать, to talk) without wickedness but *razumet*[44]; do not *svirepovat'*

---

40. Peteltsvaig 2015, 5.

41. "Owning God in heart" in the original text is "верующий" which derives from to have a credo, principles rather than to believe like "I know God is up there." Rhetorically, in the Kievan Rus' eloquent tradition, a rhetor should own God in heart to deliver a treatise/moral directive, not having any opponent in mind. Instead, the purpose was to nurture so there was no need to persuade or conquer someone's mind.

42. Tongue is a literal translation of *yazyik* (язык, tongue) in this case, but, to English, it's better to translate "language" because Monomakh was mostly talking about how a highly moral speaker would be like.

43. *Smirenije* (смирение, meekness) is an important rhetorical category, along with harmony and abstinence. In Monomakh's testament, *smirenije* means "*bezymjannaja blagodat [=blagost']* (безыменная благодать = благость, goodness), which, in the English-medium form, may represent being with "nameless glory." However, nameless is not merely about an absence of a name but also inability to express in words.

44. *Razumet'* (разуметь) (to understand) is an abstract Old Church Slavoc verb that is much deeper than "understand» or "comprehend." It used to mean to mindfully achieve a *smysl* [meaning of something in its context and by its reader and creator].

(свиреповать, be furious) with a word, do not *hulit'* in *beseda* (беседа, a talk), and do not laugh much…hold eyes down but *dusha* (душа, a soul) upright.

3. As I sat upon my sledge, I *pomyslil* (помысел, gave a pure thought) in my *dusha* (душа, a soul) and gave prayers to God, who has led me, a sinner, even to this day. My children or someone else, listening to this *gramotKa*, do not laugh, but if it is *luba* (люба, close to like) to someone, let him[45] accept it with the heart and not be lazy but work.

4. First of all, for the sake of God and of your soul, feel fear of God in your heart and be generous by almsgiving, because it is the beginning of any good deed. If this *gramotKa* (грамотка, rule book) is not *luba* (люба, close to like) to someone, let them not laugh but, instead, say: on a long journey, sitting on a sleigh, he told absurdity.

5. Do not judge me, my children or someone, who will read it: I do not praise myself or my courage but praise God and glorify His mercy for saving me, sinful and meager, from hazards for so many years, and creating me as not lazy and capable for all human deeds. After reading this *gramotKa* (грамотка, rule book), try for all sorts of good deeds, glorifying God with His saints. My children, do not be afraid of death, war or animals but carry out any deed that God will send your way.

---

45. See my note about gender neutrality in Russian, where I explicitly state that I deconstruct binaries in Russian when translating to English.

COMPREHENSIVE BIBLIOGRAPHY

Adrianova-Peretz, Varvara. N.d. "Essays on Poetic Genres of Ancient Rus'." Accessed on April 1, 2020. www.livelib.ru/book/1000091038-ocherki-po-istorii-russkoj-satirich-eskoj-literatury-xvii-veka-v-p-adrianovaperetts.

Alfeev, Ilarion (Metropolitan Bishop). 2014. "Molchanije" [In Russian]. *For Whom the Bell Tolls* (April). 2009. www.mgarsky-monastery.org/kolokol/1978.

Alatova, Tatyana. "Speech Culture as a Language and Culture Identity Component." *Theory of Culture* 30: 45–50. cyberleninka.ru/article/n/kultura-rechi-kak-komponent-yazykovoy-kultury-lichnosti/viewer.

Annushkin, Vladimir. 2009. "The History of Russian Rhetoric: Sources, Ideas, Authors." In *New Chapters in the History of Rhetoric,* edited by Laurent Pernot, 249–59. New York: Brill.

Annushkin, Vladimir. 2014. "Speech Culture and Rhetoric in Rhetoric Disciplines and Contemporary Speech Practices." *Language Ecology and Communicative Practice* 11 (1): 14–20.

Bakhtin, Michael. 1979. *Questions of Literature and Aesthetics.* Moscow: Progress Moscow.

Bukharkin, Pavel, Volkov, Sergey, and Matveev, Evgenij. 2013. *Rhetoric of Michael Lomonosov.* Saint Petersburg: Nestor-Historia.

Bujanova, Lyudmila. 2021. *Emotiveness and Emotions of Language: Mechanisms of Conceptualization.* Moscow: FLINTA.

Clarke, Jonathan E. M. 2019. "Narratives of Nationalism and the Conflict in Eastern Ukraine: Myth, Religion and Language." *Central and Eastern European Review* 12: 23–47.

Department of Russian as a Foreign Language. N.d. "Lectures on Speech Culture." Moscow State University.

Dixon-Kennedy, Mike. 1998. *Russian and Slavic: Myth and Legend.* Santa Barbara, CA: ABC-CLIO, Inc.

Dorofeeva, Larisa. 2010. "Pouchenije of Vladimir Monomakh as a Confession-Self-Report: The Problem of Interpretation." [In Russian]. *The Vestnik of Russian State University* 8: 97–101, cyberleninka.ru/article/n/pouchenie-vladimira-monomaha-kak-ispoved-samootchet-k-probleme-interpretatsii.

Dorofeeva, Larisa. 2014. "A Man Ideal in Russian Hagiography in XI-XVII centuries." In *Hermeneutics of Kievan Rus',* edited by Mikhail Pervushin, 191–196. Moscow: Russian Academy of Sciences.

Franklin, Simon. 2011. "Introduction." In *Sermons and Rhetoric of Kievan Rus',* edited by Simon Franklin, i–xxv. London: Harvard University Press.

Khazagerov, Georgy. 2002. *Political Rhetoric.* Moscow: Nikkolo-Media.

Khazbulaeva, Azman. N.d. "Interactive Lesson on Monomakh." Accessed on March 12, 2020. nsportal.ru/azma-pochta-azma-61mailru.

Khutorskoj, Alexander. 2001. *Contemporary Didactics.* Saint Petersburg: Piter.

Koshanskij, Nikolay. 1830, 2013. *Rhetoric.* Moscow: Imperial Academia of Sciences.

Kostromina, Elena. 2014. *Rhetoric: A Textbook.* Moscow: Direct-MEDIA.

Kostyukov, Andrey. 2018. "The Church Was Declared War." Interview by Yurij Puschaev, *Pravoslavie.* pravoslavie.ru/86691.html.

Krupinina, Nadezhda. 2022. "Literature Classes Revive Spiritual Connections between Generations." St. Pafnutij Abbey. www.pafnuty-abbey.ru/publishing/8742/.

Leschenko, Vladimir. 2003. *History of Russian Rhetoric.* Moscow: Grodno.

Lickachev, Dmitriy. N.d. "Essays on Vladimir Monomakh." literatura5.narod.ru/lihachov_sochinenija-monomaxa.html.

Limassovskij, Afanasij. N.d. "Here Comes Blagodat' into Grateful Hearts." *Pravoslavie.* pravoslavie.ru/113161.html.

Losskij, Vladimir. 2012. *Mystical Worship of Eastern Church.* The Holy Trinity-St. Sergius Lavra.

Monomakh, Vladimir. N.d. "Testament" [Pouchenije]. 1117. Republished by Pravoslavie.ru. pravoslavie.fm/mudrost/poucheniya-detyam-velikogo-knyazya-vladimira-monomaha/.

Nenarokova, Maria. 2008. "Vladimir Monomakh's Instruction: An Old Russian Pedagogic Treatise." In *What Nature Does Not Teach: Didactic Literature in the Medieval and Early-Modern Periods,* edited by Juanita Feros Ruys, 109–28. Turnout: Brepols Publishers.

Orlova, Valentina. 2010. "Nravstvennij Choice of Youth: Ideals and Reality." *Vestnik of Tomsk University of Technology* 6: 166–71. core.ac.uk/download/pdf/53067339.pdf

Orlova, Natalija. 2019. *Edges of Communication: Practical Rhetoric* [In Russian]. Moscow: DeLibri.

Orthodox Gimnasium of Sergius Radonezh. 2016. *Reading Likhachev.* Moscow: NIPK PRO Publishing.

Perevezencev, Sergey. N.d. "Vladimir Vsevolodovich Monomakh" [In Russian]. *Slovo.* portal-slovo.ru/history/35558.php.

Peteltsvaig, Asya. N.d. "The Influence of Old Church Slavonic on Russian." *Languages of the World,* www.languagesoftheworld.info/language-contact-2/influence-old-church-slavonic-russian.html.

Riazanovsky, Nicholas. 2000. *A History of Russia.* London: Oxford University Press.

Rizhskij, Ivan. 1806. *Sensitivity of Soul.* Saint Petersburg: Kharkov University Press. escriptorium.univer.kharkov.ua/handle/1237075002/1962.

Unified State Exam. N.d. "Topics to Essays for the Russian State Exam." ege-soch.ru/temy-sochinenij-ege-po-russkomu-yazy-ku/.

Vertsman, Marina. 2015. "Kikimora, Domovoi, Baccoo, and Other Strange and Spooky Creatures." New York Public Library.

Zenkin, Sergey. 2017. *The Theory of Literature: Problems and Results.* Moscow: Novoje Literaturnoje Obozrenie. iknigi.net/avtor-sergey-zenkin/146091-teoriya-literatury-problemy-i-rezultaty-sergey-zenkin/read/page-1.html.

GLOSSARY OF TERMS

Term	Translation
blagost' (благость)	close to, but not synonymous with, "glory" or "mercy." *Lit.* to express glorified attitude and deeds. Rhetorically, each interlocutor has to be merciful or pious in performing actions, thinking of their own *dusha* (soul). "Blago" [a stem] means a super-existent status of the highest universal value.
beseda (беседа)	a form of conversation that usually occurs outside of houses on superstitious or morally challenging topics. In *besedas*, one doesn't persuade but rather hears shades of voice and a slow-paced rhythm. Derived from an ancient Russian term *besedka* [arbor]. *Besedka* literally means "a sitting outside area covered with thickets of greens." The closest translation in English is "a greenery arbor." In this context, *beseda* usually occurs in a besed-ka (a canopy), as a dialogue/conversation on superstitious topics.
besedovat' (беседовать)	verb form of *beseda* (conversation, talk, dialogue)
Bezmolvije (безмолвие)	glorified silence, which metaphysically embeds a trembling heart and soul towards a sacred happening. It is compared to a silent prayer with inner ascetic doing.
dusha (душа)	technically refers to soul but has a deeper meaning in relation to eloquence. Lyudmila Bujanova claims that *dusha* extracts experience, provoking impulses of emotional spectrum that trigger *besedas* (dialogues) and *pouchenija* (treatises), although I argue that her use of "experience" is an inaccurate translation. Later in the nineteenth century, Ivan Rizhskij suggests that any poem-maker [in the general sense, any speech maker], representing *nravstvennij* (grace), "should be exalted in *dusha*, so his speech would be a furious flow, instilling flames into people's hearts." To understand "be exalted in dusha," I refer to Mikhail Bakhtin, who explains *dusha* in aesthetic terms: "an aesthetic subject is a value and can't be granted or observed; it is *I-am-for-myself*…it is a spirit of self-compassion" (italics in original) (85). Note: when I use "his," I reflect how these texts were created with a masculine-gendered language, which may be now expanded to include any gender.
Gramot[k]a	an ancient official document written by tsars and knyazs. Since they were literate and well versed in politics, literature, and mathematics, their *gramotKy* were always bookish because of an extensive use of slavisms, such as "*bozhijm promjislom*" [God's harvesting]. Another linguistic aspect is the K in the suffix of *Gramot[K]a*. *Gramota* is an official ancient Russian document, but the diminishing suffix -ka makes it a set of rules to be used daily, in the household context.

govorenije (говорение)	"saying words," which consists of a threefold process: (1) uttering words, (2) sounding forms of thoughts and ideas, and (3) communicating intentions to be perceived.
molvit'	"blurting," though this is not a literal translation. More accurately, this means freeing a mouth from water to be capable of speaking. This refers to a pagan tradition of uttering a word after swallowing consecrated water. From a Western perspective, the purpose of molvit' is not to construct a counterargument, but rather be allowed to say a word in a humble way.
nravstennij (нравственный)	masculine adjective, "moral," derived from the feminine singular noun "*nravstennost'*," which translates as "morale," but has no accurate translation on its own. *Nravstennost'* and *nravstennij* pertain to divergent axiological principles: the former pertains to inner values that guide a person's choices, socially expected in the community and beyond; the latter is mostly a socially-expected paradigm that a person has to perform to become part of a community that created certain codes of ethics and communication. *Nravstvennost'* encompasses both *dusha* and *blagost'*.
pomysly, from pomysel (помысел)	singular noun that may be translated as valleity. It is rhetorically, derived from the verb *pomyslit'* (помыслить, conceived), which means to initiate a thought. The infinitive form of *pomysel* addresses a preliminary stage of exigence, when a rhetor has only pure thoughts without deeds or ideas. In Kievan Rus' eloquence, which was deeply homiletic, the derivative *pomysly* had to be pure. Though *pomysel* refers to valleity, which may be related to intention/need, it is different from the Western concept of exigence. Unlike in the West, where a source's exigence might respond to any need or situation that requires action, in the Kievan Rus' tradition, *pomysel* triggered highly moral deeds in the name of God. On a deeper level, Orthodoxy distinguishes *mysly* (thought) from *pomysel* (valleity), but they share the same root *-mysl*. *Pomysel* is not just a fleeting thought but rather a thought that has been bothering a preacher/teacher/rhetor for some time. The purpose of a speech in the Kievan Rus' tradition could be to explore one's own battle with *pomysly*, preaching about highly moral deeds that such *pomysly* prevents one from reaching. Illarion Alfeev described *pomysly* as morally intellectual forces for reaching piety, a state of a highly moral mind. The related verb, *pomyslit'*, means to reach piety through action.
perezhivanije (переживание)	inner and spiritual worries, or an unsettling towards a sense of tranquility and peace, which symbolizes a constant, ever-evolving quest for identification and relation to God. Rhetorically, *perezhivanije* will often trigger *rassuzhdenije* (reasoning) about *nravstevnnij* (moral) topics.

pouchenije (поучение)	a written speech that forms ideals and nurtures souls and bodies, according to highly moral norms. Its close equivalent is the word "testament" or "treatise." This speech form is characterized by rhetorical questions, periphrasis, diverse tropes, and parable-like writing; it uses the imperative mood. It is about well-mannered speech deeds, and reflects the imperative mood, when a rhetor, usually committed to people's souls, fate and religion, represents the elite.
rassuzhdenije (рассуждение)	reasoning, or a functional kind of speech that can occur in three different forms: (1) description, (2) thesis proof, or (3) thinking through (*razmyshlenije*). It translates as "thinking" but is different from "reflection." Description and thesis proof are similar to the Western genres of description and persuasion, but thinking through has a meditative intent.
razmyshlenije (размышление)	similar to thinking through/about. This describes when an author intends to wander in order to understand an issue at hand and finally concludes with a thesis that sums up his main point. However, this thesis deviates from the thesis of the Western tradition, in that it does not occur at the beginning, but rather at the end of the text.
smirenije (смирени)	meekness, a feeling that Monomakh considered to be an important rhetorical feature for a highly *nravstvennij* (moral) speech, along with the features of harmony and abstinence. In Monomakh's *Testament*, *smirenije* signifies "*bezymjannaya blagodat*" (glory), which, in the English-medium form, can represent nameless glory or humility. Here, nameless is not merely about the absence of a name but about the inability to express it in words. *Smirenije* describes how the mind should be (meek, humble) while performing actions, so as to prevent any bad thoughts or deeds. This eloquent practice mirrored how Russia had been mostly silent in the Kievan Rus', deeply involved in praying and meditation. Rhetorically, it refers to a complete absence of adulation and craftiness, because the gift of speech was a prodigious enough virtue in itself.
vospitatel'nij (воспитательный)	an adjective meaning "close to educational," derived from the word "upbringing" in English. This adjective is embedded in the educational system of Russian Federation because it predisposes that each student will not only acquire knowledge but also become *vospitan*, or brought up according to the canons of Old Russian spiritual values and paternal traditions. Krupina writes that "[the *vospitatel'nij* component] fills up what a soul of a growing student urgently needs" (par. 5).

10 Turkish Rhetorics

Prefatory Introduction
Elif Guler

Turkish rhetorics refer to the rhetorical practices, perspectives, and principles developed within the material conditions and discourse communities of Turks—a collection of ethnic groups who speak languages that are part of the Turkish language family and whose ancient roots are traced back to the agricultural, pastoral, and equestrian nomad communities in Northeast, Central, and West Asia.[1] Before exploring the characteristics of Turkish rhetorics, it is worth noting that Turks have had a long and multifaceted history spanning centuries over a large geography. This makes it challenging to define the term "Türk" or determine the ethnic denominators of Turkishness—let alone provide a comprehensive overview of the Turkish rhetorical tradition. It might be helpful to begin by briefly contextualizing the cultural, ethnic, linguistic, or national denominator—Türk/Turk or Turkish—that gives the categorical name to the rhetorical tradition discussed in the following chapter.

Of the more than ten states the Turks created, the Göktürks (the Celestial Turks) constituted the first formal state to employ the word "Türk" in its name (sixth through eighth enturies CE).[2] The largest state founded by Turks was the Ottoman Empire (1299–1922 CE)—a dynastic empire that came to control the majority of Western Asia, North Africa, and Southeast Europe. By the last two centuries of this multicultural and multireligious empire, "Turks" came to denote mainly Anatolian peasants, while the ruling elite was called the Ottomans. Under the European influences of nationalism in the twentieth century, the word "Türk"

---

1. Stokes and Gorman 2009, 707–08.
2. The first written mention of Turks was found in the sixth-century Chinese records. See Taşağıl (1995, 1).

522

and Turkishness gained a new kind of significance as a national identity.[3] Today, "Turkish" usually refers to the language, culture, and people of the contemporary Turkish Republic (1923–present), a country that spreads throughout Anatolia and a part of Thrace, serving as a bridge between Asia and Europe. A related term, "Turkic" (*Türki*) is also in use to describe the Central Asian roots of modern Turkish people as well as the larger context of cultures, languages, and people of some of the contemporary central Asian countries (e.g., Azerbaijani, Kazakh, Kyrgyz, Uyghur, Uzbek, and Tatar).

Despite the fact that rhetoric must have been a significant aspect of social and political life in the geographies Turks inhabited, from their ancestral land of central Asia to the present-day Turkish Republic (i.e., Türkiye), Turkish rhetorical traditions have largely been understudied and unacknowledged as a body of texts and practices. This might be due to a myriad of complications that accompanied the Turks' vast territorial expansion (e.g., the complications created by the historically problematic nature of recordkeeping and textual archives in the Turkish case).[4] Then again, since their ancient tribal existence, Turkic communities appear to have placed a high priority on rhetorical practice. The Göktürks provided the earliest recorded evidence of the value placed on verbal communication in pre-Islamic Turkic contexts: the eighth-century CE Orkhon inscriptions. Discovered in the Orkhon Valley of contemporary Mongolia, the inscriptions constitute three four-sided stone monuments erected in honor of the notable Gokturk monarchs: Bilge Khagan, Kül Tigin (Prince Kül), and Vizier Tonyukuk. Composed in an old Turkic (runic) alphabet, the inscriptions gave voice to Bilge Khagan's messages for the Turks, addressing the members of this community for generations to come.[5] The inscriber's words on the Kul Tigin monument imply that rhetoric (i.e., the rhetorical practice of inscribing stones or the statements carved into the monuments) operates at the crux of Turks' political existence: "I have inscribed into the everlasting stone how a state can be resurrected or could be destroyed" (qtd. in Ögel 22).[6] While the primary rhetorical audience of the inscriptions was the Turkic people of an ancient period, the rhetorical act of inscribing words onto a stone—a medium that is more likely to remain through the ages compared to other elements Gokturks might have used for written communication—renders writing (or, in this case, inscribing) as the Turks' principal instrument for transcending time.[7]

---

3. Kushner 1997, 219.

4. Like many historical communities, the Turks had a long tradition of archiving textual materials. The Uyghur Turks (who lived in Northeast China and formed a khaganate starting in the eighth century) are known to be the first Turkic group to have left a legacy of archives. Furthermore, the Seljuks and the Ottomans had a strong tradition of recordkeeping. However, much of Turks' archival legacy was likely lost during natural disasters or major wars causing negligence and purge of textual materials. See Binark (1979).

5. Guler and Goksel 2019, 194–95.

6. My English translation of this quotation is based on the statement's current Turkish transliteration found in Ögel (1971).

7. Moreover, two of the stone monuments were built on top of turtle-shaped marble foundations as turtles represented long life in Turkic cultures, further emphasizing the importance of conveying to fu-

Even with the Turks' long-standing respect for rhetorical practice, an absence of Turkish sources from scholarly discussions of rhetorical traditions might also be because historical Turkish texts (oral, written, or visual) rarely delineate rhetorical terms or present a methodical formulation of rhetorical theory. The characteristics of Turkish rhetorical practices are usually embedded within the verbal or non-verbal communication traditions of Turkic or Turkish cultures. For example, ancient texts such as the Orkhon inscriptions consider *özsöz* or "plain and truthful language" the essence of rhetorical practice. The Turkish term *özsöz* comprises the word *söz* (meaning "the word") and *öz* (meaning "the essence"). This ancient view of rhetoric, as well as certain ways of address rooted in the Orkhon inscriptions, would be revived during the Turkish republican period (e.g., in Mustafa Kemal Ataturk's foundational speeches and statements where Ataturk uses rhetorical tropes drawn from the inscriptions).[1] However, rhetorical themes or definitions are usually embedded or implied in ancient, Islamic, or republican Turkish texts' overall content (or how language was used to deliver that content). Understanding the principles of rhetorical practice in Turkic/Turkish communities often necessitates a study of the rhetorical aspects of significant texts from different periods of Turkish history.[2]

The following chapter introduces such a text as a source from the Islamic period of the Turkish rhetorical tradition: Yusuf Has Hacib's *Kutadgu Bilig* (eleventh century CE, Karakhanid Empire, Central Asia). *Kutadgu Bilig* is a historically rare and unique Turkish text for its overt emphasis on the value of rhetoric—in the sense of the effective use of words. The earliest notable example of Islamic-Turkish literature, this text is primarily a collection of didactic verses that address the reader on the moral rule of law and certain aspects of daily behavior. Because it was commissioned by the Kashgar prince of the Karakhanid Empire, many Turkologists consider *Kutadgu Bilig* as a political work advising a ruler on state affairs (*siyasetnameh*). Others categorize the text as a work of *wisdom literature* advising individuals on how to lead a virtuous life. In either case, *Kutadgu Bilig* also appears as a unique reflection on Turkish culture—including Turkish oral tradition. For example, the text frequently employs rhetorical elements peculiar to the Turkish tradition (e.g., Turkish proverbs), as it displays its author's views within the context of Karakhanid Turkish culture (discussed in more detail in the following chapter's commentary).

More importantly, the appropriate use of language is one of the focal points of *Kutadgu Bilig*. The text includes two chapters dedicated to *rhetoric*—either referenced by using the Arabic term for rhetoric, *belagat* (which entered the Turkish lexicon during the Islamic period of Turkish rhetorical tradition), or discussed as the proper way to use words.[3] The text also makes

---

ture generations the words carved into the inscriptions. For their discussion on such symbolic features of the Orkhon inscriptions, see Guler and Goksel (2019, 197).

1. See Guler and Goksel (2019).

2. Ibid., 194–95.

3. "Rhetoric" has been adopted into contemporary Turkish (written in a Latin-based Turkish alphabet) as *retorik* from *rhétorique*—the French version of this ancient Greek term. The Turkish Language Association's *Contemporary Turkish Dictionary* lists two definitions for rhetoric: 1) The art of speaking

frequent references to *söz* (the word) and *dil* (denotes the Turkish word for both "tongue" and "language") in various chapters throughout its entire content. Through all these references, a certain understanding of rhetoric underwrites *Kutadgu Bilig*: the text deems the use of words or language essential to living a fulfilled life and achieving a divine form of bliss (*kut*).[4] Still, this text as not yet been discussed exclusively for its understanding of rhetoric (the purposeful use of language). The following chapter delineates some of the characteristics of Turkish rhetoric by exploring *Kutadgu Bilig* with a focus on its rhetorical perspectives, including translations of excerpts that deliberate specifically on the proper use of "the word" or "language." To this end, the chapter includes a commentary on the rhetorical aspects of *Kutadgu Bilig* as well as a partial translation of its chapters and verses that focus specifically on rhetoric.

The various parts of *Kutadgu Bilig* that focus on proper word usage allow us to consider alternative definitions and purposes of rhetoric from a historical Turkish perspective (e.g., communicating to achieve *kut*, a blessed form of happiness), which can add to our inventory of non-Western rhetorical conventions. Furthermore, the way Yusuf weaves his discussion of rhetorical notions with other virtues (e.g., knowledge, intellect, morality) is also worthy of our attention in terms of how rhetoric converges with ethical principles of a given period in the Turkish tradition. Hence, the chapter that follows includes a glossary that lists not only the terms that came to represent rhetoric in the Turkish tradition (e.g., *belâgat*) but also the terms that are considered to have close links with rhetoric within the context of *Kutadgu Bilig*. The hope is to demonstrate some of the intricate characteristics of Turkish rhetorics, while providing rhetoric scholars with an alternative source to reconsider the nature and functions of rhetoric within non-Western global contexts.

---

eloquently, the art of *hitabet* (noun, literature); 2) the study of word arts, *belagat*. The same dictionary defines *hitabet* as "the art of effective speaking" (noun, adopted from Arabic) and lists the following three definitions for *belagat*: 1) speaking well, persuasive skill (noun, old usage); 2) the study of word ats, retorik (noun, old usage); 3) the art of immaculately explaining a subject matter (noun, old usage, literature); 4) a deep, symbolic meaning hidden in something (noun, old usage, figurative expression) as in "the belagat of his silence." See "retorik," "hitabet," and "belagat" in *Güncel Türkçe Sözlük* (*Contemporary Turkish Dictionary*).

4. See Guler (2020).

10.1 Middle Turkish, 11th Century CE, Central Asia

Exploring the Rhetorical Perspectives in Yusuf Has Hacib's *Kutadgu Bilig*, Karakhanid Empire

Elif Guler

INTRODUCTION

From Turks' ancient origins in Central Asia to the establishment of modern Turkey, rhetoric (i.e., *söz söyleme sanatı or belâgat*) has been an integral part of Turkish intellectual and political life. A major example of the Turkish rhetorical tradition from its Islamic period (starting around the tenth century CE) is Yusuf Has Hacib's *Kutadgu Bilig* (1069 CE), previously translated into English as *Wisdom of Royal Glory* and roughly translated into Turkish as *Knowledge That Gives Happiness.*[5] It is worth noting here that, while it makes a skillful and a highly significant contribution to understanding the text in a Western language, Dankoff's translation of *Kutadgu Bilig* in *Wisdom of Royal Glory* includes a discussion of Yusuf's text as a Turko-Islamic adaptation of *Mirror for Princes* but has no detailed commentary on its rhetorical teachings. In addition, the newly translated portions of *Kutadgu Bilig* presented in the current chapter aim to provide a more accurate adaptation of Yusuf's text from a rhetorical perspective.

Written originally in Karakhanid-Turkish (i.e., Middle Turkish used around the tenth through the fifteenth centuries CE), *Kutadgu Bilig* is primarily a *masnavi* of about 6,645 verses. According to its surviving scribes, the author—then called Yusuf of Balasagun—wrote *Kutadgu Bilig* for the Kashgar prince, Tavghach Bughra Khan of the Karakhanid Empire, which was a Turkish Empire that reigned from 999 to 1211 CE in the Transoxiana region of Central Asia.

To date, the original manuscript of *Kutadgu Bilig* has not been recovered. The text is known through its three scribes discovered in different parts of the world:

> (1) Vienna Scribe: This first known scribe, which seems to have been made in Herat and transliterated to Uyghur-Turkish from an Arabic version of the original manuscript (1439), was retrieved and acquired by Hammer-Purgstall in Istanbul and brought to the Austrian National Library in Vienna (in the eighteenth and nineteenth centuries CE).

> (2) Cairo Scribe: This scribe, made in the Arabic script, was discovered in 1897 by Moritz, a library director in Cairo who was originally from Germany.

---

5. See Hajib and Dankoff (1983). A more direct translation of *Kutadgu Bilig* from contemporary Turkish could be *Knowledge that Leads to Divine Bliss.*

(3) Ferghana Scribe: This scribe was also written in the Arabic script (around the thirteenth century) and retrieved in Ferghana (contemporary Uzbekistan) in 1943.

Many Turkologists discussed *Kutadgu Bilig* as a political work on state affairs or *siyasetnameh* (although the world's first known example of this Persian literary genre was released later by Nizam al-Mulk in about 1090 CE). Others considered the text a work of *wisdom literature*, advising individuals on how to lead a virtuous life. While one of the focal points of *Kutadgu Bilig* is "the appropriate use of language" that the text deems essential to living a fulfilled life and achieving a divine form of bliss (*kut*), the text has not yet been discussed exclusively for its understanding of rhetoric (the purposeful use of language). With its frequent references to *söz* ("the word") and *dil* (denotes the Turkish word for both "tongue" and "language"), a certain understanding of rhetoric underwrites *Kutadgu Bilig*. This chapter explores *Kutadgu Bilig* with a specific focus on its rhetorical perspectives, including translated excerpts from the text that deliberate on the proper use of "the word" or "language."

Reşit Rahmeti Arat was the first Turkologist to complete a comparative study of its three scribes and prepare a transliteration of *Kutadgu Bilig* to the Latin-based Turkish alphabet in 1947; Arat also published a version of the text written in contemporary Turkish (i.e., Turkey-Turkish) in 1959. The translation presented in this chapter is based primarily on a later edition of Arat's work.[6]

COMMENTARY ON RHETORIC IN *KUTADGU BILIG*

This chapter will consider *Kutadgu Bilig*'s perspectives on rhetoric in the framework of the text's rhetorical situation (author, audience, purpose, message, and context). The following commentary is not meant to be a comprehensive review of the rhetorical perspectives in *Kutadgu Bilig*; rather, it aims to provide some points of entry for future discussions of this historical Turkish text's rhetoricity. Due to our rhetorical focus and the length of *Kutadgu Bilig*, the translation following the commentary includes only the parts that present the text's rhetorical perspectives. Some of the remaining parts of *Kutadgu Bilig* are reviewed in this commentary according to their discursive functions in terms of the text's rhetorical quality.

---

6. Has Hacib 1988. Other texts consulted for the critical discussion and translations in this chapter include two contemporary Turkish editions (translated from Uyghur Turkish—the origin of the Karakhanid Turkish) printed by the Turkish Ministry of Culture and Tourism. See Has Hacib and Kacalin (n.d.). See also Has Hacib and Silahdaroglu (1996). The current chapter presents an examination of these texts with an eye for *Kutadgu Bilig*'s rhetorical characteristics. As a native speaker of Turkish and someone originally from the contemporary Turkish cultural context, I produced a current translation of *Kutadgu Bilig*'s sections related to rhetoric directly from the Turkish versions of the text. In my translations, I tried to remain as faithful as possible to the original text of *Kutadgu Bilig* (including its occasionally repetitive style). I aimed to convey mainly the intended meaning (presenting it as coherently as possible) and not for achieving the text's rhyme or other stylistic characteristics.

Limited information is available about the author of *Kutadgu Bilig*, Yusuf Has Hacib (henceforth, Yusuf). As inferred from various sections of *Kutadgu Bilig* where Yusuf refers to himself and his work, the author was born in Balasagun, the winter capital of the Karakhanid Empire (present-day Kyrgyzstan). Yusuf completed *Kutadgu Bilig* in 1969 to 1970 CE. His intended primary audience for the text was Tavghach Bughra Khan (a Turkic prince in Eastern part of the Karakhanid Empire). Upon his completion and presentation of the work to the Khan, Yusuf was given the title, *Has Hacib* (the Primary Counselor).

Robert Dankoff, a Western scholar of Turkish studies, contextualizes *Kutadgu Bilig* as a didactic poem in the *mirror-for-princes* tradition (i.e., one that instructs a ruler on certain aspects of behavior and the rule of the state).[7] Other Turkologists view *Kutadgu Bilig* as a text from which all individuals can draw wisdom about different aspects of life.[8] Dankoff suggests that the content of *Kutadgu Bilig* shows a synthesis of influences from various cultures, implying that Yusuf must have studied texts of Greek philosophers like Plato and Aristotle, Persian philosopher Al-Farabi, the Qur'an, the Books of Moses, and the Biblical stories. As other Turkologists suggest and Dankoff confirms, however, *Kutadgu Bilig* is primarily a unique reflection on Turkish culture and oral tradition and its intersections with both the author's and Turkish society's beliefs, feelings, and practices—especially given its frequent employment of literary tools unique to the Turkish tradition (e.g., Turkish proverbs) in its depiction of various facets of life in the Karakhanid Empire.

The main text of *Kutadgu Bilig* presents a combination of the author's self-reflections on life (presented sometimes in prose and sometimes in verse) and an extensive allegorical poem (the masnavi) that presents the two-way conversations, debates, and letter-correspondence of four fictional personas. The majority of these discourses address the parameters of proper conduct regarding various aspects of life (the relationships between the ruler and the ruled, the proper ways a ruler or an intellectual should interact with individuals of different professions, etiquette at public gatherings, how to choose a spouse, etc). As such, the text consists of roughly eighty-two parts, each named a *bab*—a word that is also used in Turkish for the parts (*surahs*) of sacred texts like the Qur'an or the Bible. Two of these *babs* are dedicated entirely to the appropriate use of *dil* (tongue or language), and several hundreds of additional verses reference (sporadically throughout the text) to the significance of using one's *söz* or words or making statements 'properly'. In other words, as the text conveys its assumptions about the proper conduct in different areas of life, it also conveys its assumptions about the proper use of language as an essential aspect of worldly affairs.

The overarching understanding of rhetoric in *Kutadgu Bilig* seems to focus on Turkish rhetorical terms that appear specifically in the text's discussion of the use of *söz* ("the word") and *dil* ("tongue" or "language"). *Kutadgu Bilig* occasionally also denotes the word rhetoric with *belâgat*, a term that originates from Arabic (*balaghah*) and that entered the Turkish lexicon with the Islamic period of Turkish history (starting in the middle of the tenth century CE).

---

7. Khass Hajib 1983, 1.
8. Kara 2012, 9.

Belâgat refers to the ways in which oral and written language is used and studied. A review of the existing copies of *Kutadgu Bilig* shows that the text conceptualizes rhetoric primarily as the particular ways in which *söz* ('the word') and *dil* (denotes the Turkish word for both 'tongue' and 'language') should be used in daily practice. These ways are embedded and communicated through two dedicated *babs* and hundreds of additional verses devoted to deliberations on the use of *söz* and *dil*, which suggests that *Kutadgu Bilig* treats the study and the practice of rhetoric as essential to living a fulfilled life and achieving *kut* (a divine form of bliss).

With its particular focus on the notion of *kut*, *Kutadgu Bilig* digresses from an understanding of rhetoric evident in classical Greek rhetoricians' works (i.e., rhetoric as a means to persuade or as a counterpart to dialectic in the search of the truth). In addition, while *Kutadgu Bilig* considers the proper use of words a crucial aspect of a proper way of living and one that can lead to an individual's eternal bliss, it also positions the improper use of words as a possible cause of one's demise (often stated in terms of metaphors such as *losing one's head*). These and other perspectives on rhetoric in *Kutadgu Bilig*, which raise interesting questions and can provide rhetoric scholars with various points for critical discussion, are illustrated in the translations of the various verses chronologically interspersed with the following paragraphs as well as in the two *babs* on 'the tongue' (i.e., use of language) that follow this commentary.

The first eleven *babs* of *Kutadgu Bilig* function as the front matter. Since Turks had been converting to Islam in masses since the middle of the tenth century CE and have widely practiced the religion during the Karakhanid period, the influence of an Islamic understanding of divinity (belief in God and Prophet Mohammed) on *Kutadgu Bilig* is clear from its first three *babs*, which praise: (1) *Tengri*, the original word for God in Turkish (Allah was later adopted from Arabic); (2) Prophet Mohammed; and (3) the four caliphs who served after Prophet Muhammad's time.[9] The fourth *bab* is an ode to the season of spring as well as to the ruler/khan—the Kasghar prince, Tavghach Ulug Bughra Khan. The fifth *bab* discusses the seven planets and twelve constellations, alluding to them as divine creations. The front matter continues with a discussion of the fundamental importance of wisdom and intellect to human beings.

It is with the seventh *bab*, which is devoted specifically to *dil* (tongue or language), that *Kutadgu Bilig* gets exclusively rhetorical and begins to convey its understanding of the proper use of language: "The Tongue: its Merits and Demerits, its Benefits and Harms." One of the two translated *babs* that follow this commentary, "The Tongue" demonstrates a metaphorical understanding of 'language use', for example, when Yusuf alerts the reader as follows:

> 164. Behold, the tongue is a lion crouching on the threshold; O householder
> (*ey*, ev sahibi), be careful; it can devour your head.

---

9. As Dankoff suggests, although the writing in these *babs* must still be by Yusuf, they look stylistically different (in terms of their rhyme, meter, morphology, and lexicon) than the majority of the text (33–34).

This verse includes a rhetorical trope unique to Turkish rhetoric, *ey (ay* in middle Turkish*)*, found first in the earliest available Turkic texts, Gokturk Empire's Orkhon Inscriptions, from the eighth century CE. This trope is added to the opening of a statement to urge the listeners and to emphasize the point that follows.[10] The emphasis, in this case, is on the proper use of language which—in the framework of the other verses in the *bab*—seems to refer to using words sparingly and carefully as to ensure one's safety. While the seventh *bab* does not necessarily clarify how or why, it makes clear that the improper use of language leads to one's demise by "losing one's head"—which, in its historical and cultural context, could either be understood literally (i.e., to die by decapitation as a result of having made unlawful statements) or metaphorically (e.g., to lose one's professional position as a result of having made statements that discredit one's character). *Kutadgu Bilig* implies, then, that individuals have to discipline their tongue in such a way that they can communicate effectively with those who have authority and power—as those would be the ones to cause someone to lose his or her social standing or even life.

As such, another metaphorical verse in the seventh *bab* suggests that, with his or her rhetorical agency or ability to use language effectively, a communicator has the agency help others in a society with their comprehension (i.e., she can give the interlocutor the ability to "see" or understand):

> 178. utter your word consciously; let your word be an eye to the visionless (*görsüzler*), to the blind (*kör*).

> 179. The ignorant is the blind. Go, then, fool—get a share of knowledge (from those who have intellect and an eloquent tongue)!

On one hand, visionless-ness/blindness refers to ignorance and visionless/blind to those with a lack of knowledge (i.e., subject matter expertise). On the other hand, visionless-ness might also suggest a lack of intelligent foresight (often due to a lack of subject matter expertise). Those who lack the knowledge or intelligent foresight to analyze situations may fail to take appropriate actions and may even prevent others from doing so. It is also the role of a communicator, then, to use language in a way to compensate for the foresight of those lacking a vision.

Indeed, in addition to its metaphorical explanations about how language operates in society, the seventh *bab* (along with individual verses in some other *babs*) places a special emphasis on the idea of a rhetorical agency—an ability to use language effectively and control one's words wisely. This understanding of agency is implied partly, for example, when the narrator addresses his interlocutor in verse 183: "If you seek undying life (*ey hakîm*), then keep your deeds and words good." Yusuf's original Middle Turkish word for *hakîm* is *bügü*. Both *bügü*

---

10. *Ey* is still used in contemporary Turkish and is defined as an exclamation word used to get the addressee's attention and can be emphasized by stretching it out (*Ey, friend!*). *Contemporary Turkish Dictionary*, s.v. "ey," sozluk.gov.tr.

and *hakîm* originally refer to a wise person (*hikmet sahibi* in contemporary Turkish).[11] From a rhetorical perspective, *bügü or hakîm* can also be considered any individual with a rhetorical agency—especially when *Kutadgu Bilig* is read as a text for all readers to draw wisdom from. In other words, Yusuf would suggest that for an individual to consider himself a wise person (or for others to deem him to be a wise person) he should have the ability to use words effectively.[12]

Another term that appears in relation to Yusuf's deliberations on rhetorical agency is *erklig* (ability to control), which is translated as *hâkim* in contemporary Turkish adaptations of *Kutadgu Bilig*:

> 971. The ignorant should constantly keep his tongue locked up, and the knowledgeable should be able to control his tongue (*diline hâkim* in contemporary Turkish and *tilke erklig* in Middle Turkish).

Hâkim is an adjective used to conceptualize "that who is in control" or as a noun that refers to the "judge" of a judicial court.[13] Since *Kutadgu Bilig* has often been considered a political work on state affairs, Yusuf's use of *hâkim* is considered a reference to a master, a khan (which also appears in Yusuf original text in Middle Turkish as *melik* or *ilig*)—who is, indeed, the intended primary audience for *Kutadgu Bilig*. *Hâkim* is still used as part of the contemporary Turkish rhetorical phrase, *sözüne hâkim* (one who has a good command of his/her words/speech).

Not only does *Kutadgu Bilig* deem a rhetorical agency in the form of controlling one's words as one of the pillars of life, it also situates it as a means to achieve immortality when the use of language is in the form of writing. Yusuf states:

> 182. Look! One was born and dead; what remained behind is his word; the person is gone, but his words remain.[14]

> 183. If you seek undying life, O sage (*ey hakîm*), then keep your deeds and words good.

The last line of "The Tongue" acts as a transition to the eighth *bab*, which is an apology by the author that fits the Turkish rhetorical tradition of showing humility in case of a possible failure to communicate one's messages properly. The eight *bab* can also be considered a disclaimer intending to protect the author from possible discontent in the historical context,

---

11. *Hikmet* refers to wisdom. *Sahibi* means "to have."

12. In contemporary Turkish, the word will usually be written as "hakim" without the use of a *harakāt*, a mark used as a phonetic guide in the Arabic language, which predetermines the word's pronunciation and meaning.

13. See footnote 19 on the current usage of the word, "hakim."

14. In line with the Turkish language, in this and other verses, *Kutadgu Bilig* uses genderless wording, such as "kişi" which means an "individual," and the genderless pronoun "o" which means he or she and is sometimes implied in the suffix of a word. For the sake of brevity, I use "he" or "him" in reference to singular third-person pronoun (also because the intended primary audience of the text was a male prince).

as the text is presented to a prince, an absolute ruler whose opinion of the text's quality could determine the author's fate). It is worth noting that this *bab* also includes specific references to "the appropriate use of words"—references that are conflated with the value of acquiring *bilig*.

The word *bilig*, which is used in the title phrase of Yusuf's book, *Kutadgu Bilig* and rendered in contemporary Turkish as *bilgi*, means knowledge and/or wisdom. To explain the significance of the notion of *bilig* to all things in life, including rhetoric, the eight *bab* draws upon the metaphor of a pearl. That is, knowledge or wisdom is a valuable stone to be recovered; such notions are otherwise just stones that have no meaning without being discovered.

> 211. A person's heart is a bottomless sea and knowledge is the pearl that lies at the bottom.

> 212. If the person fails to bring the pearl up out of the sea— whether it is a pearl or a pebble— it makes no difference.

> 213. Gold that lies beneath the earth's bosom is only a piece of rock; when it is extracted, it becomes the signature buckle on princes' headpieces.

> 214. If the wise does not bring out knowledge upon his tongue, his knowledge may lie there forever and shed no light on its neighborhood.

> 215. Intellect and knowledge are truly fine things; if you find them, use them and you will soar up to the sky.

Taken in the context of the rest of *Kutadgu Bilig*, in Yusuf's view, *bilig* can be sourced from listening rather than speaking. It is the responsibility of the communicator to listen to the knowledgeable (*bilgili* or *bilen*, someone who has knowledge or is the expert) and the wise (*bilge*, someone who has transcended the human forms of knowledge and possesses even more foresight than any other knowledgeable person). In addition, the word that is "good" and valuable is the word which leads to action (which was alluded previously in the verse 183 that associates deeds with words).

The subsequent *babs* present short discussions on the following: the benefits of good deeds such as humility and kindness towards the public (*bab* 9), benefits of knowledge and intellect (*bab* 10), and the implications of Yusuf's title for the book and his old age (*bab* 11). The discussion in the 11th *bab* suggests that *Kutadgu Bilig* situates its messages about rhetoric within the framework of a holistic understanding of bliss or happiness (*kut*)—one that can be achieved through and embodied by all of the wisdom delivered in the text. As such, *Kutadgu Bilig* suggests, attaining *kut* requires subjecting the 'tongue' to a certain rhetorical training. Yusuf says:

> 350. I have named the book *Kutadgu*; let it endow its reader with bliss and guide (the reader).

> 351. I uttered my word and wrote the book; this book is a hand that reaches out to grasp both the worlds (this world and afterlife).

352. If a person is able to grasp both the worlds through the state (i.e., the just ruler of a state would have peace and happiness both in the world and afterlife), he will become happy (*mes'ût*); my word is accurate and honest.

The rest of *Kutadgu Bilig* revolves around the symbolism of an idealized notion of a well-rounded persona, constructed through usually the two-way dialogues of four personas, each of whom represents a critical notion symbolized by a corresponding human name in Turkish (see Table 10.1).

Table 10.1. Four personas, their roles, and the notions they represent in *Kutadgu Bilig*.

Name (Translation)	Role	Turkish Notion (Translation)
Kün Togdı (Sunrise)	Ruler	*Töre* (Rule of Law/Justice)
Ay Toldı (Moonrise)	Vizier/Sage	*Kut* (Divinely Sourced Bliss)
Odgurmış (Praised)	Sage	*Akıl* (Intellect or Wisdom)
Ögdülmiş (Awakened)	Vizier's Brother	*Akıbet* (Divine Truth/Afterlife)

These characters' dialogues reveal that a well-rounded social agent (*kişi*) carries the following characteristics:

- freed of all vices (e.g., doesn't steal, lie, drink, or gossip)
- laureated with good habits
- a devoted believer of *Tengri* (the Turkic word for God)
- a follower of justice in all dealings
- down to earth and humble
- literate in as many languages as possible
- a scholar with a good command of all sciences of the time; knowledgeable about *belâgat* (rhetoric), accounting, medicine, and so on
- skilled in archery, hunting, and playing chess
- generous and philanthropic
- compassionate and tolerant towards others
- a follower of social traditions and etiquette

The author delineates the characteristics of a well-rounded persona not in a vacuum but within the framework of a society. Participating in social life makes Yusuf's well-rounded persona a social agent and gives him a rhetorical agency (i.e., communication is a social phenomenon).

As the text focuses on the manner in which individuals should relate to each other as well as to the state, it also makes repeated references to the appropriate ways in which individuals should use words/language.

Kutadgu Bilig suggests that an ideal social agent should use words with caution and, thus, needs to discipline his or her tongue accordingly by studying language carefully. In this text's view, the purpose of rhetoric is to enlighten and guide. This purpose renders rhetoric as an essential tool in a life path that leads to *kut*, a divinely sourced bliss. Knowledge is a given condition of being able to use language or establish credibility in a society. It is only through wisdom and realizing that wisdom—through language and daily moral practice—one can be blessed with happiness, and it is ultimately the wise and happy who has credibility.

With its discourse on the use of language, Yusuf Has Hacib's *Kutadgu Bilig* demonstrates the historical value of the study and practice of rhetoric in a non-Western context. The various parts of this text that deliberate on the proper use of words, such as the two *babs* presented below, allow us to explore alternative definitions and purposes of rhetoric from a historical Turkish context (e.g., communicating to attain *kut* – a blessed form of happiness)—an exploration which can contribute to our inventory of non-Western rhetorical conventions.

Translation of Two *Babs* on Rhetoric in Yusuf Has Hacib's *Kutadgu Bilig*

The Seventh Bab—"The Tongue: Its Merits and Demerits, Its Benefits and Harms"

162. It is the tongue that serves as the interpreter of intellect and knowledge; know the value of an eloquent tongue which makes a person shine.

163. It is the tongue that gives value to a human being and through which a human being attains *kut* [divine bliss]; it is (also) the tongue that causes one to lose his esteem and, thus, lose his head.

164. Behold! The tongue is a lion crouching on the threshold; *ey*, householder, be careful! It can devour your head.

165. Listen to the words of a man who suffered from his tongue; remember and follow his words forever:

166. My tongue tortures me a great deal; let me cut my tongue so that they do not cut my head.

167. Watch your words, and you won't lose your head; hold your tongue, and you won't break your teeth.

168. The sage once stated a proverb about the tongue: *ey*, tongue owner, watch your head.

169. If you care about your safety, do not let an improper word escape your mouth.

170. A consciously made statement counts as knowledge; the statement of an ignorant person will devour his very own head.

171. I never benefited from (speaking) too many words; but it is also unbeneficial not to say anything.

172. Do not speak excessively; say the word at the right time and sparingly; in this manner, you will untie a thousand knots.

173. It is with (the use of) words that a person advanced (in life) and became a ruler (*melik*); too many words, just like a shadow, cast one's head on the ground.

174. This is what *Bilig* [Knowledge] says for the person who talks much: "he has been a chatterbox [*gevezelik etti*]"; if one says no words, however, this time *Bilig* will call him a "mute" [*ağın* in Middle Turkish; *dilsiz* in contemporary Turkish].

175. Therefore, use correct and clear language [*fasîh dil*]; if language is correct and clear [*fasîh*], it will elevate the human being.

176. Watch the tongue, and you will be watching your head; cut your word short, and your life will be longer.

177. While (what is said with) the tongue can have so many benefits, it can harm in many ways as well; one's use of language [*dil*] will sometimes be praised, and sometimes criticized.

178. Since that is the case, utter your word consciously; let your word be an eye to the visionless (*görsüzler*), to the blind.

179. The ignorant is the blind; go, then, fool—get a share of knowledge (from those who have intellect and an eloquent tongue)!

180. Look! What is born, dies; what remains behind is the word; speak good words, and you will be immortal.

181. Only two things will prevent one from aging: one is good deeds, the other good words.

182. Look! One was born, and then he died; what remained behind is his word; the person is gone, but his word remained.

183. If you seek undying life, O master [*ey hakîm*], then keep your deeds and words good.

184. My purpose to twist this tongue (of mine) so much and, sometimes, to criticize (its value) is to explain to you what a word [söz] actually entails.

185. (Note that) *Akıl* [Intellect] won't tolerate holding all of your words back, either; a person says what needs to be said; he doesn't hold that back.

186. Ey, the courageous one, I uttered this word for my son; my son is below (my level, due to age and experience); how can he possibly match up to me (with his experience).

187. Ey, son, I uttered this word for you; ey, son, I gave these advices to you.

188. If I end up being able to bequeath you gold and silver, do not even think of those as equally valuable (as these advices).

189. If you invest your silver (coins) in your (worldly) affairs, it will be used up; if you invest my words in your (worldly) affairs, you will gain silver.

190. Words are one person's true legacy to another; so much is gained by following the words that one bequeathed to another.

The Nineteenth Bab – "Moonrise Talks to the Ruler about the Virtues of the Tongue and Benefits of the Word"

955. One day, the ruler [İlig] summoned Moonrise [*Ay Toldı*]; the ruler guided him to a seat and signaled him to sit.

956. Moonrise slowly and respectfully took the seat; he fixed his eyes on the floor and made no sound.

957. The ruler said: Moonrise, speak up! Why are you so quiet? What's happened to you?

958. Moonrise said: O, master of masters (*Ey beyler beyi*), when a slave sees the face of his master, he gets too perplexed to know what to say.

959. The ruler hasn't yet ordered me to speak of anything; without his asking me (of anything), what am I supposed to say?

960. (One is supposed to) listen to the word of the knowledgeable [*bilgili*], don't object to it; do not say a word without being asked to do so.

961. That who sees a need to summon someone is also the one who is to begin speaking.

962. It would be right to call someone a savage for speaking without being asked to do so.

963. Also know that a person who speaks in front of masters [*beyler*] without being asked to do so is insane and dumb.

964. A red tongue will shorten your life; if you want peace and safety, hold your tongue tight.

965. Listen to the words of the person who is able to control [*hâkim*] his tongue; the person who can control (his use of language) lives in comfort and peace.

966. The enemy of a dark head is a red tongue; many a head the tongue has devoured and (the tongue) will yet again do so.

967. If you want to protect your head, watch your tongue; your tongue threatens your head every day.

968. The ruler said: I have completely understood what you have said. But, it is impossible for a living person not to speak at all.

969. Know that only two kinds of people will not speak: the ignorant and the mute.

970. The mute's tongue will not be able to speak; the ignorant cannot hold his tongue.

971. The ignorant should constantly keep his tongue locked up, and the knowledgeable should be "able to control his tongue" [*diline hâkim* in contemporary Turkish *and tilke erklig in* middle Turkish].

972. The word of the knowledgeable is like water to the earth; when you water the earth, crop [*nimet*] will come out of it.

973. The words of the knowledgeable will never be lacking; the water of a flowing spring will never cease to run.

974. The wise [*bilgeler*] are like watery lands; wherever they put their feet, the water will spring out of the ground there.

975. The heart of the ignorant is like sand; even if a river flows into it, it is unable to fill up or yield any crop.

976. Moonrise once again said: The ruler (already) knows that this tongue can even cost one his life.

977. As long as one shall live, is it ever possible for him not to say any words? But, he only says what is necessary; (he) doesn't hide that.

978. In order for a person to speak up, he needs to be asked about something; unless a person is asked (of anything), he should not open his mouth.

979. O Ruler [*Ey İlig*], if you think carefully about it, asking is male and answering is female.

980. A female will beget only one husband; if born, they (the female and male) can bear two children.

981. The ruler said: I've understood; all your words are true; I'll ask you about one more thing.

982. You stated the harms of the tongue, I've heard you; does it have any benefits? Say this as it is, too.

983. If now you are afraid of the harms that can come from the tongue and don't speak (at all), all your beneficial words will stay where they are and won't bring you any benefits.

984. Moonrise said: If this tongue of mine is able to do so, let me tell you; speaking has a great many benefits.

985. Out of the mouth of ignorant folk will come empty words; the wise will then (rightfully) call the ignorant a 'savage'.

986. It is the common folk who say empty and tactless words; and it is these words that will devour his head.

987. An idle statement will cause so much harm; a statement is beneficial only when it's made at the right time.

988. When the common folk's bellies are full, watch it, they will lie down like an ox; they take pleasure in and feed their bodies with idle words.

989. Those who just eat, fill their belly, and lie down as animals; what I call 'animal' here is their nature.

990. Knowledgeable people will push their bodies (for the better); they will take pleasure in knowledge and feed their souls with knowledge.

991. The body's share enters through the mouth; the soul's share, however, is true words and will enter through the ear.

992. Look, knowledge has two signs: a man will become happy with these two things.

993. One of these is the tongue [what they speak], the other is the throat [what they eat]; a person will benefit greatly from controlling these two.

994. The knowledgeable has to control his throat and tongue; there is much need for those who watch their throat and tongue.

995. The ruler: I see, that is the way it works. What is the source of speech? How many types of speech are out there?

996. Where does the speech come from and where does it go? O Sage, explain this to me.

997. What needs to be spoken and what needs to be left unspoken? What does the wise and the intellectual say about this matter?

998. Moonrise answered: The source of speech (should remain) a secret; if one has ten words, only one of these should be spoken.

999. One can be spoken; it is forbidden to say the other nine; (and) forbidden words are in fact always harmful.

1000. The ruler once more asked: How beneficial and how harmful are the words? Explain this to me.

1001. Moonrise said: Speaking has a great many benefits; if statements are made at the right place, they will elevate the slave [*kul*].

1002. Because of speech, he who is on the brown earth rises into the blue sky and assumes a place of honor.

1003. If the tongue doesn't know how to speak well, it will bring down to the ground that which was up in the sky.

1004. The ruler asked once again: What is much speech and what is little? Explain this to me, too.

1005. Moonrise said: Much speech is that which is spoken unbid and which tires the listener.

1006. Little speech is that which is said in response to what is asked and provides the needed response.

1007. As a poet in this valley once stated:

1008. Say your word well and carefully; say it only when asked to do so and keep it short.

1009. Listen more, but speak less; say your word with intellect and embellish it with knowledge.

1010. The ruler said: I understand this, too; I have yet another question. Explain this to me, too.

1011. Tell me whose speech one ought to listen, and to whom one ought to speak.

1012. Moonrise said: One ought to listen to the knowledgeable, and then should speak to the one who doesn't have knowledge.

1013. One ought to listen to the elderly for useful words and, so that they can act accordingly, ought to report these words to the younger folk.

1014. One ought to listen more, but ought to say fewer words distinctly; thus have the knowledgeable instructed me.

1015. A person does not become wise by speaking much; by listening much, the wise gains a seat of honor.

1016. Even if a person is mute, he can still become knowledgeable; but is he is deaf, he cannot acquire knowledge.

1017. The ruler asked again: I've understood that, too. I have yet another question.

1018. Should we silence the tongue or make it speak? Is it better to open up statements, or hold them back?

1019. Moonrise said: Let me sincerely present this to the ruler; if knowledge isn't communicated through the tongue, it just stays like that.

1020. It is unfair just to criticize the tongue; it has a great many aspects that need to be praised, too. The word also has aspects to praise and aspects to criticize.

1021. All living beings, all the countless crowd of living things testify to the one *Tengri* (God).

1022. Tengri created hundreds of thousands of creatures; they all praise *Tengri* with their tongues.

1023. Any human being who owns a body needs two things: one is a tongue, the other a heart.

1024. Tengri created the heart and the tongue for the sake of (speaking) true words; those whose words are crooked will forcefully be thrown into the fire.

1025. If the word is spoken truly, it provides many great benefits; a crooked word will be condemned forever.

1026. Let you tongue move only if it will speak the truth; if your statement is crooked, you should hold it back.

1027. When a person doesn't speak, they will call him a mute [*ağın* or *dilsiz*]; those who talk too much, however, will be called a chatterbox.

1028. The unreliable of human beings is that who is a chatterbox; the credible of human beings is that who is generous.

1029. The ruler heard of these words and rejoiced; he lifted his eyes to the sky and raised his hand.

1030. He thanked God, praised him much, and said: My Lord, you are merciful and great.

1031. All the good that I've ever had is from you; I (however) am a sinful and undutiful slave of yours.

1032. You have granted me with peace, worldly goods, the state, and all the other goodness in this world and, thus, all of my wishes.

1033. I cannot thank you enough for these favors; O, the Principal, may you pay the thanks (for these) to yourself.

1034. (The ruler) stopped speaking; he opened up the treasury. He dispensed much wealth to the poor and the needy.

1035. The ruler honored Moonrise; he praised (Moonrise) with his tongue and gave him gifts with his hand.

1036. He gave (Moonrise) the title of vizierate together with its seal and standard, its drum and armory suit.

1037. He gave Moonrise control over the entire country; he made the enemies bend their neck (to this will) and then withdrew.

1038. Moonrise disposed of all the affairs of state; he took advantage of his period of reign to accomplish many things.

1039. The people became rich and the state prospered; the people prayed for the ruler.

1040. The people were rescued and relieved of their troubles; the lamb and the wolf began to walk together.

1041. The entire state reached a state of peace, its governance improved; the ruler's state of happiness constantly increased.

1042. This state of peace and order lasted for a long while; all things have gotten square for the people and the state.

1043. New cities and towns were built within the state; the royal treasury was filled with gold and silver.

1044. The ruler has attained peace and prosperity; his reputation and power have spread around the world.

COMPREHENSIVE BIBLIOGRAPHY

Binark, İsmet. 1979. *Arşiv ve arşivcilik bibliyografyası = A Bibliography on Archives and Archival Studies: Türkçe ve yabancı dillerde yayınlanmış kaynaklar: Includes Turkish and Foreign sources.* Ankara: T. C. Başbakanlık Cumhuriyet Arşivi Dairesi Başkanlığı.

Guler, Elif, and Iklim Goksel. 2017. "The Pedagogical Implications of Teaching Atatürk's 'Address to the Youth' for Global Rhetoric and Civic Action in the US Writing Classroom." *Reflections: A Journal of Public Rhetoric, Civic Writing, and Service Learning* 17 (2): 69–94.

—. 2019. "Understanding Turkish Rhetoric in the Intertextuality of Two Seminal Texts: The Orkhon Inscriptions and Ataturk's *Nutuk.*" *Advances in the History of Rhetoric* 22 (2): 194–207.

Guler, Elif. 2020. "An Overview of *Kut* and *Töre* as the Pillars of the Turkish Rhetorical Tradition." In *The Routledge Handbook of Comparative World Rhetorics,* edited by Keith Lloyd, 106–15. New York: Routledge.

Güncel Türkçe Sözlük (Contemporary Turkish Dictionary). 2021. "belagat," "histabet," "retorik." Accessed March 1, 2021. Ankara: TDK. sozluk.gov.tr.

Has Hacib, Yusuf. 2015. *Kutadgu Bilig - Tipkibasim (Original Print) I—Viyana Nushasi (Vienna Scribe).* Ankara: Turk Dil Kurumu (Turkish Language Association).

Has Hacib, Yusuf, and Fikri Silahdaroğlu. 1996. *Günümüz Türkçesi İle Kutadgu Bilig Uyarlaması* (*Kutadgu Bilig Adaptation in Contemporary Turkish*). Ankara: T.C. Kültür Bakanlığı.

Has Hacib, Yusuf, and Mustafa Kacalin. N.d. *Kutadğu Bilig* (transliterated from the Uyghur script). Ankara: Turkish Ministry of Culture and Tourism. www.kultur.gov.tr.

Has Hacib, Yusuf, and Reşit Rahmeti Arat. 1988. *Kutadgu Bilig.* Ankara: Türk Tarih Kurumu Basımevi (Turkish History Association Press).

Kara, Mehmet. *Bir Başka Açıdan Kutadgu Bilig* (*Kutadgu Bilig From Another Perspective*). Istanbul: Nesil, 2012.

Khass Hajib, Yusuf and Robert Dankoff. 1983. *Wisdom of Royal Glory (Kutadgu Bilig): A Turko-Islamic Mirror for Princes.* Chicago: University of Chicago Press.

Kushner, David. 1997. "Self-Perception and Identity." *Journal of Contemporary History* 32 (2): 219–33.

Ögel, Bahattin. 1971. *Türk Kültürünün Gelisme ÇağLarı* [The Developmental Ages of Turkish Culture]. Ankara: Milli Eğitim.

Stokes, Jamie, and Anthony Gorman. 2009. *Encyclopedia of the Peoples of Africa and the Middle East.* New York: Facts on File.

Taşağıl, Ahmet. 1995. *Göktürkler* [*The Göktürks*]. Ankara: Türk Tarih Kurumu.

GLOSSARY OF TERMS

Term[15]	Translation
akıl (ukuş)	intellect; understanding; grandiose
belâgat	the use and the study of oral and written language
bilgi (bilig)	knowledge; wisdom. Also, "the word" when it is equated to substance or wisdom (the wise word).
bilgisiz	Ignorant; those who lack knowledge or wisdom; common folk
bilge	wise
dil (til)	language; tongue
dilsiz (ağın)	mute, someone who cannot speak
diline hâkim (tilke erklig)	someone who is able to control his or her tongue
Ey (Aya)	an exclamation mark that appears first in the Orkhon inscriptions (eighth century CE), the earliest available Turkish texts; still used in contemporary Turkish to add emphasis to the opening of a sentence or statement.
fasih	clean and clear (e.g., writing)
hâkim (erklig)	ability to control
İlig (melik)	the ruler
kişi	person (which *Kutadgu Bilig* links with rhetorical agency)
kut	divinely sourced bliss; royal glory; God's benediction (also used in words *kutlu* or *kutalmış* meaning "that is celebrated and blessed with God's benediction").
kutadgu	that which endows one with happiness or divine bliss
söz	word; promise; statement
özsöz	the essential word; plain and truthful language
Töre	Turkish moral rule of law (largely unwritten, oral)

15. This glossary presents both the terms that are directly about rhetoric (e.g., belâgat) and the terms that are considered to have close links with rhetoric within the context of *Kutadgu Bilig*. The words in parentheses, if applicable, present the contemporary transliterations of the original usage in middle Turkish.

CONTRIBUTORS

Leonora Anyango, PhD, is a language, culture, and education expert of international re-pute, and an applied linguist who specializes in the teaching of English as an international language. She has a vast knowledge of multiple languages, including Japanese, Kiswahili and several African languages. Her research includes, but is not limited to, multilingual writing pedagogies, African rhetoric, translation and interpretation, and she is an avid writer of creative nonfiction, which work has appeared in *Assay: Journal of Non-Fiction Studies* among others. She has published numerous book chapters and is co-editor of the upcoming *New Directions in Technology for Writing Instruction* (Spring Nature, 2023). Currently, she teaches English composition at the University of Pittsburgh.

Raed Alsawaier's PhD is from Washington State University in instructional technology and English rhetoric. As a Jordanian American, he strives to build bridges, fight Islamophobia, and spread enlightenment. He has published articles from his recently completed dissertation on the effects of gamification on learners' motivation and engagement in the college environment.

Maha Baddar is Professor of English at Pima Community College. She received her PhD in rhetoric from the University of Arizona. Her publications include "The Arabs Did Not 'Just' Translate Aristotle: Al-Farabi's Logico-Rhetorical Theory," "Toward a New Understanding of Audience in the Medieval Arabic Translation Movement: The Case of al-Kindi's 'Statement on the Soul,'" and "Texts that Travel: Translation Genres and Knowledge-Making in the Medieval Arabic Translation Movement."

Patricia Bizzell is Distinguished Professor of English Emerita at Holy Cross, where she taught courses in academic writing, rhetorical theory and practice, nineteenth-century American activist rhetorical genres, and literature in English by cultural and linguistic border crossers. Among her honors are NCTE's Outstanding Book Award for *The Rhetorical Tradition*, the Exemplar Award from the Conference on College Composition and Communication, and the 2016–2017 Cardin Chair in Humanities at Loyola University Maryland. She is a Fellow of the Rhetoric Society of America, its past president, and a two-term member of the Modern Language Association's Publication Committee, among other professional responsibilities.

Gregory Coles holds a PhD in English from The Pennsylvania State University. His research currently lies at the intersection of Kenneth Burke studies and the rhetorics of historically marginalized groups, including but not limited to feminist rhetorics, racial minority rhetorics, sexual minority rhetorics, and postcolonial rhetorics. His rhetorical scholarship has been published in *College English* and *Rhetorica*.

Trey Conner, Associate Professor at University of South Florida St. Petersburg, forms community partnerships that provide service learning opportunities for USFSP students, facilitates a welcoming classroom space for students to learn rituals of writing ranging from contemplative practices to distributed authorship, and writes about the function of chanting, song, and rhythm in diverse rhetorical and poetic traditions. He has published scholarly articles on Carnatic music, Advaita Vedanta, open source culture, and digital pedagogy. Trey remains always already engaged in a process of "infinite rehearsal" of collaboration with friends, family, students, and colleagues.

Rasha Diab is Associate Professor of Rhetoric and Writing and a faculty affiliate of the departments of English and Middle Eastern Studies at the University of Texas at Austin. Her work centers on the rhetorics of peacemaking, Arab-Islamic rhetorics, and revisionist historiography. In addition to *Shades of Ṣulḥ* (University of Pittsburgh Press, 2016), which received the Conference on College Composition and Communication (CCCC) Outstanding Book Award in the Monograph Category (2018), she has published on peacemaking rhetoric and Arab-Islamic rhetorics.

Richard Doyle, Edwin Erle Sparks Professor at The Pennsylvania State University, has authored scores of scholarly articles and seven books. He has been awarded grants from the National Science Foundation and the Mellon Foundation while winning acclaim and accolades as a classroom teacher in the US, the UK, Germany, and China. In 2002, Doyle was healed of life-long severe asthma in an Ayahuasca ceremony, and he has since devoted his life to synthesizing the world's spiritual practices into a practical, open source, and empirically verifiable pathway available to all. His most recent book is *The Genesis of Now: Self Experiments with the Bible and the End of Religion*.

Robert Eddy's PhD is from the University of Durham, England, where he studied the rhetorics of politics, science, and religion. He has directed writing programs in China and Egypt, and at Washington State University, where he is currently professor of English. Prior to WSU, he won the University of North Carolina Board of Governors' Teaching Award in 2001. He has most recently published *Writing Across Cultures* (2019, with co-author Amanda Espinosa-Aguilar) and *From Columbus to Churchill: Heroes, Villains, and Confronting Racism* (2022, with co-editor S. M. Ghazanfar).

Lahcen El Yazghi Ezzaher is Professor of English at the University of Northern Colorado. He is an accomplished scholar in histories and theories of rhetoric, theories of discourse, world literature, translation studies, and postcolonial criticism. His most recent publication, *Three Arabic Treatises on Aristotle's Rhetoric* (Southern Illinois University Press, 2015), earned a 2015 NEH fellowship and the 2017 Aldo and Jeanne Scaglione Prize for Translation of a Scholarly Study of Literature from the Modern Language Association. His articles have appeared in *Rhetorica, Advances in the History of Rhetoric, Global Academe, The Dictionary of African Biography*, and *The Encyclopedia of Literary and Cultural Theory*.

Shreelina Ghosh is Assistant Professor of English and Director of Composition at Gannon University. Ghosh has practiced the 2000-year old Odissi dance under eminent exponent, Guru Aloka Kanungo, since the age of four. She has performed widely across India and the USA, with choreographic works including *Panamami Buddham*; *Vayu: Visions of the Wind*; *Vyom: Mind of the Aether*; and *Shivaaradhana*. Her current research examines the use of technology as a tool for online and hybrid learning and explores the relationship between traditional and online pedagogical and performative practices. She is currently working on the Eastern rhetorical tradition of argumentation, the *Nyaya*.

Elif Guler is Associate Professor and Coordinator of the Professional Writing Program at Longwood University. Her research focuses on non-Western rhetorics, women's studies, and writing pedagogy. She co-edited *Foundational Practices of Online Writing Instruction*, and her essays appeared in *Advances in the History of Rhetoric*, *Reflections (A Journal of Public Rhetoric)*, *Studies in Popular Culture*, and *The Routledge Handbook of Comparative World Rhetorics*. Her article, "The Symbolic Restoration of Women's Place in Turkey's Resurrection," received the 2018 Whatley Award from the Popular Culture Association in the South.

ku'ualoha ho'omanawanui is Professor of Hawaiian Literature at the University of Hawai'i at Mānoa, and Director of Kaipuolono, a Native Hawaiian digital humanities project. Her book, *Voices of Fire: Reweaving the Literary Lei of Pele and Hi'iaka* (University of Minnesota Press, 2014) earned an honorable mention in the 2017 Modern Language Association award for best new Indigenous scholarship.

Steven B. Katz is Pearce Professor Emeritus of Professional Communication, and Professor Emeritus of English, at Clemson University. He has published six books, including the *Epistemic Music of Rhetoric*, and four co-authored editions of *Writing in the Sciences*. Of his numerous articles on Jewish rhetorics of the Hebrew alefbet, the ethics of scientific, and technical communication, one earned the NCTE Award for best article, and several others appeared in collections that won the NCTE Award for best books. He has also published hundreds of poems in a number of journals and media platforms.

Andy Kirkpatrick is a Fellow of the Australian Academy of the Humanities and Professor in the Department of Humanities, Languages and Social Sciences at Griffith University. He has published extensively on aspects of Chinese rhetoric and, with Xu Zhichang, is the author of *Chinese Rhetoric and Writing* (Parlor Press/WAC Clearinghouse, 2012). He is currently co-editing two new handbooks: *Asian Englishes* (with Kingsley Bolton as co-editor) and *Language Education Policy in Asia* (with Tony Liddicoat as co-editor).

Uma S. Krishnan is Professor of English and associate Writing Program Coordinator at Kent State University. She is also the Director of the Writing Internship Program. She is deeply interested in ethnographic studies, literacy and social practices of indigenous and ethnic groups, research methodologies, and Eastern rhetoric and literature. Krishnan's ethnographic case study on the Mumbai Dabbawalas in India led her to receive an Honorable Mention for the 2016 James Berlin Memorial Outstanding Dissertation Award at the Conference on College Composition and Communication.

Haixia Lan is Professor of English at the University of Wisconsin-La Crosse, where she teaches rhetorical invention, style, and comparative rhetoric. Author of *Aristotle and Confucius on Rhetoric and Truth: The Form and the Way,* she focuses her research on comparative rhetoric to help foster cross-cultural understanding and communication.

Keith Lloyd is Professor of English at Kent State University-Stark where he teaches undergraduate courses in composition, rhetoric, history of English, and linguistics, and a graduate course in comparative rhetoric. He has published extensively in *Rhetoric Review* and *Rhetoric Society Quarterly,* and other journals, on the historical development of rhetorics of India, with a special emphasis on the *Nyāya Sūtras,* and on permeations of this tradition into Western logics. He is editor of the *Routledge Handbook on Comparative Rhetorics,* and co-author, with Donghong Liu, of *Rhetoric and Composition Studies* published by Wuhan: Central China Normal University Press.

Anne Melfi completed her PhD in rhetoric and composition at Georgia State University. Her contribution to this collection draws on her dissertation, which was supported in part by a grant from the GSU College of Arts and Sciences, the guidance of Maharishi Mahesh Yogi, and her Master's in consciousness and the Vedic literature from Maharishi International University. Her essays appear in the *Routledge Handbook of Comparative World Rhetorics, Bodhi* journal, and *Truth to Power: Public Intellectuals In and Out of Academe.* She co-edited "An Annotated Bibliography of Global and Non-Western Rhetorics" for *Present Tense: A Journal of Rhetoric in Society.*

Georganne Nordstrom is Professor of Composition and Rhetoric and Associate Chair of the English department at the University of Hawai'i at Mānoa. She is the co-editor of *Huihui: Navigating Art and Literature in the Pacific* (University of Hawai'i Press, 2015), and author of *A Practitioners Inquiry into Collaboration: Pedagogy, Practice, and Research* (Routledge, 2021). A 2018–2019 Fulbright Scholar, Georganne is also the recipient of the 2012 Richard Braddock Award (with B. N. McDougall) and is currently serving as vice president of the International Writing Center Association.

Lana Oweidat is Associate Professor of Rhetoric and Composition at Goucher College, Baltimore, where she directs the writing center and teaches courses in writing and rhetoric. Her scholarly work, which has appeared in several journals and edited collections, tackles Arab-Islamic rhetoric, anti-Islamophobia pedagogies, multilingual composition, and tutor training. She is grateful to Goucher College for supporting her work in this collection through a summer research grant.

Maria Prikhodko holds a PhD in English Composition and TESOL from Indiana University of Pennsylvania and currently works at DePaul University, where she teaches first-year composition and rhetoric to multilingual students, as well as an upper-division course called "Writing across Borders" in collaboration with Unichristus University in Fortaleza, Brazil. Her research interests are grounded at the intersection of rhizomatic literacies, multilingualism, non-Western rhetorics, and post-materialism.

Ellen Quandahl is Associate Professor Emerita, Department of Rhetoric and Writing Studies, San Diego State University, where she directed Lower Division Writing and the Graduate Program. Her work on Aristotle and the ancient tradition, Byzantine rhetoric, Kenneth Burke, and writing studies, appears in *JAC*, *College English*, and *Rhetorica*. She is co-editor of the volume *Reclaiming Pedagogy*.

Shuv Raj Rana Bhat is an instructor of writing in the Department of English at Texas Christian University. His work has been published in *ANQ: A Quarterly Journal of Short Articles, Notes, and Reviews*; *Crosscurrents*; *SCHOLARS: Journal of Arts & Humanities*; *enculturation: a journal of rhetoric, writing, and culture*; *Present Tense: A Journal of Rhetoric in Society*; *Journal of Global Literacies, Technologies, and Emerging Pedagogies*; and *The Peer Review*. His research is grounded at the intersections of critical discourse studies, multimodal composition, antiracist, decolonial and critical pedagogies, critical stylistics and rhetorics, non-Western and postcolonial rhetorics, and language, power and ideology.

Jim Ridolfo is Associate Professor and Director of Composition at the University of Kentucky. His books include *The Available Means of Persuasion: Mapping a Theory and Pedagogy of Multimodal Public Rhetoric* (with David Sheridan and Anthony Michel), *Rhetoric and the Digital Humanities* (co-edited with William Hart-Davidson), *Digital Samaritans: Rhetorical Delivery and Engagement in the Digital Humanities*, and *Rhet Ops: Rhetoric and Information Warfare* (also co-edited with William Hart-Davidson). His work has also appeared in *JAC*; *Enculturation*; *College English*; *Kairos: A Journal of Rhetoric, Technology, and Pedagogy*; *Pedagogy: Critical Approaches to Teaching Literature, Language, Composition, and Culture*; and *Rhetoric Review*.

Brian J. Stone is Associate Professor of English and Director of Writing Programs at Indiana State University, Terre Haute, where he teaches writing, rhetoric, and medieval Celtic literature. His monograph, *The Rhetorical Arts in Late Antique and Early Medieval Ireland*, published by Amsterdam University Press in 2021, is the first study of rhetoric in early Ireland.

Jeffrey Walker is Professor Emeritus, Department of Rhetoric and Writing, University of Texas, Austin. His publications include *Bardic Ethos and the American Epic Poem* (Louisiana University Press, 1989); *Rhetoric and Poetics in Antiquity* (Oxford, 2000); *Investigating Arguments: Readings for College Writing* (a textbook, co-authored with Glen McClish, Houghton-Mifflin, 1991); and articles in *Rhetorica, Rhetoric Society Quarterly, Advances in the History of Rhetoric, Papers on Rhetoric, College English*, and other journals.

Index of Glossary Terms

Index of Names, Peoples, Places, and Religions

ABOUT THE EDITORS

Tarez Samra Graban is Associate Professor of English at Florida State University, where she teaches global rhetorics at the graduate level, teaches with transnational and comparative methodologies at the undergraduate level, and studies the rhetorical practices and archival positioning of women academics, activists, and elected leaders in southern Africa and the Middle East. Graban has published in *African Journal of Rhetoric, Gender & Language, Rhetorica, College English,* and *College Composition and Communication.* Her books include *Gen Admin: Theorizing WPA Identities in the 21st Century* (with Colin Charlton et al., Parlor Press, 2011), *Women's Irony* (Southern Illinois University Press, 2015), and *Teaching through the Archives* (edited with Wendy Hayden, Southern

Illinois University Press, 2022). With Anne Melfi and Nicole Khoury, she edited "An Annotated Bibliography of Global and Non-Western Rhetorics" (2021). From 2015 to 2018 she held a faculty research fellowship at the University of South Africa.

Hui Wu is Professor of English and Chair of the Department of Literature and Languages at the University of Texas at Tyler. An accomplished scholar recognized for comparative studies of rhetoric, global feminist rhetorics, and history of composition in a transnational context, Wu has published her studies in scholarly anthologies and selective journals in rhetoric and composition, such as *College English, Rhetoric Society Quarterly, College Composition and Communication,* and *Rhetoric Review.* One of her articles, "Lost and Found in Transnation: Modern Conceptualization of Chinese Rhetoric" won the 2010 Theresa Enos award for the best article in *Rhetoric Review.* Her books include *Once Iron Girls: Essays on*

Gender by Post-Mao Literary Women (Lexington Books, 2010), *Reading and Writing about the Disciplines: A Rhetorical Approach* (with Emily Standridge, Fountainhead Press, 2015), and *Guiguzi, China's First Treatise on Rhetoric: A Translation and Commentary* (Southern Illinois University Press, 2016).

CPSIA information can be obtained
at www.ICGtesting.com
Printed in the USA
JSHW011928121222
34685JS00003B/5

9 781643 173160